Cases and Materials on Equity and Trusts

Authors

Matthew E Carn
Adam Doyle
Christine Flutter
Jan Maltby
Katharine Matheson
Richard Quenby

Consultant Editor

Matthew E Carn

First edition July 2010

Fourth edition July 2015

Published ISBN: 9781 4727 3390 0

Previous ISBN: 9781 4727 2117 4

British Library Cataloguing-in-Publication Data
A catalogue record for this book is available
from the British Library

Published by
BPP Learning Media Ltd
BPP House, Aldine Place
London W12 8AA
www.bpp.com/learningmedia

Printed in the United Kingdom by
Charlesworth Press

Flanshaw Way
Flanshaw Lane
Wakefield
WF2 9LP

Your learning materials, published by BPP
Learning Media Ltd, are printed on paper
sourced from sustainable, managed forests.

Extracts from the Law Reports, the Weekly Law
Reports and the Industrial Cases Reports are
reproduced by permission of:

The Incorporated Council of Law Reporting for
England and Wales, Megarry House,
119 Chancery Lane, London WC2A 1PP

Extracts from the All England Reports, and other
LexisNexis titles are reproduced by permission of
LexisNexis which is a trading name of, Reed
Elsevier (UK) Limited, Registered office, 1-3 Strand,
London WC2N 5JR

Extracts from Westlaw publications (including
journal articles) are reproduced with permission of
Thomson Reuters (Legal) Limited, Registered Office,
100 Avenue Road, London NW3 3PF

Contents

A note about copyright

Dear Customer

What does the little © mean and why does it matter?

Your market-leading BPP books, course materials and e-learning materials do not write and update themselves. People write them: on their own behalf or as employees of an organisation that invests in this activity. Copyright law protects their livelihoods. It does so by creating rights over the use of the content.

Breach of copyright is a form of theft – as well as being a criminal offence in some jurisdictions, it is potentially a serious breach of professional ethics.

With current technology, things might seem a bit hazy but, basically, without the express permission of BPP Learning Media:

Photocopying our materials is a breach of copyright

Scanning, ripcasting or conversion of our digital materials into different file formats, uploading them to Facebook or e-mailing them to your friends is a breach of copyright

You can, of course, sell your books, in the form in which you have bought them – once you have finished with them. (Is this fair to your fellow students? We update for a reason.) But the e-products are sold on a single user licence basis: we do not supply 'unlock' codes to people who have bought them second-hand.

And what about outside the UK? BPP Learning Media strives to make our materials available at prices students can afford by local printing arrangements, pricing policies and partnerships which are clearly listed on our website. A tiny minority ignore this and indulge in criminal activity by illegally photocopying our material or supporting organisations that do. If they act illegally and unethically in one area, can you really trust them?

Index of Cases

A

B

C

D

E

F

G

H

I

J

K

L

M

N

O

P

R

S

T

1

Introduction to Equity and Trusts

Topic List

1.1 Why do we have 'Equity'?

Although many other legal systems have a notion of 'equity' as a process of modifying what are otherwise harsh and inflexible rules, the concept of 'Equity' as a second body of legal rules is a special anomaly of the common law world. Indeed, English law was not always structured this way, and were it not for decisions made over 700 years ago, the structure of English law would be quite different.

To understand how Equity came to exist in this way we have to go back to the reign of Henry III. At this time if you wanted to go to court you had to use a writ, or legal template, to structure your claim and bring it to court. If you could not find a suitable writ you could somehow fit your case within, then in effect you had no claim. Fortunately new writs could be created, so if there was an obvious lacuna in the law then this could, at least theoretically, be corrected.

However, by the reign of Henry III there was a growing fear that there were too many writs and that this would lead to the undeserving obtaining legal remedies and the courts being flooded with litigation. This fear reached its zenith in 1258, when the nobles presented Henry with the Provisions of Oxford. This document stipulated that the writ system should not be expanded any further.

While this provided a temporary respite for the English legal system from a flood of claims, the rigidity of having to fit your claim within a suitable writ and the inability to create new writs quickly led to ossification and unfairness within the law. Fortunately there was a final option available to litigants denied access to the court system: they could petition the king in person as the fount of all justice. With kings having to spend their time on so many other competing issues, this duty was quickly passed on to the Chancellor, who was a senior advisor and key person in running the country. Traditionally the Chancellor was also a cleric and was not only concerned with the facts of the case but also with the fate of the souls of the litigants. When he heard petitions he would therefore give his judgment in accordance with good conscience. Nevertheless the decisions made by the Chancellor in his court of Chancery did much to ameliorate the harshness of the Common Law.

By doing this, however, the Court of Chancery was brought into conflict with the Common Law courts. Until the Judicature Acts of 1873-1875, the civil courts did not have a uniform or neatly defined structure. Instead they competed between themselves for cases as a means of funding their survival. This led to a problem in that an unsuccessful claim at Common Law might be given a remedy in the Court of Chancery. The question as to which decision should prevail was finally answered in the *Earl of Oxford's Case* 21 ER 485.

The Earl of Oxford's Case in Chancery **21 ER 485**

Panel: Coke CJ

Facts: In 1574 Magdalene College, Cambridge sold some land to Benedict Spinola, who then sold it to the Earl of Oxford. This land was considerably developed and 130 houses, among other things, were constructed on the land. On or about 1612 the Master of Magdalene College tried to regain the property for the college and during this time attempted to obtain possession of one of the 130 houses by undue means. The question was whether the Court of Chancery had jurisdiction to hear the claim by the Earl of Oxford. It was held that whenever there is a conflict between the rules of Common Law and Equity, the rules of Equity should always take precedence.

CHIEF JUSTICE COKE

First, As a Right in Law cannot die, no more can Equity in Chancery die, and therefore *nullus recedat a Cancellaria sine remedio*, 4 E. 4, 11, a. Therefore the Chancery is always open, and although the Term be adjourned the Chancery is not; for Conscience and Equity is always ready to render to every one their Due, and 9 E. 4, 11, a. The Chancery is only removable at the Will of the King and Chancellor; and by 27 E. 3, 15. The Chancellor must give Account to none but only to the King and Parliament.

Decipher
Archaic language

The Cause why there is a Chancery is, for that Mens Actions are so divers and infinite, That it is impossible to make any general Law which may aptly meet with every particular Act, and not fail in some Circumstances. …

But in this Case, upon the Matter there is no Judgment, but only a Discontinuance of the Suit, which gives no Possession; and altho' to prosecute Law and Equity together be a Veration; yet voluntarily to attempt the Law in a doubtful Case, and after to resort to Equity, is neither strange nor unreasonable.

But take it as a Judgment to all Intents; then I answer,

That in this Case there is no Opposition to the Judgment; neither will the Truth or Justice of the Judgment be examined in this Court, nor any Circumstance depending thereupon; but the same is justified and approv'd; and therefore a Judgment is no Let to examine it in Equity, so as all the Truth of the Judgment, &c., be (not) examin'd. …

In Chancery upon a Recognizance, a Capias may be awarded, and the Precedents of that Court shall close up the Mouths of the Judges of the Common Law, notwithstanding the Statute of Magna Charta, cap. 29. *Quod nullus liber homo capiatur aut imprisonetur nisi per legale Judicium Parium suorum vel per Legem Terræ.* And so it was adjudged in Clement Parson's Case, 21 Eliz. in the Exchequer, which you may see in 8 Coke, 142, and 25 Eliz. in Martin and Bye's Case, and in 7 Jac. in Com. Banco, Higham's Case, and Kilway's Case vouched to be adjudged, 9 Co 29. Vide Doctor and Student, 306 a, and every Court at Westminster ought to take Notice of the Usages and Customs of the Rest of the Courts at Westminster, which are as a Law to those Courts, and of which the Common Law takes Notice. …

...The Chancellor sits in Chancery according to an absolute and uncontrolable Power, and is to judge according to that which is alledged and proved; but the Judges of the Common Law are to judge according to a strict and ordinary (or limited) Power...

There was no need to make a judgment upon the specific facts of the case as the suit had been discontinued by this stage. However, the essence of Coke CJ's judgment is that whenever there is a conflict between the Common Law and Equity, then Equity will take preference over the Common Law rules.

Following the Judicature Acts 1873-1875 we now have a single High Court, Court of Appeal and (since October 2009) Supreme Court, which have replaced the various Common Law courts and the Court of Chancery. Instead each court now has the ability to resort to equity in order to do justice between the parties. However, a consequence of Equity being a separate body of rules for so long is that there are a body of rules which have enabled a more sophisticated way of dealing with property than the Common Law allowed. This body of rules has also developed over time and has culminated in the law of trusts.

The key advantage of the trust over what can be done with property at Common Law is the flexibility with what can be done with property when a trust is used. For more detail on this, please refer to Chapter 1 of the *Equity and Trusts Manual*. Trusts nowadays play a pivotal role in the commercial world. Indeed, they are so prominent that it is practically impossible to calculate the number of trust funds in existence world wide, or the combined worth of all the assets held under these trusts. The importance of trusts has been even been noted outside of Common Law legal systems as far back as the 1930s by the noted French commentator Pierre Lepaulle. This is particularly noteworthy as France is a civil law system, in which traditionally it is impossible to have split ownership rights in the way that trustees and beneficiaries do.

Pierre Lepaulle, Traité théorique et pratique des trusts en droit interne, en droit fiscal et en droit international, Paris (1932), p.113.

Thus from settlement of the greatest of wars down to the simplest inheritance on death, from the most audacious Wall Street scheme down to the protection of grandchildren, the trust can see marching before it the motley procession of the whole of human endeavour: dreams of peace, commercial imperialism, attempts to strangle competition or to reach paradise, hatred or philanthropy, love of one's family or the desire to strip it of everything after one's death, all those in the procession being dressed either in robes or in rags, and either crowned in a halo or walking with a grin. The trust is the guardian angel of the Anglo-Saxon, accompanying him everywhere, impassively, from the cradle to the grave.

1.2 The Nature of Trustee and Beneficiary Rights in a Trust

Once a trust has been created the settlor can no longer have a role to play in the trust as a settlor specifically. The legal title has been transferred to the trustee and the equitable title is held by the beneficiary. The trustee and beneficiary are therefore the only parties within the trust relationship. As the trustee has legal title to the trust assets, this means the trustee has power as to how those assets are used, such as how they are invested, or to whom they are transferred. However, the trustee cannot deal with the trust property freely. Instead, the trustee has active duties regarding what is to be done with the trust assets. The flip side of these trustee duties are the rights of the beneficiary. The beneficiary's rights not only assert the fact the trustee is not an absolute owner of the property, but also that the ultimate control of the trust assets is in the hands of the beneficiary. The clearest example of this ultimate control is the ability of the beneficiary to collapse the trust and take trust assets as an absolute owner, even in circumstances where the settlor did not want this to happen.

Saunders v Vautier 49 ER 533

Panel: Lord Langdale MR

Facts: In his will Richard Wright left his stock in the East India Company to be held on trust for Daniel Vautier. The income generated from the stock was to be accumulated and this income together with the stock itself to be transferred to Vautier as absolute owner when he was 25. When Vautier was 21 (the age of majority at the time) he applied to receive the stock and the income. The trustee, Saunders, contested this, stating that Vautier would only become entitled to the stock and the income according to the terms of the trust. It was held that Vautier became entitled to the property of the trust as soon as he was an adult and as long as he was of full mental capacity.

> LORD LANGDALE MR
>
> I think the principle has been repeatedly acted upon; and where a legacy is directed to accumulate for a certain period, or where the payment is postponed, the legatee, if he has an absolute indefeasible interest in the legacy, is not bound to wait until the expiration of that period, but may require payment the moment he is competent to give a valid discharge.

Vautier was therefore allowed to take the stock and the income immediately, despite wishes to the contrary in Wright's will. The rule in *Saunders v Vautier* from this case is that once the beneficiary is of full age and capacity the terms of the trust should be secondary to the law's treatment of people as autonomous individuals. The law of trusts should not, therefore, treat sane adults as if they were children. Therefore, once beneficiaries are adults they should be treated as being capable of running their own affairs, including their property rights.

The strict legal principle, however, is quite narrow; taken literally the rule in *Saunders v Vautier* will only apply where the sole beneficiary is absolutely entitled to the property, is of full age and is of full mental capacity. Subsequent case law has extended the rule to trusts where there are multiple beneficiaries. By extending the rule in this way, however, two further questions arise. First, if the trust is a fixed trust, where the beneficiary has a fixed share of the trust assets, can they take absolute ownership of that specific part of the trust assets? Second, if the trust is a discretionary trust, where it is uncertain what amount of the trust assets each beneficiary will receive, can all the beneficiaries agree to take absolute ownership of the assets under the rule in *Saunders v Vautier* despite the uncertainty?

With regard to the fixed trust question, there are two High Court decisions that give some guiding principles.

Stephenson (Inspector of Taxes) v Barclays Bank Trust Co Ltd [1975] 1 WLR 882

Panel: Walton J

Statute: Finance Act 1965 s 22

Facts: In his will Sir Richard Winfrey made Barclays Bank his executors and trustees. His will provided, among other things, for annuities to be given to his daughters during their widowhood. These assets were then to be held on trust in equal shares for all of his grandchildren who were alive at the testator's death that reached the age of 21.

A subsequent deed of arrangement modified this arrangement so that an extra fund was added to the assets used by the annuities. Upon these extra assets being added to the annuities the widows would not be entitled to any of the other trust assets. The trustees did not transfer any of those assets to the grandchildren. The Inland Revenue claimed that the trust was liable to capital gains tax as a consequence of this deed of arrangement. The trustees resisted this claim, stating that since the grandchildren were not capable of overriding the terms of the trust by becoming absolute owners of the property there could be no such disposal that would attract capital gains tax.

It was held that the grandchildren were together entitled to the trust assets and therefore the trust was liable to capital gains tax.

> MR JUSTICE WALTON
>
> Now it is trite law that the persons who between them hold the entirety of the beneficial interests in any particular trust fund are as a body entitled to direct the trustees how that trust fund is to be dealt with, and this is obviously the legal territory from which that definition derives. ... I think it may be desirable to state what I conceive to be certain elementary principles.
>
> (1) In a case where the persons who between them hold the entirety of the beneficial interests in any particular trust fund are all *sui juris* and acting together, ("the beneficial interest holders"), they are entitled to direct the trustees how the trust fund may be dealt with. (2) This does not mean, however, that they can at one and the same time override

the pre-existing trusts and keep them in existence. ... (3) Nor, I think, are the beneficial interest holders entitled to direct the trustees as to the particular investment they should make of the trust fund. I think this follows for the same reasons as the above. Moreover, it appears to me that once the beneficial interest holders have determined to end the trust they are not entitled, unless by agreement, to the further services of the trustees. Those trustees can of course be compelled to hand over the entire trust assets to any person or persons selected by the beneficiaries against a proper discharge, but they cannot be compelled, unless they are in fact willing to comply with the directions, to do anything else with the trust fund which they are not in fact willing to do. (4) Of course, the rights of the beneficial interest holders are always subject to the right of the trustees to be fully protected against such matters as duty, taxes, costs or other outgoings; for example, the rent under a lease which the trustees have properly accepted as part of the trust property.

So much for the rights of the beneficial interest holders collectively. When the situation is that a single person who is sui juris has an absolutely vested beneficial interest in a share of the trust fund, his rights are not, I think, quite as extensive as those of the beneficial interest holders as a body. In general, he is entitled to have transferred to him (subject, of course, always to the same rights of the trustees as I have already mentioned above) an aliquot share of each and every asset of the trust fund which presents no difficulty so far as division is concerned. This will apply to such items as cash, money at the bank or an unsecured loan, Stock Exchange securities and the like. However, as regards land, certainly, in all cases, as regards shares in a private company in very special circumstances ... and possibly (although the logic of the addition in fact escapes me) mortgage debts ... the situation is not so simple, and even a person with a vested interest in possession in an aliquot share of the trust fund may have to wait until the land is sold, and so forth, before being able to call upon the trustees as of right to account to him for his share of the assets. ...

 Alert

Thus the conclusion of the whole matter appears to me to be that when the deed of family arrangement was executed the two grandchildren became, for the purposes of capital gains tax, jointly absolutely entitled as against the trustees of their grandfather's will trusts to the remaining residue of the estate not thereby appropriated to answer their aunts' annuities within the meaning of section 22 (5) of the Finance Act 1965, and paragraph 9 of Schedule 19 to the Finance Act 1969; and that, consequent thereupon, the trustees are, by virtue of section 25 (3), deemed for the purposes of capital gains tax to have disposed of the whole of such remaining residue and immediately reacquired the same in their capacity as trustees for a consideration equal to its market value. I have already indicated that the figure of £10,000 is purely notional, and the actual figures will now remain to be worked out by the parties.

It must be noted, as Walton J did at the end of his judgment, that on the facts of this case the trustees were only liable to capital gains tax on a few small parcels of unquoted shares and some land. However, this case is authority for the suggestion that beneficiaries of fixed trusts are able to become absolute owners of their specific part of the trust as long as there is no problem in dividing the assets. While land is clearly a type of property that is hard to divide up, another important example is shares within a private company. Therefore, where a trust has shares in a private company and one of the beneficiaries has a fixed interest in a majority of the shares, the court will not automatically allow that beneficiary to take the shares absolutely.

Lloyds Bank Plc v Duker and Others [1987] 1 WLR 1324

Panel: John Mowbray QC sitting as a deputy High Court judge

Facts: In his will Rowland Smith made Lloyds Bank his personal representative. Among his assets were 999 of 1,000 shares in a private company (Rowland Smith Hotels Ltd) that owned a hotel in Torquay. These shares were subject to a partial intestacy (some of the legatees had died without leaving any heirs to take their shares in the company) and therefore the family entered into a deed of arrangement. The testator's wife, Freda Smith, was to receive 46/80ths of the shares and the remaining amount was to be divided among the other five beneficiaries of Mr Smith's will in proportion to the amount of specified assets they were entitled to. Freda Smith wanted to become absolute owner of her shares in the company, but no transfer was made before she died. In her will she left her shares to Mr Dukar, the managing director of the company controlling the hotel. Mr Dukar then asked Lloyds Bank to transfer the shares to him absolutely. The other beneficiaries objected to this and so Lloyds Bank applied to the court as to whether it had to comply with Mr Dukar's request or whether all of the company shares should be sold on the open market. It was held that Mr Dukar was not entitled to take his shares absolutely as this would give him an unfair advantage over the other beneficiaries.

JOHN MOWBRAY QC

The whole net estate is ready for immediate distribution. I assume for the purpose of answering the question that anyone entitled to an aliquot part of such an estate as this is normally entitled to insist on a corresponding part of any easily divisible property being distributed to him as it is, rather than the whole property being sold and the money proceeds distributed. Other beneficiaries, if they like, can ask the executors to sell their parts of the property, or they can do it for themselves.

What the other beneficiaries say here is that if the shares are transferred out in the 1/80th fractions, Mr Duker will not take 46/80ths of the total value received by all the beneficiaries as a group, but much more, because a majority holding is worth more per share than a minority holding. ...

What is more, none of the minority holdings can be expected to participate in dividends for the foreseeable future, if Mr Duker takes 574 shares. That appears from a letter which his (and the company's) accountants wrote to Mrs. Arnold Smith on 13 February 1986. I shall read it. It says:

'Dear Mrs. Smith,

Palace Hotel, Torquay — Shares

"Further to our letter of 21 January, our client wishes us to provide You with further information concerning the shares in Rowland Smith Hotels Ltd. — 1. It is the opinion of the executors that the shares in the company should be allocated pro rata to the residuary legatees of the estate of Rowland Smith. 2. This opinion is supported by counsel's opinion which has been reiterated recently despite the alternative advice which has been given to some of the 'minority' beneficiaries. 3. We believe that in the light of counsel's opinion and the offer made by our client, the court would be unlikely to recommend a sale of the hotel but should it take this step there are doubts as to whether such a sale could be enforced having regard to the structure of the company. 4. Although profitability is now running at a more satisfactory level, in order to maintain the hotel in a competitive position, the directors have embarked on a number of major projects. Accordingly, profits will need to be retained in the business for the foreseeable future and shareholders are unlikely, therefore, to receive dividends during this time. 5. In view of the lack of good dividend prospects, the value of the minority shareholdings in the company is certainly substantially lower than the offer of £403 per share recently made to You by our client."

As I understand it, Mr Duker offered £403 a share to all the other beneficiaries, and has subsequently increased this offer to £510 a share. (The minority beneficiaries' counsel confirmed this on instructions.) At that price, the minority's 425 shares would be worth a total of £216750. The minority could, on any view, insist on their joint holding of 425 shares being sold as a single block, and I think that en bloc they might fetch more than that. None the less, the want of any dividends for the foreseeable future, and the inability of the buyer of any minority block to force a dividend would be bound to have a definite depressing effect on the value of the holding.

Mr Duker could not be expected to join in a winding up resolution, and he would not need dividends, because he could pay himself a salary as managing director.

So, though the state of the evidence does not enable me to make any precise finding about values, I can find this much, which is all I need for the present purpose: the value per share of a holding of 574 shares in the company is markedly higher than the value per share of a holding even of 425 shares. The result is that, if Mr Duker takes 574 shares, the value of what he takes will be markedly more than 46/80ths of the aggregate values of his and the other holdings.

Is that finding of fact enough to override what I am assuming is the normal rule by which Mr Duker would be entitled to call for a transfer of 574 of the shares? It seems clear to me that such a transfer would not be in accordance with Mr Smith's will. When he gave one half of his residuary estate to his wife and the other half to his brothers and sisters and others, he must have meant half by value. The partial intestacy does not affect the meaning of the will. No one is suggesting that the shares should be distributed otherwise than in the 1/80th fractions.

To bring about a fair division in the 1/80th fractions, according to values, it would be necessary for the bank to sell all 999 shares and distribute the money proceeds in those fractions. ...

Are the circumstances in the present case such as to require the bank to sell all 999 shares, rather than distributing 574 of them to Mr Duker? To answer this question, I need to see what kind of circumstances would exclude his normal right to have this aliquot part of the shares distributed to him. ...

...The operative reason is that, if the shares were transferred out in the 1/80th fractions, Mr Duker would get a greater value per share than the other beneficiaries and so would get more than his 46/80ths of the total value received by the beneficiaries as a body.

I have not had much help from dicta in the authorities...

I can, though, get some help from another general principle. I mean the principle that trustees are bound to hold an even hand among their beneficiaries, and not favour one as against another... Of course Mr Duker must have a larger part than the other beneficiaries. But if he takes 46/80ths of the shares he will be favoured beyond what Mr Smith intended, because his shares will each be worth more than the others. The trustees' duty to hold an even hand seems to indicate that they should sell all 999 shares instead.

 Alert

Mr Harrod pointed out that if Mr Duker's shares are sold, immediate capital gains tax will be incurred on the unrealised capital appreciation which has accrued since the death of Mrs. Smith (or it may be Mr Smith) whereas if the bank transfers them to Mr Duker as a residuary legatee no capital gains tax will be immediately payable. This is something I must take into account, though I think it might be tempered to some extent by a sale of the whole company realising more per share than even a majority holding of 574 shares. ...

In all the circumstances, to prevent the unfairness which would result from a transfer of 574 of the shares to Mr Duker, and to ensure that he takes 46/80ths of the residuary estate measured by value, I consider that the bank should not transfer any of the shares to him, but should sell all 999 on the general market, Mr Duker being left free to become a buyer.

From these cases it is clear that a fixed trust beneficiary does not have an automatic right to take a share of the trust assets absolutely by using the rule in *Saunders v Vautier*. Instead, the court has to consider whether the property can easily be divided, and whether an absolute transfer would be to the detriment of the other beneficiaries.

The comments made in *Dukar* indicate exceptions to the general rule rather than negating the rule absolutely. Therefore, fixed interest beneficiaries do theoretically have the right to exercise *Saunders v Vautier* rights, although these might be prevented from being used depending upon the type of property and the facts of the case.

The situation is less clear, however, with regard to beneficiaries under discretionary trusts. All that is directly relevant upon this point is conflicting *obiter* from two cases, which leaves an important and therefore unfortunate lacuna in the law.

Re Smith [1928] Ch 915

Panel: Romer J

Facts: Mr Aspinall left one fourth of his residuary estate to be held on discretionary trust for his widow and any children she may have. The widow, who was well beyond child bearing age, her two surviving children and the legal personal representatives of the deceased child all joined in executing a mortgage assigning all the interests they would have taken under the will. The Public Trustee went to court to see if the property under a discretionary trust was capable of being assigned in this way. It was held that as all the discretionary beneficiaries had joined together in making the assignment, the property was capable of being assigned in this way.

MR JUSTICE ROMER

... The question I have to determine is whether the Legal and General Assurance Company are now entitled to call upon the trustees to pay the whole of the income to them. It will be observed from what I have said that the whole of this share is now held by the trustees upon trusts under which they are bound to apply the whole income and eventually pay over or apply the whole capital to Mrs Aspinall and the three children or some or one of them. So far as the income is concerned they are obliged to pay it or apply it for her benefit or to pay it or apply it for the benefit of the children. So far as regards the capital they have a discretion to pay it and to apply it for her benefit and, subject to that, they must hold it upon trust for the children. Mrs Aspinall, the two surviving children and the representatives of the deceased child are between them entitled to the whole fund. In those circumstances it appears to me, notwithstanding the discretion which is reposed in the trustees, under which discretion they could select one or more of the people I have mentioned as recipients of the income, and might apply part of the capital for the benefit of Mrs Aspinall and so take it away from the children, that the four of them, if they were all living, could come to the Court and say to the trustees: "Hand over the fund to us." It appears to me that that this is in accordance ... with principle. What is the principle? As I understand it is this. Where there is a trust under which trustees have a discretion as to applying the whole or part of a fund to or for the benefit of a particular person, that particular person cannot come to the trustees, and demand the fund; for the whole fund has not been given to him but only so much as the trustees think fit to let him have. But when the trustees have no discretion as to the amount of the fund to be applied, the fact that the trustees have a discretion as to the method in which the whole of the fund shall be applied for the benefit of the particular person does not prevent that particular person from coming and saying: "Hand over the fund to me." ...

There will, consequently, be a declaration that, in the events which have happened, the plaintiff is bound to pay the whole of the income of the one-fourth to the defendant society during the lifetime of Mrs Aspinall, or until the mortgage is discharged.

 Alert

Note that since there was no taking of the property absolutely by any of the discretionary beneficiaries, this is not a case where the rule in *Saunders v Vautier* is directly used. This case is therefore strictly only an *obiter* comment upon how *Saunders*

v Vautier might apply. What is clear though is that Romer J clearly held that the fact the trust is discretionary should not interfere with the rights of the discretionary beneficiaries if they all agree to embark on a course of action with the trust property and they are all of full age and full capacity.

However, the question of whether discretionary beneficiaries have any right to trust property before they are selected by the trustees has not been consistently answered in this way.

Gartside and Another v Inland Revenue Commissioners [1968] AC 553

Panel: Lord Reid, Lord Morris of Borth-Y-Gest, Lord Hodson, Lord Guest and Lord Wilberforce

Statute: Finance Act 1940 s 43

Facts: In his will Thomas Gartside left one fourth of his residuary estate to be held on discretionary trust for his son John, John's wife if he married and any grandchildren. When John died the assets were then held on trust in equal shares for any male grandchildren who reached the age of 21 or any female grandchildren who reached the age of 21 or were married. John married and he and his wife had twin sons.

Before John died the trustees advanced £23,500 to each of the grandchildren. There was clearly a passing of property when John died, as each of the grandchildren then had a fixed share in the assets. However, the Inland Revenue claimed there was also a definite interest held by the grandchildren before John died, when the trust was a discretionary trust. Therefore, when the advancement of £23,500 was made to each grandchild, this was liable to estate duty under the Finance Act 1940 s 43.

The question before the court was strictly whether the interest each grandchild had was a 'measurable interest' within the specific ambit of the Finance Act.

It was held that as the amount was not measurable it was not liable to estate duty. However, Lords Reid and Wilberforce made comments in their judgments that can be considered relevant to the application of the rule in *Saunders v Vautier*.

LORD REID

... [A] right to require trustees to consider whether they will pay you something does not enable you to claim anything. If the trustees do decide to pay you something, you do not get it by reason of having the right to have your case considered: you get it only because the trustees have decided to give it to you. ...

LORD WILBERFORCE

I have said that no one of the discretionary beneficiaries had at the relevant time any right to receive any income, but this is not the whole of the matter. It is also necessary to appreciate that the discretionary beneficiaries taken together had no right to receive any or, a fortiori, all of the income. Two of them were infants but even if they had been of age they could not, with their parents, have called upon the trustees to pay them the income of any year; the reason being that the trustees had power to accumulate so much as they did not distribute, which might be the whole, for the possible benefit of persons unborn. To describe them as "the only people who could during the relevant period obtain any benefit from the property or have any beneficial enjoyment of it" may be misleading, unless one bears in mind that, singly or collectively, they had no right in any year to receive a penny. ...

The *obiter* suggestion of *Smith* is preferable to that of *Gartside*. This is because their Lordships' judgments were greatly influenced by the notion that further grandchildren might be born, whose rights in the property would be affected by those already alive if they were said to be able to use *Saunders v Vautier*. This particular point must be correct; if the number of beneficiaries can be increased in the future then it is not possible for them all to come together and agree to take the property absolutely. However, where the number of beneficiaries is fixed there is no risk of any beneficiaries losing out through use of *Saunders v Vautier*. The trustees have discretion as to the distribution of assets to beneficiaries, but they are limited to only being able to select from the list of beneficiaries. It is certain, therefore, that whenever a discretion is made it will benefit the class of beneficiaries as a whole. There is no reason to prevent the class, if they all agree and are of full age and mental capacity, from being able to bring the trust to an end and take the property absolutely.

Therefore, *Gartside* should be considered as useful *obiter* for an exceptional circumstance justifying deviation from the general availability of *Saunders v Vautier*, rather than authority for a blanket denial of availability of the rule itself.

1.3 An Important Distinction: Trusts and Powers

Since the beginning of the 20th century trusts have become more complex as a means of combating increasingly sophisticated rules of taxation. Fixed trust beneficiaries came to be seen as having a definite interest in the future, which could be taxed. Consequently, the discretionary trust was conceived to combat this. As tax law evolved to touch upon discretionary trusts, the reaction was to make those capable of benefiting objects of powers of appointment rather than beneficiaries.

Powers of appointment (sometimes called 'mere powers') have a number of extremely important differences from either fixed or discretionary trusts. The rules regarding powers were clarified by Templeman J in *Re Manisty's Settlement Trusts* [1974] Ch 17, which was endorsed and developed by Sir Robert Megarry V-C in *Re Hay's Settlement Trusts* [1982] 1 WLR 202.

Re Hay's Settlement Trusts [1982] 1 WLR 202

Panel: Sir Robert Megarry V-C

Facts: In clause 4 of her deed of settlement Lady Hay settled property for people or purposes as the trustees may appoint by deed within 21 years of the date the settlement was created, with the proviso that no appointment should be made to Lady Hay, any husband of hers, or any trustee or past trustee. If no appointment was made the property was to be held on trust for Lady Hay's nieces and nephews alive at the time the settlement was created.

In clause 2 of a subsequent deed of appointment Lady Hay further authorised the trustees to hold on trust any unappointed income for the benefit of 'any person or persons whatsoever or to any charity,' with the exception of the settlor, any husband of hers and any present or past trustee.

The trustees went to court to find out whether clause 4 was valid, and whether 'any person or persons whatsoever' as allowed under clause 2 was a valid class for a discretionary trust. It was found that clause 4 was valid but clause 2 of the subsequent deed was void.

SIR ROBERT MEGARRY V-C

Two provisions of these instruments are at the centre of the dispute. They are, first, the power of appointment conferred by what I have called the first main limb of clause 4 of the settlement; and, second, the discretionary trust of income under clause 2 of the deed of appointment. Under the power of appointment the trustees were to hold the trust fund on trust for "such persons or purposes" as the trustees should appoint before May 7, 1979, subject to excluding the settlor, her husband and trustees or former trustees, by virtue of the second proviso. Such a provision raises obvious questions about the enormous class of persons who were possible objects of the power: everyone in the world is included save for a handful of persons. If that power is invalid, then of course the appointment made under it must also be invalid, and no other appointment could ever have been valid. The result would therefore be that the second main limb of clause 4 would take effect, and the nieces and nephews living at the date of the settlement would have become entitled to the trust fund in equal shares *ab initio*. ...

The starting point must be to consider whether the power created by the first limb of clause 4 of the settlement is valid. ... The essential point is whether a power for trustees to appoint to anyone in the world except a handful of specified persons is valid. Such a power will be perfectly valid if given to a person who is not in a fiduciary position: the difficulty arises when it is given to trustees, for they are under certain fiduciary duties in relation to the power, and to a limited degree they are subject to the control of the courts. ...

In *Re Manisty's Settlement* [1974] Ch 17, a settlement gave trustees a discretionary power to apply the trust fund for the benefit of a small class of the settlor's near relations, save that any member of a smaller "excepted class" was to be excluded from the class of beneficiaries. The trustees were also given power at their absolute discretion to declare that any person, corporation or charity (except a member of the excepted class or a trustee) should be included in the class of beneficiaries. Templeman J. held that this power to extend the class of beneficiaries was valid. ... In general, I respectfully agree with Templeman J.

I propose to approach the matter by stages. First, it is plain that if a power of appointment is given to a person who is not in a fiduciary position, there is nothing in the width of the power which invalidates it per se. The power may be a special power with a large class of persons as objects; the power may be what is called a "hybrid" power, or an "intermediate" power, authorising appointment to anyone save a specified number or class of persons; or the power may be a general power. Whichever it is, there is nothing in the number of persons to whom an appointment may be made which will invalidate it. The difficulty comes when the power is given to trustees as such, in that the number of objects may interact with the fiduciary duties of the trustees and their control by the court. ...

That brings me to the second point, namely, the extent of the fiduciary obligations of trustees who have a mere power vested in them, and how far the court exercises control over them in relation to that power. In the case of a trust, of course, the trustee is bound to execute it, and if he does not, the court will see to its execution. A mere power is very different. Normally the trustee is not bound to exercise it, and the court will not compel him to do so. That, however, does not mean that he can simply fold his hands and ignore it, for normally he must from time to time consider whether or not to exercise the power, and the court may direct him to do this.

Alert

When he does exercise the power, he must, of course (as in the case of all trusts and powers) confine himself to what is authorised, and not go beyond it. But that is not the only restriction. Whereas a person who is not in a fiduciary position is free to exercise the power in any way that he wishes, unhampered by any fiduciary duties, a trustee to whom, as such, a power is given is bound by the duties of his office in exercising that power to do so in a responsible manner according to its purpose. It is not enough for him to refrain from acting capriciously; he must do more. He must "make such a survey of the range of objects or possible beneficiaries ..." as will enable him to carry out his fiduciary duty. He must find out "the permissible area of selection and then consider responsibly, in individual cases, whether a contemplated beneficiary was within the power and whether, in relation to other possible claimants, a particular grant was appropriate": *Re Baden (No 1)* [1971] AC 424, 449, 457 *per* Lord Wilberforce. ...

The last proposition, relating to the survey and consideration, at first sight gives rise to some difficulty. It is now well settled that no mere power is invalidated by it being impossible to ascertain every object of the power; provided the language is clear enough to make it possible to say whether any given individual is an object of the power, it need not be possible to compile a complete list of every object... .

Alert

That brings me to the third point. How is the duty of making a responsible survey and selection to be carried out in the absence of any complete list of objects? ...[P]lainly the requirements for a mere power cannot be more stringent than those for a discretionary trust, the duty, I think, may be expressed along the following lines... . The trustee must not simply proceed to exercise the power in favour of such of the objects as happen to be at hand or claim his attention. He must first consider what persons or classes of persons are objects of the power within the definition in the settlement or will. In doing this, there is no need to compile a complete list of the objects, or even to make an accurate assessment of

Alert

Alert

the number of them: what is needed is an appreciation of the width of the field, and thus whether a selection is to be made merely from a dozen or, instead, from thousands or millions... . Only when the trustee has applied his mind to the size of the problem "should he then consider in individual cases whether, in relation to other possible claimants, a particular grant is appropriate. In doing this, no doubt he should not prefer the undeserving to the deserving; but he is not required to make an exact calculation whether, as between deserving claimants, A is more deserving than B... .

If I am right in these views, the duties of a trustee which are specific to a mere power seem to be threefold. Apart from the obvious duty of obeying the trust instrument, and in particular of making no appointment that is not authorised by it, the trustee must, first, consider periodically whether or not he should exercise the power; second, consider the range of objects of the power; and third, consider the appropriateness of individual appointments. I do not assert that this list is exhaustive; but as the authorities stand it seems to me to include the essentials, so far as relevant to the case before me.

Alert

...

From what I have said it will be seen that I cannot see any ground upon which the power in question can be said to be void. Certainly it is not void for linguistic or semantic uncertainty; there is no room for doubt in the definition of those who are or are not objects of the power. Nor can I see that the power is administratively unworkable. ... Nor do I think that the power is void as being capricious. In *Re Manisty's Settlement* [1974] Ch 17, 27, Templeman J. appears to be suggesting that a power to benefit "residents of Greater London" is void as being capricious "because the terms of the power negative any sensible intention on the part of the settlor." In saying that, I do not think that the judge had in mind a case in which the settlor was, for instance, a former chairman of the Greater London Council, as subsequent words of his on that page indicate. In any case, as he pointed out earlier in the page, this consideration does not apply to intermediate powers, where no class which could be regarded as capricious has been laid down. Nor do I see how the power in the present case could be invalidated as being too vague, a possible ground of invalidity considered in *Re Manisty's Settlement*, at p. 24. Of course, if there is some real vice in a power, and there are real problems of administration or execution, the court may have to hold the power invalid: but I think that the court should be slow to do this. Dispositions ought if possible to be upheld, and the court ought not to be astute to find grounds upon which a power can be invalidated. Naturally, if it is shown that a power offends against some rule of law or equity, then it will be held to be void: but a power should not be held void upon a peradventure. In my judgment, the power conferred by clause 4 of the settlement is valid.

Alert

With that, I turn to the discretionary trust of income under clause 2 of the deed of appointment. Apart from questions of the validity of the trust per se, there is the prior question whether the settlement enabled the trustees to create such a trust, or, for that matter, the power set out in clause 1 of the deed of appointment. The power conferred by clause 4 of the settlement provides that the trustees are to hold the trust fund on trust "for such persons or purposes for such interests and with such gifts over and (if for persons) with such provisions for their respective maintenance or advancement at the discretion of the trustees or of any other persons" as the trustees shall appoint. Clause 2 of the deed of appointment provides that the trustees are to hold the trust fund on trust to pay the income "to or for the benefit of any person or persons whatsoever ... or to any charity" in such manner and shares and proportions as the trustees think fit. I need say nothing about purposes or charities as no question on them has arisen. The basic question is whether the appointment has designated the "persons" to whom the appointment is made.

Looked at as a matter of principle, my answer would be "No." There is no such person to be found in clause 2 of the deed of appointment: instead, there is merely the mechanism whereby a person or persons may be ascertained from time to time by the exercise of the discretion given to the trustees. If that mechanism is operated, then persons may emerge who will be entitled: but they will emerge not by virtue of any exercise of the power in the settlement but by virtue of the exercise of the discretion in the deed of appointment. That seems to me to be a plain case of delegation: the power in the settlement is not being exercised by appointing the persons who are to benefit but by creating a discretionary trust under which the discretionary trustees will from time to time select those who will benefit. True, the appointor under the settlement and the trustees under the discretionary trust are the same persons: but I do not think that this affects the matter. The power in the settlement is a power to appoint to persons and not a power to nominate those (whether the appointors or anyone else) who will select persons who are to benefit; and I do not see how identity in the appointors and nominators can alter the fact that the mechanisms set up by the deed of appointment differs from anything authorised by the settlement. ...

I do not think that the fact that the power is an intermediate power excludes it from the rule against delegation. On the contrary, the fact that the power is vested in trustees subjects it to that rule unless there is something in the settlement to exclude it. I can see nothing in the settlement which purports to authorise any such appointment or to exclude the normal rule against delegation. In my judgment, both on principle and on authority clause 2 of the deed of appointment is void as being an excessive execution of the power. ...

I consider that the duties of trustees under a discretionary trust are more stringent than those of trustees under a power of appointment (see, for example, *In Re Baden (No. 1)* at p. 457), and as at present advised I think that I would, if necessary, hold that an intermediate trust such as that in the present case is void as being administratively unworkable. In my view there is a difference between a power and a trust in this respect. The essence of that difference, I think, is that beneficiaries under a trust have rights of enforcement which mere objects of a power lack. ...

Sir Robert Megarry V-C held that the discretionary trust under clause 2 was void. He therefore held that, upon the expiration of the 21-year time period as set out in clause 4, the nieces and nephews that were alive at the time the settlement was created became entitled to the trust fund.

Further Reading

Penner J E, *The Law of Trusts*, (6th edition), pp 1 – 48

2

The Three Certainties

Topic List

Introduction

A trustee has a duty to look after trust property for the beneficiary, upon the terms set out by the settlor. It is therefore vital that the trustee knows the terms of the trust, the property subject to it and the beneficiary. These elements are known as the 'three certainties': certainty of words or intention to create a trust; certainty of subject matter; and certainty of object or beneficiary. If these are not sufficiently clear there are two serious consequences: first, the trustee may inadvertently breach the trust; second, the court may feel unable to assist it if it is unsure what it is being asked to enforce. Therefore, in order to be valid and enforceable, an express private trust must be sufficiently certain. A court, if asked to pronounce on the validity and enforceability of a trust, will construe the trust document as a whole. This is because it is hard to separate the certainties: they overlap, but for ease of analysis they are discussed individually.

2.1 Certainty of Intention

In deciding whether there is certainty of intention to create a trust, the court will look at the overall intention of the settlor, rather than at the exact wording. Words can of course be evidence of intention, but all of the circumstances will be considered.

In re Adams and the Kensington Vestry (1884) 27 Ch D 394

Panel: Baggally, Cotton and Lindley LJJ

Facts: In his will, George Smith left his property 'unto and to the absolute use of my wife Harriet, in full confidence that she will do what is right as to the disposal thereof between my children either in her lifetime or by will after her decease.' The question was whether Harriet was absolutely entitled to the property and thus able to sell it, or whether she held it on trust for the children.

LORD JUSTICE COTTON

...[I]t seems to me perfectly clear what the testator intended. He leaves his wife his property absolutely, but what was in his mind was this: "I am the head of the family, and it is laid upon me to provide properly for the members of my family - my children: my widow will succeed me when I die, and I wish to put her in the position I occupied as the person who is to provide for my children." Not that he entails upon her any trust so as to bind her, but he simply says, in giving her this, I express to her, and call to her attention, the moral obligation which I myself had and which I feel that she is going to discharge. The motive of the gift is, in my opinion, not a trust imposed upon her by the gift in the will. He leaves the property to her; he knows that she will do what is right, and carry out the moral obligation which he thought lay on him, and on her if she survived him, to provide for the children.

He then looked at authority and at how the courts' attitude to interpretation of dispositions had changed:

...in the later cases, especially *Lambe v Eames* and *In re Hutchinson and Tenant*, both the Court of Appeal and the late Master of the Rolls shewed a desire really to find out what, upon the true construction, was the meaning of the testator, rather than to lay hold of certain words which in other wills had been held to create a trust, although on the will before them they were satisfied that that was not the intention. I have no hesitation in saying myself, that I think some of the older authorities went a great deal too far in holding that some particular words appearing in a will were sufficient to create a trust. Undoubtedly confidence, if the rest of the context shews that a trust is intended, may make a trust, but what we have to look at is the whole of the will which we have to construe, and if the confidence is that she will do what is right as regards the disposal of the property, I cannot say that that is, on the true construction of the will, a trust imposed upon her. Having regard to the later decisions, we must not extend the old cases in any way, or rely upon the mere use of any particular words, but, considering all the words which are used, we have to see what is their true effect, and what was the intention of the testator as expressed in his will. In my opinion, here he has expressed his will in such a way as not to shew an intention of imposing a trust on the wife, but on the contrary, in my opinion, he has shewn an intention to leave the property, as he says he does, to her absolutely.

 Alert

See also *Comiskey v Bowring-Hanbury* where the same wording was analysed but a different conclusion reached as the overall context differed.

Comiskey and Others v Bowring-Hanbury and Another [1905] AC 84

Panel: The Earl of Halsbury LC, Lord Macnaghten, Lord Davey, Lord James, Lord Robertson and Lord Lindley

Facts: By his will, Mr Hanbury left all his property to his wife Ellen 'absolutely in full confidence that she will make such use of it as I should have made myself and that at her death she will devise it to such one or more of my nieces as she may think fit and in default of any disposition by her thereof by her will or testament I hereby direct that all my estate and property acquired by her under this my will shall at her death be equally divided among the surviving said nieces.'

His widow, Ellen, asked the court whether she took the property by way of absolute gift, or whether her husband had intended her to hold it on trust for his seven nieces. The Court of Appeal held, by a majority, that no trust was created and that she took the property by way of absolute gift. As the gift over to the nieces was incompatible with an absolute gift to the widow, it was invalid. The nieces appealed.

The House of Lords, by a majority, reversed this decision. Their Lordships looked at the wording in the context of the will as a whole to find that the testator intended a life interest for Ellen, and after her death his nieces were entitled to the property equally, unless Ellen selected differently.

EARL OF HALSBURY LC

... he did not contemplate that during her lifetime she would have disposed of it in any way or placed upon it such an irrevocable character, either by way of settlement or anything else, that at the time when she died herself it would have passed away from her power of disposition. ... He does contemplate that she might make a will herself, and that those words, "in default of any disposition by her thereof by her will," ought to be read with the other words, so that what he is contemplating is, first of all, that the property is to remain capable of being left by her, and, secondly, that she may have made a will, but have made no disposition of that particular property which she has come into possession of under his will.

Then, ... he gives directions. I cannot think that if it was in his mind that she was to be absolute owner and to do what she pleased with it he would, after he had given her a complete power of disposition, use such a phrase as "I hereby direct." To my mind it is clear that he is contemplating that she shall have the full use of the property during her lifetime, and that after her death one or more of his nieces is to be the object of his bounty, and if his widow does not select one or more, then they are all to share alike. That, to my mind, is the meaning of the language. I do not stop to bring in any rules of law or any canons of construction. I look at the words merely as they stand in the will, and I think the natural and ordinary meaning of those words is what I have suggested.

LORD DAVEY

The words which have been so much commented upon, "in full confidence," are, in my opinion, neutral. I think it would be impossible to regard them as technical words in any sense. They are words which may or may not create a trust, and whether they do so or not must be determined by the context of the particular will in which you find them. In the present case I do not think it necessary to determine any such question.

... Reading the will without paying any attention to legal rules, and for the purpose only of seeking the testator's intention and the meaning of the words he used, it is obvious that he did not intend that his wife should have an absolute power to dispose of the estate in her lifetime or otherwise than by her will.

... The use of the word "absolutely," as defining the amount of the estate which is given to the wife, must of course be subject to any executory limitation or any other valid limitation or exception which you find engrafted on that estate in fee simple; therefore I attach no importance, or very little importance, to the use of the word "absolutely".

 Link
See Adams

 Alert

Thus, the court held that the wife was not free to deal with the property as she chose: there was a trust imposed upon her.

Paul v Constance [1977] 1 WLR 527

Panel: Cairns, Scarman and Bridge LJJ

Facts: Mrs Paul and Mr Constance lived together in the late 1960s and early 1970s while Mr Constance was still married. He received damages for a work-related injury which, as most people did not know they were not married, he paid into a deposit account in his sole name. Other money, including joint bingo winnings, was paid in. Mrs Paul had authority to withdraw funds, and money was used for joint purchases, then the remainder was shared. Mr Constance said to Mrs Paul on several occasions, 'the money is as much mine as yours'. He died intestate and his widow was administrator of his estate. Mrs Paul claimed the money in the account, on the ground that it had been held on express trust by Mr Constance for himself and Mrs Paul. The Court of Appeal upheld the decision of the judge at first instance: Mr Constance's words were held to be a clear oral declaration of trust, for the benefit of himself and Mrs Paul.

LORD JUSTICE SCARMAN

Alert

...we are dealing with simple people, unaware of the subtleties of equity, but understanding very well indeed their own domestic situation. It is, of course, right that one should consider the various things that were said and done by the plaintiff and the deceased during their time together against their own background and in their own circumstances.

He said that technical language was not needed, but all of the facts and circumstances must be considered:

When one bears in mind the unsophisticated character of the deceased and his relationship with the plaintiff during the last few years of his life, Mr. Wilson submits that the words that he did use on more than one occasion, "This money is as much yours as mine," convey clearly a present declaration that the existing fund was as much the plaintiff's as his own. The judge accepted that conclusion. I think that he was well justified in doing so and, indeed, I think that he was right to do so. There are, as Mr. Wilson reminded us, other features in the history of the relationship between the plaintiff and the deceased which support the interpretation of those words as an express declaration of trust. I have already described the interview with the bank manager when the account was opened. I have mentioned also the putting of the "bingo" winnings into the account and the one withdrawal for the benefit of both of them.

He did, however, acknowledge that it is difficult to pinpoint a specific moment of declaration.

These principles are not confined to personal and family arrangements.

In re Kayford Limited (in liquidation) [1975] 1 WLR 279

Panel: Megarry J

Facts: A mail order company sold soft furnishings. Customers paid in advance for goods ordered. The company had financial problems and wanted to protect the customers' money. It was paid into a dormant deposit account in the company's name, which was changed to a Customers' Trust Deposit account shortly before the company went into liquidation. The liquidators wanted to know whether the money in the account was part of the company's assets, or whether it was held on trust for the customers in proportion to their contributions.

MR JUSTICE MEGARRY

There is no doubt about the so-called 'three certainties' of a trust. The subject-matter to be held on trust is clear, and so are the beneficial interests therein, as well as the beneficiaries. As for the requisite certainty of words, it is well settled that a trust can be created without using the words 'trust' or 'confidence' or the like: the question is whether in substance a sufficient intention to create a trust has been manifested. ... I feel no doubt that here a trust was created. From the outset the advice (which was accepted) was to establish a trust account at the bank. The whole purpose of what was done was to ensure that the moneys remained in the beneficial ownership of those who sent them, and a trust is the obvious means of achieving this. No doubt the general rule is that if you send money to a company for goods which are not delivered, you are merely a creditor of the company unless a trust has been created. The sender may create a trust by using appropriate words when he sends the money (though I wonder how many do this, even if they are equity lawyers), or the company may do it by taking suitable steps on or before receiving the money. If either is done, the obligations in respect of the money are transformed from contract to property, from debt to trust. Payment into a separate bank account is a useful (though by no means conclusive) indication of an intention to create a trust, but of course there is nothing to prevent the company from binding itself by a trust even if there are no effective banking arrangements.

 Alert

Although in this case the judge concluded that there was a trust, he did say, *obiter*, different considerations might apply where trade creditors were involved.

2.2 Certainty of Subject Matter

Trusts can be declared over all types of property, but the specific property to be subject to the trust must be certain.

Sprange v Barnard (1789) 2 Bro CC 585

Panel: Lord Arden MR

Facts: Susannah Sprange made a valid will: '... for my husband Thomas Sprange, to bewill to him the sum of £300, ...for his sole use; and, at his death, the remaining part of what is left, that he does not want for his own wants and use, to be divided between ...[my brother and sisters].'

Thomas Sprange applied for a declaration that he was absolutely entitled to the £300. The court held that the property subject to the purported trust was not sufficiently certain to create a valid trust, and that therefore Thomas took the money absolutely.

LORD ARDEN MR

It is contended for the persons to whom it is given in remainder, that he shall only have it for his life, and that the words are strictly mandatory on him to dispose of it in a certain way; but it is only to dispose of what he has no occasion for; therefore, the question is, whether he may not call for the whole; and it seems to me perfectly clear on all the authorities, that he may. ...The property, and the person to whom it is to be given, must be certain, in order to raise a trust. Now here, the property ... is only what shall remain at his death.... it appears to me to be a trust which would be impossible to

 Link
See also *Palmer v Simmods* and *Boyce v Boyce* both of which deal with property which is not sufficiently certain to be the subject matter of a trust.

be executed. I must, therefore, declare him to be absolutely entitled to the £300, and decree it to be transferred to him.

Palmer v Simmonds (1854) 2 Drew 221

Panel: R T Kindersley V-C

Facts: Henrietta Roscoe made a will leaving the residue of her estate to Thomas Harrison'... for his own use and benefit, as I have full confidence in him, that if he should die without lawful issue he will, after providing for his widow during her life, leave the bulk of my said residuary estate unto...[four named people] equally.'

The executors asked whether the property to be subject to the trust was sufficiently certain. The Vice Chancellor found that there was the requisite intention (an expression of 'confidence' being sufficient at the time) and certain objects. However there was no certainty of subject-matter.

R T KINDERSLEY V-C

If she had said "my residuary estate," I must, according to the cases, have held that there was a trust. But the question is whether the words "the bulk of my residuary estate" mean the same thing as "my residuary estate," or anything precise and definite. The testatrix has here used a term which is not a legal term; a term which has not in law any appropriate meaning. ...

Then there is another instance of the use of legal terms... when she wishes to describe persons to take in remainder, whether the gift over is absolute or only in certain events, she uses appropriate terms. Still more when she gives her residuary estate does she use appropriate legal terms. But when we come to the clause in question, we find her using this language: she expresses her confidence that Harrison will give "the bulk of my said residuary estate". Now what she there meant could not be her residuary estate, which she had already in clear terms given; but the bulk of it. ...Its popular meaning we all know. When a person is said to have given the bulk of his property, what is meant is not the whole but the greater part, and that is in fact consistent with its classical meaning. When, therefore, the testatrix uses that term, can I say she has used a term expressing a definite, clear, certain part of her estate, or the whole of her estate? I am bound to say she has not designated the subject as to which she expresses her confidence; and I am therefore of opinion that there is no trust created; that Harrison took absolutely, and those claiming under him now take.

Link
Refer back to
Sprange v Barnard

In re Golay's Will Trusts [1965] 1 WLR 969

Panel: Ungoed-Thomas J

Facts: In his will, Golay directed his executors to let his housekeeper enjoy one of his flats for her life and to receive a 'reasonable income' from his other properties. Although they had no difficulty choosing which flat was subject to the trust, the executors asked the court whether the direction as to 'reasonable income' was void for uncertainty. The court found that the trust was valid, because what was a reasonable income for a housekeeper can be objectively identified and is therefore certain.

MR JUSTICE UNGOED-THOMAS

It is ... submitted that what the court is concerned with in the interpretation of this will is not to ascertain what is "reasonable income" in the opinion of the court but to ascertain the testator's intention in using the words "reasonable income". The question therefore comes to this: whether the testator by the words "reasonable income" has given a sufficient indication of his intention to provide an effective determinant of what he intends so that the court in applying that determinant can give effect to the testator's intention.

Alert

Whether the yardstick of "reasonable income" were applied by trustees under a discretion given to them by a testator or applied by a court in course of interpreting and applying the words "reasonable income" in a will, the yardstick sought to be applied by the trustees in the one case and the court in the other case would be identical. The trustees might be other than the original trustees named by the testator and the trustees could even surrender their discretion to the court. It would seem to me to be drawing too fine a distinction to conclude that an objective yardstick which different persons sought to apply would be too uncertain, not because of uncertainty in the yardstick but as between those who seek to apply it.

In this case, however, the yardstick indicated by the testator is not what he or any other specified person subjectively considers to be reasonable but what he identifies objectively as "reasonable income". The court is constantly involved in making such objective assessments of what is reasonable and it is not to be deterred from doing so because subjective influences can never be wholly excluded. In my view the testator intended by "reasonable income" the yardstick which the court could and would apply in quantifying the amount so that the direction in the will is not in my view defeated by uncertainty.

Boyce v Boyce (1849) 16 Sim 476

Panel: Wigram V-C

Facts: The testator left his several houses in trust for his wife for her life. After the wife's death, his daughter Maria was to choose one of the houses to be conveyed to her. The will then stated that 'all the other of my freehold houses which my daughter Maria shall not choose and elect' were to be conveyed to the testator's other daughter Charlotte. Maria died before her father, so did not choose any house. The court held that there was no trust in favour of Charlotte as the property to be subject to the trust was uncertain. The houses therefore formed part of the testator's residuary estate. The case report explained the testator's reasoning thus, without quoting him directly:

WIGRAM V-C

[T]he gift in favour of Charlotte was a gift, not of all the testator's freehold houses situate on the North Cliff in Southwold, but of all *the other* of his freehold houses which Maria should not choose; and, therefore, it was only a gift of the houses that should remain, provided Maria should choose one of them: that no choice had been, or,

Link
Sprange v Barnard

indeed, could have been made by Maria, and, therefore, the gift in favour of Charlotte had failed.

Hunter v Moss [1994] 1 WLR 452

Panel: Dillon, Mann and Hirst LJJ

Facts: Moss held 490 ordinary shares in Moss Electrical Company Limited. Moss said to Hunter, the financial director, that he intended to give him 50 shares to put him on an equal footing with the managing director, who had bought 50 shares with bonus money. Moss had said he would hold 50 shares for Hunter and would account for all dividends. The company was sold and the question was whether the trust was void for uncertainty of subject matter. The Court of Appeal upheld the trust.

Lord Justice Dillon rejected the analogy with *Re London Wine Co (Shippers) Ltd* [1986] PCC 121 where tangible chattels were not segregated and therefore there was no certainty of subject matter.

LORD JUSTICE DILLON

That was a case in which the business of the company was that of dealers in wine and over a period it had acquired stocks of wine which were deposited in various warehouses in England. Quantities were then sold to customers by the company, but in many instances the wine remained at the warehouse. There was no appropriation – on the ground, as it were — from bulk, of any wine, to answer particular contracts. But the customer received from the company a certificate of title for wine for which he had paid which described him as the sole and beneficial owner of such-and-such wine of such-and-such a vintage. The customer was charged for storage and insurance, but specific cases were not segregated or identified. Subsequently, at a stage when large stocks of wine were held in various warehouses to the order of the company and its customers, a receiver was appointed by a debenture holder. The question that arose was whether the customers who had received these certificates of title had a good title to the quantity of wine referred to in the certificate as against the receiver appointed under a floating charge. The judge held that it could not be said that the legal title to the wine had passed to individual customers and the description of the wine did not adequately link it with any given consignment or warehouse. And, furthermore, it appeared that there was a lack of comparison at the time the certificates were issued in that, in some cases, the certificates were issued before the wine which had been ordered by the company had actually been received by the company. It seems to me that that case is a long way from the present. It is concerned with the appropriation of chattels and when the property in chattels passes. We are concerned with a declaration of trust, accepting that the legal title remained in the defendant and was not intended, at the time the trust was declared, to pass immediately to the plaintiff.

Link
See the comments on *re Wait* in the judgment of Neuberger J in *re Harvard Securities Ltd.*

He said it was crucial that the case concerned the shares of one class in one company, and that this was relevant whether that company was large, such as ICI, or small. Such gifts will not fail simply because the Testator or Donor has not indicated which of the identical shares the beneficiary is to have.

Link
See *re Harvard Securities Ltd* which was another case concerning shares on one class in one company.

Alert

Just as a person can give, by will, a specified number of his shares of a certain class in a certain company, so equally, in my judgment, he can declare himself trustee of 50 of his ordinary shares in M.E.L. or whatever the company may be and that is effective to give a beneficial proprietary interest to the beneficiary under the trust.

Re Harvard Securities Ltd (in liquidation) [1997] BCLC 369

Panel: Neuberger J

Facts: This case concerned a number of unidentified and unsegregated shares of one particular class in one particular company. Until 1988 Harvard Securities was a stockbroking investment business. It purchased shares in a US company and sold them to clients in parcels of shares. For costs and time saving reasons it did not register these parcels in the names of individual clients, but held the legal title under a nominee name. Harvard wrote to clients referring to 'your shares' being 'held to your order' by the nominee.

The liquidator of Harvard Securities wanted to know whether the shares were held by the nominee for Harvard Securities beneficially or for their clients beneficially.

In his judgment Neuberger J surveyed the authorities on certainty of subject matter, beginning with Atkins LJ in the case of *Re Wait* [1927] 1 Ch 606. Wait bought 1,000 tons of wheat and by a sub-contract he sold 500 tons to sub-purchasers. He went bankrupt without delivering the wheat to the sub-purchasers, although they had paid for it. By a majority the Court of Appeal held that there was no trust and that the subpurchasers were merely ordinary creditors.

MR JUSTICE NEUBERGER:

"He [Atkin LJ] said ([1927] 1 Ch 606 at 629-630:

Link
See the similar facts and comments in *Hunter v Moss*.

'no 500 tons of wheat have ever been ear-marked, identified or appropriated as the wheat to be delivered to the claimants under the contract. The claimants have never received any bill of loading, warrant, delivery order or any document of title representing the goods.'

He then turned to the decision of Oliver J in *Re London Wine Co*:

"In that case, a company had substantial stocks of wine in a number of warehouses. Most of these stocks had been sold to customers, who received from the company a 'Certificate of Title' in respect of the wine for which they had paid, and each such certificate described the customer as 'the sole and beneficial owner' of the wine in question. There was no appropriation from the bulk of any wine to answer any particular contracts. When receivers were appointed in respect of the company, it had sufficient stocks of wine to answer the claims of all of its customers. Oliver J held that the company did not hold any of the wine in trust for its customers, he further held that the customers had no proprietary right in respect of any of the wine, even though they had paid for the wine. He reached this conclusion even where the customer had purchased the company's total stock of a particular wine. Mirroring similar observations of Atkin LJ in *Re Wait*, Oliver J said (at 137):

'I cannot see how, for instance, a farmer who declares himself to be a trustee of two sheep (without identifying them) can be said to have created a perfect and complete trust whatever rights he may confer by such declaration as a matter of contract. And it would seem to me to be immaterial that at the time he has a flock of sheep out of which he could satisfy the interest. Of course, he could by appropriate words, declare himself to be a trustee of the specified proportion of his whole flock and thus create an equitable tenancy in common between himself and the named beneficiary ... But the *mere* declaration that a given number of animals would be held upon trust could not ... without very clear words pointing to such an intention, result in the creation of an interest ... at the time of the declaration. And where the mass from which the numerical interest is to take effect is not itself ascertainable at the date of the declaration such conclusion becomes impossible.' (Oliver J's emphasis.)

Then he considers *Re Goldcorp Exchange Ltd (in receivership)* [1995] 1 AC 74, a decision of the Privy Council where the same principle was applied to gold bullion:

In that case, the company, which dealt in bullion, sold to its customers bullion which it stored for them. Each customer received an invoice certificate verifying his ownership, and had the right to require physical delivery to his order on seven days' notice and payment of delivery charges. Although the company assured customers that it would maintain sufficient stock of bullion to meet all their demands, it failed to do so. The question which fell to be considered was whether or not the customers had any interests in the bullion owned and stored by the company.

In giving the judgment of the Privy Council, Lord Mustill began with the following observations ([1995] 1 AC 74 at 89-90):

'It is common ground that the contracts in question were for the sale of unascertained goods. For present purposes, two species of unascertained goods may be distinguished. First, there are "generic goods". These are sold on terms which preserve the seller's freedom to decide for himself how and from what source he will obtain goods answering the contractual description. Secondly, there are "goods sold ex-bulk". By this expression their Lordships denote goods which are by express stipulation to be supplied from a fixed and a pre-determined source, from within which the seller may make his own choice ... Approaching these situations a priori common sense dictates that the buyer cannot acquire title until it is known to what goods the title relates. Whether the property then passes will depend upon the intention of the parties and in particular on whether there has been a consensual appropriation of particular goods to the contract ... Their Lordships have laboured this point, about which there has been no dispute, simply to show that any attempt by the non-allocated claimant to assert that a legal title passed by virtue of the sale would have been defeated, not by some arid legal technicality but by what Lord Blackburn called "the very nature of things". The same conclusion applies, and for the same reason, to any argument that a title in equity was created by the sale, taken in isolation from the collateral promises.'

Having explained that it was strictly unnecessary to consider *Re Wait*, because that case involved a contract for a sale ex-bulk, Lord Mustill suggested that the reasoning in the whole of the judgment of Atkin LJ was 'irresistible' (see [1995] 1 AC 74 at 91).

Therefore in *Re Goldcorp* there was no trust for the customers.

Mr Justice Neuberger then turned to *Hunter v Moss*, where the distinction between tangible and intangible property was crucial to the decision that there was a valid trust of the shares. He acknowledged that as he is sitting in the High Court, he was bound by the decision in *Hunter v Moss* and refused to follow *Re Wait, Re London Wine* and *Re Goldcorp*.

Should I refuse to follow *Hunter*? In Underhill and Hayton *Law Relating to Trusts and Trustees* (15th edn, 1995) there is strong adverse criticism of the decision and reasoning in *Hunter*. It is said that Dillon LJ's reliance on the analogy of testamentary dispositions was inappropriate... .

In addition, ... the reliance by Dillon LJ on the decision in *Re Rose* appears to overlook the fact that, in the relevant document, Mr Rose had specifically identified the shares which were intended to be the subject matter of the gift... .

I see the force of these points. However, the decision in *Hunter* is binding on me, unless I am satisfied that it is per incuriam or that it has been overruled by a subsequent decision.

He explained why he could not find the decision in *Hunter v Moss* to be *per incuriam*, and why he could not find that it has been overruled. He then referred to the distinction between tangible and intangible property:

Alert

While I am not particularly convinced by the distinction, it appears to me that a more satisfactory way of distinguishing Hunter from the other cases is that it was concerned with shares, and not with chattels. First, that is a ground which is consistent with Dillon LJ's reliance on *Re Rose* (a case concerned with shares) and his ground for distinguishing *Re London Wine Co (Shippers) Ltd* (and, by implication, *Re Wait*) which, it will be remembered, he described as being 'concerned with the appropriation of chattels and when property in chattels passes'. Second, it is on this basis that the editors of *Underhill and Hayton* believe that *Hunter* is explained (although they regard it on an unsatisfactory basis). Third, the observations of Atkin LJ in *Re Wait* [1927] 1 Ch 606 at 630, referring to the 'ordinary operations of buying and selling goods' could be said to provide a policy ground for there being one rule for chattels and another for shares.

Fourth, as the editors of Meagher Gummow & Lehane *Equity Doctrines & Remedies* (3rd edn) paras 679-682 point out, the need for appropriation before any equitable interest can exist in relation to chattels can be contrasted with the absence of any such need before there can be an effective equitable assignment of an unascertained part of a whole debt or fund. This distinction is described by the editors as 'very difficult to see'; none the less, they accept that, despite the criticism to which cases such as *Re Wait* have been subjected, it is unlikely that they will be overruled. ...

The description of the sub-contracted grain in *Re Wait*, the client's wine in *Re London Wine Co (Shippers) Ltd,* and the customer's bullion in *Goldcorp* as 'an unascertained part of a mass of goods' is quite apt. It would not, however, be a sensible description of the 50 shares in *Hunter* or, indeed, the shares in the present case. Mr Halpern pointed out that it is not really possible to identify, whether physically or by words, a proportion of a debt, whereas it is possible to identify chattels (by labelling or segregation) or shares (by reference to their number); he also pointed out that part of a debt or fund is fungible with the balance. For those two reasons, he submitted that the inconsistency suggested in *Meagher Gummow & Lehane* is not valid. There is obvious force in that point, but, in the end, it seems to me that, given that the distinction exists between an assignment of part of a holding of chattels and an assignment of part of a debt or fund, the effect of the decision in *Hunter* is that, in this context, shares fall to be treated in this context in the same way as a debt or fund rather than chattels.

In all the circumstances, therefore, it seems to me that the correct way for me, at first instance, to explain the difference between the result in *Hunter*, and that in *Re Wait, Re London Wine Co (Shippers) Ltd* and *Goldcorp*, is on the ground that *Hunter* was concerned with shares as opposed to chattels."

Thus, having surveyed the authorities on unsegregated property in depth, Neuberger J concluded that, although he found it unsatisfactory that different rules apply to tangible and intangible property, he was bound by the authorities which make such a distinction. He therefore applied *Hunter v Moss*, which also concerned intangible property, and held that although the shares were identical and unsegregated, there was nevertheless certainty of subject matter and thus a valid trust.

2.3 Certainty of Objects

The 'objects' of a trust are the beneficiaries. The beneficiaries of any particular trust must be ascertainable, otherwise a court would not be able to enforce it in their favour, or prevent benefits being given to the wrong people. The test to be applied to check whether the objects are certain differs according to the type of arrangement in question. A more stringent test is applied to fixed trusts than to discretionary trusts, powers of appointment and gifts subject to conditions precedent.

2.3.1 Powers of Appointment

Re Gulbenkian's Settlement Trusts [1970] AC 508

Panel: Lord Reid, Lord Hodson, Lord Guest, Lord Upjohn and Lord Donovan

Facts: A 1929 Settlement contained a power to appoint property 'for the maintenance and personal support or benefit of all or any one or more to the exclusion of the other or others of the following persons, namely, the said Nubar Sarkis Gulbenkian and any wife and his children or remoter issue for the time being in existence whether minors or adults and any person or persons in whose house or apartments or in whose company or under whose care or control or by or with whom the said Nubar Sarkis Gulbenkian may from time to time be employed or residing.'

The House of Lords held, unanimously, that the power was valid as it could be said with certainty that any given individual is or is not a member of the class.

LORD REID

It may be true that when a mere power is given to an individual he is under no duty to exercise it or even to consider whether he should exercise it. But when a power is given to trustees as such, it appears to me that the situation must be different. A settlor [sic] or testator who entrusts a power to his trustees must be relying on them in their fiduciary capacity so they cannot simply push aside the power and refuse to consider whether it ought in their judgment to be exercised and they cannot give money to a person who is not within the classes of persons designated by the settlor: the construction of the power is for the court.

If the classes of beneficiaries are not defined with sufficient particularity to enable the court to determine whether a particular person is or is not, on the facts at a particular time, within one of the classes of beneficiaries, then the power must be bad for uncertainty. If the donee of the power (whether or not he has any duty) desires to exercise it in favour of a particular person it must be possible to determine whether that particular person is or is not within the class of objects of the power, and it must be possible to determine the validity of the power immediately it comes into operation. …

 Alert

The appellants submitted a further argument, that a power is bad for uncertainty unless it is possible to make a complete list of the possible beneficiaries at the time when it falls to be exercised. It is said that trustees cannot properly exercise their discretion unless they can survey the whole field: otherwise there might be in existence potential beneficiaries whom they might regard as more deserving than those who are known to them. In my view that cannot be right.

Lord Upjohn first of all set out the test proposed by Lord Denning MR in the same case in the Court of Appeal:

LORD UPJOHN

The Master of the Rolls ([1968] Ch. 126, 134E) propounded a test in the case of powers collateral, namely, that if you can say of one particular person meaning thereby, apparently, any one person only that he is clearly within the category the whole power is good though it may be difficult to say in other cases whether a person is or is not within the category, and he supported that view by reference to authority. … Moreover, the Master of the Rolls (at p. 133B) expressed the view that the different doctrine with regard to trust powers should be brought into line with the rule with regard to conditions precedent and powers collateral.

However Lord Upjohn rejected this broad test:

But with respect to mere powers, while the court cannot compel the trustees to exercise their powers, yet those entitled to the fund in default must clearly be entitled to restrain the trustees from exercising it save among those within the power. So the trustees or the

 Alert

court must be able to say with certainty who is within and who is without the power. It is for this reason that I find myself unable to accept the broader proposition advanced by Lord Denning M.R.

Instead, Lord Upjohn gave his own, narrower, interpretation:

If a donor (be he a settlor or testator) directs trustees to make some specified provision for "John Smith", then to give legal effect to that provision it must be possible to identify "John Smith". If the donor knows three John Smiths then by the most elementary principles of law neither the trustees nor the court in their place can give effect to that provision; neither the trustees nor the court can guess at it. It must fail for uncertainty unless of course admissible evidence is available to point to a particular John Smith as the object of the donor's bounty.

Then, taking it one stage further, suppose the donor directs that a fund or the income of a fund should be equally divided between members of a class. That class must be as defined as the individual; the court cannot guess at it. Suppose the donor directs that a fund be divided equally between "my old friends," then unless there is some admissible evidence that the donor has given some special "dictionary" meaning to that phrase which enables the trustees to identify the class with sufficient certainty, it is plainly bad as being too uncertain. Suppose that there appeared before the trustees (or the court) two or three individuals who plainly satisfied the test of being among "my old friends," the trustees could not consistently with the donor's intentions accept them as claiming the whole or any defined part of the fund. They cannot claim the whole fund for they can show no title to it unless they prove they are the only members of the class, which of course they cannot do, and so, too, by parity of reasoning they cannot claim any defined part of the fund and there is no authority in the trustees or the court to make any distribution among a smaller class than that pointed out by the donor. The principle is, in my opinion, that the donor must make his intentions sufficiently plain as to the objects of his trust and the court cannot give effect to it by misinterpreting his intentions by dividing the fund merely among those present. Secondly, and perhaps it is the more hallowed principle, the Court of Chancery, which acts in default of trustees, must know with sufficient certainty the objects of the beneficence of the donor so as to execute the trust. Then, suppose the donor does not direct an equal division of his property among the class but gives a power of selection to his trustees among the class; exactly the same principles must apply. The trustees have a duty to select the donees of the donor's bounty from among the class designated by the donor; he has not entrusted them with any power to select the donees merely from among known claimants who are within the class, for that is constituting a narrower class and the donor has given them no power to do this.

LORD DONOVAN

My Lords, where trustees are given power to make payments out of a trust fund to members of a designated class, then if the trustees have a complete discretion as to whom they shall pay the money, or as to whether they shall make any payment at all, I see no reason why the whole clause should be regarded by the law as void for

Decipher
Lord Upjohn seems to endorse the 'complete list' test, which appears contrary to what he stated earlier. However, see Lord Wilberforce in *McPhail v Doulton* who interprets the passage as *not* requiring a complete list of all possible beneficiaries.

uncertainty simply because some members of the designated class might be unascertainable. It is true that this means that such members will never even get considered as possible objects of the trustees' discretion, but I regard that result as less unfortunate than depriving all the ascertainable members of any chance of benefit. I find myself therefore in complete sympathy with the rule that provided one can say with certainty whether a given individual is or is not a member of the class, the power collateral (as it is called) does not fail altogether simply because a complete list of every member cannot be drawn up.

2.3.2 Fixed Trusts

Inland Revenue Commissioners v Broadway Cottages Trust [1955] Ch 20

Panel: Singleton, Jenkins and Hodson LJJ

Facts: The settlor settled £80,000 upon trust and directed the trustees to apply the income for the benefit of all or any of the objects set out in the trust deed. Broadway Cottages Trust was a charity mentioned in the deed, which received income and paid tax on it. The tax could only be reclaimed if it could be shown that there was a valid trust. The court held that there was not. This was a fixed trust, and to be valid, the objects had to be certain. The test for certainty of objects for a fixed trust is whether it is possible to make a complete list of the beneficiaries. In this particular case, it was not possible and the trust failed.

LORD JUSTICE JENKINS

It must, we think, follow from the appellants' concession to the effect that the class of "beneficiaries" is incapable of ascertainment, ... that the trust of the capital of the settled fund for all the beneficiaries living or existing at the termination of the appointed period, and if more than one in equal shares, must be void for uncertainty, inasmuch as there can be no division in equal shares amongst a class of persons unless all the members of the class are known.

2.3.3 Discretionary Trusts

McPhail v Doulton [1971] AC 424

Panel: Lord Reid, Lord Hodson, Lord Guest, Viscount Dilhorne and Lord Wilberforce

Facts: In 1941, Mr Baden executed a deed setting up a trust in favour of the staff of Matthew Hall & Co Limited and their 'relatives and dependants'. Clause 9(a) of the deed said:

'9. (a) The trustees shall apply the net income of the fund in making at their absolute discretion grants to or for the benefit of any of the officers and employees or ex-officers or ex-employees of the company or to any relatives or dependants of any such persons in such amounts at such times and on such conditions (if any) as they think fit'

The House of Lords, by a majority, held that Clause 9(a) constituted a trust and not a power; and that the test for determining the validity of a discretionary trust in terms of certainty of objects was that in *re Gulbenkian*: the trust would be valid if it could be said with certainty that any individual was or was not a member of the class. The 'complete list' test in *IRC v Broadway Cottages Trust* [1955] Ch 20 was overruled.

LORD WILBERFORCE

In this House, the appellants contend, and this is the first question for consideration, that the provisions of clause 9 (a) constitute a trust and not a power. If that is held to be the correct result, both sides agree that the case must return to the Chancery Division for consideration, on this footing, whether this trust is valid. But here comes a complication. In the present state of authority, the decision as to validity would turn on the question whether a complete list (or on another view a list complete for practical purposes) can be drawn up of all possible beneficiaries. This follows from the Court of Appeal's decision in *Inland Revenue Commissioners v Broadway Cottages Trust* [1955] Ch 20 as applied in later cases by which, unless this House decides otherwise, the Court of Chancery would be bound. The respondents invite your Lordships to review this decision and challenge its correctness. So the second issue which arises, if clause 9 (a) amounts to a trust, is whether the existing test for its validity is right in law and, if not, what the test ought to be.

Lord Wilberforce concluded that the arrangement was a trust:

Naturally read, the intention of the deed seems to me clear: clause 9 (a), whose language is mandatory ('shall'), creates, together with a power of selection, a trust for distribution of the income...

He then considered whether the *Broadway Cottages* 'complete list' test is the correct test, or whether it is the 'is/is not' test for powers in *Re Gulbenkian*. He started by considering whether the complete list test is appropriate, and decided that it is not:

The basis for the *Broadway Cottages* principle is stated to be that a trust cannot be valid unless, if need be, it can be executed by the court, and (though it is not quite clear from the judgment where argument ends and decision begins) that the court can only execute it by ordering an equal distribution in which every beneficiary shares. So it is necessary to examine the authority and reason for this supposed rule as to the execution of trusts by the court.

Assuming, as I am prepared to do for present purposes, that the test of validity is whether the trust can be executed by the court, it does not follow that execution is impossible unless there can be equal division.

As a matter of reason, to hold that a principle of equal division applies to trusts such as the present is certainly paradoxical. Equal division is surely the last thing the settlor ever intended: equal division among all may, probably would, produce a result beneficial to none. Why suppose that the court would lend itself to a whimsical execution? And as regards authority, I do not find that the nature of the trust, and of the

Alert

court's powers over trusts, calls for any such rigid rule. Equal division may be sensible and has been decreed, in cases of family trusts, for a limited class, here there is life in the maxim 'equality is equity,' but the cases provide numerous examples where this has not been so, and a different type of execution has been ordered, appropriate to the circumstances.

Having decided that the 'complete list' test is not appropriate for a discretionary trust, he cited early examples of discretionary trusts, family or other trusts where equal division was not ordered. He then looked at modern authorities, in particular *IRC v Broadway Cottages Trust* where the 'complete list' test was applied not only to a fixed trust of capital, which necessarily involved equal division, but also to a discretionary trust of income. The Court of Appeal in that case reasoned that the trust of income could only be executed on the basis of equal division. Lord Wilberforce did not agree with this.

Lord Wilberforce rejected any arguments which sought to suggest that the speeches in *Re Gulbenkian* (and in particular the speech of Lord Upjohn) can be interpreted as an endorsement of the complete list test in *Broadway Cottages* for a discretionary trust. He examined the pertinent passage from Lord Upjohn's speech, and commented on it:

'The trustees have a duty to select the donees of the donor's bounty from among the class designated by the donor; he has not entrusted them with any power to select the donees merely from among known claimants who are within the class, for that is constituting a narrower class and the donor has given them no power to do this' ([1970] A.C. 508 , 524).

What this does say, and I respectfully agree, is that, in the case of a trust, the trustees must select from the class. What it does not say, as I read it, or imply, is that in order to carry out their duty of selection they must have before them, or be able to get, a complete list of all possible objects.

So I think that we are free to review the *Broadway Cottages* case [1955] Ch. 20. The conclusion which I would reach, implicit in the previous discussion, is that the wide distinction between the validity test for powers and that for trust powers is unfortunate and wrong, that the rule recently fastened upon the courts by *Inland Revenue Commissioners v Broadway Cottages Trust* ought to be discarded, and that the test for the validity of trust powers ought to be similar to that accepted by this House in *In re Gulbenkian's Settlements* [1970] AC 508 for powers, namely, that the trust is valid if it can be said with certainty that any given individual is or is not a member of the class.

Assimilation of the validity test does not involve the complete assimilation of trust powers with powers. As to powers, I agree with my noble and learned friend Lord Upjohn in *In re Gulbenkian's Settlements* that although the trustees may, and normally will, be under a fiduciary duty to consider whether or in what way they should exercise their power, the court will not normally compel its exercise. It will intervene if the trustees exceed their powers, and possibly if they are proved to have exercised it capriciously. But in the case of a trust power, if the trustees do not exercise it, the court will: I respectfully adopt as to this the statement in Lord Upjohn's opinion [sic] (p. 525).

Link
See *Re Gulbenkian's Settlements*

I would venture to amplify this by saying that the court, if called upon to execute the trust power, will do so in the manner best calculated to give effect to the settlor's or testator's intentions... .

Then, as to the trustees' duty of inquiry or ascertainment, in each case the trustees ought to make such a survey of the range of objects or possible beneficiaries as will enable them to carry out their fiduciary duty... .

Two final points: first, as to the question of certainty. I desire to emphasise the distinction clearly made and explained by Lord Upjohn ([1970] AC 508, 524) between linguistic or semantic uncertainty which, if unresolved by the court, renders the gift void, and the difficulty of ascertaining the existence or whereabouts of members of the class, a matter with which the court can appropriately deal on an application for directions. There may be a third case where the meaning of the words used is clear but the definition of beneficiaries is so hopelessly wide as not to form 'anything like a class' so that the trust is administratively unworkable or in Lord Eldon's words one that cannot be executed (*Morice v Bishop of Durham*, 10 Ves.Jr. 522, 527). I hesitate to give examples for they may prejudice future cases, but perhaps 'all the residents of Greater London' will serve. I do not think that a discretionary trust for 'relatives' even of a living person falls within this category.

In the final part of his speech, above, Lord Wilberforce said that even where the three certainties are present, the trust may still fail for 'administrative unworkability'. This was the point at issue in *R v District Auditor, ex p. West Yorkshire Metropolitan County Council* [1986] RVR 24 where a purported discretionary trust for the inhabitants of West Yorkshire, although certain, was impossible to execute simply because of the sheer numbers involved. This point has caused much academic debate.

Link
See Further
Reading

Re Baden's Deed Trusts (No 2) [1973] Ch 9

Panel: Sachs, Megaw and Stamp LJJ

Facts: Following the House of Lords decision in *McPhail v Doulton*, the case was sent back to the Chancery Division for the 'is/is not' test to be applied to find whether the discretionary trust for 'relatives and dependants' was valid or void for uncertainty of objects.

Mr Justice Brightman in the Chancery Division found that the test was satisfied for 'relatives and dependants'. So did all three judges in the Court of Appeal, but they all interpreted and applied the test differently in coming to the same conclusion.

LORD JUSTICE SACHS

His general approach was that in order to be valid, there had to be conceptual certainty. To assess whether this is present, the court must have a practical common-sense approach. Once the class *as a concept* is certain, it is merely a matter of evidence as to whether someone is or is not within it. He remarked on Lord Wilberforce's speech in *McPhail v Doulton*, saying that it does *not* say that a trust is invalid simply because it is impossible to bring evidence that someone *is not* within the class. When Lord Wilberforce said that the trustees need to survey the range of possible objects/beneficiaries as to enable them to carry out their fiduciary duty, he did *not* mean that the trustees have to survey everyone – they simply need to know the size of the possible class.

The test to be applied to each of these words is: "can it be said with certainty that any given individual is or is not a member of the class?" *per* Lord Wilberforce [1971]_AC 424, 450, 454 and 456, words which reflect those of Lord Reid and Lord Upjohn in *In re Gulbenkian's Settlements* [1970] AC 508, 518, 521 and 525. …

It is first to be noted that the deed must be looked at through the eyes of a businessman seeking to advance the welfare of the employees of his firm and those so connected with the employees that a benevolent employer would wish to help them. He would not necessarily be looking at the words he uses with the same eyes as those of a man making a will. Accordingly, whether a court is considering the concept implicit in relevant words, or whether it is exercising the function of a court of construction, it should adopt that same practical and common-sense approach which was enjoined by Upjohn J. in *In re Sayer* [1957] Ch 423 , 436, and by Lord Wilberforce in the *Baden* case [1971] AC 424 , 452, and which would be used by an employer setting up such a fund.

The next point as regards approach that requires consideration is the contention, strongly pressed by Mr. Vinelott, that the court must always be able to say whether any given postulant is not within the relevant class as well as being able to say whether he is within it. In construing the words already cited from the speech of Lord Wilberforce in the *Baden* case (as well as those of Lord Reid and Lord Upjohn in the *Gulbenkian* case), it is essential to bear in mind the difference between conceptual uncertainty and evidential difficulties. That distinction is explicitly referred to by Lord Wilberforce in *In re Baden's Deed Trusts* [1971] AC 424, 457 when he said:

"… as to the question of certainty. I desire to emphasise the distinction clearly made and explained by Lord Upjohn [1970] AC 508, 524 between linguistic or semantic uncertainty which, if unresolved by the court, renders the gift void, and the difficulty of ascertaining the existence or whereabouts of members of the class, a matter with which the court can appropriately deal on an application for directions."

As Mr. Vinelott himself rightly observed, "the court is never defeated by evidential uncertainty," and it is in my judgment clear that it is conceptual certainty to which reference was made when the "is or is not a member of the class" test was enunciated. … Once the class of persons to be benefited is conceptually certain it then becomes a question of fact to be determined on evidence whether any postulant has on inquiry been proved to be within it: if he is not so proved, then he is not in it. That position remains the same whether the class to be benefited happens to be small (such as "first cousins") or large (such as "members of the X Trade Union" or "those who have served in the Royal Navy"). The suggestion that such trusts could be invalid because it might be impossible to prove of a given individual that he was not in the relevant class is wholly fallacious – and only Mr. Vinelott's persuasiveness has prevented me from saying that the contention is almost unarguable.

 Alert

It was suggested that some difficulty arises from the passage in the speech of Lord Wilberforce in the *Baden* case [1971] AC 424, 457 where he referred to the need of trustees "to make such a survey of the range of objects or possible beneficiaries as will enable them to carry out their fiduciary duty." The word "range," however, in that context has an inbuilt and obvious element of considerable elasticity, and thus provides for an almost infinitely variable range of vision suitable to the particular trust to be considered. In modern trusts of the category now under consideration it may be sufficient to know whether the range of potential postulants runs into respectively dozens, hundreds, thousands, tens of thousands or even hundreds of thousands. I cannot imagine that the above-quoted passage was intended to cast doubt, for instance, on the validity of wide-ranging discretionary trusts such as those of the Army Benevolent Fund. When looked at in the context of the rest of the speech this particular passage does not seem to me to cause any difficulty. In my judgment it refers to something quite different, to a need to provide a list of individuals or to provide a closely accurate enumeration of the numbers in the class: it relates to that width of the field from which beneficiaries may be drawn and which the trustees should have in mind so that they can adapt to it their methods of discretionary selection. Assessing in a businesslike way "the size of the problem" is what the trustees are called on to do.

Having set these principles out he then looked at whether the words 'dependants' and 'relatives' are certain, while acknowledging that it is not the function of the court to provide an exhaustive definition of the words. As regards 'dependants' he agreed with Brightman J in the Chancery Division:

I consider that the trustees, or if necessary the court, are quite capable of coming to a conclusion in any given case as to whether or not a particular candidate could properly be described as a dependant – a word that, as the judge said, "conjures up a sufficiently distinct picture". I agree, too, that any one wholly or partly dependent on the means of another is a "dependant". There is thus no conceptual uncertainty inherent in that word and the executors' contentions as to the effect of its use fail.

As regards the term 'relatives' he also agreed that this term was certain:

As regards "relatives" Brightman J., after stating, at p. 625, "It is not in dispute that a person is a relative of an ... employee ..., if both trace legal descent from a common ancestor:" a little later said: "In practice, the use of the expression 'relatives' cannot cause the slightest difficulty." With that view I agree for the reasons he gave when he correctly set out the evidential position. As regards the suggested uncertain numerative range of that concept of the word "relative" (a matter which strictly would only be relevant to the abandoned "administratively unworkable" point) and also when considering the practical side of the functions of the trustees, it is germane to note that in *In re Scarisbrick* [1951] Ch 622, Lord Evershed M.R. observed, with regard to a class of "relations," at p. 632: "That class is, in theory, capable of almost infinite expansion, but proof of relationship soon becomes extremely difficult in fact." That factor automatically narrows the field within which the trustees select. Further, a settlor using the word "relatives" in the context of this deed (which is not the same context as that of a will) would assume that the trustees would, in the exercise of their discretion, make their selection in a sensible way from the field, however wide. ...

As a footnote to this conclusion it is interesting to observe that no case was cited to us in which a court has actually decided that a trust was invalid on account of the use of that word, whatever may have been said obiter. If this is due to a tendency to construe deeds and wills so as to give effect to them rather than to invalidate trusts, that is an approach which is certainly in accord with modern thought. I would accordingly dismiss this appeal.

LORD JUSTICE MEGAW

He rejected the executors' close and narrow interpretation of the test. They had argued that the words 'or is not' had special importance, and had been included for a reason. It followed that the trust would be void if it was not possible to say with certainty that someone was not a relative of an employee. Lord Justice Megaw rejected this as completely impractical because although it may be possible to say that there is no proof that someone is a relative, it may still not be certain that he is not. He said that the trust is valid if a substantial number could be said to fall within the class. This of course raises another question as to what 'substantial' means.

The main argument of Mr. Vinelott was founded upon a strict and literal interpretation of the words in which the decision of the House of Lords in *In re Gulbenkian's Settlements* [1970] AC 508 was expressed. That decision laid down the test for the validity of powers of selection. It is relevant for the present case, because in the previous excursion of this case to the House of Lords [1971] AC 424 it was held that there is no relevant difference in the test of validity, whether the trustees are given a power of selection or, as was held by their Lordships to be the case in this trust deed, a trust for selection. The test in either case is what may be called the *Gulbenkian* test. The *Gulbenkian* test, as expressed by Lord Wilberforce at p. 450, and again in almost identical words at p. 454 is this:

"... the power is valid if it can be said with certainty whether any given individual is or is not a member of the class and does not fail simply because it is impossible to ascertain every member of the class."

The executors' argument concentrates on the words "or is not" in the first of the two limbs of the sentence quoted above: "if it can be said with certainty whether any given individual is *or is not* a member of the class." It is said that those words have been used deliberately, and have only one possible meaning; and that, however startling or drastic or unsatisfactory the result may be – and Mr. Vinelott does not shrink from saying that the consequence is drastic – this court is bound to give effect to the words used in the House of Lords' definition of the test. It would be quite impracticable for the trustees to ascertain in many cases whether a particular person was *not* a relative of an employee. The most that could be said is: "There is no proof that he is a relative." But there would still be no "certainty" that such a person was not a relative. Hence, so it is said, the test laid down by the House of Lords is not satisfied, and the trust is void. For it cannot be said with certainty, in relation to any individual, that he is not a relative.

I do not think it was contemplated that the words "or is not" would produce that result. It would, as I see it, involve an inconsistency with the latter part of the same sentence: "does not fail simply because it is impossible to ascertain every member of the class". The executors' contention, in substance and reality, is that it does fail "simply because it is impossible to ascertain every member of the class."

...

In my judgment, much too great emphasis is placed in the executors' argument on the words "or is not." To my mind, the test is satisfied if, as regards at least a substantial number of objects, it can be said with certainty that they fall within the trust; even though, as regards a substantial number of other persons, if they ever for some fanciful reason fell to be considered, the answer would have to be, not "they are outside the trust," but "it is not proven whether they are in or out." What is a "substantial number" may well be a question of common sense and of degree in relation to the particular trust: particularly where, as here, it would be fantasy, to use a mild word, to suggest that any practical difficulty would arise in the fair, proper and sensible administration of this trust in respect of relatives and dependants.

 Alert

Lord Justice Megaw, like Sachs LJ, agreed with Brightman J's definition of 'relatives' as people who can trace their legal descent through a common ancestor. He thus found that the class was conceptually certain and upheld the trust.

LORD JUSTICE STAMP

He said that for the class to be conceptually certain, its size must be known. He felt that it is not possible to know the boundaries of a class of 'relatives' as defined by Sachs LJ and Megaw LJ. Instead, he defined 'relatives' more narrowly as 'next of kin'. Having done that, he decided that the class was then conceptually certain. He said that the true application of the is/is not test is to show that a given individual is or is not within the class. He said that it was possible in this case to do that if relatives was defined as 'next of kin' and on that basis upheld the trust.

Clearly Lord Wilberforce in expressing the view that the test of validity of a discretionary trust ought to be similar to that accepted by the House of Lords in the *Gulbenkian* case did not take the view that it was sufficient that you could find individuals who were clearly members of the class; for he himself remarked, towards the end of his speech as to the trustees' duty of inquiring or ascertaining, that in each case the trustees ought to make such a survey of the range of objects or possible beneficiaries as will enable them to carry out their fiduciary duty. It is not enough that trustees should do nothing but distribute the fund among those objects of the trust who happen to be at hand or present themselves. ... the trustees ought to make such a survey of the range of objects or possible beneficiaries as will enable them to carry out their fiduciary duty... But, as I understand it, having made the appropriate survey, it matters not that it is not complete or fails to yield a result enabling you to lay out a list or particulars of every single beneficiary. Having done the best they can, the trustees may proceed upon the basis similar to that adopted by the court where all the beneficiaries cannot be ascertained and distribute upon the footing that they have been... .

Validity or invalidity is to depend upon whether you can say of any individual - and the accent must be upon that word "any," for it is not simply the individual whose claim you are considering who is spoken of - "is or is not a member of the class," for only thus can you make a survey of the range of objects or possible beneficiaries.

 Alert

If the matter rested there, it would in my judgment follow that, treating the word "relatives" as meaning descendants from a common ancestor, a trust for distribution such as is here in question would not be valid. Any "survey of the range of the objects or possible beneficiaries" would certainly be incomplete, and I am able to discern no principle upon which such a survey could be conducted or where it should start or finish. The most you could do, so far as regards relatives, would be to find individuals who are clearly members of the class – the test which was accepted in the Court of Appeal, but rejected in the House of Lords, in the *Gulbenkian* case.

However, if the narrower meaning of relatives, as 'next of kin' is adopted, it *is* possible to make a survey of the class:

The class of beneficiaries thus becomes a clearly defined class and there is no difficulty in determining whether a given individual is within it or without it.

Finally, he looked at whether 'dependants' as a concept is certain, and found that it is:

The only other challenge to the validity of the trust is directed against the use of the word "dependants" which it is said introduces a linguistic or semantic uncertainty. That in the context the word connotes financial dependence I do not doubt, and although in a given case there may be a doubt whether there be a sufficient degree of dependence to satisfy the qualification of being a "dependant," that is a question which can be determined by the court and does not introduce linguistic uncertainty.

2.3.4 Gifts Subject to a Condition Precedent

Re Allen [1953] Ch 810

Panel: Evershed MR, Birkett and Romer LJJ

Facts: This case involved a gift subject to a condition precedent. The testator, Allen, left certain property to the eldest of the sons of his nephew Francis, 'who shall be a member of the Church of England and an adherent to the doctrine of that Church.' There was a gift over. The question for the Court of Appeal was whether the gift was void for uncertainty of objects.

EVERSHED MR

The Master of the Rolls discussed the appropriate test to be applied and drew a distinction between conditions subsequent and conditions precedent. Conditions subsequent are conditions which may bring to an end an interest which has already vested in a donee. For gifts subject to such conditions, the object or class of objects must be capable of exact description. However, the test is different for gifts subject to a condition precedent. These are gifts where the condition must be performed before the gift can vest. Here, it is not necessary to have a complete list of possible donees: the class should not necessarily be capable of exact description.

All that the claiming devisee has to do is at the relevant date to establish, if he can, that he satisfies the condition or qualification whatever be the appropriate test. If the formula is such as to involve questions of degree (as, prima facie, is implicit in any requirement of "adherence" or "attachment" to a particular faith or creed), the uncertainty of the test contemplated may well invalidate the formula as a condition subsequent but will not, in my judgment, necessarily do so in the case of a condition precedent; for if the claimant he [sic] able to satisfy any, or at least any reasonable test, is he disentitled to the benefit of the gift? The essential difference which, I think, exists, and to which I have alluded, was well illustrated by Mr. Hunter-Brown in the course of argument. A condition subsequent divesting an estate vested in A if A at some relevant date should not be a tall man would, as it seems to me, be held void for uncertainty. For tallness being a matter of degree, by what standard is it, for the supposed purposes, to be judged? If "tallness" is achieved by being above the "average" height, then what average is contemplated? The average of A's town or neighbourhood, the average of Englishmen, the average of all mankind? and would a man in height above the average, say of all Englishmen, by however small a fraction of an inch, be called "tall" in any ordinary sense? But questions of this kind, which might be fatal to the supposed formula as a condition subsequent, might have no application in the case of a condition precedent or qualification; for a claimant who was 6ft. 6ins. tall might fairly say that he satisfied the testator's requirement judged by any reasonable standard.

It may well be that, in a case such as I have supposed, very difficult questions might arise, for example, if the claimant proved that he was a man very slightly above the average height of Englishmen. The court would then have to decide on the facts and on the construction of the bequest (for example, that by "tall" the testator had meant "lofty") whether the claimant satisfied the requirements of the testator and had established his claim to the gift. But I am not persuaded that where a formula constitutes a condition precedent or a qualification it is right for the court to declare the condition or qualification void for uncertainty so as thereby to defeat all possible claimants to the gift unless the terms of the condition or qualification are such that it is impossible to give them any meaning at all, or such that they involve repugnancies or inconsistencies in the possible tests which they postulate, as distinct, for example, from mere problems of degree.

 Alert

He concluded:

> ... in the case of a will it is in general the function and duty of a court to construe the testator's language with reasonable liberality and to try, if it can, to give sensible effect to the intention he has expressed. To this general rule conditions subsequent seem to me to be an exception. The requirement that it must be known with certainty from the outset what are the exact events which will cause a forfeiture or divesting (to borrow once again the language of Lord Russell) seems to me to be founded on principles well established by authority but peculiarly applicable to provisions for forfeiting or divesting an estate or interest previously conferred.

Having stated these principles he concluded that the two parts of the formula set out in the will were valid, although he acknowledged that the second part was more problematic.

Re Barlow's Will Trust [1979] 1 All ER 296

Panel: Browne-Wilkinson J

Facts: Helen Barlow had a large collection of pictures, some of which she bequeathed to specific people in her will. Her executors were directed to allow any of her family and friends who wished to do so to buy one of the remaining pictures. The executors asked the court whether this direction was void for uncertainty.

MR JUSTICE BROWNE-WILKINSON

First of all, the judge drew attention to the arguments on either side:

> Those arguing against the validity of the gift in favour of the friends contend that, in the absence of any guidance from the testatrix, the question "Who were her friends?" is incapable of being answered. The word is said to be "conceptually uncertain" since there are so many different degrees of friendship and it is impossible to say which degree the testatrix had in mind. In support of this argument they rely on Lord Upjohn's remarks in *In re Gulbenkian's Settlements* [1970] AC 508, and the decision of the House of Lords in *In re Baden's Deed Trusts* [1971] AC 424, to the effect that it must be possible to say who is within and who without the class of friends. They say that since the testatrix intended all her friends to have the opportunity to acquire a picture, it is necessary to be able to ascertain with certainty all the members of that class.

> Mr. Shillingford, who argued in favour of the validity of the gift, contended that the test laid down in the *Gulbenkian* and *Baden* cases was not applicable to this case; the test, he says, is that laid down by the Court of Appeal in *In re Allen, decd.* [1953] Ch 810, as appropriate in cases where the validity of a condition precedent or description is in issue, namely, that the gift is valid if it is possible to say of one or more persons that he or they undoubtedly qualify even though it may be difficult to say of others whether or not they qualify.

He stressed that this case was not the type of case where it is necessary to decide all the members of the class:

The distinction between the Gulbenkian test and the In re Allen test is, in my judgment, well exemplified by the word "friends". The word has a great range of meanings; indeed, its exact meaning probably varies slightly from person to person. Some would include only those with whom they had been on intimate terms over a long period; others would include acquaintances whom they liked. Some would include people with whom their relationship was primarily one of business; others would not. Indeed, many people, if asked to draw up a complete list of their friends, would probably have some difficulty in deciding whether certain of the people they knew were really "friends" as opposed to "acquaintances". Therefore, if the nature of the gift was such that it was legally necessary to draw up a complete list of "friends" of the testatrix, or to be able to say of any person that "he is not a friend", the whole gift would probably fail even as to those who, by any conceivable test, were friends.

But in the case of a gift of a kind which does not require one to establish all the members of the class (e.g. "a gift of £10 to each of my friends"), it may be possible to say of some people that on any test, they qualify. Thus in In re Allen, dec'd, at p. 817, Sir Raymond Evershed M.R. took the example of a gift to X "if he is a tall man"; a man 6 ft. 6 ins. tall could be said on any reasonable basis to satisfy the test, although it might be impossible to say whether a man, say, 5 ft. 10 ins. high satisfied the requirement.

He decided that the case before him was not a gift to a particular class, but a series of possible gifts to individuals who answered the description of friend by any reasonable test. The judge helpfully set out some ideas as to how one determines who is a friend.

The effect of clause 5 (a) is to confer on friends of the testatrix a series of options to purchase. Although it is obviously desirable as a practical matter that steps should be taken to inform those entitled to the options of their rights, it is common ground that there is no legal necessity to do so. Therefore, each person coming forward to exercise the option has to prove that he is a friend; it is not legally necessary, in my judgment, to discover who all the friends are. In order to decide whether an individual is entitled to purchase, all that is required is that the executors should be able to say of that individual whether he has proved that he is a friend. The word "friend," therefore, is a description or qualification of the option holder.

Alert

It was suggested that by allowing undoubted friends to take I would be altering the testatrix's intentions. It is said that she intended all her friends to have a chance to buy any given picture, and since some people she might have regarded as friends will not be able to apply, the number of competitors for that picture will be reduced. This may be so; but I cannot regard this factor as making it legally necessary to establish the whole class of friends. The testatrix's intention was that a friend should acquire a picture. My decision gives effect to that intention.

I therefore hold that the disposition does not fail for uncertainty, but that anyone who can prove that by any reasonable test he or she must have been a friend of the testatrix is entitled to exercise the option. Without seeking to lay down any exhaustive definition of such test, it may be helpful if I indicate certain minimum requirements: (a) the

Alert

relationship must have been a long-standing one. (b) The relationship must have been a social relationship as opposed to a business or professional relationship. (c) Although there may have been long periods when circumstances prevented the testatrix and the applicant from meeting, when circumstances did permit they must have met frequently. If in any case the executors entertain any real doubt whether an applicant qualifies, they can apply to the court to decide the issue.

He then cited authority to show 'friends' is an uncertain concept in a trust context:

Secondly, in *In re Lloyd's Trust Instruments* (unreported), June 24, 1970 , but extracts from which are to be found in *Brown v Gould* [1972] Ch.53 Megarry J. stated, at p. 57:

"If there is a trust for 'my old friends,' all concerned are faced with uncertainty as to the concept or idea enshrined in those words. It may not be difficult to resolve that 'old' means not 'aged' but 'of long standing'; but then there is the question of how long is 'long'. Friendship, too, is a concept with almost infinite shades of meaning. Where the concept is uncertain, the gift is void. Where the concept is certain, then mere difficulty in tracing and discovering those who are entitled normally does not invalidate the gift."

Further Reading

Penner J E, *The Law of Trusts,* (5th edition), Chapter 7

Hardcastle, I M, 'Administrative Unworkability – a reassessment of an abiding problem', 1990 Conv 24

Harpum, C, 'Administrative Unworkability and Purpose Trusts', 1986 CLJ 391 pp 391 – 393

Hayton, D, 'Uncertainty and the Subject-matter of Trusts', 1994 LQR 335

3

Formalities

Topic List

Introduction

When discussing formalities within the law in general we are describing a set of rules required for a transaction to have legal effect. Within equity and trusts, however, the word takes on a more specific definition. In this context formalities are the rules that must be followed before a party can either acquire rights as a beneficiary, or transfer an equitable interest on to another party. This definition is therefore beneficiary focussed and should be contrasted with the transfer of legal title from one party to another (which is covered in the chapter on Constitution).

To fully understand how the rules on formalities work it is necessary to understand the background reasons why they were created. The various statutory sections concerning formalities are there to rectify potential specific legal problems, which is why the requirements of each section are not exactly the same. The four main reasons for formalities and rules of constitution have been stated in an academic article, which has been universally praised.

Informal trusts and third parties, J.D. Feltham, Conv. 1987, July-August, 246-252, at 248-249

Such requirements have been analysed to have (a) a ritual or cautionary function, requiring a donor to pause and give due consideration to the transfer, (b) a protective function, safeguarding against undue influence and impositions, (c) an evidentiary function, providing reliable evidence of the creation of the trust as a guard against false claims, a guide to the location of beneficial ownership which constitutes a link in the chain of beneficial entitlement and a source of knowledge of the details of the trust, and (d) a channelling function, standardising transactions in an effective way. The purpose of such requirements, particularly (a) and (c), is defeated if equity treats the transaction as effective notwithstanding that the formalities are not complied with. Moreover there is no longer a sanction to ensure an impetus to comply with the relevant formal requirements.

These requirements highlighted by Feltham, especially (c), are important for considering the application of the Law of Property Act 1925 s 53(1)(c) to dispositions of an equitable interest.

3.1 Creation of Trusts of Land

The general rule for creation of trusts is that they do not have to comply with any formalities; so long as the three certainties are present this will suffice. However, to create an enforceable trust of land the requirements in the Law of Property Act 1925 s 53(1)(b) have to be complied with. This section specifically requires that a declaration of a trust of land has to be evidenced in writing that is signed by the settlor or the settlor's authorised agent. If this written document does not exist, the trust exists but is unenforceable. However, since the requirement is only for evidence of the existence of the trust, a document that is subsequently written and signed will make a trust of land enforceable from the date the trust was created.

Re Vandervell's Trusts (No 2) [1974] Ch 269

Panel: Lord Denning MR, Stephenson and Lawton LJJ

Statute: Law of Property Act 1925 s 53(1)(b)

Facts: The facts of this case are not directly relevant to the application of s 53(1)(b). However, it is submitted that the judgment by Lord Denning MR makes the clearest distinction between declarations of trusts generally and declarations of trusts of land.

LORD DENNING MR

But, as soon as the option was exercised and the shares registered in the trustees' name, there was created a valid trust of the shares in favour of the children's settlement. Not being a trust of land, it could be created without any writing. A trust of personalty can be created without writing. Both Mr. Vandervell and the trustee company had done everything which needed to be done to make the settlement of these shares binding on them. So there was a valid trust...

The entire panel of the Court of Appeal allowed the appeal as this was a creation of a trust of shares, which fell outside of the ambit of s 53(1)(b).

Trusts of land can be created without writing where they come within the ambit of s 53(2), which exempts resulting or constructive trusts from the writing requirements of s 53(1)(b).

Hodgson v Marks [1971] Ch 892

Panel: Russell, Buckley and Cairns LJJ

Statute: Law of Property Act 1925 s 53(1)(b)

Facts: Mrs Hodgson was an elderly widow who had Mr Evans as her lodger. Mrs Hodgson transferred legal title of her house to Mr Evans to prevent her nephew from turning Mr Evans out of the house. Mr Evans then sold the house to Mr Marks, who had acquired a registered mortgage from a building society to finance the purchase. Mrs Hodgson knew nothing of the sale or of the existence of Mr Marks. When she found out what had happened Mrs Hodgson sued Mr Marks and the building society, and asked the court to reconvey the house to her free of the mortgage. It was held Mrs Hodgson had a beneficial interest in the house under a resulting trust, which fell within s 53(2) and therefore did not need to be evidenced in writing.

LORD JUSTICE RUSSELL

I turn next to the question whether section 53(1) of the Law of Property Act 1925 prevents the assertion by the plaintiff of her entitlement in equity to the house. Let me first assume that, contrary to the view expressed by the judge, Mr. Marks is not debarred from relying upon the section, and the express oral arrangement or declaration of trust between the plaintiff and Mr. Evans found by the judge was not effective as such. Nevertheless, the evidence is clear that the transfer was not intended to operate as a gift, and, in those circumstances, I do not see why there was not a resulting trust of the beneficial interest to the plaintiff, which would not, of course, be affected by section 53 (1). ... If an attempted express trust fails, that seems to me just the occasion for implication of a resulting trust, whether the failure be due to uncertainty, or perpetuity, or lack of form. It would be a strange outcome if the plaintiff were to lose her beneficial interest because her evidence had not been confined to negativing a gift but had additionally moved into a field forbidden by section 53 (1) for lack of writing.

3.2 Disposition of an Equitable Interest

It is extremely important to note that s 53(1)(b) only applies to the creation of trusts, while s 53(1)(c) applies to the disposition of equitable interests. In other words, s 53(1)(c) only applies to situations where a trust has already been created. Therefore, the two paragraphs are mutually exclusive; you cannot use both paragraphs for the same specific transfer.

Grey v Inland Revenue Commissioners [1960] AC 1

Panel: Viscount Simonds, Lord Radcliffe, Lord Cohen and Lord Keith of Avonholm. Lord Reid was present at the hearing in the Appellate Committee.

Statutes: Law of Property Act 1925 s 53(1)(c); Statute of Frauds 1677 s 9

Facts: In an attempt to avoid paying stamp duty on the transfer of 18,000 shares from himself to his grandchildren, Mr Hunter entered into a convoluted scheme of transfer. First, he created six trusts in favour of his grandchildren, with Mr Grey as one of the trustees. Each trust had as its subject matter a nominal sum so that it could come into existence. Second, Mr Hunter got the same trustees to hold the 18,000 shares with him as the beneficiary. As a third step Mr Hunter then orally instructed the trustees to hold the 18,000 shares in equal shares according to the terms of the trusts for the grandchildren. Finally, five weeks after this oral instruction, Mr Hunter and the trustees executed six deeds (one for each trust) in which the oral instruction was evidenced as having transferred the equitable interest from Mr Hunter to his grandchildren.

The issue before the House of Lords was whether this type of transfer came within the meaning of 'disposition' in the Law of Property Act 1925 s 53(1)(c). It was agreed by the parties before the hearing that if the oral instruction had been ineffective then the shares had been transferred by the deed, and as such their Lordships did not consider this specific issue at length in their judgments. It was held there was an effective disposition of the equitable interest that was liable to be taxed.

VISCOUNT SIMONDS

These facts give rise to the plain question whether the oral directions given by Mr. Hunter, which are recited in each of the instruments, were effective or were, having regard to section 53 (1) (c) of the Law of Property Act, 1925 , wholly ineffective. In the former event the instruments would not, and in the latter would, be chargeable with a valorem duty.

Section 53 (1) of the Act is as follows "Subject to the provisions hereinafter contained with respect to the creation of interest in land by parol, ... (c) a disposition of an equitable interest or trust subsisting at the time of the disposition, must be in writing signed by the person disposing of the same, or by his agent thereunto lawfully authorised in writing or by will."

Briefly, then, were the several oral directions given by Mr. Hunter dispositions by him of the equitable interest in the shares held by the appellants as nominees for him?

If the word "disposition" is given its natural meaning, it cannot, I think, be denied that a direction given by Mr. Hunter, whereby the beneficial interest in the shares theretofore vested in him became vested in another or others, is a disposition. But it is contended by the appellants that the word "disposition" is to be given a narrower meaning and (so far as relates to *inter vivos* transactions) be read as if it were synonymous with "grants and assignments" and that, given this meaning, it does not cover such a direction as was given in this case. As I am clearly of the opinion, which I understand to be shared by your Lordships, that there is no justification for giving the word "disposition" a narrower meaning than it ordinarily bears, it will be unnecessary to discuss the interesting problem that would otherwise arise. ...

 Alert

LORD RADCLIFFE

My Lords, if there is nothing more in this appeal than the short question whether the oral direction that Mr. Hunter gave to his trustees on February 18, 1955, amounted in any ordinary sense of the words to a "disposition of an equitable interest or trust subsisting at the time of the disposition," I do not feel any doubt as to my answer. I think that it did. Whether we describe what happened in technical or in more general terms the full equitable interest in the 18,000 shares concerned, which at that time was his, was (subject to any statutory invalidity) diverted by his direction from his ownership into the beneficial ownership of the various equitable owners, present and future, entitled under his six existing settlements. ...

In my opinion, it is a very nice question whether a parol declaration of trust of this kind was or was not within the mischief of section 9 of the Statute of Frauds. The point has never, I believe, been decided and perhaps it never will be. Certainly it was long established as law that while a declaration of trust respecting land or any interest therein required writing to be effective, a declaration of trust respecting personalty did not. Moreover, there is warrant for saying that a direction to his trustee by the equitable owner of trust property prescribing new trusts of that property was a declaration of trust. But it does not necessarily follow from that that such a direction, if the effect of it was to determine completely or *pro tanto* the subsisting equitable interest of the maker of the direction, was not also a grant or assignment for the purposes of section 9 and therefore required writing for its validity. Something had to happen to that equitable interest in order to displace it in favour of the new interests created by the direction: and it would be at any rate logical to treat the direction as being an assignment of the subsisting interest to the new beneficiary or beneficiaries or, in other cases, a release or surrender of it to the trustee. ...

For these reasons I think that there is no direct link between section 53(1)(c) of the Act of 1925 and section 9 of the Statute of Frauds. The link was broken by the changes introduced by the amending Act of 1924, and it was those changes, not the original statute, that section 53 must be taken as consolidating. If so, it is inadmissible to allow the construction of the word "disposition" in the new Act to be limited or controlled by any meaning attributed to the words "grant" or "assignment" in section 9 of the old Act.

Their Lordships were all in agreement that the appeal should be dismissed. The Court of Appeal decision ([1958] Ch 690), in which it was held that the deed evidencing the oral instruction was sufficient signed writing for the transaction, was therefore upheld. Since this was a written document, it was subject to stamp duty that Mr Hunter was liable to pay.

Consequently, it would appear that this decision is *ratio* for the proposition that writing evidencing an earlier void oral disposition of an equitable interest will make the disposition valid. It is respectfully submitted that this reasoning is flawed. A strict reading of s 53(1)(c) reveals that signed writing is required to dispose of an equitable interest at the time of disposition, not later. Furthermore, the consequence of not having this signed writing is that the disposition is void; it is automatically of no legal effect. Unlike s 53(1)(b), where the result of not fulfilling the formalities is that the trust is unenforceable but still exists, failing to fulfil s 53(1)(c) strictly means we should say there has been no disposition at all. Subsequent writing is therefore not sufficient.

The outcome of *Grey*, therefore, should have been that the deed evidencing the oral transfer should not have been treated as signed writing fulfilling s 53(1)(c). This would have meant that Mr Hunter was still the beneficiary of the shares, but it would also have meant that Mr Hunter would not have been liable to pay stamp duty.

Vandervell v Inland Revenue Commissioners [1967] 2 AC 291

Panel: Lord Reid, Lord Pearce, Lord Upjohn, Lord Donovan and Lord Wilberforce

Statutes: Law of Property Act 1925 s 53(1)(c); Statute of Frauds 1677 s 9

Facts: Mr Vandervell was a successful engineer and had, amongst other things, his own private company, Vandervell Products Limited ('VPL'). He had nearly all the shares (100,000) in this company, which were held on bare trust with him as beneficiary and the National Provincial Bank as the trustee. Mr Vandervell wanted to create a professorship of Pharmacology with the Royal College of Surgeons ('RCS'). Meanwhile he also had a trustee company, Vandervell Trustees Ltd.

Following negotiations with the RCS, Mr Vandervell orally instructed the National Provincial Bank to transfer legal title of the shares to the RCS. The RCS were intended to be absolute owners of the shares, so that when Mr Vandervell declared dividends of the shares they could be retained by the RCS to fund the professorship.

When negotiating the funding of this professorship with the RCS, it was agreed that Vandervell Trustees Ltd would be granted a right to purchase the shares for £5,000 at any time within five years of giving the shares to the RCS. After three years Vandervell

Trustees Ltd exercised the right to buy the shares, but it was not stated who they were trustees for.

The first argument before the House of Lords was whether this type of transfer counted as a 'disposition' under s 53(1)(c). If the transfer made when Mr Vandervell instructed the National Provincial Bank to transfer legal title of the shares to the RCS came within s 53(1)(c) then it was a taxable disposition. If it did not come within the ambit of s 53(1)(c) then there was no tax liability on that specific transfer. If this transfer was not taxable, then the second argument before the House of Lords was that Mr Vandervell was liable to pay tax on the shares when Vandervell Trustees Ltd took legal title of the shares, as there were no appointed beneficiaries of the trust. It was held that the transfer of the shares was not a transfer coming within the ambit of s 53(1)(c). However, Mr Vandervell had not specified for whom Vandervell Trustees Ltd was holding the shares on trust. Consequently, he had an interest in those shares under a resulting trust and therefore he was liable to be taxed on that interest.

LORD UPJOHN

There are two points to be considered, completely different, each in a watertight compartment. ...

...[T]he object of the section, as was the object of the old Statute of Frauds, is to prevent hidden oral transactions in equitable interests in fraud of those truly entitled, and making it difficult, if not impossible, for the trustees to ascertain who are in truth his beneficiaries. But when the beneficial owner owns the whole beneficial estate and is in a position to give directions to his bare trustee with regard to the legal as well as the equitable estate there can be no possible ground for invoking the section where the beneficial owner wants to deal with the legal estate as well as the equitable estate.

 Alert

I cannot agree with Diplock L.J. that prima facie a transfer of the legal estate carries with it the absolute beneficial interest in the property transferred; this plainly is not so, e.g., the transfer may be on a change of trustee; it is a matter of intention in each case. But if the intention of the beneficial owner in directing the trustee to transfer the legal estate to X is that X should be the beneficial owner I can see no reason for any further document or further words in the document assigning the legal estate also expressly transferring the beneficial interest; the greater includes the less. X may be wise to secure some evidence that the beneficial owner intended him to take the beneficial interest in case his beneficial title is challenged at a later date but it certainly cannot, in my opinion, be a statutory requirement that to effect its passing there must be some writing under section 53(1)(c).

 Decipher

Counsel for the Crown admitted that where the legal and beneficial estate was vested in the legal owner and he desired to transfer the whole legal and beneficial estate to another he did not have to do more than transfer the legal estate and he did not have to comply with section 53(1)(c); and I can see no relevant difference between that case and this.

As I have said, that section is, in my opinion, directed to cases where dealings with the equitable estate are divorced from the legal estate and I do not think any of their

Lordships in Grey ... had in mind the case before your Lordships. To hold the contrary would make assignments unnecessarily complicated; if there had to be assignments in express terms of both legal and equitable interests that would make the section more productive of injustice than the supposed evils it was intended to prevent. ...

I think the Court Of Appeal reached a correct conclusion on this point, which was not raised before Plowman J.

I turn, then, to the second point.

My Lords, we have had much argument on the law of resulting trusts. I do not think that any questions of the principles of law to be applied give rise to any difficulty or are in doubt (except possibly as to their application to an option to purchase). I believe all your Lordships and the judges in the court below are at one upon the general principles. The difficulty, and it is very great, lies in the application of those well-settled principles to the facts of the case.

Link
See chapter on Resulting Trusts

So I will be as brief as I can upon the principles. Where A transfers, or directs a trustee for him to transfer, the legal estate in property to B otherwise than for valuable consideration it is a question of the intention of A in making the transfer whether B was to take beneficially or on trust and, if the latter, on what trusts. If, as a matter of construction of the document transferring the legal estate, it is possible to discern A's intentions, that is an end of the matter and no extraneous evidence is admissible to correct and qualify his intentions so ascertained.

But if, as in this case (a common form share transfer), the document is silent, then there is said to arise a resulting trust in favour of A. ...

If A intends to give away all his beneficial interest in a piece of property and thinks he has done so but, by some mistake or accident or failure to comply with the requirements of the law, he has failed to do so, either wholly or partially, there will, by operation of law, be a resulting trust for him of the beneficial interest of which he had failed effectually to dispose. If the beneficial interest was in A and he fails to give it away effectively to another or others or on charitable trusts it must remain in him. Early references to Equity, like Nature, abhorring a vacuum, are delightful but unnecessary. Let me give an example close to this case.

A the beneficial owner informs his trustees that he wants forthwith to get rid of his interest in the property and instructs him to hold the property forthwith upon such trusts as he will hereafter direct; that beneficial interest, notwithstanding the expressed intention and belief of A that he has thereby parted with his whole beneficial interest in the property, will inevitably remain in him for he has not given the property away effectively to or for the benefit of others. As Plowman J said [in the HC judgment]: "As I see it, a man does not cease to own property simply by saying 'I don't want it'. If he tries to give it away the question must always be, has he succeeded in doing so or not?" ...

LORD WILBERFORCE

Lord Wilberforce first found Mr Vandervell to be a beneficiary under a resulting trust for the same reasons as Lord Upjohn and then considered the s 53(1)(c) point.

> There remains the alternative point taken by the Crown that in any event, by virtue of section 53(1)(c) of the Law of Property Act, 1925, the appellant never effectively disposed of the beneficial interest in the shares to the Royal College of Surgeons. This argument I cannot accept. Section 53(1)(c), a successor to the dormant section 9 of the Statute of Frauds, has recently received a new lease of life as an instrument in the hands of the Revenue. The subsection, which has twice recently brought litigants to this House (*Grey v Inland Revenue Commissioners; Oughtred v Inland Revenue Commissioners*), is certainly not easy to apply to the varied transactions in equitable interests which now occur. However, in this case no problem arises. The shares in question, the 100,000 "A" shares in Vandervell Products Ltd., were, prior to November 14, 1958, registered in the name of the National Provincial Bank Ltd. upon trust for the appellant absolutely. On November 14, 1958, the appellant's solicitor received from the bank a blank transfer of the shares, executed by the bank, and the share certificate. So at this stage the appellant was the absolute master of the shares and only needed to insert his name as transferee in the transfer and to register it to become the full legal owner. He was also the owner in equity. On November 19, 1958, the solicitor ... handed the transfer to the college which, in due course, sealed it and obtained registration of the shares in the college's name. The case should then be regarded as one in which the appellant himself has, with the intention to make a gift, put the college in a position to become the legal owner of the shares, which the college in fact became. ... No separate transfer, therefore, of the equitable interest ever came to or needed to be made and there is no room for the operation of the subsection. What the position would have been had there simply been an oral direction to the legal owner (viz. the bank) to transfer the shares to the college, followed by such a transfer, but without any document in writing signed by Mr. Vandervell as equitable owner, is not a matter which calls for consideration here. The Crown's argument on this point fails but, for the reasons earlier given, I would dismiss the appeal.

 Alert

Mr Vandervell therefore succeeded on the s 53(1)(c) part of this case, as it was held that s 53(1)(c) did not apply to a situation where an absolutely entitled beneficiary instructs the trustee to make a third party the absolute owner of the property. However, due to poor planning by Mr Vandervell as to who should be the ultimate beneficiaries of the VPL shares, he became the beneficiary of the shares under a resulting trust and was therefore liable to pay the tax on the dividends, even though he had not received a penny of the dividends himself.

The decision in *Vandervell* has traditionally been seen by many academics as controversial and contradictory to *Grey*. However, it is submitted that the judgments of Lords Upjohn and Wilberforce are sound. Lord Upjohn (with whom Lords Pearce and Donovan agreed) has clearly taken a purposive interpretation of s 53(1)(c) in looking at the reasons behind why the paragraph is there, rather than merely looking at the words. If his analysis that the paragraph is to prevent fraud is accepted, then there clearly is no risk of fraud on any beneficiaries in a situation like *Vandervell*; when the

RCS received the shares, they did so as absolute owners and therefore there was no beneficiary.

Alternatively, Lord Wilberforce's reasoning is that Mr Vandervell had effectively collapsed the trust by using his rights under *Saunders v Vautier* 49 ER 282 (which he was perfectly entitled to do as the absolutely entitled beneficiary). This is because Mr Vandervell's solicitor received a blank share transfer form from the National Provincial Bank. Completion of this form is one of the requirements for transferring legal title of shares. Since Mr Vandervell had equitable title to the shares and the solicitor was his agent, in essence at this point both equitable and legal interests in the shares had been combined at this point, before the share transfer form was completed in favour of the RCS. It is absolutely correct to say that if Vandervell had exercised his *Saunders v Vautier* rights and then transferred absolute title of the shares to the RCS then this would not come within s 53(1)(c). If that is the case, following Lord Wilberforce's judgment it is a logical step that s 53(1)(c) does not apply in *Vandervell* type situations either.

Link
See Chapter 1

It is submitted that either interpretation is perfectly valid and therefore there is good justification for why s 53(1)(c) is not applicable in this situation.

3.2.1 Other situations where s 53(1)(c) of the Law of Property Act 1925 will not apply

It is important to note that pursuant to s 53(2) of the Law of Property Act 1925, neither s 53(1)(b) nor s 53(1)(c) apply to resulting, implied or constructive trusts. A common scenario where a constructive trust arises is when there is a contract for a type of property of which equity will grant specific performance if there is a breach. A type of property that is frequently subject to this type of contract is shares in a private company.

Neville v Wilson [1997] Ch 144

Panel: Nourse, Rose and Aldous LJJ

Statute: Law of Property Act 1925 s 53(1)(c)

Facts: Before he died, Mr Neville had a private company, J E Neville Ltd ('J.E.N'). During Mr Neville's lifetime J.E.N acquired the shares of another company, Universal Engineering Co (Ellesmere Port) Ltd ('U.E.C.'). After Mr Neville's death J.E.N. was informally liquidated and treated as defunct. U.E.C. meanwhile continued to be profitably run. Two of Mr Neville's children, Joseph Neville and Eileen Hill, were shareholders of J.E.N. with another of Mr Neville's children, Lillian Wilson, and two members of her family, Courtney Wilson and Jonathan Wilson. The two factions of the family fell out. Joseph and Eileen sued the other faction as to whether the informal dissolution of J.E.N. led to a disposal of J.E.N.'s equitable interest in U.E.C. If there had been a valid disposal of the equitable interest, then all of the family members shared the interest in U.E.C. as shareholders of J.E.N. when it existed. If there had not been a valid disposal, then the shares would go to the Crown as *bona vacantia* when J.E.N. was informally dissolved.

It was held that as this was a contract to sell property that was subject to the remedy of specific performance, a constructive trust was created regarding the shares. As the shares were subject to a constructive trust, they came within the ambit of s 53(2). The requirements of s 53(1)(c) were not necessary and therefore no signed writing was required for the transfer to be valid. Consequently, the shares went to the family members, not the Crown.

LORD JUSTICE NOURSE

Here again we think that common sense comes into play. It is an undisputed fact that after 1969 J.E.N. was treated by all concerned as being defunct. From that it is reasonable to infer that its shareholders, in making their agreement, intended that it should not be left with any assets. To put it in another way, it is reasonable to infer that they would have given an affirmative answer to the question whether they intended their agreement to apply to all assets whether known or unknown. …

We are therefore of the opinion that in about April 1969 the shareholders of J.E.N. entered into an agreement with one another for the informal liquidation of J.E.N. as contended for by Mr. Jacob and thus, as part of it, for the division of J.E.N.'s equitable interest in the 120 ordinary shares in U.E.C. registered in the names of the widow and Mr. Wilson amongst themselves, as Mr. Hyde put it, "on a shareholding basis," in other words, in proportions corresponding to their existing shareholdings. … In consequence J.E.N.'s equitable interest in the shares would, as the plaintiffs now claim, be divided amongst the shareholders in the proportions 104 for the trustees of the will of the testator and four each for the widow, Mr. Neville, Mrs. Hill and Mrs. Wilson.

The effect of the agreement, more closely analysed, was that each shareholder agreed to assign his interest in the other shares of J.E.N.'s equitable interest in exchange for the assignment by the other shareholders of their interests in his own aliquot share. Each individual agreement having been a disposition of a subsisting equitable interest not made in writing, there then arises the question whether it was rendered ineffectual by section 53 of the Law of Property Act 1925…

The simple view of the present case is that the effect of each individual agreement was to constitute the shareholder an implied or constructive trustee for the other shareholders, so that the requirement for writing contained in subsection (1)(c) of section 53 was dispensed with by subsection (2). That was the view taken by Upjohn J. [1958] Ch. 383 at first instance and by Lord Radcliffe in the House of Lords in *Oughtred v Inland Revenue Commissioners* [1960] A.C. 206 . In order to see whether it is open to us to adopt it in this court, we must give careful consideration to those views and to the other speeches in the House of Lords.

 Alert

Lord Justice Nourse then proceeded to give a thorough analysis of *Oughtred*, a case that does not give a clear conclusion as to whether s 53(1)(c) applies to this situation or not. He therefore felt able to adopt the reasoning of Lord Radcliffe in his dissenting judgment in *Oughtred*.

The views of their Lordships as to the effect of section 53 can be summarised as follows. Lord Radcliffe, agreeing with Upjohn J., thought that subsection (2) applied. He gave reasons for that view. Lord Cohen and Lord Denning thought that it did not. Although neither of them gave reasons... Keith and Lord Jenkins expressed no view either way. ...

We do not think that there is anything in the speeches in the House of Lords which prevents us from holding that the effect of each individual agreement was to constitute the shareholder an implied or constructive trustee for the other shareholders. In this respect we are of the opinion that the analysis of Lord Radcliffe, based on the proposition that a specifically enforceable agreement to assign an interest in property creates an equitable interest in the assignee, was unquestionably correct... A greater difficulty is caused by Lord Denning's outright rejection of the application of section 53(2), with which Lord Cohen appears to have agreed.

Alert

So far as it is material to the present case, what subsection (2) says is that subsection (1)(c) does not affect the creation or operation of implied or constructive trusts. Just as in *Oughtred v Inland Revenue Commissioners* [1960] A.C. 206 the son's oral agreement created a constructive trust in favour of the mother, so here each shareholder's oral or implied agreement created an implied or constructive trust in favour of the other shareholders. Why then should subsection (2) not apply? No convincing reason was suggested in argument and none has occurred to us since. Moreover, to deny its application in this case would be to restrict the effect of general words when no restriction is called for, and to lay the ground for fine distinctions in the future. With all the respect which is due to those who have thought to the contrary, we hold that subsection (2) applies to an agreement such as we have in this case.

For these reasons we have come to the conclusion that the agreement entered into by the shareholders of J.E.N. in about April 1969 was not rendered ineffectual by section 53 of the Act of 1925. The plaintiffs' alternative claim succeeds and they are entitled to relief accordingly. That means that J.E.N.'s equitable interest in the 120 shares did not vest in the Crown as *bona vacantia* in 1970.

3.3 Theories upon the Application of s 53(1)(c) to Sub-Trusts

An area of considerable debate within formalities is the application of s 53(1)(c) to sub-trusts. A sub-trust occurs when a beneficiary becomes a trustee of their equitable interest for another person, who becomes the sub-beneficiary. Three theories have been posited upon this issue, all of which are arguably correct yet have weaknesses. For the purposes of clarity, each theory will be labelled in relation to the academic who forwarded it.

3.3.1 The Hayton theory

This theory was first posited by David Hayton in his casebook *Nathan & Marshall: Cases and Commentary on the Law of Trusts* (6th Ed. 1975), p.54. Hayton bases his theory upon Victorian cases that were decided long before s 53(1)(c) was drafted. It must be noted at the outset that these cases therefore do not directly answer the question of the precise application of s 53(1)(c), and therefore are only applied to this question by analogy. However, Hayton submits that the principles from these cases should still decide when a disposition of an equitable interest occurs in sub-trusts.

Hayton believes there are two possible types of sub-trust, one which comes within s 53(1)(c), the other does not.

One type of sub-trust is where the beneficiary attempts to create a trust of only part of the equitable interest for a sub-beneficiary. In this situation the beneficiary still has an active role in what is happening with the trust and so all that is happening is the creation of a new trust. Consequently, the only section that could apply is s 53(1)(b) if the subject matter of this new trust is land.

Onslow v Wallis 41 ER 1361

Panel: Lord Cottenham LC

Statute: No relevant statute was directly cited in this case, although this case is used to show how s 53(1)(c) of the Law of Property Act 1925 applies.

Facts: Louisa Sarel was the beneficiary of a trust of, among other things, some freehold land. In her will trust she declared a trust of this land with Sir Henry Onslow as trustee with the duty of selling property to pay off her estate debts. The trustee of the original trust, Mr Wallis, went to court to see whether he or Sir Henry Onslow was entitled to the surplus assets of this trust after the debts had been paid off, as there appeared to be no beneficiary capable of having any interest under either an express or resulting trust. It was held that Sir Henry Onslow was entitled to the surplus assets.

LORD COTTENHAM LC

No case similar to the present has been cited, and, indeed, none has occurred, where property being on trust, the owner has given it to somebody else... In the instance before me the original owner undoubtedly had a right, as against the trustee, to direct what he should do with the property. The testatrix having a right to do what she pleased with the beneficial interest directs by her will the legal estate to be conveyed, or at least gives the property to the trustees of her will. The question, then, is whether the Defendant, who appears to be the trustee of the legal estate, has any right to enquire for what purpose the trustees of the will are to hold the property. It is a gift, in trust it is true, but it is the appointment of persons who are to stand in the place of the original owner as against the trustee. ... Suppose the testatrix had simply transferred the property, appointing new trustees, and directing the existing trustees to convey to them; could the trustee of the legal estate have in this case disputed the title of the trustees under the will because they might or might not have the means of carrying into effect the trusts of the will? ...

This, then, seems to me to be a case... so far as the Defendant Wallis is concerned, and, therefore, the direction of the Vice-Chancellor for a conveyance under the terms of the will is, I think, proper, and the decree must be affirmed...

What Lord Cottenham LC is in essence holding that since Sir Henry Onslow had outstanding duties with regards to the property, the property should be transferred to him and he could keep the excess. If we take the rules from this case in relation to s 53(1)(c), as Sir Henry Onslow had active duties to perform, this was just the creation of a new trust. This new trust was created from property of the original trust but did not use up all the property from the original trust. Consequently, the original trust was still in existence and there had not been a 'disposition' coming within s 53(1)(c).

Hayton contrasts this scenario to the situation where the beneficiary has declared a sub-trust of all of the beneficiary's equitable interest. In the latter scenario, the beneficiary has given away all of the equitable interest to the sub-beneficiary. To all intents and purposes, therefore, the beneficiary has ceased to have a role to play in the trust and therefore drops out of the picture. By dropping out of the picture, the trustee now holds the property directly for the sub-beneficiary and therefore the beneficiary must have disposed of the equitable interest. This scenario therefore needs to comply with s 53(1)(c) if the disposition is to be valid.

Re Lashmar [1891] 1 Ch 258

Panel: Lindley, Bowne and Fry LJJ

Facts: Peter Lashmar made a will in which William Penfold was to be trustee and Charles Lashmar was the beneficiary. Charles Lashmar made a will making John Moody his trustee of the trusts he had created in favour of Jane Lashmar for life, for his son George Hartnup until he was 21 and remainder to George Hartnup's heirs. Jane Lashmar predeceased Charles Lashmar and George Hartnup had already attained the age of 21 and had then died intestate, leaving no heirs. The question before the court was which trustee should have the property. It was held that as Mr Moody had no more role to play with regard to the trust Mr Penfold was entitled to have the trust property.

LORD JUSTICE LINDLEY

In this case a controversy has arisen as to which of two trustees is to keep certain property which was not intended for either of them. Mr Penfold is in the happy position of having got it, and the question is whether anybody is entitled to take it away from him, and, in particular, whether Mr Moody is entitled to take it away from him. ...

The question arises in this way. Under the will of Peter Lashmar, which was dated in 1858, Charles Lashmar was entitled to an equitable reversion in fee in certain property, the legal estate of which was vested in William Penfold, who was the surviving trustee of Peter Lashmar's will. Charles Lashmar made a will, which I will shortly read. [His Lordship then stated this will, and continued] Now the question is, upon that will, what interest (if any) the surviving trustee, William Moody, takes in this property; and I cannot find, after spelling over the will with all the care I can, that he is, or rather was, anything more than a bare trustee for George Hartnup. It is quite obvious that, as soon as Mrs Jane Lashmar *(sic)*, the surviving tenant for life, died, and George Hartnup attained twenty-one, that Moody had no duty whatever to perform. He had a power of sale during the life of the tenant for life, and also during the minority of George Hartnup; but after the tenant for life was dead, and Hartnup had attained twenty-one, he was simply a bare trustee, having no duty whatever to perform. Now, supposing that which is not the fact, that the testator had been entitled to the legal estate in this property, it appears to me that the legal estate to that property would, after the death of the widow, have vested in George Hartnup, and not in this trustee. ...

...upon the true construction of this will, Moody, the trustee under it, having no duty whatever to discharge, and having nothing on earth to do with the property, cannot take the house in question from Penfold, who has got it. It appears to me that the true way to regard this will is to look through Moody as nobody. So it comes to this. The property is in Penfold on trust for nobody at all. Therefore, he keeps it; and accordingly the appeal must be allowed. ...

I think, perhaps, I ought to say with respect to Onslow v Wallis, on which I think Mr Justice Kekewich decided this case, that there the trustee had duties to perform, and if this gentleman had any duties to perform our decision would have been the other way. It is because he has none that we decide as we have done.

Alert

As a trustee with no duties Mr Moody dropped out of the picture and therefore had no more of a role to play. If this is considered with regard to s 53(1)(c), as all the trust property had been taken out of the original trust, there is nothing left of this original trust. Consequently there is a 'disposition' of the trust property and therefore s 53(1)(c) will apply.

While Hayton does appear to have authority on his side, it is undeniable that this authority has been extremely stretched and can be seen as being artificially interpreted. For this reason, his arguments are not the last word on this matter.

3.3.2 The Green theory

A vehement critique of the Hayton theory has been given by Brian Green in this article, discussed below.

Oughtred and Vandervell – A Contextual Reappraisal, (1984) 47 MLR 385 at 396-399

Analytically, a declaration of trust over a subsisting equitable interest operates by way of sub-trust so as to carve out a subsidiary equitable interest from the original equitable proprietary right: beneficial interest following such subsidiary equitable right as is created, but with the superior equitable interest remaining formally vested in the declarant. A declaration cannot, by definition, constitute a disposition of the entirety of the interest hitherto present in the declarant, for if the declaration is to be effective as a declaration, the declarant must retain some proprietary right which can form the subject matter for the sub-trust created by him. All declarations (by beneficial owners) clearly entail a complete or pro tanto disposition of equitable interest by the declarant in diminution of the value of his estate. But, at most, a declaration of trust over a subsisting equitable interest involves a disposition "out of" that interest, not a disposition of the interest itself – and it is to dispositions of subsisting equitable interests, not to dispositions "out of" such interests, that the literal words of section 53(1)(c) are addressed.

One influential writer has expressed the view that, in deciding whether a "declaration of trust" over a subsisting equitable interest falls within section 53(1)(c), it is necessary to distinguish between declarations under which the declarant purports to reserve to himself an active role as trustee of the derivative equitable interest established by him, and declarations whereby the declarant renders himself a bare trustee for others. The former case is said to fall outside section 53(1)(c), whilst the latter is said to be within it on the basis that the declarant having no further role to play simply "drops out of the picture" from the moment of the declaration onwards. ... In this writer's submission, however, this somewhat inelegant distinction between declarations within section 53(1)(c) and declarations without it, whatever its intuitive appeal, is certainly not justified by the nineteenth-century authorities marshalled in its support. ...

As to the nineteenth century authorities, both Onslow and Lashmar involved a somewhat unusual dispute between two sets of trustees as to entitlement to property in the complete absence of any persons who could claim to be beneficially entitled behind their respective trusts, there being no room for the doctrine of resulting trusts to break the impasse, with the real argument being as to which of the trustees was to get a windfall. In both cases T1 held for B absolutely and B had died leaving his estate to T2 as trustee. In Onslow, T2 was to realise the property in question and pay certain debts which did not exhaust the trust estate, B having failed ever to communicate to T2 what was to be done with the remainder. In Lashmar, T2 was to hold upon trusts which failed. Unsurprisingly, Lord Cottenham L.C. found for T2 in Onslow on the basis that he had outstanding duties to fulfil over the disputed property whereas T1 had none; whilst in Lashmar, the Court of Appeal held in favour of T1 on the basis that, T2 having no outstanding responsibilities in repsepct of the property either, there was no reason to prefer him to T1 in disturbance of the status quo. Had it been decided in Onslow that T1 could resist T2's suit on consenting to meet the outstanding debts himself, T2 being ignored on the basis that (if properly described as a trustee at all) he was a bare trustee for B's creditors, it might be arguable that Onslow was at least instructive on the declaration of the bare trust point. As it is, it is irrelevant; and Lashmar only more so. ...

In the light of Onslow v Wallis, it is difficult to resist the conclusion that if T1 holds property exclusively governed by a bare sub-trust under which T2 is trustee for X, T1 would not be able to resist a claim by T2 that T1 pass the property over to him. When all is said, it should be X, not some arbitrary doctrine of law, that determines when, if at all, T2 drops out of the picture. ... If X directs T2 to step aside, or opposes T2's attempts to call in the property from T1, X's wishes must prevail. But until such an occurrence (or until T2 deliberately assigns his outstanding bare equitable to X) T2 is still around to accept a conveyance of the legal estate at some future date and to hold to X's order from that time onwards.

If one abandons the notion of declarants who have constituted themselves as bare trustees of subsisting equitable interests "dropping out of the picture," the question of whether a declaration of trust over a subsisting equitable interest needs to comply with section 53(1)(c) admits of a uniform answer whatever the complexities of the trusts declared. The orthodoxy is that such declarations are outside section 53(1)(c), but there is no authority which directly supports this view, and in its absence this writer would make the following plea on behalf of the contrary position. It has already been noted that the characteristic which makes a subsisting equitable interest worthy of protection is the beneficial interest attached to it. When looked at in this way, it will readily be seen that assignments and declarations of trust, both of which have the effect of extinguishing the beneficial interest in the owner of a hitherto subsisting equitable interest, are equally deserving of formal protection. And both should be caught by section 53(1)(c) by adopting the notion of a declaration of trust working a "part-disposal" of a subsisting equitable interest, a disposal of the beneficial part of the bundle of hitherto subsisting equitable rights. (In this connection one might enlist Viscount Simonds' judgment in Grey as supportive of the view that it is to dispositions of beneficial interests that section 53(1)(c) is addressed.) Adopting this view, one would escape the absurd suggestion that a declaration of trust shifting beneficial ownership lies outside section 53(1)(c), whilst a subsequent assignment of the declarant's outstanding valueless equitable rights falls within it. ...

While Green has some valid points when he criticises the Hayton theory, he unfortunately does not submit any authority to justify his own argument apart from the definition of 'disposition' that Viscount Simonds gave in his judgment in *Grey*. Consequently it can be argued that this theory is hypothetical and will not automatically be followed by the courts.

3.3.3 The Penner theory

The third theory has been submitted by James Penner in his textbook *The Law of Trusts* (first edition 2000). In a similar vein to Green, Penner believes that the Hayton theory is a 'slender reed upon which to rest a difference in the requirement of writing'. However, unlike Green, Penner submits that it is just not possible for a beneficiary to drop out of the picture. Even if a beneficiary has declared a sub-trust of the entire equitable interest, the trustee will still have duties toward the beneficiary specifically, and therefore would be fully entitled to distribute trust property directly to the beneficiary according to the terms of the main trust. It would then be for the beneficiary as trustee of the sub-trust to distribute assets to the sub-beneficiary. Indeed, if the trustee decided to distribute assets directly to the sub-beneficiary, it could be said that the trustee was interfering in a trust to which the trustee was not a party.

This interpretation of sub-trusts, albeit without direct reference to the original author of the theory, has recently been considered *obiter* by the Court of Appeal.

Nelson v Greening & Sykes (Builders) Ltd [2007] EWCA Civ 1358, [2008] 1 EGLR 59

Panel: Ward, Wall and Lawrence Collins LJJ

Statute: Law of Property Act 1925 s 53(1)(c)

Facts: This case focusses upon the application of the Charging Orders Act 1979 s 2 to a contract for the sale of land. A side effect of creation of the contract of the land between Greening & Sykes and Mr Nelson was that a constructive trust was created in favour of Mr Nelson. Mr Nelson in turn passed the benefit of this contract on to his associate Ms Hanley, for whom he was a nominee. In essence, Mr Nelson held his interest under the contract on trust for Ms Hanley. One of the questions before the court was whether Mr Nelson holding his interest on trust for Ms Hanley was a disposition of an equitable interest. It was held that there was no disposition of Mr Nelson's interest.

LORD JUSTICE LAWRENCE COLLINS

Lord Justice Lawrence Collins first considered the traditional case-law distinction before going on to consider the rules in regard to the facts of the case before him.

Alert

57 These authorities do not bind this court to hold that as a matter of law an intermediate trustee ceases to be a trustee. I accept the submission for G&S that saying... that the practical effect [of Mr Nelson holding the property on sub-trust for Ms Hanley] would seem to amount to or be capable of amounting to the "getting rid" of the trust of the equitable interest then subsisting, is not the same as saying that as a matter of law it does get rid of the intermediate trust. What he was saying was that in the case of a trust and sub-trust of personal property the trustees may decide that as a matter of practicality it is more convenient to deal directly with the beneficiary of the sub-trust.

58 But in any event it seems to me that the authorities have no application to a case where the trust property is the purchaser's interest in land created by the existence of an executory contract for sale and purchase. ...

In summary Lawrence Collins LJ is stating that even if all the property of a trust has been placed on a sub-trust, this does not mean that the original trust has come to an end. The trustee of the original trust still has duties regarding that trust to the beneficiary; even though the sub-trust has been created these duties continue to exist. The argument therefore is that despite the sub-trust being declared over all of the trust assets, this does not destroy the original trustee-beneficiary relationship and therefore there has been no 'disposition' of trust assets.

It must be noted, however, that the comments by Lawrence Collins LJ were considered to have no general effect upon the rules of sub-trusts generally. Instead the statements made were in the context of a commercial relationship. These comments, in regard to the general law, are therefore obiter. Consequently, just like the theory submitted by Green, there is no direct authority to support this theory.

The law is therefore in an uncertain state as to how it should develop in this area. Each of the three theories that have been submitted is supportable and it will be for future judgments to actively consider the merits of each and ultimately find the prevailing view.

Further Reading

Penner J E, *The Law of Trusts*, (6th edition), pp 132 – 153

Hayton D and Mitchell C, *Hayton & Marshall Commentary and Cases on The Law of Trusts and Equitable Remedies*, (12th edition), pp 71 – 87

4

Constitution

4.1 Constitution

To constitute a trust, legal title must be vested in the trustee(s). If the settlor intends to make himself the sole trustee, there is no need for a transfer of legal title and the trust is fully effective once he has made a valid self declaration of trust (which can be informal except in the case of land – see Chapter 3 on formalities). If the settlor intends to use another/others as trustee(s), he must transfer the legal title to them, using the correct method for the type of property being transferred. Until legal title vests in the trustee(s), the trust is incompletely constituted and, as the cases below demonstrate, the intended beneficiary is unable to enforce the trust if, as is usual, he is a volunteer – equity will not assist a volunteer. Similar principles apply to making outright gifts: until legal title is correctly vested in the intended donee, the gift is incomplete and equity will not perfect an imperfect gift or assist the donee as a volunteer. Some of the cases extracted in this chapter involve incompletely constituted trusts and some involve incomplete gifts. The leading case is *Milroy v Lord*, which we will discuss first.

Milroy v Lord (1862) 4 De Gex, Fisher & Jones 264, 45 ER 1185

Panel: Knight Bruce and Turner LJJ

Facts: Thomas Medley executed a deed purporting to transfer shares in a certain bank to Samuel Lord to hold on trust for the plaintiffs. No transfer of the shares into Lord's name was ever made in the books of the bank, as required by the bank's constitution, and they remained in Medley's name until his death. The judge held that the shares were bound by the trusts. Medley's personal representative (one of the defendants) appealed. It was held that there was no valid trust of the shares.

LORD JUSTICE TURNER

...Under the circumstances of this case it would be difficult not to feel a strong disposition to give effect to this settlement to the fullest extent, and certainly I have spared no pains to find the means of doing so, consistently with what I apprehend to be the law of the Court; but, after full and anxious consideration, I find myself unable to do so. I take the law of this Court to be well settled, that, in order to render a voluntary settlement valid and effectual, the settler must have done everything which, according to the nature of the property comprised in the settlement, was necessary to be done in order to transfer the property and render the settlement binding upon him. He may of course do this by actually transferring the property to the persons for whom he intends to provide, and the provision will then be effectual, and it will be equally effectual if he transfers the property to a trustee for the purposes of the settlement, or declares that he himself holds it in trust for those purposes; and if the property be personal, the trust may, as I apprehend, be declared either in writing or by parol; but, in order to render the settlement binding, one or other of these modes must, as I understand the law of this Court, be resorted to, for there is no equity in this Court to perfect an imperfect gift. The cases I think go further to this extent, that if the settlement is intended to be effectuated by one of the modes to which I have referred, the Court will not give effect to it by applying another of those modes. If it is intended to take effect by transfer, the Court

Alert

Alert

Alert

will not hold the intended transfer to operate as a declaration of trust, for then every imperfect instrument would be made effectual by being converted into a perfect trust. ...

...Now it is plain that it was not the purpose of this settlement, or the intention of the settlor, to constitute himself a trustee of the bank shares. The intention was that the trust should be vested in the Defendant Samuel Lord, and I think therefore that we should not be justified in holding that by the settlement, or by any parol declaration made by the settlor, he himself became a trustee of these shares for the purposes of the settlement. By doing so we should be converting the settlement or the parol declaration to a purpose wholly different from that which was intended to be effected by it, and, as I have said, creating a perfect trust out of an imperfect transaction.

...The decree must be altered accordingly... .

This case illustrates the vital importance of correctly transferring legal title. It also shows that, if legal title is not correctly transferred, equity will not rescue the failed trust (or gift) by holding that the settlor has made himself a trustee, as that was never his intention. This point is also illustrated by the next two cases, which show how harshly the rule can operate. While *Milroy v Lord* related to an intended trust, the following case related to a failed gift.

Jones v Lock (1865-66) LR 1 Ch App 25

Panel: Lord Cranworth LC

Facts: Robert Jones had received a cheque for £900 (payable to him) in payment of a mortgage and had told his solicitor that he intended to add £100 to it and invest it for the benefit of his nine-month old son. On being asked if he had brought his son a gift on his return from a business trip, he fetched the £900 cheque and put it in his son's hands saying 'I give this to baby'. He then put the cheque in a safe stating that he was going to put it away for his son. Robert Jones died a few days later, having told his solicitor that he intended to alter his will to provide for his son. His will (made before the son's birth) left most of his estate to his children from a previous marriage. The son's mother brought a claim for £900 on his behalf against the estate. The judge held that there was a valid declaration of trust for the son. The other children appealed. It was held that there was no valid gift or declaration of trust.

LORD CRANWORTH LC

...I regret to say that I cannot bring myself to think that, either on principle or on authority, there has been any gift or any valid declaration of trust. ... If I give any chattel that, of course, passes by delivery, and if I say, expressly or impliedly, that I constitute myself a trustee of personality, that is a trust executed, and capable of being enforced without consideration. ...[T]he authorities cited before me ... all turn upon the question, whether what has been said was a declaration of trust or an imperfect gift. In the latter case the parties would receive no aid from a Court of equity if they claimed as volunteers. But when there has been a declaration of trust, then it will be enforced, whether there has been consideration or not. Therefore the question in each case is one of fact; has there been a gift or not, or has there been a declaration of trust or not?

I should have every inclination to sustain this gift, but unfortunately I am unable to do so; the case turns on the very short question whether Jones intended to make a declaration that he held the property in trust for the child; and I cannot come to any other conclusion than that he did not. I think it would be of very dangerous example if loose conversations of this sort, in important transactions of this kind, should have the effect of declarations of trust.

...[T]he testator would have been very much surprised if he had been told that he had parted with the £900, and could no longer dispose of it. It all turns upon the facts, which do not lead me to the conclusion that the testator meant to deprive himself of all property in the note, or to declare himself a trustee of the money for the child. I extremely regret this result, because it is obvious that, by the act of God, this unfortunate child has been deprived of a provision which his father meant to make for him.

Richards v Delbridge (1874) LR 18 Eq 11

Panel: Sir George Jessel MR

Facts: A grandfather was the leaseholder of business premises and endorsed a memorandum on the lease to the effect that he gave the lease and his business stock-in-trade to his grandson, who was under the age of majority. He then arranged for the lease to be delivered to the grandson's mother. The grandfather died soon afterwards and an action was brought on behalf of the grandson claiming that there was a valid declaration of trust in his favour of the lease, goodwill and stock-in-trade. It was held that the ineffectual transfer could not be upheld as a declaration of trust, as the grandfather had not intended to declare himself a trustee.

SIR GEORGE JESSEL MR

...The principle is a very simple one. A man may transfer his property, without valuable consideration, in one of two ways: he may either do such acts as amount is (sic) law to a conveyance or assignment of the property, and thus completely divest himself of the legal ownership, in which case the person who by those acts acquires the property takes it beneficially, or on trust, as the case may be; or the legal owner of the property may, by one or other of the modes recognised as amounting to a valid declaration of trust, constitute himself a trustee, and, without an actual transfer of the legal title, may so deal with the property as to deprive himself of its beneficial ownership, and declare that he will hold it from that time forward on trust for the other person. It is true he need not use the words, "I declare myself a trustee", but he must do something which is equivalent to it, and use expressions which have that meaning; for, however anxious the Court may be to carry out a man's intention, it is not at liberty to construe words otherwise than according to their proper meaning. ...

The true distinction appears to me to be plain, and beyond dispute: for a man to make himself a trustee there must be an expression of intention to become a trustee, whereas words of present gift shew an intention to give over property to another, and not retain it in the donor's own hands for any purpose, fiduciary or otherwise.

 Alert

In *Milroy v Lord*, Lord Justice Turner, after referring to the two modes of making a voluntary settlement valid and effectual, adds these words:

"The cases, I think, go further, to this extent, that if the settlement is intended to be effectuated by one of the modes to which I have referred, the Court will not give effect to it by applying another of those modes. If it is intended to take effect by transfer, the Court will not hold the intended transfer to operate as a declaration of trust, for then every imperfect instrument would be made effectual by being converted into a perfect trust."

It appears to me that that sentence contains the whole law on the subject. ...

I must, therefore, [find for the defendants]... .

These three cases can be contrasted with the case of *T Choithram International SA and others v Pagarani and others* [2001] 1 WLR 1, where the Privy Council felt able, on the somewhat unusual facts, to find a valid trust from a seemingly imperfect gift. In contrast to the three cases extracted above, the settlor in this case *did* intend to make himself a trustee.

T Choithram International SA and others v Pagarani and others [2001] 1 WLR 1

Panel: Lord Browne-Wilkinson, Lord Jauncey of Tullichettle, Lord Clyde, Lord Hobhouse of Woodborough and Lord Millett

Facts: Thakurdas Choithram Pagarani (TCP) was the majority shareholder in a number of companies. Rather than drawing profits from the companies, he built up credits on accounts with them. Having made generous provision for his family, he intended to leave much of his remaining wealth to charity and, after being diagnosed with cancer, he executed a trust deed setting up a charitable Foundation with himself as one of the trustees. After signing the trust deed, he said words to the effect that he was giving his shares and wealth in the companies to the Foundation and he instructed the accountant to the companies to make the transfers. TCP then held meetings of the Boards of Directors of the companies and of the Trustees of the Foundation at which he confirmed that he had gifted his wealth to the Foundation. The accountant altered some entries in the company books to show the Foundation as creditor in place of TCP; he gave instructions for his assistant to make similar alterations in respect of other credit balances but this was not done until after TCP's death. TCP did not execute any share transfer forms but, after his death, the Trustees of the Foundation were registered as shareholders in his place.

His first wife and their children challenged the validity of those gifts to the Foundation which had not been completed before TCP's death. The Court of Appeal of the British Virgin Islands upheld the judge's decision to the effect that TCP's actions were insufficient to constitute a completed gift to the Foundation. The defendants appealed to the Privy Council.

It was held that TCP's words of gift were essentially words of gift on trust and so the deposit balances and shares were held on the trusts of the Foundation trust deed.

LORD BROWNE-WILKINSON

...The case again raises, but with a new twist, the question "when is a gift completed". ...

In order to have made an effective gift of his shares and deposit balances to the foundation TCP must have intended to make an immediate gift... .

...[T]heir Lordships are satisfied that that was TCP's intention. Perhaps the most telling evidence of all is the minutes of the companies' meetings... . ... They record that the directors of each of the four companies, who in each case included TCP, "acknowledge and confirm that the trustees of the [foundation] are henceforth the holders of the shares and assets in the company gifted to the [foundation] by Mr T C Pagarani". Those minutes were signed by TCP. It is hard to imagine a clearer statement of what TCP understood to be the position, ie that he had already given outright to the foundation all his interests in the company balances and the shares.

...[T]he judge ... founded his decision on the ground that the requirements laid down in *Milroy v Lord* (1862) 4 De GF & J 264 had not been satisfied. ...

Their Lordships ... turn to the central and most important question: on the basis that TCP intended to make an immediate absolute gift "to the foundation" but had not vested the gifted property in all the trustees of the foundation, are the trusts of the foundation trust deed enforceable against the deposits and the shares or is this (as the judge and the Court of Appeal held) a case where there has been an imperfect gift which cannot be enforced against TCP's estate whatever TCP's intentions.

The judge and the Court of Appeal understandably took the view that a perfect gift could only be made in one of two ways, viz (a) by a transfer of the gifted asset to the donee, accompanied by an intention in the donor to make a gift; or (b) by the donor declaring himself to be a trustee of the gifted property for the donee. In case (a), the donor has to have done everything necessary to be done which is within his own power to do in order to transfer the gifted asset to the donee. If the donor has not done so, the gift is incomplete since the donee has no equity to perfect an imperfect gift: *Milroy v Lord* 4 De GF & J 264; *Richards v Delbridge* (1874) LR 18 Eq 11; *In re Rose; Midland Bank Executor and Trustee Co Ltd v Rose* [1949] Ch 78; *In re Rose; Rose v Inland Revenue Comrs* [1952] Ch 499. Moreover, the court will not give a benevolent construction so as to treat ineffective words of outright gift as taking effect as if the donor had declared himself a trustee for the donee: *Milroy v Lord* 4 De GF & J 264. So, it is said, in this case TCP used words of gift to the foundation (not words declaring himself a trustee): unless he transferred the shares and deposits so as to vest title in all the trustees, he had not done all that he could in order to effect the gift. It therefore fails. Further it is said that it is not possible to treat TCP's words of gift as a declaration of trust because they make no reference to trusts. Therefore the case does not fall within either of the possible methods by which a complete gift can be made and the gift fails.

Though it is understandable that the courts below should have reached this conclusion since the case does not fall squarely within either of the methods normally stated as being the only possible ways of making a gift, their Lordships do not agree with that conclusion. The facts of this case are novel and raise a new point. It is necessary to make an analysis of the rules of equity as to complete gifts. Although equity will not aid a volunteer, it will not strive officiously to defeat a gift. This case falls between the two common form situations mentioned above. Although the words used by TCP are those normally appropriate to an outright gift—"I give to X"—in the present context there is no breach of the principle in Milroy v Lord if the words of TCP's gift (ie to the foundation) are given their only possible meaning in this context. The foundation has no legal existence apart from the trust declared by the foundation trust deed. Therefore the words "I give to the foundation" can only mean "I give to the trustees of the foundation trust deed to be held by them on the trusts of foundation trust deed". Although the words are apparently words of outright gift they are essentially words of gift on trust.

 Alert

But, it is said, TCP vested the properties not in all the trustees of the foundation but only in one, ie TCP. Since equity will not aid a volunteer, how can a court order be obtained vesting the gifted property in the whole body of trustees on the trusts of the foundation. Again, this represents an over-simplified view of the rules of equity. ...[B]eneficiaries under a trust, although volunteers, can enforce the trust against the trustees. Once a trust relationship is established between trustee and beneficiary, the fact that a beneficiary has given no value is irrelevant. It is for this reason that the type of perfected gift referred to in class (b) above is effective since the donor has constituted himself a trustee for the donee who can as a matter of trust law enforce that trust.

What then is the position here where the trust property is vested in one of the body of trustees, viz TCP? In their Lordship's view there should be no question. TCP has, in the most solemn circumstances, declared that he is giving (and later that he has given) property to a trust which he himself has established and of which he has appointed himself to be a trustee. All this occurs at one composite transaction taking place on 17 February. There can in principle be no distinction between the case where the donor declares himself to be sole trustee for a donee or a purpose and the case where he declares himself to be one of the trustees for that donee or purpose. In both cases his conscience is affected and it would be unconscionable and contrary to the principles of equity to allow such a donor to resile from his gift. Say, in the present case, that TCP had survived and tried to change his mind by denying the gift. In their Lordship's view it is impossible to believe that he could validly deny that he was a trustee for the purposes of the foundation in the light of all the steps that he had taken to assert that position and to assert his trusteeship. In their Lordship's judgment in the absence of special factors where one out of a larger body of trustees has the trust property vested in him he is bound by the trust and must give effect to it by transferring the trust property into the name of all the trustees. ...

 Alert

 Link
See also the case of *Pennington v Waine* (below) where the Court of Appeal referred to the concept of unconscionability.

 Alert

Their Lordships will therefore humbly advise Her Majesty that the appeal ought to be allowed and the action dismissed on the grounds that at TCP's death the deposit balances and the shares in the companies were held on the trusts of the foundation trust deed and the same are now validly vested in the trustees of the foundation.

It could be argued that this case is confined to the particular facts – TCP was treated as declaring himself to be a trustee, albeit one of several trustees, and therefore bound by his declaration. However, the idea of it being unconscionable for the donor to change his mind and resile from the gift is arguably a wider concept and this was picked up by the Court of Appeal in the case of *Pennington and another v Waine and others* [2002] 1 WLR 2075.

A number of principles have emerged to mitigate the harshness of the rules laid down in *Milroy v Lord*. One is the principle from *Re Rose, Rose v Inland Revenue Commissioners* [1952] Ch 499. It will be recalled that, in *Milroy v Lord,* it was said that the settlor must have done *everything necessary* in order to transfer the property and make the settlement binding on him. The precise meaning of this was explored in *Re Rose*, where it was held to mean only that the settlor must have done *everything that he himself could do* to transfer legal title. This prevents trusts or gifts from failing merely because something remains to be done by a third party.

The case involved both an attempted outright gift and an attempted transfer on trust and Lord Evershed MR stated that he would confine himself to discussing the gift, as a decision on that would necessarily involve a similar decision in relation to the trust.

In re Rose, Rose v Inland Revenue Commissioners [1952] Ch 499

Panel: Lord Evershed MR, Jenkins and Morris LJJ

Facts: On 30 March 1943, Mr Rose executed two transfers of shares in a private company. One transferred shares to his wife by way of gift. The other transferred shares to his wife and another person as trustees for Mr Rose's wife and son. The transfers and share certificates were delivered to the transferees but were only registered by the company on 30 June 1943. Mr Rose died in 1947 and it was vital that the transfers were effective before 10 April 1943 if estate duty on the shares was to be avoided. The judge held that estate duty was not payable. The Crown appealed. It was held that once the settlor had done everything in his power to transfer the shares, he was a trustee of the shares for the transferees and so no estate duty was payable in respect of them.

LORD EVERSHED MR

...[The transfer] was in form in exact correspondence with the requirements of the company's regulations; ... On its execution the deed of transfer was, beyond question, delivered to the transferee, together with the certificate relative to those shares. It follows, therefore, that so far as lay in his power, the deceased did all that he could – he followed carefully and precisely the obligations imposed on a proposing transferor ... – to divest himself then and there ... of all his interest, legal and equitable, in the ... shares. ...

...I will now go to the case of *Milroy v Lord*, which is in truth the foundation of the Crown's argument; since it is on that case that depends the proposition that, if this document was intended to operate as a transfer, effect cannot be given to what may be thought to have been the intention behind it by treating it as operating as a declaration of trust. It is necessary to examine the case with a little care because, being a decision of this court, it is binding on us. ...

Mr. Pennycuick has mostly founded his argument on the passage in the judgment of Turner L.J.

The Master of the Rolls then cited a passage, extracted above.

Those last few sentences form the gist of the Crown's argument and on it is founded the broad, general proposition that if a document is expressed as, and on the face of it intended to operate as, a transfer, it cannot in any respect take effect by way of trust... In my judgment, that statement is too broad and involves too great a simplification of the problem; and is not warranted by authority. I agree that if a man purporting to transfer property executes documents which are not apt to effect that purpose, the court cannot then extract from those documents some quite different transaction and say that they were intended merely to operate as a declaration of trust, which ex facie they were not; but if a document is apt and proper to transfer the property – is in truth the appropriate way in which the property must be transferred – then it does not seem to me to follow from the statement of Turner L.J. that, as a result, either during some limited period or otherwise, a trust may not arise, for the purpose of giving effect to the transfer. ... And, for my part, I do not think that the case of *Milroy v Lord* is an authority which compels this court to hold that in this case – where, in the terms of Turner L.J.'s judgment, the settlor did everything which, according to the nature of the property comprised in the settlement, was necessary to be done by him in order to transfer the property – the result necessarily negatives the conclusion that, pending registration, the settlor was a trustee of the legal interest for the transferee.

The view of the limitations of *Milroy v Lord*, which I have tried to express, was much better expressed by Jenkins J. in the recent case which also bears the same name of *In re Rose* (though that is a coincidence). ...[I]n that case, Rose ... had executed (as had this Mr. Rose) a transfer in appropriate form and handed the transfer and the certificate to Hook; but, at the time of his death, the transfer had not been registered. ... [M]y brother considered the case of *Milroy v Lord*, and in regard to it he used this language; "I was referred on that to the well known case of *Milroy v Lord*, and also to the recent case of *In re Fry*. Those cases, as I understand them, turn on the fact that the deceased donor had not done all in his power, according to the nature of the property given, to vest the legal interest in the property in the donee. In such circumstances it is, of course, well settled that there is no equity to complete the imperfect gift. If any act remained to be done by the donor to complete the gift at the date of the donor's death the court will not compel his personal representatives to do that act and the gift remains incomplete and fails. In *Milroy v Lord* the imperfection was due to the fact that the wrong form of transfer was used for the purpose of transferring certain bank shares. The document was not the appropriate document to pass any interest in the property at all." Then he refers to *In re Fry*, which is another illustration. "In this case, as I understand it, the testator had done everything in his power to divest himself of the shares in question to Mr. Hook. He had executed a transfer. It is not suggested that the transfer was not in accordance with the company's regulations. He had handed that transfer together with the certificate to Mr. Hook. There was nothing else the testator could do." I venture respectfully to adopt the whole of the passage I have read which, in my judgment, is a correct statement of the law. If that be so, then it seems to me that it cannot be asserted on the authority of *Milroy v Lord*, and I venture to think it also cannot be asserted as a matter of logic and good sense or principle, that because, by the regulations of the company, there had to be a gap before Mrs. Rose could, as between herself and the company, claim the rights which the shares gave her vis-à-vis the company, the deceased was not in the meantime a trustee for her of all his rights and benefits under the shares ... and if the deceased had received a dividend between execution and registration and Mrs. Rose had claimed to have that dividend handed to her, what would have been the the deceased's answer? ... How could he, in the face of his own statement under seal, deny the proposition that he had, on March 30, 1943, transferred the shares to his wife? – and by the phrase "transfer the shares" surely must be meant transfer to her "the shares and all my right title and interest thereunder."...

...If, as I have said, the phrase "transfer the shares" is taken to be and to mean a transfer of all rights and interests in them, then I can see nothing contrary to the law in a man saying that so long as, pending registration, the legal estate remains in the donor, he was, by the necessary effect of his own deed, a trustee of that legal estate. ... I would dismiss the appeals.

LORD JUSTICE JENKINS

...On the deceased executing the transfers and handing them over, together with the relative share certificates, to the transferees or their agent, the matter, then, stood thus: The deceased had done all in his power to divest himself of and to transfer to the transferees the whole of his right, title and interest, legal and equitable, in the shares in question. He had ... done all he could, in appropriate form, to transfer the whole of his interest, but so far as the legal title was concerned, it was not in his power himself to effect the actual transfer of that, inasmuch as it could only be conferred on the transferees in its perfect form by registration of the transfers. But he had, in my judgment, transferred to the transferees the right to be placed on the register in his stead as the owners of the shares, subject to the directors' power to refuse registration.

...[I]t seems to me plain enough that this gift or disposition must have been made on the date when the deceased executed instruments of transfer and delivered them, with the certificates, to the transferees.

...I can understand that in given circumstances a gift might, rightly or wrongly, be claimed to be incomplete because it could be recalled by the donor. If here it could be said that the deceased, had he changed his mind at any moment before registration, could, by the taking of appropriate proceedings, recall the transfers and recover the certificates and restrain the directors of the company from registering the transfers, then I would understand the proposition that the gift was incomplete, inasmuch as the property had never passed irrevocably to the donees. ... It seems to me impossible to suppose that any such action could have been brought by the deceased in this case with any prospect of success. ...

I agree with my Lord that the case of *Milroy v Lord* by no means covers the question with which we have to deal in the present case. If the deceased had in truth transferred the whole of his interest in these shares so far as he could transfer the same, ... in my view, ... his only remaining interest consisted in the fact that his name still stood on the register as holder of the shares; but having parted in fact with the whole of his beneficial interest, ... in my view the effect ... must be that, pending registration, the deceased was in the position of a trustee of the legal title in the shares for the transferees. ...

In my view, in order to arrive at a right conclusion in this case, it is necessary to keep clear and distinct the position as between transferor and transferee and the position as between transferee and the company. It is, no doubt, true that the rights conferred by shares are all rights against the company, and it is no doubt true that, in the case of a company with ordinary regulations, no person can exercise his rights as a shareholder vis-à-vis the company or be recognized by the company as member unless and until he is placed on the register of members. But in my view it is a fallacy to adduce from that the conclusion that there can be no complete gift of shares as between transferor and transferee unless and until the transferee is placed on the register. In my view, a transfer ... in the form appropriate under the company's regulations, coupled with delivery of the transfer and certificate to the transferee, does suffice, as between transferor and transferee, to constitute the transferee the beneficial owner of the shares, and the circumstance that the transferee must do a further act in the form of applying for and obtaining registration in order to get in and perfect his legal title, having been equipped by the transferor with all that is necessary to enable him to do so, does not prevent the transfer from operating, in accordance with its terms as between the transferor and transferee, and making the transferee the beneficial owner. ...

 Alert

For these reasons, as well as those given by my Lord, I am of the opinion that the learned judge came to a right conclusion in this case, and that the shares ... did not attract duty... .

LORD JUSTICE MORRIS

I am in agreement with the judgments which my Lords have delivered.

The case of *Re Rose, Rose v IRC* is authority for treating both gifts and transfers on trust as complete in equity where the settlor has done all in his power to transfer title. The case was subjected to some criticism. There were suggestions that it was inconsistent with *Milroy v Lord* in treating the settlor as a trustee for the intervening period, when it was not his intention to be a trustee. However, the principle is now well established and was applied to a gift of registered land in the following case, which rejected the idea of any inconsistency with *Milroy v Lord*.

Mascall v Mascall (1985) 50 P & CR 119

Panel: Lawton, Browne-Wilkinson LJJ and Sir Denys Buckley

Facts: A father executed a transfer of a house to his son by way of gift. He handed the transfer to the son and also handed him the land certificate relating to the house. The son's solicitors sent the transfer to the Stamp Office and, while it was there, the father and son had a very serious quarrel and the father decided that he did not want to go through with the transfer of the house. The father applied for a declaration that the transfer was void. The deputy judge held that there had been a gift of the house to the (defendant) son. The (plaintiff) father appealed. It was held that the gift was complete as the plaintiff had done everything in his power to transfer the house and it was for the defendant to ask the Land Registry to register him as owner.

LORD JUSTICE LAWTON

...[I]t seems to me that ... in *Milroy v Lord* the Chancery Court of Appeal proceeded on the basis that the settlor had not done everything that was necessary to give the legal title to Mr. Lord.

The first person to appreciate that *Milroy v Lord* did not have the effect which it was often thought to have had, namely that everything had to be done before a gift could be perfected, was Jenkins J. in *Re Rose, Midland Bank Executor and Trustee Co Ltd v Rose*...

His Lordship then cited extracts from the judgment of Jenkins J in that case and explained:

It was on that principle as to whether the donor had done everything in his power to effect the transfer of the legal interest to the donee that Jenkins J. decided in favour of the donee.

The same problem arose in *Re Rose, Rose v Inland Revenue Commissioners*... Jenkins L.J. pointed out that the statement that a failed transfer cannot be construed in any circumstances as a trust was a statement which was much too wide. He qualified the proposition by saying that, if the effect in law is that the donor holds the legal interest for the benefit of the donee, in those circumstances there is a trust to which the court will give effect.

In my judgment, that is the situation here. The plaintiff had done everything in his power to transfer the house to the defendant. He had intended to do it. He had handed over the land certificate. He had executed the transfer and all that remained was for the defendant, in the ordinary way of conveyancing, to submit the transfer for stamping and then to ask the Land Registry to register his title. Mr. Pearson sought to say that, in relation to registered land, if not to unregistered land, the plaintiff could have done more because he himself ... could have asked the Land Registry to register the transfer and he had not done so; therefore he had not done everything within his power. In my judgment, that is a fallacious argument. He had done everything in his power in the ordinary way of the transfer of registered property and, in the ordinary way, it was for the defendant to get the Land Registry to register him as the proprietor of the property. In those circumstances, it seems to me that the deputy judge's judgment was correct and I would dismiss the appeal.

LORD JUSTICE BROWNE-WILKINSON

...Gifts can be made by a donor either direct to the donee or to a trustee for donees. In either case the property, the subject-matter of the gift, has to be vested in the donee or the trustee for the donee. The settlor can achieve that broadly in two different ways. First, he can transfer the gifted property itself. Secondly, he can declare himself a trustee of the gifted property for the benefit of the donee. In the present case, a declaration of trust of that kind by the plaintiff for the benefit of the defendant simply does not arise. The only question is: Has there been a sufficient transfer of the land to the defendant?

The basic principle underlying all the cases is that equity will not come to the aid of a volunteer. Therefore, if a donee needs to get an order from a court of equity in order to complete his title, he will not get it. If, on the other hand, the donee has under his control everything necessary to constitute his title completely without any further assistance from the donor, the donee needs no assistance from equity and the gift is complete. It is on that principle, which is laid down in *Re Rose*, that in equity it is held that a gift is complete as soon as the settlor or donor has done everything that the donor has to do, that is to say, as soon as the donee has within his control all those things necessary to enable him, the donee, to complete his title.

 Alert

...[I]n my judgment, *Milroy v Lord* is entirely consistent with *Re Rose*. ... The principle set out by Turner L.J. in his judgment is often treated as being a general proposition that everything must have been done which was necessary to complete the legal transfer of property. But ... I can see nothing in that [judgment] requiring that all formalities necessary to complete a legal transfer have to be carried through. Turner L.J. is saying the settlor must have done everything it is necessary for him to do. For those reasons, I can see no inconsistency in the authorities.

In this case, the plaintiff executed a transfer and put it within the control of the defendant together with the land certificate. He had done everything necessary to complete the transaction so far as he, the plaintiff, was concerned. The gift was in equity complete. ...

...I too, would dismiss the appeal.

SIR DENYS BUCKLEY

I agree with both the judgments... .

It can be seen that Browne-Wilkinson LJ regarded *Re Rose* and *Milroy v Lord* as consistent with each other. The second paragraph in the extract from his judgment suggests that the donee must have under his control everything necessary to complete his title. Following *Re Rose* and *Mascall*, it was generally assumed that, for a gift or trust to be regarded as complete in equity, the settlor must have parted with the documents so that there was nothing further he could do and it was out of his power to change his mind. However, in the case of *Pennington and another v Waine and others* [2002] 1 WLR 2075, the Court of Appeal held that handing over the documents was not always necessary. Picking up on comments in *Chothram v Pagarani*, the Court of Appeal held that in some circumstances it might be unconscionable for the settlor to change his mind.

Pennington and another v Waine and others [2002] 1 WLR 2075

Panel: Schiemann, Clarke and Arden LJJ

Facts: Ada Crampton owned 75% of the shares in Crampton Bros. Ltd (the company). In 1998, just over a month before her death, she executed a transfer form transferring 400 shares by way of gift to her nephew Harold Crampton. She handed the completed form to Mr Pennington, who was a partner in the company's auditors and the form was placed on the file of the company. Ada told Harold that she was giving him some shares and that she wanted him to become a director of the company. The company's articles required directors to hold at least one share. In October, Mr Pennington sent Harold a form to sign, consenting to act as a director, and his accompanying letter explained that Ada had instructed him to arrange the transfer of 400 shares to Harold and stated that this required no action on Harold's part. Harold signed the consent form and Ada countersigned it. In November 1998, Ada executed a will making gifts of the rest of her shareholding and making no reference to the 400 shares. No further action was taken regarding the stock transfer form before Ada's death in November. Ada's executors brought an action against a number of defendants including Harold. The judge held that the gift was effective and Ada had transferred the beneficial interest in the shares to Harold. Some of the other defendants appealed.

It was held that, although the transfer form had not been handed to Harold, a stage had been reached where it would have been unconscionable for Ada to recall the gift, so the beneficial interest had passed to Harold.

LADY JUSTICE ARDEN

...The judge held that Mr Pennington was not the company's agent when he received the form of transfer signed by Ada.

[In other words, the form was not treated as having been delivered to the company. Mr Pennington was, in effect, holding it as Ada's agent.]

...I will refer to the decision of Jenkins J in In *re Rose* [1949] Ch 78 as *Midland Bank Executor and Trustee Co Ltd v Rose* and to the decision of this court in the (unconnected) case of *In re Rose* [1952] Ch 499 as *Rose v Inland Revenue Comrs*.

...[T]he principle that equity will not assist a volunteer at first sight looks like a hard-edged rule of law not permitting much argument or exception. Historically the emergence of the principle may have been due to the need for equity to follow the law rather than an intuitive development of equity. The principle against imperfectly constituted gifts led to harsh and seemingly paradoxical results. Before long, equity had tempered the wind to the shorn lamb (i e the donee). It did so on more than one occasion and in more than one way.

First it was held that an incompletely constituted gift could be upheld if the gift had been completed to such an extent that the donee could enforce his right to the shares as against third parties without forcing the donor to take any further step. Accordingly, if a share transfer has been executed by the donor and duly presented to the company for registration, the donee would be entitled, if necessary, to apply to the court for an order for rectification of the share register...

That exception was extended in *Rose v Inland Revenue Comrs* [1952] Ch 499 and other cases by holding that for this exception to apply it was not necessary that the donor should have done all that it was necessary to be done to complete the gift, short of registration of the transfer. On the contrary it was sufficient if the donor had done all that it was necessary for him or her to do.

There is a logical difficulty with this particular exception because it assumes that there is a clear answer to the question, when does an equitable assignment of a share take place? ... The equitable assignment clearly occurs at some stage before the shares are registered. But does it occur when the share transfer is executed, or when the share transfer is delivered to the transferee, or when the transfer is lodged for registration ... or the directors resolve that the transfer should be registered? I return to this point below.

According to counsel's researches, the situation in the present case has not arisen in any reported cases before. I note that in her recent work, *Personal Property Law, Text, Cases and Materials* (2000), p 241 Professor Sarah Worthington takes it as at (sic) axiomatic that:

"notwithstanding any demonstrable intention to make a gift, there will be no effective gift in equity if the donor simply places matters (such as completed transfer forms accompanied by the relevant share certificates) in the hands of the donor's agents. In those circumstances the donor remains at liberty to recall the gift simply by revoking the instructions previously given to the agent. The donor has not done all that is necessary, and the donee is not in a position to control completion of the transfer. It follows that the intended gift will not be regarded as complete either at law or in equity."

Secondly equity has tempered the wind (of the principle that equity will not assist a volunteer) to the shorn lamb (the donee) by utilising the constructive trust. This does not constitute a declaration of trust and thus does not fall foul of the principle (see *Milroy v Lord* 4 De GF & J 264 and *Jones v Lock* LR 1 Ch App 25) that an imperfectly constituted gift is not saved by being treated as a declaration of trust. Thus, for example, in *T Choithram International SA v Pagarini* (sic) [2001] 1 WLR 1 the Privy Council held that the assets which the donor gave to the foundation of which he was one of the trustees were held upon trust to vest the same in all the trustees of the foundation on the terms of the trusts of the foundation. This particular trust obligation was not a term of the express trust constituting the foundation but a constructive trust adjunct to it. So, too, in *Rose v Inland Revenue Comrs* [1952] Ch 499, the Court of Appeal held that the beneficial interest in the shares passed when the share transfers were delivered to the transferee, and that consequently the transferor was a trustee of the legal estate in the shares from that date. ...

I will need to return to this point below.

Thirdly equity has tempered the wind to the shorn lamb by applying a benevolent construction to words of gift. As explained above an imperfect gift is not saved by being treated as a declaration of trust. But where a court of equity is satisfied that the donor had an intention to make an immediate gift, the court will construe the words which the donor used as words effecting a gift or declaring a trust if they can fairly bear that meaning and otherwise the gift will fail. This point can also be illustrated by reference to *T Choithram International SA v Pagarini* (sic) [2001] 1 WLR 1. ... The Privy Council held that the gift to "the foundation" could only properly be construed as a gift to the purposes declared by the trust deed and administered by the trustees. Lord Browne-Wilkinson giving the judgment of the Privy Council [stated]: [Her Ladyship cited a passage from *Choithram v Pagarani*, extracted above]

Link
See *Choithram v Pagarani* (above).

Accordingly the principle that, where a gift is imperfectly constituted, the court will not hold it to operate as a declaration of trust, does not prevent the court from construing it to be a trust if that interpretation is permissible as a matter of construction, which may be a benevolent construction. ...

The cases to which counsel have referred us do not reveal any, or any consistent single policy consideration behind the rule that the court will not perfect an imperfect gift. The objectives of the rule obviously include ensuring that donors do not by acting voluntarily act unwisely in a way that they may subsequently regret. This objective is furthered by permitting donors to change their minds at any time before it becomes completely constituted. This is a paternalistic objective, which can outweigh the respect to be given to the donor's original intention as gifts are often held by the courts to be incompletely constituted despite the clearest intention of the donor to make the gift. ... There must also be, in the interests of legal certainty, a clearly ascertainable point in time at which it can be said that the gift was completed, and this point in time must be arrived at on a principled basis.

There are countervailing policy considerations which would militate in favour of holding a gift to be completely constituted. These would include effectuating, rather than frustrating, the clear and continuing intention of the donor, and preventing the donor from acting in a manner which is unconscionable. ...[B]oth these policy considerations are evident in *T Choithram International SA v Pagarini* (sic) [2001] 1 WLR 1. It does not seem to me that this consideration is inconsistent with what Jenkins LJ said in *In re McArdle*, decd [1951] Ch 669. His point was that there is nothing unconscionable in simply (without more) changing your mind. That is also the point which Professor Worthington makes in the passage I have cited.

Link
See the reference to this concept by Lord Browne-Wilkinson in *Choithram v Pagarani* (above).

If one proceeds on the basis that a principle which animates the answer to the question whether an apparently incomplete gift is to be treated as completely constituted is that a donor will not be permitted to change his or her mind if it would be unconscionable, in the eyes of equity, vis-a-vis the donee to do so, what is the position here? There can be no comprehensive list of factors which makes it unconscionable for the donor to

Alert

change his or her mind: it must depend on the court's evaluation of all the relevant considerations. What then are the relevant facts here? Ada made the gift of her own free will: there is no finding that she was not competent to do this. She not only told Harold about the gift and signed a form of transfer which she delivered to Mr Pennington for him to secure registration: her agent also told Harold that he need take no action. In addition Harold agreed to become a director of the company ..., which he could not do without shares being transferred to him. If Ada had changed her mind on (say) 10 November 1998, in my judgment the court could properly have concluded that it was too late for her to do this as by that date Harold signed the form ...[agreeing to become a director], the last of the events identified above, to occur.

There is next the pure question of law: was it necessary for Ada deliver (sic) the form of transfer to Harold? ... In *Rose v Inland Revenue Comrs* [1952] Ch 499 the issue was whether the gift was perfected by 10 April 1943, by which date the donor had executed the declarations of gift and delivered the share transfers to reflect the gifts to the transferees. Argument was not therefore directed to the question whether a beneficial interest in the shares passed on the dates of the declarations of trust or on the date on which the share transfers were handed over. For my own part I do not consider that it was necessary to the conclusions of Sir Raymond Evershed MR that the gift should have taken effect before the transfers were delivered to the transferees. ... [I]f this were the view of Sir Raymond Evershed MR it seems to me that it would not ... be possible to reconcile it with *Milroy v Lord* 4 De GF & J 264, and in particular with the principle that the court will not convert an imperfect gift into a declaration of trust. There could not be a constructive trust until the gift was perfected. The conclusion of Jenkins LJ was predicated on the basis that delivery of the transfer to the donee was necessary and had occurred. Likewise the decision of this court in *Mascall v Mascall* 50 P & CR 119 ... [was] predicated on the same basis. ... Accordingly the ratio of *Rose v Inland Revenue Comrs* [1952] Ch 499 was as I read it that the gifts of shares in that case were completely constituted when the donor executed share transfers and delivered them to the transferees even though they were not registered in the register of members of the company until a later date.

However, that conclusion as to the ratio in *Rose v Inland Revenue Comrs* does not mean that this appeal must be decided in the appellant's favour. Even if I am correct in my view that the Court of Appeal took the view in *Rose v Inland Revenue Comrs* that delivery of the share transfers was there required, it does not follow that delivery cannot in some circumstances be dispensed with. Here, there was a clear finding that Ada intended to make an immediate gift. Harold was informed of it. Moreover, I have already expressed the view that a stage was reached when it would have been unconscionable for Ada to recall the gift. It follows that it would also have been unconscionable for her personal representatives to refuse to hand over the share transfer to Harold after her death. In those circumstances, in my judgment, delivery of the share transfer before her death was unnecessary so far as perfection of the gift was concerned.

 Alert

It is not necessary to decide the case simply on that basis. After the share transfers were executed Mr Pennington wrote to Harold on Ada's instructions informing him of the gift and stating that there was no action that he needed to take. I would also decide this appeal in favour of the respondent on this further basis. If I am wrong in the view that delivery of the share transfers to the company or the donee is required and is not dispensed with by reason of the fact that it would be unconscionable for Ada's personal representatives to refuse to hand the transfers over to Harold, the words used by Mr Pennington should be construed as meaning that Ada and, through her, Mr Pennington became agent for Harold for the purpose of submitting the share transfer to the company. This is an application of the principle of benevolent construction to give effect to Ada's clear wishes. Only in that way could the result "This requires no action on your part" and an effective gift be achieved. Harold did not question this assurance and must be taken to have proceeded to act on the basis that it would be honoured.

...Nothing in this judgment is intended to detract from the requirement that a donor should comply with any formalities required by the law to be complied with by him or her, such as, in the case of a gift of shares, the completion of an instrument of transfer or, in the case of a gift of land, the requirements of ... the Law of Property (Miscellaneous Provisions) Act 1989 or, in the case of a gift of a chattel, delivery of the chattel. ...

In the circumstances I would dismiss the appeal.

Lord Justice Schiemann, in dismissing the appeal, agreed with the reasons given by Arden LJ. Lord Justice Clarke decided the case the same way but on a slightly different basis. However, he also expressed agreement with the majority view in the following terms.

LORD JUSTICE CLARKE

...It is certainly true that Ada could have done more. She could have delivered the transfer form to Harold or to the company. She could indeed have applied to the company to enter Harold's name in its register of members...

[A]lthough I know that hard cases make bad law, I would have expected Harold to be entitled ... to the 400 shares apparently transferred by stock transfer form... I should add that, if unconscionability is the test, I agree with Arden LJ that it would have been unconscionable of Ada, as at the time of her death (if not earlier), to assert that the beneficial interest in the 400 shares had not passed to Harold. It would certainly be unconscionable of the estate to seek to resile from the transfer after Ada's death because, as at her death, she plainly intended Harold to own the shares. ...

Later in his judgment, he said:

As Arden LJ has observed, Lord Browne-Wilkinson [in Choithram v Pagarani]... highlighted the contrast between the maxim that equity will not aid a volunteer and the maxim that it will not strive officiously to defeat a gift. It seems to me that if equity refuses to aid Harold on the facts of this case, it will prefer the former maxim to the latter, whereas all the circumstances of the case lead to the conclusion that it should give effect to the gift which Ada intended. ...

In her judgment, Arden LJ refers to conflicting policy considerations.

Although the outcome of this case seems to accord with the settlor's intentions, there are difficulties with the decision. It is not easy to predict when a court might consider it unconscionable for a settlor to change his mind.

There is also a question as to how the idea of it being unconscionable for a donor to change his mind relates to the more established doctrine of proprietary estoppel, where a person may be prevented from going back on a promise or assurance, relating to property, which has been relied on by another to his detriment as, for example, in the case of *Gillett v Holt* [2001] Ch 210.

In addition to the cases above which illustrate ways in which the strict rule from *Milroy v Lord* may be mitigated, the rule in *Strong v Bird* (1874) LR 18 Eq 315 and the concept of *donatio mortis causa* are two well-established exceptions to the general rule that equity will not perfect an imperfect gift.

The rule in *Strong v Bird* stems from the case of that name and has been developed in a number of cases. The key point is that a failure to perfect legal title may be cured if the intended recipient becomes the personal representative because, as such, the legal title vests in him.

Strong v Bird (1874) LR 18 Eq 315

Panel: Sir George Jessel MR

Facts: Mrs Bird lived with her step-son (the defendant) and paid him a quarterly sum for her board and lodging. The step-son borrowed a sum of money from her and it was agreed that it would be repaid by her deducting £100 a quarter from her quarterly payments. She deducted £100 from each of her next two payments but then said that she forgave the debt and made no further deductions. She died four years later, having appointed the step-son as her sole executor. One of her next of kin claimed that the step-son owed the balance of the debt to the estate. It was held that the debt was released at law by the debtor becoming executor and the debtor was not liable in equity because of the continuing intention to forgive the debt.

SIR GEORGE JESSEL MR

...Upon these facts, I consider it to be clear that whether Mrs. Bird did or did not give in law, she intended to do so. The question is, Did the law allow her to make this a complete gift without doing more than she actually did?

First of all, it is said, and said quite accurately, that the mere saying by a creditor to a debtor, "I forgive you the debt," will not operate as a release at law. ... [I]n a case where the thing which is the subject of donation is transferable or releasable at law, the legal transfer or release shall take place. The gift is not perfect until what has been generally called a change of the property at law has taken place. Allowing that rule to operate to its full extent, what occurred was this. The donor, or the alleged donor, had made her will, and by that will had appointed Mr. Bird, the alleged donee, executor. After her death he proved the will, and the legal effect of that was to release the debt in law, and therefore the condition which is required, namely, that the release shall be perfect at law, was complied with by the testatrix making him executor. It is not necessary that the legal change shall knowingly be made by the donor with a view to carry out the gift. It may be made for another purpose; but if the gift is clear, and there is to be no recall of the gift, and no intention to recall it, ... there is no reason why the legal instrument should not have its legal effect. ...[W]hen a testator makes his debtor executor, and thereby releases the debt at law, he is no longer liable at law. It is said that he would be liable in this Court: and so he would, unless he could shew some reason for not being made liable. Then what does he shew here? Why he proves to the satisfaction of the Court a continuing intention to give; and it appears to me that there being the continuing intention to give, and there being a legal act which transferred the ownership or released the obligation – for it is the same thing – the transaction is perfected, and he does not want the aid of a Court of Equity to carry it out, or to make it complete, because it is complete already, and there is no equity against him to take the property away from him.

On that ground I shall hold that this gentleman had a perfect title to the £900... .

The case related to perfecting the release of a debt, and also discussed the perfecting of gifts, where the debtor or donee is executor to the creditor or donor. As executor, he acquires legal title which puts right the previous defect. Providing the intention to forgive the debt or make the gift continued until the creditor or donor's death, the debtor cannot be required to pay the debt and the donee can keep the gift. The principle was applied to perfecting a gift in the case described below.

In re Stewart, Stewart v McLaughlin [1908] 2 Ch 251

Panel: Neville J

Facts: Dr Stewart informed his wife that he had bought bonds for her and handed her an envelope which contained a letter from his brokers confirming the purchase. However, the gift was not completed prior to Dr Stewart's death. The wife was appointed an executrix. It was held that the wife was entitled to the bonds, as the principle of *Strong v Bird* could be used to perfect imperfect gifts and applied whether or not the donee was the sole executor.

MR JUSTICE NEVILLE

...The intention of the testator to give the bonds being ... proved, does the fact that the wife was appointed executrix give validity to what, unless it can be supported as a declaration of trust, would be an imperfect and invalid gift? I think it does, the case, in my opinion, being within the principle of *Strong v Bird*, which is a decision of the late Sir George Jessel that has remained unchallenged for upwards of thirty years and has been followed in several cases. It purports to lay down a principle of general application, and I think I am bound to apply that principle to the present case. The decision is, as I understand it, to the following effect: that where a testator has expressed the intention of making a gift of personal estate belonging to him to one who upon his death becomes his executor, the intention continuing unchanged, the executor

Alert

is entitled to hold the property for his own benefit. The reasoning by which the conclusion is reached is of a double character – first, that the vesting of the property in the executor at the testator's death completes the imperfect gift made in the lifetime, and, secondly, that the intention of the testator to give the beneficial interest to the executor is sufficient to countervail the equity of beneficiaries under the will, the testator having vested the legal estate in the executor. The whole of the property in the personal estate in the eye of the law vesting in each executor, it seems to me immaterial whether the donee is the only executor or one of several; nor do I think the rule is confined to cases of the release of a debt owing by the donee. The intention to give, however, must not be an intention of testamentary benefaction, although the intended donee is the executor, for in that case the rule cannot apply, the prescribed formalities for testamentary disposition not having been observed... I think, therefore, that the plaintiff is entitled ... to the ... bonds... .

Alert

The above case shows that the rule can apply even where the donee is not the sole executor. The case of *Re James* [1935] Ch 449 applied the rule to a donee acquiring title as administrator, although this was regarded, *obiter dicta*, as doubtful in *Re Gonin* [1979] Ch 16.

The next case examines in more detail the requirements of the rule in *Strong v Bird* as to the donor's intention, and stresses the need for an intention to make an immediate gift, which must continue unchanged until death.

In re Freeland, Jackson v Rodgers [1952] Ch 110

Panel: Lord Evershed MR, Jenkins and Morris LJJ

Facts: The plaintiff, Mrs Jackson, claimed that, in the spring of 1949, her friend Mrs Freeland gave her her Hillman motor car. The car was not handed over to the plaintiff and was not then in running order. The plaintiff's evidence was that Mrs Freeland had said she would let her have the car as soon as she could get it on the road. Several months later, Mrs Freeland wrote to the plaintiff explaining that another friend's car had broken down and that she was lending the car to this other friend (Mrs Rodgers) for a few months, but that she was not going back on her word to let the plaintiff have it if she would like it. Mrs Freeland lent the car to Mrs Rodgers after having it put in order. Mrs Freeland died in April 1950, having appointed Mrs Jackson and Mrs Rodgers as executrices of her will, executed in June 1949. The plaintiff (Mrs Jackson) sought a declaration that she owned the car and that the defendant (Mrs Rodgers) be ordered to deliver it to her. The judge held that the gift to the plaintiff had been perfected and the defendant appealed. It was held that the rule in *Strong v Bird* does not apply where the intention is to make a gift in the future, rather than a present intention to make an immediate gift.

LORD EVERSHED MR

...[T]he transactions with which we are concerned took place in the spring of 1949. The plaintiff's allegation is that in that spring the testatrix gave to her the Hillman motor car, that is to say, "gave" it in the popular sense of the term, meaning to make then and there a gift of it, such gift being, however, in the eye of the law imperfect, because it was not accompanied by actual manual delivery or its equivalent; and the plaintiff says that that imperfection is, by reason of the so-called rule in *Strong v Bird*, cured by the circumstance that the plaintiff was appointed personal representative of the testatrix.

...The bare and simple proposition which is associated with the case of *Strong v Bird*, namely, that an imperfect gift may be perfected by the subsequent appointment of the donee as personal representative, disguises an important distinction. In the headnote to the case of *In re Stewart* the principle is stated thus: "The principle laid down by Jessel M.R. in *Strong v Bird* – that where a testator has expressed in his lifetime an intention to give personal estate belonging to him to one who becomes his executor, the intention to give continuing, the donee is entitled to hold the property for his own benefit - is not confined to the release of a debt; and it is immaterial whether the donee is the only executor or one of several."

That summary of the decision of Jessel M.R. seems to me to be equivocal; for the words "an intention to give" may mean either one of two things: they may mean an intention of giving, that is to say, an intention to do that which at the time of doing it was meant to be a gift out and out; or they may mean an intention to make a gift in the future, which is in effect a promise, not enforceable in the eyes of the law, to make a gift thereafter.

 Alert

I am quite satisfied that the doctrine enunciated in *Strong v Bird* does not apply to the latter of the two types of case. There must, for the application of this doctrine, be an intention of giving, as distinct from an intention to give. ...

The question, then, is whether it is established that the testatrix, at the relevant date, intended to make an absolute gift to the plaintiff of this motor car, a gift which was only imperfect in the eye of the law because of the technicality of the absence of the transfer of possession, manual delivery or its equivalent, which the law requires to perfect such a gift. ...

In relation to the letter written to Mrs Jackson, which the judge had treated as favourable to her claim, his Lordship said:

It is all in the future.

It may be that you could have a case in which a gift might be absolute, though immediate possession by the donee might be postponed. I need not discuss to what extent the two conceptions are possible as a matter of broad general theory, but prima facie, if I make an absolute gift, or purport to do so, of some chattel, and then assert a right to use it, not merely to keep it for custody, but to use it for such purposes as I think fit, on such terms as I think fit, and for such time as I think fit, it seems to me that the assertion of that right is not consistent with an absolute gift, though it may well be consistent with a promise to give at some future date. ...

LORD JUSTICE JENKINS

I agree. In order to succeed in this case the plaintiff had to prove that there was on the part of the testatrix a present intention to make an immediate gift to her, the plaintiff, of the motor car in question, and that that intention survived until the date of the testatrix's death. ...

It seems to me that th[e] conversation as reported by the plaintiff ... is consistent with a promise by the testatrix to give the car to the plaintiff when the car had been put into running order, and if that were the true construction of this conversation it would not, in my view, suffice to satisfy the requirements for the application of the rule in *Strong v Bird*.

...[T]he car was put in running order, and it was lent to the defendant...

In my view, the lending of the car to the defendant, albeit with the consent of the plaintiff, is really fatal to the plaintiff's claim that there was a continuing intention to make an immediate gift. ...[T]he principle of *Strong v Bird* ... is confined, in my view, to cases where nothing remains to be done but the mere formality of transfer, in order to perfect what was intended by the testator or testatrix to be an immediate gift, inter vivos, and surely there can be no room for its application in a case where there is an intention to give, but the gift is not completed because the intending donor desires first of all to apply the subject-matter of the contemplated or promised gift to some other purpose. ...

Accordingly, for the reasons I have endeavoured to express, as well as those stated by my Lord, I agree that this appeal should be allowed.

Lord Justice Morris also reached the conclusion that the appeal should be allowed on the basis that there was an intention to give in the future.

As has been seen above, the rule in *Strong v Bird* can apply to perfect a gift as well as to perfect the release of a debt. There seems no reason why it should not also apply to perfectly constitute a trust if the intended trustee acquires legal title as executor. The following case related to the constitution of a trust where the trustee acquired legal title indirectly. The rule in *Strong v Bird* was mentioned but the situation was not precisely the same, as the trustee obtained legal title as trustee of another family trust, rather than as executor.

In re Ralli's Will Trusts, Calvocoressi v Rodocanachi and Another, In Re Ralli's Marriage Settlement [1964] Ch 288

Panel: Buckley J

Facts: A.P.Ralli left his residuary estate on trust for his wife for life, the remainder to his two daughters, Irene and Helen, in equal shares. Some years later, Helen executed a marriage settlement, settling her existing and after-acquired property on trust for herself for life with remainder (if, as happened, she died without issue) to Irene's children. Helen also covenanted that she would transfer existing and after-acquired property to the trustees of the marriage settlement. Helen never assigned to the trustees her remainder interest under her father's will trust and she died several years before her mother, ie before her remainder interest fell into possession. The plaintiff had at some point become a trustee of the father's (A.P.Ralli's) will trust and, as the sole surviving trustee both of that trust and of Helen's marriage settlement, he brought an action to ascertain whether he should hold Helen's remainder interest for Irene's children, under the marriage settlement.

It was held that he held it on the trust of the marriage settlement. As legal title had come (without impropriety) into his hands, the trust became completely constituted and the means by which he acquired title were irrelevant.

MR JUSTICE BUCKLEY

In this case I have to consider whether certain investments which are now standing in the plaintiff's name, representing one-half of the residuary estate of the late Ambrose Pandia Ralli (whom I will call "the testator"), form in the events which have happened part of the estate of the testator's daughter Helen ... or are held upon the trusts of Helen's marriage settlement.

In the argument before me the plaintiff has supported the view that in the events which have happened Helen's half of the testator's residue is held on the trusts of the settlement. The defendants have contended that, the covenant to settle the property in question being executory and unenforceable for the benefit of Irene's children as mere volunteers outside the marriage consideration, the share of residue belongs by operation of the trusts of the will to Helen's estate. ...

The plaintiff, on the other hand, contends that, as he already holds the fund, no question of his having to enforce the covenant arises. The fund, having come without impropriety into his hands, is now, he says, impressed in his hands with the trusts upon which he ought to hold it under the settlement; and because of the covenant it does not lie in the mouth of the defendants to say that he should hold the fund in trust for Helen's estate. ...

Sir Milner Holland, for the plaintiff, says that the capacity in which the trustee has become possessed of the fund is irrelevant. Thus in *Strong v Bird* an imperfect gift was held to be completed by the donee obtaining probate of the donor's will of which he was executor. ... Similarly in *In re James* a grant of administration to two administrators was held to perfect an imperfect gift by the intestate to one of them... .

In my judgment the circumstance that the plaintiff holds the fund because he was appointed a trustee of the will is irrelevant. He is at law the owner of the fund, and the means by which he became so have no effect upon the quality of his legal ownership. The question is: For whom, if anyone, does he hold the fund in equity? In other words, who can successfully assert an equity against him disentitling him to stand upon his legal right? It seems to me to be indisputable that Helen, if she were alive, could not do so, for she has solemnly covenanted under seal to assign the fund to the plaintiff, and the defendants can stand in no better position. It is, of course, true that the object of the covenant was not that the plaintiff should retain the property for his own benefit, but that he should hold it on the trusts of the settlement. It is also true that, if it were

 Alert

necessary to enforce performance of the covenant, equity would not assist the beneficiaries under the settlement, because they are mere volunteers; and that for the same reason the plaintiff, as trustee of the settlement, would not be bound to enforce the covenant and would not be constrained by the court to do so, and indeed, it seems, might be constrained by the court not to do so. As matters stand, however, there is no occasion to invoke the assistance of equity to enforce the performance of the covenant. It is for the defendants to invoke the assistance of equity to make good their claim to the fund. To do so successfully they must show that the plaintiff cannot conscientiously withhold it from them. When they seek to do this, he can point to the covenant which, in my judgment, relieves him from any fiduciary obligation he would otherwise owe to the defendants as Helen's representatives. ...

Had someone other than the plaintiff been the trustee of the will and held the fund, the result of this part of the case would, in my judgment, have been different; and it may seem strange that the rights of the parties should depend upon the appointment of the plaintiff as a trustee of the will in 1946, which for present purposes may have been a quite fortuitous event. The result, however, in my judgment, flows – and flows, I think, quite rationally – from the consideration that the rules of equity derive from the tenderness of a court of equity for the consciences of the parties. ... In the circumstances of the present case ... it is not unconscientious in the plaintiff to withhold from Helen's estate the fund which Helen covenanted that he should receive: on the contrary, it would have been unconscientious in Helen to seek to deprive the plaintiff of that fund, and her personal representatives can be in no better position. The inadequacy of the volunteers' equity against Helen and her estate consequently is irrelevant, for that equity does not come into play... .

For these reasons I am of opinion that in the events which have happened the plaintiff now holds the fund in question on the trusts of the marriage settlement, and I will so declare.

The effect of this judgment is that a trust can become constituted if the legal title to the intended trust property vests in the trustee by any legitimate means. In the case itself, it vested in the trustee in his capacity as trustee of a different family trust. However, the case has been subjected to some criticism. The judge referred to the rule in *Strong v Bird* by way of analogy but did not allude to the requirements regarding intention that apply to that rule.

A further exception by which gifts can be perfected is by way of *donatio mortis causa* (plural: *donationes mortis causa*). The next case is often cited as setting out the essential requirements for this.

Cain v Moon [1896] 2 QB 283

Panel: Lord Russell of Killowen CJ and Wills J

Facts: The deceased deposited money at a bank and received a deposit note, which she handed to her mother (the defendant) in 1893. Five days before her death in 1895, she told her mother that, if she died, the deposit note was for her. The deceased's husband, as administrator, sued to recover the deposit note. The judge held that there was a valid *donatio mortis causa*. The plaintiff appealed. It was held that all the conditions for a valid *donatio mortis causa* had been complied with.

LORD RUSSELL OF KILLOWEN CJ

...[F]or an effectual *donatio mortis causâ* three things must combine: first, the gift or donation must have been made in contemplation, though not necessarily in expectation, of death; secondly, there must have been delivery to the donee of the subject-matter of the gift; and, thirdly, the gift must be made under such circumstances as shew that the thing is to revert to the donor in case he should recover. This last requirement is sometimes put somewhat differently, and it is said that the gift must be made under circumstances shewing that it is to take effect only if the death of the donor follows; it is not necessary to say which way of putting it is the better. ...

Alert

...Now, two of the three conditions of a good *donatio mortis causâ* existed here, for the gift was made in contemplation of death, and with the intention that it should revert to the donor in case of her recovery; but it is said that the third essential condition of such a gift was not satisfied, because there was no delivery. ... If, when the defendant visited her daughter in her last illness, she had had the note in her purse, and, when her daughter expressed her intention of benefiting her, she had handed the note to her, and the latter had handed it back accompanied with the language which she did in fact use, the case would be unarguable: because this form was not gone through, is the transaction to be deprived of the character of a *donatio mortis causâ* which it would otherwise have borne? I think not. I concede that there must be a delivery to the person to be benefited of the subject of the donatio mortis causâ; but, in my judgment, there s no reason why an antecedent delivery should not be effective. ... I think, therefore, that in the present case all the conditions legally necessary for an effective *donatio mortis causâ* were complied with, and this appeal must, consequently, be dismissed.

Alert

MR JUSTICE WILLS

I am of the same opinion. ...

In the next case, the Court of Appeal examined the issue of what needs to be 'delivered'.

Birch v Treasury Solicitor [1951] Ch 298

Panel: Lord Evershed MR, Asquith and Jenkins LJJ

Facts: The deceased had a serious accident, was admitted to hospital and died just over a month later. Shortly before her death, she instructed one of the plaintiffs to go to her home and find a handbag containing her bank books, saying she wanted the two plaintiffs (husband and wife) to have the money at the banks if anything happened to her. The plaintiffs claimed the money in the banks by way of *donatio mortis causa*. The judge dismissed the claim and the plaintiffs appealed. It was held that there was a valid *donatio mortis causa* of the money in the accounts by delivery of the deposit books.

LORD EVERSHED MR

The judgment which I am about to read is that of the court...

Th[e] evidence establishes beyond question that certain prerequisites of a valid *donatio mortis causa* were fulfilled. The gift, if otherwise valid, was made in contemplation of death; and was to take effect conditionally on death occurring and in that event only.
...

The English Law in regard to *donationes mortis causa* ... is in many respects anomalous. It was indeed questioned at one time whether the old decisions supporting *donationes mortis causa* were consistent with the Wills Act, 1837, on the ground that they are in a sense testamentary in that full effect is not given to them until the donor's death. Being before that date incomplete, the gifts are then (unlike other gifts or trusts) rendered perfect and complete by the law. "A *donatio mortis causa*", said Buckley, J., in *In re Beaumont*, "is a singular form of gift. It may be said to be of an amphibious nature being a gift which is neither entirely *inter vivos* nor testamentary. It is an act *inter vivos* by which the donee is to have the absolute title to the subject of the gift not at once but if the donor dies. If the donor dies the title becomes absolute not under but as against his executor. ..."

Because of these peculiar characteristics the courts will examine any case of alleged *donatio mortis causa* and reject it if in truth what is alleged as a *donatio* is an attempt to make ... a will ... not complying with the forms required by the Wills Act. Such, as we read it, was the case of *Reddel v Dobree*, where the donor stipulated that the box delivered to the claimant should be returned to him, the donor, every three months, thereby preserving to the donor an effective dominion over the contents which he could change from time to time. For the same reasons it is of the essence of a valid *donatio* that there should be ... delivery in fact of the thing given to the donee. As Lord Hardwicke observed in the course of his judgment in *Ward v Turner*, mere symbolic delivery will not suffice. It might, therefore, be supposed that there could be a valid *donatio* only of such subject matters as were capable of actual manual delivery. But this is clearly not the law. Thus (as Lord Hardwicke himself noted) where the thing given is of a bulky nature, the handing to the donee of the key of the box or place where the thing is kept will be sufficient and is not to be regarded as merely symbolic. So Lord Hardwicke summed the matter up by stating that it is impossible to make a *donatio mortis causa* "without a transfer or something amounting to that".

The question then is, where actual transfer does not or cannot take place, what will "amount to that"? As a matter of principle the indicia of title, as distinct from mere evidence of title, the document or thing the possession or production of which entitles the possessor to the money or property purported to be given, should satisfy Lord

Hardwicke's condition. On this ground, in our judgment, the validity of a donation of money standing to the donor's credit in a Post Office Savings Bank deposit, or a mortgage debt, should be sustained; and it appears to us irrelevant in such cases whether all the terms of the contract out of which a chose in action arises are stated in the document of title.

...As Buckley, J., stated in *In re Beaumont*: "in order that the gift may be valid it must, I think, be shown that the donor handed over either property or the indicia of title to property which belonged to him. His own cheque is not property; it is only a revocable order, such that if the banker acts on it, the donee will have the money to which it relates".

...[I]n *In re Dillon*, ... Cotton, L.J. [said]: "The case of *Duffield v Elwes* shows that there may be a good *donatio mortis causa* of an instrument which does not pass by delivery, and that the executors of the donor are trustees for the donee for the purpose of giving effect to the gift. ..."

Alert

...[W]e think that the real test is whether the instrument "amounts to a transfer" as being the essential indicia or evidence of title, possession or production of which entitles the possessor to the money or property purported to be given.

We must not, however, be taken to be casting any doubt upon the correctness of the decision in *Delgoffe v Fader*, for, as the judge observed upon the evidence before him, the deposit book there in question "was in no way essential to be produced if the depositor had required to withdraw her money". ...

What, then, is the evidence in this case as to the necessity for production of the books upon any withdrawal - for this, in the view we take, is the essential matter? In each case upon the face of the deposit book such production was beyond doubt made a term or condition of the deposit. ...

...We think accordingly that the book[s were] and [are] the essential indicia of title and that delivery of the book[s] "amounted to transfer" of the chose[s] in action.

The result is that, in our judgment, the plaintiffs are entitled to succeed... .

In the case which follows, the doctrine of *donatio mortis causa* was, for the first time, applied to a gift of land. (In an older House of Lords case, there had been *dicta* to the effect that the doctrine did not apply to land.) The judgment in this case explains how the established requirements for a valid *donatio mortis causa* can be applied in the case of land.

Sen v Headley [1991] Ch 425

Panel: Purchas, Nourse and Leggatt LJJ

Facts: Mr Hewett owned an unregistered freehold house. He and Mrs Sen had lived together for about 10 years from 1954 to 1964 and had remained close friends from then until Mr Hewett's death in December 1986. In November 1986, Mr Hewett was admitted to hospital suffering from terminal cancer and Mrs Sen visited him daily and looked after his house, to which she had always had a set of keys. At his request, she took him a bunch of keys from the sideboard drawer. Three days before he died, he told her 'The house is yours, Margaret. You have the keys. They are in your bag. The deeds are in the steel box'. After he died, Mrs Sen found in her bag the bunch of keys she had taken to him in hospital. One key was the only key to the locked steel box containing the house deeds and she found this box shortly after he died. Mrs Sen, as plaintiff, claimed that there had been a valid gift of the house. The judged dismissed her claim and the plaintiff appealed. Lord Justice Nourse gave the judgment of the Court of Appeal, holding that land is capable of passing by way of *donatio mortis causa* and that the three general requirements for such a gift had been met.

LORD JUSTICE NOURSE

Donationes mortis causa may be said to have been an anomaly in our law, both for their immunity to ... the Wills Act 1837 (7 Will. 4 & 1 Vict. c. 26) and as exceptions to the rule that there is no equity to perfect an imperfect gift. ...

There have been several judicial statements of what, in general terms, is necessary to constitute a donatio mortis causa: *Cain v Moon* [1896] 2 QB 283, 286 (Lord Russell of Killowen C.J.); *In re Craven's Estate* [1937] Ch 423, 426 (Farwell J.); and *Delgoffe v Fader* [1939] Ch 922, 927 (Luxmoore L.J.). Regard must also be had to what was said by this court in *Birch v Treasury Solicitor* [1951] Ch 298, the most authoritative of the modern decisions. If the question whether the subject matter is capable of passing by way of donatio mortis causa is put on one side, the three general requirements for such a gift may be stated very much as they are stated in *Snell's Equity*, 29th ed.(1990), pp. 380-383. First, the gift must be made in contemplation, although not necessarily in expectation, of impending death. Secondly, the gift must be made upon the condition that it is to be absolute and perfected only on the donor's death, being revocable until that event occurs and ineffective if it does not. Thirdly, there must be a delivery of the subject matter of the gift, or the essential indicia of title thereto, which amounts to a parting with dominion and not mere physical possession over the subject matter of the gift.

 Alert

...Mummery J. [at the trial] ... found no difficulty in holding that the first and second requirements were satisfied on the evidence and that part of his decision has not been questioned. He said [1990] Ch. 728, 736:

"The real difficulty in this case is caused by the third requirement which raises acutely the question whether it can ever be complied with in the case of real property when all that has occurred is an informal delivery of title deeds, or the means of access to the title deeds, accompanied by oral words of gift."

...The sufficiency of delivery in the case of a chose in action was considered at length in the judgment of this court ... in *Birch v Treasury Solicitor* [1951] Ch. 298, where it was held that there had been *donationes mortis causa* of the money standing in four accounts, by the delivery of a Post Office Savings Bank book and three other bank books of various descriptions. ...

...This court held ... that there had to be a transfer "or something amounting to that," that delivery must be made of "the essential indicia... of title, possession or production of which entitles the possessor to the money or property purported to be given;" see [1951] Ch 298, 308 and 311.

It cannot be doubted that title deeds are the essential indicia of title to unregistered land. Moreover, on the facts found by the judge, there was here a constructive delivery of the title deeds ... equivalent to an actual handing of them by Mr. Hewett to Mrs. Sen and it could not be suggested that Mr. Hewett did not part with dominion over the deeds. The two questions which remain to be decided are, first, whether Mr. Hewett parted with dominion over the house; secondly, if he did, whether land is capable of passing by way of a *donatio mortis causa*.

We have traced the need for there to be a parting with dominion over the subject matter of the gift, i.e. with the ability to control it, to the judgment of Lord Kenyon C.J. in *Hawkins v Blewitt* (1798) 2 Esp. 663, where he said:

"In the case of a *donatio mortis causa*, possession must be immediately given. That has been done here; a delivery has taken place; but it is also necessary that by parting with the possession, the deceased should also part with the dominion over it. That has not been done here."

A similar view was taken in *Reddel v Dobree* (1839) 10 Sim. 244 and *In re Johnson* (1905) 92 LT 357. In each of those three cases the alleged donor delivered a locked box to the alleged donee and either retained or took back the key to it; in *Reddel v Dobree* he also reserved and exercised a right to take back the box. In each of them it was held that the alleged donor had retained dominion over the box and that there had been no *donatio mortis causa*.

It appears therefore that the need for there to be a parting with dominion was first identified in cases where the subject matter of the gift was a locked box and its contents. In *Birch v Treasury Solicitor* [1951] Ch 298 as we have seen, a similar need was recognised where the subject matter of the gift was a chose in action. Without in any way questioning that need, we think it appropriate to observe that a parting with dominion over an intangible thing such as a chose in action is necessarily different from a parting with dominion over a tangible thing such as a locked box and its contents. We think that in the former case a parting with dominion over the essential indicia of title will ex hypothesi usually be enough. ...

...We therefore respectfully disagree with the judge's view ... that a delivery of title deeds can never amount to a parting with dominion over the land. As appears from *Birch v Treasury Solicitor* [1951] Ch 298, the question is one to be decided on the facts of the individual case.

 Alert

We do not suggest that there might never be a state of facts where there was a parting with dominion over the essential indicia of title to a chose in action but nevertheless a retention of dominion over the chose itself... . ...It is true that in the eyes of the law Mr. Hewett, by keeping his own set of keys to the house, retained possession of it. But the benefits which thereby accrued to him were wholly theoretical. He uttered the words of gift, without reservation, two days after his readmission to hospital, when he knew that he did not have long to live and when there could have been no practical possibility of his ever returning home. He had parted with dominion over the title deeds. Mrs. Sen had her own set of keys to the house and was in effective control of it. In all the circumstances of the case, we do not believe that the law requires us to hold that Mr. Hewett did not part with dominion over the house. We hold that he did.

Having now decided that the third of the general requirements for a donatio mortis causa was satisfied in this case, we come to the more general question whether land is capable of passing by way of such a gift. ...

His Lordship referred to the formalities for declaring trusts of land contained in the Law of Property Act 1925 s 53(1)(b) and continued:

Section 53(2) is in these terms: "This section does not affect the creation or operation of resulting, implied or constructive trusts."

...In general it may be said that the constructive trust has been a ready means of developing our property law in modern times and that the process is a continuing one.

Let it be agreed that the doctrine is anomalous. Anomalies do not justify anomalous exceptions. ... [I]t is apparent that to make a distinction in the case of land would be to make just such an exception. A *donatio mortis causa* of land is neither moe nor less anomalous than any other. Every such gift is a circumvention of the Wills Act 1837. Why should the additional statutory formalities for the creation and transmission of interests in land be regarded as some larger obstacle? The only step which has to be taken is to extend the application of the implied or constructive trust arising on the donor's death... . ...

We hold that land is capable of passing by way of a donatio mortis causa and that the three general requirements for such a gift were satisfied in this case. We therefore allow Mrs. Sen's appeal.

 Alert

Further Reading

Margaret Halliwell, 'Perfecting imperfect gifts and trusts: have we reached the end of the Chancellor's foot?', [2003] *67 Conveyancer* 192

5

Secret Trusts

Topic List

Introduction

Generally, anyone who wishes to create a trust to take effect on his or her death must make sure that the trust is sufficiently certain: a clear intention to create a trust must be expressed in the will, and there must be certainty of object and subject-matter. The testator must also comply with the rules on formalities and constitution. The formalities to be followed are set out in Wills Act 1837 s 9: in writing, signed by the testator and witnessed correctly. Constitution of the trust happens on death, when the legal title to all of the property vests in the trustees by operation of law.

There are, however, some situations in which a person may wish to set up a trust upon death without revealing the details in his or her will. For example, historically, a testator may have wished to provide for his mistress and illegitimate children without anyone else knowing.

The courts have recognised the validity of certain trusts which do not comply with the formalities in Wills Act s 9. Some trusts are known as fully secret trusts, because their existence and terms are not obvious from reading the will: it appears that there is an absolute gift to the secret trustee. Other trusts are mentioned in the will but the terms of the trust are not fully disclosed. These are known as half secret trusts.

There are stringent rules which must be obeyed before these trusts are valid, and there are differences in the rules applicable to fully secret trusts and to half secret trusts.

5.1 The Justification for Upholding Secret Trusts

The justification for recognising the fully secret trust was the prevention of fraud on the part of the secret trustee. As the existence of the trust was not apparent on the face of the will, it was open to the secret trustee to use the Wills Act 1837 to say that, as the testator had not complied with the statutory provisions, the secret trustee took the property absolutely.

McCormick v Grogan (1869) LR 4 HL 82

Panel: Lord Hatherley LC, Lord Westbury, Lord Colonsay and Lord Cairns

Facts: The testator made a will leaving his estate to Grogan. After he had made the will, the testator told Grogan this. Grogan was surprised, but the testator told him he would have it no other way. He told him where to find the will and that there was a letter with it. After the death, Grogan found the letter which contained the names of many people and stated 'I do not wish you to act strictly on the foregoing instructions, but leave it to your own good judgement to do as you think I would, if living...'. Grogan paid many of the gifts itemised in the letter, but not all of them. McCormick, who had not received anything although he was mentioned in the letter, sought a declaration that there was a secret trust in his favour.

The House of Lords said that a secret trust could be enforced where the alleged trustee is perpetuating a fraud on the testator and the intended beneficiary. The fraud arises when he refuses to carry out his obligations on the basis that the formalities in the Wills Act s 9 had not been complied with and that therefore the trust had not been properly set up. However, the House of Lords in this case held that there was no secret trust: the testator had not intended to impose a trust on Grogan. Further, Grogan had genuinely believed that he had good reason to exclude McCormick and therefore there was no bad conscience on his part.

LORD HATHERLEY LC

Now this doctrine has been established, no doubt, a long time since upon a sound foundation with reference to the jurisdiction of Courts of Equity to interpose in all cases of fraud; and therefore if, for example, an heir said to a person who was competent to dispose of his property by will, "Do not dispose of it by will, I undertake to carry into effect all such wishes as you may communicate to me." And if the testator, acting on that representation, did not dispose of his property by will, and the heir has kept the property for himself, without carrying those instructions into effect, the Court of Equity has interposed on the ground of the fraud thus committed by the heir in inducing the testator to die intestate, upon the faith of the heir's representations that he would carry all such wishes as were confided to him into effect. ...

So again, if a legatee states to the testator that upon the testator's confiding his property, apparently disposing of it, to him, the legatee, by a regular and formal instrument, he will carry into effect all such intentions as the testator shall confide to him, then that legatee, although he apparently may be held in law to take the whole interest, shall have fastened upon his conscience the trust of carrying into full effect those instructions which he received upon such representations as I have described. ... Such an undertaking or promise on the part of the legatee has been held, in some cases, to be capable of being inferred from the conduct of the person when secret instructions have been communicated to him by the testator, which conduct has been held by the Court to be equivalent to an undertaking or promise on his part that he will abide by the instructions so communicated to him.

But this doctrine evidently requires to be carefully restricted within proper limits. It is in itself a doctrine which involves a wide departure from the policy which induced the Legislature to pass the Statute of Frauds, and it is only in clear cases of fraud that this doctrine has been applied—cases in which the Court has been persuaded that there has been a fraudulent inducement held out on the part of the apparent beneficiary in order to lead the testator to confide to him the duty which he so undertook to perform.

His Lordship then reviewed the evidence and found that there was no trust, and no fraud on the testator's intention:

...this gentleman did, to a certain extent, carry into effect the arrangements described in this letter of instructions. ... Finding himself thus placed in a position which was in no way of his own seeking, and finding this letter of his friend, he has, to the best of his judgment, carried those instructions into effect, with the desire, doubtless, of doing that which he would think it right and reasonable to do, though under no possible legal obligation to effectuate intentions which were not properly and legally conveyed to him.

Lord Westbury also emphasised the rationale for upholding secret trusts: The prevention of fraud on the intentions of the testator. Like Lord Hatherley LC, he found that there was no fraud in this particular case.

LORD WESTBURY

...if an individual on his deathbed, or at any other time, is persuaded by his heir-at-law, or his next of kin, to abstain from making a will, or if the same individual, having made a will, communicates the disposition to the person on the face of the will benefited by that disposition, but, at the same time, says to that individual that he has a purpose to answer which he has not expressed in the will, but which he depends on the disponee to carry into effect, and the disponee assents to it, either expressly, or by any mode of action which the disponee knows must give to the testator the impression and belief that he fully assents to the request, then, undoubtedly, the heir-at-law in the one case, and the disponee in the other, will be converted into trustees, simply on the principle that an individual shall not be benefited by his own personal fraud.

This justification had been used before in *Wallgrave v Tebbs* (1855) 2 K&J 313. It was subsequently reiterated for fully secret trusts in *Blackwell v Blackwell* [1929] AC 318, although the remarks are *obiter*, as the case concerned a half secret trust (it is discussed fully later in this chapter in the section on half secret trusts). With half secret trusts, the existence of the trust was clear, so fraud was an insufficient reason to uphold them. The justification in these cases was that the trust arose outside or 'dehors' the will, and did not therefore have to comply with the Wills Act 1837 s 9.

Link
See *Blackwell v Blackwell*

Re Gardner [1923] 2 Ch 230

Panel: Romer J

Facts: The testatrix in her will gave property to her husband 'knowing he will carry out my wishes'. At that time, those words were sufficient to show an intention to create a trust. The testatrix then signed a memorandum, setting out what she wanted her husband to do, but she did not execute it formally, so it did not operate as a valid codicil. The question was whether there was a valid trust. If there was, one third of the property went to the estate of a beneficiary who had predeceased the testatrix. The judge held that a trust arose when there was communication and acceptance during the testatrix's lifetime: it therefore arose dehors or 'outside of' the will.

MR JUSTICE ROMER

I cannot see why a trust for the benefit of individuals engrafted upon property given to the donee by a will or by means of an intestacy should be treated as a gift made to those individuals by the will of the donor any more than it should be so treated where the property has been given to the donee by the donor in his lifetime. The principle has nothing to do with the fact that the gift has been made by one method rather than by

Alert

another. Apart from authority I should without hesitation say that in the present case the husband held the corpus of the property upon trust for the two nieces and the nephew, notwithstanding the fact that the niece predeceased the testatrix. The rights of the parties appear to me to be exactly the same as though the husband, after the memorandum had been communicated to him by the testatrix in the year 1909, had executed a declaration of trust binding himself to hold any property that should come to him upon his wife's partial intestacy upon trust as specified in the memorandum.

This reasoning creates a difficulty in that the trust was not in fact completely constituted until the death of the testatrix as the legal title to the property did not vest in the trustee until the death had occurred. This however did not seem to worry the courts and the 'dehors the will' theory was discussed again in *Blackwell v Blackwell* and in the following case.

Link
to *Blackwell v Blackwell*, passage marked C

Re Young [1951] Ch 344

Panel: Danckwerts J

Facts: The testator made a will containing a fully secret trust. The testator's chauffeur was one of the beneficiaries under that trust. He was also one of the witnesses to the will. Under the Wills Act 1837 s 15, a gift to a beneficiary who witnesses the will fails. The question here was whether the gift given by way of secret trust failed. The court upheld the trust on the basis that it arose outside of the will, so it was irrelevant that the chauffeur witnessed the will.

MR JUSTICE DANCKWERTS

The widow has testified that the testator's intention, as communicated to her, was that the man who had been employed by the testator for many years as chauffeur and general factotum should receive a legacy of £2,000. The chauffeur was one of the two attesting witnesses to the will, and if he takes the legacy under the terms of the will the result of s.15 of the Wills Act, 1837, is to make his legacy ineffective. The question is whether he takes the legacy under the will. Mr. Christie, on behalf of the next-of-kin, referred to In re Fleetwood (15 Ch D 594), a case of a secret trust, decided by Hall, V.-C., where it was held that, as a woman intended to be a beneficiary was one of the attesting witnesses to the fourth codicil, the trust for her failed as to her beneficial interest, as it would have done, Hall, V.-C., said, had it been declared in the codicil. It appears that the point was not argued in that particular case, which was concerned with a number of other points; and it seems to me that that particular decision is contrary to principle. The whole theory of the formation of a secret trust is that the Wills Act has nothing to do with the matter because the forms required by the Wills Act are entirely disregarded, since the persons do not take by virtue of the gift in the will, but by virtue of the secret trusts imposed upon the beneficiary, who does in fact take under the will.

Alert

Having explained why he thinks that the decision in *In re Fleetwood* was per incuriam, Danckwerts J continued:

It seems to me that according to ... *In re Gardner*, every consideration connected with this principle requires me to reach the conclusion that a beneficiary under a secret trust does not take under the will, and that he is not, therefore, affected by s.15 of the Wills Act, 1837. Accordingly, the legacy intended for Thomas Cobb, though given in an indirect manner, is effective and he has not forfeited it.

Upholding secret and half secret trusts has thus been justified by case law. There has however been much academic debate and the practice has been criticised as being outmoded.

Challinor, E., 'Debunking the myth of secret trusts?' 2005 LQR 492

On analysing the 'dehors the will' theory she says:

I submit that a closer analysis of this temptingly neat theory reveals it to be flawed. The theory claims that secret trusts are governed by the law of trusts and not that of probate, and yet these trusts involve a departure from the usual rules pertaining to trusts. For in upholding secret trusts, the courts are allowing trusts to bind after-acquired property, and under the normal rules of trusts it is impossible to declare an immediate trust of future property, or a trust which binds such property as and when it is received.

On the fraud theory, she comments:

In fully-secret trusts, unless evidence of the trust is admitted contrary to the provisions of the Wills Act, the intended trustee will be able to take the property beneficially and will profit from his own misconduct, so this justification for the enforcement of these trusts on this basis does seem valid. Here equity would be acting in a way with which we are familiar in other areas of the law, such as in *Rochefouchauld v Boustead*.

However, this original and narrow conception of the "fraud theory" does not explain the existence of half-secret trusts. In such a trust, the intended trustee takes the property as trustee on the face of the will, and there is no possibility of him taking beneficially even if the court declined to admit evidence of the terms of the trust. He would hold the property on resulting trust for residue or next of kin. Moreover, even in cases of fully-secret trusts, the case law exhibits examples of where any justification on the basis of a "*malus animus*" is no longer valid. The "fraud theory" has been extended in an attempt to encompass a justification of half-secret trusts and the modern case law. Hodge argues that it is not the personal fraud of the purported legatee, but a general fraud committed upon the testator and the beneficiaries by reason of the failure to observe the intentions of the former and of the destruction of the beneficial interests of the latter, which secret trusts seek to avoid.

...

In *Blackwell v Blackwell*, Lord Buckmaster also adopted this wider version of the fraud argument (Lord Hailsham L.C. concurring), claiming that "the personal benefit of the legatee cannot be the sole determining factor in considering the admissibility of the evidence" that if a clear promise is made by the intended trustee, inducing a gift to be made in his will, "the trustee is not at liberty to suppress the evidence of the trust and thus destroy the whole object of its creation, in fraud on the beneficiaries." While *Blackwell v Blackwell* was a case concerning a half-secret trust, it is clear that this reasoning was intended to apply equally to fully-secret trusts.

However, there does exist a huge flaw in extending the theory this far; it amounts to no more than a bald assertion that a testator's wishes should be respected even if he has put them into effect in a manner that is not acceptable (that is, not in compliance with s.9 of the Wills Act). In many cases the true intention of the testator cannot be put into place, and purported beneficiaries under ineffective wills are routinely deprived of property which testators or settlors would desire them to have, simply because trusts and wills have not been put into effect in the proper manner. The tradition equitable maxim that "equity will not permit a statute to be used as an instrument of fraud" must be adapted to something more like "equity will not allow a statute to be used so as to renege on a promise" if it is to fit with the situations envisaged in *Blackwell v Blackwell*. As Critchley has pointed out, this widening of the fraud theory focuses "on potential, rather than actual, wrongdoing ... the policy aim underlying (it) is thus proactive (or preventative) rather than reactive (or curative)". The very mild form of fraud which it envisages does not justify equitable intervention in the face of strict statutory provisions in the same way that a *malus animus* does.

Link
See Critchley's article in Further Reading

In order to recap, the two principal arguments which have been advanced in order to justify and explain the existence of secret trusts do not seem to give the all-embracing and logical explanations which they purport to provide. It seems that the doctrine developed organically, changing on a case to case basis in order to suit the particular situations which arose.

Concluding that the doctrine is difficult to justify, she says:

Here, the continued existence of secret trusts seems to be divorced from the initial contexts in which it first operated. Changes in society have rendered the need for secrecy largely obsolete. Gifts for charity no longer require it, and a desire to provide for objects which someone would not wish to reveal can be achieved more efficiently by other means. [Challinor suggests that a bank account could be opened in the beneficiary's name.]

We must admit, with Moffatt, that: "today it is more likely that a secret trust will be used by the indecisive rather than secretive testator" such as was with the testatrix in *Snowden, Re*; allowing such testators to avoid the expensive and tiresome process required under the Wills Act. However, as Watkin has pointed out, this is obviously no valid justification for the departure from a clear legislative intent. The role of equity seems, in this area, to have been expanded too far. The present situation is much more like that described in the contention made in this question; the trusts are used as a covert device to avoid formalities. Secret trusts, then, are a relic of older days and their continued existence seems an anomaly. Even commentators who argue that there are no sound justifications for the existence of secret trusts, tend to argue that the doctrine is "too well established to be disturbed" or they reassure us that "we should not be too alarmed" for, "the probability is that few testators wish to rely on them and hence they do not constitute a serious threat to the practice of formal will making".

Link
See article by Meager which is extracted at the end of the chapter

Conclusion

I would disagree, arguing that these reasons are not sufficient to demand the continued existence of secret trusts. There is much to be said for an abolition, or at least a fundamental revision, of the law relating to them, as the law is confused, and justifications for the distinctions between the two types of secret trusts are difficult to find. They serve a very limited social purpose and fraud would be better prevented by an insistence upon compliance with the requirements of the Wills Act.

5.2 Secret Trusts and Certainty

Kasperbauer and another v Griffith and others [2000] 1 WTLR 333

Panel: Peter Gibson, Aldous LJJ and Harman J

Facts: In his will, Mr Griffith left a freehold property, Lower Hazel House, to his widow Rosemary. At a family meeting prior to his death, Mr Griffith explained that he wanted to benefit his two children, and that in order to avoid inheritance tax, he did not intend to write his wishes down. He said that Rosemary 'knew what she had to do' with the house. After his death, his son and daughter claimed that Rosemary held the house on secret trust for them. The Court of Appeal agreed with the judge at first instance that there was no intention to create a trust. Rosemary took the house absolutely.

LORD JUSTICE PETER GIBSON

First, he quoted the explanation of the doctrine of secret trusts by Nourse J in *In re Cleaver, decd*, [1981] 1 WLR 939.

"The principle of all these cases is that a court of equity will not permit a person to whom property is transferred by way of gift, but on the faith of an agreement or clear understanding that it is to be dealt with in a particular way for the benefit of a third person, to deal with that property inconsistently with that agreement or understanding. If he attempts to do so after having received the benefit of the gift equity will intervene by imposing a constructive trust on the property which is the subject matter of the agreement or understanding...

 Alert

I would emphasise that the agreement or understanding must be such as to impose on the donee a legally binding obligation to deal with the property in the particular way and that the other two certainties, namely, those as to the subject matter of the trust and the persons intended to benefit under it are as essential to this species of trust as they are to any other."

He then set out the requirements for a valid fully secret trust:

... the authorities make plain that what is needed is (i) an intention by the testator to create a trust, satisfying the traditional requirement of three certainties (that is to say certain language in imperative form, certain subject-matter and certain objects or beneficiaries); (ii) the communication of the trust to the legatee, and (iii) acceptance of the trust by the legatee, which acceptance can take the form of silent acquiescence. The crucial question in the present case is whether there was that intention and, as Mr Justice Brightman said in *Ottaway v Norman* [1972] Ch 698, ... it is an essential element that the testator must intend to subject the legatee to an obligation in favour of the intended beneficiary. That will be evidenced by appropriately imperative, as distinct from precatory, language. Similarly in *In re Snowden*, decd [1979] Ch 528, ... Sir Robert Megarry V.-C., in considering whether a secret trust was imposed on a legatee by an arrangement, raised the question at page 534:

"In particular, did it impose a trust, or did it amount to a mere moral or family obligation?"

The judge emphasised that once the appropriate elements are found, a secret trust will be imposed by the court by way of constructive trust:

Whilst I of course accept that, once the essential elements of a secret trust are found to be present, equity acts to prevent fraud or other unconscionable conduct by imposing a constructive trust, I emphasise the need to fulfil those essential requirements.

 Link
See also the Express / Constructive trusts section in this chapter

After surveying the evidence, including the solicitor's attendance notes, he concluded:

To my mind the phrase which the testator repeated, that the widow knew what she had to do, is equivocal and is at least consistent with the belief and intention on the part of the testator that his expressed intentions imposed only a moral obligation on her. Plainly there was evidence on which the judge could reach that conclusion. It is to my mind strongly supported by Dr Burrows' [the solicitor's] attendance notes and her oral evidence. True it is that Dr Burrows was never told of the meeting on 14 February. Nevertheless the words used by the testator, recorded in the attendance note of 9 March 1993, of an outright gift coupled with the testator's realisation that it was up to the widow whether to pass a share back to Rhodri and Sian after the testator's death and his feeling that she would do so, are plainly indicative of the fact that the testator regarded the obligation on the widow to be only a moral one. It is supported too by the language used by the testator to Mr Havens [a friend] that there had to be a certain amount of trust. There was ample evidence before the judge on which he could reach his conclusion that the testator did not intend to impose an enforceable obligation on the widow.

5.3 Fully Secret Trusts

As stated above, not only must there be an intention to create a trust, but the trust must be communicated to the intended trustee and accepted by him or her. Unless this is done, the trustee's conscience is not affected by trusteeship and he takes the property as an absolute gift. In the case of a fully secret trust, the existence of, terms of, and property subject to the trust must be communicated before death, generally to all trustees.

5.3.1 Communication

Wallgrave v Tebbs (1855) 2 K&J 313

Panel: Sir W Page Wood V-C

Facts: In his will, William Coles left £12,000 and some freehold property to Tebbs and Martin. Coles had thought about whether these gifts should be applied for charitable purposes, and he had had a letter drawn up setting out his ideas, but had never signed it. Tebbs and Martin knew nothing about this letter until after Coles' death, nor had they promised to carry out his wishes. Wallgrave, Coles' executor, wanted the money to be applied for the charitable purposes, but Tebbs and Martin claimed that they took it absolutely because no trust had been created. The court agreed: there was no trust as there had been no communication of its existence during the testator's lifetime.

SIR W PAGE-WOOD V-C

Where a person, knowing that a testator in making a disposition in his favour intends it to be applied for purposes other than his own benefit, either expressly promises, or by silence implies, that he will carry the testator's intention into effect, and the property is left to him upon the faith of that promise or undertaking, it is in effect a case of trust; and, in such a case, the Court will not allow the devisee to set up the Statute of Frauds, or rather the Statute of Wills, by which the Statute of Frauds is now, in this respect, superseded; and for this reason: the devisee by his conduct has induced the testator to leave him the property; and, as Lord Justice Turner says in *Russell v Jackson*, (10 Hare, 211) no one can doubt that, if the devisee had stated that he would not carry into effect the intentions of the testator, the disposition in his favour would not have been found in the will. But in this the Court does not violate the spirit of the statute: but for the same end, namely, prevention of fraud, it engrafts the trust on the devise, by admitting evidence which the statute would in terms exclude, in order to prevent a party from applying property to a purpose foreign to that for which he undertook to hold it.

But the question here is totally different. Here there has been no such promise or undertaking on the part of the devisees. Here the devisees knew nothing of the testator's intention until after his death. That the testator desired, and was most anxious, to have his intentions carried out is clear. But it is equally clear that he has suppressed everything illegal. He has abstained from creating, either by his will or otherwise, any trust upon which this Court can possibly fix. Upon the face of the will the parties take indisputably for their own benefit. Can I possibly hold that the gift is void? If I knew perfectly well that a testator in making me a bequest, absolute on the face of the will, intended it to be applied for the benefit of a natural child, of whom he was not known to be the father, provided that intention had not been communicated to me during the testator's life, the validity of the bequest as an absolute bequest to me could not be questioned.

He applied that reasoning to the facts before him:

In the present case there is no trust created. It is impossible for the Court to look upon a document which is excluded by the statute; and, such evidence being excluded, the case is reduced to one in which the testator has relied solely on the honor of the devisees, who, as far as this Court is concerned, are left perfectly at liberty to apply the property to their own purposes.

In re Maddock [1902] 2 Ch 220

Panel: Collins MR; Stirling and Cozens-Hardy LJJ

Facts: Sarah Maddock made a will in which she left the residue of her estate to Susan Washington absolutely. A few days afterwards, Maddock executed a memorandum, which did not comply with the relevant formalities so as to be a valid codicil to the will. The memorandum instructed the trustees to hold part of the residue on trust. Maddock communicated the contents of the memorandum to Washington before her death and Washington accepted that she held the residue on trust. It was held that there was a binding trust, and that the property subject to the trust could not be used to pay the debts of the estate.

The Master of the Rolls applied *Wallgrave v Tebbs*.

COLLINS MR

The obligation ... has, it would seem, as between the legatee, who under such circumstances accepts the legacy, and the persons designated by the testator as beneficiaries, the character of a trust. But the right of the latter is wholly dependent on whether the legatee accepts the legacy with knowledge of the mandate, and no right for them arises at all unless and until the legatee has, with notice, accepted the legacy. A personal relation is then established between these two parties, without reference to others, and, as between them, would seem to have the incidents of a trust.

LORD JUSTICE STIRLING:

...as between Miss Washington and the beneficiaries under the memorandum, the savings have been separated in favour of those beneficiaries from the general mass of the testator's estate, and made subject to the disposition expressed in the memorandum. *Primâ facie*, therefore, it seems to me that, as between Miss Washington and those beneficiaries, ... that the savings ought (as between that property and the other property given to Miss Washington) to be held exempted from the charges which fall primarily on the personal estate not specifically bequeathed.

The memorandum itself when carefully examined seems to me to contain much which serves to indicate that this was the meaning of the testatrix. She states that she leaves the document "with her will": she desires the fund to be invested by her trustees. In my opinion, this indicates her meaning to be that the memorandum should (as between the beneficiaries thereunder and Miss Washington) be taken as forming part of her testamentary disposition, and that (as between the same parties) the memorandum should take effect as if it had been a duly executed codicil, and the like consequences as regards the administration of the estate must follow.

Lord Justice Cozens-Hardy agreed that there was a secret trust:

LORD JUSTICE COZENS-HARDY

It is clear that no unattested document can be admitted to probate or treated as part of the will. It is established that a devisee or legatee, who is entitled absolutely upon the terms of the will, is in no way affected by the existence of a document shewing that he was not intended to enjoy beneficially, if he had no knowledge of the document until after the death of the testator. Such a memorandum may or may not influence him as a man of honour, but no legal effect can be given to it. If, however, the devisee or legatee is informed of the testator's intention, either before the will in his favour is made or at any time afterwards before the testator's death, different considerations arise. It is sometimes said that under such circumstances a trust is created in favour of the beneficiaries under the memorandum.

[He makes some obiter comments on what would happen to the trust if the secret trustee were to predecease the testator, or disclaim:]

Now, the so-called trust does not affect the property except by reason of a personal obligation binding the individual devisee or legatee. If he renounces and disclaims, or dies in the lifetime of the testator, the persons claiming under the memorandum can take nothing against the heir-at-law or next of kin or residuary devisee or legatee.

Link
See *Blackwell v Blackwell*

Thus, a secret trust may fail if the secret trustee predeceases the testator or disclaims the gift, in exactly the same way that an absolute gift will fail in the same circumstances. The opposite view was taken by Lord Buckmaster in *Blackwell v Blackwell* which is set out later in this chapter. He suggested, obiter, that a trustee in a fully secret trust will not be permitted to renounce the gift and thereby defeat the trust. He did not, however, say what would happen in the event of the trustee predeceasing the testator.

Decipher
Note that the judges appear to contradict each other.

It is unclear what happens in the case of a half secret trust, although the general equitable principle that a court will not permit a trust to fail for want of a trustee may operate.

Re Boyes (1884) 26 Ch D 531

Panel: Kay J

Facts: Boyes wished to provide for Nell Brown (his lover), and their child. He instructed his solicitor, Carritt, to prepare a will in which he left his estate to Carritt absolutely. Carritt was to hold the estate subject to directions which Boyes would give him later. After Boyes' death, two letters were found, leaving £25 to Carritt and the rest to Nell. At no time did Carritt argue that this was an absolute gift to him: he always acknowledged that he held the property on trust. Boyes' legitimate next of kin argued that because Carritt did not know the terms of the trust during Boyes' lifetime, he held the estate on resulting trust for them. The court reluctantly agreed.

MR JUSTICE KAY

There is another well-known class of cases where no trust appears on the face of the will, but the testator has been induced to make the will, or, having made it, has been induced not to revoke it by a promise on the part of the devisee or legatee to deal with the property, or some part of it in a specified manner. In these cases the Court has compelled discovery and performance of the promise, treating it as a trust binding the conscience of the donee, on the ground that otherwise a fraud would be committed, because it is to be presumed that if it had not been for such promise the testator would not have made or would have revoked the gift. ...

But no case has ever yet decided that a testator can by imposing a trust upon his devisee or legatee, the objects of which he does not communicate to him, enable himself to evade the Statute of Wills by declaring those objects in an unattested paper found after his death.

The essence of all those decisions is that the devisee or legatee accepts a particular trust which thereupon becomes binding upon him, and which it would be a fraud in him not to carry into effect.

If the trust was not declared when the will was made, it is essential in order to make it binding, that it should be communicated to the devisee or legatee in the testator's lifetime and that he should accept that particular trust. It may possibly be that he would be bound if the trust had been put in writing and placed in his hands in a sealed envelope, and he had engaged that he would hold the property given to him by the will upon the trust so declared although he did not know the actual terms of the trust: *McCormick v Grogan* . ...

The legatee might be a trustee, but the trust declared by such an unattested paper would not be good. For this purpose there is no difference whether the devisee or legatee is declared to be a trustee on the face of the will, or by an engagement with the testator not appearing on the will. The devisee or legatee cannot by accepting an indefinite trust enable the testator to make an unattested codicil.

I cannot help regretting that the testator's intention of bounty should fail by reason of an informality of this kind, but in my opinion it would be a serious innovation upon the law relating to testamentary instruments if this were to be established as a trust in her favour.

Re Stead [1900] 1 Ch 237

Panel: Farwell J

Facts: Maria Stead made a will leaving the residue of her estate to Mrs Witham and Mrs Andrew as joint tenants absolutely. Mrs Witham alleged that Maria had, after executing her will, told her that she and Mrs Andrew would hold the residue subject to a trust in favour of Maria's nephew and charities. Maria left her will unchanged, on the basis that Mrs Witham had consented to carry out the trust, and in confidence that Mrs Andrew would also carry out her obligations under the trust. Mrs Andrew denied that she was bound by the secret trust as she did not know about it until after Maria's death. The judge surveyed the authorities and found the state of the law to be unsatisfactory and difficult to justify. The general rule is that only those to whom the trust is communicated are bound by the trust. The exception is that if the gift is to joint tenants, both are bound if the communication took place prior to the execution of the will. In this case, as the communication took place after the execution of the will to joint tenants, Mrs Andrew was not bound by the trust and took a half share absolutely.

> **MR JUSTICE FARWELL**
>
> If A. induces B. either to make, or to leave unrevoked, a will leaving property to A. and C. as tenants in common, by expressly promising, or tacitly consenting, that he and C. will carry out the testator's wishes, and C. knows nothing of the matter until after A.'s death, A. is bound, but C. is not bound: *Tee v Ferris* 2 K&J 357; the reason stated being, that to hold otherwise would enable one beneficiary to deprive the rest of their benefits by setting up a secret trust. If, however, the gift were to A. and C. as joint tenants, the authorities have established a distinction between those cases in which the will is made on the faith of an antecedent promise by A. and those in which the will is left unrevoked on the faith of a subsequent promise. In the former case, the trust binds both A. and C.: *Russell v Jackson* 10 Hare 204; *Jones v Badley* LR 3 Ch 362; the reason stated being that no person can claim an interest under a fraud committed by another; in the latter case A. and not C. is bound: *Burney v Macdonald* 15 Sim 6 and *Moss v Cooper* 1 J&H 352, the reason stated being that the gift is not tainted with any fraud in procuring the execution of the will. Personally I am unable to see any difference between a gift made on the faith of an antecedent promise and a gift left unrevoked on the faith of a subsequent promise to carry out the testator's wishes; but apparently a distinction has been made by the various judges who have had to consider the question. I am bound, therefore, to decide in accordance with these authorities, and accordingly I hold that the defendant Mrs. Andrew is not bound by any trust.

It is unclear whether the principle in *Re Stead* applies to secret trusts of land, and to half secret trusts of any type of property. Trustees must hold the legal title in a trust of land as joint tenants (Law of Property Act 1925 s 1(6)). Therefore, it appears that there is no scope for the application of the principle, as there is no possibility of the trustees holding land as tenants in common. Further, in *Re Stead* communication took place after the execution of the will. Where there is a half secret trust, communication must take place before the execution of the will so it is doubtful whether the principle can apply.

5.3.2 Acceptance

In addition to communication of the trust, the secret trustee must accept the trust; either expressly, or impliedly by conduct or silence.

Moss v Cooper (1861) 1 J&H 352

Panel: Sir W Page Wood V-C

Facts: The testator wanted to give the residue of his estate to charity. He made a will giving it to Mr Gawthorn, Mr Sedman and Mr Owen absolutely, with a memorandum containing the testator's suggestions for dividing it in favour of various charities. The will and memorandum were communicated by Gawthorn to the others without any express acceptance or refusal of the trust. Sedman later said he would try to carry out the testator's wishes as far as he could; Owen did not say anything; Gawthorn predeceased the testator. It was argued that as Sedman and Owen had not accepted the trust and their consciences had therefore not been affected, they could take absolutely. The court disagreed. Sedman had specifically accepted; Owen's acceptance could be inferred from his silence.

SIR W PAGE WOOD V-C

...To fasten any trust upon an absolute bequest of property, it is necessary to prove knowledge on the part of the legatee of the intended trust, and acquiescence, either by words of consent or by silence, when the intention is communicated to him. ...

Alert

Here it is said that the testator intended to give the legatees full and complete control over the property. On the face of the will he did; but the question is whether, behind that intention, he had not a further desire to secure as far as possible their obedience to his wishes. ...

If, immediately after making his will (for a bargain before the will is not at all essential), the testator had invited Gawthorn, Owen and Sedman to his house, and had said to them, "Here is my will, made in this form, because I am told that the property must be put entirely at your disposal; but I want a promise from you to dispose of it in a particular way:" and if they, by their silence, led him to believe they would so apply it, I apprehend it is quite clear that a trust would be created, and that it is altogether immaterial whether the promise is made before or after the execution of the will, that being a revocable instrument. The legatees, as soon as they learned the intention of the testator, would be bound to elect whether they would undertake the trust or not. If they are silent, the trust, if legal, must be executed, and if not, the gift will altogether fail.

Alert

Once the trust has been communicated and accepted, and the testator relies on that acceptance by making the will accordingly, or by changing it, or by not making a will at all, the secret trust is valid and the trustee is bound. Usually, the secret trustee is obliged to deal with the relevant property in accordance with the testator's wishes, during their lifetimes. However, the obligation may be for the trustee to make a will in a particular way.

Ottaway v Norman [1972] Ch 698

Panel: Brightman J

Facts: Ottaway left his house and contents to Eva Hodges by his will. There was ample evidence of conversations during which Ottaway communicated his intention that she dispose of the property by will in favour of Ottaway's son and his wife. She agreed and made a will in appropriate terms, but some years afterwards made a new one leaving it to Norman. The son and wife sought a declaration that there had been an intention to create a trust, communication, acceptance and reliance, and therefore Eva was not at liberty to gift the property elsewhere in her will. The court held that there was a valid secret trust and Eva's conscience was bound. It did not matter that there was no deliberate fraud on Eva's part, nor was it relevant how Ottaway's intention was to be carried out: there was no distinction to be drawn between an obligation to transfer property *inter vivos* or by will.

MR JUSTICE BRIGHTMAN

The general principle can, for present purposes, be sufficiently explained by reference to two cases. In *In re Gardner* [1920] 2 Ch 523 a testatrix had given all her estate to her husband for his use and benefit during his life "knowing that he will carry out my wishes". Four days later she signed a memorandum expressing the wish that what she described as "the money I leave to my husband" should on his death be equally divided among certain named beneficiaries. She died in 1919 possessed of a personal estate only, and her husband died four days later. After his death his wife's will and the memorandum were found in his safe, and there was parol evidence that shortly after the execution of the will the testatrix had said in his presence that her property after his death was to be equally divided between the named beneficiaries, and that he assented thereto. ...

Warrington L.J. said, at p. 530:

"The question is really this: Can the husband, who, as a result of the particular form in which the testamentary disposition of the wife is made, takes at law for his own benefit the corpus of her personal estate, properly refuse to carry into effect a wish as to the disposition of that property expressed to him by the wife before her death and assented to and accepted by him? The principle upon which the jurisdiction of the court is based is stated, in extremely clear language, by Lord Davey in *French v French* [1902] 1 IR 172: 'The basis of the jurisdiction' – that is the jurisdiction to which I have referred– 'is of course that the testator has died, leaving the property by his will in a particular manner on the faith and in reliance upon an express or implied promise by the legatee to fulfil his wishes, and your Lordships will at once see that it makes no difference whatever whether the will be made before the communication to the legatee or afterwards, because, as was said, I think, by Vice-Chancellor Turner in one of the cases which were cited, the presumption is that the testator would have revoked his will and made another disposition if he had not relied upon the promise, express or implied, made by the legatee to fulfil his wishes.

The second case referred to by Brightman J is *Blackwell v Blackwell* [1929] AC 318. He refers to a passage from the speech of Viscount Sumner, set out below.

He also quotes Lord Warrington of Clyffe, also set out below.

He then concludes:

It will be convenient to call the person upon whom such a trust is imposed the "primary donee" and the beneficiary under that trust the "secondary donee." The essential elements which must be proved to exist are: (i) the intention of the testator to subject the primary donee to an obligation in favour of the secondary donee; (ii) communication of that intention to the primary donee; and (iii) the acceptance of that obligation by the primary donee either expressly or by acquiescence. It is immaterial whether these elements precede or succeed the will of the donor. I am informed that there is no recent reported case where the obligation imposed on the primary donee is an obligation to make a will in favour of the secondary donee as distinct from some form of inter vivos transfer. But it does not seem to me that there can really be any distinction which can validly be taken on behalf of the defendant in the present case. The basis of the doctrine of a secret trust is the obligation imposed on the conscience of the primary donee and it does not seem to me that there is any materiality in the machinery by which the donor intends that that obligation shall be carried out.

 Link

See the section in this chapter on Express / Constructive trusts

5.4 Half Secret Trusts

Half secret trusts differ from fully secret trusts in that it is clear on the face of the will that a trust exists, but the terms of that trust are kept secret. The rules have developed in a piecemeal fashion, with the rules on timing of communication differing from those for fully secret trusts.

Blackwell v Blackwell [1929] AC 318

Panel: Lord Hailsham LC, Viscount Sumner, Lord Buckmaster, Lord Carson and Lord Warrington of Clyffe

Facts: John Blackwell validly executed a codicil to his will, giving £12,000 to five people to apply the income and pay the capital 'for the purposes indicated by me to them'. He told the trustees, before the execution of the codicil, that the objects of the trust were a lady and her son, but the exact details were not put in writing until afterwards. Blackwell's widow and son, the residuary legatees, brought an action to test whether the trust was valid. The House of Lords recognised the concept of the half secret trust, and held that the trust was valid, justifying it on two grounds: first, that 'fraud' included failure to carry out the testator's wishes; and second, that the trust did not arise under the will, but outside or 'dehors', and that therefore the provisions of the Wills Act were irrelevant.

LORD BUCKMASTER

His lordship made some *obiter* comments on whether a fully secret trustee can renounce the gift and defeat the trust:

...In the case where no trusts are mentioned the legatee might defeat the whole purpose by renouncing the legacy and the breach of trust would not in that case enure to his own benefit, but I entertain no doubt that the Court, having once admitted the evidence of the trust, would interfere to prevent its defeat.

He then gave judicial recognition to the half secret trust as a concept for the first time:

…a testator having been induced to make a gift on trust in his will in reliance on the clear promise by the trustee that such trust will be executed in favour of certain named persons, the trustee is not at liberty to suppress the evidence of the trust and thus destroy the whole object of its creation, in fraud of the beneficiaries.

He surveyed the authorities culminating in an examination of *In re Fleetwood* (15 Ch D 594):

I omit the detailed examination of other cases, for they are all carefully considered and dealt with by Hall V.-C. in the case of *In re Fleetwood*, an authority which indisputably covers the present case if it be accurately decided. In that case the testatrix left to a named person all her personalty, "to be applied as I have requested him to do." The request was made out and the named trustee jotted down in the presence of the testatrix the names of the persons and the amounts which the testatrix

desired to give and, after this, the codicil was executed. The point raised was the same as in the present case – namely, that when the trusteeship appears upon the instrument the trust must be for the next of kin or residuary legatees and that the Wills Act prevented effect being given to a trust to be effected by parol evidence. The learned Vice-Chancellor went through all the cases, including the case of *McCormick v Grogan*, and decided that the trusts should be executed. That decision has never been definitely disapproved in any decided case, for the statements in *Le Page v Gardom* 84 LJ Ch 749 and *In re Gardner* are mere dicta in cases where the point raised here was not material, and, in my opinion, it was in fact followed in *In re Huxtable* [1902] 2 Ch 793. In that case a testatrix bequeathed a sum of £4000 [to her trustee] "for the charitable purposes agreed upon between us". The testatrix had, in fact, verbally communicated to the legatee her intention to leave him the sum of £4000, the income of which he was to apply during his life for the relief of sick and necessitous persons being members of the Church of England and that he was to dispose of the principal as his own property. Farwell J. admitted the evidence, including that which conferred upon the trustee power of disposing of the principal after his death. The Court of Appeal held that the evidence was admissible as to the trusts of the £4000, which, upon the face of the will, was wholly given for charitable purposes but was not admissible for the purpose of providing for the £4000 after the death of the trustee, since the will had given the whole £4000, and such evidence would contradict the will. All the learned Lords Justice agreed that the affidavit of the trustee was admissible for the purpose of showing what were the charitable purposes but for no further purpose. There is nothing in the judgments that shows that this decision was affected by the fact that the gift was a charitable gift, nor on principle can I see that such distinction could be maintained, for, if a general charitable purpose only were disclosed by the will, a scheme might be prepared for carrying it into effect, and unless evidence were admitted the testatrix's specific instructions could have been disregarded; but they were not, they were distinctly carried out.

I agree with the Court of Appeal in thinking that this also is an authority in support of the doctrine laid down in *In re Fleetwood*. In these circumstances, even if the antecedent decisions had been less definite, it would require a very clear conviction that *In re Fleetwood* was wrongly decided to render it right and proper that it should now be overruled.

... In my opinion, however, *In re Fleetwood* was not wrongly decided. It was decided in accordance with the series of authorities by which the law was established and which it is now too late to question or to overrule.

VISCOUNT SUMNER

In itself the doctrine of equity, by which parol evidence is admissible to prove what is called "fraud" in connection with secret trusts, and effect is given to such trusts when established, would not seem to conflict with any of the Acts under which from time to time the Legislature has regulated the right of testamentary disposition. A Court of conscience finds a man in the position of an absolute legal owner of a sum of money, which has been bequeathed to him under a valid will, and it declares that, on proof of certain facts relating to the motives and actions of the testator, it will not allow the legal owner to exercise his legal right to do what he will with his own. This seems to be a perfectly normal exercise of general equitable jurisdiction. The facts commonly but not necessarily involve some immoral and selfish conduct on the part of the legal owner. The necessary elements, on which the question turns, are intention, communication, and acquiescence. The testator intends his absolute gift to be employed as he and not as the donee desires; he tells the proposed donee of this intention and, either by express promise or by the tacit promise, which is signified by acquiescence, the proposed donee encourages him to bequeath the money in the faith that his intentions will be carried out. The special circumstance, that the gift is by bequest only makes this rule a special case of the exercise of a general jurisdiction, but in its application to a bequest the doctrine must in principle rest on the assumption that the will has first operated according to its terms. It is because there is no one to whom the law can give relief in the premises, that relief, if any, must be sought in equity. So far, and in the bare case of a legacy absolute on the face of it, I do not see how the statute-law relating to the form of a valid will is concerned at all, and the expressions, in which the doctrine has been habitually described, seem to bear this out. For the prevention of fraud equity fastens on the conscience of the legatee a trust, a trust, that is, which otherwise would be inoperative; in other words it makes him do what the will in itself has nothing to do with; it lets him take what the will gives him and then makes him apply it, as the Court of conscience directs, and it does so in order to give effect to wishes of the testator, which would not otherwise be effectual.

To this two circumstances must be added to bring the present case to the test of the general doctrine, first, that the will states on its face that the legacy is given on trust but does not state what the trusts are, and further contains a residuary bequest, and, second, that the legatees are acting with perfect honesty, seek no advantage to themselves, and only desire, if the Court will permit them, to do what in other circumstances the Court would have fastened it on their conscience to perform.

Since the current of decisions down to *In re Fleetwood* and *In re Huxtable* has established that the principles of equity apply equally when these circumstances are

Decipher

Note that Dankwerts J in *re Young* takes the opposite view.

Link

See *Ottaway v Norman*

present as in cases where they are not, the material question is whether and how the Wills Act affects this case. It seems to me that, apart from legislation, the application of the principle of equity, which was made in Fleetwood's and Huxtable's cases, was logical, and was justified by the same considerations as in the cases of fraud and absolute gifts. Why should equity forbid an honest trustee to give effect to his promise, made to a deceased testator, and compel him to pay another legatee, about whom it is quite certain that the testator did not mean to make him the object of this bounty? In both cases the testator's wishes are incompletely expressed in his will. Why should equity, over a mere matter of words, give effect to them in one case and frustrate them in the other? No doubt the words "in trust" prevent the legatee from taking beneficially, whether they have simply been declared in conversation or written in the will, but the fraud, when the trustee, so called in the will, is also the residuary legatee, is the same as when he is only declared a trustee by word of mouth accepted by him. I recoil from interfering with decisions of long standing, which reject this anomaly, unless constrained by statute.

LORD WARRINGTON OF CLYFFE

It has long been settled that if a gift be made to a person or persons in terms absolutely but in fact upon a trust communicated to the legatee and accepted by him, the legatee would be bound to give effect to the trust, on the principle that the gift may be presumed to have been made on the faith of his acceptance of the trust, and a refusal after the death of the testator to give effect to it would be a fraud on the part of the legatee. Of course in these cases the trust is proved by parol evidence, and such evidence is clearly admissible. It is also settled that in such cases it is immaterial whether the trust is communicated and accepted before or after the execution of the will, inasmuch as in the latter case the testator, if it had not been accepted, might have revoked the will.

Further in *Moss v Cooper* Wood V.-C. said: "If, on the faith of a promise by A., a gift is made in favour of A. and B., the promise is fastened on to the gift to both, for B. cannot profit by A.'s fraud".

I think the principle on which this doctrine is founded is that the parol evidence is not adduced for the purpose of altering or affecting the will itself, the legatee still takes under the will, but is under a personal obligation the breach of which would be a fraud on the testator: *Cullen v Attorney-General for Ireland* (1866) LR 1 HL 190.

The question is whether the same principle applies where, as in the present case, the fact that the gift is upon trust is mentioned in the will, though the terms of the trust can only be established by parol.

Eve J. and the Court of Appeal (the Master of the Rolls and Lawrence and Russell L.JJ.) have answered the question in the affirmative, basing their decisions on the judgment of Hall V.-C. in *In re Fleetwood*, the Court of Appeal also expressing the view that that judgment was followed by the Court of Appeal in *In re Huxtable*.

I confess to having felt considerable doubt during the argument whether to apply the principle in such a case as the present would not be to give validity to a parol will in spite of the provisions first of the Statute of Frauds and secondly of the Wills Act. Subsequent reflection however and a careful perusal of the judgment of Hall V.-C. in In re Fleetwood, wherein the earlier authorities under both statutes are cited and discussed, have satisfied me that that case and, in consequence, the present case in the Courts below were rightly decided. I think the solution is to be found by bearing in mind that what is enforced is not a trust imposed by the will, but one arising from the acceptance by the legatee of a trust, communicated to him by the testator, on the faith of which acceptance the will was made or left unrevoked, as the case might be. If the evidence had merely established who were the persons and what were the purposes indicated it would in my opinion have been inadmissible, as to admit it would be to allow the making of a will by parol. It is the fact of the acceptance of the personal obligation which is the essential feature, and the rest of the evidence is merely for the purpose of ascertaining the nature of that obligation.

Re Colin Cooper [1939] Ch 811

Panel: Sir Wilfred Greene MR; Clauson and Goddard LJJ

Facts: Cooper made a will leaving £5000 to two trustees 'upon trusts which I have already communicated to them'. He had in fact communicated the trusts. He fell ill while on a game shoot in Africa and two days before his death made a new will, which included the following wording: 'The sum of £5000 bequeathed to my trustees in the will now cancelled is to be increased to £10,000, they knowing my wishes regarding this sum'. The trustees did not know about this increase until after Cooper's death. The court had to decide how much money was held subject to the trust. It said that the trust of £5000 was valid as it had been communicated during the testator's lifetime (and before the will was executed, which is an additional requirement for a half secret trust).

SIR WILFRED GREENE MR

In this case it is not possible to give effect to what the testator obviously desired, because he has not taken the steps which the law requires to enable that desire to become effective. He was minded to make a disposition by means of what is commonly called a secret trust, as he was not disposed to set out upon the face of his will or upon the face of some identifiable document described in his will the dispositions which he desired to make; accordingly he adopted the familiar device of bequeathing a legacy in favour of named persons which they were to hold as trustees, but the actual trusts upon which they were to hold it had been communicated by him to them and accepted by them in his lifetime. In order that a disposition which it is desired to make by that process can be effective it is necessary that the intention of the testator be communicated to the trustees, that the trustees accept the instructions of the testator, and that acting on the faith of that acceptance, he makes the gift or, if it is a gift which has been already made, leaves it unrevoked.

He applied *Blackwell v Blackwell* (above):

It seems to me that upon the facts of this case it is impossible to say that the acceptance by the trustees of the onus of trusteeship in relation to the first and earlier legacy is something which must be treated as having been repeated in reference to the second legacy or the increased legacy, whichever way one chooses to describe it. In order that a secret trust might be made effective with regard to that added sum in my opinion precisely the same factors were necessary as were required to validate the original trusts, namely, communication, acceptance or acquiescence, and the making of the will on the faith of such acceptance or acquiescence. None of these elements, as I have said, were present. It is not possible, in my opinion, to treat the figure of £5000 in relation to which the consent of the trustees was originally obtained as something of no essential importance. I cannot myself see that the arrangement between the testator and the trustees can be construed as though it had meant "£5000 or whatever sum I may hereafter choose to bequeath". That is not what was said and it was not with regard to any sum other than the £5000 that the consciences of the trustees (to use a technical phrase) were burdened.

Re Keen [1937] Ch 236

Panel: Lord Wright MR; Romer and Greene LJJ

Facts: By clause 5 of his will, Keen gave £10,000 to his trustees to be held 'upon trust and disposed of by them … as may be notified by me … during my lifetime'. He did not execute the will until August 1932. Before that, in March 1932, he had handed over a sealed envelope containing instructions to be opened on his death, that the money was to be used to benefit a lady, G. The court had to decide whether there was a valid half-secret trust. The Court of Appeal found that although it was acceptable to communicate the terms of the trust in a sealed envelope, in this instance the communication had been before the will was executed and was therefore inconsistent with the wording of the will and the trust therefore failed.

Link
See the comments of Kay J in *re Boyes*.

LORD WRIGHT MR

The judge at first instance had said that the identity of the lady should have been disclosed to the trustees during Keen's lifetime. Lord Wright disagreed and said:

The summons came before Farwell J., who decided adversely to the claims of the lady on the short ground that she could not prove that she was a person notified to the trustees by the testator during his lifetime within the words of clause 5. His opinion seems to be that the clause required the name and identity of the lady to be expressly disclosed to the trustees during the testator's lifetime so that it was not sufficient to place these particulars in the physical possession of the trustees or one of them in the form of a memorandum which they were not to read till the testator's death.

I am unable to accept this conclusion, which appears to me to put too narrow a construction on the word "notified" as used in clause 5 in all the circumstances of the case. To take a parallel, a ship which sails under sealed orders, is sailing under orders though the exact terms are not ascertained by the captain till later. I note that the case

Alert

of a trust put into writing which is placed in the trustees' hands in a sealed envelope, was hypothetically treated by Kay J. as possibly constituting a communication in a case of this nature: *In re Boyes*. This, so far as it goes, seems to support my conclusion. The trustees had the means of knowledge available whenever it became necessary and proper to open the envelope.

Having decided that the communication by that means was in principle valid, his Lordship went on to consider whether it was admissible in this particular case. He decided that it was not, for two reasons: first, that the will referred to future communication, and the communication in question had already been made, so there was inconsistency. Second, it is not permissible in half secret trust arrangements, to refer to future communications. Communication of the terms of the trust must take place before or contemporaneously with the will.

He distinguished *Blackwell v Blackwell*:

There was in that case a bequest to trustees to apply the income "for the purposes indicated by me and at any time to pay part of the corpus to such person or persons indicated by me as they think fit, the balance to fall into the residuary estate". The testator had by parol at or before the execution of the will indicated or defined the nature of the trust and the beneficiaries and the trustees had accepted the trust on those terms. It was held that parol evidence was admissible to explain the trusts and to prove that the trustees had accepted the legacy on the condition of fulfilling them. The trusts were accordingly, when thus established, proper to be enforced by the Court. There was, it was held, in such a case no conflict between the express terms of the will and the actual trusts intended...

He went on to consider the judgment of Lord Sumner in *Blackwell v Blackwell*:

But he goes on to add qualifications which are essentially relevant for the determination of the present case. These are qualifications which flow from the circumstance that the will is not completely silent as to the trust, as is the case in wills of the type discussed in *McCormick v Grogan*, but does in express terms indicate that there is a trust. The qualifications are thus stated by Lord Sumner: "The limits, beyond which the rules as to unspecified trusts must not be carried, have often been discussed. A testator cannot reserve to himself a power of making future unwitnessed dispositions by merely naming a trustee and leaving the purposes of the trust to be supplied afterwards, nor can a legatee give testamentary validity to an unexecuted codicil by accepting an indefinite trust, never communicated to him in the testator's lifetime... *In re Boyes* ... To hold otherwise would indeed be to enable the testator to 'give the go-by' to the requirements of the Wills Act, because he did not choose to comply with them."

 Alert

As in my judgment clause 5 should be considered as contemplating future dispositions and as reserving to the testator the power of making such dispositions without a duly attested codicil simply by notifying them during his lifetime, the principles laid down by Lord Sumner must be fatal to the appellant's claim.

There has been criticism of the difference in the rules on communication for secret and half secret trusts, but *Re Keen* has been followed in *Re Bateman's Will Trust* [1970] 1 WLR 1463.

Re Bateman's Will Trusts [1970] 1 WLR 1463

Panel: Pennycuick V-C

Facts: By clause 7 of his will, Bateman left £24,000 to his trustees and directed them to pay the income to 'such persons and in such proportions as shall be stated by me in a sealed letter on my own handwriting addressed to my trustees'. The question was whether the trusts were valid. The court applied *re Keen* and held that there was no trust as it was clearly envisaged, by the wording of the will, that Bateman would give the trustees a letter in the future.

PENNYCUICK V-C

It will be remembered that the direction in that clause is to set aside a sum of £24,000 and pay the income "to such persons and in such proportions as shall be stated by me in a sealed letter ... to my trustees". Now those words are, on their plain meaning, future. There is no evidence as to whether a sealed letter had been written and addressed to the trustees by the testator at the date that he made his will. The only thing that does appear clear is that after his death some sealed letter, or at any rate some document, was in existence upon which the trustees acted. However, whatever the facts, the terms of the direction in clause 7 are plainly future. The direction is to pay the income "to such persons and in such proportions as shall be stated by me in a sealed letter." Those words clearly, I think, import that the testator may, in the future, after the date of the will, give a sealed letter to his trustees. It is impossible to confine the words to a sealed letter already so given. If that is the true construction of the wording it is not in dispute that the direction is invalid.

Wilde, D., 'Secret and semi-secret trusts: justifying distinctions between the two', 1995 Conv. 366

In this article, Wilde argues against those who criticise the differences in the rules on the validity of secret and half secret trusts. He says that the reason that both types of trust are enforced is prevention of fraud. The differences in the rules can, he argues, be justified on the basis that a solicitor is less likely to be involved in the creation of a fully secret trust, and therefore extensive protections should be given to those dispositions:

... a fully secret trust is typically liable to arise where a benefactor is, understandably, only dimly aware of the need for formality in desired arrangements, and where, accordingly, no recourse to legal advice is made. A fully secret trust can be set up without a solicitor ever being instructed to draw up any will; and even where a solicitor is instructed to draw up a will, it might easily be that the solicitor is kept completely ignorant of the secret trust to operate in conjunction with it, which trust might be put in place before or after the making of the will. This is not necessarily the case with a fully secret trust. It may be that a fully secret trust is used as a conveyancing device with the benefit of full legal advice. But, it is a common situation that the law must allow for in its regulation of fully secret trusts that, quite understandably, no legal advice is taken. However, a semi-secret trust always appears on the face of a will. It is difficult to imagine how one might obtain empirical proof, but it seems reasonable to assume that the overwhelming majority of wills are drawn up by solicitors; and, insofar as some people make wills without instructing a solicitor, that they are aware they are drawing up a formal legal document with a complex of law affecting its operation, and that they are consequently taking a risk in not consulting a solicitor. Accordingly, semi-secret trusts always arise in a situation where a solicitor is consulted and is made aware by the terms of the will that the trust is being set up; or, at least, in a very few cases, where the risk of not consulting a solicitor is deliberately taken.

Thus, the introduction of substantive legal rules whose observance was to be necessary to the validity of fully secret trusts would operate harshly on the benefactor operating in the dark with respect to their existence. There would not necessarily be any solicitor to advise the benefactor to observe them. Testamentary intentions would be liable to be defeated by such rules, when it is a major function of the secret trust doctrine to rescue a benefactor who has acted in understandable ignorance of rules. This would not be true where a fully secret trust was used as a conveyancing device on legal advice, but it would be unworkable to set up a separate set of legal rules for this situation, operating when some unspecifiable degree of legal advice had been obtained. So, minimal regulation of fully secret trusts generally is desirable. However, in the case of semi-secret trusts, there always is – or, at the very least, there is a realisation that there ought to be – a solicitor consulted, so that it is appropriate to lay down legal rules substantively limiting the recognition of semi-secret trusts, which the solicitor is in a position to advise the benefactor to observe, provided those rules serve some legally valuable purpose. ...

Where there is a failure to observe these special rules limiting the recognition of semi-secret trusts, the courts are able to say that the proximate cause of the failure of the trust is not the fraud of the trustee, but rather the disregard of legal rules in a context where legal advice was taken or where the taking of proper legal advice was known to be appropriate. Should a solicitor fail to advise observance, the redress of the intended beneficiary on the failure of the trust – admittedly not perfect redress, since it depends upon awareness of the right (but then so do many other legal remedies) – is an action in negligence for damages against the solicitor.

Turning, then, to an attempted justification, one by one, of the distinctions drawn by the courts between secret and semi-secret trusts.

Declaration prior to or contemporaneously with will

In the case of a fully secret trust, the courts require only that the trust be declared at any time before the death of the benefactor. In the case of a semi-secret trust, however, the courts require that the trust must be declared before or contemporaneously with the execution of the will by the terms of which the property is left upon the unspecified trust; and, moreover, the terms of the will must not contemplate the possibility of any later new declaration (even where the only actual declaration was a prior or contemporaneous one); otherwise the trust fails, and there is a resulting trust for the residuary beneficiary or successor upon intestacy. This is the most widely criticised of the distinctions drawn between secret and semi-secret trusts. Certainly it cannot be supported upon the ground stated by the courts. However, it is suggested that the rule does have a value. A solicitor is obliged to advise the settlor that the terms of the trust must be finalised at the date of the will, and that they cannot be varied thereafter without a new will. Unless, unusually, the settlor wishes to keep the terms of the trust secret even from the solicitor, there is then no risk of a declaration of trust being made which is not under the supervision of a solicitor, as could easily happen were the settlor instead left free to declare or vary the trust at will at any time later. The scrutiny of a solicitor should ensure that the trust is valid in all respects, not just in terms of the rules relating to semi-secret trusts, that it is sufficiently certain and so on; that a suitable record is made to evidence the terms of the trust; and that the trust is drawn up with the benefit of general advice as to the prudence of the provision made which a solicitor should be peculiarly competent to give, as to such matters as tax implications. In these respects, the rule is in the interests of the settlor: securing the general validity of the trust, facilitating its proof, and ensuring that it is the most desirable provision the settlor can make for the intended beneficiary generally.

This rule should not, therefore, be viewed simply as an arbitrary trap liable to frustrate the intentions of a benefactor. It should operate towards the fullest achievement of those intentions, provided a competent solicitor is instructed; and where a solicitor fails to observe this rule, the intended beneficiary can sue for compensation.

It is true that the rule inhibits the benefactor who is not so much interested in secrecy, but rather in flexibility, wishing to make frequent informal changes of mind. But there is much to be said for the view that while a desire for secrecy is a legitimate motive for setting up a semi-secret trust, a desire for such flexibility is not a motive the law should indulge.

5.5 Secret Trusts: Express or Constructive?

There is no clear answer as to whether secret trusts are express or constructive. If express, there are difficulties for secret trusts of land as, to be valid, express trusts of land must be evidenced in signed writing (Law of Property Act 1925 s 53(1)(b)). It would, however, seem logical for half secret trusts, which are evident on the face of the will, to be treated as express trusts. This seems to be the interpretation in *Re Baillie* (1886) 2 TLR 660 where a half secret trust of land was unenforceable without written evidence. It must be noted, however, that this case was decided before the concept of a half secret trust had been fully recognised.

If the justification for upholding fully secret trusts is prevention of fraud, it follows that the trust is constructive, as it is imposed by the court. Constructive trusts do not need to comply with any formalities to be valid (Law of Property Act 1925 s 53(2)). There is judicial support for this interpretation in *Ottaway v Norman* and *Kasperbauer v Griffith*. *Ottaway v Norman*, upheld a fully secret trust of land even though it was not evidenced in signed writing. Section 53(1)(b) was, however, not considered by the court.

Link
For a different approach which rejects the express and constructive trust interpretations, see the article by Perrins referred to in the Further Reading section at the end of this chapter.

5.6 Secret Trusts in the Modern World

Despite the seminal cases on this topic being decided in a very different social era, when skeletons were kept very firmly in cupboards, the secret trust does have relevance in today's world.

Gold v Hill [1999] 1 FLR 54

Panel: Carnwath J

Facts: Mr Gilbert had left his wife and was living with another woman, Carol, and her two children. In his will, he left everything to his wife, but he took out life insurance intending to benefit Carol and the children in the event of his death. He nominated Mr Gold, his solicitor, as beneficiary to receive the policy proceeds. He later had informal conversations with Mr Gold in which he told him of the insurance arrangement and urged Mr Gold to 'look after Carol and the kids'. At no time did Mr Gold seek to take the proceeds for himself: he sought a declaration that he did in fact hold the proceeds on trust for Carol.

MR JUSTICE CARNWATH

The judge dismissed arguments to the effect that Mr Gold held on resulting trust for the wife as beneficiary under the will. Those arguments he set out as follows:

> ...there is no reason to doubt that Mr Gilbert intended to nominate Mr Gold. The question is in what capacity, and for what purposes, he intended Mr Gold to receive the money, and whether what he did is effective to achieve that intention. He submits that the natural interpretation of the document is that Mr Gilbert intended Mr Gold to take in his capacity as executor of a will that he intended to make, but never did. There are two possible consequences: either the nomination fails because the condition to which it was subject was never fulfilled; or it is effective, but Mr Gold holds the proceeds on resulting trust for the deceased. In either event the funds would become part of his estate to be dealt with in accordance with his will.

The judge dismissed these arguments and agreed with the arguments presented on behalf of Mr Gold, that he held the funds for Carol by way of an arrangement analogous to a secret trust:

> The nomination, like a testamentary disposition, does not transfer or create any interest until death. It is consistent with the principle of *Blackwell v Blackwell* that the nominee should take under the rules of the policy, but then be required to 'apply it as the court of conscience directs' and so 'to give effect to the wishes of the testator'. Such doubts as there may be, in the case of testamentary dispositions, as to the effectiveness of an intention communicated after the execution of the will, appear to be derived from the particular rules applying to wills. There is no reason why they should create similar difficulties in the case of nominations. Since the nomination has no effect until the time of death, it should be sufficient that the nature of the trust is sufficiently communicated prior to that time.

Meager, R., 'Secret trusts – do they have a future?', 2003 Conveyancer and Property Lawyer, 203

This article analyses the findings of a survey of practitioners to ascertain attitudes to and the levels of use of fully-secret and half-secret trusts in November 2001.

Link
See the article by Challinor where it is argued that these trusts are outmoded.

Respondents were first required to indicate whether their clients had ever asked them about making a secret testamentary bequest and 35 per cent of the respondents stated that they had. This is a substantial proportion and the finding indicates that there is a genuine requirement amongst testators to be able to effect a bequest secretly, although it is not singularly demonstrative that secret trusts are required as there are of course other means by which to make a discreet bequest, depending upon the level of secrecy required.

Respondents were then asked whether they had been involved in the creation of fully secret or half-secret trusts and 16 per cent had been involved in the creation of the former and 20 per cent in the latter. The respondents were not required to state on how many occasions they had been involved in the creation of secret trusts but some clearly indicated that it had been on multiple occasions....

The information derived from the next question is more indicative of the respondents' own perceptions of secret trusts as they were asked whether they had ever advised a client that a secret trust would be a suitable "instrument" to fulfil their clients' requirements. Thirteen per cent of the respondents had advised clients that a fully secret trust would be appropriate and 23 per cent that a half-secret trust would be. Interestingly, fewer practitioners had advocated the use of a fully secret trust than had assisted in the creation of one, but more had advised clients about the appropriateness of half-secret trusts than had created one.

Whilst the responses to this question offer some insight into the legal practitioners' perception of the appropriateness of secret trusts for the purpose of facilitating secret bequests, it is not conclusive. One respondent wrote that "he has never used or come across such a trust but would be prepared to use one if the right circumstances arose". This response automatically raises the possibility, or some might even argue probability, that whilst some respondents stated that they had neither advised clients as to the suitability of secret trusts nor assisted in the creation of one, this is not necessarily indicative that those responding in the negative would not be prepared to advocate their use. Furthermore, it may be suggestive that secret trusts are used more rarely in every day practice not because they are deemed unreliable or potentially problematic, but because too little is understood about their construction and possible use, reflecting a lack of education of the practitioners themselves.

The questionnaire then asked for information about whether respondents, advising clients about means by which to effect secret bequests, had suggested devices other than secret trusts, and 27 per cent had. This response further supports earlier findings in which it had been concluded that there is clearly a genuine requirement among testators to make secret bequests. ...

The final question in the purely quantitative section of the survey asked, in response to the preceding question, which option their clients chose. Twenty-nine per cent chose a secret trust, 52 per cent chose another device and 19 per cent chose none of the options.10 This finding reinforces previously drawn conclusions that there is a genuine requirement among testators to make secret bequests and that both varieties of secret trust, as well as other means, are being used to achieve this end.

The article then discusses the perceptions of secret trusts within the targeted section of the legal profession. Meager concludes:

There is clearly a demand for an instrument which enables testators to make bequests secretly. A substantial proportion of the survey sample of legal practitioners were also of the opinion that there are many circumstances in which the use of a secret trust may be appropriate.

Secret trusts appear to be viewed with cynicism because of the insurmountable problems which can potentially arise should the trustee choose to fraudulently deny the existence of the trust. What has perhaps been largely overlooked is the power that legal practitioners have to ensure that this situation does not arise. There appears to be very little reason why they should not advise their clients to construct a document attesting to the existence and the terms of the trust and lodging it with the solicitor who holds the will.

Whilst this would inevitably result in there being a limited amount of publicity, it would be less public than any ensuing litigation to establish the existence of the trust. ...

On reflection, the secret trust is perhaps potentially more useful than it has ever been given credit for, particularly given the diverse variety of circumstances in which respondents considered their use may be appropriate. With a limited amount of administration, which would pose no real threat to the secret nature of the trust, it could be constructed in such a way as to make it no less secure and dependable than any other form of trust instrument. By constructing fully secret trusts in such a way as to make it impossible for a secret trustee to avoid the duty which he has accepted, it would perhaps be no longer necessary for half-secret trusts to exist.

The greatest hurdle to overcome, it would seem, is to assure legal practitioners of the potential reliability of such a device, carefully constructed. Perhaps it would be appropriate to review the education of potential legal practitioners to advise them on ways of avoiding the problems most commonly associated with the use of secret trusts, thus equipping them to better cater for their clients' requirements. ...

Further Reading

Penner J E, *The Law of Trusts*, (5th edition), Chapter 6, pp 148 – 160

Critchley, P, Instruments of fraud, testamentary dispositions, and the doctrine of secret trusts, 1999 LQR 631

Kincaid, D, The tangled web: the relationship between a secret trust and the will, 2000 LQR 420

Perrins, B, Secret trusts: The key to the Dehors, 1985 Conv 248

6

Private Purpose Trusts

Topic List

Introduction

Ordinarily, a trust must be for the benefit of a legal person (ie an individual or a company), not for a purpose. This is known as 'the beneficiary principle'. A trust for a purpose will be invalid unless:

(a)   The purpose is charitable (charitable trusts are covered in Chapter 8);

or

(b)

    (i)   The purpose falls within one of anomalous *Re Endacott* exceptions; or
    (ii)   The purpose falls within the *Re Denley* principle.

Trusts which fall within (b) are known as private purpose trusts. For a private purpose trust to be valid it must also:

* Comply with the perpetuity period; and
* Be sufficiently certain and not be purely capricious.

In some instances, even though it may appear that a trust for a purpose has been created, it may be possible to interpret the expression of purpose as a mere indication of motive for what is in fact an absolute gift, to which the rules regarding private purposes trusts do not therefore apply.

 Link
See the discussion of motive cases below.

6.1 The Beneficiary Principle

The beneficiary principle derives from the first-instance decision in *Morice v Bishop of Durham* (1804) 9 Ves JR 399, where Sir William Grant MR held that the trust was void because it was a non-charitable purpose trust.

Morice v Bishop of Durham (1804) 9 Ves JR 399

Panel: Sir William Grant MR

Facts: By her will the testatrix left her entire personal estate to the Bishop of Durham on trust to pay her debts and certain legacies and then to use what remained for '... such objects of benevolence and liberality as [he] in his own discretion should most approve of ...'.

> SIR WILLIAM GRANT MR
>
> The only question is whether the trust upon which the residue of the personal estate is bequeathed be a trust for charitable purposes. That the residue is left on some trust and not for the personal benefit of the bishop is clear from the words of the will, and is admitted by his lordship who expressly disclaims any beneficial interest. That it is a trust, unless it be of a charitable nature, too indefinite to be executed by this court, has not been, and cannot be, denied. There can be no trust over the exercise of which this court will not assume a control, for an uncontrollable power of disposition would be ownership and not trust. If there be a clear trust, but for uncertain objects, the property

that is the subject of the trust is undisposed of, and the benefit of such trust must result to those to whom the law gives the ownership in default of disposition by the former owner. But this doctrine does not hold good with regard to trusts for charity. Every other trust must have a definite object. There must be somebody in whose favour the court can decree performance. But it is now settled upon authority which it is too late to controvert that, where a charitable purpose is expressed, however general, the bequest shall not fail on account of the uncertainty of the object. The particular mode of application will be directed by the King in some cases, in others by this court.

Alert

Is this a trust for charity? Do purposes of liberality and benevolence mean the same as objects of charity? That word in its widest sense denotes all the good affections men ought to bear towards each other; in its most restricted and common sense relief of the poor. In neither of these senses is it employed in this court. Here its signification is derived chiefly from the statute 43 Eliz, c 4 [relating to charitable gifts]. Those purposes are considered charitable which that statute enumerates or which by analogies are deemed within its spirit and intendment, and to some such purpose every bequest to charity generally shall be applied. But, it is clear, liberality and benevolence can find numberless objects not included in that statute in the largest construction of it. The use of the word "charitable" seems to have been purposely avoided in this will in order to leave the bishop the most unrestrained discretion. Supposing the uncertainty of the trust no objection to its validity, could it be contended to be an abuse of the trust to employ this fund upon objects which all mankind would allow to be objects of liberality and benevolence though not to be said, in the language of this court, to be objects also of charity? By what rule of construction could it be said that all objects of liberality and benevolence are excluded which do not fall within the statute of Elizabeth? The question is not whether he may not apply it upon purposes strictly charitable, but whether he is bound so to apply it? I am not aware of any case in which the bequest has been held charitable where the testator has not either used that word to denote his general purpose or specified some particular purpose, which this court has determined to be charitable in its nature. All the cases upon that subject are to be found in the report of *Moggridge v Thackwell* (1807) 13 Ves 416. *Browne v Yeall* 7 Ves 47 I should have thought a much more doubtful case. There was ground for contending that the particular purpose specified was charitable in itself, according the decisions of this court, and it was described by the testator as a charitable design. But here there is no specific purpose pointed out to which the residue is to be applied. The words "charity" and "charitable" do not occur: the words used are not synonymous: the trusts may be completely executed without bestowing any part of this residue upon purposes strictly charitable. The residue, therefore, cannot be said to be given to charitable purposes, and, as the trust is too indefinite to be disposed of to any other purpose, it follows that the residue remains undisposed of and must be distributed among the next of kin of the testatrix.

Once it had been decided that the trust created by the bequest was not charitable, it could only be valid if it had a 'definite object', ie 'somebody in whose favour the court can decree specific performance'. As no such person could be identified, the gift failed.

A further illustration of the beneficiary principle is to be found in the case of *Re Astor's Settlement Trusts* [1952] Ch 534, in which Astor J held that various purpose trusts were void as not being for the benefit of individuals.

Re Astor's Settlement Trusts, Astor v Schofield & Ors [1952] Ch 534

Panel: Roxburgh J

Facts: The settlor established a discretionary trust under which the trust income was to be used for a variety of purposes, including the 'establishment maintenance and improvement of good understanding sympathy and co-operation between nations, especially the nations of the English speaking world and also between different sections of people in any nation or community', ... 'preservation of the independence and integrity of newspapers ...[and]... the Press', ... 'the protection of newspapers ... from being absorbed or controlled by combines' ... [and] ... 'the restoration ... of the independence of ... writers in newspapers.'

MR JUSTICE ROXBURGH

The question upon which I [have to decide] is whether the non-charitable trusts of income ... are void ... on two grounds: (1) that they are not trusts for the benefit of individuals; (2) that they are void for uncertainty.

Lord Parker considered the first of these two questions in his speech in *Bowman v Secular Society Ltd* [1917] AC 406 and I will cite two important passages. The first is: "The question whether a trust be legal or illegal or be in accordance with or contrary to the policy of the law, only arises when it has been determined that a trust has been created, and is then only part of the larger question whether the trust is enforceable. For, as will presently appear, trusts may be unenforceable and therefore void, not only because they are illegal or contrary to the policy of the law, but for other reasons." The second is: "A trust to be valid must be for the benefit of individuals, which this is certainly not, or must be in that class of gifts for the benefit of the public which the courts in this country recognize as charitable in the legal as opposed to the popular sense of that term." ...

The typical case of a trust is one in which the legal owner of property is constrained by a court of equity so to deal with it as to give effect to the equitable rights of another. These equitable rights have been hammered out in the process of litigation in which a claimant on equitable grounds has successfully asserted rights against a legal owner or other person in control of property. Prima facie, therefore, a trustee would not be expected to be subject to an equitable obligation unless there was somebody who could enforce a correlative equitable right, and the nature and extent of that obligation would be worked out in proceedings for enforcement. At an early stage, however, the courts were confronted with attempts to create trusts for charitable purposes which there was no equitable owner to enforce. Lord Eldon explained in *Attorney-General v Brown* (1818) 1 Swans 265, 290 how this difficulty was dealt with: "It is the duty of a court of equity, a main part, originally almost the whole, of its jurisdiction, to administer trusts; to protect not the visible owner, who alone can proceed at law, but the individual equitably, though not legally, entitled. From this principle has arisen the practice of administering the trust of a public charity: persons possessed of funds appropriated to such purposes are within the general rule; but no one being entitled by an immediate and peculiar interest to prefer a complaint, who is to compel the performance of their obligations, and to enforce their responsibility? It is the duty of the King, as parens patriae, to protect property devoted to charitable uses; and that duty is executed by the officer who represents the Crown for all forensic purposes. On this foundation rests the right of the Attorney-General in such cases to obtain by information the interposition of a court of equity. ..." But if the purposes are not charitable, great difficulties arise both in theory and in practice. In theory, because having regard to the historical origins of equity it is difficult to visualize the growth of equitable obligations which nobody can enforce, and in practice, because it is not possible to contemplate with equanimity the creation of large funds devoted to non-charitable purposes which no court and no department of state can control, or in the case of maladministration reform. Therefore, Lord Parker's second proposition would prima facie appear to be well founded. Moreover, it gains no little support from the practical considerations that no officer has ever been constituted to take, in the case of non-charitable purposes, the position held by the Attorney-General in connexion with charitable purposes, and no case has been found in the reports in which the court has ever directly enforced a non-charitable purpose against a trustee. Indeed where, as in the present case, the only beneficiaries are purposes and an at present unascertainable person, it is difficult to see who could initiate such proceedings. If the purposes are valid trusts, the settlors have retained no beneficial interest and could not initiate them. It was suggested that the trustees might proceed ex parte to enforce the trusts against themselves. I doubt that, but at any rate nobody could enforce the trusts against them. ... Lord Parker's two propositions ... [are not new] but merely re-echoed what Sir William Grant had said as Master of the Rolls in *Morice v The Bishop of Durham* as long ago as 1804: "There must be somebody, in whose favour the court can decree performance." The position was recently restated by Harman J in *In re Wood* [1949] Ch 498, 501: "A gift on trust must have a *cestui que* trust," and this seems to be in accord with principle. ... [There is nothing to] justify the conclusion that a Court of Equity will recognize as an equitable obligation affecting the income of large funds in the hands of trustees a direction to apply it in furtherance of enumerated non-charitable purposes in a manner which no court or department can control or enforce.

 Decipher
'Cestui que trust' means 'beneficiary'.

The second ground on which the relevant trusts are challenged is uncertainty. If (contrary to my view) an enumeration of purposes outside the realm of charities can take the place of an enumeration of beneficiaries, the purposes must, in my judgment, be stated in phrases which embody definite concepts, and the means by which the trustees are to try to attain them must also be prescribed with a sufficient degree of certainty. The test to be applied is stated by Lord Eldon LC in *Morice v Bishop of Durham* as follows (10 Ves 539):

"*As it is a maxim, that the execution of a trust shall be under the control of the court, it must be of such a nature, that it can be under that control; so that the administration of it can be reviewed by the court; or, if the trustee dies, the court itself can execute the trust: a trust therefore, which, in case of maladministration could be reformed; and a due administration directed; and then, unless the subject and the objects can be ascertained, upon principles, familiar in other cases, it must be decided, that the court can neither reform maladministration, nor direct a due administration."* ...

Applying this test, I find many uncertain phrases in the enumeration of [these] purposes ... eg, "different sections of people in any nation or community", ... "integrity of the Press", ... "combines" ... [and] "the restoration ... of the independence of ... writers in newspapers ..." . The purposes must be so defined that, if the trustees surrendered their discretion, the court could carry out the purposes declared... . But how ... could I decree in what manner the trusts ... were to be performed? The settlement gives no guidance at all. ... Accordingly, in my judgment, the trusts ... are void also for uncertainty.

But while I have reached my decision on two separate grounds, both, I think, have their origin in a single principle, namely, that a court of equity does not recognize as valid a trust which it cannot both enforce and control. This seems to me to be good equity and good sense.

Alert

This decision re-affirmed the principle first enunciated in *Morice* that a trust for a non-charitable purpose which does not have someone who is capable of enforcing it *must* be invalid – 'a gift on trust must have a cestui que trust' – because the law will not countenance a private purpose trust that cannot be controlled or enforced by a beneficiary in the same way that a charitable trust can be controlled and enforced by the Attorney-General.

It can also be seen that even if the beneficiary principle had been satisfied, Roxburgh J would have decided that the trusts still failed for lack of certainty as to the purposes for which they had been established, which in turn would have made it impossible for the court to determine whether the trustees had sufficiently complied with their obligations under the trusts.

Link
See Uncertain or Capricious Trusts below.

6.2 Anomalous Exceptions

Despite the decision in *Morice*, many private purpose trusts were subsequently upheld by the courts, including the House of Lords, even though they quite clearly failed to comply with the beneficiary principle.

6.2.1 Trusts for the Erection and Maintenance of Monuments and Graves

In *Musset v Bingle* [1876] WN 170 a testator gave £300 for the erection of a monument. This purpose trust was upheld.

The discussion in this case assumed without adverse comment that a trust for the *erection* of a monument was a valid purpose trust. The only issue was as to perpetuity, which the judge resolved on the basis that he was simply prepared to assume that the work needed to erect the monument would inevitably be completed within the perpetuity period.

In Musset the will also contained a bequest of £200 to be held upon trust and used for the maintenance of the monument. This was held to be void for perpetuity, since the trust might endure for longer than the perpetuity period.

Link
See Perpetuity below

In *Re Hooper* [1932] 1 Ch 38, a trust for the maintenance of family graves, vaults and monuments was also upheld.

In re Hooper, Parker v Ward [1932] 1 Ch 38

Panel: Maugham J

Facts: The testator left a sum of money to trustees upon trust 'so far as they legally can do so ... [to] ... provide for the care and upkeep of' various family graves, vaults and monuments.

MR JUSTICE MAUGHAM

This point is one to my mind of doubt, and I should have felt some difficulty in deciding it if it were not for *Pirbright v Salwey* [1896] WN 86, a decision of Stirling J, which unfortunately is reported, as far as I know, only in the Weekly Notes. The report is as follows: "A testator, after expressing his wish to be buried in the inclosure in which his child lay in the churchyard of E, bequeathed to the rector and churchwardens for the time being of the parish church 800*l.* Consols, to be invested in their joint names, the interest and dividends to be derived therefrom to be applied, so long as the law for the time being permitted, in keeping up the inclosure and decorating the same with flowers: *Held*, that the gift was valid for at least a period of 21 years from the testator's death, and semble that it was not charitable."

That was a decision arrived at by Stirling J, after argument by very eminent counsel. The case does not appear to have attracted much attention in text-books, but it does not appear to have been commented upon adversely, and I shall follow it.

The trustees here have the sum of 1000*l.* which they have to hold upon trust to "invest the same and to the intent that so far as they legally can do so and in any manner that they may in their discretion arrange they will out of the annual income thereof" ... [for the stated purposes] ... which have to be done expressly according to an arrangement made in the discretion of the trustees and so far as they legally can do so. I do not think that is distinguishable from the phrase "so long as the law for the time being permits" and the conclusion at which I arrive, following the decision I have mentioned, is that this trust is valid for a period of twenty-one years from the testator's death so far as regards the ... upkeep of graves or vaults or monuments in the churchyard or in the cemetery.

Alert

Again, as with *Musset v Bingle*, the discussion in this case assumed that a trust for the maintenance of family graves, vaults and monuments was a valid purpose trust. The debate centred primarily upon whether the trust was void for perpetuity.

6.2.2 Trusts for the Saying of Private Masses

In *Bourne and Another v Kean and Others* [1919] AC 815, the House of Lords upheld a purpose trust for the saying of private masses.

Bourne and Another v Kean and Others [1919] AC 815

Panel: Lord Birkenhead LC, Lord Buckmaster, Lord Atkinson, Lord Parmoor, and Lord Wrenbury

Facts: The testator left the bulk of his estate to various Roman Catholic orders for the saying of private masses for the repose of his soul. The principal issues for determination were: (i) whether the saying of private masses in accordance with the Roman Catholic faith was illegal under statute, following the Reformation, as a 'superstitious use'; and (ii) if not, whether there was any reason at common law why a trust for the saying of such masses might not be upheld.

LORD BIRKENHEAD LC

My Lords, ... after the most anxious consideration, [I have come] to several conclusions:

(1)   That at common law masses for the dead were not illegal, but on the contrary that dispositions of property to be devoted to procuring masses to be said or sung were recognized both by common law and by statute.

(2)   That at the date of the passing of 1 Edw.6, c.14, no Act or provision having the force of an Act had made masses illegal.

(3)   That 1 Edw.6, c.14, did not itself make masses illegal, or provide that property might not thereafter be given for the purpose of procuring masses to be said or sung. It merely confiscated property then held for such and similar purposes. Subsequent legislation was passed to confiscate property afterwards settled to such uses. This is certainly true of 1 Eliz. c.24, and may be true of 1 Geo.1, c.50.

(4)   That, as a result of the Acts of Uniformity, 1549 and 1559, masses became illegal. The saying or singing of masses was a penal offence from 1581 to 1791, and no Court could enforce uses or trusts intended to be devoted to such uses.

(5)   That neither contemporaneous exposition of the statute 1 Edw.6, c.14, nor any doctrine closely related to it in point of date, placed upon it the construction adopted in *West v Shuttleworth*. ...

(6)   That the substratum of the decisions which held such uses and trusts invalid perished as a consequence of the passing of the Catholic Relief Act 1829, and thereafter your Lordships may give free play to the principle cessante ratione legis cessat lex ipsa.

(7)   That the current of decisions which held that such uses and trusts are ipso facto superstitious and void begins with *West v Shuttleworth*, and is due to a misunderstanding of the old cases. ...

The conclusion therefore, so far as I am concerned, is that a gift for masses for the souls of the dead ceased to be impressed with the stamp of superstitious use when Roman Catholicism was again permitted to be openly professed in this country, and that thenceforth it could not be deemed illegal.

 Alert

The conclusion therefore, was that trusts for the saying of masses had always been lawful at common law, and had only been prohibited by statute for a period between the Uniformity Act 1559 (or possibly the Uniformity Act 1549) and the Catholic Relief Act 1829. It therefore followed, in the opinion of a majority of the House, that the gift in the present case was valid. Their Lordships do not appear to have discussed the possibility that the gift was invalid for non-compliance with the beneficiary principle.

6.2.3 Trusts for the Maintenance of Particular Animals

In *Re Dean, Cooper-Dean v Stevens* [1889] 41 Ch D 552, a trust for the future upkeep of the testator's horses and hounds was held to be valid.

Re Dean, Cooper-Dean v Stevens [1889] 41 Ch D 552

Panel: North J

Facts: The testator gave an annuity of £750 per year to his trustees for a period of 50 years to allow them to maintain such of his horses and hounds as were living at his death.

MR JUSTICE NORTH

The first question is as to the validity of the provision made by the testator in favour of his horses and dogs. It is said that it is not valid; because (for this is the principal ground upon which it is put) neither a horse nor a dog could enforce the trust; and there is no person who could enforce it. It is obviously not a charity, because it is intended for the benefit of the particular animals mentioned and not for the benefit of animals generally, and it is quite distinguishable from the gift made in a subsequent part of the will to the Royal Society for the Prevention of Cruelty to Animals, which may well be a charity. In my opinion this provision for the particular horses and hounds referred to in the will is not, in any sense, a charity, and, if it were, of course the whole gift would fail, because it is a gift of an annuity arising out of land alone. But, in my opinion, as it is not a charity, there is nothing in the fact that the annuity arises out of land to prevent its being a good gift.

Then it is said, that there is no cestui que trust who can enforce the trust, and, that the Court will not recognise a trust unless it is capable of being enforced by some one. I do not assent to that view. There is not the least doubt that a man may if he pleases, give a legacy to trustees, upon trust to apply it in erecting a monument to himself, either in a church or in a churchyard, or even in unconsecrated ground, and I am not aware that such a trust is in any way invalid, although it is difficult to say who would be the cestui que trust of the monument. In the same way I know of nothing to prevent a gift of a sum of money to trustees, upon trust to apply it for the repair of such a monument. In my opinion such a trust would be good, although the testator must be careful to limit the time for which it is to last, because, as it is not a charitable trust, unless it is to come to an end within the limits fixed by the rule against perpetuities, it would be illegal. But a trust to lay out a certain sum in building a monument, and the gift of another sum in trust to apply the same to keeping that monument in repair, say, for ten years, is, in my opinion, a perfectly good trust, although I do not see who could ask the Court to enforce it. If persons beneficially interested in the estate could do so, then the present Plaintiff can do so; but, if such persons could not enforce the trust, still it cannot be said that the trust must fail because there is no one who can actively enforce it.

Is there then anything illegal or obnoxious to the law in the nature of the provision, that is, in the fact that it is not for human beings, but for horses and dogs? ... It is clearly settled by authority that a charity may be established for the benefit of horses and dogs, and, therefore, the making of a provision for horses and dogs, which is not a charity, cannot of itself be obnoxious to the law, provided, of course, that it is not to last for too long a period. ... There is nothing, therefore, in my opinion, to make the provision for the testator's horses and dogs void.

Mr Justice North was clearly of the view that a trust for the maintenance of particular animals was not capable of being a charitable trust but was nonetheless a valid private purpose trust. Although he expressly referred to the fact that such a trust must not 'last for too long a period', the judgment does not reveal on what basis the judge thought that this requirement was satisfied.

Link
See Perpetuity below

6.2.4 Miscellaneous Cases – Foxhunting

In *Re Thompson, Public Trustee v Lloyd* [1934] Ch 342, Clauson J upheld a trust for 'the promotion and furthering of fox-hunting'.

Re Thompson, Public Trustee v Lloyd [1934] Ch 342

Panel: Clauson J

Facts: The testator bequeathed a legacy to a friend to be applied by him in such manner as he should in his absolute discretion think fit towards the promotion and furthering of fox-hunting.

MR JUSTICE CLAUSON

The testator ... bequeathed a legacy of 1000*l.* to his friend ... to be applied by him in such manner as he should in his absolute discretion think fit towards the promotion and furthering of fox-hunting. In the first place, it is clear that Mr Lloyd [the friend] is not entitled to the legacy for his own benefit nor indeed does he so claim it, but he is anxious to carry out the testator's expressed wishes, if and so far as he lawfully may do so. No argument has been put forward which could justify the Court in holding this gift to be a gift in favour of charity, although it may well be that a gift for the benefit of animals generally is a charitable gift: but it seems to me plain that I cannot construe the object for which this legacy was given as being for the benefit of animals generally. In my judgment the object of the gift has been defined with sufficient clearness and is of a nature to which effect can be given. The proper way for me to deal with the matter will be, not to make, as it is asked by the summons, a general declaration, but, following the example of Knight Bruce V-C in *Pettingall v Pettingall*, to order that, upon the defendant Mr Lloyd giving an undertaking (which I understand he is willing to give) to apply the legacy when received by him towards the object expressed in the testator's will, the plaintiffs do pay to the defendant Mr Lloyd the legacy of 1000*l.*; and that, in case the legacy should be applied by him otherwise than towards the promotion and furthering of fox-hunting, the residuary legatees are to be at liberty to apply.

Alert

This judgment illustrates a number of points:

(a)   A trust for the promotion and furtherance of fox-hunting is a valid private purpose trust.

(b)   A private purpose trust is dependent for its fulfilment – given that there is no beneficiary who can enforce it – upon the willingness of the trustee to carry out the purpose, hence the reference to the undertaking which the trustee (Mr Lloyd) was willing to give. (Because of this dependence upon the trustee for performance of the trust, private purpose trusts are also referred to as 'trusts of imperfect obligation'.)

(c)   Although there would be no beneficiary of the purpose trust who could ensure that the trust was performed correctly, the due performance by the trustee of his obligations would always be monitored by the residuary legatees, who would be entitled have the trust 'terminated' (and as a result receive the balance of the legacy of £1,000 which remained unspent) in the event of any breach. The judge therefore granted them the opportunity of bringing such a breach to the court's attention by giving them liberty to apply.

Such a trust, if established today, might well be void for illegality, given the provisions of the Hunting Act 2004.

In *Re Astor* (above), Roxburgh J considered the validity of these anomalous exceptions.

MR JUSTICE ROXBURGH

...These cases I must now consider. First of all, there is a group relating to horses, dogs, graves and monuments, among which I was referred to *Pettingall v Pettingall* 11 LJ Ch 176; ... *In re Dean* 41 Ch D 552; *Pirbright v Salwey* [1896] WN 86; and *In re Hooper* [1932] 1 Ch 38.

In *Pettingall v Pettingall* a testator made the following bequest by his will: "'Having a favourite black mare, I hereby bequeath, that at my death, £50 per annum be paid for her keep in some park in England or Wales; her shoes to be taken off, and she never to be ridden or put in harness; and that my executor consider himself in honour bound to fulfil my wish, and see that she will be well provided for, and removable at his will. At her death all payment to cease.' It being admitted that a bequest in favour of an animal was valid, two questions were made: first, as to the form of the decree on this point; and secondly, as to the disposition of the surplus not required for the mare. Knight Bruce V-C said, that so much of the £50 as would be required to keep the mare comfortably, should be applied by the executor, and that he was entitled to the surplus. He must give full information, whenever required, respecting the mare; and if the mare were not properly attended to, any of the parties interested in the residue might apply to the court. The decree on this point ought to be, that £50 a year should be paid to the executor during the life of the mare, or until further order; he undertaking to maintain her comfortably; with liberty for all parties to apply." The points which I wish to make are (1) that it was there admitted that a bequest in favour of an animal was valid, and (2) that there were persons interested in residue who having regard to the decree made would have had no difficulty in getting the terms of the "bequest" enforced. ...

In *In re Dean* a testator ... charged his said freehold estates with the payment to his trustees, for the term of 50 years, if any of [his] horses and hounds should so long live, of an annual sum of £750. And he declared that his trustees should apply the said annual sum in the maintenance of the horses and hounds for the time being living, and in maintaining the stables, kennels and buildings inhabited by the said animals in such condition of repair as his trustees might deem fit ... . North J said: "Then it is said, that there is no cestui que trust who can enforce the trust, and that the court will not recognize a trust unless it is capable of being enforced by someone. I do not assent to that view. There is not the least doubt that a man may if he pleases, give a legacy to trustees, upon trust to apply it in erecting a monument to himself, either in a church or in a churchyard, or even in unconsecrated ground, and I am not aware that such a trust is in any way invalid, although it is difficult to say who would be the cestui que trust of the monument. In the same way I know of nothing to prevent a gift of a sum of money to trustees, upon trust to apply it for the repair of such a monument. In my opinion such a trust would be good, although the testator must be careful to limit the time for which it is to last, because, as it is not a charitable trust, unless it is to come to an end within the limits fixed by the rule against perpetuities, it would be illegal. But a trust to lay out a certain sum in building a monument, and the gift of another sum in trust to apply the same to keeping that monument in repair, say, for ten years, is, in my opinion, a perfectly good trust, although I do not see who could ask the court to enforce it. If persons beneficially interested in the estate could do so, then the present plaintiff can do so; but, if such persons could not enforce the trust, still it cannot be said that the trust must fail because there is no one who can actively enforce it." ... North J did undoubtedly uphold the particular directions, whether or not they could be "actively enforced." But putting it at its highest, he merely held that there were certain classes of trusts, of which this was one, in which that objection was not fatal. He did not suggest that it was not generally fatal outside the realms of charity.

In *Pirbright v Salwey* a testator ... bequeathed to the rector and churchwardens of the parish church £800 Consols, the interest and dividends to be derived therefrom to be applied, so long as the law for the time being permitted, in keeping up the inclosure and decorating the same with flowers. It was held that the gift was valid for at least a period of 21 years from the testator's death, and semble that it was not charitable.

In *In re Hooper* a testator bequeathed to his executors and trustees money out of the income of which to provide, so far as they legally could do so, for the care and upkeep of certain graves, a vault and certain monuments. Maugham J said: "This point is one to my mind of doubt, and I should have felt some difficulty in deciding it if it were not for *Pirbright v Salwey*. ... That was a decision arrived at by Stirling J, after argument by very eminent counsel. The case does not appear to have attracted much attention in textbooks, but it does not appear to have been commented upon adversely, and I shall follow it." In this case, and probably also in *Pirbright v Salwey*, there was a residuary legatee to bring before the court any failure to comply with the directions. But I think that Maugham J regarded them both as exceptions from general principle.

Last in this group is *In re Thompson*. I have included it in this group because, although it relates to the furtherance of foxhunting and thus moves away from the subject-matter of the group and much nearer to the present case, it is expressly founded on *Pettingall v Pettingall*, and it is indeed a most instructive case. The testator bequeathed a legacy of £1,000 to a friend to be applied by him in such manner as he should think fit towards the promotion and furthering of foxhunting, and devised and bequeathed his residuary estate to Trinity Hall in the University of Cambridge. ... When counsel, during the course of the argument, observed, "True, there is no cestui que trust who can enforce the application of the legacy, but that is immaterial: *In re Dean*. The object to which the legacy is to be applied is sufficiently defined to be enforced," Clauson J interposed: "The college, as residuary legatees, seem to have an interest in the legacy, as, but for the trust for its application, they would be entitled to it. The procedure adopted by Knight Bruce V-C in *Pettingall v Pettingall* ... might be followed in this case." And in his judgment he said: "In my judgment the object of the gift has been defined with sufficient clearness and is of a nature to which effect can be given. The proper way for me to deal with the matter will be, not to make, as it is asked by the summons, a general declaration, but following the example of Knight Bruce V-C in *Pettingall v Pettingall*, to order that, upon the defendant Mr Lloyd ... giving an undertaking (which I understand he is willing to give) to apply the legacy when received by him towards the object expressed in the testator's will, the plaintiffs do pay to the defendant Mr Lloyd the legacy of £1,000; and that, in case the legacy should be applied by him otherwise than towards the promotion and furthering of foxhunting, the residuary legatees are to be at liberty to apply." I understand Clauson J to have held in effect that there was somebody who could enforce the purpose indicated because the college, as residuary legatees, would be entitled to the legacy but for the trust for its application and they could apply to the court to prevent any misapplication or breach of the undertaking given by Mr Lloyd. I infer from what he said that he would not have upheld the validity of this non-charitable purpose if there had been no residuary legatee, and no possibility of making such an order as was made in *Pettingall v Pettingall*.

Let me then sum up the position so far. On the one side there are Lord Parker's two propositions with which I began. These were not new, but merely re-echoed what Sir

William Grant had said as Master of the Rolls in *Morice v The Bishop of Durham* as long ago as 1804: "There must be somebody, in whose favour the court can decree performance." The position was recently restated by Harman J in *In re Wood* [1949] Ch 498: "A gift on trust must have a cestui que trust," and this seems to be in accord with principle. On the other side is a group of cases relating to horses and dogs, graves and monuments - matters arising under wills and intimately connected with the deceased - in which the courts have found means of escape from these general propositions and also *In re Thompson* ... which I have endeavoured to explain. ... [They] may, I think, properly be regarded as anomalous and exceptional and in no way destructive of the proposition which traces descent from or through Sir William Grant through Lord Parker to Harman J. Perhaps the late Sir Arthur Underhill was right in suggesting that they may be concessions to human weakness or sentiment (see Law of Trusts, 8th ed., p 79). They cannot, in my judgment, of themselves (and no other justification has been suggested to me) justify the conclusion that a Court of Equity will recognize as an equitable obligation affecting the income of large funds in the hands of trustees a direction to apply it in furtherance of enumerated non-charitable purposes in a manner which no court or department can control or enforce. I hold that the trusts here in question are void ... .

 Alert

Having reviewed the many cases since *Morice* which did not accord with the beneficiary principle, Roxburgh J concluded that they were 'anomalous and exceptional'. In his view the correct position in law, which he traced from *Morice* through to *In re Wood*, was that a non-charitable purpose trust could not be valid in the absence of 'somebody, in whose favour the court can decree performance'.

In *Re Endacott, deceased* [1960] Ch 262, the Court of Appeal had the opportunity to consider the rule in *Morice*, the many anomalous exceptions which had been sanctioned over the intervening years, and the 'return to orthodoxy' represented by the decision of Roxburgh J in *Re Astor*. The Court of Appeal affirmed the orthodox view and held that a trust 'for the purpose of providing some useful memorial to myself' was void as a non-charitable purpose trust.

Re Endacott, deceased, Corpe v Endacott [1960] Ch 262

Panel: Lord Evershed MR, Sellers and Harman LJJ

Facts: A testator gave his residuary estate to the North Tawton Parish Council 'for the purpose of providing some useful memorial to myself ...'.

LORD EVERSHED MR

By his will ... the testator ... made ... the following residuary gift: "Everything else I leave to North Tawton Devon Parish Council for the purpose of providing some useful memorial to myself ... ."

Mr Arnold, for the parish council, has put his case on two broad distinct grounds. He has first said that the words "for the purpose of providing some useful memorial to myself" merely indicated the reason why the testator had made this gift, but did not,

 Link
See below the discussion under 'Motive cases' as to apparent purpose trusts actually taking effect as absolute gifts.

and were not intended to, impose any obligation upon the parish council, with the result that the gift should be treated as a gift out and out to the parish council.

Alternatively, Mr Arnold has argued on the footing that the words (contrary to his first contention) do impose a trust or obligation of some kind, though it is to be noted that it has not been suggested that such a trust would offend the rule against perpetuities. But, on this alternative basis, the argument has diverged thus: First, if the trust be not (upon its true interpretation) a charitable trust, still it is said to be of a public nature and valid and effective, on the ground that it falls within a class of cases which have been referred to as "anomalous," and which were recited by Roxburgh J conveniently in his recent decision in the case of *In re Astor's Settlement Trusts* [1952] Ch 534 ... . The contention is that this case, falling within that so-called anomalous class, must be treated as effective, being of a public character and being also such that, by appropriate machinery, it can be properly controlled by the court. ...

Then, alternatively, it is said the trusts are in truth charitable, and the argument on this alternative again diverges. First of all, it has been submitted that a parish council (and, of course, this particular parish council) is, according to its statutory constitution, limited, at any rate quoad any gifts of this kind which it receives, to charitable functions and activities. If that is right, then it is said that the gift to such a body stamps (and, if necessary, qualifies) the nature of the trusts which are declared, and that they should, accordingly, be taken as being and intended to be within the scope of the (charitable) statutory activities or powers. Secondly (and this was a point particularly put to us by Mr Buckley for the Attorney-General), it is said that, whether the parish council be or be not a body confined in activity to charitable purposes, the true view of the meaning of these vital words "for the purpose of providing some useful memorial to myself" is that they are, as a matter of language, equivalent to a trust for the benefit of the local inhabitants of North Tawton Parish and therefore, according to authority, charitable.

Those, broadly, are the contentions; and I will deal at once and briefly with the first point, namely: Was the language which I have quoted intended to impose an obligation, or was it merely expository? That matter I can deal with briefly, because it is, after all, a matter of mere construction. It will, therefore, be convenient if I state at once what my view is of the meaning of these words "for the purpose of providing some useful memorial to myself"; and ... I do not think that these words were merely expository. In my judgment, they were intended to impose an obligation in the nature of a trust. In my judgment, the object of these words, the trust, the obligation, which the testator intended them to impose was this: that the council were, with his money (and subject, of course, to the obligation about the widow), to create a memorial to himself. His first idea was (and I am not saying that it was either foolish or ignoble) that there should thereafter be in North Tawton, Devon, a memorial to himself; but that the memorial was to have this quality, that it was to be useful; and that I take to mean that it was intended that it should have the quality of utility rather than ornament. Though I do not think aesthetic or ornamental considerations were excluded, still his purpose was that the memorial, whatever form it took and whether material or not, should be useful; and, by way again of anticipation of my answer to Mr Buckley, I cannot see that it was necessarily to be useful only to the inhabitants of North Tawton.

I have stated my view of the construction and that view answers the first point. It follows that this was not a gift out and out to the North Tawton Parish Council. My view of the intention of those words also carries with it the answer to many of the other points that have arisen. I go further and say that, in the end of all, this case should be decided on the grounds ... that here was a specific obligation sought to be imposed, specific in this sense, that it was to be for the purpose of providing a memorial for this testator having the quality of utility, something obviously that could not be confined to charitable purposes, but no doubt having the quality also that it served a public purpose of some kind. In my judgment this view of the words does carry with it the result, with all respect to the learning which has been put before us, that to hold it valid would be for this court to go beyond (and appreciably beyond) the tenor of the decided cases on these difficult subjects.

I come then to Mr. Arnold's alternative ground. ... It is convenient and perhaps logical to take first the point that the parish council being, it is said, confined to charitable activities so far as is relevant, then this gift must take its character by reflection of that fact. I am unable to accept that argument. The cases, of which *In re Rumball, decd* [1956] Ch 105 ... in this court is the most recent, illustrate at any rate this proposition that gifts to persons holding a particular office, and particularly an ecclesiastical office, if they are not to be treated as gifts to the holder of that office in his personal capacity, are taken to be gifts to be applied for the purposes for which the office is held. The vicar or the cardinal archbishop (to take references from two cases) receives the gift and disposes of it (as it is said) virtute officii, and the nature of the officium is such that the duties, the trusts, must be ecclesiastical and therefore charitable. If that is accepted, then general words which follow may be regarded either as merely emphasising the fact that the gift is to the ecclesiastical officer virtute officii or possibly, as intended, not only to do that but also to limit to some extent the scope of his possible disposition, within the scope of his office, of those funds. No decided case, so far as we are aware, has applied that principle to such a body as a parish council. If it were shown perfectly clearly that every activity of a parish council, at any rate so far as gifts were concerned, must be of a charitable character, it might follow that a similar reasoning would apply; but I am not satisfied that it is true to say of a parish council that it is confined in its activities to charitable activities, or that it is so confined as regards any gifts it may receive. I do not forget the argument that you might give something to a vicar not personally, but having attached to it an obligation to apply it for purposes which were outside his ecclesiastical duties, but I cannot find in this case any true analogy to that kind of illustration. There is here a gift to this parish council for the purpose which I have stated, and the relevance of the matter must be (the purpose being a very wide one and not on the face of it charitable): Is the nature of a parish council's activities so clearly defined as being of a charitable character as to impose an essential limitation on the words which I have already tried to construe?

We were referred to section 268 of the Local Government Act, 1933. That deals with acceptance of gifts by local authorities and (so far as relevant) provides: "Subject to the provisions of this section, a local authority may accept, hold and administer any gift ... for any local public purpose, or for the benefit of the inhabitants of the area," etc. I have no doubt (and I do not think Mr Arnold really contended to the contrary) that the words "for any local public purpose" cannot be confined in that context to charitable purposes. ... The words "local public purposes" are not, according to our law, regarded as being exclusively charitable; and, even against the background of the Local Government Act of 1894, I think it is plain that local public purposes in section 268 of the Act of 1933 are not only charitable purposes. But I do not forget the point that this section deals with acceptance of gifts and would not necessarily colour the general activities of a parish council, though I venture for my part to think that if, in the case of gifts, it is made plain that a parish council can apply them to non-charitable as well as charitable purposes, it is a severe obstacle in Mr Arnold's way. ...

I now turn to Mr Arnold's alternative argument based on the view that there is here a trust and a trust of a public character, but not a charitable trust. What he says is, that the trust is in line with the trusts which were rendered effective in those cases which I have called "anomalous," and many of which are referred to in Roxburgh J's decision, beginning with *Pettingall v Pettingall* (1842) 11 LJ Ch 176. I include in that list cases such as the three to which we have had our attention particularly drawn today. The argument is that assuming the non-charitable but public nature of this trust, still it is of a character which the court can efficiently, and will, enforce. It must be said that these cases are of a somewhat anomalous kind. They are classified in the recent book written by Mr J H C Morris and Professor Barton Leach, The Rule Against Perpetuities (1956) (p 298). "We proceed," say the authors, "to examine these 'anomalous' exceptions. It will "be found that they fall into the following groups: (1) trusts for the erection or maintenance of monuments or graves; (2) trusts for the saying of masses, in jurisdictions where such trusts are not regarded as charitable; (3) trusts for the maintenance of particular animals; (4) trusts for the benefit of unincorporated associations (though this group is more doubtful); (5) miscellaneous cases." I am prepared to accept, for the purposes of the argument, that it does not matter that the trusts here are attached to residue and not to a legacy; that is to say, it does not matter that the persons who would come to the court and either complain if the trusts were not being carried out, or claim the money on the footing that they had not been carried out, are next-of-kin rather than residuary legatees. Still, in my judgment, the scope of these cases (and I can call them anomalous because they have been so called both in the book of Mr Morris and Professor Barton Leach and in the course of the argument) ought not to be extended. So to do would be to validate almost limitless heads of non-charitable trusts, even though they were not (strictly speaking) public trusts, so long only as the question of perpetuities did not arise; and, in my judgment, that result would be out of harmony with the principles of our law. No principle perhaps has greater sanction or authority behind it than the general proposition that a trust by English law, not being a charitable trust, in order to be effective, must have ascertained or ascertainable beneficiaries. These cases constitute an exception to that general rule. The general rule, having such authority as that of Lord Eldon, Lord Parker and my predecessor, Lord Greene MR, behind it, was most recently referred to in the Privy Council in *Leahy v Attorney-General for New South Wales* [1959] AC 457 ... .

I therefore, so far as this case is concerned, conclude (having already stated my view of the meaning of the words) that, though this trust is specific, in the sense that it

 Alert

indicates a purpose capable of expression, yet it is of far too wide and uncertain a nature to qualify within the class of cases cited. It would go far beyond any fair analogy to any of those decisions. I do not wish to take time by much example, particularly because I am not unmindful of having already said that I do not wish to add to the future burden of citation; but, merely by way of example, take trusts for the maintenance of memorials, I refer to *In re Hooper* [1932] 1 Ch 38. That was a case where the purpose of the bequest was to provide for the care and upkeep of certain graves, a vault and monuments. Maugham J said: "This point is one, to my mind, of doubt, and I should have felt some difficulty in deciding it if it were not for *Pirbright v Salwey* [1896] WN 86. That was a decision arrived at by Stirling J after argument by very eminent counsel. The case does not appear to have attracted much attention in textbooks, but it does not appear to have been commented upon adversely, and I shall follow it." It may be said that other cases in regard to monuments, which were closely on the facts in line, might similarly follow the decision of Stirling J, but this case, as I construe the purposes of the gift, is very different from *In re Hooper*. ...

Those, then, are my reasons for the conclusion which I stated at the beginning of this judgment, that in my view Danckwerts J rightly decided the case, and I therefore would dismiss the appeal.

LORD JUSTICE HARMAN

I agree. At first sight, my mind recoiled from the possibility of this gift being held valid, and I have not seen any cause in the course of the hearing to resile from that view. One must first construe the will; and my view of that is that this testator, as my Lord has said, intended by his will to provide himself with a memorial in his native town. He added that the memorial to himself should also be useful. ... So read, it seems to me apparent that the law cannot uphold the will, unless connected with the fabric of a church, without throwing over every kind of authority on this subject. A gift for public purposes in the parish of North Tawton, a gift for patriotic purposes, a gift for benevolent purposes, are all, as we all know, universally now held to be bad. How, then, shall it be held that a gift for useful purposes is good without upsetting the whole structure so elaborately built up and ... so firmly established? I cannot think that charity has anything to do with this bequest. As for establishing it without the crutch of charity, I applaud the orthodox sentiments expressed by Roxburgh J in the *Astor* case, and I think, as I think he did, that though one knows there have been decisions at times which are not really to be satisfactorily classified, but are perhaps merely occasions when Homer has nodded, at any rate these cases stand by themselves and ought not to be increased in number, nor indeed followed, except where the one is exactly like another. Whether it would be better that some authority now should say those cases were wrong, this perhaps is not the moment to consider. At any rate, I cannot think a case of this kind, the case of providing outside a church an unspecified and unidentified memorial, is the kind of instance which should be allowed to add to those troublesome, anomalous and aberrant cases.

In my judgment, Danckwerts J came to the right conclusion, and this appeal ought to be dismissed.

In *Re Endacott* the Court of Appeal therefore:

(a) re-affirmed the necessity for a private purpose trust to comply with the beneficiary principle in order for it to be valid;

(b) identified four categories of 'anomalous' private purpose trust which had been 'wrongly' upheld in the 150 years since *Morice* but which it would not be right to overrule given the length of time for which they had stood unchallenged, namely:

   (i) Trusts for the erection and maintenance of monuments and graves (eg *Re Hooper* [1932] 1 Ch 38);

   (ii) Trusts for the saying of private masses (eg *Bourne v Keane* [1919] AC 815);

   (iii) Trusts for the maintenance of particular animals (eg *Pettingall v Pettingall* (1842) 11 LJ Ch 176; *Re Dean* [1889] 41 Ch D 552); and

   (iv) Miscellaneous cases – of which the one most frequently cited is *Re Thompson* (see above).

(c) made clear that no further exceptions were to be allowed.

The result is that any trust (whenever created) which falls fairly and squarely within one of the anomalous purposes sanctioned in *Re Endacott* will be valid. However, any other private purpose trust will not be valid unless it falls within the Re Denley exception.

Link
See Trusts for Persons below.

6.3 Perpetuity

Even if a private purpose trust falls within one of the *Re Endacott* exceptions (see above), nonetheless it will still be invalid if it infringes the rule against perpetuity.

The rule against perpetuity (also known as the rule against inalienability) is a common law rule which exists to prevent property from being held for a non-charitable purpose which may never end. The rule requires that it must be possible to say, at the moment that the trust is created, that it will definitely come to an end before the expiry of the 'the perpetuity period'. This is achieved by stating that the purpose is to be carried on for the duration of the perpetuity period, but then the trust fund is to be distributed elsewhere.

Under common law, 'the perpetuity period' is defined as the lifetime of any relevant life (or lives) in being plus 21 years. 'Life in being' simply means any person now born or in the womb.

The person establishing the trust may nominate a life in being of their own choosing. They may choose a named individual or (which is quite common) they may identify the person simply as a member of a particular class – eg 'the last survivor of the issue of Queen Victoria living at my death' (if the trust is created by a will). This is known as a 'royal lives' clause. [Queen Victoria is often chosen because she had nine children, who themselves had a further 40 children; so over the ensuing years the class of relevant lives in being has become very large, thereby optimising the chances that the applicable perpetuity period will last for many years.]

If at the date of the testator's death the youngest living descendant of Queen Victoria is 10 years old, and that person lives to the age of 90, the relevant perpetuity period is calculated as follows:

Lifetime of relevant life in being (90 years – 10 years)   =   80   years

Plus

Additional period of 21 years   =   21   years

Total: 101 years

If no relevant life in being is specified, then the common law applies a 'default' perpetuity period of 21 years. The trust must expressly limit the duration to this period.

Of course, it is in the very nature of the anomalous purpose trusts discussed above that they do not have an ascertainable beneficiary and so, in the absence of a nominated 'relevant life in being' the applicable perpetuity period in relation to them will usually be 21 years.

This time constraint can present problems where the purpose trust is for an ongoing activity such as the maintenance of monuments and graves or the maintenance of animals. In *Re Hooper* (above) the testator had not nominated a relevant life in being, but had stated that the trustees were only to carry out the purpose '... so far as they legally can do so ...'. Mr Justice Maugham felt able to treat that phrase as being indistinguishable from the phrase 'so long as the law for the time being permits' which had been upheld in *Pirbright v Salwey*, and therefore sufficient to import a perpetuity period of 21 years, per Maugham J:

> This point is one to my mind of doubt, and I should have felt some difficulty in deciding it if it were not for *Pirbright v Salwey* [1896] WN 86, a decision of Stirling J ... The case does not appear to have attracted much attention in text-books, but it does not appear to have been commented upon adversely, and I shall follow it.
>
> The trustees ... [may only act] ... so far as they legally can do so. I do not think that is distinguishable from the phrase "so long as the law for the time being permits" and the conclusion at which I arrive, following the decision I have mentioned, is that this trust is valid for a period of twenty-one years from the testator's death so far as regards the ... upkeep of graves or vaults or monuments in the churchyard or in the cemetery.

But in the absence of such 'saving' words, any such trust will fail for perpetuity. So in *Musset v Bingle* (above), the trust for maintenance of the monument was void for perpetuity as no perpetuity period was specified. But the trust for the erection of the monument was valid, because it was assumed that the monument would be erected within the perpetuity period.

Note that it is in fact possible to ensure that a monument or grave is maintained for a period considerably in excess of 21 years under the Parish Councils and Burial Authorities (Miscellaneous Provisions) Act s 1, which provides that a burial authority may agree, upon payment of a sum, to maintain a monument or grave for a period not exceeding 99 years.

The decision in *Re Dean* (above), however, is more difficult to reconcile with the need for compliance with the perpetuity period. This is particularly so given that the life of the animal in question cannot be a 'relevant life in being' (only human lives qualify as 'relevant' lives), nor is regard to be taken of the fact that many animals do not have a natural lifespan of more than 21 years: see the Irish case of *Re Kelly* [1932] IR 255.

6.4 Uncertain or Capricious Trusts

Even though a purpose trust may be allowed as an exception to the beneficiary principle and the rule against perpetuity, the law will not uphold a purpose trust if it is too vague or if it is too capricious, (ie if it is devoid of any beneficial use or purpose).

As stated above, in *Re Astor*, for example, Roxburgh J would have declined to enforce the trusts in issue on the additional ground that the trust obligations were too vague.

An example of a trust which was considered to be too capricious to be worthy of enforcement is to be found in *Brown v Burdett* (1882) 21 Ch D 667.

Brown v Burdett (1882) 21 Ch D 667

Panel: Bacon V-C

Facts: The testatrix devised a freehold house, yard, garden, and outbuildings, to trustees and their heirs, upon trust to block up all the rooms of the house (except four rooms in which she directed that a housekeeper and his wife should be placed in occupation), and the coach-house, for twenty years; and subject thereto upon trust for a named beneficiary. She directed her trustees to visit the house and premises once in every three months to see that the trusts were effectually carried out, and declared that if any trustee should neglect or refuse to carry out the trusts aforesaid, any real or personal estate given or intended to be given to him by the will should go elsewhere.

> BACON V-C
>
> I think I must "unseal" this useless, undisposed of property.
>
> There will be a declaration that the house and premises were undisposed of by the will
> ...

The court refused to give effect to a trust whose purpose was useless, and so declared that the property had not been disposed of by the will.

6.5 *Re Denley* – Trusts for Persons

The decision of Goff J in *Re Denley's Trust Deed* [1969] 1 Ch 373 suggests that there may be a category of purpose trust which will be valid even though it does not satisfy the beneficiary principle or fall within one of the *Re Endacott* exceptions: a purpose trust which is expressed to be for the benefit of ascertainable individuals.

Re Denley's Trust Deed, Holman & Ors v H H Martyn & Co Ltd & Ors [1969] 1 Ch 373

Panel: Goff J

Facts: The settlor settled certain land upon trustees to be used as a sports ground 'primarily for the benefit of the employees of the company and secondarily for the benefit of such other person or persons (if any) as the trustees may allow to use the same ...'. The use of the land as a sports ground was expressly limited to the perpetuity period. Mr Justice Goff upheld the trust.

MR JUSTICE GOFF

[Counsel] has argued that the trust ... in the present case is ... a purpose trust, that is, a trust for providing recreation, which he submits is void on the beneficiary principle... . [I]n my judgment the beneficiary principle of In re Astor's Settlement Trusts which was approved in In re Endacott, decd ... is confined to purpose or object trusts which are abstract or impersonal. The objection is not that the trust is for a purpose or object per se, but that there is no beneficiary or cestui que trust. ... Where, then, the trust, though expressed as a purpose, is directly or indirectly for the benefit of an individual or individuals, it seems to me that it is in general outside the mischief of the beneficiary principle. The trust in the present case is limited in point of time so as to avoid any infringement of the rule against perpetuities and, for the reasons I have given, it does not offend against the beneficiary principle; and unless, therefore, it be void for uncertainty, it is a valid trust. ... As it is a private trust and not a charitable one, it is clear that, however it be regarded, the individuals for whose benefit it is designed must be ascertained or capable of ascertainment at any given time: see *Inland Revenue Commissioners v Broadway Cottages Trust* [1955] Ch 20. It is conceded that "the employees of the company"..., which must mean for the time being, are so ascertained or ascertainable, but [counsel] submits that the inclusion in the class of "such other person or persons (if any) as the trustees may allow" is fatal, and that the qualification "secondarily" in relation to such persons does not help. In my judgment, however, this is not so. ...[T]he provision as to "other persons" is not a trust but a power operating in partial defeasance of the trust in favour of the employees which it does not therefore make uncertain. Moreover, as it is a power, it is not necessary that the trustees should know all possible objects in whose favour it is exercisable: see *In re Gulbenkian's Settlements* [1968] Ch 126. Therefore, in my judgment, it is a valid power. ... Another question, perhaps of difficulty, might arise, if the trustees purported to admit not to a given individual or individuals but a class which they failed to specify with certainty, whether in such a case this would import uncertainty into and invalidate the whole trust or would be merely an invalid exercise of the power; but, as that has not in fact occurred, I need not consider it. There is, however, one other aspect of uncertainty which has caused me some concern; that is, whether this is in its nature a trust which the court can control, for, as Lord Eldon LC said in *Morice v Bishop of Durham* (1805) 10 Ves 522:

 Alert

> "As it is a maxim, that the execution of a trust shall be under the control of the court, it must be of such a nature, that it can be under that control; so that the administration of it can be reviewed by the court; or, if the trustee dies, the court itself can execute the trust: a trust therefore, which, in case of mal-administration could be reformed; and a due administration directed; and then, unless the subject and the objects can be ascertained, upon principles, familiar in other cases, it must be decided, that the court can neither reform maladministration, nor direct a due administration."

> The difficulty I have felt is that there may well be times when some of the employees wish to use the sports club for one purpose while others desire to use it at the same time for some other purpose of such natures that the two cannot be carried on together. The trustees could, of course, control this by making rules and regulations ..., but they might not. In any case, the employees would probably agree amongst themselves, but I cannot assume that they would. If there were an impasse, the court could not resolve it, because it clearly could not either exercise the trustees' power to make rules or settle a scheme, this being a non-charitable trust: see In re Astor's Settlement Trusts [1952] Ch 534. In my judgment, however, it would not be right to hold the trust void on this ground. The court can, as it seems to me, execute the trust both negatively by restraining any improper disposition or use of the land, and positively by ordering the trustees to allow the employees and such other persons (if any) as they may admit to use the land for the purpose of a recreation or sports ground. Any difficulty there might be in practice in the beneficial enjoyment of the land by those entitled to use it is, I think, really beside the point. The same kind of problem is equally capable of arising in the case of a trust to permit a number of persons - for example, all the unmarried children of a testator or settlor - to use or occupy a house or to have the use of certain chattels; nor can I assume that in such cases agreement between the parties concerned would be more likely, even if that be a sufficient distinction, yet no one would suggest, I fancy, that such a trust would be void. In my judgment, therefore, the [trust is] valid ...

The essence of Goff J's decision is that even if a purpose trust does not have a beneficiary, it may nonetheless still be valid provided that it is directly or indirectly for the benefit of an ascertained or ascertainable individual or individuals. On this reasoning, In Re Astor's Settlement Trusts and Re Endacott could be distinguished on the ground that they had involved trusts which were purely for purposes which were 'abstract or impersonal'.

Applying the judge's test, it could readily be ascertained whether an individual was or was not an employee of the relevant company. However, there was a further complication, in that the terms of the trust allowed the trustees to permit 'such other person or persons (if any) as the trustees may allow' to use the sports ground. This appeared to mean that the sports ground might be used by persons who were not ascertained or ascertainable – their identity would never be known until they were actually selected by the trustees. The judge dealt with this problem by saying that the trustees were not under a trust obligation to allow use by such third parties, but merely had a power to do so, and that such a power, even if implemented, did not affect the validity of the trust.

This decision has been the subject of debate and criticism, and its correctness is open to question. It was accepted as correct by Sir Robert Megarry V-C in *Re Northern Developments (Holdings)* (1978), unreported (but referred to by Sir Peter Millett in 'Quistclose Trusts' (1985) 101 LQR 280). However, in *Re Grant's Will Trusts* [1980] 1 WLR 361, Vinelott J characterised the facts of *Re Denley* as not being concerned with a purpose trust at all, but involving simply a discretionary trust under which the trustees had a discretion to apply property for use by a defined class of beneficiaries, namely the employees of the company, per Vinelott J:

> I can see no distinction in principle between a trust to permit a class defined by reference to employment to use and enjoy land in accordance with rules to be made at the discretion of trustees on the one hand, and, on the other hand, a trust to distribute income at the discretion of trustees amongst a class, defined by reference to, for example, relationship to the settlor. In both cases the benefit to be taken by any member of the class is at the discretion of the trustees, but any member of the class can apply to the court to compel the trustees to administer the trust in accordance with its terms.

And in *Re Horley Town Football Club* [2006] All ER (D) 34, Lawrence Collins J observed (by way of implicit criticism) that

> Goff J appears to have equated the beneficiary principle with the question of enforceability and not with the issue of equitable ownership ... there are difficulties with regard to [the] termination of such a trust which make [*Re Denley*] an unsafe basis for decision: see Thomas and Hudson, The Law of Trusts (2004), para 6.21.

6.6 Motive Cases

As stated above, it is sometimes the case that what appears at first sight to be a purpose trust is in fact an absolute gift, with the 'purpose' being no more than a mere expression of non-binding motive on the part of the testator as to the reason for making the gift. This is a matter of construction of the particular disposition.

In *Re Andrew's Trust* [1905] 2 Ch 48, the court applied this construction to a trust fund which had been established by friends of the deceased in order to pay for the education of his infant children. The court upheld the trust as being for the children absolutely.

Re Andrew's Trust [1905] 2 Ch 48

Panel: Kekewich J

Facts: A fund was subscribed by the friends of a deceased clergyman for the education of his children, all of whom were then infants. The trust deed stated that the money was not intended for the exclusive use of any one of them in particular, nor for equal division among them, but as deemed necessary to defray the expenses of all, and solely in the matter of education. The education of the children was paid for partly out of the trust fund and partly out of monies respectively coming to them under their father's will. When all the children had grown up there remained a portion of the trust fund which was unapplied, and an issue arose as to whether it belonged to the friends upon resulting trust or to the children.

MR JUSTICE KEKEWICH

The Court is asked to determine how these shares and dividends ought to be dealt with, all the children being still alive and of full age. ...

I have been referred by counsel for the applicants to *In re Trusts of the Abbott Fund* [1900] 2 Ch 326, but it is absolutely different from the case now before the Court. There a fund had been raised for the maintenance and support of two distressed ladies, and on the death of the survivor there was still money in the hands of the trustees. Stirling J held that there was a resulting trust of this balance for the subscribers. He did not think that the ladies ever became absolute owners of the fund, and probably no one reading the case is likely to differ from that conclusion. Here I am dealing with different facts, including the fact that the children are still alive, and I do not think myself much guided, and certainly not in the slightest degree bound, by the authority of that case.

It seems to me that the guiding principle is to be found in several authorities examined by Wood V-C in ... *In re Sanderson's Trust* 3 K & J 497 – and the judgment of the Vice-Chancellor in that case. One passage may be usefully cited: "There are two classes of cases between which the general distinction is sufficiently clear, although the precise line of demarcation is occasionally somewhat difficult to ascertain. If a gross sum be given, or if the whole income of the property be given, and a special purpose be assigned for that gift, this Court always regards the gift as absolute, and the purpose merely as the motive of the gift, and therefore holds that the gift takes effect as to the whole sum or the whole income, as the case may be." Here the only specified object was the education of the children. But I deem myself entitled to construe "education" in the broadest possible sense, and not to consider the purpose exhausted because the children have attained such ages that education in the vulgar sense is no longer necessary. Even if it be construed in the narrower sense it is, in Wood V-C's language, merely the motive of the gift, and the intention must be taken to have been to provide for the children in the manner (they all being then infants) most useful.

Alert

Therefore ... I am prepared to hold that the shares and accumulated dividends belong to the children, and the only remaining question is in what proportions do they take. The [trust deed] states that the fund was not subscribed for equal division, but was intended to defray the expenses of all as deemed necessary, and apparently the trustees of the fund exercised their discretion in dividing the money so far as it was divided at all. But there is no longer room for discretion, and I think the only safe course is to hold that the children are entitled to what remains in equal shares.

Mr Justice Kekewich referred to well-established authority for the proposition that an absolute gift to which an expression of purpose had been attached does not lose its true character as a gift so as to become a trust for a purpose instead. The advantage of this construction, of course, is that such a gift is not then subject at all to the rules governing purpose trusts.

The decision in *Re Andrew's Trust* was approved in more recent times by the Court of Appeal in *Re Osoba (deceased), Osoba v Osoba and others* [1979] 1 WLR 247 where the Court of Appeal felt able to construe an apparent purpose trust as an absolute gift.

Re Osoba (deceased), Osoba v Osoba and others [1979] 1 WLR 247

Panel: Buckley, Goff, Eveleigh LJJ

Facts: The testator gave a fund to his wife upon trust for her maintenance, for the training of his daughter, Abiola, up to University grade and for the maintenance of his aged mother. After his daughter had completed her University education and his widow and mother had died, the question arose as to who was entitled to the fund. The Court of Appeal held that the fund was held on trust for the three women absolutely; and thus the daughter was now entitled absolutely, the widow and mother having died.

LORD JUSTICE GOFF

...Sir Robert Megarry V-C [the judge below] devoted a not inconsiderable part of his judgment to an attempt to reconcile *Re Abbott Fund Trusts* [1900] 2 Ch 326 with *Re Andrew's Trust* [1905] 2 Ch 48 and to seeing which more nearly approximates to the present case. But I do not think it was really necessary for him, nor do I consider it necessary for us, to embark on any such exercise. Both cases may well have been right on their particular facts, but as Sir Robert Megarry V-C himself correctly pointed out, what has to be done in this case is to construe the will of the testator and endeavour to ascertain his intention from the words he has used, of course, in the light of such knowledge of relevant facts as we know he must have had. Those cases are relevant for present purposes so far only as they lay down any principle of construction which is applicable to the testator's will. *Re Abbott* does not, I think, do this at all. ...

Re Andrew's Trust [1905] 2 Ch 48, on the other hand, did establish a principle of construction, or rather applied one then already long established in these terms:

'There are two classes of cases between which the general distinction is sufficiently clear, although the precise line of demarcation is occasionally somewhat difficult to ascertain. If a gross sum be given, or if the whole income of the property be given, and a special purpose be assigned for that gift, this Court always regards the gift as absolute, and the purpose merely as the motive of the gift, and therefore holds that the gift takes effect as to the whole sum or the whole income as the case may be.'

Kekewich J was there himself citing from the judgment of Page Wood V-C in *Re Sanderson's Trust* ((1857) 3 K & J 497 at 503).

In my judgment the decision in the case depends on the ambit of that principle and of another one similar thereto, of which *Barlow v Grant* (1684) 1 Vern 255 is an early example, and their applicability to the testator's language in the present case. Page Wood V-C said in *Re Sanderson* ... that the principle is always applied. That, I think, was putting it too high as it is not a rule of law, but, in the absence of context, to which of course it must yield, or perhaps very special circumstances, it is a long established and oft applied principle which I would not seek to whittle away. Of course, it is possible to imagine examples where the application of the principle would appear to be ridiculous, and a number were suggested in argument. If and when such a case does in fact arise it can be argued and decided, for as I have said, the principle in *Re Sanderson* ... is not a rule of law, but in all ordinary circumstances and in the absence of a contrary context, it must in my view be applied.

The initial question of construction is, then, whether the words in this residuary clause do indicate an intention to make a gift with a superadded expression of purpose, and I start with this, that where there is but one beneficiary and the purpose is that of maintenance or education, that is tantamount to a gift to the beneficiary and the purpose is accordingly disregarded: see, for example, *Webb v Kelly* ((1839) 9 Sim 469 at 472), where Shadwell V-C said: 'I think that a gift for the maintenance and education of the legatee is an absolute gift ...'; and *Lewes v Lewes* ((1848) 16 Sim 266 at 267), where Shadwell V-C said: 'I think that there is no sensible way of dealing with this case except by taking the words "for the maintenance, clothing and education" to be equivalent to "for the benefit of the children".' If, therefore, the trust had been simply to be used for her, that is the widow's, maintenance, it seems to me that the principle of *Re Sanderson's Trust* ... , and *Barlow v Grant*, must be applied, and she would have taken the whole residue absolutely.

Then it seems to me that as a matter of construction it can make no difference that the trust was to use the property for the maintenance of the aged mother as well, for the intention to make an absolute gift is the same, albeit it is made to two people, not one only. Thus in *Presant and Presant v Goodwin*, the principle was applied to a bequest of 'all my remaining property to be invested and appropriated to the education of my sister Juliana's children as shall seem most meet and beneficial to them by the executor and executrix of this my will, recommending to them that the boys receive a classical education to fit them for the learned professions, and the girls to fit them for the purpose of teaching in respectable private families, or in schools of the first respectability'. See also per Lord Macnaghten, giving the judgment of the Privy Council in *Williams v Papworth*.

So the crux of the matter is the inclusion of 'the training of my daughter Abiola up to University grade'. ...

So in the end the primary question is short and straightforward, namely whether ... because the purpose in Abiola's case is different from that in the other two, and unlike maintenance is definitely finite though the beneficiary be still alive, the *Re Sanderson* principle is excluded, or whether ... the trust creates an absolute gift to the three named beneficiaries. ...

Having regard to Abiola's age at the date of the will, the purpose in her case is one which the testator could well have contemplated would, or might, exhaust a fair proportion of the fund. It is, moreover, one conferring an extensive and continuing benefit on Abiola, and it seems to me it is at least as much a provision for her benefit

Alert

which ought to be treated as a gift with a superadded purpose which should be disregarded, as the provision for placing out the beneficiary as an apprentice: see *Barlow v Grant* which I have already mentioned, and *Barton v Cooke*, or that of purchasing a commission in *Cope v Wilmot* ((1772); see 1 Coll 381 at 396. ...

Sir Robert Megarry V-C ... said:

'In those circumstances I should be reluctant to read his will as showing an intention that once his daughter's training up to university level was at an end she was to have nothing more, and there should be no further testamentary provision for her. I do not think that the words relating to using the residue for Abiola's training and the maintenance of the widow show that any residue not required for these purposes was to be withheld from Abiola and the widow.'

Subject to the observation that the will also provided for the mother, I would respectfully agree with that view. ...

In my judgment, therefore, on its true construction ... the will created a trust for the benefit of the widow, the daughter and the mother absolutely. ... [The] fact that the gift is to the widow in trust does not, as it seems to me, in any way prevent the named beneficiaries, including herself, from taking an absolute beneficial interest as joint tenants, or tenants in common, under the trust.

LORD JUSTICE BUCKLEY

...Had the trust for the daughter's benefit been the only trust declared in respect of the testator's residue, she would in my judgment have become entitled to the whole residue beneficially on the testator's death.

The principle of construction which applies in such cases is explained in Roper on Legacies 4th Edn (1847), p 646, where I find this:

'Where a legacy is given to a person to answer a particular purpose to which it becomes impossible to appropriate it, but from no fault of the legatee, he would be entitled to the money; as in instances of a sum of money being left for the benefit of an infant as an apprentice fee and he is never placed in the situation or character of an apprentice; or where a legacy is given to a person to assist him in defraying the expenses necessary to secure priest's orders and he becomes a lunatic—in each case the legacy will vest at the testator's death, and upon this principle: it is considered that the property was intended for the legatee at all events, and that the mode directed for its application was merely a secondary consideration and independent of the gift.'

If a testator has given the whole of a fund, whether of capital or income, to a beneficiary, whether directly or through the medium of a trustee, he is regarded, in the absence of any contra-indication, as having manifested an intention to benefit that person to the full extent of the subject-matter, notwithstanding that he may have expressly stated that the gift is made for a particular purpose, which may prove to be impossible of performance or which may not exhaust the subject-matter. This is because the testator has given the whole fund; he has not given so much of the fund as will suffice or be required to achieve the purpose, nor so much of the fund as a trustee or

Alert

anyone else should determine, but the whole fund. This must be reconciled with the testator's having specified the purpose for which the gift is made. This reconciliation is achieved by treating the reference to the purpose as merely a statement of the testator's motive in making the gift. Any other interpretation of the gift would frustrate the testator's expressed intention that the whole subject-matter shall be applied for the benefit of the beneficiary. These considerations have, I think, added force where the subject-matter is the testator's residue, so that any failure of the gift would result in intestacy. The specified purpose is regarded as of less significance than the dispositive act of the testator, which sets the measure of the extent to which the testator intends to benefit the beneficiary. ...

Accordingly, in my judgment, the trust declared by ... the testator's will must take effect as a trust for all the three ladies absolutely.

Both Goff and Buckley LJJ construed the will as making an absolute gift of the property in question to the three named beneficiaries. They felt able to do this because it was entirely possible that the whole of the fund might have been needed to meet the needs of the three beneficiaries, which was inconsistent with the notion that the fund was to be used for a limited purpose and then applied elsewhere. The statement that the fund was to be used for maintenance or training (as the case might be), did not alter the position – those words were to be construed as a non-binding explanation of the testator's motive for making the gift.

Further Reading

Watt, Gary *Trusts and Equity*. (2nd edition) Oxford University Press

Martin, Jill *Hanbury and Martin: Modern Equity*. (17th edition) Sweet & Maxwell Ltd

Hayton and Mitchell: Cases and Commentary on Trusts and Equitable Remedies (12th edition)

Emery C T, 'The Most Hallowed Principle: Certainty of Beneficiaries of Trusts and Powers of Appointment', (1982) 98 LQR 551

Sir Peter Millett, 'Quistclose Trusts', (1985) 101 LQR 280

Brown, James, 'What are we to do with testamentary trusts of imperfect obligation?', (2007) 71 Conv 148

7

Unincorporated Associations

Topic List

Introduction

The law recognises individuals and companies as having separate legal personalities. Amongst other things, the concept of separate legal personality invests the 'person' in question with the ability to own property or to hold it on trust.

However, legal persons (both individual and corporate) often join together in the pursuit of common purposes, such as sporting, political or other activities. They often form clubs or other organisations in order to do so. Collectively, these are known as unincorporated associations.

7.1 What is an Unincorporated Association?

The essential characteristics of an unincorporated association were explained by Lawton LJ in *Conservative and Unionist Central Office v Burrell (Inspector of Taxes)* [1982] 1 WLR 522.

Conservative and Unionist Central Office v Burrell (Inspector of Taxes) **[1982] 1 WLR 522**

Panel: Lawton, Brightman and Fox LJJ

Facts: For many years the Conservative and Unionist Party (the Party) has consisted of three elements, namely (i) the Parliamentary Party, ie the members of both Houses of Parliament who take the Conservative whip, (ii) the individual members of numerous constituency associations, the umbrella organisation for which is the National Union of Conservative and Unionist Associations, and (iii) the party headquarters, known as Central Office, which administers the party's affairs, including receiving all moneys raised by the constituency associations, investing and managing the party's funds and then distributing those funds in accordance with the directions of the party leader. Central Office was assessed to corporation tax in relation to the income which it received from the Party's funds on the basis that it was an 'unincorporated association' and so fell within the extended definition of 'company' contained in Income and Corporation Taxes Act 1970 s 526(5). Central Office contended that (i) it was not itself an unincorporated association, but simply an administrative unit of the Party, (ii) even if the national union were an unincorporated association the funds did not belong to it because they were administered by Central Office, and so the national union could not be a taxable person, and (iii) the Party itself was an amorphous combination of various elements which lacked the characteristics of an unincorporated association, with the result that if the funds were owned by the Party the income arising from those funds was not assessable to corporation tax. The Court of Appeal held that the Party was not an unincorporated association.

LORD JUSTICE LAWTON

It was agreed before us that the Central Office was nothing more than an administrative unit of the [Party]. ... Both parties to this appeal asked the court to consider the legal nature of the [Party]. If it is an unincorporated association, corporation tax has to be paid on the income identified in the Party income and expenditure accounts for the relevant years as 'investment income and interest'. If it is not such an association, income tax will have to be paid on this income. ... The reason why the [Party] is contesting the assessments to corporation tax which have been made on it is that for the relevant years the rates at which corporation tax was charged were much higher than the rates for income tax. ...

I infer that by 'unincorporated association' in this context Parliament meant two or more persons bound together for one or more common purposes, not being business purposes, by mutual undertakings, each having mutual duties and obligations, in an organisation which has rules which identify in whom control of it and its funds rests and on what terms and which can be joined or left at will. ...

 Alert

The Crown's main argument, however, was based on the proposition that the [Party's] unquestioned, valid control of funds could only be possible in law if it were an unincorporated association. The officers of the [Party] who receive donations, legacies and constituency association quota subscriptions for [Party] purposes could not hold them as trustees since the law does not recognise trusts for non-charitable purposes. Clearly they could not use the funds for their own purposes. The only form of holding which made legal sense, so it was submitted, was that they held the funds for the benefit of the members of the party, being an unincorporated association, to be used by them for the [Party's] purposes. I reject this argument for three reasons: first, because I find this working back kind of argument a most unsatisfactory way of establishing the existence of an association which could only have come into existence as the result of an agreement between two or more persons; second, because it disregards the history of the central funds; and, third, because it ignores what most people intend when they make donations to central funds. I have had the benefit of reading in draft Brightman LJ's analysis of the legal nature of a donation to Central Office central funds. I agree with what he will say.

LORD JUSTICE BRIGHTMAN

... So in the present case it seems to me that the status of a contribution to the Conservative Party central funds is this. The contributor draws a cheque (for example) in favour of, or hands it to, the [constituency association] treasurers. The treasurers are impliedly authorised by the contributor to present the cheque for encashment and to add the contribution to Central Office funds. Central Office funds are the subject matter of a mandate which permits them to be used for the purposes of the Conservative Party as directed by the leader of the party. The contributor cannot demand his money back once it has been added to Central Office funds. He could object if Central Office funds were used or threatened to be use otherwise than in accordance with their declared purposes, unless it is correct to say, on ordinary accounting principles, that his contribution has already passed out of Central Office funds.

This discussion of mandates, and complaining contributors, is all very remote and theoretical. No contributor to Central Office funds will view his contribution in this way, or contemplate even the remotest prospect of legal action on his part. He believes he is making an out and out contribution or gift to a political party. And so he is in practical terms. The only justification for embarking on a close analysis of the situation is the challenge, which was thrown down by counsel for the Crown ... to suggest ... [that the only] legal framework which fits the undoubted fact that funds are held by the Central Office and are administered for the use and benefit of the Conservative Party, [is] that the Conservative Party is an unincorporated association.

I see no legal difficulty in the mandate theory. It is not necessary to invent an unincorporated association in order to explain the situation.

7.2 Different Interpretations of Gifts to Unincorporated Associations

Property is often gifted to unincorporated associations. This presents two distinct sets of problems:

(a) If the gift is regarded as an attempt to transfer ownership to the unincorporated association in its own name, the gift must fail because an unincorporated association has no separate legal personality and so cannot own property in its own name; but

(b) If the gift is construed as a trust for the purposes of the association, then unless the unincorporated association is charitable, the gift may well fail for the reasons identified in Chapter 6 on Private purpose trusts, namely breach of the beneficiary principle, breach of the rule against perpetuity, or uncertainty.

To enable such gifts to be upheld, the courts have developed a number of differing ways of interpreting gifts to unincorporated associations

7.2.1 Gift for present members beneficially

This is one of the oldest bases for upholding a gift to unincorporated association. On this interpretation, a gift to an unincorporated association is treated as a gift to each of the individual members of the association.

However, this interpretation is only appropriate where the circumstances, and in particular the subject matter of the property, lend themselves to it. In *Leahy v A-G for New South Wales* [1959] AC 457 the Privy Council considered this interpretation but held that it did not apply on the facts.

Leahy v A-G for New South Wales [1959] AC 457

Panel: Viscount Simonds, Lord Morton of Henryton, Lord Cohen, Lord Somervell of Harrow and Lord Denning

Facts: The testator left a property, which consisted of a 730 acre farm, upon trust for the nuns or brothers of various non-charitable religious orders. One of the issues which fell to be decided was whether the gift under the will took effect as an immediate gift of the property to the nuns and brothers in those orders. The Privy Council advised that it did not.

VISCOUNT SIMONDS

The ... difficulty of solving ... [this question] ... arises out of the artificial and anomalous conception of an unincorporated society which, though it is not a separate entity in law, is yet for many purposes regarded as a continuing entity and, however inaccurately, as something other than an aggregate of its members. In law a gift to such a society simpliciter (ie, where, to use the words of Lord Parker in *Bowman v Secular Society Ltd* [1917] AC 406, neither the circumstances of the gift nor the directions given nor the objects expressed impose on the donee the character of a trustee) is nothing else than a gift to its members at the date of the gift as joint tenants or tenants in common. ... If it is a gift to individuals, each of them is entitled to his distributive share (unless he has previously bound himself by the rules of the society that it shall be devoted to some other purpose).

The question then appears to be whether, even if the gift to a selected Order ... is prima facie a gift to the individual members of that Order, there are other considerations arising out of the terms of the will, or the nature of the society, its organisation and rules, or the subject-matter of the gift which should lead the court to conclude that, though prima facie the gift is an absolute one (absolute both in quality of estate and in freedom from restriction) to individual nuns, yet it is invalid because it is in the nature of an endowment and tends to a perpetuity or for any other reason. ...

 Alert

The prima facie validity of such a gift (by which term their Lordships intend a bequest or demise) is a convenient starting point for the examination of the relevant law. For as Lord Tomlin (sitting at first instance in the Chancery Division) said in *In re Ogden* [1933] Ch 678, a gift to a voluntary association of persons for the general purposes of the association is an absolute gift and prima facie a good gift. He was echoing the words of Lord Parker in *Bowman's* case that a gift to an unincorporated association for the attainment of its purposes "may ... be upheld as an absolute gift to its members." These words must receive careful consideration, for it is to be noted that it is because the gift can be upheld as a gift to the individual members that it is valid, even though it is given for the general purposes of the association. If the words "for the general purposes of the association" were held to import a trust, the question would have to be asked, what is the trust and who are the beneficiaries? A gift can be made to persons (including a corporation) but it cannot be made to a purpose or to an object: so also, a trust may be created for the benefit of persons as cestuis que trust but not for a purpose or object unless the purpose or object be charitable. For a purpose or object cannot sue, but, if it be charitable, the Attorney-General can sue to enforce it. ... It is therefore by disregarding the words "for the general purposes of the association" (which are assumed not to be charitable purposes) and treating the gift as an absolute gift to individuals that it can be sustained. The same conclusion had been reached 50 years before in *Cocks v Manners* (1871) LR 12 Eq 574, where a bequest of a share of residue to the "Dominican Convent at Carisbrooke (payable to the Superior for the time being)" was held a valid gift to the individual members of that society. In that case no difficulty was created by the addition of words which might suggest that the community as a whole, not its members individually, should be the beneficiary. ...

 Link
See 'Trusts for the general purposes of the association' below

The cases that have been referred to (and many others might have been referred to in the courts of Australia, England and Ireland) are all cases in which gifts have been upheld as valid either on the ground that, where a society has been named as legatee, its members could demand that the gift should be dealt with as they should together think fit; or on the ground that a trust had been established (as in *In re Drummond*) which did not create a perpetuity. It will be sufficient to mention one only of the cases in which a different conclusion has been reached, before coming to a recent decision of the House of Lords which must be regarded as of paramount authority. In *Carne v Long* (1860) 2 De GF & J 75 the testator devised his mansion-house after the death of his wife to the trustees of the Penzance Public Library to hold to them and their successors for ever for the use, benefit, maintenance and support of the said library. It appeared that the library was established and kept on foot by the subscriptions of certain inhabitants of Penzance, that the subscribers were elected by ballot and the library managed by officers chosen from amongst themselves by the subscribers, that the property in the books and everything else belonging to the library was vested in trustees for the subscribers and that it was provided that the institution should not be broken up so long as 10 members remained. It was urged that the gift was to a number of private persons and there were in truth no other beneficiaries. But Campbell LC rejected the plea in words which, often though they have been cited, will bear repetition: "If the devise had been in favour of the existing members of the society, and they had been at liberty to dispose of the property as they might think fit, then it might, I think, have been a lawful disposition and not tending to a perpetuity. But looking to the language of the rules of this society, it is clear that the library was intended to be a perpetual institution, and the testator must be presumed to have known what the regulations were." This was perhaps a clear case where both from the terms of the gift and the nature of the society a perpetuity was indicated.

[I] must now turn to the recent case of *In re Macaulay's Estate*, which appears to be reported only in a footnote to *In re Price* [1943] Ch 422. There the gift was to the Folkestone Lodge of the Theosophical Society absolutely for the maintenance and improvement of the Theosophical Lodge at Folkestone. It was assumed that the donee, "the Lodge," was a body of persons. The decision of the House of Lords ... was that the gift was invalid. ... A passage from the judgment of Lord Hanworth MR (which has been obtained from the records) may usefully be cited. He said: "The problem may be stated in this way. If the gift is in truth to the present members of the society described by their society name so that they have the beneficial use of the property and can, if they please, alienate and put the proceeds in their own pocket, then there is a present gift to individuals which is good: but if the gift is intended for the good not only of the present but of future members so that the present members are in the position of trustees and have no right to appropriate the property or its proceeds for their personal benefit then the gift is invalid. ..."

... At the risk of repetition their Lordships would point out that, if a gift is made to individuals, whether under their own names or in the name of their society, and the conclusion is reached that they are not intended to take beneficially, then they take as trustees. If so, it must be ascertained who are the beneficiaries. If at the death of the testator the class of beneficiaries is fixed and ascertained or ascertainable within the limit of the rule against perpetuities, all is well. If it is not so fixed and not so ascertainable the trust must fail. Of such a trust no better example could be found than a gift to an Order for the benefit of a community of nuns, once it is established that the community is not confined to living and ascertained persons. A wider question is opened if it appears that the trust is not for persons but for a non-charitable purpose. As has been pointed out, no one can enforce such a trust.

It must now be asked, then, whether in the present case there are sufficient indications to displace the prima facie conclusion that the gift ... is to the individual members of the selected Order ... at the date of the testator's death so that they can together dispose of it as they think fit. It appears to their Lordships that such indications are ample.

 Alert

In the first place, it is not altogether irrelevant that the gift is in terms upon trust for a selected Order. It is true that this can in law be regarded as a trust in favour of each and every member of the Order. But at least the form of the gift is not to the members, and it may be questioned whether the testator understood the niceties of the law. In the second place, the members of the selected Order may be numerous, very numerous perhaps, and they may be spread over the world. If the gift is to the individuals it is to all the members who were living at the death of the testator, but only to them. It is not easy to believe that the testator intended an "immediate beneficial legacy" ... to such a body of beneficiaries. ... In the third place, the subject-matter of the gift cannot be ignored. It appears from the evidence filed in the suit that Elmslea is a grazing property of about 730 acres, with a furnished homestead containing 20 rooms and a number of outbuildings. With the greatest respect to those judges who have taken a different view, their Lordships do not find it possible to regard all the individual members of an Order as intended to become the beneficial owners of such a property. Little or no evidence has been given about the organisation and rules of the several Orders, but it is at least permissible to doubt whether it is a common feature of them, that all their members regard themselves or are to be regarded as having the capacity of (say) the Corps of Commissionaires (see *In re Clarke*) to put an end to their association and distribute its assets. On the contrary, it seems reasonably clear that, however little the testator understood the effect in law of a gift to an unincorporated body of persons by their society name, his intention was to create a trust, not merely for the benefit of the existing members of the selected Order, but for its benefit as a continuing society and for the furtherance of its work. ... "

7.2.2 Gift to members subject to the rules of the association

This interpretation, known as the 'contractual analysis' represents the 'prevailing view' under which gifts in favour of an unincorporated association may be upheld. On this interpretation, a gift to an unincorporated association is treated as a gift to each of the individual members of the association, *but* (and in contrast to the previous interpretation) the members do not 'pocket' their share immediately. Instead, they take the gift subject to their mutual duties and obligations under the membership rules of the association.

Artistic Upholstery Ltd v Art Forma (Furniture) Ltd [1999] 4 All ER 277

Panel: Lawrence Collins QC sitting as a deputy judge of the High Court

Facts: The claimant (Artistic) was one of the members of an unincorporated association (the Guild). For many years the Guild had organised trade exhibitions on behalf of its members under the name 'Long Point'. The defendant (Art Forma) was a former member of the Guild. Following its expulsion from the Guild, it had registered the name 'Long Point' as a trade mark. Artistic brought proceedings on behalf of itself and all the other members of the Guild to restrain Art Forma from using the name 'Long Point' in connection with its business. This raised the question as to whether an unincorporated association could own intellectual property, which required a consideration of the nature of an unincorporated association and the legal basis (if any) on which it could hold property of any kind. The judge endorsed the contractual analysis and held that intellectual property was capable of being owned by an unincorporated association.

LAWRENCE COLLINS QC sitting as a deputy judge of the High Court

... An unincorporated association is not, of course, a legal person. In *Currie v Barton* (1988) Times, 12 February, O'Connor LJ said, in relation to unincorporated associations, the law ... 'does not recognise that those bodies have any corporate or separate legal existence. They cannot be sued or sue in their own names. You cannot make a contract with the body, because in law it does not exist. It consists of all its members.'

The rights of members as between themselves are contractual. In *Re Bucks Constabulary Widows' and Orphans' Fund Friendly Society, Thompson v Holdsworth (No 2)* [1979] 1 WLR 936, Walton J said that judicial opinion ... 'is now firmly set along the lines that the interests and rights of persons who are members of any type of unincorporated association are governed exclusively by contract, that is to say rights between themselves and their rights to any surplus assets.'

Walton J had followed Re Recher's Will Trusts, National Westminster Bank Ltd v National Anti-Vivisection Society Ltd [1972] Ch 526, where Brightman J said, in the context of an association formed for a non-charitable purposes:

'Such an association of persons is bound ... to have some sort of constitution; ie the rights and liabilities of the members of the association will inevitably depend on some form of contract inter se, usually evidenced by a set of rules.'

Since there are substantial associations with a large (and changing) membership, holding property in the form of subscriptions or donations or association premises, it has been necessary to develop a legal analysis which will provide a practical solution to the problem that an unincorporated association, as such, has no capacity to hold property. Several solutions have been developed, including treating the members as holding as joint tenants, or having trustees holding on trust for the members or for the purposes of the association. But the prevailing view is that, at least where there are no

Link
See the extract from *Re Recher* below.

Alert

171

appointed trustees to hold the property of the association, or where a transfer of property has not been accompanied by a valid declaration of trust, personal property will be held under the express or implied terms of the contract of the members inter se. Thus in *Re Recher's Will Trusts*, when the association received a donation which was not accompanied by words which purported to impose a trust, the gift took effect 'in favour of the existing members of the association as an accretion to the funds which are the subject-matter of the contract which such members have made inter se' ... . Brightman J followed the decision of Cross J in *Neville Estates Ltd v Madden* [1962] Ch 832 ... , who had analysed the proprietary effects of a gift to an unincorporated association; one of the ways in which it could take effect was as a gift to the members not as joint tenants, but subject to their rights and liabilities towards one another as members of the association: in such a case the member could not sever his share.

In the *Bucks Constabulary case* ... Walton J applied *Re Recher's Will Trusts* in the context of a friendly society and said:

'... all unincorporated societies rest in contract to this extent, that there is an implied contract between all the members inter se governed by the rules of the society. In default of any rule to the contrary, and it will seldom if ever be that there is such a rule, when a member ceases to be a member of the association he ipso facto ceases to have any interest in its funds.'

Consequently, even though an unincorporated association as such cannot hold property because it is not a legal person, property can be held by the members subject to the express or implied terms of the contract into which they enter with one another upon becoming members. ...

It follows from the authorities to which I have referred, and from the constitution and rules of the guild, that if the goodwill which is the foundation of a claim in passing off is to be regarded as property (as it plainly is ...), then an unincorporated association, such as the guild, through its members, may own goodwill which could found an action in passing off. The goodwill is held by the members as their property in that capacity in accordance with the constitution and rules.

So, in the absence of any evidence that the property is intended to be held upon trust, a gift to an unincorporated association should ordinarily be interpreted as a gift to the members subject to the rules of the association.

However, there will be circumstances where such an interpretation is not possible, for example where:

- The association has ceased to exist: see *In re Recher's Will Trusts National Westminster Bank Ltd v National Anti-Vivisection Society Ltd and Others* [1972] Ch 526.

- The association has no identifiable rules – in *Leahy*, for example, there was little or no evidence as to the rules of the relevant Orders.

- The rules of the association do not give it a sufficient degree of control over its assets: see *Re Grant's Will Trusts* [1980] 1 WLR 360 below.

In re Recher's Will Trusts National Westminster Bank Ltd v National Anti-Vivisection Society Ltd and Others [1972] Ch 526

Panel: Brightman J

Facts: By her will, the testatrix left a portion of her residuary estate to an unincorporated association ('the London & Provincial Anti-Vivisection Society') which had ceased to exist by the time of her death because its affairs had been transferred to a larger association ('the National Anti-Vivisection Society'). The issue for determination was whether the gift was held for the surviving association or whether it failed. The court held that the gift failed.

MR JUSTICE BRIGHTMAN

Having reached the conclusion that the gift in question is not a gift to the members of the London & Provincial society at the date of death, as joint tenants or tenants in common, so as to entitle a member as of right to a distributive share, nor an attempted gift to present and future members beneficially, and is not a gift in trust for the purposes of the society, I must now consider how otherwise, if at all, it is capable of taking effect. ...

A trust for non-charitable purposes, as distinct from a trust for individuals, is clearly void because there is no beneficiary. It does not, however, follow that persons cannot band themselves together as an association or society, pay subscriptions and validly devote their funds in pursuit of some lawful non-charitable purpose. An obvious example is a members' social club. But it is not essential that the members should only intend to secure direct personal advantages to themselves. The association may be one in which personal advantages to the members are combined with the pursuit of some outside purpose. Or the association may be one which offers no personal benefit at all to the members, the funds of the association being applied exclusively to the pursuit of some outside purpose. Such an association of persons is bound, I would think, to have some sort of constitution; that is to say, the rights and liabilities of the members of the association will inevitably depend on some form of contract inter se, usually evidenced by a set of rules. In the present case it appears to me clear that the life members, the ordinary members and the associate members of the London & Provincial society were bound together by a contract inter se. Any such member was entitled to the rights and subject to the liabilities defined by the rules. If the committee acted contrary to the rules, an individual member would be entitled to take proceedings in the courts to compel observance of the rules or to recover damages for any loss he had suffered as a result of the breach of contract. As and when a member paid his subscription to the association, he would be subjecting his money to the disposition and expenditure thereof laid down by the rules. That is to say, the member would be bound to permit, and entitled to require, the honorary trustees and other members of the society to deal with that subscription in accordance with the lawful directions of the committee. Those directions would include the expenditure of that subscription, as part of the general funds of the association, in furthering the objects of the association. The resultant situation, on analysis, is that the London & Provincial society represented an organisation of individuals bound together by a contract under which their subscriptions became, as it were, mandated towards a certain type of expenditure ... . Just as the two parties to a bi-partite bargain can vary or terminate their contract by mutual assent, so it must follow that the life members, ordinary members and associate members of the London & Provincial society could, at any moment of time, by unanimous agreement (or by majority vote, if the rules so prescribe), vary or terminate their multi-partite contract. There would be no limit to the type of variation or termination to which all might agree. There is no private trust or trust for charitable purposes or other trust to hinder the process. It follows that if all members agreed, they could decide to wind up the London & Provincial society and divide the net assets among themselves beneficially. No one would have any locus standi to stop them so doing. The contract is the same as any other contract and concerns only those who are parties to it, that is to say, the members of the society.

The funds of such an association may, of course, be derived not only from the subscriptions of the contracting parties but also from donations from non-contracting parties and legacies from persons who have died. In the case of a donation which is not accompanied by any words which purport to impose a trust, it seems to me that the gift takes effect in favour of the existing members of the association as an accretion to the funds which are the subject-matter of the contract which such members have made inter se, and falls to be dealt with in precisely the same way as the funds which the members themselves have subscribed. So, in the case of a legacy. In the absence of words which purport to impose a trust, the legacy is a gift to the members beneficially, not as joint tenants or as tenants in common so as to entitle each member to an immediate distributive share, but as an accretion to the funds which are the subject-matter of the contract which the members have made inter se.

In my judgment the legacy in the present case to the London & Provincial society ought to be construed as a legacy of that type, that is to say, a legacy to the members beneficially as an accretion to the funds subject to the contract which they had made inter se. Of course, the testatrix did not intend the members of the society to divide her bounty between themselves, and doubtless she was ignorant of that remote but theoretical possibility. Her knowledge or absence of knowledge of the true legal analysis of the gift is irrelevant. The legacy is accordingly in my view valid, subject only to the effect of the [dissolution of the London & Provincial society]. ...

In my judgment the London & Provincial society was dissolved on January 1, 1957, and the contract theretofore binding persons together, under the name and according to the rules of the London & Provincial society, was terminated. The position after 1956 was that all the members of the London & Provincial society lost their rights and shed their obligations under that contract, and some of such persons, namely, the life and ordinary members of the London & Provincial society (or those who wished) automatically acceded to another association of persons who were then bound together by another contract, namely, the National society, and assumed the rights and obligations attaching to members of that association. What I find in the will is a gift to the members of the London & Provincial society as an accretion to the funds subject to the contract between such members. In my judgment, I am not entitled to construe that gift as a gift to the members of a different association as an accretion to the funds subject to a different contract. ...

Re Grant's Will Trusts [1980] 1 WLR 360

Panel: Vinelott J

Facts: By his will, the testator made a gift of a property to the Chertsey and Walton Constituency Labour Party (CLP) for use as its headquarters. The rules governing CLP were in the model form issued by the national Labour Party (NLP). Those rules could be changed at any time by NLP and CLP was obliged to conform to any changes. One of the rules provided that a constituency party could not deal with any property, nor make any changes to its rules, without the approval of NLP. Mr Justice Vinelott held that in those circumstances CLP lacked the necessary degree of control over its own assets to permit the contractual analysis to be applied.

MR JUSTICE VINELOTT

The question raised by the summons is whether the gift in the will of the testator's real and personal estate is a valid gift, or is void for uncertainty or for perpetuity or otherwise; and if it is a valid gift who are the persons entitled to benefit thereunder.

Before turning to this question, it will be convenient to explain what are in my judgment the principles which govern the validity of a gift to an unincorporated association. A convenient starting point is a passage in the decision of Cross J in *Neville Estates Ltd v Madden* ([1962] Ch 832, [1961] 3 All ER 769) which is often cited:

'The question of the construction and effect of gifts to or in trust for unincorporated associations was recently considered by the Privy Council in *Leahy v Attorney General for New South Wales*. The position, as I understand it, is as follows. Such a gift may take effect in one or other of three quite different ways. In the first place, it may, on its true construction, be a gift to the members of the association at the relevant date as joint tenants, so that any member can sever his share and claim it whether or not he continues to be a member of the association. Secondly, it may be a gift to the existing members not as joint tenants, but subject to their respective contractual rights and liabilities towards one another as members of the association. In such a case a member cannot sever his share. It will accrue to the other members on his death or resignation, even though such members include persons who became members after the gift took effect. If this is the effect of the gift, it will not be open to objection on the score of perpetuity or uncertainty unless there is something in its terms or circumstances or in the rules of the association which precludes the members at any given time from dividing the subject of the gift between them on the footing that they are solely entitled to it in equity. Thirdly, the terms or circumstances of the gift or the rules of the association may show that the property in question is not to be at the disposal of the members for the time being, but is to be held in trust for or applied for the purposes of the association as a quasi-corporate entity. In this case the gift will fail unless the association is a charitable body. If the gift is of the second class, i.e., one which the members of the association for the time being are entitled to divide among themselves, then, even if the objects of the association are in themselves charitable, the gift would not, I think, be a charitable gift.'

This statement, though it may require amplification in the light of subsequent authorities, is still as I see it an accurate statement of the law.

In a case in the first category, that is a gift which, on its true construction, is a gift to members of an association who take as joint tenants, any member being able to sever his share, the association is used in effect as a convenient label or definition of the class which is intended to take; but, the class being ascertained, each member takes as joint tenant free from any contractual fetter. So, for instance, a testator might give a legacy or share of residue to a dining or social club of which he had been a member with the intention of giving to each of the other members an interest as joint tenant, capable of being severed, in the subject-matter of the gift. Cases within this category are relatively uncommon. A gift to an association will be more frequently found to fall within the second category. There the gift is to members of an association, but the property is given as an accretion to the funds of the association so that the property becomes subject to the contract (normally evidenced by the rules of the association) which governs the rights of the members inter se. Each member is thus in a position to ensure that the subject matter of the gift is applied in accordance with the rules of the association, in the same way as any other funds of the association. This category is well illustrated by the decision of Brightman J in *Re Recher's Will Trusts*. ...

It must, as I see it, be a necessary characteristic of any gift within the second category that the members of the association can by an appropriate majority (if the rules so provide), or acting unanimously if they do not, alter their rules so as to provide that the funds, or part of them, shall be applied for some new purpose, or even distributed amongst the members for their own benefit. For the validity of a gift within this category rests essentially on the fact that the testator has set out to further a purpose by making a gift to the members of an association formed for the furtherance of that purpose in the expectation that, although the members at the date when the gift takes effect will be free, by a majority if the rules so provide or acting unanimously if they do not, to dispose of the fund in any way they may think fit, they and any future members of the association will not in fact do so but will employ the property in the furtherance of the purpose of the association and will honour any special condition attached to the gift.

 Alert

Turning to the third category, the testator may seek to further the purpose by giving a legacy to an association as a quasi-corporate entity, that is to present and future members indefinitely, or by purporting to impose a trust. In the former case the gift will fail for perpetuity, unless confined within an appropriate period; though if it is so confined and if the members for the time being within the perpetuity period are free to alter the purposes for which the property is to be used and to distribute the income amongst themselves it will not, as I see it, fail on any other ground. In the latter case, the gift will fail on the ground that the court cannot compel the use of the property in furtherance of a stated purpose unless, of course, the purpose is a charitable one. ...

I have also been referred to the recent decision of Goff J in *Re Denley's Trust Deed*. There by cl 2 of a trust deed trustees were given powers of sale over land held by them and were directed to hold the land while unsold during a defined perpetuity period on trust ...

Goff J, having held that the words '... secondarily for the benefit of such other person or persons (if any) as the trustees may allow to use the same' conferred on the trustees a power operating in partial defeasance of a trust in favour of the employees, held that the trust deed created a valid trust for the benefit of the employees, the benefit being the right to use the land subject to and in accordance with the rules made by the trustees. That case on a proper analysis, in my judgment, falls altogether outside the categories of gifts to unincorporated associations and purpose trusts. I can see no distinction in principle between a trust to permit a class defined by reference to employment to use and enjoy land in accordance with rules to be made at the discretion of trustees on the one hand, and, on the other hand, a trust to distribute income at the discretion of trustees amongst a class, defined by reference to, for example, relationship to the settlor. In both cases the benefit to be taken by any member of the class is at the discretion of the trustees, but any member of the class can apply to the court to compel the trustees to administer the trust in accordance with its terms. As Goff J pointed out ([1968] 3 All ER 65 at 72, [1969] 1 Ch 373 at 388):

'The same kind of problem is equally capable of arising in the case of a trust to permit a number of persons - for example, all the unmarried children of a testator or settlor - to use or occupy a house, or to have the use of certain chattels; nor can I assume that in such cases agreement between the parties concerned would be more likely, even if that be a sufficient distinction, yet no one would suggest, I fancy, that such a trust would be void.' ...

Reading the gift in the will in the light of the rules governing the Chertsey and Walton Constituency Labour Party, it is in my judgment impossible to construe the gift as a gift made to the members of the Chertsey and Walton Constituency Labour Party at the date of the testator's death with the intention that it should belong to them as a collection of individuals, though in the expectation that they and any other members subsequently admitted would ensure that it was in fact used for what in broad terms has been labelled 'headquarters' purposes' of the Chertsey and Walton Constituency Labour Party.

I base this conclusion on two grounds. First, the members of [the Chertsey and Walton Constituency Labour Party] do not control the property, given by subscription or otherwise, to ... [it]. The rules which govern [the Chertsey and Walton Constituency Labour Party] are capable of being altered by an outside body which could direct an alteration under which the general committee of [the Chertsey and Walton Constituency Labour Party] would be bound to transfer any property for the time being held for the benefit of [the Chertsey and Walton Constituency Labour Party] to [the national Labour Party] for national purposes. The members of [the Chertsey and Walton Constituency Labour Party] could not alter the rules so as to make the property bequeathed by the testator applicable for some purpose other than that provided by the rules; nor could they direct that property to be divided amongst themselves beneficially.

Brightman J observed in *Re Recher's Will Trusts* ([1971] 3 All ER 401 at 405, [1972] Ch 526 at 536) that: 'It would astonish a layman to be told there was a difficulty in his giving a legacy to an unincorporated non-charitable society which he had or could have supported without trouble during his lifetime.' The answer to this apparent paradox is, it seems to me, that subscriptions by members of the Chertsey and Walton CLP must be taken as made on terms that they will be applied by the general committee in accordance with the rules for the time being, including any modifications imposed by the annual party conference or the NEC. In the event of the dissolution of the Chertsey and Walton CLP any remaining fund representing subscriptions would (as the rules now stand) be held on a resulting trust for the original subscribers. Thus although the members of the CLP may not be able themselves to alter the purposes for which a fund representing subscriptions is to be used or to alter the rules so as to make such a fund divisible amongst themselves the ultimate proprietary right of the original subscribers remains. There is, therefore, no perpetuity and no non-charitable purpose trust. But if that analysis of the terms on which subscriptions are held is correct, it is fatal to the argument that the gift in the testator's will should be construed as a gift to the members of the Chertsey and Walton CLP at the testator's death, subject to a direction not amounting to a trust that it be used for headquarters' purposes. Equally it is in my judgment impossible, in particular having regard to the gift over to the national Labour Party, to read the gift as a gift to the members of the national Labour Party at the testator's death, with a direction not amounting to a trust, that the national party permit it to be used by the Chertsey and Walton CLP for headquarters' purposes.

That first ground is of itself conclusive, but there is another ground which reinforces this conclusion. The gift is not in terms a gift to the Chertsey and Walton CLP, but to the Labour Party Property Committee, who are to hold the property for the benefit of, that is in trust for, the Chertsey headquarters of the Chertsey and Walton CLP. The fact that a gift is a gift to trustees and not in terms to an unincorporated association militates against construing it as a gift to the members of the association at the date when the gift takes effect, and against construing the words indicating the purposes for which the property is to be used as expressing the testator's intention or motive in making the gift and not as imposing any trust. This was, indeed, one of the considerations which led the Privy Council in Leahy's case to hold that the gift '... upon trust for such Order of Nuns of the Catholic Church or the Christian Brothers as my Executors and Trustees should select' would, apart from the Australian equivalent of the Charitable Trusts (Validation) Act 1954, have been invalid.

I am, therefore, compelled to the conclusion that the gift of the testator's estate fails, and that his estate accordingly devolves as on intestacy."

The contractual analysis presupposes that the members of an unincorporated association are bound together by rules which they are able to determine and which allow them to 'own' or 'share in' the association's property in whatever manner they choose. This essential element of internal control or self-determination was clearly absent in *Re Grant*, because the facts established that the constituency party did not have control over its rules nor, as a consequence, over any property which it owned.

As a result, the contractual analysis could not be invoked to uphold the validity of the gift.

Re Horley Town Football Club, Hunt and another v McLaren and others [2006] EWHC 2386 (Ch), [2006] WTLR 1817

Panel: Lawrence Collins J

Facts: Horley Town FC (the Club) was an unincorporated association. The Club's trustees held its ground, clubhouse and other assets upon trust for the Club for a defined perpetuity period. The membership was divided into full members, temporary members and associate members. Guests and visitors were entitled to temporary membership, whereas associate membership was available to anyone who was a member 'of any independently constituted club invited to use the facilities' of the Club. The various categories of membership appeared to have been created to ensure compliance with the then licensing laws. Full members were each entitled to one vote at annual general meetings, whereas associate members were restricted to one vote per independently constituted club. The court was required to determine to whom the Club's assets would belong upon expiry of the perpetuity period. The judge held that the assets belonged to the full members alone.

MR JUSTICE LAWRENCE COLLINS

I am satisfied that the Deed should be construed as a gift to the Club, as a "contract-holding" gift to the Club and its members for the time being within category (2) in *Neville Estates v Madden*.

If the gift is construed in this way, perpetuity is not a problem, because the gift to the members is not, on a true construction, contingent, under the rule in *Boraston's* case: Hawkins and Ryder, Construction of Wills, paras 20-40 et seq. The interests of the members of the Club under cl 3 nevertheless vest immediately. Their interests as members devolve with the other Club property under the Club rules. Nor can the gift be characterised as uncertain.

As Vinelott J said in *Re Grant's Will Trusts* ... it is a necessary characteristic of any [such] gift ... that the members of the association can, in accordance with the rules, direct that the funds should be applied to some new purpose or distributed among the members for their own benefit.

I do not consider that it matters that the Rules were changed in 2000 to confer a right to vote on a body which is not itself a member, namely the club of which Associate Members are members. This is far from the case of *Re Grant's Will Trusts*, where Vinelott J held that the influence of a body (not itself a member) on the rules and the destination of Club property was fatal to the argument that a gift should be analysed as one within the second class identified in *Neville Estates v Madden*. ...

The next question is the identity of the persons who hold the beneficial interest. I am satisfied that the beneficial ownership is in the current full members (and not the temporary or associate members), and is held on bare trust for them. The members hold subject to the current rules, and could unanimously or by AGM call for the assets to be

Alert

Link
See Distribution of assets below.

transferred. Adult and senior members are entitled to share in distribution on per capita basis.

In my judgment I should adopt the same approach as Sir Robert Megarry in taking a "broad sword" and applying fairness and common sense. In my judgment it does not make a difference that in the present case the Rules say in r 4 that the Club shall consist of "members and temporary members"; or in r 5 provide that Associate Members will enjoy the same rights as full members except those relating to voting rights; or that r 15 gives a right to vote to "independently constituted clubs enjoying Associate Membership". I would accept that a mere inequality in voting rights would not mean that a category of members is excluded altogether from any entitlement to the surplus assets of the association upon its dissolution. But the associate members in the present case have no effective rights and it would be wholly unrealistic to treat the introduction of associate members by amendment of the Rules as a transfer of the Club's property to them.

The consequence would be that the beneficial ownership is held on bare trust for the members, who could either unanimously or at an AGM call for the assets to be transferred.

All the sets of Rules, including the 2004 Rules, provide for amendment of the Rules by AGM. The members may agree to dissolve the Club and to distribute the assets amongst themselves or the association may be wound up by the court: *Re Lead Co's Workmen's Fund Society* [1904] 2 Ch 196; *Neville Estates v Madden* [1962] Ch 832, 849; *Re Recher* [1972] Ch 526, 538-539. The Rules do not specify how the Club's assets are to be distributed following dissolution. In the absence of any rule to the contrary, there is to be implied into the rules of the Club a rule to the effect that the surplus funds of the Club should be divided on a dissolution amongst the members of the Club, and this distribution will normally be per capita among the members (irrespective of length of membership or the amount of subscriptions paid) but may reflect different classes of membership: *Re Sick and Funeral Society of St John's Sunday School, Golcar* [1973] Ch 51, at 60, [1972] 2 All ER 439, [1972] 2 WLR 962; *Re Bucks Constabulary Widows' and Orphans' Fund Friendly Society (No 2)* [1979] 1 WLR 936, at 952; *Re GKN Bolts & Nuts Ltd etc Sports & Social Club* [1982] 1 WLR 774, at 778.

In the light of these decisions and in the light of my conclusion on temporary and associate members, the persons entitled to share in a distribution would be the adult and senior members of the Club on a per capita basis.

It is not necessary to consider whether the gift took effect as a *Re Denley* trust for the benefit of the members for the time being of the Club. The existence of the Associate Members and temporary members would not in itself prevent the adoption of such a construction: the existence of those members could properly be overlooked on the basis that they are not within the class of persons for whose benefit the property is held upon trust. But there are difficulties with regard to termination of such a trust which make it an unsafe basis for decision: see Thomas and Hudson, The Law of Trusts (2004), para 6.21."

Although the judge deals with the point rather briefly, and does not offer any specific reasons for his decision on this point, his conclusion is clear enough: the mere fact that the membership of the Club included other clubs, each with their own rules and members, did not breach the 'control' requirement set out in *Re Grant*. It seems probable that the judge recognised that in this case the full members retained effective voting power over the association's property because the number of associate members was very small compared to the number of full members, whereas in *Re Grant* the members of the constituency Labour party (who were the equivalent of the full members in this case) had *no* effective voting rights at all over constituency property.

7.2.3 Trust for present and future members

It is possible, at least in theory, for a gift to be made to the members of an unincorporated association as trustees upon trust for themselves and future members of the association – this possibility was referred to (but rejected on the facts) in *Leahy*. It was also discussed in *Neville Estates v Madden* and *Re Grant*.

7.2.4 Trust for the general purposes of the association

Some older cases appeared simply to assume that a trust for private (ie non-charitable) purposes was valid, subject only to compliance with the rule against perpetuity. However, as discussed in Chapter 6, private purpose trusts must comply with both the beneficiary principle *and* the rule against perpetuity.

This dual requirement was confirmed by Viscount Simonds in *Leahy*. So a gift to a non-charitable unincorporated association cannot be upheld as a trust for the general purposes of the association.

7.3 *Re Denley* Purpose Trust

However, as also discussed in Chapter 6, there is one species of private purpose trust which may not fall foul of the beneficiary principle, namely a Re Denley purpose trust, ie a purpose trust which is directly or indirectly for the benefit of an ascertainable individual or individuals.

Link
See *Re Denley* in Chapter 6

The *Re Denley* approach was applied to unincorporated associations in *Re Lipinski's Will Trusts, Gosschalk v Levy* [1976] Ch 235.

Re Lipinski's Will Trusts, Gosschalk v Levy [1976] Ch 235

Panel: Oliver J

Facts: By his will, the testator bequeathed part of his residuary estate to trustees on trust as to one half for the Hull Judeans (Maccabi) Association, which provided social, cultural and sporting activities for Jewish youth in Hull, to be used in constructing and/or improving new buildings for the association. The gift was valid.

JUSTICE OLIVER MR

... [T]his is a gift to an unincorporated non-charitable association. Such a gift, if it is an absolute and beneficial one, is of course perfectly good see, for instance, the gift to the Corps of Commissionaires in *In re Clarke* [1901] 2 Ch 110. What I have to consider, however, is the effect of the specification by the testator of the purposes for which the legacy was to be applied. ...

The principles applicable to this type of case were stated by Cross J in *Neville Estates Ltd v Madden* [1962] Ch 832, 849, and they are conveniently summarised in Tudor, Charities, 6th ed. (1967), p 150, where it is said:

"In *Neville Estates Ltd v Madden* Cross J expressed the opinion (which is respectfully accepted as correct) that every such gift might, according to the actual words used, be construed in one of three quite different ways: (a) As a gift to the members of the association at the date of the gift as joint tenants so that any member could sever his share and claim it whether or not he continued to be a member. (b) As a gift to the members of the association at the date of the gift not as joint tenants, but subject to their contractual rights and liabilities towards one another as members of the association. In such a case a member cannot sever his share. It will accrue to the other members on his death or resignation, even though such members include persons who become members after the gift took effect. If this is the effect of the gift, it will not be open to objection on the score of perpetuity or uncertainty unless there is something in its terms or circumstances or in the rules of the association which precludes the members at any given time from dividing the subject of the gift between them on the footing that they are solely entitled to it in equity. (c) The terms or circumstances of the gift or the rules of the association may show that the property in question - ie, the subject of the gift - is not to be at the disposal of the members for the time being but is to be held in trust for or applied for the purposes of the association as a quasi-corporate entity. In this case the gift will fail unless the association is a charitable body."

That summary may require, I think, a certain amount of qualification in the light of subsequent authority, but for present purposes I can adopt it as a working guide. Mr Blackburne, for the next-of-kin, argues that the gift in the present case clearly does not fall within the first category, and that the addition of the specific direction as to its employment by the association prevents it from falling into the second category. This is, therefore, he says, a purpose trust and fails both for that reason and because the purpose is perpetuitous. He relies upon this passage from the judgment of the Board in *Leahy v Attorney-General for New South Wales* [1959] AC 457, 478:

"If the words 'for the general purposes of the association' were held to import a trust, the question would have to be asked, what is the trust and who are the beneficiaries? A gift can be made to persons (including a corporation) but it cannot be made to a purpose or to an object: so also, a trust may be created for the benefit of persons as cestuis que trust but not for a purpose or object unless the purpose or object be charitable. For a purpose or object cannot sue, but, if it be charitable, the Attorney-General can sue to enforce it."

Mr Blackburne points out, first, that the gift is in memory of the testator's late wife (which, he says, suggests an intention to create a permanent memorial or endowment); secondly, that the gift is solely for a particular purpose (which would militate strongly against any suggestion that the donees could wind up and pocket the money themselves, even though their constitution may enable them to do so); and, thirdly, that the gift contemplates expenditure on "improvements," which connotes a degree of continuity or permanence. All this, he says, shows that what the testator had in mind was a permanent endowment in memory of his late wife.

For my part, I think that very little turns upon the testator's having expressed the gift as being in memory of his late wife. I see nothing in this expression which suggests any intention to create a permanent endowment. It indicates merely, I think, a tribute which the testator wished to pay, and it is not without significance that this self-same tribute appeared in the earlier will in which he made an absolute and outright gift to the association. The evidential value of this in the context of a construction summons may be open to doubt, and I place no reliance upon it. It does, however, seem to me that nothing is to be derived from these words beyond the fact that the testator wished the association to know that his bounty was a tribute to his late wife.

I accept, however, Mr Blackburne's submission that the designation of the sole purpose of the gift makes it impossible to construe the gift as one falling into the first of Cross J's categories, even if that were otherwise possible. But I am not impressed by the argument that the gift shows an intention of continuity. Mr Blackburne prays in aid *In re Macaulay's Estate* [1943] Ch 435 which is reported as a note to *In re Price* [1943] Ch 422, where the gift was for the "maintenance and improvement of the Theosophical Lodge at Folkestone." The House of Lords held that it failed for perpetuity, the donee being a non-charitable body. But it is clear from the speeches of both Lord Buckmaster and Lord Tomlin that their Lordships derived the intention of continuity from the reference to "maintenance." Here it is quite evident that the association was to be free to spend the capital of the legacy. ...

But that is not the end of the matter. If the gift were to the association simpliciter, it would, I think, clearly fall within the second category of Cross J's categories. At first sight, however, there appears to be a difficulty in arguing that the gift is to members of the association subject to their contractual rights inter se when there is a specific direction or limitation sought to be imposed upon those contractual rights as to the manner in which the subject matter of the gift is to be dealt with. This, says Mr Blackburne, is a pure "purpose trust" and is invalid on that ground, quite apart from any question of perpetuity. I am not sure, however, that it is sufficient merely to demonstrate that a trust is a "purpose" trust. ...

There would seem to me to be, as a matter of common sense, a clear distinction between the case where a purpose is prescribed which is clearly intended for the benefit of ascertained or ascertainable beneficiaries, particularly where those beneficiaries have the power to make the capital their own, and the case where no beneficiary at all is intended (for instance, a memorial to a favourite pet) or where the beneficiaries are unascertainable: as in the case, for instance, of *In re Price* [1943] Ch

422. If a valid gift may be made to an unincorporated body as a simple accretion to the funds which are the subject matter of the contract which the members have made inter se – and *Neville Estates Ltd v Madden* [1962] Ch 832 and *In re Recher's Will Trusts* [1972] Ch 526 show that it may - I do not really see why such a gift, which specifies a purpose which is within the powers of the association and of which the members of the association are the beneficiaries, should fail. Why are not the beneficiaries able to enforce the trust or, indeed, in the exercise of their contractual rights, to terminate the trust for their own benefit? Where the donee association is itself the beneficiary of the prescribed purpose, there seems to me to be the strongest argument in common sense for saying that the gift should be construed as an absolute one within the second category - the more so where, if the purpose is carried out, the members can by appropriate action vest the resulting property in themselves, for here the trustees and the beneficiaries are the same persons.

 Alert

Is such a distinction as I have suggested borne out by the authorities? The answer is, I think, "not in terms," until recently. But the cases appear to me to be at least consistent with this. For instance, *In re Clarke* [1901] 2 Ch 110 (the case of the Corps of Commissionaires); *In re Drummond* [1914] 2 Ch 90 (the case of the Old Bradfordians) and *In re Taylor* [1940] Ch 481 (the case of the Midland Bank Staff Association), in all of which the testator had prescribed purposes for which the gifts were to be used, and in all of which the gifts were upheld, were all cases where there were ascertainable beneficiaries; whereas in *In re Wood* [1949] Ch 498 and *Leahy's* case (where the gifts failed) there were none. *In re Price* is perhaps out of line, because there there was no ascertained beneficiary and yet Cohen J was prepared to uphold the gift even on the supposition that (contrary to his own conclusion) the purpose was non-charitable. But, as I have mentioned, the point about the trust being a purpose trust was not argued before him.

A striking case which seems to be not far from the present is *In re Turkington* [1937] 4 All ER 501, where the gift was to a masonic lodge "as a fund to build a suitable temple in Stafford." The members of the lodge being both the trustees and the beneficiaries of the temple, Luxmoore J construed the gift as an absolute one to the members of the lodge for the time being.

Directly in point is the more recent decision of Goff J in *In re Denley's Trust Deed* [1969] 1 Ch 373 where the question arose as to the validity of a deed under which land was held by trustees as a sports ground:

"primary for the benefit of employees of [a particular company] and secondarily for the benefit of such other person or persons ... as the trustees may allow to use the same..."

The latter provision was construed by Goff J as a power and not a trust. The same deed conferred on the employees a right to use and enjoy the land subject to regulations made by the trustees. Goff J held that the rule against enforceability of non-charitable "purpose or object" trusts was confined to those which were abstract or impersonal in nature where there was no beneficiary or cestui que trust. A trust which, though expressed as a purpose, was directly or indirectly for the benefit of an individual or individuals was valid provided that those individuals were ascertainable at any one time and the trust was not otherwise void for uncertainty. Goff J said, at p 382:

"I think there may be a purpose or object trust, the carrying out of which would benefit an individual or individuals, where that benefit is so indirect or intangible or which is otherwise so framed as not to give those persons any locus standi to apply to the court to enforce the trust, in which case the beneficiary principle would, as it seems to me, apply to invalidate the trust, quite apart from any question of uncertainty or perpetuity. Such cases can be considered if and when they arise. The present is not, in my judgment, of that character, and it will be seen that clause 2 (d) of the trust deed expressly states that, subject to any rules and regulations made by the trustees, the employees of the company shall be entitled to the use and enjoyment of the land. Apart from this possible exception, in my judgment the beneficiary principle of *In re Astor's Settlement Trusts* [1952] Ch 534, which was approved in *In re Endacott, decd* [1960] Ch 232 – see particularly by Harman LJ, at p. 250 – is confined to purpose or object trusts which are abstract or impersonal. The objection is not that the trust is for a purpose or object per se, but that there is no beneficiary or cestui que trust.... Where, then, the trust, though expressed as a purpose, is directly or indirectly for the benefit of an individual or individuals, it seems to me that it is in general outside the mischief of the beneficiary principle."

I respectfully adopt this, as it seems to me to accord both with authority and with common sense. ...

I have already said that, in my judgment, no question of perpetuity arises here ... . There is an additional factor. This is a case in which, under the constitution of the association, the members could, by the appropriate majority, alter their constitution so as to provide, if they wished, for the division of the association's assets among themselves. This has, I think, a significance. I have considered whether anything turns in this case upon the testator's direction that the legacy shall be used "solely" for one or other of the specified purposes. Mr Rossdale has referred me to a number of cases where legacies have been bequeathed for particular purposes and in which the beneficiaries have been held entitled to override the purpose, even though expressed in mandatory terms.

Perhaps the most striking in the present context is *In re Bowes* [1896] 1 Ch 507, where money was directed to be laid out in the planting of trees on a settled estate. That was a "purpose" trust, but there were ascertainable beneficiaries, the owners for the time being of the estate; and North J. held that the persons entitled to the settled estate were entitled to have the money whether or not it was laid out as directed by the testator. He says, at p 510:

"Then, the sole question is where this money is to go to. Of course, it is a perfectly good legacy. There is nothing illegal in the matter, and the direction to plant might easily be carried out; but it is not necessarily capable of being performed, because the owner of the estate might say he would not have any trees planted upon it at all. If that were the line he took, and he did not contend for anything more than that, the legacy would fail; but he says he does not refuse to have trees planted upon it; he is content that trees should be planted upon some part of it; but the legacy has not failed. If it were necessary to uphold it, the trees can be planted upon the whole of it until the fund is exhausted. Therefore, there is nothing illegal in the gift itself; but the owners of the estate now say: 'It is a very disadvantageous way of spending this money; the money is to be spent for our benefit, and that of no one else; it was not intended for any purpose other than our benefit and that of the estate. That is no reason why it should be thrown away by doing what is not for our benefit, instead of being given to us, who want to have the enjoyment of it.' I think their contention is right. I think the fund is devoted to improving the estate, and improving the estate for the benefit of the persons who are absolutely entitled to it."

I can see no reason why the same reasoning should not apply in the present case simply because the beneficiary is an unincorporated non-charitable association. I do not think the fact that the testator has directed the application "solely" for the specified purpose adds any legal force to the direction. The beneficiaries, the members of the association for the time being, are the persons who could enforce the purpose and they must, as it seems to me, be entitled not to enforce it or, indeed, to vary it.

Alert

Thus, it seems to me that whether one treats the gift as a "purpose" trust or as an absolute gift with a superadded direction or, on the analogy of *In re Turkington* [1937] 4 All ER 501 as a gift where the trustees and the beneficiaries are the same persons, all roads lead to the same conclusion.

In my judgment, the gift is a valid gift ...

In the opinion of Oliver J, the gift was valid because the trust which it imposed was for the benefit of ascertainable individuals, namely the members of the association. The direction that the gift was to be used "solely" for building or improvement works could be ignored because it had no legal force, thus leaving the members of the association free to use the gift for any other purpose in accordance with the rules of the association.

Many commentators would agree that the reasoning of Oliver J is perhaps difficult to follow. In particular, in various passages of his judgment he appears to equate a purpose trust for the benefit of ascertainable individual members of an unincorporated association as being the equivalent of a gift to those members subject to the rules of the association. The better view, it is suggested, is to treat the *Re Denley* approach and the contractual analysis as separate interpretations.

7.4 Distribution of Surplus Assets

The interpretation which is applied to validate the capacity in which an unincorporated association is able to accept and own property also dictates the manner in which that property will be distributed when the affairs of the association are wound up following its dissolution.

Thus, if the property has been held on a *Re Denley* purpose trust (or theoretically a trust for present and future members), the property falls be returned to the original contributors on a resulting trust basis. If, on the other hand, the property has been held on the contractual basis, the property falls to be distributed between the members in accordance with the rules of the association.

7.4.1 Distribution on a contractual basis

Where property is held by the members of an unincorporated association subject to the rules of the association, applicable principles as regards distribution are set out in *Re Bucks Constabulary Widows' and Orphans' Fund Friendly Society; Thompson v Holdsworth and others (No 2)* [1979] 1 Ch 1.

Re Bucks Constabulary Widows' and Orphans' Fund Friendly Society; Thompson v Holdsworth and others (No 2) [1979] 1 Ch 1

Panel: Walton J

Facts: The subject society existed to administer a fund which had been established primarily to provide, by voluntary contributions from its members, for the relief of widows and orphans of deceased members of the Bucks Constabulary. The fund rules made no provision for the distribution of its assets in the event of the society being wound up. In April 1968 the Bucks Constabulary was amalgamated with other constabularies to form the Thames Valley Constabulary and a resolution was passed to wind up the society. A proposal that the fund's surplus assets should be transferred to the benevolent fund of the Thames Valley Constabulary was held to be unlawful, so the trustee of the fund applied to the court to determine whether (i) the surplus assets should be distributed among the persons who were members of the society at the date of its dissolution or whether, as the Crown claimed, they should pass to the Crown as bona vacantia, and (ii) if the assets were to be distributed among the members, whether they should be distributed in equal shares or in proportion to the subscriptions respectively paid by the persons who were members of the society at the date of its dissolution. Consistently with the contractual approach, Walton J held that the surplus assets should be distributed in accordance with the terms of the rules, or any subsequent agreement between the members. Failing that, the surplus should be distributed equally.

MR JUSTICE WALTON

I ... adopt the analysis made by Brightman J in *Re Recher's Will Trust* [1972] Ch 526

[Mr Justice Walton quoted from Brightman J and continued]

All this doubtless seems quite elementary, but it appears to me to have been lost sight of to some extent in some of the [later] decisions ... in relation to the destination on dissolution of the funds of unincorporated associations.

[Having concluded that the fund was indeed held on a *Re Recher* contractual basis, the judge continued]

[The] question ... now... [arises], consequent on my previous decision that in fact the surplus funds of this friendly society belong to its members, first of all as to whether those surplus funds ought to be distributed basically between such members in equal shares, or, alternatively, in proportion to the subscriptions respectively paid by the persons who were the members of the friendly society at the date of the dissolution thereof.

I think that there is no doubt that ... judicial opinion has been hardening and is now firmly set along the lines that the interests and rights of persons who are members of any type of unincorporated association are governed exclusively by contract, that is to say the rights between themselves and their rights to any surplus assets. ...

That being the case, prima facie there can be no doubt at all but that the distribution is on the basis of equality, because, as between a number of people contractually interested in a fund, there is no other method of distribution if no other method is provided by the terms of the contract, and it is not for one moment suggested here that there is any other method of distribution provided by the contract. ...

Alert

So, where property is held on a contractual basis, it will be distributed:

(a)   In accordance with the terms of the contract; or

(b)   If there are no such terms, as the members agree; or

(c)   If there is no such agreement, as the court directs (which will usually result in an equal division between the existing members).

Of course, not all members of an unincorporated association are necessarily equal. As appears from the facts of Re Horley Town, members may be 'full', 'temporary', 'associate' or enjoy a myriad number of other labels. In the extract cited above in relation to distribution of assets, Lawrence Collins J considered that only the 'full' members, ie those with full rights to use the association's facilities and those with full voting rights, had any right to participate in a distribution of the association's property.

Link
See the extract from *Re Horley Town* above".

7.5 Bona Vacantia or One Surviving Member

Where an unincorporated association has become moribund and there are no members to whom a distribution can be made, the association's property will pass to the Crown (or the Duchies of Lancaster and Cornwall, according to the location of the property) as bona vacantia: *Cunnack v Edwards* [1896] 2 Ch 697

However, for so long as there is at least one surviving member, that member may claim the association's surplus assets.

Hanchett-Stamford v Attorney General and others [2009] Ch 173

Panel: Lewison J

Facts: The Performing and Captive Animals Defence League (the league) was founded in 1914. Over the years the league acquired a substantial portfolio of stocks, shares and property. However, the membership declined to the point where, in 2006, only two life members remained, namely the claimant and her husband. Following the death of the husband, the court was required to determine: (i) whether the league was a charity; (ii) according to the answer to (i), what should happen to its assets. Having found that the association was not a charity, Lewison J directed that the association's property belonged to the claimant alone.

MR JUSTICE LEWISON

... The league has never been incorporated. It is therefore an unincorporated association. Accordingly, unless its assets are held on charitable trusts, they belong in some sense to its members for the time being. I will need to examine this generalisation more closely in due course. If, on the other hand, its assets are held on charitable trusts then none of the members of the league can have a claim to beneficial ownership of them. ... I conclude ... that the league was not and never became a charity.

... In my judgment under normal circumstances a gift to an unincorporated association will fall into the second of Cross J's categories [in *Neville Estates v Madden*]. It is, in Brightman J's words [1972] Ch 526, 539:

"an accretion to the funds which are the subject matter of the contract which such members have made inter se, and falls to be dealt with in precisely the same way as the funds which the members themselves have subscribed." ...

The thread that runs through all [the] cases is that the property of an unincorporated association is the property of its members, but that they are contractually precluded from severing their share except in accordance with the rules of the association; and that, on its dissolution, those who are members at the time are entitled to the assets free from any such contractual restrictions. It is true that this is not a joint tenancy according to the classical model; but since any collective ownership of property must be a species of joint tenancy or tenancy in common, this kind of collective ownership must, in my judgment, be a subspecies of joint tenancy, albeit taking effect subject to any contractual restrictions applicable as between members. In some cases (such as *Cunnack v Edwards* [1895] 1 Ch 489, [1896] 2 Ch 679) those contractual restrictions may be such as to exclude any possibility of a future claim. In others they may not. The cases are united in saying that on a dissolution the members of a dissolved association have a beneficial interest in its assets, and Lord Denning MR goes as far as to say that it is a "beneficial equitable joint tenancy". I cannot see why the legal principle should be any different if the reason for the dissolution is the permanent cessation of the association's activities or the fall in its membership to below two. The same principle ought also to hold if the contractual restrictions are abrogated or varied by agreement of the members. I do not find in the authorities considered by Walton J [in *In re Bucks Constabulary Widows' and Orphans' Fund Friendly Society (No 2)* [1979] 1 WLR 936] anything that binds me to hold that where there is one identifiable and living member of an unincorporated association that has ceased to exist, the assets formerly held by or for that association pass to the Crown as bona vacantia. In addition, article 1 of the First Protocol of the European Convention for the Protection of Human Rights and Fundamental Freedoms guarantees the peaceful enjoyment of possessions. It says: "No one shall be deprived of his possessions except in the public interest and subject to the conditions provided for by law ..."

Alert

On the face of it for one of two members of an unincorporated association to be deprived of his share in the assets of the association by reason of the death of the other of them, and without any compensation, appears to be a breach of this article. It is also difficult to see what public interest is served by the appropriation by the state of that member's share in the association's assets. This, in my judgment, provides another reason why the conclusion that a sole surviving member of an unincorporated association, while still alive, cannot claim its assets is unacceptable.

I therefore respectfully decline to follow Walton J's obiter dictum that a sole surviving member of an unincorporated association cannot claim the assets of the association, and that they vest in the Crown as bona vacantia. I might add that the Attorney General suggested in argument, without arguing in favour of one outcome, that there were three possible outcomes: first, that the last surviving member is entitled to the assets; secondly, that the assets are held jointly between the last surviving member and the estate of the member whose death caused the dissolution; thirdly, that the assets were ownerless or bona vacantia. For the reasons I have given, I conclude the first outcome is correct and I reject the second and third.

Further reading

Griffiths, Gerwyn Ll H. 'Another twist in the tale – unincorporated associations and the distribution of surplus funds' ConvPL Issue 5 (2009) 428

Gardner, S. 'A detail in the construction of gifts to unincorporated associations' [1998] Conv 8

Rickett, C. 'Unincorporated associations and their dissolution' [1980] CLJ 88

Gravells, N. 'Gifts to unincorporated associations: where there is a will there is a way' (1977) 40 MLR 231

8

Charitable Trusts

Topic List

Introduction

Charitable purpose trusts enjoy several advantages which give them a special status not accorded to non-charitable purpose trusts. Trusts for purposes are generally void as they do not satisfy the 'beneficiary principle'. This rule does not apply to charities because the Attorney-General can enforce them. Provided that a general charitable intention can be shown, the purposes need not be certain as the Charity Commissioners or the court can draw up a scheme for the application of the funds. Charities are exempt from the perpetuity rules against inalienability and, to an extent, the rule against remoteness of vesting. An initial gift to charity *is* subject to that rule, but a gift over from one charity to another is exempt. Charities also enjoy huge tax advantages. Not surprisingly, therefore, there are strict rules which must be complied with before an organisation can be registered as a charity, or a trust upheld as a charitable trust. In brief, these are:

(a) The purpose must be charitable. The 'Heads of Charity' referred to in the next section are relevant here;

(b) There must be an identifiable benefit to the public or a sufficient section of the public;

(c) The objects must be wholly and exclusively charitable.

8.1 The Heads of Charity

Before the enactment of the Charities Act 2006 ('the CA 2006'), in order to be charitable, a trust had to fall within the spirit of the preamble to the Charitable Uses Act 1601, often referred to as the Statute of Elizabeth. The purposes set out there were classified by Lord Macnaghten in *Commissioners for Special Purposes of Income Tax v Pemsel* [1891] AC 531 into four 'heads of charity' namely: trusts for the relief of poverty; trusts for the advancement of education; trusts for the advancement of religion; and trusts for other purposes beneficial to the community. The CA 2006 sets out twelve charitable purposes and s 2(4) includes purposes recognised as charitable under existing law. Thus, the previous 'heads of charity' and the case law relating to them are still relevant.

The following are extracts of some leading case examples of charitable purposes.

8.1.1 Trusts for the Advancement of Education

The advancement of education was recognised as a charitable purpose by the Statue of Elizabeth, by Lord Macnaghten's classification, and now under the CA 2006 s2(2)(b). It has been interpreted much more widely than education in its formal, conventional sense, to include arts and culture. In 1972 it was extended in *Incorporated Council of Law Reporting for England and Wales v AG* [1972] Ch 73 to incorporate improving any useful branch of human knowledge and its public dissemination. Now, as it has been given its own separate category under the CA 2006, it is unclear how widely 'education' will be interpreted in future.

In re Hopkins' Will Trusts [1965] Ch 669

Panel: Wilberforce J

Facts: By her will, Evelyn Hopkins left one-third of her estate to the Francis Bacon Society, whose objects were to encourage study of the life, works and influence of Bacon, and to encourage the study of evidence in favour of him being the true author of some of the plays ascribed to Shakespeare. The gift was to be applied towards the finding of the Bacon/Shakespeare manuscripts, or, if they had been found by the date of the testatrix's death, for the general work and propaganda of the Society. This was held to be a valid educational charitable trust. Mr Justice Wilberforce first examined the wording of the will closely and concluded that the purpose was certain. He then looked at the evidence as to whether the purpose was futile as, if it were, the court would be justified in declaring the trust invalid. Only then did he turn to the question of whether the purpose was charitable.

MR JUSTICE WILBERFORCE

On this evidence, should the conclusion be reached that the search for the Bacon-Shakespeare manuscripts is so manifestly futile that the court should not allow this bequest to be spent upon it as upon an object devoid of the possibility of any result? I think not. The evidence shows that the discovery of any manuscript of the plays is unlikely; but so are many discoveries before they are made (one may think of the Codex Sinaiticus, or the Tomb of Tutankhamen, or the Dead Sea Scrolls); I do not think that that degree of improbability has been reached which justifies the court in placing an initial interdict on the testatrix's benefaction.

I come, then, to the only question of law: is the gift of a charitable character? The society has put its case in the alternative under the two headings of education and of general benefit to the community and has argued separately for each. This compartmentalisation is derived from the accepted classification into four groups of the miscellany found in the Statute of Elizabeth... but the somewhat ossificatory classification to which it gave rise survives in the decided cases. It is unsatisfactory because the frontiers of "educational purposes" (as of the other divisions) have been extended and are not easy to trace with precision, and because, under the fourth head, it has been held necessary for the court to find a benefit to the public within the spirit and intendment of the obsolete Elizabethan statute. The difficulty of achieving that, while at the same time keeping the law's view of what is charitable reasonably in line with modern requirements, explains what Lord Simonds accepted as the case-to-case approach of the courts: see *National Anti-Vivisection Society v. Inland* Revenue Commissioners. There are, in fact, examples of accepted charities which do not decisively fit into one rather than the other category. Examples are institutes for scientific research (see the *National Anti-Vivisection* case, *per* Lord Wright), museums (see *In re Pinion*), the preservation of ancient cottages *(In re Cranstoun,)* and even the

Link
See Political Trusts section below

promotion of Shakespearian drama *(In re Shakespeare Memorial Theatre Trust)*. The present may be such a case.

Accepting, as I have the authority of Lord Simonds for so doing, that the court must decide each case as best it can, on the evidence available to it, as to benefit, and within the moving spirit of decided cases, it would seem to me that a bequest for the purpose of search, or research, for the original manuscripts of England's greatest dramatist (whoever he was) would be well within the law's conception of charitable purposes. The discovery of such manuscripts, or of one such manuscript, would be of the highest value to history and to literature. It is objected, against this, that as we already have the text of the plays, from an almost contemporary date, the discovery of a manuscript would add nothing worth while. This I utterly decline to accept. Without any undue exercise of the imagination, it would surely be a reasonable expectation that the revelation of a manuscript would contribute, probably decisively, to a solution of the authorship problem, and this alone is benefit enough. It might also lead to improvements in the text. It might lead to more accurate dating.

He then turned to the arguments for the next of kin, relying on *In re Shaw* [1957] 1 WLR 729 where it was held that a gift was not educational if it simply added to knowledge without being 'combined with teaching or education'.

The words "combined with teaching or education," though well explaining what the judge had in mind when he rejected the gift in *Shaw's* case, are not easy to interpret in relation to other facts. I should be unwilling to treat them as meaning that the promotion of academic research is not a charitable purpose unless the researcher were engaged in teaching or education in the conventional meaning; and I am encouraged in this view by some words of Lord Greene M.R. in *In re Compton*. The testatrix there had forbidden the income of the bequest to be used for research, and Lord Greene M.R. treated this as a negative definition of the education to be provided. It would, he said, exclude a grant to enable a beneficiary to conduct research on some point of history or science. This shows that Lord Greene M.R. considered that historic research might fall within the description of "education." I think, therefore, that the word "education" as used by Harman J. in *In re Shaw, decd.; Public Trustee v. Day* must be used in a wide sense, certainly extending beyond teaching, and that the requirement is that, in order to be charitable, research must either be of educational value to the researcher or must be so directed as to lead to something which will pass into the store of educational material, or so as to improve the sum of communicable knowledge in an area which education may cover - education in this last context extending to the formation of literary taste and appreciation (compare *Royal Choral Society v. Inland Revenue Commissioners*). Whether or not the test is wider than this, it is, as I have stated it, amply wide enough to include the purposes of the gift in this case. ... I accept that research of a private character, for the benefit only of the members of a society, would not normally be educational - or otherwise charitable – ... but I do not think that the research in the present case can be said to be of a private character, for it is inherently inevitable, and manifestly intended, that the result of any discovery should be published to the world.

8.1.2 Trusts for the Advancement of Religion

In re South Place Ethical Society [1980] 1 WLR 1565

Panel: Dillon J

Facts: The South Place Religious Society held land and a chapel on the trusts declared by an 1825 deed for use 'for the public worship of one God'. In 1887, using powers conferred by the 1825 deed, the society abandoned prayer, changed its name to South Place Ethical Society and changed the objects to 'the study and dissemination of ethical principles and the cultivation of a rational religious sentiment'. The trustees sought a declaration as to whether the objects were charitable, or whether the trustees had a duty to apply the assets cy-près because the current objects were no longer charitable. It was held that the objects were not for the advancement of religion. Beginning his judgment, Dillon J explained that the society members were sincere people of integrity, agnostic rather than atheist. He explained that the society's beliefs were an aspect of Humanism, idealising the ethical principles of truth, beauty and love rather than believing in anything supernatural. The objects of the society involved the study and dissemination of these principles through public meetings, lectures, musical and social activities.

MR JUSTICE DILLON

Of course it has long been established that a trust can be valid and charitable as for the advancement of religion, although the religion which is sought to be advanced is not the Christian religion. In *Bowman v Secular Society Ltd* [1917] AC 406, Lord Parker of Waddington gave a very clear and valuable summary of the history of the approach of the law to religious charitable trusts at pp. 448 to 450. He said, at p. 449: "It would seem to follow that a trust for the purpose of any kind of monotheistic theism would be a good charitable trust."...

The Society argued that religion does not have to be dependent on the belief in any god: sincere belief in ethical qualities is equally sacred and the advancement of such beliefs advances religion. The judge surveyed the American authorities which suggested that the society would be accepted as a body established for the advancement of religion and concluded:

In a free country – and I have no reason to suppose that this country is less free than the United States of America – it is natural that the court should desire not to discriminate between beliefs deeply and sincerely held, whether they are beliefs in a god or in the excellence of man or in ethical principles or in Platonism or some other scheme of philosophy. But I do not see that that warrants extending the meaning of the word "religion" so as to embrace all other beliefs and philosophies. Religion, as I see it, is concerned with man's relations with God, and ethics are concerned with man's relations with man. The two are not the same, and are not made the same by sincere inquiry into the question: what is God? If reason leads people not to accept Christianity or any known religion, but they do believe in the excellence of qualities such as truth, beauty and love, or believe in the platonic concept of the ideal, their beliefs may be to

Alert

them the equivalent of a religion, but viewed objectively they are not religion. The ground of the opinion of the court, in the United States Supreme Court, that any belief occupying in the life of its possessor a place parallel to that occupied by belief in God in the minds of theists prompts the comment that parallels, by definition, never meet.

In *Bowman v Secular Society Ltd* [1917] AC 406, 445 Lord Parker of Waddington in commenting on one of the objects of the society in that case, namely to promote the principle that human conduct should be based upon natural knowledge and not upon supernatural belief, and that human welfare in this world is the proper end of all thought and action, said of that object, at p. 445:

"It is not a religious trust, for it relegates religion to a region in which it is to have no influence on human conduct."

That comment seems to me to be equally applicable to the objects of the society in the present case, and it is not to be answered in my judgment by attempting to extend the meaning of religion. Lord Parker of Waddington has used the word "in its natural and accustomed sense." Again, in *United Grand Lodge of Ancient Free and Accepted Masons of England v Holborn Borough Council* [1957] 1 WLR 1080, Donovan J. in delivering the judgment of the Divisional Court, after commenting that freemasonary held out certain standards of truth and justice by which masons were urged to regulate their conduct, and commenting that, in particular, masons were urged to be reverent, honest, compassionate, loyal, temperate, benevolent and chaste, said, at p. 1090: "Admirable though these objects are it seems to us impossible to say that they add up to the advancement of religion." Therefore I take the view that the objects of this society are not for the advancement of religion.

There is a further point. It seems to me that two of the essential attributes of religion are faith and worship; faith in a god and worship of that god. This is supported by the definitions of religion given in the *Oxford English Dictionary* (1914), …

 Alert

In *Reg. v Registrar General, Ex parte Segerdal* [1970] 2 QB 697, which was concerned with the so-called Church of Scientology, Buckley L.J. said, at p. 709:

"Worship I take to be something which must have some at least of the following characteristics: submission to the object worshipped, veneration of that object, praise, thanksgiving, prayer or intercession."

He went on to say that, looking at the wedding ceremony of the scientologists, he could find nothing in the form of ceremony which would not be appropriate in a purely civil, non-religious ceremony such as is conducted in a register office, and that it contained none of the elements which he has suggested are necessary elements of worship. He then said:

"I do not say that you would need to find every element in every act which could properly be described as worship, but when you find an act which contains none of those elements it cannot, in my judgment, answer to the description of an act of worship."

The society really accepts that worship by that definition, which in my view is the correct definition in considering whether a body is charitable for the advancement of religion, is not practised by the society, because, indeed, it is not possible to worship in that way a mere ethical or philosophical ideal.

He rejected the society's concept of 'natural' worship, which consisted of appreciating and finding emotional and spiritual fulfilment in nature, music and any kind of aesthetic experience. Although the trust was not a charitable trust for the advancement of religion, it was upheld as being for the advancement of education and for the public benefit.

Church of Scientology's Application for Registration as a Charity [2005] WTLR 1151

Panel: The Charity Commissioners for England and Wales

Facts: In considering an application for registration as a charity by the Church of Scientology, the Board of Commissioners considered, amongst other things, whether it was established for the advancement of religion and if so, whether it was for the public benefit. They took into account the principles of the European Convention on Human Rights Articles 9 and 14. Scientology is based exclusively on the research, writing and lectures of Ron Hubbard, which include fundamental principles through which people can realise their natural spiritual potential. The path outlined by Hubbard must be followed closely if this is to be achieved. The core practices of Scientology are auditing and training. Auditing involves addressing past painful experiences, thereby attaining increased awareness, capability and spiritual transformation. Training is intensive study through which a person learns to be an auditor.

The Commissioners decided that the Church of Scientology was not registrable because it was not a religion for the purposes of charity law. Although Scientology acknowledges a supreme being, its nature is not fully developed. Further, as auditing and training involve private counselling and study, they are more like education and training than religious practice, as they lack essential veneration and reverence. The Commissioners elaborated on what would be classed as a religion within charity law.

The Commissioners noted that English charity law has developed empirically, within the context of the traditional Western monotheistic religions, although it has long embraced monotheistic religions other than Christianity and Judaism. Within that context, the following general principles are firmly established:

(i)   Trusts for the advancement of religion take effect as charities without assessment by the court of the worth or value of the beliefs in question, unless the tenets of a particular sect inculcate doctrines adverse to the very foundations of all religion and/or subversive of all morality.

(ii)   The law does not prefer one religion to another and as between religions the law stands neutral, but it assumes that any religion is at least likely to be better than none.

(iii)   In deciding whether a gift is for the advancement of religion, the court does not concern itself with the truth of the religion, a matter which is not susceptible of proof. This does not mean that the court will recognise as a religion everything that chooses to call itself a religion. But when once the religion is recognised by the court as a religion, the beneficial nature of a gift for its advancement will prima facie be assumed.

(iv)   In addition, in order to be charitable, the trust must not only be for the advancement of religion, it must also be of public benefit. This is a question of fact which must be answered by the court in the same manner as any other question of fact, ie by means of evidence cognizable by the court. In the absence of evidence to the contrary, public benefit is presumed.

Given these judicial principles, the Commissioners found it understandable that the English courts have resisted closely defining what it is that makes some belief systems religious and other not. However, the Commissioners accepted that there are some characteristics of religion which can be discerned from the legal authorities:

1.   Belief in a god or a deity or supreme being – *R v Registrar General ex parte Segerdal* (Lord Denning).

2.   Reverence and recognition of the dominant power and control of any entity or being outside their own body and life (i.e. outside the body and life of the follower of that religion) – *Segerdal* (Wian LJ).

3.   Two of the essential attributes of religion are faith and worship: faith in a god and worship of that god – *South Place Ethical Society* (Dillon J). The Commissioners noted that Hubert Picarda QC writes that religion involves not merely faith of a particular kind, but also worship, and states that the essential ingredient of worship is found in the definition of Webster's New International dictionary which defines religion as "service and adoration of God or a god as expressed in a form of worship."

4.   A trust for the purpose of any kind of monotheistic theism would be a good charitable trust – *Bowman v Secular Society* (Lord Parker of Waddington)

5.   Worship must have at least some of the following characteristics: submission to the object worshipped, veneration of that object, praise, thanksgiving, prayer or intercession – *Segerdal* (Buckley LJ).

6.   It would not seem to be possible to worship in this way (ie with reverence) a mere ethical or philosophical ideal – *South Place Ethical Society* (Dillon J)

7.   Promotion of religion includes "the observances that serve to promote and manifest it." – *Keren Kayemeth Le Jisroel v IRC* (Lord Hanworth MR).

8.   There must be a promotion of the religion, meaning "the promotion of spiritual teaching in a wide sense, and the maintenance of the doctrines on which it rests, and the observances that serve to promote and manifest it." – *Keren Kayemeth Le Jisroel v IRC* (Lord Hanworth MR). This would include observance of

particular common standards, practices or codes of conduct as stipulated in particular scriptures or teachings.

9. To advance religion means "to promote it, to spread the message ever wider among mankind; to take some positive steps to sustain and increase religious belief and these things are done in a variety of ways which may be comprehensively described as pastoral and missionary" – *United Grand Lodge v Holborn BC* (Donovan J).

10. Promotion of religion includes a missionary element or other charitable work through which the beliefs of the religion are advanced – *United Grand Lodge v Holborn BC* (Donovan J).

11. Public benefit is a necessary element in religious trusts as it is in other charitable trusts – *Coats v Gilmour* (Lord Greene MR).

Having *considered* these characteristics, the Commissioners concluded that the definition of a religion in English charity law was characterised by a belief in a supreme being and an expression of that belief through worship. The cases also make clear that there must be advancement or promotion of the religion. ...

The Commissioners noted that the *Segerdal* and *South Place Ethical Society* cases in particular, referring to the requirement of a god or deity have traditionally been regarded as decisive of the principle that theism (belief in a god) is a necessary criterion of religion for the purposes of charity law. Both cases suggest that religion in charity law is characterised by:

- Faith in the personal, creator god of the traditional monotheistic religions, having existence outside the body and life of the votary, and

- Worship of that deity in the form of formalised expressions of supplication, veneration, praise and intercession, as traditionally practised in monotheistic religions.

Against those criteria, the Commissioners noted that Scientology claims to acknowledge a supreme being which may have created the world. This supreme being ("infinity", the Eighth dynamic, the "allness of all"), is according to the expert opinion submitted by CoS in support of its application, a thoroughly impersonal abstract conception, more analogous to eastern enlightenment and realisation, which Scientologists recognise as the ultimate ground of being but of which they are reluctant to claim complete understanding.

Whilst the Commissioners noted that CoS's application stated that Scientology acknowledges a supreme being, the Commissioners concluded that the supreme being did not appear to be of kind indicated by the decided cases.

The Commissioners also noted CoS's submission that the activities of auditing and training constitute its worship, this argument being supported by the expert opinion submitted by CoS. However, the Commissioners were unable to accept that the practices of auditing and training were akin to or comparable with the acts of worship

Alert

see also Dillon J's comments in *South Place Ethical* case

indicated by the English cases – praise, veneration, prayer, thanksgiving, intercession, submission to the object worshipped.

As the Commissioners had concluded that Scientology was not charitable they had no need to consider whether it was for the public benefit. They did however do so, and stated that 'public benefit' is an essential element of charity law, and is presumed where the purpose is for the advancement of religion. This presumption has now been abolished by the CA 2006.

8.1.3 Trusts for sports and games

In re Dupree's Deed Trusts [1945] Ch 16

Panel: Vaisey J

Facts: A trust fund of £5000 was established with the income to be used to promote an annual chess tournament for boys under 21 living in Portsmouth. The trustees sought a declaration as to whether this was a valid charitable trust on the basis that it was for the advancement of education. It was upheld, although the judge expressed unease at laying down any hard and fast rules as to where the line should be drawn on the educational value of sports and games.

MR JUSTICE VAISEY

The game of chess (which, by those who follow it, as well, perhaps, as by those who do not follow it, is regarded as something rather more than a mere game) is an institution with a very long history behind it, and it possesses the somewhat notable feature that it is essentially a game of skill into which elements of chance enter, if at all, only to a negligible extent. It is a game which, I suppose, is played all over the civilized world. I have some evidence which enables me to say – and, indeed, I think I might have said it even without that evidence – that the nature of the game is such as to encourage the qualities of foresight, concentration, memory and ingenuity. Even unguided by actual evidence, I should not have been surprised if the conclusion could have been reached that the game is essentially one which does possess an educational value.

There are many pursuits possessing an educational value which may be followed to excess, and the matter is in no way concluded by any such consideration. Chess players may become so obsessed by the interest of their pursuit that they may neglect other duties, but the same thing may be said of those who range the mysterious country of the higher mathematics or indulge in the study of classical authors. I am not surprised to learn from the evidence that there are schoolmasters and persons actually concerned with the business of education who regard the playing of chess as something of so much value educationally that in some places it is actually a part of a school curriculum. ...

I think that the case before me may be a little near the line, and I decide it without attempting to lay down any general propositions. One feels, perhaps, that one is on rather a slippery slope. If chess, why not draughts? If draughts, why not bezique, and so on, through to bridge and whist, and, by another route, to stamp collecting and the acquisition of birds' eggs? Those pursuits will have to be dealt with if and when they come up for consideration in connexion with the problem whether or no [sic] there is in existence an educational charitable trust. Nor do I say whether, if this trust had been without a geographical limitation, if it had been for the promotion of chess playing in vacuo or at large, the area of what is regarded as charitable would or would not have been over-stepped. Having regard to the evidence before me and to what is known about the game of chess by everybody, and, in particular, to the fact that the encouragement of chess playing here is for the benefit of young persons living within a well-defined area, and also that it is of the essence of the constitution of the trusteeship that two of the trustees should be persons closely connected with educational activities in the borough, I think I am bound, in the present case, to hold that there is a good charitable trust, and answer the question by declaring that the trusts constituted by the deed of June 30, 1932, are valid charitable trusts.

The Recreational Charities Act 1958 ('the RCA 1958') sets out the circumstances in which trusts for the provision of recreational facilities are deemed to be charitable. Amateur sports are now a charitable purpose under the CA 2006.

Guild v Inland Revenue Commissioners [1992] AC 310

Panel: Lord Keith of Kinkel, Lord Roskill, Lord Griffiths, Lord Jauncey of Tullichettle and Lord Lowry

Facts: James Russell left the residue of his estate to the town council of North Berwick 'for the use in connection with the sports centre in North Berwick or some similar purpose in connection with sport'. The Inland Revenue claimed tax on the transfer, but the executor argued that it was exempt from tax under the Finance Acts as it was charitable within the meaning of the RCA 1958. The House of Lords held that it was charitable and thus exempt from tax: no element of deprivation was required to be shown in order for a purpose to be charitable under the RCA 1958.

LORD KEITH OF KINKEL

In the course of his argument in relation to the first branch of the bequest counsel for the commissioners accepted that it assisted in the provision of facilities for recreation or other leisure time occupation within the meaning of subsection (1) of section 1 of the Act, and also that the requirement of public benefit in the proviso to the subsection was satisfied. It was further accepted that the facilities of the sports centre were available to the public at large so that the condition of subsection (2)(b)(ii) was satisfied. It was maintained, however, that these facilities were not provided "in the interests of social welfare" as required by subsection (1), because they did not meet the condition laid down in subsection (2)(a), namely that they should be "provided with the object of improving the conditions of life for the persons for whom the facilities are primarily intended." The reason why it was said that this condition was not met was that on a proper construction it involved that the facilities should be provided with the object of meeting a need for such facilities in people who suffered from a position of relative social disadvantage. Reliance was placed on a passage from the judgment of Walton J. in *Inland Revenue Commissioners v McMullen* [1978] 1 WLR 664. That was a case where the Football Association had set up a trust to provide facilities to encourage pupils of schools and universities in the United Kingdom to play association football and other games and sports. Walton J. held that the trust was not valid as one for the advancement of education nor did it satisfy section 1 of the Act of 1958. He said, at p.675, in relation to the words "social welfare" in subsection (1):

"In my view, however, these words in themselves indicate that there is some kind of deprivation - not, of course, by any means necessarily of money - which falls to be alleviated; and I think that this is made even clearer by the terms of subsection (2)(a). The facilities must be provided with the object of improving the conditions of life for persons for whom the facilities are primarily intended. In other words, they must be to some extent and in some way deprived persons."

When the case went to the Court of Appeal [1979] 1 W.L.R. 130 the majority (Stamp and Orr L.JJ.) affirmed the judgment of Walton J. on both points, but Bridge L.J. dissented. As regards the Recreational Charities Act 1958 point he said, "...Save in the sense that the interests of social welfare can only be served by the meeting of some social need, I cannot accept the judge's view that the interests of social welfare can only be served in relation to some 'deprived' class. The judge found this view reinforced by the requirement of subsection (2)(a) of section 1 that the facilities must be provided 'with the object of improving the conditions of life for the persons for whom the facilities are primarily intended; ...' Here again I can see no reason to conclude that only the deprived can have their conditions of life improved. Hyde Park improves the conditions of life for residents in Mayfair and Belgravia as much as for those in Pimlico or the Portobello Road, and the village hall may improve the conditions of life for the squire and his family as well as for the cottagers. The persons for whom the facilities here are primarily intended are pupils of schools and universities, as defined in the trust deed, and these facilities are in my judgment unquestionably to be provided with the object of improving their conditions of life. ... There cannot surely be any doubt that young persons as part of their education do need facilities for organised games and sports both by reason of their youth and by reason of their social and economic circumstances. They cannot provide such facilities for themselves but are dependent on what is provided for them."

In the House of Lords [1981] A.C. 1 [*IRC v* McMullen] the case was decided against the Crown upon the ground that the trust was one for the advancement of education, opinion being reserved on the point under the Recreational Charities Act 1958.

Although the House of Lords did not decide *IRC v McMullen* on the RCA 1958 point, in *Guild v IRC* Lord Keith of Kinkel specifically addressed the issue:

The fact is that persons in all walks of life and all kinds of social circumstances may have their conditions of life improved by the provision of recreational facilities of suitable character. The proviso requiring public benefit excludes facilities of an undesirable nature. In my opinion the view expressed by Bridge L.J. in *Inland Revenue Commissioners v McMullen* is clearly correct...

I would therefore reject the argument that the facilities are not provided in the interests of social welfare unless they are provided with the object of improving the conditions of life for persons who suffer from some form of social disadvantage. It suffices if they are provided with the object of improving the conditions of life for members of the community generally.

8.2 Public Benefit

As well as being for a recognised charitable purpose within CA 2006 s 2(2), there must be an element of public benefit: s 3. Before the enactment of CA 2006, there was a presumption of public benefit where the trust was for the relief of poverty, advancement of education or advancement of religion. This presumption has been abolished by s 3(2). However, existing law, particularly the cases on the 4th head of charity ('other purposes beneficial to the community'), may assist by giving an example of what the public benefit of a particular trust might be. The benefits must be capable of being identified, defined or described. The leading case in this area is *Gilmour v Coats* [1949] AC 426.

Gilmour v Coats [1949] AC 426

Panel: Lord Simonds, Lord du Parcq, Lord Normand, Lord Morton of Henryton and Lord Reid

Facts: £500 was given on trust for the purposes of a Carmelite Priory in Notting Hill, London, if those purposes were charitable. The Priory was a community of cloistered nuns who spent all of their time in prayer, penance and contemplation and took no part in outside works. It was argued that this conferred a benefit on the public both through intercessionary prayers and through edification by the example of lives devoted to prayer. The trustees asked how they should apply the trust fund. The House of Lords held that the purposes of the Priory were not charitable as there was no element of public benefit shown. In his leading opinion, Lord Simonds turned first to the question whether there is any proof that intercessionary prayer benefits the public. He acknowledged that cloistered communities, though they have existed for a long time, have never been upheld as charitable, so looking back over early law is not a useful exercise.

LORD SIMONDS

... There may be circumstances in which the court will in a later age hold an object not to be charitable which has in earlier ages been held to possess that virtue. and the converse case may be possible. That degree of uncertainty in the law must be admitted. But I would ask your Lordships to say that it is only a radical change of circumstances, established by sufficient evidence, that should compel the court to accept a new view of this matter. Let me then examine briefly the law as it is to-day and, having done so, ask what are the compelling reasons for a change. I need not go

Link
see Chapter 7, *Leahy v A-G for New South Wales*

beyond the case of *Cocks v Manners* which was decided nearly eighty years ago by Wickens V.-C. In that case the testatrix left her residuary estate between a number of religious institutions, one of them being the Dominican Convent at Carisbrooke, a community not differing in any material respect from the community of nuns now under consideration. The learned judge who was, I suppose, as deeply versed in this branch of the law as any judge before or since (for he had been for many years junior counsel to the Attorney-General in equity cases), used these words, which I venture to repeat, though they have already been cited in the courts below:

"On the Act [sc. the Statute of Elizabeth] unaffected by authority I should certainly hold that the gift to the Dominican Convent is neither within the letter nor the spirit of it; and no decision has been referred to which compels me to adopt a different conclusion. A voluntary association of women for the purpose of working out their own salvation by religious exercises and self-denial seems to me to have none of the requisites of a charitable institution, whether the word 'charitable' is used in its popular sense or in its legal sense. It is said, in some of the cases, that religious purposes are charitable, but that can only be true as to religious services tending directly or indirectly towards the instruction or the edification of the public; an annuity to an individual, so long as he spent his time in retirement and constant devotion, would not be charitable, nor would a gift to ten persons, so long as they lived together in retirement and performed acts of devotion, be charitable. Therefore the gift to the Dominican Convent is not, in my opinion, a gift on a charitable trust."

No case, said the learned Vice-Chancellor, had been cited to compel him to come to a contrary conclusion, nor has any such case been cited to your Lordships. Nor have my own researches discovered one. ...

Although evidence was given by the Archbishop of Westminster that the doctrine of the Roman Catholic Church was that intercessionary prayers conferred a benefit on the public, Lord Simonds refused to give it more than negligible weight as the benefit was incapable of proof.

My Lords, I would speak with all respect and reverence of those who spend their lives in cloistered piety, and in this House of Lords Spiritual and Temporal, which daily commences its proceedings with intercessory prayers, how can I deny that the Divine Being may in His wisdom think fit to answer them? But, my Lords, whether I affirm or deny, whether I believe or disbelieve, what has that to do with the proof which the court demands that a particular purpose satisfies the test of benefit to the community? Here is something which is manifestly not susceptible of proof. But, then it is said, this is a matter not of proof but of belief: for the value of intercessory prayer is a tenet of the Catholic faith, therefore in such prayer there is benefit to the community. But it is just at this "therefore" that I must pause. It is, no doubt, true that the advancement of religion is, generally speaking, one of the heads of charity. But it does not follow from this that the court must accept as proved whatever a particular church believes. The faithful must embrace their faith believing where they cannot prove: the court can act only on proof. A gift to two or ten or a hundred cloistered nuns in the belief that their prayers will benefit the world at large does not from that belief alone derive validity any more than does the belief of any other donor for any other purpose.

He then considered the second argument in favour of public benefit: edification by example.

It is in my opinion sufficient to say that this is something too vague and intangible to satisfy the prescribed test. The test of public benefit has, I think, been developed in the last two centuries. To-day it is beyond doubt that that element must be present. No court would be rash enough to attempt to define precisely or exhaustively what its content must be. But it would assume a burden which it could not discharge if now for the first time it admitted into the category of public benefit something so indirect, remote, imponderable and, I would add, controversial as the benefit which may be derived by others from the example of pious lives. ...

It was also argued that the element of public benefit was satisfied as qualification for membership of the community was open to any woman in the world. Lord Simonds applied established case law to reject this argument.

Questions arise as to whether the element of public benefit is satisfied where a trust is restricted to certain sections of society. This was considered in *Inland Revenue Commissioners v Baddeley* [1955] AC 572. The key considerations appear to be who is capable of benefiting, rather than who is actually benefiting, and whether the restriction to a section of society is reasonable. This in turn depends on the purpose of the charity. So the public benefit requirement can differ according to differing charitable aims.

Link

See The Charity Commissioners Guidance on Public Benefit in Further Reading.

Inland Revenue Commissioners v Baddeley [1955] AC 572

Panel: Lord Tucker, Viscount Simonds, Lord Porter, Lord Reid and Lord Somervell of Harrow

Facts: Two pieces of land were conveyed to the trustees of the Newtown Mission Church on similar terms. The first was to be used 'for the promotion of the religious social and physical well-being of persons resident in the County Boroughs of West Ham and Leyton... by the provision of facilities for religious services and instruction and for the social and physical training and recreation' of members of the church, or people likely to become members and of insufficient means otherwise to enjoy them. The second was playing fields to be used for the 'moral' rather than 'religious' well-being of the same people. The question was whether the purposes were charitable because if they were, the transfer deeds attracted a much lower rate of duty than would otherwise have been the case. The court (Lord Reid dissenting) first decided that the purposes of the trusts were not 'wholly and exclusively charitable', and that they failed on this basis. The judges then considered the element of 'public benefit' and sought to clarify exactly what this meant.

VISCOUNT SIMONDS

Suppose that, contrary to the view that I have expressed, the trust would be a valid charitable trust, if the beneficiaries were the community at large or a section of the community defined by some geographical limits, is it the less a valid trust if it is confined to members or potential members of a particular church within a limited geographical area?

The starting point of the argument must be, that this charity (if it be a charity) falls within the fourth class in Lord Macnaghten's classification. It must therefore be a trust which is, to use the words of Sir Samuel Romilly in *Morice v Bishop of Durham*, of "general public utility," and the question is what these words mean. ...But it is said that if a charity falls within the fourth class, it must be for the benefit of the whole community or at least of all the inhabitants of a sufficient area. and it has been urged with much force that, if, as Lord Greene said in *In re Strakosch*, this fourth class is represented in the preamble to the Statute of Elizabeth by the repair of bridges, etc., and possibly by the maintenance of Houses of Correction, the class of beneficiaries or potential beneficiaries cannot be further narrowed down. Some confusion has arisen from the fact that a trust of general public utility, however general and however public, cannot be of equal utility to all and may be of immediate utility to few. A sea wall, the prototype of this class in the preamble, is of remote, if any, utility to those who live in the heart of the Midlands. But there is no doubt that a trust for the maintenance of sea walls generally or along a particular stretch of coast is a good charitable trust. Nor, as it appears to me, is the validity of a trust affected by the fact that by its very nature only a limited number of people are likely to avail themselves, or are perhaps even capable of availing themselves, of its benefits. It is easy, for instance, to imagine a charity which has for its object some form of child welfare, of which the immediate beneficiaries could only be persons of tender age. Yet this would satisfy any test of general public utility. It may be said that it would satisfy the test because the indirect benefit of such a charity would extend far beyond its direct beneficiaries, and that aspect of the matter has probably not been out of sight. Indirect benefit is certainly an aspect which must have influenced the decision of the "cruelty to animal" cases. But, I doubt whether this sort of rationalization helps to explain a branch of the law which has developed empirically and by analogy upon analogy.

It is, however, in my opinion, particularly important in cases falling within the fourth category to keep firmly in mind the necessity of the element of general public utility, and I would not relax this rule. For here is a slippery slope. In the case under appeal the intended beneficiaries are a class within a class; they are those of the inhabitants of a particular area who are members of a particular church: the area is comparatively large and populous and the members may be numerous. But, if this trust is charitable for them, does it cease to be charitable as the area narrows down and the numbers diminish? Suppose the area is confined to a single street and the beneficiaries to those whose creed commands few adherents: or suppose the class is one that is determined not by religious belief but by membership of a particular profession or by pursuit of a particular trade. These were considerations which influenced the House in the recent case of *Oppenheim*. That was a case of an educational trust, but I think that they have

Alert

even greater weight in the case of trusts which by their nominal classification depend for their validity upon general public utility.

It is pertinent, then, to ask how far your Lordships might regard yourselves bound by authority to hold the trusts now under review valid charitable trusts, if the only question in issue was the sufficiency of the public element. ...Relevant [on this point] is the case of *Verge v Somerville*. In that case, in which the issue was as to the validity of a gift "to the trustees of the Repatriation Fund or other similar fund for the benefit of New South Wales returned soldiers," Lord Wrenbury, delivering the judgment of the Judicial Committee, said that, to be a charity, a trust must be "for the benefit of the community or of an appreciably important class of the community. The inhabitants," he said, "of a parish or town or any particular class of such inhabitants, may, for instance, be the objects of such a gift, but private individuals, or a fluctuating body of private individuals, cannot." Here, my Lords, are two expressions: "an appreciably important class of the community" and "any particular class of such inhabitants," to which in any case it is not easy to give a precise quantitative or qualitative meaning. But I think that in the consideration of them the difficulty has sometimes been increased by failing to observe the distinction, at which I hinted earlier in this opinion, between a form of relief extended to the whole community yet by its very nature advantageous only to the few and a form of relief accorded to a selected few out of a larger number equally willing and able to take advantage of it. Of the former type repatriated New South Wales soldiers would serve as a clear example. To me it would not seem arguable that they did not form an adequate class of the community for the purpose of the particular charity that was being established. It was with this type of case that Lord Wrenbury was dealing, and his words are apt to deal with it. Somewhat different considerations arise if the form, which the purporting charity takes, is something of general utility which is nevertheless made available not to the whole public but only to a selected body of the public - an important class of the public it may be. For example, a bridge which is available for all the public may undoubtedly be a charity and it is indifferent how many people use it. But confine its use to a selected number of persons, however numerous and important: it is then clearly not a charity. It is not of general public utility: for it does not serve the public purpose which its nature qualifies it to serve.

Alert

Alert

Oppenheim v Tobacco Securities [1951] AC 297

Panel: Lord Simonds, Lord Normand, Lord Oaksey, Lord Morton of Henryton and Lord Macdermott

Facts: A trust fund was established with the income and capital to be used for 'the education of children of employees or former employees of British-American Tobacco Company Limited ... or any of its subsidiary or allied companies in such manner and according to such schemes or rules or regulations as the acting trustees shall in their absolute discretion from time to time think fit...'. There were over 100,000 employees and former employees who were potential beneficiaries of the trust find. The question was whether the trust benefited a sufficient section of the public to make it charitable. The court (Lord MacDermott dissenting) held that it did not. In the leading opinion, Lord Simonds began by acknowledging that no clear answer as to what constitutes 'public benefit' could be given, but that there must be an element of public benefit in trusts for educational purposes.

LORD SIMONDS

If I may begin at the bottom of the scale, a trust established by a father for the education of his son is not a charity. The public element, as I will call it, is not supplied by the fact that from that son's education all may benefit. At the other end of the scale the establishment of a college or university is beyond doubt a charity. "Schools of learning and free schools and scholars of universities" are the very words of the preamble to the Statute of Elizabeth. So also the endowment of a college, university or school by the creation of scholarships or bursaries is a charity and none the less because competition may be limited to a particular class of persons. It is upon this ground, as Lord Greene, M.R., pointed out in *In re Compton*, that the so-called Founder's Kin cases can be rested. The difficulty arises where the trust is not for the benefit of any institution either then existing or by the terms of the trust to be brought into existence, but for the benefit of a class of persons at large. Then the question is whether that class of persons can be regarded as such a "section of the community" as to satisfy the test of public benefit. These words "section of the community" have no special sanctity, but they conveniently indicate first, that the possible (I emphasize the word "possible") beneficiaries must not be numerically negligible, and secondly, that the quality which distinguishes them from other members of the community, so that they form by themselves a section of it, must be a quality which does not depend on their relationship to a particular individual. It is for this reason that a trust for the education of members of a family or, as in *In re Compton*, of a number of families cannot be regarded as charitable. A group of persons may be numerous but, if the nexus between them is their personal relationship to a single propositus or to several propositi, they are neither the community nor a section of the community for charitable purposes.

 Alert

I come, then, to the present case where the class of beneficiaries is numerous but the difficulty arises in regard to their common and distinguishing quality. That quality is being children of employees of one or other of a group of companies. I can make no distinction between children of employees and the employees themselves. In both cases the common quality is found in employment by particular employers. The latter of the two cases by which the Court of Appeal held itself to be bound, *In re Hobourn Aero Components Ld.'s Air Raid Distress Fund*, is a direct authority for saying that such a common quality does not constitute its possessors a section of the public for charitable purposes. In the former case, *In re Compton*, Lord Greene, M.R., had by way of illustration placed members of a family and employees of a particular employer on the same footing, finding neither in common kinship nor in common employment the sort of nexus which is sufficient. ... It appears to me that it would be an extension, for which there is no justification in principle or authority, to regard common employment as a quality which constitutes those employed a section of the community. It must not, I think, be forgotten that charitable institutions enjoy rare and increasing privileges, and that the claim to come within that privileged class should be clearly established. ...

Learned counsel for the appellant sought to fortify his case by pointing to the anomalies that would ensue from the rejection of his argument. For, he said, admittedly those who follow a profession or calling, clergymen, lawyers, colliers, tobacco-workers and so on, are a section of the public; how strange then it would be if, as in the case of railwaymen, those who follow a particular calling are all employed by one employer. Would a trust for the education of railwaymen be charitable, but a trust for the education of men employed on the railways by the Transport Board not be charitable? and what of service of the Crown whether in the civil service or the armed forces? Is there a difference between soldiers and soldiers of the King? My Lords, I am not impressed by this sort of argument and will consider on its merits, if the occasion should arise, the case where the description of the occupation and the employment is in effect the same, where in a word, if you know what a man does, you know who employs him to do it. It is to me a far more cogent argument, as it was to my noble and learned friend in the *Hobourn* case, that if a section of the public is constituted by the personal relation of employment, it is impossible to say that it is not constituted by 1,000 as by 100,000 employees, and, if by 1,000, then by 100, and, if by 100, then by 10.

Lord Simonds refused to harmonise the law on educational purpose trusts with the 'poor relations' cases where public benefit is presumed to be present. The 'poor relations' cases are a separate line of the law which has developed independently and are beyond the scope of this Chapter.

LORD NORMAND

... The fact that the children of the employees and not the employees themselves are the beneficiaries does not help the appellants, for there is no public element in the relationship of parent and child. The common attribute that each parent has a contract of service with the same employer remains for consideration. A contract of service is in a high degree personal, and it constitutes a personal and private relationship between the parties. Whatever the number of the employees in the service of the same employer each still stands independently in this personal and private relationship to the employer.

...

In principle I am unable to say that any public element can be born out of the several private contracts between a particular employer and his employees. The appellant would not boldly submit that when the common employer employed two servants the public element at once emerged. He said it was a question of degree and the courts must take account of the number of employees, the magnitude of the sum settled by the truster, the size of the employers' undertaking, the non-contractual personal relationships (or their absence) between the employer and his employees, and other circumstances. I am unable to find any logical principles in these submissions. ...The appellant's argument would lead to a degree of uncertainty in this branch of the law which only compelling authority or logical necessity would induce me to accept.

8.3 Wholly and Exclusively Charitable

The purpose of the trust must not only be charitable: it must be wholly and exclusively charitable. This causes problems where the testator has given a fund for purposes which are charitable *or* for purposes which are not, as the trustees might apply the fund wholly for purposes other than purely charitable ones. If they could, the trust will be void unless it can be said to be a valid non-charitable purpose trust. But if the testator leaves a fund for 'charitable *and* benevolent' purposes, those purposes are exclusively charitable, as the purposes must not only be benevolent: they must *also* be charitable. If the language of the trust permits, it may be possible to sever the charitable from the non-charitable gift and apply part of the fund to the charitable purpose, as in *Salusbury v Denton* (1857) 3 K&J 529.

Chichester Diocesan Fund and Board of Finance v Simpson [1944] AC 341

Panel: Viscount Simon LC, Lord Macmillan, Lord Wright, Lord Porter and Lord Simonds

Facts: Caleb Diplock left the residue of his estate to his executors and directed them to apply it 'for such charitable institution or institutions or benevolent objects' as they in their absolute discretion select. After the estate had been distributed among 139 benevolent institutions, the next of kin claimed to be entitled to the residue on the basis that the charitable trusts were void and the money was therefore held on resulting trust for them on intestacy. The House of Lords held that the gift of the residue was void for uncertainty and did not fall within the 'charitable' exception as it was not exclusively for charitable purposes.

LORD SIMONDS

… I approach this will, as I approach any other will, with the resolve to find the testator's intention from the language that he has used. When I have found it, I consider its effect. If there is an ambiguity, it may be that I am at liberty to choose that construction which will give legal effect to the instrument rather than that which will invalidate it. Where the testator's words would, if no question of invalidity arose, leave no doubt in my mind, I am not at liberty to create an ambiguity in order then to place what is sometimes called a benignant construction on the will.

My Lords, the words for your consideration are "charitable or benevolent." The question is whether, in the context in which they are found in this will, these words give to the executors a choice of objects extending beyond that which the law recognizes as charitable. If they do not, that is the end of the matter. The trust is a good charitable trust. If they do, it appears to be conceded by counsel for the appellant institution that the trust is invalid, but, in deference to the argument of the Attorney-General, who invited your Lordships to take a different view, I must say a few words at a later stage. My Lords, of those three words your Lordships will have no doubt what the first, "charitable," means. It is a term of art with a technical meaning and that is the meaning which the testator must be assumed to have intended. If it were not so, if in this will "charitable" were to be given, not its legal, but some popular, meaning, it would not be possible to establish the validity of the bequest. The last of the three words "benevolent" is not a term of art. In its ordinary meaning it has a range in some respects far less wide than legal charity, in others somewhat wider. It is, at least, clear that the two words, the one here used in its technical meaning, the other having only, and, accordingly, here used in, a popular meaning, are by no means coterminous. These two words are joined or separated by the word "or," a particle, of which the primary function is to co-ordinate two or more words between which there is an alternative. It is, I think, the only word in our language apt to have this effect. Its primary and ordinary meaning is the same, whether or not the first alternative is preceded by the word "either."

My Lords, averting my mind from the possible ill effects of an alternative choice between objects "charitable" and objects "benevolent," I cannot doubt that the plain meaning of the testator's words is that he has given this choice, and that, if he intended to give it, he could have used no words more apt to do so. Is there, then, anything in the context which narrows the area of choice by giving to the words "or benevolent" some other meaning than that which they primarily and naturally have? And if so, what is the other meaning which is to be given to them?

He examined the contention that 'or' was not to be used in its ordinary meaning, but as an explanatory word, equivalent to 'otherwise called'. This interpretation would mean that 'benevolent' means the same as charitable so the trust could be interpreted as being wholly charitable. His Lordship refused to accept this interpretation.

Then it was suggested that the words "or benevolent" should be construed as equivalent to "provided such objects are also of a benevolent character" that is to say, the objects must be charitable but of that order of charity which is commonly called benevolent. I think that this is only a roundabout way of saying that "or" should be read as "and," that the objects of choice must have the two characteristics of charitable and benevolent. It is possible that a context may justify so drastic a change as that involved in reading the disjunctive as conjunctive. I turn then to the context to see what justification it affords for reading the relevant words in any but their natural meaning. Reading and re-reading them, as your Lordships have so often done in the course of this case, I can find nothing which justifies such a departure. ... On the plain reading of this will I could only come to the conclusion that the testator intended exclusively to benefit charitable objects if I excised the words "or benevolent" which he has used. That I cannot do.

Coming to the conclusion that, on the true construction of this will, the executors may, if they think fit, distribute the testator's estate among objects which are benevolent but not charitable, I then ask what is in law the effect of such a disposition. My Lords, it may not have come as so rude a shock to some of your Lordships as it did to me to hear it suggested that there could be any doubt but that it is utterly invalid, but, in fact, the learned Attorney-General, if I understood his argument, categorically invited your Lordships to hold that a bequest for charitable or benevolent objects simpliciter is in English law a good and effective bequest, and urged that *In re Jarman's Estate* which decided the contrary should be over-ruled. In other words, his contention was that to enlarge the executors' area of choice so as to include benevolent objects which are not charitable with objects which are charitable does not make the whole gift fail for uncertainty. I do not see how, if his proposition is a sound one, it could be limited to the introduction of benevolent objects. Philanthropic objects, liberal objects, perhaps patriotic or public objects, must come within the scope of this new doctrine. Nor, if a gift for charitable or benevolent objects is valid, could it be any longer contended with any show of logic that a gift for benevolent objects alone is invalid. My Lords, I suggest that this proposition runs counter to authority and principle.

Salusbury v Denton (1857) 3 K&J 529

Panel: Sir Page Wood V-C

Facts: Mr Burroughs left part of the proceeds of an insurance policy upon trust for his wife, directing that she was to apply part either during her life or by her will, 'to the foundation of a charity school or such other charitable endowment for the benefit of the poor of Offley as she may prefer…'. The remainder was to be held for the benefit of relatives. Mr Burroughs directed his wife to choose how the fund should be split between these charitable and non-charitable purposes. She died without appointing, and without making a will. The question for the court was whether the fund could be severed and the charitable purpose upheld. It was held that it was possible to sever the gift and uphold the charitable purpose where the words show an intention to create separate funds, as here. The fund was divided into two equal parts, on the basis that equality is equity.

Link

See *Chichester* where there was an either/or case – it was possible to give the whole fund to the non-charitable purpose

SIR PAGE WOOD V-C

The first question that was argued was whether, as to the part intended by the testator for charitable purposes, the gift was or was not void; and as to this part of the case I have no doubt, as I said at the close of the argument, that it was not void, because under the terms of the will the widow had an option — she was at liberty to apply that part "to the foundation of a charity school, *or* such other charitable endowment," as in the will mentioned. And whatever may be the effect of the words "foundation of a charity school" occurring in the first branch of that alternative it is clear as to the second — the foundation of a charitable endowment — that a bequest for such a purpose would be a lawful bequest…

The judge then turned to the question whether the bequest was void for uncertainty on the basis that the testator had not specified which part should be applied for charitable purposes and which for private purposes, referring to two apparently conflicting cases:

The first of these — the case of *Doyley* v *The Attorney-General* — was very similar to the present. There the property in question was bequeathed in trust for certain purposes, and, subject thereto, the trustees and the survivor of them, and the heirs and executors of the survivor, were to dispose of it to such of his relations of his mother's side who were most deserving, and in such manner as they thought fit, *and* for such charitable uses and purposes as they should also think most proper and convenient; and the Master of the Rolls (Sir Joseph Jekyll) directed that one-half of the estate should go to the testator's relatives on the mother's side, and the other half to charitable uses; the known rule that equality is equity being, as he said, the best measure to go by.

It appears to me that there is no possibility of distinguishing that case from the present; for there can be no substantial difference between a direction to dispose of property to such relations and for such charitable purposes as the trustees should think most proper, and a direction like the present, to apply "a part" to such charitable purposes "and the remainder" among relatives with a like discretion. The two cases cannot be distinguished.

The case of *Down v Worrall* (1 My. & Kee. 561) will be found on examination not to conflict with that to which I have last referred. In *Down v Worrall* the testator left part of his residuary personal estate to his trustees to settle it either to or for charitable or pious purposes, at their discretion, or otherwise for the separate benefit of his sister and all or any of her children, in such manner as his trustees should think fit. And there it was held that a sum which remained at the decease of the surviving trustee, and which had not been applied either to charitable purposes or for the benefit of the testator's sister and her children, was undisposed of, and belonged to the testator's next of kin.

Now, whether that case can or cannot be reconciled with all the others on this subject, it is very clearly distinguished from the present: for it is one thing to direct a trustee to give *a part* of a fund to one set of objects *and the remainder* to another, and it is a distinct thing to direct him to give "either" to one set of objects "or" to another. *Down v Worrall* was a case of the latter description. There the trustees could give all to either of the objects. This is a case of the former description. Here the trustee was bound to give a part to each.

Link
see *Chichester*

I am therefore of opinion that, even if the case of *Down v Worrall* can be reconciled with the other authorities on this subject, it cannot affect my decision in the case before me. Here there is a plain direction to the widow to give a part to the charitable purposes referred to in the will as she may think fit, and the remainder among the testator's relatives as she may direct. And the widow having died without exercising that discretion, the moiety in question must be divided equally.

8.4 Trusts for Political Purposes

If the main object of an organisation is political, it cannot be said to be for charitable purposes. The following cases consider what 'counts' as political. Both cases contain lengthy dicta on 'public benefit' but these extracts focus on the issue of whether political purposes can be charitable.

National Anti-Vivisection Society v Inland Revenue Commissioners [1948] AC 31

Panel: Viscount Simon, Lord Wright, Lord Porter, Lord Simonds and Lord Normand

Facts: The National Anti-Vivisection Society had the main aim of changing the law to ban vivisection, campaigning for the repeal of the Cruelty to Animals Act 1876 which allowed experiments on live animals without anaesthetic in certain circumstances. The

Society claimed exemption from income tax on the basis that it was established for charitable purposes only, which gave it exemption under the Income Tax Act 1918. The court held that the society was not charitable for two reasons: first, the main object was political in that it campaigned for a change in the law; second, because any benefit to public morals was outweighed by the detriment to medical science and public health.

LORD SIMONDS

The first and shorter point is whether a main purpose of the society is of such a political character that the court cannot regard it as charitable. To this point little attention was directed in the courts below. It is mentioned only in the judgment of the learned Master of the Rolls. As will appear in the course of this opinion, it is worthy of more serious debate. ...

My Lords, on the first point the learned Master of the Rolls cites in his judgment a passage from the speech of Lord Parker in *Bowman v Secular Society, Ld*:

"A trust for the attainment of political objects has always been held invalid, not because it is illegal .... but because the court has no means of judging whether a proposed change in the law will or will not be for the public benefit."

 Alert

Lord Parker is here considering the possibility of a valid charitable trust and nothing else and when he says "has always been held invalid" he means "has always been held not to be a valid charitable trust." The learned Master of the Rolls found this authoritative statement upon a branch of the law, with which no one was more familiar than Lord Parker, to be inapplicable to the present case for two reasons, first, because he felt difficulty in applying the words to "a change in the law which is in common parlance a 'non-political' question," and secondly, because he thought they could not in any case apply, when the desired legislation is "merely ancillary to the attainment of what is ex hypothesi a good charitable object."

My Lords, if I may deal with this second reason first, I cannot agree that in this case an alteration in the law is merely ancillary to the attainment of a good charitable object. In a sense no doubt, since legislation is not an end in itself, every law may be regarded as ancillary to the object which its provisions are intended to achieve. But that is not the sense in which it is said that a society has a political object. Here the finding of the commissioners is itself conclusive. "We are satisfied," they say, "that the main object of the society is the total abolition of vivisection .... and (for that purpose) the repeal of the Cruelty to Animals Act, 1876 , and the substitution of a new enactment prohibiting vivisection altogether." This is a finding that the main purpose of the society is the compulsory abolition of vivisection by Act of Parliament. What else can it mean? and how else can it be supposed that vivisection is to be abolished? Abolition and suppression are words that connote some form of compulsion. It can only be by Act of Parliament that that element can be supplied. ...

My Lords, I see no reason for supposing that Lord Parker in the cited passage used the expression "political objects" in any narrow sense or was confining it to objects of acute political controversy. On the contrary he was, I think, propounding familiar doctrine, nowhere better stated than in a text-book, [*Tyssen on Charitable Bequests*] ...

Lord Parker uses slightly different language but means the same thing, when he says that the court has no means of judging whether a proposed change in the law will or will not be for the public benefit. It is not for the court to judge and the court has no means of judging. The same question may be looked at from a slightly different angle. One of the tests, and a crucial test, whether a trust is charitable, lies in the competence of the court to control and reform it. ...But, my Lords, is it for a moment to be supposed that it is the function of the Attorney-General on behalf of the Crown to intervene and demand that a trust shall be established and administered by the court, the object of which is to alter the law in a manner highly prejudicial, as he and His Majesty's Government may think, to the welfare of the state? This very case would serve as an example, if upon the footing that it was a charitable trust it became the duty of the Attorney-General on account of its maladministration to intervene. There is undoubtedly a paucity of judicial authority on this point. ...But in truth the reason of the thing appears to me so clear that I neither expect nor require much authority. I conclude upon this part of the case that a main object of the society is political and for that reason the society is not established for charitable purposes only.

McGovern v Attorney General [1982] Ch 321

Panel: Slade J

Facts: The human rights organisation Amnesty International was advised that certain of its purposes were charitable and in 1977 the Amnesty International Trust Declaration was executed. The purposes were stated to be the relief of needy people who had recently been prisoners of conscience, and their families; attempting to secure the release of others; and procuring the abolition of torture. They applied to register the trust as a charity. The Charity Commissioners refused this as the main object of the trust was political: to procure a change in government policy and alter the law both in the UK and abroad. The judge accepted that the relief of human suffering could in principle be charitable within the spirit of the preamble to the Statute of Elizabeth, but that in itself was not sufficient: there must also be an element of public benefit. He surveyed the 'political purposes' cases at length.

MR JUSTICE SLADE

...[T]he court will not regard as charitable a trust of which a main object is to procure an alteration of the law of the United Kingdom for one or both of two reasons: first, the court will ordinarily have no sufficient means of judging as a matter of evidence whether the proposed change will or will not be for the public benefit. Secondly, even if the evidence suffices to enable it to form a prima facie opinion that a change in the law is desirable, it must still decide the case on the principle that the law is right as it stands, since to do otherwise would usurp the functions of the legislature. ...

 Alert

Thus far, the only types of political trust to which I have directed specific attention have been those of which a main object is to procure a change in the law of this country.

The principles established by *Bowman's case* [1917] AC 406 and the *National Anti-Vivisection Society* case [1948] AC 31 will render such trusts non-charitable whether or not they are of a party-political nature. Conversely, however, several cases cited to me illustrate that trusts of which a main object is to promote the interests of a particular political party in this country fail to achieve charitable status, even though they are not directed towards any particular change in English law: see, for example, *Bonar Law Memorial Trust v Inland Revenue Commissioners* (1933) 17 TC 508, and *In re Hopkinson, decd.* [1949] 1 All ER 346. In my judgment any such trusts are plainly "political trusts" within the spirit, if not the letter, of Lord Parker of Waddington's pronouncement, and the same reasons for the court's refusing to enforce them would apply, but a fortiori. Since their nature would ex hypothesi be very controversial, the court could be faced with even greater difficulties in determining whether the objects of the trust would be for the public benefit; correspondingly, it would be at even greater risk of encroaching on the functions of the legislature and prejudicing its reputation for political impartiality, if it were to promote such objects by enforcing the trust.

I now turn to consider the status of a trust of which a main object is to secure the alteration of the laws of a *foreign* country. The mere fact that the trust was intended to be carried out abroad would not by itself necessarily deprive it of charitable status. ... The point with which I am at present concerned is whether a trust of which a direct and main object is to secure a change in the laws of a foreign country can *ever* be regarded as charitable under English law. Though I do not think that any authority cited to me precisely covers the point, I have come to the clear conclusion that it cannot.

... There is no obligation on the court to decide on the principle that any foreign law is ex hypothesi right as it stands; it is not obliged for all purposes to blind itself to what it may regard as the injustice of a particular foreign law.

In my judgment, however, there remain overwhelming reasons why such a trust still cannot be regarded as charitable. All the reasoning of Lord Parker of Waddington in *Bowman v Secular Society Ltd* [1917] AC 406 seems to me to apply a fortiori in such a case. A fortiori the court will have no adequate means of judging whether a proposed change in the law of a foreign country will or will not be for the public benefit. ...[T]he community which has to be considered in this context, even in the case of a trust to be executed abroad, is the community of the United Kingdom. Assuming that this is the right test, the court in applying it would still be bound to take account of the probable effects of attempts to procure the proposed legislation, or of its actual enactment, on the inhabitants of the country concerned, which would doubtless have a history and social structure quite different from that of the United Kingdom. Whatever might be its view as to the content of the relevant law from the standpoint of an English lawyer, it would, I think, have no satisfactory means of judging such probable effects upon the local community.

Furthermore, before ascribing charitable status to an English trust of which a main object was to secure the alteration of a foreign law, the court would also, I conceive, be bound to consider the consequences for this country as a matter of public policy. In a number of such cases there would arise a substantial prima facie risk that such a trust, if enforced, could prejudice the relations of this country with the foreign country concerned: ... For all these reasons, I conclude that a trust of which a main purpose is to procure a change in the laws of a foreign country is a trust for the attainment of political objects within the spirit of Lord Parker of Waddington's pronouncement and, as such, is non-charitable.

... If a principal purpose of a trust is to procure a reversal of government policy or of particular administrative decisions of governmental authorities, does it constitute a trust for political purposes falling within the spirit of Lord Parker's pronouncement? In my judgment it does. If a trust of this nature is to be executed in England, the court will ordinarily have no sufficient means of determining whether the desired reversal would be beneficial to the public, and in any event could not properly encroach on the functions of the executive, acting intra vires, by holding that it should be acting in some other manner. If it is a trust which is to be executed abroad, the court will not have sufficient means of satisfactorily judging, as a matter of evidence, whether the proposed reversal would be beneficial to the community in the relevant sense, after all its consequences, local and international, had been taken into account. ...

I think one is again driven to the conclusion that trusts of the nature now under discussion, which are to be executed abroad, cannot qualify as charities any more than if they are to be executed in this country. The court, in considering whether particular methods of carrying out or reforming them would be for the public benefit, would be faced with an inescapable dilemma, of which a hypothetical example may be given. It appears from the Amnesty International Report 1978, p. 270, that Islamic law sanctions the death penalty for certain well-defined offences, namely, murder, adultery and brigandage. Let it be supposed that a trust were created of which the object was to secure the abolition of the death penalty for adultery in those countries where Islamic law applies, and to secure a reprieve for those persons who have been sentenced to death for this offence. The court, when invited to enforce or to reform such a trust, would either have to apply English standards as to public benefit, which would not necessarily be at all appropriate in the local conditions, or would have to attempt to apply local standards, of which it knew little or nothing. An English court would not, it seems to me, be competent either to control or reform a trust of this nature, and it would not be appropriate that it should attempt to do so.

This is limited to trusts of which the *purposes* are political. The fact that the trustees may employ political *means* in furthering the non-political purposes will not necessarily render it non-charitable.

Further Reading

Charities Act 2006 Explanatory Notes

Charity Commission Guidance on Public Benefit, 16.1 2008

Charity Commission Guidance on acceptable political campaigning by charities

9

Resulting Trusts

Topic List

Introduction

Unlike express trusts, which arise as a consequence of the settlor's express intention for property to be held on trust, resulting and constructive trusts arise by operation of law. What this essentially means is that despite a lack of adherence to the rules regarding formalities and constitution, the courts will imply a trust to come into existence in various situations.

As the noted academic Birks clarified in his work on English Private Law, the word 'resulting' in the context of resulting trusts derives from the Latin word *resilare*, which means to 'jump back'. A resulting trust therefore describes the situation where beneficial interest in the property jumps back to the person who was absolute owner of the property immediately before legal title was transferred to the trustee.

9.1 Types of Resulting Trust

An attempt to categorise the situations in which a resulting trust comes in to existence was made by Megarry J in *Re Vandervell's Trusts (No 2)* [1974] Ch 269.

Re Vandervell's Trusts (No 2) [1974] Ch 269

Panel: Megarry J

Statute: Law of Property Act 1925 s 53(1)(c)

Facts: After the resulting trust of the shares in his company was found in favour of Mr Vandervell in *Vandervell v Inland Revenue Commissioners* [1967] 2 AC 291, Mr Vandervell had these shares registered for the benefit of his children. He then exercised his control over the company by declaring dividends over the shares that eventually amounted to over a million pounds, which were held on trust for his children. As a belt and braces approach to ensure the Inland Revenue Commissioners did not think that he had any interest in the shares, Vandervell then executed a deed stating all interest in the shares and any dividends had been assigned and released from his ownership.

Link
See Chapter 3

Having thought he had provided for his children Vandervell subsequently changed his will, leaving the majority of his estate to his second wife, with only a small amount of the estate going to the children. Vandervell died a short time later.

After his death, the executors of Vandervell's will argued that nothing done regarding the shares had displaced Vandervell's interest in them. Therefore they had not been held on trust for his children, but instead made up part of his estate. Consequently, his second wife was entitled to the shares.

It was held that the second wife was entitled to the shares. However, it must be noted that this decision was reversed in the Court of Appeal. The relevant part of this High Court judgment is how resulting trusts can be categorised, which received no adverse comment from the Court of Appeal.

MR JUSTICE MEGARRY

... It seems to me that the relevant points on resulting trusts may be put in a series of propositions which, so far as not directly supported, appear at least to be consistent with Lord Wilberforce's speech, and reconcilable with the true intent of Lord Upjohn's speech, though it may not be with all his words on a literal reading. The propositions are the broadest of generalisations, and do not purport to cover the exceptions and qualifications that doubtless exist. Nevertheless, these generalisations at least provide a starting point for the classification of a corner of equity which might benefit from some attempt at classification. The propositions are as follows.

(1) If a transaction fails to make any effective disposition of any interest it does nothing. This is so at law and in equity, and has nothing to do with resulting trusts.

(2) Normally the mere existence of some unexpressed intention in the breast of the owner of the property does nothing: there must at least be some expression of that intention before it can effect any result. To yearn is not to transfer.

(3) Before any doctrine of resulting trust can come into play, there must at least be some effective transaction which transfers or creates some interest in property.

(4) Where A effectually transfers to B (or creates in his favour) any interest in any property, whether legal or equitable, a resulting trust for A may arise in two distinct classes of case. For simplicity, I shall confine my statement to cases in which the transfer or creation is made without B providing any valuable consideration, and where no presumption of advancement can arise; and I shall state the position for transfers without specific mention of the creation of new interests.

(a) The first class of case is where the transfer to B is not made on any trust. If, of course, it appears from the transfer that B is intended to hold on certain trusts, that will be decisive, and the case is not within this category; and similarly if it appears that B is intended to take beneficially. But in other cases there is the rebuttable presumption that B holds on a resulting trust for A, The question is not one of the automatic consequences of a dispositive failure by A, but one of presumption: the property has been carried to B, and from the absence of consideration and any presumption of advancement B is presumed not only to hold the entire interest on trust, but also to hold the beneficial interest for A absolutely. The presumption thus establishes both that A is to take on trust and also what that trust is. Such resulting trusts may be called "presumed resulting trusts."

(b) The second class of case is where the transfer to B is made on trusts which leave some or all of the beneficial interest undisposed of. Here B automatically holds on a resulting trust for A to the extent that the beneficial interest has not been carried to him or others. The resulting trust here does not depend on any intentions or presumptions, but is the automatic consequence of A's failure to dispose of what is vested in him. Since *ex hypothesi* the transfer is on trust, the resulting trust does not establish the trust but merely carries back to A the beneficial interest that has not been disposed of. Such resulting trusts may be called "automatic resulting trusts."

(5) Where trustees hold property in trust for A, and it is they who, at A's direction, make the transfer to B, similar principles apply, even though on the face of the transaction the transferor appears to be the trustee and not A. If the transfer to B is on trust, B will hold any beneficial interest that has not been effectually disposed of on an automatic resulting trust for the true transferor, A. If the transfer to B is not on trust, there will be a rebuttable presumption that B holds on a resulting trust for A.

In essence Megarry J held that resulting trusts arose in two different scenarios. The first scenario can be categorized as 'presumed' resulting trusts. In this type of resulting trust there is a rebuttable presumption that where property is placed in the name of another person, that person will hold it on trust for the original owner. The second scenario can be categorized as 'automatic' resulting trusts. This type of resulting trust arises where there is a failure to dispose of the beneficial interest, either when the trust has been constituted but equitable title has not passed from the original absolute owner, or when there are assets remaining when the trust has come to an end.

This categorisation was doubted, however, in *Westdeutsche Landesbank Girozentrale v Islington LBC* [1996] AC 669.

Westdeutsche Landesbank Girozentrale v Islington LBC [1996] AC 669

Panel: Lord Goff of Chieveley, Lord Browne-Wilkinson, Lord Slynn of Hadley, Lord Woolf and Lord Lloyd of Berwick

Statute: Senior Courts Act 1981 s 35A

Facts: The local authority was one of many that borrowed money from a bank to supplement what it had received from central government in a complex transaction known as a credit swap agreement. These agreements were subsequently found to be void as local authorities did not have the powers to enter into them. The bank attempted to recover the sum of £1,145,525 from the local authority. The Court of Appeal held the bank was entitled to the money plus compound interest. The local authority appealed this on the ground that compound interest was only payable if there was a trust relationship between the bank and the local authority.

It was held that there was no trust relationship and therefore the bank only had a personal claim to the money. Consequently, only simple interest was payable on the sum lent to the local authority.

LORD BROWNE-WILKINSON

This is not a case where the bank had any equitable interest which pre-dated receipt by the local authority of the upfront payment. Therefore, in order to show that the local authority became a trustee, the bank must demonstrate circumstances which raised a trust for the first time either at the date on which the local authority received the money or at the date on which payment into the mixed account was made. Counsel for the bank specifically disavowed any claim based on a constructive trust. This was plainly right because the local authority had no relevant knowledge sufficient to raise a constructive trust at any time before the moneys, upon the bank account going into overdraft, became untraceable. ... Therefore, as the argument for the bank recognised, the only possible trust which could be established was a resulting trust arising from the circumstances in which the local authority received the upfront payment.

Under existing law a resulting trust arises in two sets of circumstances: (A) where A makes a voluntary payment to B or pays (wholly or in part) for the purchase of property which is vested either in B alone or in the joint names of A and B, there is a presumption that A did not intend to make a gift to B: the money or property is held on trust for A (if he is the sole provider of the money) or in the case of a joint purchase by A and B in shares proportionate to their contributions. It is important to stress that this is only a *presumption*, which presumption is easily rebutted either by the counter-presumption of advancement or by direct evidence of A's intention to make an outright transfer... . (B) Where A transfers property to B *on express trusts*, but the trusts declared do not exhaust the whole beneficial interest... . Both types of resulting trust are traditionally regarded as examples of trusts giving effect to the common intention of the parties. A resulting trust is not imposed by law against the intentions of the trustee (as is a constructive trust) but gives effect to his presumed intention. Megarry J in *Re Vandervell's Trusts (No. 2)* suggests that a resulting trust of type (B) does not depend on intention but operates automatically. I am not convinced that this is right. If the settlor has expressly, or by necessary implication, abandoned any beneficial interest in the trust property, there is in my view no resulting trust: the undisposed-of equitable interest vests in the Crown as *bona vacantia*...

Alert

Applying these conventional principles of resulting trust to the present case, the bank's claim must fail. There was no transfer of money to the local authority on express trusts: therefore a resulting trust of type (B) above could not arise. As to type (A) above, any presumption of resulting trust is rebutted since it is demonstrated that the bank paid, and the local authority received, the upfront payment with the intention that the moneys so paid should become the absolute property of the local authority. It is true that the parties were under a misapprehension that the payment was made in pursuance of a valid contract. But that does not alter the actual intentions of the parties at the date the payment was made or the moneys were mixed in the bank account.

As no trust was found, these statements are strictly *obiter*. Furthermore, the statement on resulting trusts made by Lord Browne-Wilkinson can be criticized as being conceptually wrong. These criticisms can be split into two categories.

Firstly, Lord Browne-Wilkinson has suggested that where there are undisposed of assets that would come within an 'automatic' resulting trust under Megarry J's classification, these would go as *bona vacantia* to the Crown. Whilst there is some High Court authority that agrees with this, such as *Re West Sussex Constabulary's Widows, Children and Benevolent (1930) Fund Trusts* [1971] Ch 1, there is House of lords authority in *Vandervell v Inland Revenue Commissioners* that property will be found to go on resulting trust to the original owner rather than to the Crown *bona vacantia*. Indeed, on the facts Vandervell wanted anybody but himself to be the beneficial owner of the shares, yet the House of Lords held that he would be the beneficiary of a resulting trust.

Link
See Chapter 3 and 7

The second point of criticism of Lord Browne-Wilkinson's judgment is his statement that resulting trusts give effect to the common intention of the parties. With respect, this must be wrong. There is House of Lords authority, such as *McPhail v Doulton* [1971] AC 424, that states the overriding considerations of the Court are to give effect to the intentions of the settlor. Therefore only the settlor's intentions are relevant.

Link
See Chapter 2

It is therefore submitted that the classification given by Megarry J in *Re Vandervell's Trusts (No 2)* is to be preferred over Lord Browne-Wilkinson's *obiter* comments.

9.2 'Presumed' Resulting Trusts

To see how 'presumed' resulting trusts operate, please refer to *Bull v Bull* [1955] QB 234 in Chapter 10 of the casebook.

9.3 'Automatic' Resulting Trusts

A clear example of how 'automatic' resulting trusts work can be seen in *Vandervell v Inland Revenue Commissioners*. In this case, due to the fact there was no specified beneficiary of the shares, there was no valid declaration of trust due to a lack of certainty of object. However, another example of when an 'automatic' resulting trust will be found is in commercial practice, following a line of cases starting with *Barclays Bank v Quistclose Investments Ltd* [1970] AC 567.

Barclays Bank v Quistclose Investments Ltd [1970] AC 567

Panel: Lord Reid, Lord Morris of Borth-Y-Gest, Lord Guest, Lord Pearce and Lord Wilberforce

Facts: Rolls Razor was a company that was in serious financial difficulties. It had an overdraft with Barclays Bank of about £484,000. Rolls Razor negotiated with the financier Sir Isaac Woolfson for a loan of £1,000,000. The financier was willing to lend the money as long as Rolls Razor was able to source money for a dividend it had declared as a means of inspiring investor confidence. Rolls Razor procured a loan for £209,719 8s 3d from Quistclose on the condition the money was to be paid into a separate bank account and was only to be used for the purpose of paying the dividend.

The money was duly paid into a separate bank account set up by Barclays. After the account was created, Rolls Razor sent a letter to Barclays recording the agreement between Rolls Razor and Barclays bank that the money was to be used solely to pay the dividend. Subsequently, the cheque from Quistclose was paid into the account and cleared.

Before the dividend could be paid Rolls Razors went into voluntary liquidation. Barclays claimed the money in the account for the dividend to pay off part of the dividend. Quistclose went to court claiming that, since the dividend could no longer be paid, the money should return to Quistclose under a resulting trust.

It was held that there was a trust of the money given to pay the dividend. Since Rolls Razor was now in voluntary liquidation the money was now on trust for Quistclose instead of being available to pay Rolls Razor's debts.

LORD WILBERFORCE

Two questions arise, both of which must be answered favourably to the respondents if they are to recover the money from the bank. The first is whether as between the respondents and Rolls Razor Ltd. the terms upon which the loan was made were such as to impress upon the sum of £209,719 8s. 6d. a trust in their favour in the event of the dividend not being paid. The second is whether, in that event, the bank had such notice of the trust or of the circumstances giving rise to it as to make the trust binding upon them.

It is not difficult to establish precisely upon what terms the money was advanced by the respondents to Rolls Razor Ltd There is no doubt that the loan was made specifically in order to enable Rolls Razor Ltd to pay the dividend. There is equally, in my opinion, no doubt that the loan was made only so as to enable Rolls Razor Ltd to pay the dividend and for no other purpose. This follows quite clearly from the terms of the letter of Rolls Razor Ltd to the bank of July 15, 1964, which letter, before transmission to the bank, was sent to the respondents under open cover in order that the cheque might be (as it was) enclosed in it. The mutual intention of the respondents and of Rolls Razor Ltd, and the essence of the bargain, was that the sum advanced should not become part of the assets of Rolls Razor Ltd, but should be used exclusively for payment of a particular class of its creditors, namely, those entitled to the dividend. A necessary consequence from this, by process simply of interpretation, must be that if, for any reason, the dividend could not be paid, the money was to be returned to the respondents: the word "only" or "exclusively" can have no other meaning or effect.

That arrangements of this character for the payment of a person's creditors by a third person, give rise to a relationship of a fiduciary character or trust, in favour, as a primary trust, of the creditors, and secondarily, if the primary trust fails, of the third person, has been recognised in a series of cases over some 150 years. ...

The second, and main, argument for the appellant was of a more sophisticated character. The transaction, it was said, between the respondents and Rolls Razor Ltd, was one of loan, giving rise to a legal action of debt. This necessarily excluded the implication of any trust, enforceable in equity, in the respondents' favour: a transaction may attract one action or the other, it could not admit of both.

My Lords, I must say that I find this argument unattractive. Let us see what it involves. It means that the law does not permit an arrangement to be made by which one person agrees to advance money to another, on terms that the money is to be used exclusively to pay debts of the latter, and if, and so far as not so used, rather than becoming a general asset of the latter available to his creditors at large, is to be returned to the lender. The lender is obliged, in such a case, because he is a lender, to accept, whatever the mutual wishes of lender and borrower may be, that the money he was willing to make available for one purpose only shall be freely available for others of the borrower's creditors for whom he has not the slightest desire to provide.

I should be surprised if an argument of this kind – so conceptualist in character - had ever been accepted. In truth it has plainly been rejected by the eminent judges who from 1819 onwards have permitted arrangements of this type to be enforced, and have approved them as being for the benefit of creditors and all concerned. There is surely no difficulty in recognising the co-existence in one transaction of legal and equitable rights and remedies: when the money is advanced, the lender acquires an equitable right to see that it is applied for the primary designated purpose... if the primary purpose cannot be carried out, the question arises if a secondary purpose (i.e., repayment to the lender) has been agreed, expressly or by implication: if it has, the remedies of equity may be invoked to give effect to it, if it has not (and the money is intended to fall within the general fund of the debtor's assets) then there is the appropriate remedy for recovery of a loan. I can appreciate no reason why the flexible interplay of law and equity cannot let in these practical arrangements, and other variations if desired: it would be to the discredit of both systems if they could not. In the present case the intention to create a secondary trust for the benefit of the lender, to arise if the primary trust, to pay the dividend, could not be carried out, is clear and I can find no reason why the law should not give effect to it.

I pass to the second question, that of notice. ... It is common ground, and I think right, that a mere request to put the money into a separate account is not sufficient to constitute notice. But on July 15, 1964, the bank, when it received the cheque, also received the covering letter of that date which I have set out above: previously there had been the telephone conversation between Mr Goldbart and Mr Parker, to which I have also referred. From these there is no doubt that the bank was told that the money had been provided on loan by a third person and was to be used only for the purpose of paying the dividend. This was sufficient to give them notice that it was trust money and not assets of Rolls Razor Ltd.

Quistclose was therefore able to claim the money as beneficiaries of a resulting trust and the case established that where money has been lent for a specific purpose and the money was paid into a separate bank account, then if some or all of the money was not used for the specified purpose it was held on resulting trust for the lender. If the money was used for a specified purpose, however, the trust relationship came to an end and the relationship between the lender and the debtor was that of an ordinary unsecured loan.

This has the important consequence of affecting the ability of the lender to get the money back. Once the money has been used as specified, the lender no longer has the advantage of a proprietary claim against the money. The lender will not be able to take priority over the ordinary unsecured creditors of the debtor. Instead, the lender must share with all the other debtor's creditors what assets are available if the debtor becomes insolvent. The harsh practicality of this is that an unsecured creditor sees little, if any, return for the money that was originally lent if the debtor becomes insolvent.

Whilst the finding of the existence of this type of trust has clear commercial advantages to those wanting to engage in credit relationships, there are elements of uncertainty as to how these types of trust apply. This first major issue is how Lord Wilberforce described how *Quistclose* trusts work. If we accept his belief that *Quistclose* trusts start as a primary trust, then we have to accept that the primary trust could possibly be to fulfil a purpose, such as the paying off of a dividend in *Quistclose* itself. This is inherently problematic as it would allow private purpose trusts to exist outside of the limitations described in *Re Endacott* [1960] Ch 232. The courts have therefore tried to find alternative interpretations for how *Quistclose* trusts operate.

Link
See Chapter 6

Twinsectra v Yardley and Others [2002] 2 AC 164

Panel: Lord Slynn of Hadley, Lord Steyn, Lord Hoffmann, Lord Hutton and Lord Millett

Facts: Mr Yardley wanted to obtain a loan of £1,000,000 to purchase some land. Both Mr Yardley and his solicitor Mr Leach made applications for loans to various parties. Eventually they were successful in that Twinsectra was willing to lend the entire sum. However, Twinsectra wanted a solicitor's personal undertaking from Mr Leach to protect Twinsectra in the event of Yardley defaulting on the loan. Mr Leach was unwilling to agree to such an undertaking so Mr Yardley contacted a second solicitor, Mr Sims. Mr Sims was willing to provide an undertaking, as he had worked with Mr Yardley in the past and owed Mr Yardley about $1,500,000. The loan was agreed with the agreement that the money was to be used for the sole purpose of acquiring property and that the money was to be retained by Mr Sims until Mr Yardley acquired the property.

The money was consequently paid to Mr Sims, who in breach of his undertaking transferred the money to Mr Leach. Mr Sims faxed a copy of the undertaking to Mr Leach, but since the undertaking had no reference to Mr Leach at all he felt he was not bound by what it said. Mr Leach therefore felt he was merely holding the money subject to Mr Yardley's instruction, and when Mr Yardley asked for the money Mr Leach transferred it to him. Mr Yardley then began to spend some of the money contrary to the instructions in the undertaking. Mr Yardley defaulted on the loan and Twinsectra tried to claim their money back, firstly through a proprietary claim for whatever money remained in Mr Yardley's account and secondly against Mr Leach for assisting a breach of trust.

Link
See Chapter 16

It was held that there was a *Quistclose* trust of the money and therefore whatever money was left in Mr Yardley's account that was identifiable as belonging to Twinsectra was subject to a resulting trust. Twinsectra were therefore able to take priority over Mr Yardley's unsecured creditors in claiming this part of the loan money back.

LORD MILLETT

52 My Lords, there are two issues in this appeal. The first is concerned with the nature of the so-called "Quistclose trust" and the requirements for its creation. The second arises only if the first is answered adversely to the appellant. It is whether his conduct rendered him liable for having assisted in a breach of trust. ...

68 Money advanced by way of loan normally becomes the property of the borrower. He is free to apply the money as he chooses, and save to the extent to which he may have taken security for repayment the lender takes the risk of the borrower's insolvency. But it is well established that a loan to a borrower for a specific purpose where the borrower is not free to apply the money for any other purpose gives rise to fiduciary obligations on the part of the borrower which a court of equity will enforce. In the earlier cases the purpose was to enable the borrower to pay his creditors or some of them, but the principle is not limited to such cases.

69 Such arrangements are commonly described as creating "a Quistclose trust", after the well known decision of the House in Quistclose Investments Ltd v Rolls Razor Ltd [1970] AC 567 in which Lord Wilberforce confirmed the validity of such arrangements and explained their legal consequences. When the money is advanced, the lender acquires a right, enforceable in equity, to see that it is applied for the stated purpose, or more accurately to prevent its application for any other purpose. This prevents the borrower from obtaining any beneficial interest in the money, at least while the designated purpose is still capable of being carried out. Once the purpose has been carried out, the lender has his normal remedy in debt. If for any reason the purpose cannot be carried out, the question arises whether the money falls within the general fund of the borrower's assets, in which case it passes to his trustee in bankruptcy in the event of his insolvency and the lender is merely a loan creditor; or whether it is held on a resulting trust for the lender. This depends on the intention of the parties collected from the terms of the arrangement and the circumstances of the case.

70 In the present case Twinsectra contends that paragraphs 1 and 2 of the undertaking which Mr Sims signed on 24 December created a Quistclose trust. Mr Leach denies this and advances a number of objections to the existence of a trust. He says that Twinsectra lacked the necessary intention to create a trust, and relies on evidence that Twinsectra looked exclusively to Mr Sims' personal undertaking to repay the loan as its security for repayment. He says that commercial life would be impossible if trusts were lightly inferred from slight material, and that it is not enough to agree that a loan is to be made for a particular purpose. There must be something more, for example, a requirement that the money be paid into a segregated account, before it is appropriate to infer that a trust has been created. In the present case the money was paid into Mr Sims' client account, but that is sufficiently explained by the fact that it was not Mr Sims' money but his client's; it provides no basis for an inference that the money was held in trust for anyone other than Mr Yardley. Then it is said that a trust requires certainty of objects and this was lacking, for the stated purpose "to be applied in the purchase of property" is too uncertain to be enforced. Finally it is said that no trust in favour of Twinsectra could arise prior to the failure of the stated purpose, and this did not occur until the money was misapplied by Mr Yardley's companies.

Intention

71 The first two objections are soon disposed of. A settlor must, of course, possess the necessary intention to create a trust, but his subjective intentions are irrelevant. If he enters into arrangements which have the effect of creating a trust, it is not necessary

that he should appreciate that they do so; it is sufficient that he intends to enter into them. Whether paragraphs 1 and 2 of the undertaking created a *Quistclose* trust turns on the true construction of those paragraphs.

72 The fact that Twinsectra relied for its security exclusively on Mr Sims's personal liability to repay goes to Twinsectra's subjective intention and is not relevant to the construction of the undertaking, but it is in any case not inconsistent with the trust alleged. Arrangements of this kind are not intended to provide security for repayment of the loan, but to prevent the money from being applied otherwise than in accordance with the lender's wishes. If the money is properly applied the loan is unsecured. This was true of all the decided cases, including the *Quistclose* case itself.

The effect of the undertaking

73 A *Quistclose* trust does not necessarily arise merely because money is paid for a particular purpose. A lender will often inquire into the purpose for which a loan is sought in order to decide whether he would be justified in making it. He may be said to lend the money for the purpose in question, but this is not enough to create a trust; once lent the money is at the free disposal of the borrower. Similarly payments in advance for goods or services are paid for a particular purpose, but such payments do not ordinarily create a trust. The money is intended to be at the free disposal of the supplier and may be used as part of his cashflow. Commercial life would be impossible if this were not the case.

74 The question in every case is whether the parties intended the money to be at the free disposal of the recipient. ...

75 In the present case paragraphs 1 and 2 of the undertaking are crystal clear. Mr Sims undertook that the money would be used solely for the acquisition of property *and for no other purpose*; and was to be retained by his firm until so applied. It would not be held by Mr Sims simply to Mr Yardley's order; and it would not be at Mr Yardley's free disposition. Any payment by Mr Sims of the money, whether to Mr Yardley or anyone else, otherwise than for the acquisition of property would constitute a breach of trust. ...

The nature of the trust

77 ... They call for an exploration of the true nature of the *Quistclose* trust, and in particular the location of the beneficial interest while the purpose is still capable of being carried out.

78 This has been the subject of much academic debate. The starting point is provided by two passages in Lord Wilberforce's speech in the *Quistclose* case [1970] AC 567. ...

79 ... [T]here are two successive trusts, a primary trust for payment to identifiable beneficiaries, such as creditors or shareholders, and a secondary trust in favour of the lender arising on the failure of the primary trust. But there are formidable difficulties in this analysis, which has little academic support. What if the primary trust is not for identifiable persons, but as in the present case to carry out an abstract purpose?

Where in such a case is the beneficial interest pending the application of the money for the stated purpose or the failure of the purpose? There are four possibilities: (i) in the lender; (ii) in the borrower; (iii) in the contemplated beneficiary; or (iv) in suspense.

80 (i) *The lender*. In "The *Quistclose* Trust: Who Can Enforce It?" (1985) 101 LQR, 269, I argued that the beneficial interest remained throughout in the lender. This analysis has received considerable though not universal academic support... .

81 On this analysis, the *Quistclose* trust is a simple commercial arrangement akin (as Professor Bridge observes) to a retention of title clause (though with a different object) which enables the borrower to have recourse to the lender's money for a particular purpose without entrenching on the lender's property rights more than necessary to enable the purpose to be achieved. The money remains the property of the lender unless and until it is applied in accordance with his directions, and insofar as it is not so applied it must be returned to him. I am disposed, perhaps pre-disposed, to think that this is the only analysis which is consistent both with orthodox trust law and with commercial reality. Before reaching a concluded view that it should be adopted, however, I must consider the alternatives.

82 (ii) *The borrower*. It is plain that the beneficial interest is not vested unconditionally in the borrower so as to leave the money at his free disposal. That would defeat the whole purpose of the arrangements, which is to prevent the money from passing to the borrower's trustee in bankruptcy in the event of his insolvency. It would also be inconsistent with all the decided cases where the contest was between the lender and the borrower's trustee in bankruptcy, as well as with the *Quistclose* case itself... .

85 (iii) In the contemplated beneficiary. In the *Quistclose* case itself [1970] AC 567, as in all the reported cases which preceded it, either the primary purpose had been carried out and the contest was between the borrower's trustee in bankruptcy or liquidator and the person or persons to whom the borrower had paid the money; or it was treated as having failed, and the contest was between the borrower's trustee-in-bankruptcy and the lender. It was not necessary to explore the position while the primary purpose was still capable of being carried out and Lord Wilberforce's observations must be read in that light. ...

87 There are several difficulties with this analysis. In the first place, Lord Wilberforce's reference to *Re Rogers* 8 Morr 243 makes it plain that the equitable right he had in mind was not a mandatory order to compel performance, but a negative injunction to restrain improper application of the money; for neither Lindley LJ nor Kay LJ recognised more than this. In the second place, the object of the arrangements was to enable the subsidiary to continue trading, and this would necessarily involve it in incurring further liabilities to trade creditors. Accordingly the application of the fund was not confined to existing creditors at the date when the fund was established. The company secretary was given to understand that the purpose of the arrangements was to keep the subsidiary trading, and that the fund was "as good as share capital". Thus the purpose of the arrangements was not, as in other cases, to enable the debtor to avoid bankruptcy by paying off existing creditors, but to enable the debtor to continue trading by providing it with working capital with which to incur fresh liabilities. There is

a powerful argument for saying that the result of the arrangements was to vest a beneficial interest in the subsidiary from the start. If so, then this was not a *Quistclose* trust at all.

88 In the third place, it seems unlikely that the banks' object was to benefit the creditors (who included the Inland Revenue) except indirectly. The banks had their own commercial interests to protect by enabling the subsidiary to trade out of its difficulties. If so, then the primary trust cannot be supported as a valid non- charitable purpose trust: see *Re Grant's Will Trusts, Harris v Anderson* [1980] 1 WLR 360 and cf. *Re Denley's Trust Deed* [1969] 1 Ch 373.

 Link see Chapter 6

89 The most serious objection to this approach is exemplified by the facts of the present case. In several of the cases the primary trust was for an abstract purpose with no one but the lender to enforce performance or restrain misapplication of the money. In *Edwards v Glyn* (1859) 2 E & E 29 the money was advanced to a bank to enable the bank to meet a run. In *Re EVTR, Gilbert v Barber* [1987] BCLC 646 it was advanced "for the sole purpose of buying new equipment". ... The present case is another example. It is simply not possible to hold money on trust to acquire unspecified property from an unspecified vendor at an unspecified time. There is no reason to make an arbitrary distinction between money paid for an abstract purpose and money paid for a purpose which can be said to benefit an ascertained class of beneficiaries, and the cases rightly draw no such distinction. Any analysis of the *Quistclose* trust must be able to accommodate gifts and loans for an abstract purpose.

90 (iv) *In suspense*. As Peter Gibson J pointed out in *Carreras Rothmans Ltd v Freeman Matthews Treasure Ltd* [1985] Ch 207, 223 the effect of adopting Sir Robert Megarry V-C's analysis is to leave the beneficial interest in suspense until the stated purpose is carried out or fails. The difficulty with this (apart from its unorthodoxy) is that it fails to have regard to the role which the resulting trust plays in equity's scheme of things, or to explain why the money is not simply held on a resulting trust for the lender. ...

93 (v) *The Court of Appeal's analysis*. The Court of Appeal were content to treat the beneficial interest as in suspense, or (following Dr Chambers's analysis) to hold that it was in the borrower, the lender having merely a contractual right enforceable by injunction to prevent misapplication. Potter LJ put it in these terms [1999] Lloyd's Rep Bank 438, 456, para 75:

> "The purpose imposed at the time of the advance creates an enforceable restriction on the borrower's use of the money. Although the lender's right to enforce the restriction is treated as arising on the basis of a 'trust', the use of that word does not enlarge the lender's interest in the fund. The borrower is entitled to the beneficial use of the money, subject to the lender's right to prevent its misuse; the lender's limited interest in the fund is sufficient to prevent its use for other than the special purpose for which it was advanced."

This analysis, with respect, is difficult to reconcile with the court's actual decision in so far as it granted Twinsectra a proprietary remedy against Mr Yardley's companies as recipients of the misapplied funds. Unless the money belonged to Twinsectra immediately before its misapplication, there is no basis on which a proprietary remedy against third party recipients can be justified.

94 Dr Chambers's "novel view" (as it has been described) is that the arrangements do not create a trust at all; the borrower receives the entire beneficial ownership in the money subject only to a contractual right in the lender to prevent the money being used otherwise than for the stated purpose. If the purpose fails, a resulting trust in the lender springs into being. In fact, he argues for a kind of restrictive covenant enforceable by negative injunction yet creating property rights in the money. But restrictive covenants, which began life as negative easements, are part of our land law. Contractual obligations do not run with money or a chose in action like money in a bank account.

95 Dr Chambers's analysis has attracted academic comment, both favourable and unfavourable. For my own part, I do not think that it can survive the criticism levelled against it... . It provides no solution to cases of non-contractual payment; is inconsistent with Lord Wilberforce's description of the borrower's obligation as fiduciary and not merely contractual; fails to explain the evidential significance of a requirement that the money should be kept in a separate account; cannot easily be reconciled with the availability of proprietary remedies against third parties; and while the existence of a mere equity to prevent misapplication would be sufficient to prevent the money from being available for distribution to the creditors on the borrower's insolvency (because the trustee in bankruptcy has no greater rights than his bankrupt) it would not prevail over secured creditors. If the bank in the *Quistclose* case [1970] AC 567 had held a floating charge (as it probably did) and had appointed a receiver, the adoption of Dr Chambers's analysis should have led to a different outcome.

96 Thus all the alternative solutions have their difficulties. But there are two problems which they fail to solve, but which are easily solved if the beneficial interest remains throughout in the lender. One arises from the fact, well established by the authorities, that the primary trust is enforceable by the lender. But on what basis can he enforce it? He cannot do so as the beneficiary under the secondary trust, for if the primary purpose is fulfilled there is no secondary trust... . He cannot do so as settlor, for a settlor who retains no beneficial interest cannot enforce the trust which he has created.

97 Dr Chambers insists that the lender has merely a right to prevent the misapplication of the money, and attributes this to his contractual right to specific performance of a condition of the contract of loan. As I have already pointed out, this provides no solution where the arrangement is non-contractual. But Lord Wilberforce clearly based the borrower's obligation on an equitable or fiduciary basis and not a contractual one. He was concerned to justify the co-existence of equity's exclusive jurisdiction with the common law action for debt. Basing equity's intervention on its auxiliary jurisdiction to restrain a breach of contract would not have enabled the lender to succeed against the bank, which was a third party to the contract. There is only one explanation of the lender's fiduciary right to enforce the primary trust which can be reconciled with basic principle: he can do so because he is the beneficiary.

98 The other problem is concerned with the basis on which the primary trust is said to have failed in several of the cases ... and the *Quistclose* case itself [1970] AC 567.

Given that the money did not belong to the borrower in either case, the borrower's insolvency should not have prevented the money from being paid in the manner contemplated. A man cannot pay some only of his creditors once he has been adjudicated bankrupt, but a third party can. A company cannot pay a dividend once it has gone into liquidation, but there is nothing to stop a third party from paying the disappointed shareholders. The reason why the purpose failed in each case must be because the lender's object in making the money available was to save the borrower from bankruptcy in the one case and collapse in the other. But this in itself is not enough. A trust does not fail merely because the settlor's purpose in creating it has been frustrated: the trust must become illegal or impossible to perform. The settlor's motives must not be confused with the purpose of the trust; the frustration of the former does not by itself cause the failure of the latter. But if the borrower is treated as holding the money on a resulting trust for the lender but with power (or in some cases a duty) to carry out the lender's revocable mandate, and the lender's object in giving the mandate is frustrated, he is entitled to revoke the mandate and demand the return of money which never ceased to be his beneficially. ...

99 ... I do not think that subtle distinctions should be made between "true" *Quistclose* trusts and trusts which are merely analogous to them. It depends on how widely or narrowly you choose to define the *Quistclose* trust. There is clearly a wide range of situations in which the parties enter into a commercial arrangement which permits one party to have a limited use of the other's money for a stated purpose, is not free to apply it for any other purpose, and must return it if for any reason the purpose cannot be carried out. The arrangement between the purchaser's solicitor and the purchaser's mortgagee is an example of just such an arrangement. All such arrangements should if possible be susceptible to the same analysis.

 Alert

100 As Sherlock Holmes reminded Dr Watson, when you have eliminated the impossible, whatever remains, however improbable, must be the truth. I would reject all the alternative analyses, which I find unconvincing for the reasons I have endeavoured to explain, and hold the *Quistclose* trust to be an entirely orthodox example of the kind of default trust known as a resulting trust. The lender pays the money to the borrower by way of loan, but he does not part with the entire beneficial interest in the money, and in so far as he does not it is held on a resulting trust for the lender from the outset. Contrary to the opinion of the Court of Appeal, it is the borrower who has a very limited use of the money, being obliged to apply it for the stated purpose or return it. He has no beneficial interest in the money, which remains throughout in the lender subject only to the borrower's power or duty to apply the money in accordance with the lender's instructions. When the purpose fails, the money is returnable to the lender, not under some new trust in his favour which only comes into being on the failure of the purpose, but because the resulting trust in his favour is no longer subject to any power on the part of the borrower to make use of the money. Whether the borrower is obliged to apply the money for the stated purpose or merely at liberty to do so, and whether the lender can countermand the borrower's mandate while it is still capable of being carried out, must depend on the circumstances of the particular case.

Certainty

101 After this over-long exposition, it is possible to dispose of the remaining objections to the creation of a *Quistclose* trust very shortly. A trust must have certainty of objects. But the only trust is the resulting trust for the lender. The borrower is authorised (or directed) to apply the money for a stated purpose, but this is a mere power and does not constitute a purpose trust. Provided the power is stated with sufficient clarity for the court to be able to determine whether it is still capable of being carried out or whether the money has been misapplied, it is sufficiently certain to be enforced. ...

Conclusion

103 In my opinion the Court of Appeal were correct to find that the terms of paragraphs 1 and 2 of the undertaking created a *Quistclose* trust. The money was never at Mr Yardley's free disposal. It was never held to his order by Mr Sims. The money belonged throughout to Twinsectra, subject only to Mr Yardley's right to apply it for the acquisition of property. Twinsectra parted with the money to Mr Sims, relying on him to ensure that the money was properly applied or returned to it. Mr Sims act in paying the money over to Mr Leach was a breach of trust, but it did not in itself render the money incapable of being applied for the stated purpose. In so far as Mr Leach applied the money in the acquisition of property, the purpose was achieved.

Lord Millett's analysis is undeniably deeply impressive for its level of detail and consideration of a wide range of possible interpretations of how *Quistclose* trusts operate. Furthermore, from a pragmatic perspective it is *ratio* for how to interpret *Quistclose* trusts and the basis for discussing *Quistclose* trusts in this chapter.

However, this analysis has not been universally accepted as properly explaining why *Quistclose* trusts work. For a further analysis, see James Penner's work in the further reading.

The second issue with *Quistclose* trusts, as highlighted by *Twinsectra v Yardley*, is that such trusts have been found in situations that do not exactly correspond to the scenario of *Quistclose* itself. *Twinsectra v Yardley* and the following three cases show how the limits of *Quistclose* trusts have been teased out by the subsequent caselaw.

Re Chelsea Cloisters Ltd (In liquidation) (1981) 41 P & CR 98

Panel: Lord Denning MR, Bridge and Oliver LJJ

Facts: The landlords of a block of flats granted an underlease to a company, Chelsea Cloisters, who subsequently managed the block. Part of these managerial responsibilities entailed granting furnished and unfurnished tenancies. Under clause 1 of a tenancy agreement between the company and a tenant, the tenant had to pay a deposit to cover any damages or compensation to the company. If the deposit was not required at the end of the tenancy it was to be paid back to the now former tenant.

Initially there was no formal arrangement for how these tenancy moneys were managed, but in 1974 the company fell into financial difficulty and a chartered accountant was employed to supervise how the company was run. The accountant subsequently opened a separate bank account that was designated specifically for the tenant deposit moneys. All deposits made from June 1974 were paid into this account.

In November 1974 the underlease expired and the landlords took over the block of flats. The company subsequently went into liquidation. The liquidator went to court to find out whether the money in the tenant deposit account belonged to the landlords to hold on trust for the tenants or the creditors of the company.

It was held that in the beginning there was merely a contractual relationship between the company and the tenants. However, from the moment moneys were paid into the separate bank account, combined with the nature of clause 1 of the tenancy agreement, there was a trust for the tenants. The landlords were therefore entitled to the money to hold on trust, together with any interest accrued upon it.

LORD DENNING MR

Mr Parker first suggested that these sums paid by way of a deposit were impressed with a trust from the very beginning. He said that they were deposited as a security with the tenants having an equity to the return of any balance. I do not think that is correct. I think these deposits were made contractually with an obligation to repay the whole or some lesser sum. There was no trust at the beginning... .

 Alert

The second way in which Mr Parker put it was on the special conduct of Mr Iredale in setting up the tenants' deposit account when he took over. The question to be answered is, what is the proper inference to be drawn from the nature of the transaction? It does not matter what the transaction was called. The question is what was the nature of it. ...

It is important to have regard to Mr Iredale's affidavit when he says what the nature of this transaction was. It is given in paragraphs 12 and 13:

> 12. On August 14, 1974, I arranged for the company to open a separate bank account designated "tenants' deposit account," and gave instructions that all future deposits were to be paid into that account. This was a practical step, designed to ensure that the deposits would not be spent as part of the company's general cash flow, as had happened in the past. I was also concerned that I and my firm could be open to criticism if deposits were spent in this way and the company was then unable to make refunds to tenants. Nothing was said to the tenants about the new account.

> 13. I regarded the tenants' deposit account as available only for repaying the deposit of any tenant who had paid a deposit on or after June 18, 1974. For about a fortnight after June 18, I continued to repay the deposits of earlier tenants out of the general funds of the company. But I had to stop this soon after the receiver was appointed, because the company was receiving no income.

To my mind it is as plain as can be that Mr Iredale realised that the company was in a hopeless position: it had no money to pay anybody: and there was a danger that these deposits might fall into the hands of the other creditors of the company, contrary to the justice of the case. So, he thought that all these deposits, which the tenants had paid, and which they were entitled to have back under the terms of their agreements, ought to be kept as a separate fund to be secure against other creditors, and to be made available only to the tenants.

On the principles I have stated, it seems to me that the nature of this transaction was inevitably such as to create a trust of those moneys—from June 18 to November 16— on the terms of the original arrangements. They were to be held until the end of each tenancy. At the end of each tenancy, the dilapidations were to be calculated. If there were no dilapidations, the whole deposit was to go back to the tenants. If there were dilapidations, there were to be deductions accordingly. That seems to me to be the nature of the trust. That being the nature of the trust, it seems to me that there is nothing to go to the general body of creditors here.

Alert

LORD JUSTICE BRIDGE

"This"—that is to say, the opening of a separate bank account—"was a practical step, designed to ensure that the deposits would not be spent as part of the company's general cash flow." That is entirely consistent with an intention to keep these funds from the general funds of the company in order that they should not be swallowed up by the general funds of the company. The second critical statement was this: "I was also concerned that I and my firm could be open to criticism if deposits were spent in this way"—that is to say, if they were absorbed in the general funds of the company and spent as if they were available to be treated as part of the general funds of the company. Why was Mr Iredale apprehensive of criticism of himself and his firm? It surely can only have been that he at that time regarded the company, whose affairs he was managing, as being either under a moral or perhaps a legal duty to treat the tenants' deposits as impressed with some sort of beneficial interest in favour of the tenants and to ensure that sufficient funds were available to meet the tenants' claims to recover the deposits as and when those claims were made. It may even be that Mr Iredale supposed that the terms of clause 1 of the tenancy agreement had in fact impressed these deposits with a trust. That would have left unresolved the question arising out of the terms of that agreement. But, if he was mistaken in that belief, it would not—as Mr Parker has satisfied me in his reply—have prevented his intention from being effective, if his intention in setting aside what he believed to be trust moneys was to ensure that they were available for what he believed to be the trust purposes.

Alert

LORD JUSTICE OLIVER

I should add this, that I was bothered at one time by this point, that, when the account was opened on August 14, 1974, there was paid into it the sum of £11,000, being the amount which had been received by Mr Iredale since June 18 when he became a signatory on the company's account in respect of deposits by tenants. The argument presented by Mr Unwin as regards this was that, if a trust was created, would this not in fact involve that Mr Iredale had in mind the possibility that the company would be unable to meet its obligations and thus constitute a refund to the tenants a fraudulent preference? It is suggested that that is an unlikely intention to ascribe to a chartered accountant of Mr Iredale's experience. It seems to me that the answer is that it is not suggested that there was an express trust here in the sense that Mr Iredale consciously

Alert

said "I am going to create a trust." The question is, what is the result of what was done in the light of what Mr Iredale has said was his intention? He told the court in his affidavit what his intention was, and the funds paid in on August 14, 1974, cannot, I think, have been paid in with any different intention from the intention in respect of the funds subsequently paid in.

This case is important as a *Quistclose* trust was found despite there being no instruction by the original owner of the money, that is to say, the tenants. For this reason the concerns as highlighted by Bridge and Oliver LJJ are extremely pertinent. Every time a *Quistclose* trust is found it means that the beneficiaries of such a trust have proprietary rights to the money. It could be argued that such persons are only entitled to rights as strong as these if they intended themselves to have them; whether a trust is found or not should depend upon the intention of the original absolute owner of the property as to what should be done with regard to rights in the property.

Carreras Rothmans Ltd v Freeman Mathews Treasure Ltd and Another [1985] Ch 207

Panel: Peter Gibson J

Facts: Carreras Rothmans produced cigarettes and tobacco, which they extensively advertised. They employed Freeman Matthews Treasure as their advertising agents. As part of the advertising plan, the agents acquired advertising space in publications and on bill boards. They negotiated favourable rates for this advertising space and incurred debts in acquiring it. Carreras Rothmans then paid the advertising agents in time so that they could pay off the debts incurred for acquiring the advertising space.

In 1982 the advertising company fell into financial difficulty and, at Carreras Rothman's suggestion, the money for acquiring the advertising space was paid into a separate bank account from July 1983. Pursuant to this Carreras Rothmans made a payment of £597,128.72 to cover the cost for the June advertising, but the advertising agent went into voluntary liquidation before the advertising space was paid for. The liquidator froze all of the advertising agency's bank accounts and the third party publishers reacted by refusing to publish the adverts for Carreras Rothmans until the June advertising had been paid for. Carreras Rothmans paid off the June advertising and claimed the money in the segregated bank account from the liquidator.

It was held that Carreras Rothmans was entitled to the money in the account under a *Quistclose* trust.

MR JUSTICE PETER GIBSON

The July agreement was plainly intended to vary the contractual position of the parties as to how, as the contract letter put it, payments made by the plaintiff to the defendant for purely onwards transmission, in effect, to the third party creditors, would be dealt with. If one looks objectively at the genesis of the variation, the plaintiff was concerned about the adverse effect on it if the defendant, which the plaintiff knew to have financial problems, ceased trading and the third party creditors of the defendant were not paid at a time when the defendant had been put in funds by the plaintiff. The objective was accurately described by Mr. Higgs in his informal letter of 19 July as to protect the interests of the plaintiff and the third parties. For this purpose a special account was to be set up with a special designation. The moneys payable by the plaintiff were to be paid not to the defendant beneficially but directly into that account so that the defendant was never free to deal as it pleased with the moneys so paid. The moneys were to be used only for the specific purpose of paying the third parties and as the cheque letter indicated, the amount paid matched the specific invoices presented by the defendant to the plaintiff. The account was intended to be little more than a conduit pipe, but the intention was plain that whilst in the conduit pipe the moneys should be protected. There was even a provision covering the possibility (though what actual situation it was intended to meet it is hard to conceive) that there might be a balance left after payment and in that event the balance was to be paid to the plaintiff and not kept by the defendant. It was thus clearly intended that the moneys once paid would never become the property of the defendant. That was the last thing the plaintiff wanted in view of its concern about the defendant's financial position. As a further precaution the bank was to be put on notice of the conditions and purpose of the account. I infer that this was to prevent the bank attempting to exercise any rights of set off against the moneys in the account.

Only two matters were relied on as indicating that no trust was intended. One was the consideration fee; but the presence of consideration does not negative a trust. The other was the express reference in the penultimate paragraph in relation to placements and forward media options with which was contrasted the absence of the word "trust" in relation to the moneys in the account. But I regard that as of minimal significance when I consider all the other indications as to the capacity in which the defendant was to hold any moneys in the account. In my judgment even in the absence of authority it is manifest that the defendant was intended to act in relation to those moneys in a fiduciary capacity only.

There is of course ample authority that moneys paid by A to B for a specific purpose which has been made known to B are clothed with a trust. In the *Quistclose* case [1970] AC 567, 580 Lord Wilberforce referred to the recognition, in a series of cases over some 150 years, that arrangements for the payment of a person's creditors by a third person gives rise to

> "a relationship of a fiduciary character or trust, in favour, as a primary trust, of the creditors, and secondarily, if the primary trust fails, of the third person ..."

Lord Wilberforce in describing the facts of the *Quistclose* case said a little earlier on p. 580 that the mutual intention of the provider of the moneys and of the recipient of the moneys and the essence of the bargain was that the moneys should not become part of the assets of the recipient but should be used exclusively for payment of a particular class of its creditors. That description seems to me to be apt in relation to the facts of the present case too. ...

 Alert

It is of course true that there are factual differences between the *Quistclose* case and the present case. The transaction there was one of loan with no contractual obligation on the part of the lender to make payment prior to the agreement for the loan. In the present case there is no loan but there is an antecedent debt owed by the plaintiff. I doubt if it is helpful to analyse the *Quistclose* type of case in terms of the constituent parts of a conventional settlement, though it may of course be crucial to ascertain in whose favour the secondary trust operates (as in the *Quistclose* case itself) and who has an enforceable right. In my judgment the principle in all these cases is that equity fastens on the conscience of the person who receives from another property transferred for a specific purpose only and not therefore for the recipient's own purposes, so that such person will not be permitted to treat the property as his own or to use it for other than the stated purpose. Most of the cases in this line are cases where there has been an agreement for consideration so that in one sense each party has contributed to providing the property. But if the common intention is that property is transferred for a specific purpose and not so as to become the property of the transferee, the transferee cannot keep the property if for any reason that purpose cannot be fulfilled. I am left in no doubt that the provider of the moneys in the present case was the plaintiff. True it is that its own witnesses said that if the defendant had not agreed to the terms of the contract letter, the plaintiff would not have broken its contract but would have paid its debt to the defendant, but the fact remains that the plaintiff made its payment on the terms of that letter and the defendant received the moneys only for the stipulated purpose. That purpose was expressed to relate only to the moneys in the account. In my judgment therefore the plaintiff can be equated with the lender in *Quistclose* as having an enforceable right to compel the carrying out of the primary trust. ...

 Alert

In my judgment therefore a trust was created by the July agreement, the trust was completely constituted by the payment of moneys into the special account and the plaintiff as the provider of the moneys has an equitable right to an order for the carrying out by the defendant of the trust.

Two of the key issues in Peter Gibson J's judgment are firstly, that it was vital in finding a *Quistclose* trust that the money was paid into a separate bank account. However, in *Re EVTR Ltd* (1987) 3 BCC 389 the fact the money was paid into the company's general bank account was not fatal to finding a *Quistclose* trust. Secondly, it was also reported that a specific purpose had been stated for how the money was used. However, it is important to note that this has not been found to be essential in every *Quistclose* trusts case. Please refer to *Re Chelsea Cloisters Ltd (In liquidation)* (1981) 41 P & CR 98 above and see also *Cooper v PRG Powerhouse Ltd* [2008] 2 All ER (Comm) 964.

Re EVTR Ltd (1987) 3 BCC 389

Panel: Dillon, Woolf and Bingham LJJ

Facts: Mr Barber, a former employee of EVTR, won nearly £250,000 on a premium bonds win. He wanted to help his former company, which was in financial difficulties. He lent £60,000 to EVTR for the purpose of acquiring equipment from a manufacturer, Quantel. Since this sum was insufficient to purchase the equipment outright, EVTR agreed to lease the equipment from a leasing company, Concord. The new equipment would take seven months to arrive. In the meantime, some temporary equipment was leased to EVTR through Concord. The £60,000 was paid by EVTR as a deposit against the cost of the permanent equipment, in order to get the temporary equipment on loan.

Before the new equipment was delivered, receivers were appointed to administer EVTR. EVTR ceased trading and the leasing company took the temporary equipment back. Since EVTR never received the new equipment, the leasing company returned the £60,000, with a reduction for an agreed sum for EVTR's breach of contract and loss of interest.

The issue before the Court was whether the money was a company asset, and therefore should be used to meet the claims of EVTR's creditors, or whether the money was held under a *Quistclose* trust for Mr Barber.

Despite the money being used to hire equipment, it was held that the fact the permanent equipment had never arrived meant that there was a *Quistclose* trust of the money.

LORD JUSTICE DILLON

In the present case the £60,000 was released by Knapp-Fishers to the company on the appellant's instructions for a specific purpose only, namely the sole purpose of buying new equipment. Accordingly, I have no doubt, in the light of *Quistclose*, that, if the company had gone into liquidation, or the receivers had been appointed, and the scheme had become abortive before the £60,000 had been disbursed by the company, the appellant would have been entitled to recover his full £60,000, as between himself and the company, on the footing that it was impliedly held by the company on a resulting trust for him as the particular purpose of the loan had failed.

At the other end of the spectrum, if after the £60,000 had been expended by the company as it was, the Encore system had been duly delivered to, and accepted by, the company, there could be no doubt that the appellant's only right would have been as an unsecured creditor of the company for the £60,000. There would have been no question of the Encore system, or any interest in it, being held on any sort of trust for the appellant, and if, after it had been delivered and installed, the company had sold the system, the appellant could have had no claim whatsoever to the proceeds of sale as trust moneys held in trust for him.

The present case lies on its facts between those two extremes of the spectrum. Other scenarios between the extremes could equally be written, e.g. if, after the £60,000 had been paid by the company, Quantel had been enjoined by a third party from supplying the Encore system on the ground that the Encore system infringed patent rights or copyright of the third party and Quantel had thereupon refunded the £60,000, or if the Encore system was supplied but proved totally useless for its purpose and was therefore rejected and the money was returned.

The deputy judge took the view that the trust concept was spent when the £60,000 was paid out by the company. But he considered that the correctness of that view could be tested by an analogy which, with all respect to him, was false. He considered – rightly on the facts – that, had Concord or Quantel gone into liquidation after cashing the cheque or bankers' draft issued by the company, it could not have been argued that the proceeds of the cheque or bankers' draft were other than part of their general assets; but that is a false analogy, in that Concord and Quantel had no notice of any trust in favour of the appellant, whereas the company did have notice, and it was the company and not Concord or Quantel which was bound as to the manner in which the £60,000 could be used. ...

On *Quistclose* principles, a resulting trust in favour of the provider of the money arises when money is provided for a particular purpose only, and that purpose fails. In the present case, the purpose for which the £60,000 was provided by the appellant to the company was, as appears from the authority to Knapp-Fishers, the purpose of the company's buying new equipment. But in any realistic sense of the words that purpose has failed in that the company has never acquired any new equipment, whether the Encore system which was then in mind or anything else. True it is that the £60,000 was paid out by the company with a view to the acquisition of new equipment, but that was only at half-time, and I do not see why the final whistle should be blown at half-time. The proposed acquisition proved abortive and a large part of the £60,000 has therefore been repaid by the payees. The repayments were made because of, or on account of, the payments which made up the £60,000 and those were payments of trust moneys. It is a long established principle of equity that, if a person who is a trustee receives money or property because of, or in respect of, trust property, he will hold what he receives as a constructive trustee on the trusts of the original trust property. ... It follows, in my judgment, that the repayments made to the receivers are subject to the same trusts as the original £60,000 in the hands of the company. There is now, of course, no question of the £48,536 being applied in the purchase of new equipment for the company, and accordingly, in my judgment, it is now held on a resulting trust for the appellant. ...

The company did of course have the benefit for some months of the loan of the temporary equipment. Therefore, at any rate as between the company and Quantel, there was not a total failure of consideration so far as the company was concerned. But, even assuming (contrary to submissions made by counsel for the appellant) that the appellant was at the material times aware of the loan of the temporary equipment, the loan of the temporary equipment was merely ancillary to the purchase of the Encore system to cover the gap until the Encore system was available to be delivered to the company. On the way matters developed, it was the Encore system, and not the temporary system, that the company was to purchase, and the company never got the Encore system.

LORD JUSTICE BINGHAM

It would, I think, strike most people as very hard if Mr Barber were in this situation to be confined to a claim as an unsecured creditor of the company. While it is literally true that the fund which he provided was applied to the stipulated purpose, the object of the payment was not achieved and that was why the balance was repaid to the receivers. My doubt has been whether the law as it stands enables effect to be given to what I can see as the common fairness of the situation. Our attention has not, I think,

 Alert

been drawn to any case closely analogous to the present. But the company certainly held the fund on trust in the first instance.

9.4 Conclusion on *Quistclose* Trusts

The cases post-*Quistclose* show that *Quistclose* trusts have been found in a far wider range of scenarios than would have been suggested by reading Lord Wilberforce's judgment in *Quistclose* alone. Sadly, however, these cases do not all speak with one voice and the only certainty we do have is that some deviation from the original *Quistclose* requirements will not be fatal to finding a trust, but ignoring those requirements to too great a degree will preclude the existence of a trust. This lack of clarity leads to a great deal of uncertainty as to how far the envelope can be pushed and it appears that currently much depends upon the facts of each case and how they are presented in court. The problem with this is that whilst the beneficiaries of a *Quistclose* trust have a proprietary right to the money and are therefore 'winners' every time such a trust is found, it leads to the inevitable consequence of the unsecured creditors always losing out.

If the law is to allow this to happen it must be able to justify when *Quistclose* trusts can be found and why they exist. Otherwise there is always the risk of this area of law becoming unprincipled, impracticable and unfair. To ensure we reach this happy state, a considered analysis of the cases will be required in future decisions.

Further Reading

Parker and Mellows: The Modern Law of Trusts, 9th edition, A J Oakley, pp 316-321

Glister, *The nature of Quistclose trusts: classification and reconciliation*, C.L.J. 2004, 63(3), pp 632-655

The Law of Trusts, J E Penner, 6th edition, pp 248-256

Swadling (Ed.), *The Quistclose Trust*, 2004 (Hart), Chapter 3

10

Implied Trusts
of the Home

Topic List

Introduction

The law of trusts has proven to be of particular importance when dealing with cases regarding the home. It is uncommon for those living together to expressly declare that the home is to be held on trust for one or both of the parties in compliance with the Law of Property Act (LPA) 1925 s 53(1)(b). It has instead been left to the courts to use their powers under the LPA 1925 s 53(2) to imply a trust in favour of the party claiming a beneficial interest.

While the trust has been used in the case of spouses or civil partners, for both of those situations legislation provides a framework for the court's decision. Increasingly, however, unmarried co-habitees have applied to the courts claiming beneficial interests in the home and it is in this field particularly that implied trusts have adapted to changing social and economic conditions.

10.1 Implied Trusts of Land

When dealing with the issue of cohabitation the courts will first see if there is an express declaration as to the beneficial interests of the parties. In order to comply with LPA 1925 s 53(1)(b) this must be evidenced in writing and signed by the person or persons creating the trust. If these formalities have not been complied with or no express trust is found then the courts will instead need to look to implied trusts for a possible solution.

Gissing v Gissing **[1971] AC 886**

Panel: Lord Reid, Lord Morris of Borth-y-Gest, Viscount Dilhorne, Lord Pearson and Lord Diplock

Statute: Law of Property Act 1925 s 53(1)(b), (2)

Facts: The claimant and defendant had married while both were in employment and a house was subsequently purchased as the matrimonial home in the name of the defendant alone. While the claimant had not financially contributed to the purchase, she did spend her own money on family clothes, furniture, and the garden. Following a number of years of marriage, the defendant left the claimant, who subsequently sued for a share in the matrimonial home. The issue was whether she could claim a beneficial interest under an implied trust.

It was held that despite expenditures of her own money on the house and family, the claimant was unable to establish a common intention to share the house with her husband. She had not contributed to the purchase price either initially or through mortgage payments and there was no evidence of any express discussions between the parties relating to beneficial ownership.

LORD DIPLOCK

...I did, however, differ from the majority of the members of your Lordships' House who were parties to the decision in *Pettitt v Pettitt* in that I saw no reason in law why the fact that the spouses had not applied their minds at all to the question of how the beneficial interest in a family asset should be held at the time when it was acquired should prevent the court from giving effect to a common intention on this matter which it was satisfied that they would have formed as reasonable persons if they had actually thought about it at that time. I must now accept the majority decision that, put in this form at any rate, this is not the law.

In all the previous cases about the beneficial interests of spouses in the matrimonial home the arguments and judgments have been directed to the question whether or not an agreement between the parties as to their respective interests can be established on the available evidence. This approach to the legal problem involved is in most cases adequate, but it passes over the first stage in the analysis of the problem, viz., the role of the agreement itself in the creation of an equitable estate in real property. In the instant appeal, I think it is desirable to start at the first stage.

Any claim to a beneficial interest in land by a person, whether spouse or stranger, in whom the legal estate in the land is not vested must be based upon the proposition that the person in whom the legal estate is vested holds it as trustee upon trust to give effect to the beneficial interest of the claimant as cestui que trust [beneficiary]. The legal principles applicable to the claim are those of the English law of trusts and in particular, in the kind of dispute between spouses that comes before the courts, the law relating to the creation and operation of 'resulting, implied or constructive trusts.' Where the trust is expressly declared in the instrument by which the legal estate is transferred to the trustee or by a written declaration of trust by the trustee, the court must give effect to it. But to constitute a valid declaration of trust by way of gift of a beneficial interest in land to a cestui que trust the declaration is required by section 53 (1)[b] of the Law of Property Act, 1925, to be in writing. If it is not in writing it can only take effect as a resulting, implied or constructive trust to which that section has no application.

A resulting, implied or constructive trust - and it is unnecessary for present purposes to distinguish between these three classes of trust - is created by a transaction between the trustee and the cestui que trust in connection with the acquisition by the trustee of a legal estate in land, whenever the trustee has so conducted himself that it would be inequitable to allow him to deny to the cestui que trust a beneficial interest in the land acquired. and he will be held so to have conducted himself if by his words or conduct he has induced the cestui que trust to act to his own detriment in the reasonable belief that by so acting he was acquiring a beneficial interest in the land.

This is why it has been repeatedly said in the context of disputes between spouses as to their respective beneficial interests in the matrimonial home, that if at the time of its acquisition and transfer of the legal estate into the name of one or other of them an express agreement has been made between them as to the way in which the beneficial interest shall be held - notwithstanding the absence of any written declaration of trust. Strictly speaking this states the principle too widely, for if the agreement did not provide for anything to be done by the spouse in whom the legal estate was not to be vested, it would be a merely voluntary declaration of trust and unenforceable for want of writing. But in the express oral agreements contemplated by these dicta it has been assumed sub silentio that they provide for the spouse in whom the legal estate in the matrimonial home is not vested to do something to facilitate its acquisition, by contributing to the purchase price or to the deposit or the mortgage instalments when it is purchased upon mortgage or to make some other material sacrifice by way of contribution to or economy in the general family expenditure. What the court gives effect to is the trust resulting or implied from the common intention expressed in the oral agreement between the spouses that if each acts in the manner provided for in the agreement the beneficial interests in the matrimonial home shall be held as they have agreed.

An express agreement between spouses as to their respective beneficial interests in land conveyed into the name of one of them obviates the need for showing that the conduct of the spouse into whose name the land was conveyed was intended to induce the other spouse to act to his or her detriment upon the faith of the promise of a specified beneficial interest in the land and that the other spouse so acted with the intention of acquiring that beneficial interest. The agreement itself discloses the common intention required to create a resulting, implied or constructive trust.

But parties to a transaction in connection with the acquisition of land may well have formed a common intention that the beneficial interest in the land shall be vested in them jointly without having used express words to communicate this intention to one another; or their recollections of the words used may be imperfect or conflicting by the time any dispute arises. In such a case – a common one where the parties are spouses whose marriage has broken down – it may be possible to infer their common intention from their conduct.

As in so many branches of English law in which legal rights and obligations depend upon the intentions of the parties to a transaction, the relevant intention of each party is the intention which was reasonably understood by the other party to be manifested by that party's words or conduct notwithstanding that he did not consciously formulate that intention in his own mind or even acted with some different intention which he did not communicate to the other party. On the other hand, he is not bound by any inference which the other party draws as to his intention unless that inference is one which can reasonably be drawn from his words or conduct. It is in this sense that in the branch of English law relating to constructive, implied or resulting trusts effect is given to the inferences as to the intentions of parties to a transaction which a reasonable man would draw from their words or conduct and not to any subjective intention or absence of intention which was not made manifest at the time of the transaction itself. It is for the court to determine what those inferences are. ...

 Alert

Where in any of the circumstances described above contributions, direct or indirect, have been made to the mortgage instalments by the spouse into whose name the matrimonial home has not been conveyed, and the court can infer from their conduct a common intention that the contributing spouse should be entitled to some beneficial interest in the matrimonial home, what effect is to be given to that intention if there is no evidence that they in fact reached any express agreement as to what the respective share of each spouse should be?

I take it to be clear that if the court is satisfied that it was the common intention of both spouses that the contributing wife should have a share in the beneficial interest and that her contributions were made upon this understanding, the court in the exercise of its equitable jurisdiction would not permit the husband in whom the legal estate was vested and who had accepted the benefit of the contributions to take the whole beneficial interest merely because at the time the wife made her contributions there had been no express agreement as to how her share in it was to be quantified.

 Alert

In such a case the court must first do its best to discover from the conduct of the spouses whether any inference can reasonably be drawn as to the probable common understanding about the amount of the share of the contributing spouse upon which each must have acted in doing what each did, even though that understanding was never expressly stated by one spouse to the other or even consciously formulated in words by either of them independently. It is only if no such inference can be drawn that the court is driven to apply as a rule of law, and not as an inference of fact, the maxim "equality is equity," and to hold that the beneficial interest belongs to the spouses in equal shares.

The same result however may often be reached as an inference of fact. The instalments of a mortgage to a building society are generally repayable over a period of many years. During that period, as both must be aware, the ability of each spouse to contribute to the instalments out of their separate earning is likely to alter, particularly in the case of the wife if any children are born of the marriage. If the contribution of the wife in the early part of the period of repayment is substantial but is not an identifiable and uniform proportion of each instalment, because her contributions are indirect or, if direct, are made irregularly, it may be a reasonable inference that their common intention at the time of acquisition of the matrimonial home was that the beneficial interest should be held by them in equal shares and that each should contribute to the cost of its acquisition whatever amounts each could afford in the varying exigencies of family life to be expected during the period of repayment. In the social conditions of today this would be a natural enough common intention of a young couple who were both earning when the house was acquired but who contemplated having children whose birth and rearing in their infancy would necessarily affect the future earning capacity of the wife.

The relative size of their respective contributions to the instalments in the early part of the period of repayment, or later if a subsequent reduction in the wife's contribution is not to be accounted for by a reduction in her earnings due to motherhood or some other cause from which the husband benefits as well, may make it a more probable inference that the wife's share in the beneficial interest was intended to be in some proportion other than one-half. And there is nothing inherently improbable in their acting on the understanding that the wife should be entitled to a share which was not to be quantified immediately upon the acquisition of the home but should be left to be determined when the mortgage was repaid or the property disposed of, on the basis of what would be fair having regard to the total contributions, direct or indirect, which each spouse had made by that date. Where this was the most likely inference from their conduct it would be for the court to give effect to that common intention of the parties by determining what in all the circumstances was a fair share.

Difficult as they are to solve, however, these problems as to the amount of the share of a spouse in the beneficial interest in a matrimonial home where the legal estate is vested solely in the other spouse, only arise in cases where the court is satisfied by the words or conduct of the parties that it was their common intention that the beneficial interest was not to belong solely to the spouse in whom the legal estate was vested but was to be shared between them in some proportion or other. ...

 Alert

On what then is the wife's claim based? In 1951 when the house was purchased she spent about £190 on buying furniture and a cooker and refrigerator for it. She also paid about £30 for improving the lawn. As furniture and household doorbells are depreciating assets whereas houses have turned out to be appreciating assets it may be that she would have been wise to have devoted her savings to acquiring an interest in the freehold; but this may not have been so apparent in 1951 as it has now become. The court is not entitled to infer a common intention to this effect from the mere fact that she provided chattels for joint use in the new matrimonial home; and there is nothing else in the conduct of the parties at the time of the purchase or thereafter which supports such an inference. There is no suggestion that the wife's efforts or her earnings made it possible for the husband to raise the initial loan or the mortgage or that her relieving her husband from the expense of buying clothing for herself and for their son was undertaken in order to enable him the better to meet the mortgage installments (sic) or to repay the loan. The picture presented by the evidence is one of husband and wife retaining their separate proprietary interests in property whether real or personal purchased with their separate savings and is inconsistent with any common intention at the time of the purchase of the matrimonial home that the wife, who neither then nor thereafter contributed anything to its purchase price or assumed any liability for it, should nevertheless be entitled to a beneficial interest in it.

Both Buckley J. and Edmund Davies L.J. in his dissenting judgment in the Court of Appeal felt unable on this evidence to draw an inference that there was any common intention that the wife should have any beneficial interest in the house. I think that they were right. Like them I, too, come to this conclusion with regret, because it may well be that had husband and wife discussed the matter in 1951 when the house was bought he would have been willing for her to have a share in it if she wanted to. But this is speculation, and if such an arrangement had been made between them there might well have also been a different allocation of the household expenses between them in the ensuing years. ...

Gissing v Gissing establishes that implied trusts may be used with regard to beneficial interests in the absence of any express declaration to satisfy LPA 1925 s 53(1). It is also a good example of the presumption that, where legal title is in one name only, the beneficial ownership belongs to that person alone and the other party is required to show a common intention that they should have a beneficial interest. While it was dealing with a matrimonial case, subsequent authorities expanded upon *Gissing,* and carried forward its observations regarding use of the implied trust. The first type of implied trust that we shall look at is the resulting trust.

10.2 Resulting Trusts

The simplest form of implied trust is the resulting trust, where a beneficial interest is implied through contribution to the purchase price of the home by the party claiming the interest. The presumed intention of the contributing party would be, therefore, that they would obtain a beneficial interest in the home unless it can be established that they advanced the money (i.e. gifted it) or loaned it to the other party.

Bull v Bull [1955] 1 QB 234

Panel: Denning, Hodson and Parker LJJ

Facts: A house was purchased in the sole name of a son, the majority of the price coming from him but the balance having been paid by his mother. It was agreed that they would share occupation of the home. Several years later the son married and it was agreed that the mother would occupy two rooms in the house and the son and his wife the remainder. Arguments soon arose, however, and the son served notice to quit on his mother, who refused to leave. The matter proceeded to court and the question arose as to who had the beneficial interest in the home.

It was held that the mother held her share in the house as a tenant in common under a resulting trust and could enforce her interest against her son. He could not, therefore, turn her out or force a sale of the house without her consent unless the court granted such an order.

LORD JUSTICE DENNING

...The judge [at first instance] has found that the mother did contribute a substantial amount towards the house and that she did not intend to make a gift of that money to her son. There was therefore no presumption of advancement, but a resulting trust in her favour. Furthermore, the judge has found that, when the house was bought, it was the intention of both mother and son that it, although taken in the son's name, should be a home for them both. He has held that in these circumstances the son cannot turn the mother out now as if she was a trespasser; and that his only remedy is by application to a court of equity. The son appeals to this court.

Similar circumstances must often arise in families, but strangely enough there is no authority on the point. The son is of course the legal owner of the house; but the mother and son are, I think, equitable tenants in common. Each is entitled in equity to an undivided share in the house, the share of each being in proportion to his or her respective contribution. The rights of equitable tenants in common as between themselves have never, so far as I know, been defined; but there is plenty of authority about the rights of legal owners in common. Each of them is entitled to the possession of the land and to the use and enjoyment of it in a proper manner. Neither can turn out the other; but if one of them should take more than his proper share the injured party can bring an action for an account. If one of them should go so far as to oust the other he is guilty of a trespass: see *Jacobs v Seward*. Such being the rights of legal tenants in common, I think that the rights of equitable owners in common are the same, save only for such differences as are necessarily consequent on the interest being equitable and not legal. It is well known that equity follows the law; and it does so in these cases about tenants in common as in others. ...

In the simplest cases, therefore, a contribution to the purchase price will give rise to a resulting trust in proportion to this contribution. This contribution has always needed to be at the time of acquisition of the home but some doubt was cast upon this by the case of *Tinsley v Milligan* [1994] 1 AC 340 though compare *Curley v Parkes* [2004] EWCA Civ 1515, [2005] 1 P & CR DG15 and *Samad v Thompson* [2008] EWHC 2809 (Ch), [2008] NPC 125.

Laskar v Laskar [2008] EWCA Civ 347, [2008] 1 WLR 2695

Panel: Lord Neuberger of Abbotsbury, Tuckey and Rimer LJJ

Facts: A mother was tenant of a council property, which she subsequently purchased at a considerable discount from the local authority. A small amount of money was provided by her daughter and the daughter's name was also placed upon the legal title for the purpose of securing a mortgage. Both parties moved out of the property and let it out instead, the mortgage payments being made by the mother from this income. The mother remained responsible for maintenance of the house. The mother-daughter relationship broke down, however, and the daughter claimed a 50% stake in the house as a joint tenant.

It was held that, as the house in question was not a family home but rather purchased as an investment, the resulting trust rather than the constructive trust was the appropriate vehicle for deciding the claim. The mortgage should be treated as a joint contribution as it was in both names and instalments were paid from the income of the property. As such, the daughter's share was 33%.

LORD NEUBERGER OF ABBOTSBURY

The presumption of joint ownership

...12 The arguments which the claimant advances as to the beneficial ownership of the property are threefold. First, that the judge should not have concluded that the presumption that a house which is jointly owned in law is beneficially owned in equal shares was rebutted on the facts of this case. In other words it is said that there is a presumption that the beneficial interests were the same as the legal interests, and that that presumption was not rebutted in this case. ...

15 The claimant contends that the reasoning of the majority of the House of Lords in *Stack v Dowden* [2007] 2 AC 432 compels a finding in the present case that the beneficial ownership of the property was held in equal shares by the parties. As

Chadwick LJ pointed out when giving permission to appeal, the *Stack* case was decided after Judge Levy gave his decision in this case. In the *Stack* case the two parties who purchased the house in question were living together in a long-term sexual relationship, and had children when they purchased the house, which they intended to be, and indeed was occupied as, their family home. It is by no means clear to me that the approach laid down by Baroness Hale of Richmond in that case was intended to apply in a case such as this. In this case, although the parties were mother and daughter and not in that sense in an arm's length commercial relationship, they had independent lives, and, as I have already indicated, the purchase of the property was not really for the purpose of providing a home for them. The daughter hardly lived there at the time it was purchased, and did not live there much if at all afterwards, and the mother did not live there for long. The property was purchased primarily as an investment.

16 Lady Hale's speech began by identifying the problem to be addressed as relating to "a cohabiting couple": see para 40 (and see para 14 of the speech of Lord Walker of Gestingthorpe). But a number of the remarks in the course of her speech indicate that her reasoning was intended to apply to other personal relationships, at least where the property is purchased as a home for two (or indeed more than two) people who are the legal owners: see especially, at para 58, with the reference to "the domestic consumer context". Accordingly I think Judge Behrens was right to conclude in *Adekunle v Ritchie* [2007] WTLR 1505 in the Leeds County Court that the reasoning in the *Stack* case applied to a case where a house was purchased by a mother and a son in joint names as a home for them both.

17 It was argued that this case was midway between the cohabitation cases of co-ownership where property is bought for living in, such as the *Stack* case, and arm's length commercial cases of co-ownership, where property is bought for development or letting. In the latter sort of case, the reasoning in *Stack v Dowden* would not be appropriate and the resulting trust presumption still appears to apply. In this case, the primary purpose of the purchase of the property was as an investment, not as a home. In other words this was a purchase which, at least primarily, was not in "the domestic consumer context" but in a commercial context. To my mind it would not be right to apply the reasoning in *Stack v Dowden* to such a case as this, where the parties primarily purchased the property as an investment for rental income and capital appreciation, even where their relationship is a familial one. ...

The reasoning of Lord Neuberger, therefore, is that the resulting trust is still the appropriate vehicle for situations not specifically dealing with a family home. *Laskar v Laskar* was comparable to a commercial transaction and, where the land was used as an investment, then the approach of Baroness Hale in Stack v Dowden was not appropriate. Shares were limited to proportions based upon direct financial contributions.

10.3 Constructive Trusts

The rigidity of the resulting trust has led the courts to develop the constructive trust as a tool for dealing with beneficial ownership of the home instead. In many cases one party will not have contributed to the original purchase, either through deposit or monies secured by way of mortgage, or will not have their name on the legal title. The focus of the courts will, therefore, be to discern the intentions of the parties, specifically a common intention to share the home beneficially despite the lack of a financial contribution to the purchase price.

10.3.1 Legal Title in One Name Only

Lloyds Bank v Rosset [1991] 1 AC 107

Panel: Lord Bridge of Harwich, Lord Griffiths, Lord Ackner, Lord Oliver of Aylmerton and Lord Jauncey of Tullichettle

Statutes: Law of Property Act 1925 s 53(1), (2)

Facts: A semi-derelict property was purchased by a husband, using trust money, for the purpose of becoming the matrimonial home for him and his wife. The trustee, however, required that the property be registered in the name of the husband alone. Prior to completion the husband charged the property to the bank as security for a loan, without the knowledge or consent of his wife, who had also begun renovation works on the house. When the bank later claimed possession the wife claimed a beneficial interest in the house. As there was no express agreement between the parties as to how the house should be shared the courts needed to look at whether one could be inferred from her conduct or from the nature of the house itself, being the matrimonial home. It was held that the wife had no interest in the property as she had not contributed to either the purchase or later mortgage instalments. While she had supervised building works this was not sufficient to give rise to any beneficial interest. In the absence of an express agreement her conduct was insufficient for the court to find a beneficial interest.

LORD BRIDGE OF HARWICH

...The first and fundamental question which must always be resolved is whether, independently of any inference to be drawn from the conduct of the parties in the course of sharing the house as their home and managing their joint affairs, there has at any time prior to acquisition, or exceptionally at some later date, been any agreement, arrangement or understanding reached between them that the property is to be shared beneficially. The finding of an agreement or arrangement to share in this sense can only, I think, be based on evidence of express discussions between the partners, however imperfectly remembered and however imprecise their terms may have been. Once a finding to this effect is made it will only be necessary for the partner asserting a claim to a beneficial interest against the partner entitled to the legal estate to show that he or she has acted to his or her detriment or significantly altered his or her position in

 Alert

reliance on the agreement in order to give rise to a constructive trust or a proprietary estoppel.

In sharp contrast with this situation is the very different one where there is no evidence to support a finding of an agreement or arrangement to share, however reasonable it might have been for the parties to reach such an arrangement if they had applied their minds to the question, and where the court must rely entirely on the conduct of the parties both as the basis from which to infer a common intention to share the property beneficially and as the conduct relied on to give rise to a constructive trust. In this situation direct contributions to the purchase price by the partner who is not the legal owner, whether initially or by payment of mortgage instalments, will readily justify the inference necessary to the creation of a constructive trust. But, as I read the authorities, it is at least extremely doubtful whether anything less will do. ...

Outstanding examples on the other hand of cases giving rise to situations in the first category are *Eves v Eves* [1975] 1 WLR 1338 and *Grant v Edwards* [1986] Ch 638. In both these cases, where the parties who had cohabited were unmarried, the female partner had been clearly led by the male partner to believe, when they set up home together, that the property would belong to them jointly. In *Eves v Eves* the male partner had told the female partner that the only reason why the property was to be acquired in his name alone was because she was under 21 and that, but for her age, he would have had the house put into their joint names. He admitted in evidence that this was simply an 'excuse.' Similarly in *Grant v Edwards* the female partner was told by the male partner that the only reason for not acquiring the property in joint names was because she was involved in divorce proceedings and that, if the property were acquired jointly, this might operate to her prejudice in those proceedings. ...

The judgment of Lord Bridge is extremely important with regard to codification of implied trusts of the home and it clearly sets out what will be required for a constructive trust.

10.3.2 Express Common Intention Constructive Trusts

As Lord Bridge stated in *Lloyds Bank v Rosset*, above, if there is evidence of express discussions between the parties regarding beneficial interests in the property then an agreement to share the house beneficially may be found under an express common intention constructive trust. Coupled with this agreement is the requirement for detrimental reliance, which must also be satisfied before a beneficial interest may be found.

Grant v Edwards [1986] Ch 638

Panel: Sir Nicolas Browne-Wilkinson V-C, Mustill and Nourse LJJ

Facts: The defendant purchased a house in the names of himself and his brother, in which both he and the claimant resided. The brother had no beneficial interest in the home but was included for the purpose of securing a mortgage. The claimant made no contribution to either the purchase price or mortgage instalments, which were paid by the defendant. She was informed, however, that her name had not been put on the legal title as it would have adversely affected her current divorce proceedings. Substantial outgoings and expenses were paid by the claimant and an insurance payout on the home was paid into their joint account. Upon separation the claimant claimed a share in the home. It was held that she was entitled to a 50% share in the house through her beneficial interest under a trust.

LORD JUSTICE NOURSE

...In most of these cases the fundamental, and invariably the most difficult, question is to decide whether there was the necessary common intention, being something which can only be inferred from the conduct of the parties, almost always from the expenditure incurred by them respectively. In this regard the court has to look for expenditure which is referable to the acquisition of the house: see *per* Fox L.J. in *Burns v Burns* [1984] Ch 317, 328H-329C. If it is found to have been incurred, such expenditure will perform the twofold function of establishing the common intention and showing that the claimant has acted upon it.

There is another and rarer class of case, of which the present may be one, where, although there has been no writing, the parties have orally declared themselves in such a way as to make their common intention plain. Here the court does not have to look for conduct from which the intention can be inferred, but only for conduct which amounts to an acting upon it by the claimant. And although that conduct can undoubtedly be the incurring of expenditure which is referable to the acquisition of the house, it need not necessarily be so.

The clearest example of this rarer class of case is *Eves v Eves* [1975] 1 WLR 1338. That was a case of an unmarried couple where the conveyance of the house was taken in the name of the man alone. At the time of the purchase he told the woman that if she had been 21 years of age, he would have put the house into their joint names, because it was to be their joint home. He admitted in evidence that that was an excuse for not putting the house into their joint names, and this court inferred that there was an understanding between them, or a common intention, that the woman was to have some sort of proprietary interest in it; otherwise no excuse would have been needed. After they had moved in, the woman did extensive decorative work to the downstairs rooms and generally cleaned the whole house. She painted the brickwork of the front of the house. She also broke up with a 14-lb. sledge hammer the concrete surface which covered the whole of the front garden and disposed of the rubble into a skip, worked in the back garden and, together with the man, demolished a shed there and put up a new shed. She also prepared the front garden for turfing. Pennycuick V.-C. at first instance, being unable to find any link between the common intention and the woman's activities after the purchase, held that she had not acquired a beneficial interest in the house. On an appeal to this court the decision was unanimously reversed, by Lord Denning M.R. on a ground which I respectfully think was at variance with the principles stated in *Gissing v Gissing* [1971] AC 886 and by Browne L.J. and

Brightman J. on a ground which was stated by Brightman J. [1975] 1 WLR 1338, 1345:

> "The defendant clearly led the plaintiff to believe that she was to have some undefined interest in the property, and that her name was only omitted from the conveyance because of her age. This, of course, is not enough by itself to create a beneficial interest in her favour; there would at best be a mere 'voluntary declaration of trust' which would be 'unenforceable for want of writing': *per* Lord Diplock in *Gissing v Gissing* [1971] AC 886, 905. If, however, it was part of the bargain between the parties, expressed or to be implied, that the plaintiff should contribute her labour towards the reparation of a house in which she was to have some beneficial interest, then I think that the arrangement becomes one to which the law can give effect. This seems to be consistent with the reasoning of the speeches in *Gissing v Gissing*."...

So what sort of conduct is required? In my judgment it must be conduct on which the woman could not reasonably have been expected to embark unless she was to have an interest in the house. If she was not to have such an interest, she could reasonably be expected to go and live with her lover, but not, for example, to wield a 14-lb. sledge hammer in the front garden. In adopting the latter kind of conduct she is seen to act to her detriment on the faith of the common intention. ...

Alert

From the above facts and figures it is in my view an inevitable inference that the very substantial contribution which the plaintiff made out of her earnings after August 1972 to the housekeeping and to the feeding and to the bringing up of the children enabled the defendant to keep down the instalments payable under both mortgages out of his own income and, moreover, that he could not have done that if he had had to bear the whole of the other expenses as well. ...

Was the conduct of the plaintiff in making substantial indirect contributions to the instalments payable under both mortgages conduct upon which she could not reasonably have been expected to embark unless she was to have an interest in the house? I answer that question in the affirmative. I cannot see upon what other basis she could reasonably have been expected to give the defendant such substantial assistance in paying off mortgages on his house. I therefore conclude that the plaintiff did act to her detriment on the faith of the common intention between her and the defendant that she was to have some sort of proprietary interest in the house. ...

Alert

LORD JUSTICE MUSTILL

...Turning to the facts, the first question is whether there was an explicit bargain or a common intention at the moment of acquisition to the effect that the plaintiff should have a beneficial interest in the house. Strictly speaking, there was not. There was no discussion as to the quid pro quo, if any, which the plaintiff was to provide. Nor was there any common intention, for it is found that the defendant never intended the plaintiff to have a share. The reason given for placing the brother's name on the title was simply an untruthful excuse for not doing at once what he never meant to do at all.

This is not, however, fatal to the claim. Whatever the defendant's actual intention, the nature of the excuse which he gave must have led the plaintiff to believe that she would in the future have her name on the title, and this in turn would justify her in concluding that she had from the outset some kind of right to the house. The... defendant's conduct must now preclude him from denying that it is sufficiently analogous to these categories to make the relevant principles apply. ...

Finally, there remains the question whether the conduct of the plaintiff can be regarded as referable to the bargain or intention thus construed. On the facts as analysed by Nourse L.J. I consider that it can. Accordingly, the conditions are satisfied for the creation of an interest, and for the reasons given by Nourse L.J. I agree that the interest should be quantified at 50 per cent. I would therefore allow the appeal.

SIR NICOLAS BROWNE-WILKINSON V-C

I agree. In my judgment, there has been a tendency over the years to distort the principles as laid down in the speech of Lord Diplock in *Gissing v Gissing* [1971] AC 886 by concentrating on only part of his reasoning. For present purposes, his speech can be treated as falling into three sections: the first deals with the nature of the substantive right; the second with the proof of the existence of that right; the third with the quantification of that right.

1. The nature of the substantive right: [1971] A.C. 886, 905B-G

If the legal estate in the joint home is vested in only one of the parties ("the legal owner") the other party ("the claimant"), in order to establish a beneficial interest, has to establish a constructive trust by showing that it would be inequitable for the legal owner to claim sole beneficial ownership. This requires two matters to be demonstrated: (a) that there was a common intention that both should have a beneficial interest; (b) that the claimant has acted to his or her detriment on the basis of that common intention.

2. The proof of the common intention

(a) Direct evidence (p. 905H). It is clear that mere agreement between the parties that both are to have beneficial interests is sufficient to prove the necessary common intention. Other passages in the speech point to the admissibility and relevance of other possible forms of direct evidence of such intention: see pp. 907C and 908C.

(b) Inferred common intention (pp. 906A-908D). Lord Diplock points out that, even where parties have not used express words to communicate their intention (and therefore there is no direct evidence), the court can infer from their actions an intention that they shall both have an interest in the house. This part of his speech concentrates on the types of evidence from which the courts are most often asked to infer such intention viz. contributions (direct and indirect) to the deposit, the mortgage instalments or general housekeeping expenses. In this section of the speech, he analyses what types of expenditure are capable of constituting evidence of such common intention: he does not say that if the intention is proved in some other way such contributions are essential to establish the trust.

3. The quantification of the right (pp. 908D-909)

Once it has been established that the parties had a common intention that both should have a beneficial interest and that the claimant has acted to his detriment, the question may still remain "what is the extent of the claimant's beneficial interest?" This last section of Lord Diplock's speech shows that here again the direct and indirect contributions made by the parties to the cost of acquisition may be crucially important.

If this analysis is correct, contributions made by the claimant may be relevant for four different purposes, viz.: (1) in the absence of direct evidence of intention, as evidence from which the parties' intentions can be inferred; (2) as corroboration of direct evidence of intention; (3) to show that the claimant has acted to his or her detriment in reliance on the common intention: Lord Diplock's speech does not deal directly with the nature of the detriment to be shown; (4) to quantify the extent of the beneficial interest. ...

But as Lord Diplock's speech in *Gissing v Gissing* [1971] AC 886, 905D and the decision in *Midland Bank Plc v Dobson* (unreported) make clear, mere common intention by itself is not enough: the claimant has also to prove that she has acted to her detriment in the reasonable belief by so acting she was acquiring a beneficial interest.

There is little guidance in the authorities on constructive trusts as to what is necessary to prove that the claimant so acted to her detriment. What "link" has to be shown between the common intention and the actions relied on? Does there have to be positive evidence that the claimant did the acts in conscious reliance on the common intention? Does the court have to be satisfied that she would not have done the acts relied on but for the common intention, e.g. would not the claimant have contributed to household expenses out of affection for the legal owner and as part of their joint life together even if she had no interest in the house? Do the acts relied on as a detriment have to be inherently referable to the house, e.g. contribution to the purchase or physical labour on the house?

I do not think it is necessary to express any concluded view on these questions in order to decide this case. *Eves v Eves* [1975] 1 WLR 1338 indicates that there has to be some "link" between the common intention and the acts relied on as a detriment. In that case the acts relied on did inherently relate to the house (viz. the work the claimant did to the house) and from this the Court of Appeal felt able to infer that the acts were done in reliance on the common intention. So, in this case, as the analysis of Nourse L.J. makes clear, the plaintiff's contributions to the household expenses were essentially linked to the payment of the mortgage instalments by the defendant: without the plaintiff's contributions, the defendant's means were insufficient to keep up the mortgage payments. In my judgment where the claimant has made payments which, whether directly or indirectly, have been used to discharge the mortgage instalments, this is a sufficient link between the detriment suffered by the claimant and the common intention. The court can infer that she would not have made such payments were it not for her belief that she had an interest in the house. On this ground therefore I find that the plaintiff has acted to her detriment in reliance on the common intention that she had

Alert

a beneficial interest in the house and accordingly that she has established such beneficial interest. ...

In many cases of the present sort, it is impossible to say whether or not the claimant would have done the acts relied on as a detriment even if she thought she had no interest in the house. Setting up house together, having a baby, making payments to general housekeeping expenses (not strictly necessary to enable the mortgage to be paid) may all be referable to the mutual love and affection of the parties and not specifically referable to the claimant's belief that she has an interest in the house. As at present advised, once it has been shown that there was a common intention that the claimant should have an interest in the house, any act done by her to her detriment relating to the joint lives of the parties is, in my judgment, sufficient detriment to qualify. The acts do not have to be inherently referable to the house: see *Jones (A. E.) v Jones (F.W.)* [1977] 1 WLR 438 and *Pascoe v Turner* [1979] 1 WLR 431. The holding out to the claimant that she had a beneficial interest in the house is an act of such a nature as to be part of the inducement to her to do the acts relied on. Accordingly, in the absence of evidence to the contrary, the right inference is that the claimant acted in reliance on such holding out and the burden lies on the legal owner to show that she did not do so: see *Greasley v Cooke* [1980] 1 WLR 1306 . ...

Taking into account the fact that the house was intended to be the joint property, the contributions to the common expenditure and the payment of the fire insurance moneys into the joint account, I agree that the plaintiff is entitled to a half interest in the house.

Taking into account the express agreement between the parties, therefore, the court was able to find an express common intention constructive trust when coupled with the evidence of detrimental reliance on the part of the claimant. This resulted in a finding of a beneficial interest in her favour. This is not always the case, however, and there are occasions when the evidence of express agreement or detriment is held to be insufficient to give rise to an express common intention constructive trust. For an example of this see the case of *James v Thomas* [2008] 1 FLR 1598. For a further case on detrimental reliance see *Parris v Williams* [2009] 1 P & CR 9.

10.4 Inferred Common Intention Constructive Trust

In the absence of express agreement between the parties regarding beneficial interests in the home, the courts may infer an intention to share based purely on the conduct of the parties. The inferred common intention constructive trust may arise, traditionally, if one pays substantial mortgage repayments, something that we have already seen in the case of *Lloyds Bank v Rosset* per Lord Bridge, above. However, over recent years, cases have developed whereby other contributing factors may be taken into account in order to allow the courts to infer a common intention to share the home beneficially between the parties. In addition to those cases listed below also see *Le Foe v Le Foe* [2001] EWCA Civ 1870.

10.4.1 Legal Title in Joint Names

Stack v Dowden [2007] 2 AC 432

Panel: Lord Hoffmann, Lord Hope of Craighead, Lord Walker of Gestingthorpe, Baroness Hale of Richmond and Lord Neuberger of Abbotsbury

Facts: A home was purchased in the sole name of the respondent (D). She earned substantially more money than the appellant (S) and, as such, paid all of the mortgage payments together with a large proportion of the household bills. A great number of improvements were also made to the house and it eventually sold for three times its original purchase price. A new home was purchased in the names of both parties but over two thirds was provided by way of a bank account in the respondent's sole name including the equity from the sale of their first home. Mortgage repayments for the balance were paid by both parties but approximately 60 per cent were provided by the respondent. For the entirety of this period the appellant and respondent kept separate bank accounts and made separate transactions with regard to savings and investments. Upon separation the appellant claimed an interest in the house.

It was held that because both parties were on the legal title the presumption was that it was to be held in equal beneficial shares. This could be rebutted by the party claiming unequal shares, however. The respondent was able to do so because she had provided a larger amount of the purchase price and had also kept her financial assets, investments, and interests separate from the appellant. This was enough to indicate that an unequal distribution of assets was intended and the respondent was given a higher share.

LORD HOPE OF CRAIGHEAD

4 The cases can be broken down into those where there is a single legal ownership and those where there is joint legal ownership. There must be consistency of approach between these two cases, a point to which my noble and learned friend, Lord Neuberger of Abbotsbury, has drawn our attention. I think that consistency is to be found by deciding where the onus lies if a party wishes to show that the beneficial ownership is different from the legal ownership. I agree with Baroness Hale that this is achieved by taking sole beneficial ownership as the starting point in the first case and by taking joint beneficial ownership as the starting point in the other. In this context joint beneficial ownership means property is assumed to be held by the beneficial owners equally. So in a case of sole legal ownership the onus is on the party who wishes to show that he has any beneficial interest at all, and if so what that interest is. In a case of joint legal ownership it is on the party who wishes to show that the beneficial interests are divided other than equally. ...

11 In a case such as this, where the parties had already been living together for about 18 years and had four children when 114 Chatsworth Road was purchased in joint names and payments on the mortgage secured on that property were in effect contributed to by each of them equally, there would have been much to be said for adhering to the presumption of English law that the beneficial interests were divided

between them equally. But I do not think that it is possible to ignore the fact that the contributions which they made to the purchase of that property were not equal. The relative extent of those contributions provides the best guide as to where their beneficial interests lay, in the absence of compelling evidence that by the end of their relationship they did indeed intend to share the beneficial interests equally. The evidence does not go that far. On the contrary, while they pooled their resources in the running of the household, in larger matters they maintained their financial independence from each other throughout their relationship.

12 The result might have been different if greater weight could have been given to the inclusion in the transfer of the standard-form receipt clause. But English property law does not permit this, for the reasons explained in *Mortgage Corpn v Shaire* [2001] Ch 743, 753. I think that indirect contributions, such as making improvements which added significant value to the property, or a complete pooling of resources in both time and money so that it did not matter who paid for what during their relationship, ought to be taken into account as well as financial contributions made directly towards the purchase of the property. I would endorse Chadwick LJ's view in *Oxley v Hiscock* [2005] Fam 211, para 69 that regard should be had to the whole course of dealing between them in relation to the property. But the evidence in this case shows that there never was a stage when both parties intended that their beneficial interests in the property should be shared equally. Taking a broad view of the matter, therefore, I agree that the order that the Court of Appeal made provides the fairest result that can be achieved in the circumstances. ...

LORD WALKER OF GESTINGTHORPE

25 [In *Lloyds Bank plc v Rosset*] Lord Bridge then asked himself whether it was worthwhile to add any general remarks by way of illumination of the law. He limited himself to drawing attention to one "critical distinction". If, at p 132 e – g, there is to be a finding of an actual "agreement, arrangement, or understanding" between the parties it must "be based on evidence of express discussions between the partners, however imperfectly remembered and however imprecise their terms may have been". Lord Bridge continued, at pp 132–133:

> "In sharp contrast with this situation is the very different one where there is no evidence to support a finding of an agreement or arrangement to share, however reasonable it might have been for the parties to reach such an arrangement if they had applied their minds to the question, and where the court must rely entirely on the conduct of the parties both as to the basis from which to infer a common intention to share the property beneficially and as the conduct relied on to give rise to a constructive trust. In this situation direct contributions to the purchase price by the partner who is not the legal owner, whether initially or by payment of mortgage instalments, will readily justify the inference necessary to the creation of a constructive trust. But, as I read the authorities, it is at least extremely doubtful whether anything less will do."

In concurring in this passage the House was unanimously, if unostentiously (sic), agreeing that a "common intention" trust could be inferred even when there was no evidence of an actual agreement. Apart from two bare references, at p 132 g and p 133 f, to "a constructive trust or a proprietary estoppel" Lord Bridge did not refer to the elaborate arguments of counsel, at pp 110–125, addressed to him as to the varieties and interaction of these two concepts.

26 Lord Bridge's extreme doubt "whether anything less will do" was certainly consistent with many first-instance and Court of Appeal decisions, but I respectfully doubt whether it took full account of the views (conflicting though they were) expressed in *Gissing v Gissing* [1971] AC 886 (see especially Lord Reid, at pp 896 g –897 b, and Lord Diplock, at p 909 d – h). It has attracted some trenchant criticism from scholars as potentially productive of injustice: see *Gray & Gray, Elements of Land Law*, 4th ed, paras 10.132–10.137, the last paragraph being headed "A More Optimistic Future". Whether or not Lord Bridge's observation was justified in 1990, in my opinion the law has moved on, and your Lordships should move it a little more in the same direction, while bearing in mind that the Law Commission may soon come forward with proposals which, if enacted by Parliament, may recast the law in this area. ...

Alert

33 In the ordinary domestic case where there are joint legal owners there will be a heavy burden in establishing to the court's satisfaction that an intention to keep a sort of balance-sheet of contributions actually existed, or should be inferred, or imputed to the parties. The presumption will be that equity follows the law. In such cases the court should not readily embark on the sort of detailed examination of the parties' relationship and finances that was attempted (with limited success) in this case. I agree with Lady Hale that this is, on its facts, an exceptional case.

34 In those cases (it is to be hoped, a diminishing number) in which such an examination is required the court should in my opinion take a broad view of what contributions are to be taken into account. In *Gissing v Gissing* [1971] AC 886, 909 g, Lord Diplock referred to an adjustment of expenditure "referable to the acquisition of the house." "Referable" is a word of wide and uncertain meaning. It would not assist the development of the law to go back to the sort of difficulties that arose in connection with the doctrine of part performance, where the act of part performance relied on had to be "uniquely referable" to a contract of the sort alleged: see *Steadman v Steadman* [1976] AC 536. Now that almost all houses and flats are bought with mortgage finance, and the average period of ownership of a residence is a great deal shorter than the contractual term of the mortgage secured on it, the process of buying a house does very often continue, in a real sense, throughout the period of its ownership. The law should recognise that by taking a wide view of what is capable of counting as a contribution towards the acquisition of a residence, while remaining sceptical of the value of alleged improvements that are really insignificant, or elaborate arguments (suggestive of creative accounting) as to how the family finances were arranged.

35 That is in my view the way in which the law can be seen developing through a considerable number of decisions of the Court of Appeal, of which I would single out *Grant v Edwards* [1986] Ch 638 (before *Lloyds Bank plc v Rosset* [1991] 1 AC 107) and then *Stokes v Anderson* [1991] 1 FLR 391, *Midland Bank plc v Cooke* [1995] 2 All ER 562 and *Oxley v Hiscock* [2005] Fam 211. In the last-mentioned case

Chadwick LJ summarised the law as follows, at para 69, Lord Bridge's "second category" cases):

> "But, in a case where there is no evidence of any discussion between them as to the amount of the share which each was to have-and even in a case where the evidence is that there was no discussion on that point-the question still requires an answer. It must now be accepted that (at least in this court and below) the answer is that each is entitled to that share which the court considers fair having regard to the whole course of dealing between them in relation to the property. And, in that context, 'the whole course of dealing between them in relation to the property' includes the arrangements which they make from time to time in order to meet the outgoings (for example, mortgage contributions, council tax and utilities, repairs, insurance and housekeeping) which have to be met if they are to live in the property as their home."

36 That summary was directed at cases where there is a single legal owner. In relation to such cases the summary, with its wide reference to "the whole course of dealing between them in relation to the property", is in my opinion a correct statement of the law, subject to the qualifications in paras 61 et seq of Lady Hale's opinion. I would only add that Chadwick LJ did not refer to contributions in kind in the form of manual labour on improvements, possibly because that was not an issue in that case. For reasons already mentioned, I would include contributions in kind by way of manual labour, provided that they are significant. ...

BARONESS HALE OF RICHMOND

56 Just as the starting point where there is sole legal ownership is sole beneficial ownership, the starting point where there is joint legal ownership is joint beneficial ownership. The onus is upon the person seeking to show that the beneficial ownership is different from the legal ownership. So in sole ownership cases it is upon the non-owner to show that he has any interest at all. In joint ownership cases, it is upon the joint owner who claims to have other than a joint beneficial interest. ...

 Alert

58 The issue as it has been framed before us is whether a conveyance into joint names indicates only that each party is intended to have some beneficial interest but says nothing about the nature and extent of that beneficial interest, or whether a conveyance into joint names establishes a prime facie case of joint and equal beneficial interests until the contrary is shown. For the reasons already stated, at least in the domestic consumer context, a conveyance into joint names indicates both legal and beneficial joint tenancy, unless and until the contrary is proved.

 Alert

59 The question is, how, if at all, is the contrary to be proved? Is the starting point the presumption of resulting trust, under which shares are held in proportion to the parties' financial contributions to the acquisition of the property, unless the contributor or contributors can be shown to have had a contrary intention? Or is it that the contrary can be proved by looking at all the relevant circumstances in order to discern the parties' common intention?

...

68 The burden will therefore be on the person seeking to show that the parties did intend their beneficial interests to be different from their legal interests, and in what way. ...

69 In law, "context is everything" and the domestic context is very different from the commercial world. Each case will turn on its own facts. Many more factors than financial contributions may be relevant to divining the parties' true intentions. These include: any advice or discussions at the time of the transfer which cast light upon their intentions then; the reasons why the home was acquired in their joint names; the reasons why (if it be the case) the survivor was authorised to give a receipt for the capital moneys; the purpose for which the home was acquired; the nature of the parties' relationship; whether they had children for whom they both had responsibility to provide a home; how the purchase was financed, both initially and subsequently; how the parties arranged their finances, whether separately or together or a bit of both; how they discharged the outgoings on the property and their other household expenses. When a couple are joint owners of the home and jointly liable for the mortgage, the inferences to be drawn from who pays for what may be very different from the inferences to be drawn when only one is owner of the home. The arithmetical calculation of how much was paid by each is also likely to be less important. It will be easier to draw the inference that they intended that each should contribute as much to the household as they reasonably could and that they would share the eventual benefit or burden equally. The parties' individual characters and personalities may also be a factor in deciding where their true intentions lay. In the cohabitation context, mercenary considerations may be more to the fore than they would be in marriage, but it should not be assumed that they always take pride of place over natural love and affection. At the end of the day, having taken all this into account, cases in which the joint legal owners are to be taken to have intended that their beneficial interests should be different from their legal interests will be very unusual.

70 This is not, of course, an exhaustive list. There may also be reason to conclude that, whatever the parties' intentions at the outset, these have now changed. An example might be where one party has financed (or constructed himself) an extension or substantial improvement to the property, so that what they have now is significantly different from what they had then. ...

Applying the law to the facts

86 The starting point is that it is for Ms Dowden to show that the common intention, when taking a conveyance of the house into their joint names or thereafter, was that they should hold the property otherwise than as beneficial joint tenants. Unfortunately, we lack precise findings on many of the factors relevant to answering that question, because the judge addressed himself to "looking at the parties' entire course of conduct together". He looked at their relationship rather than the matters which were particularly relevant to their intentions about this property. He founded his conclusion on the length and nature of their relationship, which he repeatedly referred to as a partnership, despite the fact that they had maintained separate finances throughout their time together. With the best will in the world, and acknowledging the problems of

making more precise findings on many issues after this length of time, this is not an adequate answer to the question. It amounts to little more than saying that these people were in a relationship for 27 years and had four children together. During this time Mr Stack made unquantifiable indirect contributions to the acquisition and improvement of one house and quantifiable direct contributions to the acquisition of another. Both co-operated in looking after the home and bringing up their children. ...

92 This is, therefore, a very unusual case. There cannot be many unmarried couples who have lived together for as long as this, who have had four children together, and whose affairs have been kept as rigidly separate as this couple's affairs were kept. This is all strongly indicative that they did not intend their shares, even in the property which was put into both their names, to be equal (still less that they intended a beneficial joint tenancy with the right of survivorship should one of them die before it was severed). Before the Court of Appeal, Ms Dowden contended for a 65% share and in my view she has made good her case for that. ...

Despite the eloquent view espoused by Baroness Hale, Lord Neuberger was less impressed with the logic that had been applied to both the present case and the law of implied trusts of the home in general. Dissenting, he went on to give his own opinion regarding the facts in issue.

LORD NEUBERGER OF ABBOTSBURY

103 In the present type of case, while the number of unmarried cohabitants has increased very substantially over the past 50 (and even more over the past 20) years, the change has been one of degree, and does not, in my view, justify a departure from established legal principles. I agree with Griffiths LJ (see *Bernard v Josephs* [1982] Ch 391, 402) that the applicable principles are the same whether the parties are married or not, although the nature of the relationship will bear on the inferences to be drawn from their discussions and actions. ...

Beneficial ownership on acquisition: where there is no evidence

...

109 In the absence of any relevant evidence other than the fact that the property, whether a house or a flat, acquired as a home for the legal co-owners is in joint names, the beneficial ownership will also be joint, so that it is held in equal shares. This can be said to result from the maxims that equity follows the law and equality is equity. On a less technical, and some might say more practical, approach, it can also be justified on the basis that any other solution would be arbitrary or capricious.

110 Where the only additional relevant evidence to the fact that the property has been acquired in joint names is the extent of each party's contribution to the purchase price, the beneficial ownership at the time of acquisition will be held, in my view, in the same proportions as the contributions to the purchase price. That is the resulting trust solution. The only realistic alternative in such a case would be to adhere to the joint ownership solution. There is an argument to support the view that equal shares should still be the rule in cohabitation cases, on the basis that it may be what many parties may expect if

they purchase a home in joint names, even with different contributions. However, I consider that the resulting trust solution is correct in such circumstances. ...

113 There are also practical reasons for rejecting equality and supporting the resulting trust solution. The property may be bought in joint names for reasons which cast no light on the parties' intentions with regard to beneficial ownership. It may be the solicitor's decision or assumption, the lender's preference for the security of two borrowers, or the happenstance of how the initial contact with the solicitor was made. ...

146 In other words, where the resulting trust presumption (or indeed any other basis of apportionment) applies at the date of acquisition, I am unpersuaded that (save perhaps in a most unusual case) anything other than subsequent discussions, statements or actions, which can fairly be said to imply a positive intention to depart from that apportionment, will do to justify a change in the way in which the beneficial interest is owned. To say that factors such as a long relationship, children, a joint bank account, and sharing daily outgoings of themselves are enough, or even of potential central importance, appears to me not merely wrong in principle, but a recipe for uncertainty, subjectivity, and a long and expensive examination of facts. ...

Stack v Dowden dealt with a situation where the home was in the name of both parties. For a case where the home was in the name of one party only, see *Holman v Howes* [2007] EWCA Civ 877, [2008] 1 FLR 1217, an express common intention constructive trust case where the holistic approach espoused by Baroness Hale in *Stack v Dowden* was approved *obiter dicta*. Further, *Stack v Dowden* principles were applied in *Abbott v Abbott* [2007] UKPC 53, [2008] 1 FLR 1451 to an inferred common intention constructive trust case where legal title was in one name only.

Abbott v Abbott [2007] UKPC 53, [2008] 1 FLR 1451

Panel: Lord Bingham of Cornhill, Lord Walker of Gestingthorpe, Baroness Hale of Richmond, Lord Carswell and Lord Neuberger of Abbotsbury

Facts: The parties were given a piece of land in Antigua by the defendant's mother for the purpose of building their matrimonial home. This was conveyed into the defendant's name alone. The money to build the house was secured by gifts and a series of loans, which were subsequently turned into mortgages. These were secured by the defendant in his sole name but the claimant was also jointly and severally liable for the sums. Income was paid into a joint account, from which the mortgage repayments were made. Upon dissolution of the marriage the claimant claimed a beneficial share in the home. It was held that the land provided by the defendant's mother was to be considered as a gift to both parties rather than just to the defendant. Since the mortgage taken out over the house was in both names there was also a clear intention to share the house beneficially. Furthermore, the factors to be taken into consideration regarding quantification of beneficial shares in the land had moved on since *Lloyds Bank v Rosset*, which had been given too much weight by the Court of Appeal. As the parties had made mortgage repayments out of their joint account and had shared liability for the mortgage equally it was appropriate to award equal division of the house.

BARONESS HALE OF RICHMOND

4 There are, of course, two separate questions: first, was it intended that the parties should share the beneficial interest in a property conveyed to one of them only; and second, if it was so intended, in what proportions was it intended that they share the beneficial interest? There are two separate concepts which may help in answering those questions, explained by Peter Gibson LJ in *Drake v Whipp* [1996] 1 FLR 826, 827:

> "A potent source of confusion, to my mind, has been suggestions that it matters not whether the terminology used is that of the constructive trust, to which the intention, actual or imputed, of the parties is crucial, or that of the resulting trust which operates as a presumed intention of the contributing party in the absence of rebutting evidence of actual intention."

It is now clear that the constructive trust is generally the more appropriate tool of analysis in most matrimonial cases. ...

 Alert

5 ...Lord Walker pointed out [in *Stack v Dowden*], at para 25, that although Lord Bridge had drawn a sharp contrast between cases in which there had been some prior agreement to share and those where there had not, he and all the other members of the House were "unanimously, if unostentatiously, agreeing that a 'common intention' trust could be inferred even when there was no evidence of an actual agreement". Lord Walker went on to comment, in para 26:

> "Lord Bridge's extreme doubt 'whether anything less will do' was certainly consistent with many first-instance and Court of Appeal decisions, but I respectfully doubt whether it took full account of the views (conflicting though they were) expressed in *Gissing v Gissing* (see especially Lord Reid [1971] AC 886 at pp 896G-897B and Lord Diplock at p 909D-H). It has attracted some trenchant criticism from scholars as potentially productive of injustice (see *Gray & Gray*, Elements of Land Law, 4th ed [(2005)], paras 10.132 to 10.137, the last paragraph being headed 'A More Optimistic Future'). Whether or not Lord Bridge's observation was justified in 1990, in my opinion the law has moved on, and your Lordships should move it a little more in the same direction ..."

6 Lord Walker, Lord Hoffmann and Lord Hope of Craighead all agreed with my own opinion, in which I summed the matter up thus at para 60:

> "The law has indeed moved on in response to changing social and economic conditions. The search is to ascertain the parties' shared intentions, actual, inferred or imputed, with respect to the property in the light of their whole course of conduct in relation to it."

The House also approved a passage from the Law Commission's discussion paper on *Sharing Homes* (2002, Law Com No 278, para 4.27):

"If the question really is one of the parties' 'common intention', we believe that there is much to be said for adopting what has been called a 'holistic approach' to quantification, undertaking a survey of the whole course of dealing between the parties and taking account of all conduct which throws light on the question what shares were intended."

...

The matrimonial home: applying the law to the facts

...

17 It has been said more than once in the English courts that if a parent gives financial assistance to a newly married couple to acquire their matrimonial home, the usual inference is that it was intended as a gift to both of them rather than to one alone: see *McHardy and Sons (A Firm) v Warren* [1994] 2 FLR 338, at 340; *Midland Bank plc v Cooke* [1995] 4 All ER 562, at 570. It might be doubted whether such an inference could so readily be drawn in other countries where the culture may be different. But this was a Caribbean judge, albeit from a different small Caribbean island, and it is certainly not for us to say that it was an inference which he was not entitled to draw.

 Alert

18 Furthermore, it was supported by the behaviour of both parties throughout the marriage until it broke down. Not only did they organise their finances entirely jointly, having only a joint bank account into which everything was paid and from which everything was paid. They also undertook joint liability for the repayment of the mortgage loan and interest. This has always been regarded as a significant factor: see *Hyett v Stanley* [2003] EWCA Civ 942, [2004] 1 FLR 394. Yet the Court of Appeal appear to have attached no weight to it at all.

19 Finally, it must be borne in mind that the husband accepted in the course of his evidence that the wife did have a beneficial interest in the home, although he disputed the amount. The Court of Appeal appears to have attached undue significance to the dictum of Lord Bridge in *Lloyd's Bank plc v Rosset*, in particular as to what conduct is to be taken into account in quantifying an acknowledged beneficial interest. The law has indeed moved on since then. The parties' whole course of conduct in relation to the property must be taken into account in determining their shared intentions as to its ownership.

 Alert

20 For all those reasons, the Board is of the view that the Court of Appeal should not have interfered with the findings of the learned trial judge on the beneficial ownership of the matrimonial home. ...

28 The Board will therefore humbly advise Her Majesty that the appeal should be allowed in respect of the house and the furniture. There should be a declaration that the husband holds the house in trust for them both in equal shares. There should also be an order that the house be sold and the proceeds divided equally, subject to an adjustment in favour of the wife for 20% of the costs of acquiring the furniture.

It seems clear, therefore, that Baroness Hale intended the factors discussed in *Stack v Dowden* to apply to inferred common intention constructive trusts where legal title is in one name only. Subsequent cases have asserted that, since *Stack v Dowden*, a common intention to share ownership in a sole name case can be inferred from the whole course of conduct. However, in most cases, the court has held that the particular conduct of the claimant on the facts did not suffice for this purpose. It is arguably a pity that, in the case that follows, the Supreme Court did not take the opportunity to offer more *obiter* guidance on the kind of conduct needed to infer an intention for the non-legal owner to have an interest. The court did, however, make clear its view that the same principles apply to *quantifying* interests in all cases of common intention trusts, whether the legal title is in sole or joint names. Although this is *obiter dicta* in relation to sole name cases, it is at the top end of the persuasive scale.

Jones v Kernott [2012] 1 AC 776

Panel: Lord Walker of Gestingthorpe, Baroness Hale of Richmond, Lord Kerr of Tonaghmore, Lord Wilson JJSC, Lord Collins of Mapesbury

Facts: The appellant (J) and respondent (K) met in 1980. Both worked and their incomes were similar. J bought a mobile home in her sole name in 1981 and K moved in with her in 1983. In 1985, J sold the mobile home and the couple bought a property in their joint names for £30,000. The £6,000 deposit was paid from the sale proceeds of the mobile home and the balance came from a mortgage in their joint names. K paid £100 a week towards household expenses and J paid the mortgage and other household bills out of their joint resources. In 1986, they took out a joint loan of £2,000 to build an extension and K did some of the work and paid friends and relatives to do other work on it. The trial judge found that the extension probably increased the value of the property from £30,000 to £44,000. K moved out in 1993 and J continued to live there with their two children and paid all the outgoings. The parties tried unsuccessfully to sell the property in 1995. At some point, they agreed to cash in a joint life insurance policy and they divided the proceeds, so that K could use his share as a deposit on a home. The judge found that K was able to afford his home because he had not contributed to the joint property or made any significant contribution to the support of his children for the past 14½ years. The judge held that the parties' intentions as to their beneficial interests had changed after they separated and ordered that the joint property be divided as to 90% for J and 10% for K. K appealed to the High Court, where Mr Nicholas Strauss QC held that the change in intention could readily be inferred or imputed from the parties' conduct and that, in the absence of words or conduct indicating how their shares should alter, the appropriate criterion was what he considered fair and just. The judge's assessment could be justified as such. K then appealed to the Court of Appeal, which allowed the appeal, holding that there was nothing to indicate that the parties' intentions had changed and that they owned the property as tenants in common in equal shares. J then appealed to the Supreme Court, which reversed the decision of the Court of Appeal and restored the order made by the judge.

LORD WALKER OF GESTINGTHORPE and BARONESS HALE OF RICHMOND JJSC ...

2 The decision in *Stack v Dowden* has ... attracted a good deal of comment. ... This appeal provides an opportunity for some clarification.

Stack v Dowden [2007] 2 AC 432 ...

8 The curious feature of the decided cases up until then had been that, once an intention to share ownership had been established, the courts had tended to adopt a more flexible and "holistic" approach to the quantification of the parties' shares in cases of sole legal ownership than they had in cases of joint legal ownership. In the former, they had adopted a concept of the "common intention" constructive trust which depends upon the shared intentions of the parties. In the latter, they had tended to analyse the matter in terms of a resulting trust, which depends upon the law's presumption as to the intention of the party who makes a financial contribution to the purchase. ...

9 The leading opinion in the House of Lords was that of Lady Hale. ...

10 ...[In] the case of a house transferred into ... joint names ... she held that there is a presumption that the beneficial interests coincide with the legal estate. ...

13 ...[I]f the task [of seeking to show that the parties intended their beneficial interests to be different from their legal interests] is embarked upon, it is to ascertain the parties' common intentions as to what their shares in the property would be, in the light of their whole course of conduct in relation to it: Lady Hale, at para 60. It is the way in which this point was made which seems to have caused the most difficulty in the lower courts. The difficulty is well illustrated in Lord Wilson JSC's judgment, at paras 85-87, which read the judgment in a way which we would not read it. It matters not which reading is correct. It does matter that any confusion is resolved.

14 It was also accepted that the parties' common intentions might change over time... .

15 At its simplest the principle in *Stack v Dowden* is that a "common intention" trust, for the cohabitants' home to belong to them jointly in equity as well as on the proprietorship register, is the default option in joint names cases. The trust can be classified as a constructive trust, but it is not at odds with the parties' legal ownership. ...

A single regime?

16 ...[W]e recognise that a "common intention" trust is of central importance to "joint names" as well as "single names" cases... . Nevertheless it is important to point out that the starting point for analysis is different in the two situations. That is so even though it may be necessary to enquire into the varied circumstances and reasons why a house or flat has been acquired in a single name or in joint names... .

17 The starting point is different because the claimant whose name is not on the proprietorship register has the burden of establishing some sort of implied trust, normally what is now termed a "common intention" constructive trust. The claimant whose name is on the register starts (in the absence of an express declaration of trust in different terms...) with the presumption (or assumption) of a beneficial joint tenancy. ...

The competing presumption: a resulting trust? ...

Link

See Lord Wilson's judgment below

25 The time has come to make it clear, in line with *Stack v Dowden* [2007] 2 AC 432 (see also *Abbott v Abbott* [2008] 1 FLR 1451), that in the case of the purchase of a house or flat in joint names for joint occupation by a married or unmarried couple, where both are responsible for any mortgage, there is no presumption of a resulting trust arising from their having contributed to the deposit (or indeed the rest of the purchase) in unequal shares. The presumption is that the parties intended a joint tenancy both in law and in equity. But that presumption can of course be rebutted by evidence of a contrary intention, which may more readily be shown where the parties did not share their financial resources.

Inference or imputation?

26 In *Stack v Dowden* [2007] 2 AC 432 Lord Neuberger observed, at paras 125-126:

"125. While an intention may be inferred as well as express, it may not, at least in my opinion, be imputed. ...

"126. An inferred intention is one which is objectively deduced to be the subjective actual intention of the parties, in the light of their actions and statements. An imputed intention is one which is attributed to the parties, even though no such actual intention can be deduced from their actions and statements, and even though they had no such intention. Imputation involves concluding what the parties would have intended, whereas inference involves concluding what they did intend."

Rimer LJ made some similar observations in the Court of Appeal in this case... .

 Alert

31 In deference to the comments of Lord Neuberger and Rimer LJ, we accept that the search is primarily to ascertain the parties' actual shared intentions, whether expressed or to be inferred from their conduct. However, there are at least two exceptions. The first, which is not this case, is where the classic resulting trust presumption applies. Indeed, this would be rare in a domestic context, but might perhaps arise where domestic partners were also business partners: see *Stack v Dowden*, para 32. The second, which for reasons which will appear later is in our view also not this case but will arise much more frequently, is where it is clear that the beneficial interests are to be shared, but it is impossible to divine a common intention as to the proportions in which they are to be shared. In those two situations, the court is driven to impute an intention to the parties which they may never have had.

32 Lord Diplock, in *Gissing v Gissing* [1971] AC 886, 909, pointed out that, once the court was satisfied that it was the parties' common intention that the beneficial interest was to be shared in some proportion or other, the court might have to give effect to that common intention by determining what in all the circumstances was a fair share. And it is that thought which is picked up in the subsequent cases, culminating in the judgment of Chadwick LJ in *Oxley v Hiscock* [2005] Fam 211, paras 65, 66 and 69, and in particular the passage in para 69 which was given qualified approval in *Stack v Dowden*: "the answer is that each is entitled to that share which the court considers fair having regard to the whole course of dealing between them in relation to the property."

33 Chadwick LJ was not there saying that fairness was the criterion for determining whether or not the property should be shared, but he was saying that the court might have to impute an intention to the parties as to the proportions in which the property would be shared. ...

34 However, while the conceptual difference between inferring and imputing is clear, the difference in practice may not be so great. ... The law recognizes that a legitimate inference may not correspond to an individual's subjective state of mind. ...

Lord Walker and Baroness Hale summarised the facts and proceedings in the lower courts.

These proceedings ...

In referring to the decision of the Court of Appeal, they stated:

45 Rimer LJ, in the majority, held that there was nothing to indicate that the parties' intentions had changed after their separation. A crucial part of his reasoning was his interpretation of the decision in *Stack v Dowden*: that it did not "enable courts to find, by way of the imputation route, an intention where none was expressly uttered nor inferentially formed": para 77. Wall LJ also concluded that he could not infer an intention to change the beneficial interests from the parties' conduct: paras 57, 58.

Discussion

46 It is always salutary to be confronted with the ambiguities which later emerge in what seemed at the time to be comparatively clear language. The primary search must always be for what the parties actually intended, to be deduced objectively from their words and their actions. If that can be discovered, then, as Mr Nicholas Strauss QC pointed out in the High Court, it is not open to a court to impose a solution upon them in contradiction to those intentions, merely because the court thinks it fair to do so.

47 ...[W]here the parties already share the beneficial interest, and the question is what their interests are and whether their interests have changed, the court will try to deduce what their actual intentions were at the relevant time. ... But if it cannot deduce exactly what shares were intended, it may have no alternative but to ask what their intentions as reasonable and just people would have been had they thought about it at the time. This is a fallback position which some courts may not welcome, but the court has a duty to come to a conclusion on the dispute put before it.

48 In this case, there is no need to impute an intention that the parties' beneficial interests would change, because the judge made a finding that the intentions of the parties did in fact change. At the outset, their intention was to provide a home for themselves and their progeny. But thereafter their intentions did change significantly. He did not go into detail, but the inferences are not difficult to draw. They separated in October 1993. No doubt in many such cases, there is a period of uncertainty about where the parties will live and what they will do about the home which they used to share. This home was put on the market in late 1995 but failed to sell. Around that time a new plan was formed. The life insurance policy was cashed in and Mr Kernott was

able to buy a new home for himself. He would not have been able to do this had he still had to contribute towards the mortgage, endowment policy and other outgoings on 39 Badger Hall Avenue. The logical inference is that they intended that his interest in Badger Hall Avenue should crystallise then. Just as he would have the sole benefit of any capital gain in his own home, Ms Jones would have the sole benefit of any capital gain in Badger Hall Avenue. In so far as the judge did not in so many words infer that this was their intention, it is clearly the intention which reasonable people would have had had they thought about it at the time. But in our view it is an intention which he both could and should have inferred from their conduct.

49 A rough calculation on this basis produces a result so close to that which the judge produced that it would be wrong for an appellate court to interfere. ...

Conclusion

51 In summary, therefore, the following are the principles applicable in a case such as this, where a family home is bought in the joint names of a cohabiting couple who are both responsible for any mortgage, but without any express declaration of their beneficial interests. (1) The starting point is that equity follows the law and they are joint tenants both in law and in equity. (2) That presumption can be displaced by showing (a) that the parties had a different common intention at the time when they acquired the home, or (b) that they later formed the common intention that their respective shares would change. (3) Their common intention is to be deduced objectively from their conduct... . Examples of the sort of evidence which might be relevant to drawing such inferences are given in Stack v Dowden [2007] 2 AC 432, para 69. (4) In those cases where it is clear either (a) that the parties did not intend joint tenancy at the outset, or (b) had changed their original intention, but it is not possible to ascertain by direct evidence or by inference what their actual intention was as to the shares in which they would own the property, "the answer is that each is entitled to that share which the court considers fair having regard to the whole course of dealing between them in relation to the property": Chadwick LJ in Oxley v Hiscock [2005] Fam 211, para 69. In our judgment, "the whole course of dealing ... in relation to the property" should be given a broad meaning, enabling a similar range of factors to be taken into account as may be relevant to ascertaining the parties' actual intentions. (5) Each case will turn on its own facts. Financial contributions are relevant but there are many other factors which may enable the court to decide what shares were either intended (as in case (3)) or fair (as in case (4)).

52 This case is not concerned with a family home which is put into the name of one party only. The starting point is different. The first issue is whether it was intended that the other party have any beneficial interest in the property at all. If he does, the second issue is what that interest is. There is no presumption of joint beneficial ownership. But their common intention has once again to be deduced objectively from their conduct. If the evidence shows a common intention to share beneficial ownership but does not show what shares were intended, the court will have to proceed as at para 51(4) and (5) above.

Link
Contrast the views of Lord Kerr at para 77 and Lord Wilson at para 89

Alert

Alert

53 The assumptions as to human motivation, which led the courts to impute particular intentions by way of the resulting trust, are not appropriate to the ascertainment of beneficial interests in a family home. Whether they remain appropriate in other contexts is not the issue in this case.

54 It follows that we would allow this appeal and restore the order of the judge.

LORD COLLINS OF MAPESBURY

55 I agree that the appeal should be allowed for the reasons given in the joint judgment of Lord Walker of Gestingthorpe and Baroness Hale of Richmond JJSC. ...

57 The absence of legislative intervention ... made it necessary for the judiciary to respond by adapting old principles to new situations. That has not been an easy task. ...

64 I agree ... that authority justifies the conceptual approach of Lord Walker and Baroness Hale JJSC that, in joint names cases, the common intention to displace the presumption of equality can, in the absence of express agreement, be inferred (rather than imputed: see para 31 of the joint judgment) from their conduct, and where, in such a case, it is not possible to ascertain or infer what share was intended, each will be entitled to a fair share in the light of the whole course of dealing between them in relation to the property.

65 That said, it is my view that in the present context the difference between inference and imputation will hardly ever matter (as Lord Walker and Baroness Hale JJSC recognise at para 34), and that what is one person's inference will be another person's imputation. ...

LORD KERR OF TONAGHMORE JSC

67 I agree that this appeal should be allowed. There are differences of some significance in the reasoning that underlies the joint judgment of Lord Walker of Gestingthorpe and Baroness Hale of Richmond JJSC and that contained in Lord Wilson JSC's judgment. I agree with Lord Collins of Mapesbury that these are both terminological and conceptual. I am less inclined to agree, however, that the divergence in reasoning is unlikely to make a difference in practice. While it may well be that the outcome in many cases will be the same, whether one infers an intention or imputes it, that does not mean that the process by which the result is arrived at is more or less the same. Indeed, it seems to me that a markedly and obviously different mode of analysis will generally be required. ...

68 The following appear to be the areas of agreement. (i) In joint names' cases, the starting point is ... the presumption that the parties are joint tenants and are thus entitled to equal shares. (ii) That presumption can be displaced by showing (a) that the parties had a different common intention at the time when they acquired the home or (b) that they later formed the common intention that their respective shares would change. (iii) The common intention, if it can be inferred, is to be deduced objectively from the parties' conduct. (iv) Where the intention as to the division of the property cannot be inferred, each is entitled to that share which the court considers fair. In

considering the question of what is fair the court should have regard to the whole course of dealing between the parties.

69 The areas of disagreement appear to be these: (a) is there sufficient evidence in the present case from which the parties' intentions can be inferred? (b) is the difference between inferring and imputing an intention likely to be great as a matter of general practice?

How far should the court go in seeking to infer actual intention as to shares?

70 At para 32 above Lord Walker and Baroness Hale JJSC have quoted the important judgment of Chadwick LJ in *Oxley v Hiscock* [2005] Fam 211 and at para 51(4) have said that, on the authority of what was said in para 69 of *Oxley's* case, where it is not possible to ascertain what the actual intention of the parties was as to the shares in which they would own the property, each is entitled to the share which the court considers fair having regard to the whole course of dealing between them in relation to the property. This, I believe, casts the test somewhat differently from the way that it was formulated by Chadwick LJ. ...

71 Chadwick LJ did not confine the circumstances in which an intention is to be imputed to those where it was impossible to infer an intention. Rather, he considered that it was proper–and necessary–to impute it when there had been no discussion about the amounts of the shares that each was to have or where there was no evidence of such a discussion. Lord Walker and Baroness Hale JJSC have pointed out that *Oxley v Hiscock* received qualified approval in *Stack v Dowden* [2007] 2 AC 432. It seems clear, however, that there was no approval of the notion that an intention should be imputed where there had been no discussion between the parties... .

72 It is hardly controversial to suggest that the parties' intention should be given effect to where it can be ascertained and that, although discussions between them will always be the most reliable basis on which to draw an inference as to that intention, these are not the only circumstances in which that exercise will be possible. There is a natural inclination to prefer inferring an intention to imputing one. If the parties' intention can be inferred, the court is not imposing a solution. ... I believe that the court should anxiously examine the circumstances in order, where possible, to ascertain the parties' intention but it should not be reluctant to recognise, when it is appropriate to do so, that inference of an intention is not possible and that imputation of an intention is the only course to follow.

73 ...There are reasons to question the appropriateness of the notion of imputation in this area but, if it is correct to use this as a concept, I strongly favour the way in which it was described by Lord Neuberger in Stack v Dowden... .

74 ...In many ways, it would be preferable to have a stark choice between deciding whether it is possible to deduce what their intention was and, where it is not, deciding what is fair, without elliptical references to what their intention might have - or should have - been. But imputing intention has entered the lexicon of this area of law and it is probably impossible to discard it now.

Link
see para 26 where this is quoted

75 ...As soon as it is clear that inferring an intention is not possible, the focus of the court's attention should be squarely on what is fair... .

Is there sufficient evidence in the present case from which the parties' intentions can be inferred?

76 Lord Walker and Baroness Hale JJSC have concluded that the failure of the parties to sell their home in Badger Hall Avenue in late 1995, leading as it did to the cashing in of the life insurance policy, meant that Mr Kernott intended that his interest in the Badger Hall Avenue property should crystallise then. That may indeed have been his intention but, for my part, I would find it difficult to *infer* that it actually was what he then intended. ...[T]he bare facts of his departure from the family home and acquisition of another property are a slender foundation on which to conclude that he had entirely abandoned whatever stake he had in the previously shared property.

77 On the other hand, I would have no difficulty in concluding ... that it was eminently fair that the property should be divided between the parties in the shares decreed by Judge Dedman. Like Lord Wilson JSC, therefore, I would prefer to allow this appeal on the basis that it is impossible to infer that the parties intended that their shares in the property be apportioned as the judge considered they should be but that such an intention should be imputed to them.

LORD WILSON JSC

78 ...I warmly applaud the development of the law of equity, spear-headed by Baroness Hale of Richmond and Lord Walker of Gestingthorpe in their speeches in *Stack v Dowden* [2007] 2 AC 432, and reiterated in their judgment in the present appeal, that the common intention which impresses a constructive trust upon the legal ownership of the family home can be *imputed* to the parties to the relationship.

Lord Wilson cited the passage from *Stack v Dowden* where Lord Neuberger distinguished between inference and imputation and continued:

82 In *Oxley v Hiscock* ...[t]he home had been held in Mr Hiscock's sole name so, for Chadwick LJ, the first question was whether Mrs Oxley could establish that they had nevertheless had a common intention that she should have some beneficial share in it. In the present case, however, the home is held in the joint names of the parties so, for us, the first question is whether Ms Jones can establish that they nevertheless had (albeit not necessarily at the outset) a common intention that the beneficial shares of herself and Mr Kernott should be in some proportions other than joint and equal. The second question, which arises in the event only of an affirmative answer to the first, is to determine the proportions in which the beneficial shares are held.

83 In relation to the second question Chadwick LJ concluded, in his summary at para 69, that, where there was no evidence of any discussion between the parties as to the proportions in which their beneficial shares in the family home were to be held, each was "entitled to that share which the court considers fair having regard to the whole course of dealing between them in relation to the property"; ... because "what the court is doing, in cases of this nature, is to supply or impute a common intention as to the parties' respective shares (in circumstances in which there was, in fact, no common

Link
See Lord Wilson at para 89 and contrast the view of Lord Walker and Baroness Hale at para 48

Link
See para 26 where this is quoted

intention) on the basis of that which ... is shown to be fair." Emboldened by developments in the case law ... Chadwick LJ thus saw fit to reassert the power to impute. ...

84 The analysis by Chadwick LJ of the proper approach to the second question was correct. In paras 31 and 51(4) above Lord Walker and Baroness Hale JJSC reiterate that, although its preference is always to collect from the evidence an expressed or inferred intention, common to the parties, about the proportions in which their shares are to be held, equity will, if collection of it proves impossible, impute to them the requisite intention. Before us is a case in which Judge Dedman, the trial judge, found–and, was entitled on the evidence to find–that the common intention required by the first question could be inferred. Thus the case does not require us to consider whether modern equity allows the intention required by the first question also to be imputed if it is not otherwise identifiable. That question will merit careful thought.

 Alert

85 In para 61 of her ground-breaking speech in *Stack v Dowden* Lady Hale quoted, with emphasis, the words of Chadwick LJ in para 69 of *Oxley v Hiscock*, which I have quoted in para 83 above. Then she quoted a passage from a Discussion Paper published by the Law Commission in July 2002 and entitled *Sharing Homes* about the proper approach to identifying the proportions which "were intended". Finally she added four sentences to each of which, in quoting them as follows, I take the liberty of attributing a number:

"[1] That may be the preferable way of expressing what is essentially the same thought, for two reasons. [2] First, it emphasises that the search is still for the result which reflects what the parties must, in the light of their conduct, be taken to have intended. [3] Second, therefore, it does not enable the court to abandon that search in favour of the result which the court itself considers fair. [4] For the court to impose its own view of what is fair upon the situation in which the parties find themselves would be to return to the days before *Pettitt v Pettitt* [1970] AC 777... ."

86 I leave on one side Lady Hale's first sentence although, whereas Chadwick LJ was identifying the criterion for imputing the common intention, the context of the passage in the Discussion Paper suggests that the Law Commission was postulating a criterion for inferring it. On any view Lady Hale's second sentence is helpful; and, by her reference to what the parties must, in the light of their conduct, be taken to have intended (as opposed to what they did intend), Lady Hale made clear that, by then, she was addressing the power to resort to imputation. Lady Hale's fourth sentence has been neatly explained–by Mr Nicholas Strauss QC ... who determined the first appeal in these proceedings... –as being that, in the event that the evidence were to suggest that, whether by expression or by inference, the parties intended that the beneficial interests in the home should be held in certain proportions, equity would not "impose" different proportions upon them; and, at para 46 above, Lord Walker and Baroness Hale JJSC endorse Mr Strauss QC's explanation.

 Link
but see para 13 where Lord Walker and Baroness Hale state that Lord Wilson reads the judgment in a way that they would not

87 The problem has lain in Lady Hale's third sentence. Where equity is driven to impute the common intention, how can it do so other than by search for the result which the court itself considers fair? The sentence was not obiter dictum so rightly, under our

system, judges below the level of this court have been unable to ignore it. Even in these proceedings judges in the courts below have wrestled with it. .... In his judgment on the second appeal Rimer LJ went so far as to suggest, at para 77, that Lady Hale's third sentence must have meant that, contrary to appearances, she had not intended to recognise a power to impute a common intention at all.

88 I respectfully disagree with Lady Hale's third sentence.

89 Lord Walker and Baroness Hale JJSC observe, at para 34 above, that in practice the difference between inferring and imputing a common intention to the parties may not be great. I consider that, as a generalisation, their observation goes too far–at least if the court is to take (as in my view it should) an ordinarily rigorous approach to the task of inference. Indeed in the present case they conclude, at paras 48 and 49, that, in relation to Chadwick LJ's second question the proper inference from the evidence, which, if he did not draw, the trial judge should have drawn, was that the parties came to intend that the proportions of the beneficial interests in the home should be held on a basis which in effect equates to 90% to Ms Jones and to 10% to Mr Kernott... . As it happens, reflective perhaps of the more rigorous approach to the task of inference which I prefer, I regard it, as did Mr Strauss QC ... as more realistic, in the light of the evidence before the judge, to conclude that inference is impossible but to proceed to impute to the parties the intention that it should be held on a basis which equates to those proportions. At all events I readily concur in the result which Lord Walker and Baroness Hale JJSC propose.

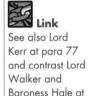

Link
See also Lord Kerr at para 77 and contrast Lord Walker and Baroness Hale at para 48

10.5 Conclusion

In *Stack v Dowden*, Lord Neuberger states that it is for parliament and not the courts to overhaul the complexities and inconsistencies that plague this area of law. Yet this does not seem to be forthcoming and so we must turn to cases such as *Stack v Dowden* and *Jones v Kernott* to point us in the correct direction with regard to implied trusts of the home.

This is a complex and uncertain area of law that has continually adapted to the changing social and economic environment in which the courts find themselves. While the resulting trust is a well-established principle it is very strict in its application and does not often reflect the practical situations or predicaments in which parties claiming beneficial interests find themselves. Constructive trusts, therefore, have had and will continue to have a key role to play in this field. They are, however, problematic and have arguably introduced a large amount of uncertainty into this field. Unlike a resulting trust, should one go to court it will be very difficult to predict with any accuracy what outcome might arise. This is a particularly dynamic area of law, however, and future developments may provide a semblance of clarity to what is currently clouded by ambiguity.

Further Reading

Barnes, Luke: '*Stack v Dowden*: The Principles in Practice'. *Family Law Week*, May 2007

Bridge, Stuart: 'Cohabitation: The Law Commission's Recommendations for Reform'. *Family Law Week*, August 2007

Fotheringham, John. 'Cohabitation Reform: The Scottish Experience'. *Family Law Week*, May 2008

Pettit, Philip H. *Equity and the Law of Trusts*: 11th Edition. Oxford University Press, 2009. Chapters 8 – 10.

Piška, Nick: 'Ambulatory trusts and the family home: Jones v Kernott'. (2010) 1 TLI 24.

Oakley, A.J. *Parker and Mellows: The Modern Law of Trusts*: 9th edition. Sweet & Maxwell, London, 2008. Chapters 9-10

11

Fiduciary Duties

Topic List

11.1 What is a Fiduciary Duty?

A fiduciary duty is a legal obligation on the part of one person (the fiduciary) to act in the best interests of another person (the principal).

Fiduciary duties exist independently of any other form of duty which the fiduciary may owe to the principal. A trustee, for example, will owe the following duties to a beneficiary:

▸ **Trust duties** – these are duties which relate to the management and administration of the trust's affairs, eg the duty to keep accurate records, or to act even-handedly as between beneficiaries.

▸ **Statutory duties** – these are duties which statute imposes upon a trustee, eg the duty of care which is imposed by Trustee Act 2000 s 1.

▸ **Fiduciary duties** – these are so-called 'overarching' duties which equity imposes upon the fiduciary because of the special relationship of trust which he occupies as regards the principal.

Equally, a fiduciary may owe contractual duties to his principal in addition to fiduciary duties, according to the nature of the particular relationship between the fiduciary and the principal.

11.2 The Relationships Which Give Rise to a Fiduciary Duty

A fiduciary duty arises where a relationship of 'trust and confidence', sometimes also characterised as a relationship of 'good faith' or 'loyalty', exists between the principal and the fiduciary.

There is no comprehensive list of the relationships which give rise to the existence of fiduciary duties under common law. Some relationships are automatically fiduciary, eg:

- Trustee and beneficiary

- Solicitor and client

- Agent and principal

- Company director and company (although this duty has now been codified by Companies Act 2000 s 170(1))

- Business partner and co-partners

Other relationships, eg between a family member and an elderly relative, or between a company director and the company's shareholders, or between co-venturers in a joint property venture, will be characterised as fiduciary if the particular circumstances of the case establish that the relationship in question possesses the requisite characteristics of trust and confidence, good faith or loyalty. Each case turns upon its own facts.

11.3 The Duties of a Fiduciary

Although the duties of a fiduciary have been differently articulated on a number of occasions, there are two themes which consistently emerge from the cases, the classic exposition of which appears from *Bray v Ford* [1896] AC 44.

Bray v Ford [1896] AC 44

Panel: Lord Halsbury LC, Lord Watson, Lord Herschell and Lord Shand

Facts: The respondent (Ford) was a governor of the Yorkshire College. He also acted as solicitor to the College, in which capacity he received payment for his services. The appellant (Bray) circulated a letter in which he alleged that in receiving payment Ford had 'illegally and improperly' taken advantage of his position as a fiduciary. Ford brought a libel action against Bray. A critical issue in the case was whether Bray's accusation was justified, ie was he correct in saying that, as a fiduciary, Ford was not entitled to charge for his services.

LORD HERSCHELL

It is an inflexible rule of a Court of Equity that a person in a fiduciary position, such as the respondent's, is not, unless otherwise expressly provided, entitled to make a profit; he is not allowed to put himself in a position where his interest and duty conflict. It does not appear to me that this rule is, as has been said, founded upon principles of morality. I regard it rather as based on the consideration that, human nature being what it is, there is danger, in such circumstances, of the person holding a fiduciary position being swayed by interest rather than by duty, and thus prejudicing those whom he was bound to protect.

Link
See also Authorised Remuneration, Section 6.

So:

- A fiduciary must not put himself in a position of actual or potential conflict with the interests of the principal. Potential conflict arises where there is a realistic possibility of a potential conflict rather than a mere theoretical prospect.

- A fiduciary must not derive personal profit from his position as a fiduciary.

Link
See the extract from Imageview Management v Jack below.

A more modern, and possibly wider, formulation of the duties of a fiduciary was given by Millett LJ in *Bristol and West Building Society v Mothew* [1998] Ch 1.

Bristol and West Building Society v Mothew [1998] Ch 1

Panel: Staughton, Millett and Otton LJJ

Facts: The defendant solicitor acted for the claimant in relation to a mortgage advance on a property which the claimant subsequently repossessed and sold for less than the amount outstanding under the mortgage. Prior to completion of the mortgage, the defendant had failed to inform the claimant that the borrowers were funding part of the balance of the purchase price by way of a second mortgage. The claimant alleged that this failure amounted to a breach of fiduciary duty (as well as a breach of the defendant's contractual and tortious duties to it) with the result that the defendant was liable for the whole of the claimant's loss, without the claimant having to prove that it would not have proceeded with the advance if it had been told the true position. The Court of Appeal held that, although the solicitor had acted in breach of his contractual and tortuous duties to the claimant, he had not acted in breach of any fiduciary duty.

LORD JUSTICE MILLETT

The expression "fiduciary duty" is properly confined to those duties which are peculiar to fiduciaries and the breach of which attracts legal consequences differing from those consequent upon the breach of other duties. Unless the expression is so limited it is lacking in practical utility. In this sense it is obvious that not every breach of duty by a fiduciary is a breach of fiduciary duty. I would endorse the observations of Southin J in *Girardet v Crease & Co* (1987) 11 BCLR (2d) 361, 362:

"The word 'fiduciary' is flung around now as if it applied to all breaches of duty by solicitors, directors of companies and so forth. ...That a lawyer can commit a breach of the special duty [of a fiduciary] ... by entering into a contract with the client without full disclosure ...and so forth is clear. But to say that simple carelessness in giving advice is such a breach is a perversion of words. ...It is similarly inappropriate to apply the expression to the obligation of a trustee or other fiduciary to use proper skill and care in the discharge of his duties. If it is confined to cases where the fiduciary nature of the duty has special legal consequences, then the fact that the source of the duty is to be found in equity rather than the common law does not make it a fiduciary duty. ..."

I respectfully agree, and endorse the comment of Ipp J in *Permanent Building Society v Wheeler* (1994) 14 ACSR 109, 157:

"It is essential to bear in mind that the existence of a fiduciary relationship does not mean that every duty owed by a fiduciary to the beneficiary is a fiduciary duty. In particular, a trustee's duty to exercise reasonable care, though equitable, is not specifically a fiduciary duty. ... The director's duty to exercise care and skill has nothing to do with any position of disadvantage or vulnerability on the part of the company. It is not a duty that stems from the requirements of trust and confidence imposed on a fiduciary. In my opinion, that duty is not a fiduciary duty, although it is a duty actionable in the equitable jurisdiction of this court. ..."

... This leaves those duties which are special to fiduciaries and which attract those remedies which are peculiar to the equitable jurisdiction and are primarily restitutionary or restorative rather than compensatory. A fiduciary is someone who has undertaken to act for or on behalf of another in a particular matter in circumstances which give rise to a relationship of trust and confidence. The distinguishing obligation of a fiduciary is the obligation of loyalty. The principal is entitled to the single-minded loyalty of his fiduciary. This core liability has several facets. A fiduciary must act in good faith; he must not make a profit out of his trust; he must not place himself in a position where his duty and his interest may conflict; he may not act for his own benefit or the benefit of a third person without the informed consent of his principal. This is not intended to be an exhaustive list, but it is sufficient to indicate the nature of fiduciary obligations. They are the defining characteristics of the fiduciary. As Dr Finn pointed

 Alert

out in his classic work Fiduciary Obligations (1977), p 2, he is not subject to fiduciary obligations because he is a fiduciary; it is because he is subject to them that he is a fiduciary.

The nature of the obligation determines the nature of the breach. The various obligations of a fiduciary merely reflect different aspects of his core duties of loyalty and fidelity. Breach of fiduciary obligation, therefore, connotes disloyalty or infidelity. Mere incompetence is not enough. A servant who loyally does his incompetent best for his master is not unfaithful and is not guilty of a breach of fiduciary duty."

11.4 The 'No Conflict' Rule

The 'no conflict' rule has given rise to a number of sub-rules, including the 'self-dealing rule' and the 'fair dealing' rule.

Right Reverend Hollis (Bishop of Portsmouth) and others v Rolfe and others [2008] All ER (D) 295 (Jul)

Panel: Evans-Lombe J

Facts: The claimants alleged that the defendants had sold a property which had been held on charitable trusts to some of their number in circumstances which amounted to a breach of the 'no-conflict' rule.

MR JUSTICE EVANS-LOMBE

There are in fact three rules. There is what one may call the "primitive self-dealing rule" which does not require any trust or fiduciary relationship but results from the fact that no-one can contract with himself and any attempt to do so is ineffective.

The second rule, usually referred to as the "self-dealing rule", is "that if a trustee sells the trust property to himself, the sale is voidable by any beneficiary ex debito justitiae, however fair the transaction." See *Tito v Waddell (No 2)* [1977] Ch 106 at 241.

The third rule, commonly known as the "fair dealing rule", is "that if a trustee purchases the beneficial interest of any of his beneficiaries, the transaction is not voidable ex debito justitiae, but can be set aside by the beneficiary unless the trustee can show that he has taken no advantage of his position and has made full disclosure to the beneficiary, and that the transaction is fair and honest." See *Tito v Waddell* ibid at 241.

 Decipher ex debito justitiae" means "as of right" or "as a matter of principle"

The relationship between the self-dealing rule and the fair-dealing rule, and also the applicability of those rules to an acquisition of trust property by a company in which a trustee holds a controlling interest, was considered by Vinelott J in *Re Thompson's Settlement, Thompson v Thompson* [1986] Ch 99.

Re Thompson's Settlement, Thompson v Thompson [1986] Ch 99

Panel: Vinelott J

Facts: The settlor had created a settlement under which two farms, one in England and the other in Scotland, were held upon trust for his two sons (Wilfrid and Jack), who were two of the three trustees of the settlement. The two farms were let to a company ('the old company') of which the settlor's wife and his two sons were the directors. Following the settlor's death it was agreed that each son should take one of the farms. The proposal was that the farm in England would be transferred to a partnership between Wilfrid and his two children, whilst the farm in Scotland would be transferred to a farming company ('the new company') which was controlled by Jack and his wife. In anticipation of the formal transfer of the land to the partnership and the new company respectively, which had to await the outcome of various valuation issues, the leases of the two farms were assigned to or vested in the partnership and the new company. It was held that those transactions were unlawful.

MR JUSTICE VINELOTT

The scope of the self-dealing rule and the relationship between that rule and the fair-dealing rule were explained by Sir Robert Megarry V-C in *Tito v Waddell (No 2)* [1977] Ch 106, 240:

"Self-dealing and fair-dealing. Let me revert briefly to the subject of the rules about self-dealing and fair-dealing, though on the view I take I doubt if much turns on this. ... The self-dealing rule is (to put it very shortly) that if a trustee sells the trust property to himself, the sale is voidable by any beneficiary *ex debito justitiae*, however fair the transaction. The fair-dealing rule is (again putting it very shortly) that if a trustee purchases the beneficial interest of any of his beneficiaries, the transaction is not voidable *ex debito justitiae* but can be set aside by the beneficiary unless the trustee can show that he has taken no advantage of his position and has made full disclosure to the beneficiary, and that the transaction is fair and honest. ... I can well see that both rules ... have a common origin in that equity is astute to prevent a trustee from abusing his position or profiting from his trust: the shepherd must not become a wolf. But subject to that, it seems to me that for all practical purposes there are two rules: the consequences are different, and the property and the transactions which invoke the rules are different."

...The classic statement of the [self-dealing] rule is to be found in the judgment of Lord Eldon LC in *Ex parte Lacey* (1802) 6 Ves Jun 625, a case where the assignee in bankruptcy of a bankrupt's estate purchased a part of the estate. Having stated the rule that a trustee undertakes to manage the trust property for his beneficiaries and not for the benefit and advantage of himself he explained the reason for the rule, at p 626a:

"I disavow that interpretation of Lord Rosslyn's doctrine, that the trustee must make advantage. I say, whether he makes advantage, or not, if the connection does not satisfactorily appear to have been dissolved, it is in the choice of the *cestuy que trusts* whether they will take back the property, or not; if the trustee has made no advantage. It is founded upon this; that though you may see in a particular case, that he has not

 Decipher
'Cestuy que trusts' means 'beneficiary

made advantage, it is utterly impossible to examine upon satisfactory evidence in the power of the court, by which I mean, in the power of the parties, in ninety-nine cases out of a hundred, whether he has made advantage or not."

The only other case to which I need refer is *Holder v Holder* [1968] Ch 353. ...The relevant facts are that the third defendant, Victor Holder, was appointed one of the executors of his father's will. He was already tenant of two farms owned by the testator. After the death of the testator Victor performed some acts which it was later conceded were acts of administration which precluded him from renouncing office as executor. Later he executed a purported renunciation. Probate was granted to two of the other executors named in the will. They put the two farms of which he was tenant up for sale by auction. At the auction, which was attended by most of the members of the family, Victor, through an agent, bid successfully for the farms. The farms were conveyed to him after some delay. The plaintiff, another son of the testator, started an action to set aside the conveyance to Victor. Cross J, after referring to the rule that an executor who renounces probate before he has done any acts of administration may buy any part of the testator's property from the proving executors, declined to apply the rule to the purchase by Victor. His decision was reversed by the Court of Appeal. Harman LJ said, at p 391:

"The judge decided in favour of the plaintiff on this point because Victor at the time of the sale was himself still in a fiduciary position and like any other trustee could not purchase the trust property. I feel the force of this argument, but doubt its validity in the very special circumstances of this case. The reason for the rule is that a man may not be both vendor and purchaser; but Victor was never in that position here. He took no part in instructing the valuer who fixed the reserves or in the preparations for the auction. Everyone in the family knew that he was not a seller but a buyer. In this case Victor never assumed the duties of an executor. It is true that he concurred in 'signing a few cheques for trivial sums and endorsing a few insurance policies, but he never, so far as appears, interfered in any way with the administration of the estate. It is true he managed the farms, but he did that as tenant and not as executor. He acquired no special knowledge as executor. What he knew he knew as tenant of the farms. Another reason lying behind the rule is that there must never be a conflict of duty and interest, but in fact there was none here in the case of Victor, who made no secret throughout that he intended to buy. ... [The] acts were only technically acts of intermeddling and I find no case where the circumstances are parallel. Of course, I feel the force of the judge's reasoning that if Victor remained an executor he is within the rule, but in a case where the reasons behind the rule do not exist I do not feel bound to apply it. ..."

[The] first submission [is] that the self-dealing rule has no application to a sale by trustees to a company, although if any of the trustees has an interest in the company, the transaction falls within the fair-dealing rule. [Counsel] founded this submission on the well-known case of *Farrar v Farrars Ltd* (1888) 40 Ch D 395. In that case three mortgagees were in possession of the mortgaged property. One of them, J R Farrar, was also solicitor to the mortgagees. The property was sold to a company which was to some extent promoted by J R Farrar and in which he took a small shareholding and

Link
For the significance of this fact see the commentary below.

for which he also acted as solicitor. He took no part in the negotiations. An action to set aside the transaction failed. Lindley LJ said, at pp. 409-410:

"A sale by a person to a corporation of which he is a member is not, either in form or in substance, a sale by a person to himself. To hold that it is, would be to ignore the principle which lies at the root of the legal idea of a corporate body, and that idea is that the corporate body is distinct from the persons composing it. A sale by a member of a corporation to the corporation itself is in every sense a sale valid in equity as well as at law. There is no authority for saying that such a sale is not warranted by an ordinary power of sale, and in our opinion, such a sale is warranted by such a power, and does not fall within the rule to which we have at present referred. But although this is true, it is obvious that a sale by a person to an incorporated company of which he is a member may be invalid upon various grounds, although it may not be reached by the rule which prevents a man from selling to himself or to a trustee for himself. Such a sale may, for example, be fraudulent and at an undervalue or it may be made under circumstances which throw upon the purchasing company the burden of proving the validity of the transaction, and the company may be unable to prove it."

Later he observed, at p. 410:

"But the sale cannot be set aside on the simple ground that Mr Farrar was a trustee for sale, and was a promoter of and shareholder in the company which purchased from him. It is necessary to see what his duties to his mortgagors were, and what he really did."

Then at the end of his judgment he said, at p 415:

"Mr Farrar was not a trustee selling to himself, or to others for him, nor was he buying directly or indirectly for himself, and although a sale by a mortgagee to a company promoted by himself, of which he is the solicitor, and in which he has shares, is one which the company must prove to have been bona fide, and at a price at which the mortgagees could properly sell, yet if such proves to be the fact, there is no rule of law which compels the court to set aside the sale. *Ex parte Lacey* does not require the court to hold the sale invalid, however fair and honest it may be, although the judgment in that case does throw upon the company the burden of shewing that the sale was fair and honest."

I do not think that this case assists Mr Price. [Jack] was not at the material time simply a shareholder of the new company. He and his wife were directors of the new company and he was its managing director. Their duty as directors was to further the interests of the new company in which, as it happened, they held a majority of the shares at the time of the purported assignment of the lease of the [Scottish farm]. The position as between the trustees ... and the directors of the new company is the same as it would have been if [Jack] had been a trustee of a settlement instead of a director of a company. ...[Wilfrid], of course, as a partner in a farming partnership was clearly precluded from dealing with himself as one of the trustees ... .

[The] other and more radical submission [which is] founded upon *Holder v Holder* [1968] Ch 353 [is] that the self-dealing rule only applies to a sale by trustees to one of their number, alone or jointly with others, or to a purchase by trustees from one of their number, alone or jointly with others, and to analogous dealings with trust property or trust moneys such as the grant of a lease by or to trustees. He founded that submission upon the statement by Harman LJ, at p 391, that "The reason for the rule is that a man may not be both vendor and purchaser..." He submitted that in the instant case the only dealings analogous to the sale of property were the assignments or purported assignments of the leases which were never themselves trust property. He submitted that in such a case the fair-dealing rule applies (because it is founded on the principle that a man must not put himself in a position where his duty and interest conflict and because in relation to the trustees it was their duty to consider whether to consent to the assignments) but not the self-dealing rule which only applies if there is a sale or purchase by trustees or something analogous to it. I do not think that the self-dealing rule can be so confined. It is clear that the self-dealing rule is an application of the wider principle that a man must not put himself in a position where duty and interest conflict or where his duty to one conflicts with his duty to another ... . The principle is applied stringently in cases where a trustee concurs in a transaction which cannot be carried into effect without his concurrence and who also has an interest in or owes a fiduciary duty to another in relation to the same transaction. The transaction cannot stand if challenged by a beneficiary because in the absence of an express provision in the trust instrument the beneficiaries are entitled to require that the trustees act unanimously and that each brings to bear a mind unclouded by any contrary interest or duty in deciding whether it is in the interest of the beneficiaries that the trustees concur in it.

The same principle also applies, but less stringently, in a case within the fair-dealing rule, such as the purchase by a trustee of a beneficiary's beneficial interest. There, there are genuinely two parties to the transaction and it will be allowed to stand if freely entered into and if the trustee took no advantage from his position or from any knowledge acquired from it.

In the instant case the concurrence of the trustees ... was required if the leases were to be assigned to or new tenancies created in favour of the new company and the partnership. The beneficiaries were entitled to ask that the trustees should give unprejudiced consideration to the question whether they should refuse to concur in the assignments in the expectation that a surrender of the leases might be negotiated from the old company and the estates sold or let on the open market.

The decision of the Court of Appeal in *Holder v Holder* [1968] Ch 353 does not in my judgment assist [the trustees]. The reason why, in the words of Harman LJ, the rule did not apply was that Victor, though he might technically have been made an executor notwithstanding the purported renunciation, had never acted as executor in a way which could be taken to amount to acceptance of a duty to act in the interests of the beneficiaries under his father's will.

The following points emerge from this decision:

(a)   The 'self-dealing' rule and the 'fair dealing' rule are distinct, though they both derive from the 'no conflict' rule.

(b)   A trustee will, it appears, not infringe the self-dealing rule if, as in *Holder*, his acts as trustee have been so inconsequential that it is not right in all the circumstances to treat him as being a trustee for the purposes of the rule.

(c)   A sale to a company in which the trustee holds a controlling interest amounts to a sale to the trustee.

(d)   The position will be different where the trustee has only a small or minority shareholding: *Farrar*. However, where the trustee holds only a minority interest it will still be for the company to show that the trustee took all reasonable steps to obtain the best price.

11.5 The 'No Profit' Rule

This rule is applied very strictly. It applies to any form of payment or advantage which a fiduciary receives as a result of the position which he holds.

11.5.1 Bribes and secret commissions received by a trustee

Williams v Barton [1927] 2 Ch 9

Panel: Russell J

Facts: The defendant, one of two trustees of a will, was employed as a clerk by a firm of stockbrokers on the terms that his salary should consist of half the commission earned by the firm on business introduced by him. On the defendant's recommendation, the firm was employed to value the testator's securities. The firm's charges were paid out of the testator's estate and, in accordance with its contract with the defendant, the firm paid him half the fees received. The defendant took no part in making the valuations or in fixing the fees to be charged. His co-trustee brought an action claiming that the defendant was bound to treat the fees paid to him as part of the testator's estate. It was held that the defendant had acted in breach of fiduciary duty and was liable to account for the fee.

MR JUSTICE RUSSELL

It is a well established and salutary rule of equity that a trustee may not make a profit out of his trust. A person who has the management of property as a trustee is not permitted to gain any profit by availing himself of his position, and will be a constructive trustee of any such profit for the benefit of the persons equitably entitled to the property. On the same principle a trustee has no right to charge for his time and trouble. The rule is thus stated by Lord Herschell in *Bray v Ford* [1896] AC 44: "It is an inflexible rule of a Court of Equity that a person in a fiduciary position .... is not, unless otherwise expressly provided, entitled to make a profit; he is not allowed to put himself in a position where his interest and duty conflict." It was argued on behalf of the defendant that the case was altogether outside that rule of equity, because the sums received by the defendant were merely parts of his salary paid to him by his employers under the contract of service and were not of a character for which he was liable to account.

The point is not an easy one and there is little, if any, authority to assist in its determination. The situation is an unusual one and the contract of service presents the following peculiar features. The remuneration has no relation to the services, which the defendant has to render to his employers. The defendant, while bound to render the services, might get no remuneration at all if he introduced no work, or introduced none which was acceptable to his employers. The amount of his remuneration depends (subject to his employers' acceptance of orders) upon his own efforts, but upon efforts not in relation to the work which he is engaged to do. Any increase of his remuneration rests with him.

From this it seems to me evident that the case falls within the mischief which is sought to be prevented by the rule. The case is clearly one where his duty as trustee and his interest in an increased remuneration are in direct conflict. As a trustee it is his duty to give the estate the benefit of his unfettered advice in choosing the stockbrokers to act for the estate; as the recipient of half the fees to be earned by [the firm] on work introduced by him his obvious interest is to choose or recommend them for the job.

In the event that has happened they have been chosen, and chosen because the defendant was a trustee, with the result that half of what the estate pays must necessarily pass through them to the defendant as part of his remuneration for other services rendered, but as an addition to the remuneration which he would otherwise have received for those self-same services. The services rendered remain unchanged, but the remuneration for them has been increased. He has increased his remuneration by virtue of his trusteeship. In my opinion this increase of remuneration is a profit made by the defendant out of and by reason of his trusteeship, which he would not have made but for his position as trustee.

 Alert

11.5.2 Directors' fees

Where the property of a trust includes shares in a company, the ownership of which entitles the trustees to appoint the directors of that company, the trustees cannot appoint themselves as directors and draw fees or salary as a consequence, although they may recover out-of-pocket expenses.

In re Macadam, Dallow v Codd [1946] Ch 73

Panel: Cohen J

Facts: A trust fund consisted of shares in a limited company which had been formed by the testator. The company's articles of association empowered the trustees, as holders of all the shares in the company, to appoint two directors. The trustees appointed themselves as directors and received directors' fees. They were held to have acted in breach of fiduciary duty in receiving those fees.

MR JUSTICE COHEN

The question has been raised whether the [trustees] are entitled to retain the directors' fees received by them from the company or whether they are accountable to the trust estate for the sums received by them as remuneration in respect of the office of director. I desire to say at once that nobody suggested any impropriety on their part in regard to this remuneration. The question was asked purely as one of law whether, having regard to all the provisions of the material documents, on general principles of law, they are accountable or not. .... The principle, I think, is well stated in a passage from the speech of Lord Herschell in *Bray v Ford* ... as follows: "It is an inflexible rule of a court of equity that a person in a fiduciary position .... is not, unless otherwise expressly provided, entitled to make a profit; he is not allowed to put himself in a position where his interest and duty conflict. ...

The ... nearest ... case to the present - although it is a much stronger case than the one I have to decide – is *Williams v Barton* ... .

That case is ... much stronger than the present case, because, first, the profit in a sense came directly out of the estate, and, secondly, because it was a profit earned in a sense without any work done by him. I think that the root of the matter really is: Did [the trustee] acquire the position in respect of which he drew the remuneration by virtue of his position as trustee? In the present case there can be no doubt that the only way in which the [trustees] became directors was by exercise of the powers vested in the trustees of the will under ... the articles of association of the company. The principle is one which has always been regarded as of the greatest importance in these courts, and I do not think I ought to do anything to weaken it. As I have said, although the remuneration was remuneration for services as director of the company, the opportunity to receive that remuneration was gained as a result of the exercise of a discretion vested in the trustees, and they had put themselves in a position where their interest and duty conflicted. In those circumstances, I do not think this court can allow them to make a profit out of doing so, and I do not think the liability to account for a profit can be confined to cases where the profit is derived directly from the trust estate. I leave over the matter of the exact wording of the order, because I do not want to do anything to prejudice the question whether, in the circumstances, I ought not to allow the plaintiffs to retain the whole or a part of the remuneration. If I can be satisfied (and that is the point I had not considered) that they were the best persons to be directors, I do not think it would be right for me to expect them to do the extra work for nothing.

Alert

Link
See Authorised Remuneration below.

Mr Justice Cohen decided that:

(a)   The 'no profit' rule is engaged whenever a trustee derives a benefit or advantage by virtue of his position as trustee;

(b)   It is irrelevant that the 'profit' does not come at the expense of the trust but is derived from elsewhere; and

(c)   It is may nonetheless be appropriate (see the discussion of 'Authorised remuneration') to allow a trustee who has made a profit to receive some reward for his services.

11.5.3 Exploiting opportunities

A fiduciary must not make a profit from an opportunity which only comes his way because of his fiduciary position. The prohibition applies regardless of whether the fiduciary's exploitation of the opportunity also benefits his principal, and also regardless of the fact that the principal could not have exploited the opportunity so as to make the profit.

Boardman v Phipps [1967] 2 AC 46

Panel: Viscount Dilhorne, Lord Cohen, Lord Hodson, Lord Guest and Lord Upjohn

Facts: A trust fund owned 8,000 of the 30,000 shares in a private company. One of the appellants (B) was the solicitor to the trust. As the result of an inquiry by the company as to whether the trustees would be willing to sell the trust shares to the company, B made various enquires into the company's affairs. Those enquiries enabled B to obtain a considerable amount of information regarding the financial position of the company. B, along with one of the other beneficiaries (P), also an appellant, formed the view that a re-organisation of the company's business would substantially improve the position of its shareholders. Having been unable to persuade the board to accept their proposals for re-organisation, B and P set about acquiring the remaining 22,000 shares for themselves (at no time did the trust have sufficient funds to acquire the shares). Having bought the vast majority of those shares, B and P were able to take control of the company and secure the re-organisation which they had proposed. This significantly improved the dividend and capital value of the shares, to the benefit of the trust as much as to B and P. Following the sale by B and P of their shares at a very substantial profit, the other beneficiaries brought proceedings in which they called upon B and P to account to the trust for the profit which they had made. It was held that B and P had acted in breach of fiduciary duty and were therefore liable to account for that profit.

LORD COHEN

Wilberforce J and, in the Court of Appeal, both Lord Denning MR and Pearson LJ, based their decision in favour of the respondent on the decision of your Lordships' House in *Regal (Hastings) Ltd v Gulliver* [1967] 2 AC 134. I turn, therefore, to consider that case ... in particular ... a passage in the speech of Lord Russell of Killowen where he says:

"The rule of equity which insists on those, who by use of a fiduciary position make a profit, being liable to account for that profit, in no way depends on fraud, or absence of bona fides, or upon such questions or considerations as whether the profit would or should otherwise have gone to the plaintiff, or whether the profiteer was under a duty to obtain the source of the profit for the plaintiff, or whether he took a risk or acted as he did for the benefit of the plaintiff, or whether the plaintiff has in fact been damaged or benefited by his action. The liability arises from the mere fact of a profit having, in the stated circumstances, been made."

[and also] a passage in the speech of Lord Wright, where he says:

"That question can be briefly stated to be whether an agent, a director, a trustee or other person in an analogous fiduciary position, when a demand is made upon him by the person to whom he stands in the fiduciary relationship to account for profits acquired by him by reason of his fiduciary position, and by reason of the opportunity and the knowledge, or either, resulting from it, is entitled to defeat the claim upon any ground save that he made profits with the knowledge and assent of the other person. The most usual and typical case of this nature is that of principal and agent. The rule in such cases is compendiously expressed to be that an agent must account for net profits secretly (that is, without the knowledge of his principal) acquired by him in the course of his agency. The authorities show how manifold and various are the applications of the rule. It does not depend on fraud or corruption."

...In that case the profit arose through the application by four of the directors of Regal for shares in a subsidiary company which it had been the original intention of the board should be subscribed for by Regal. Regal had not the requisite money available but there was no question of it being ultra vires Regal to subscribe for the shares. In the circumstances Lord Russell of Killowen said:

"I have no hesitation in coming to the conclusion, upon the facts of this case, that these shares, when acquired by the directors, were acquired by reason, and only by reason of the fact that they were directors of Regal, and in the course of their execution of that office."

He goes on to consider whether the four directors were in a fiduciary relationship to Regal and concludes that they were. Accordingly, they were held accountable.

In the case before your Lordships it seems to me clear that the appellants throughout were obtaining information from the company [on behalf of the trustees] for the purpose [of extracting information as to the company's business] but it does not necessarily follow that the appellants were thereby debarred from acquiring shares in the company for themselves. They were bound to give the information to the trustees but they could not exclude it from their own minds. ...[The] mere use of any knowledge or opportunity which comes to the trustee or agent in the course of his trusteeship or agency does not necessarily make him liable to account. In the present case had the company been a public company and had the appellants bought the shares on the market, they would not, I think, have been accountable. But the company is a private company and not only the information but the opportunity to purchase these shares came to them through the introduction which [B was given] to the board of the company and ... when the discussions [moved on] to the proposed split-up of the company's undertaking it was solely on behalf of the trustees that [B] was purporting to negotiate with the board of the company. ...

[The] fact [is] that the appellants obtained both the information which satisfied them that the purchase of the shares would be a good investment and the opportunity of acquiring them as a result of acting for certain purposes on behalf of the trustees. Information is, of course, not property in the strict sense of that word and, as I have

 Alert

already stated, it does not necessarily follow that because an agent acquired information and opportunity while acting in a fiduciary capacity he is accountable to his principals for any profit that comes his way as the result of the use he makes of that information and opportunity. His liability to account must depend on the facts of the case. In the present case much of the information came the appellants' way when [B] was acting on behalf of the trustees ... and the opportunity of bidding for the shares came because he purported for all purposes except for making the bid to be acting on behalf of the owners of the 8,000 shares in the company. In these circumstances it seems to me that the principle of the *Regal* case applies and that the courts below came to the right conclusion.

That is enough to dispose of the case but I would add that an agent is, in my opinion, liable to account for profits he makes out of trust property if there is a possibility of conflict between his interest and his duty to his principal. [B and P] were not general agents of the trustees but they were their agents for certain limited purposes. The information they had obtained and the opportunity to purchase the 21,986 shares afforded them by their relations with the directors of the company ... were not property in the strict sense but that information and that opportunity they owed to their representing themselves as agents for the holders of the 8,000 shares held by the trustees. In these circumstances they could not, I think, use that information and that opportunity to purchase the shares for themselves if there was any possibility that the trustees might wish to acquire them for the trust. [B] was the solicitor whom the trustees were in the habit of consulting if they wanted legal advice ... [and he] would not have been able to give unprejudiced advice if he had been consulted by the trustees and was at the same time negotiating for the purchase of the shares on behalf of himself and [P]. In other words, there was, in my opinion, at the crucial date ... a possibility of a conflict between his interest and his duty.

Link
See the discussion of remedies (below).

In making these observations I have referred to the fact that [B] was the solicitor to the trust. [P] was only a beneficiary and was not as such debarred from bidding for the shares, but no attempt was made in the courts below to differentiate between them. Had such an attempt been made it would very likely have failed as [P] left the negotiations largely to [B] and it might well be held that if [B] was disqualified from bidding [P] could not be in a better position. ...

I desire to repeat that the integrity of the appellants is not in doubt. They acted with complete honesty throughout and the respondent is a fortunate man in that the rigour of equity enables him to participate in the profits which have accrued as the result of the action taken by the appellants ... in purchasing the shares at their own risk. As the last paragraph of his judgment clearly shows, the trial judge evidently shared this view. He directed an inquiry as to what sum is proper to be allowed to the appellants or either of them in respect of his work and skill in obtaining the said shares and the profits in respect thereof. The trial judge concluded by expressing the opinion that payment should be on a liberal scale. With that observation I respectfully agree."

Link
See Authorised Remuneration below.

Although the defendants were ordered to account for the profits which they had made, they were, however, allowed payment for their services on a liberal scale.

Lord Cohen's speech illustrates the following propositions:

(a)   A fiduciary's liability to account for profit has nothing to do with fraud, dishonesty or bad faith; it flows from the very nature of the fiduciary relationship.

(b)   A fiduciary can use knowledge which he has obtained *by virtue of* his fiduciary position *only* for the benefit of his principal. Hence Lord Cohen's reference to the fact that if the company had been publicly listed, such that Boardman had obtained all the relevant information from its publicly-filed accounts, then no liability to account would have arisen.

(c)   Where the fiduciary's actions yield a profit both for his principal as well as himself, he may be entitled to be paid for his skill and effort in achieving the profit for the principal, notwithstanding his breach of fiduciary duty. see Authorised remuneration.

11.6 Authorised Remuneration

11.6.1 The inherent jurisdiction

The court has an inherent jurisdiction to authorise the payment of remuneration to express trustees, constructive trustees and other fiduciaries. However, the power to authorise remuneration is to be exercised sparingly. In particular, it should not offer any encouragement to trustees to act in breach of duty

Guinness plc v Saunders [1990] 2 AC 663

Panel: Lord Keith of Kinkel, Lord Brandon of Oakbrook, Lord Templeman, Lord Griffiths and Lord Goff of Chieveley

Facts: The plaintiff company had made a takeover bid for one of its competitors. The two defendants and a third person, who were directors of the plaintiff and the only members of its remuneration committee, agreed to pay the second defendant (W) 0.2 per cent of the ultimate value of the bid for his services in providing advice and services in connection with the bid. That decision was not authorised by the plaintiff's board of directors. Following successful completion of the bid, in relation to which W carried out a significant amount of work, W received the agreed payment, which amounted to £5.2m. On discovering the facts, the plaintiff claimed recovery of the money on the ground that W had received the payment in breach of his fiduciary duty as a director, in that he had not disclosed his interest in the agreement to the plaintiffs' directors as required by Companies Act 1985 s 317(1). W claimed that he should be allowed remuneration for the work which he had performed, but his claim was rejected.

LORD GOFF DF CHIEVELEY

The leading authorities ... demonstrate that the directors of a company, like other fiduciaries, must not put themselves in a position where there is a conflict between their personal interests and their duties as fiduciaries, and are for that reason precluded from contracting with the company for their services except in circumstances authorised by the articles of association. Similarly, just as trustees are not entitled, in the absence of an appropriate provision in the trust deed, to remuneration for their services as trustees, so directors are not entitled to remuneration for their services as directors except as provided by the articles of association.

...But the principle does not altogether exclude the possibility that an equitable allowance might be made in respect of services rendered. That such an allowance may be made to a trustee for work performed by him for the benefit of the trust, even though he was not in the circumstances entitled to remuneration under the terms of the trust deed, is now well established ... [see *Boardman v Phipps*]. Wilberforce J directed that, when accounting for such profits, not merely should a deduction be made for expenditure which was necessary to enable the profit to be realised, but also a liberal allowance or credit should be made for their work and skill. His reasoning was ...

"Moreover, account must naturally be taken of the expenditure which was necessary to enable the profit to be realised. But, in addition to expenditure, should not the defendants be given an allowance or credit for their work and skill? This is a subject on which authority is scanty; but Cohen J, in *In re Macadam* [1946] Ch 73, gave his support to an allowance of this kind to trustees for their services in acting as directors of a company. It seems to me that this transaction, ie, the acquisition of a controlling interest in the company, was one of a special character calling for the exercise of a particular kind of professional skill. If Boardman had not assumed the role of seeing it through, the beneficiaries would have had to employ (and would, had they been well advised, have employed) an expert to do it for them. If the trustees had come to the court asking for liberty to employ such a person, they would in all probability have been authorised to do so, and to remunerate the person in question. It seems to me that it would be inequitable now for the beneficiaries to step in and take the profit without paying for the skill and labour which has produced it." ...

It will be observed that the decision to make the allowance was founded upon the simple proposition that "it would be inequitable now for the beneficiaries to step in and take the profit without paying for the skill and labour which has produced it." Ex hypothesi, such an allowance was not in the circumstances authorised by the terms of the trust deed; furthermore it was held that there had not been full and proper disclosure by the two defendants to the successful plaintiff beneficiary. The inequity was found in the simple proposition that the beneficiaries were taking the profit although, if Mr Boardman (the solicitor) had not done the work, they would have had to employ an expert to do the work for them in order to earn that profit.

The decision has to be reconciled with the fundamental principle that a trustee is not entitled to remuneration for services rendered by him to the trust except as expressly provided in the trust deed. Strictly speaking, it is irreconcilable with the rule as so stated. It seems to me therefore that it can only be reconciled with it to the extent that the exercise of the equitable jurisdiction does not conflict with the policy underlying the rule. And, as I see it, such a conflict will only be avoided if the exercise of the jurisdiction is restricted to those cases where it cannot have the effect of encouraging

 Alert

trustees in any way to put themselves in a position where their interests conflict with their duties as trustees.

Not only was the equity underlying Mr Boardman's claim ... clear and, indeed, overwhelming; but the exercise of the jurisdiction to award an allowance in the unusual circumstances of that case could not provide any encouragement to trustees to put themselves in a position where their duties as trustees conflicted with their interests. The present case is, however, very different. Whether any such an allowance might ever be granted by a court of equity in the case of a director of a company, as opposed to a trustee, is a point which has yet to be decided; and I must reserve the question whether the jurisdiction could be exercised in such a case, which may be said to involve interference by the court in the administration of a company's affairs when the company is not being wound up. In any event, however, like my noble and learned friend, Lord Templeman, I cannot see any possibility of such jurisdiction being exercised in the present case. I proceed, of course, on the basis that ... [W] acted throughout in complete good faith. But the simple fact remains that, by agreeing to provide his services in return for a substantial fee the size of which was dependent upon the amount of a successful bid by Guinness, ... [he] was most plainly putting himself in a position in which his interests were in stark conflict with his duty as a director. Furthermore, for such services as he rendered, it is still open to the board of Guinness (if it thinks fit, having had a full opportunity to investigate the circumstances of the case) to award ... [him] appropriate remuneration. In all the circumstances of the case, I cannot think that this is a case in which a court of equity (assuming that it has jurisdiction to do so in the case of a director of a company) would order ... that an equitable allowance be made to ... [W] for his services.

11.7 Remedies for Breach of Fiduciary Duty

A fiduciary who acts in breach of the 'no profit' rule can be required to 'disgorge' that profit to his principal, who may pursue either a personal or a proprietary remedy in order to recover it.

11.7.1 Account

The personal remedy of an account entitles the principal to require the fiduciary to pay over an amount equal to the profit which the fiduciary has received.

Equity defines 'profit' as including *all* the benefit which the fiduciary has received during the course of the fiduciary relationship, and not merely the benefit which flows directly from the breach of fiduciary duty. The extent as well as the rigour of this rule are illustrated by the recent decisions of the Court of Appeal in *Murad v Al-Saraj* [2005] All ER (D) 503 (Jul) and *Imageview Management Ltd v Jack* [2009] 2 All ER 666.

Murad v Al-Saraj [2005] All ER (D) 503 (Jul)

Panel: Clarke, Jonathan Parker and Arden LJJ

Facts: The first defendant persuaded the claimants to enter into a joint venture with him for the purchase of a hotel, under which they would divide any capital profit from the resale of the hotel as to 50 per cent for him and 50 per cent for the claimants. It was common ground on the hearing of this appeal that (i) the first defendant had owed a fiduciary duty to the claimants in relation to that venture, (ii) he had acted in breach of that duty by, amongst other things, procuring the payment to himself of a commission of £369,000 from the seller of the hotel and (iii) had he made full disclosure, the claimants would still have participated in the joint venture but would have negotiated a greater share of the capital profit for themselves. At trial, the judge held that the consequence of the first defendant's breach of duty was that he was liable to account for the whole of his share of any capital profit which might be made when the hotel was sold. The first defendant appealed on the ground that his liability should be limited to the difference between the 50 per cent share which had actually been agreed and the lower share which he would have been forced to agree if he had made full disclosure. The majority (Parker and Arden LJJ) took the traditional approach, which was that Mr Al-Saraj had to account for any 'profit' (or benefit) which he derived from his position as a fiduciary as a consequence of his breach of fiduciary duty.

LORD JUSTICE JONATHAN PARKER

...Mr Al-Saraj contends that ... the judge was wrong in law to hold him liable to account for all the profits which he made from the joint venture, but rather that he should be held accountable only for the difference between his agreed 50 per cent share of the capital profits and such lesser share as he would have had if he had made full disclosure (that is to say, the share he had would have had but for his deliberate breach of his fiduciary obligations).

In my judgment, that contention is directly contrary to long-standing authority in this jurisdiction.

I start with the well-known passage in the judgment of Sir W M James LJ in *Parker v McKenna* (1874) LR 10 Ch App 96, where he said this:

"I do not think it is necessary, but it appears to me very important, that we should concur in laying down again and again the general principle that in this Court no agent in the course of his agency, in the matter of his agency, can be allowed to make any profit without the knowledge and consent of his principal; that that rule is an inflexible rule, and must be applied inexorably by this Court, which is not entitled, in my judgment, to receive evidence, or suggestion, or argument as to whether the principal did or did not suffer any injury in fact by reason of the dealing of the agent; for the safety of mankind requires that no agent shall be able to put his principal to the danger of such an inquiry as that."

In the same case, Lord Cairns LC said this (at p118):

"Now, the rule of this Court, as I understand it, as to agents, is not a technical or arbitrary rule. It is a rule founded upon the highest and truest principles of morality. No man can in this Court, acting as agent, be allowed to put himself in a position in which his interest and his duty will be in conflict. .... The Court will not inquire, and is not in a position to ascertain, whether the bank has lost or not lost by the acts of its directors. All that the Court has to do is examine whether a profit has been made by an agent, without the knowledge of his principal, in the course and execution of his agency, and the Court finds, in my opinion, that these agents in the course of their agency have made a profit, and for that profit they must, in my opinion, account to their principal."

 Alert

To similar effect is the following passage from the speech of Lord Russell of Killowen *Regal (Hastings) Ltd v Gulliver* [1967] 2 AC 134 at 144G-145A:

"The rule of equity which insists on those, who by use of a fiduciary position make a profit, being liable to account for that profit, in no way depends on fraud, or absence of bona fides; or upon such questions or considerations as whether the profits would or should otherwise have gone to the plaintiff, or whether the profiteer was under a duty to obtain the source of the profit for the plaintiff, or whether he took a risk and acted as he did for the benefit of the plaintiff, or whether the plaintiff has in fact been damaged or benefited by his action. The liability arises from the mere fact of a profit having, in the stated circumstances, been made. The profiteer, however honest and well-intentioned, cannot escape the risk of being called upon to account." ...

In ... [*Gwembe Valley Development Co Ltd & Anor v Koshy* [2004] BCLC 131] ... Mummery LJ, giving the judgment of the Court of Appeal, said this (at paragraph 145):

"In considering ... whether the director should account for unauthorised profits, what would have happened, if the required disclosure had been made, is irrelevant."

As Lord Eldon made clear in *Ex parte James* (1803) 8 Ves 337 at 345, one of the policy reasons behind equity's "inflexible rule" (for convenience I will refer to it hereafter as "the 'no conflict' rule") is the perceived difficulty in determining what might have happened but for the fact that the fiduciary had placed himself in a position of conflict (a point also made by Lord Wright in the passage in his speech in *Boardman v Phipps* referred to above). Another policy reason for the 'no conflict' rule is the need to deter fiduciaries from placing themselves in positions of conflict (see, eg, *Bray v Ford* [1896] AC 44 at 51 per Lord Herschell).

It is thus clear on authority, in my judgment, that the 'no conflict' rule is neither compensatory nor restitutionary: rather, it is designed to strip the fiduciary of the unauthorised profits he has made whilst he is in a position of conflict. As Lord Keith observed in *Attorney-General v Guardian Newspapers Ltd (No 2)* [1990] 1 AC 109, at 262E-F, the remedy of an account of profits:

 Alert

"... is, in my opinion, more satisfactorily to be attributed to the principle that no one should be permitted to gain from his own wrongdoing".

I therefore conclude, on the basis of long-standing authority, that Mr Al-Saraj's liability to account extends to the entirety of the profits which he made from the joint venture."

Imageview Management Ltd v Jack [2009] 2 All ER 666

Panel: Mummery, Dyson and Jacob LJJ

Facts: The defendant (J) was a professional footballer and an international for Trinidad and Tobago. He wished to play professionally in Britain and appointed the claimant (IML) as his agent to negotiate terms with interested clubs. The agency contract entitled IML to a percentage of J's salary if such a contract was secured. IML found a club who were interested in giving J a contract, but would only do so once he had obtained a work permit. IML entered into a secret deal with the club, under which the club paid IML a fee of £3,000 for obtaining that work permit. The 'true cost' to IML of obtaining the work permit was only £750. Once the work permit had been obtained by IML, J signed for the club. For several months J paid fees to IML under the agency contract, but stopped doing so when he found out about the work permit contract. IML brought proceedings against J for unpaid agency fees and J counterclaimed both for the agency fees he had already paid as well as the full £3,000 received by IML from the club or, in the alternative, the 'excess' of £2,250 which represented the difference between £3,000 and the real value of the work done. The Court of Appeal held that J was entitled both to the £3,000 received by IML and also to repayment of all the agency fees which he had paid to date.

LORD JUSTICE JACOB

Unless there was a breach of duty ... Mr Jack is liable for the unpaid balance of the fees. Was the undisclosed side deal [in relation to the work permit] 'none of Mr Jack's business'? [The courts below have] held that it was indeed Mr Jack's business: it was not [IML's] private and separate arrangement.

The basis for such a finding was that IML in negotiating a deal for itself had a clear conflict of interest. Put shortly, it is possible that the more it got for itself, the less there would or could be for Mr Jack. Moreover it gave IML an interest in Mr Jack signing for [the club] as opposed to some other club where no side deal for IML was possible.

There is no answer to this. The law imposes on agents high standards. Footballers' agents are not exempt from these. An agent's own personal interests come entirely second to the interest of his client. If you undertake to act for a man you must act 100%, body and soul, for him. You must act as if you were him. You must not allow your own interest to get in the way without telling him. An undisclosed but realistic possibility of a conflict of interest is a breach of your duty of good faith to your client. That duty should not cause an agent any problem. All he or she has to do to avoid being in breach of duty is to make full disclosure. Any agent who is doubtful about his position would do well to do just that – the mere fact that he has doubts will generally be a message from his conscience. ...

 Alert

This is a case of a secret profit obtained because [IML] was Mr Jack's agent. And there was a breach of a fiduciary duty because of a real conflict of interest. That in itself would be enough, but there is more: the profit was not only greater than the work done [in relation to the work permit] but was related to the very contract which was being negotiated for Mr Jack [with the club]. Once a conflict of interest is shown ... the right to remuneration goes.

It flies in the face of reality to say that once the terms of Mr Jack's contract [with the club] had been negotiated in principle they could not be reopened. Suppose, for instance, IML had, after negotiating [the] £3,000 fee, said to [the club]: 'Well that shows you are willing to pay more to get Mr Jack playing for you. How about reducing my fee and giving it to my client, Mr Jack?' As Mr Jack's agent [IML] had an interest in saying just that; [its] own interest was in saying nothing. He had 'a temptation not faithfully to perform his duty to his employer' (see per Cotton LJ in *Boston Deep Sea Fishing and Ice Co v Ansell* (1888) 39 Ch D 339 at 357. Of course, since he never said anything, we shall never know what [the club] would have done. Nor do we need to ('[i]t is impossible to gauge ... what the plaintiff has lost', per Lord Alverstone CJ in *Andrews v Ramsay & Co* [1903] 2 KB 635 at 637-638).

Finally in relation to this point and indeed the further points about the appropriate remedies I should mention what was something of a constant refrain from [counsel for IML]. It was this: Mr Jack got the benefit of the contract negotiated for him. Why should he not have to pay for it? Why should he have the benefit of the agent's work for nothing at all?

The answer is twofold. First, it has already been given in the cases, and second, there are sound policy reasons as to why.

As far as the cases are concerned, I have already cited enough to show that the principle is established, see for instance Atkin LJ in *Keppel v Wheeler* [1927] 1 KB 577 at 592 ('forfeit any right to remuneration at all'), Lord Alverstone CJ in *Andrews v Ramsay & Co* [1903] 2 KB 635 at 637 ('not entitled to recover any commission'), Wills J in *Andrews v Ramsay & Co* at 638 ('[t]he case ought to be the same whether the commission has already been paid or whether the agent has to sue for it') and Scrutton LJ in *Rhodes v Macalister* (1924) 29 Com Cas 19 at 28 ('The result may actually be that the employer makes money out of the fact that the agent has taken commission').

The policy reason runs as follows. We are here concerned not with merely damages such as those for a tort or breach of contract but with what the remedy should be when the agent has betrayed the trust reposed in him - notions of equity and conscience are brought into play. Necessarily such a betrayal may not come to light. If all the agent has to pay if and when he is found out are damages the temptation to betray the trust reposed in him is all the greater. So the strict rule is there as a real deterrent to betrayal. As Scrutton LJ said in *Rhodes v Macalister* at 28: 'The more that principle is enforced, the better for the honesty of commercial transactions.'

Accordingly, as the courts below held, there was a breach of fiduciary duty here. The cases I have cited make it plain that where there is such a breach commission is forfeit – so Mr Jack need pay no more agency fees and is entitled to repayment of the fees paid by him.

 Alert

The £3,000 was a secret profit made by a fiduciary. On normal equitable principles it is recoverable, subject to the possibility ... of a reasonable remuneration deduction. ...

What then are the principles which govern a deduction when a fiduciary has received a secret profit in breach of his duty of fidelity?

The basic principle is beyond dispute ... 'A fiduciary is bound to account for any profit that he or she has received in breach of fiduciary duty.'

Snell's Equity (31st edn, 2005, para 7-131) ... sets out the general rules about when an allowance for skill and effort will be made:

'A fiduciary who has acted in breach of fiduciary duty and against whom an account of profits is ordered, may nevertheless be given an allowance for skill and effort employed in obtaining the profit which he has to disgorge where "it would be inequitable now for the beneficiaries to step in and take the profit without paying for the skill and labour which has produced it." This power is exercised sparingly, out of concern not to encourage fiduciaries to act in breach of fiduciary duty. It will not likely be used where the fiduciary has been involved in surreptitious dealing ... although strictly speaking, it is not ruled out simply because the fiduciary can be criticised in the circumstances. The fiduciary bears the onus of convincing the court that an accounting of his or her entire profits is inappropriate in the circumstances ... .'

[Counsel for IML] did not contest any of this. ... [He] took us to *O'Sullivan v Management Agency and Music Ltd* [1985] QB 428 at 468 where Fox LJ said: 'Nor do I think that the principle [of making an allowance] is only applicable in cases where the conduct of the fiduciary cannot be criticised. I think that the justice of the individual case must be considered on the facts of that case.' ... But Fox LJ went on to say: 'Accordingly, where there has been dishonesty or surreptitious dealing or other improper conduct ... it might be appropriate to refuse relief; but that will depend on the circumstances.' The present case is, of course, one of surreptitious dealing.

Murad v Al-Saraj [2005] EWCA Civ 959, [2005] 32 LS Gaz R 31 [contains] the warning of the High Court of Australia in *Warman International Ltd v Dwyer* (1995) 182 CLR 544 that the remedy of an account should not be allowed to become a vehicle for the unjust enrichment of the plaintiff.

But ... the work involved [in obtaining the work permit] was never anything Mr Jack was expecting to pay for. It was something which he surely knew had to be done before he could play. But it was not a benefit which accrued to him financially. How [the club] arranged for the permit was simply a matter for [the club].

So ... I cannot see any reason for exercising the power – one to be exercised sparingly – to make an allowance. The onus of justifying the allowance is far from discharged. So I would dismiss this appeal in its entirety."

Link

The quotation is from the judgment of Wilberforce J in *Phipps v Boardman* [1964] 1 WLR 993 at 1018.

This decision sets out the legal and policy reasons why a fiduciary will be stripped of all profit if he commits a breach of fiduciary duty. Not only does the rule reflect the fact that it is impossible to know what deal might have been struck between the principal and the fiduciary if the principal had known of all the facts, but it also serves 'pour encourager les autres'.

11.7.2 Constructive Trust

The proprietary remedy of a constructive trust entitles the principal to claim that the fiduciary holds the profit on constructive trust for him. In accordance with established principles, this remedy: (a) survives the insolvency of the fiduciary; and (b) allows the principal to trace the profit if it is applied by the fiduciary in the acquisition of other property. Tracing is covered in Chapter 15.

A proprietary remedy is the preferred claim where the fiduciary still holds the profit or any substitute property.

A-G for Hong Kong v Reid [1994] 1 AC 324

Panel: Lord Templeman, Lord Goff of Chieveley, Lord Lowry, Lord Lloyd of Berwick and Sir Thomas Eichelbaum

Facts: The defendant (R), the former Acting Director of Public Prosecutions in Hong Kong, had been found guilty of accepting bribes and was ordered to repay the amount of those bribes to the Crown. The Crown's case was that R had used the bribes to buy three properties in New Zealand. The Attorney-General for Hong Kong lodged temporary caveats in New Zealand against the titles to the properties as a prelude to forcing the sale of them. He subsequently applied to the High Court of New Zealand to renew those caveats, but the application was refused on the ground that the Crown had no equitable interest in the properties. The Court of Appeal of New Zealand dismissed the Attorney-General's appeal. The Privy Council held that the money received by R was subject to a constructive trust in favour of the Crown, with the result that any property acquired by the use of that money was similarly held on trust for the Crown.

LORD TEMPLEMAN delivering the advice of the Board

When a bribe is offered and accepted in money or in kind, the money or property constituting the bribe belongs in law to the recipient. Money paid to the false fiduciary belongs to him. The legal estate in freehold property conveyed to the false fiduciary by way of bribe vests in him. Equity, however, which acts in personam, insists that it is unconscionable for a fiduciary to obtain and retain a benefit in breach of duty. The provider of a bribe cannot recover it because he committed a criminal offence when he paid the bribe. The false fiduciary who received the bribe in breach of duty must pay and account for the bribe to the person to whom that duty was owed. In the present case, as soon as the first respondent received a bribe in breach of the duties he owed to the Government of Hong Kong, he became a debtor in equity to the Crown for the amount of that bribe. So much is admitted. But if the bribe consists of property which increases in value or if a cash bribe is invested advantageously, the false fiduciary will receive a benefit from his breach of duty unless he is accountable not only for the original amount or value of the bribe but also for the increased value of the property representing the bribe. As soon as the bribe was received it should have been paid or transferred instanter to the person who suffered from the breach of duty. Equity considers as done that which ought to have been done. As soon as the bribe was received, whether in cash or in kind, the false fiduciary held the bribe on a constructive trust for the person injured. Two objections have been raised to this analysis. First it is said that if the fiduciary is in equity a debtor to the person injured, he cannot also be a trustee of the bribe. But there is no reason why equity should not provide two remedies, so long as they do not result in double recovery. If the property representing the bribe exceeds the original bribe in value, the fiduciary cannot retain the benefit of the increase in value which he obtained solely as a result of his breach of duty. Secondly, it is said that if the false fiduciary holds property representing the bribe in trust for the person injured, and if the false fiduciary is or becomes insolvent, the unsecured creditors of the false fiduciary will be deprived of their right to share in the proceeds of that property. But the unsecured creditors cannot be in a better position than their debtor. The authorities show that property acquired by a trustee innocently but in breach of trust and the property from time to time representing the same belong in equity to the cestui que trust and not to the trustee personally whether he is solvent or insolvent. Property acquired by a trustee as a result of a criminal breach of trust and the property from time to time representing the same must also belong in equity to his cestui que trust and not to the trustee whether he is solvent or insolvent.

When a bribe is accepted by a fiduciary in breach of his duty then he holds that bribe in trust for the person to whom the duty was owed. If the property representing the bribe decreases in value the fiduciary must pay the difference between that value and the initial amount of the bribe because he should not have accepted the bribe or incurred the risk of loss. If the property increases in value, the fiduciary is not entitled to any surplus in excess of the initial value of the bribe because he is not allowed by any means to make a profit out of a breach of duty. ...

[However, it] has always been assumed and asserted that the law on the subject of bribes was definitively settled by the decision of the Court of Appeal in *Lister & Co v Stubbs* (1890) 45 Ch D 1.

In that case the plaintiffs, Lister & Co, employed the defendant, Stubbs, as their servant to purchase goods for the firm. Stubbs, on behalf of the firm, bought goods from Varley & Co and received from Varley & Co bribes amounting to £5,541. The bribes were invested by Stubbs in freehold properties and investments. His masters, the firm Lister & Co, sought and failed to obtain an interlocutory injunction restraining Stubbs from disposing of these assets pending the trial of the action in which they sought, inter alia, £5,541 and damages. In the Court of Appeal the first judgment was given by Cotton LJ who had been party to the decision in *Metropolitan Bank v Heiron*, 5 Ex D 319. He was powerfully supported by the judgment of Lindley LJ and by the equally powerful concurrence of Bowen LJ. Cotton LJ said, at p 12, that the bribe could not be said to be the money of the plaintiffs. He seemed to be reluctant to grant an interlocutory judgment which would provide security for a debt before that debt had been established. Lindley LJ said, at p 15, that the relationship between the plaintiffs, Lister &

> **Decipher**
>
> 'Instanter' means 'immediately'

Co, as masters and the defendant, Stubbs, as servant who had betrayed his trust and received a bribe:

"...is that of debtor and creditor; it is not that of trustee and cestui que trust. We are asked to hold that it is - which would involve consequences which, I confess, startle me. One consequence, of course, would be that, if Stubbs were to become bankrupt, this property acquired by him with the money paid to him by Messrs Varley would be withdrawn from the mass of his creditors and be handed over bodily to Lister & Co. Can that be right? Another consequence would be that, if the appellants are right, Lister & Co could compel Stubbs to account to them, not only for the money with interest, but for all the profits which he might have made by embarking in trade with it. Can that be right?"

For the reasons which have already been advanced their Lordships would respectfully answer both these questions in the affirmative. If a trustee mistakenly invests moneys which he ought to pay over to his cestui que trust and then becomes bankrupt, the moneys together with any profit which has accrued from the investment are withdrawn from the unsecured creditors as soon as the mistake is discovered. A fortiori if a trustee commits a crime by accepting a bribe which he ought to pay over to his cestui que trust, the bribe and any profit made therefrom should be withdrawn from the unsecured creditors as soon as the crime is discovered.

The decision in *Lister & Co v Stubbs* is not consistent with the principles that a fiduciary must not be allowed to benefit from his own breach of duty, that the fiduciary should account for the bribe as soon as he receives it and that equity regards as done that which ought to be done. From these principles it would appear to follow that the bribe and the property from time to time representing the bribe are held on a constructive trust for the person injured. A fiduciary remains personally liable for the amount of the bribe if, in the event, the value of the property then recovered by the injured person proved to be less than that amount.

 Alert

Lord Templeman gave the only speech. He gave short shrift to the argument, which formed the basis of the decision in *Lister* (above) that the recipient of a bribe is only under a personal obligation to repay the bribe. It was clear, in his view, that where a fiduciary owns property which has been acquired by using the profit which the fiduciary has unlawfully acquired by virtue of his breach of duty, that property is held upon constructive trust for the principal.

Sinclair Investments (UK) Ltd v Versailles Trade Finance Ltd (in administrative receivership) and others [2012] Ch. 453

Panel: Lord Neuberger of Abbotsbury MR; Richards, Hughes LJJ

Facts: Sinclair Investments (UK) Ltd paid money to Trading Partners Ltd (TPL) to carry out trades in goods. The director was a Mr Cushnie, who transferred these funds to a subsidiary company called Versailles Trade Finance Ltd (VTFL). Rather than engage in factoring, however, VTF fraudulently used the funds to pay profits to wealthy investors in TPL; the funds were also circulated around other subsidiary companies of Mr Cushnie so that they appeared extremely profitable. As a result of the frauds, the share prices of Mr Cushnie's companies rose significantly. Mr Cushnie subsequently sold his shares in TPL for £28.69m. Of this money, £9.19m went to VTFL and £11.47m to Royal Bank of Scotland. £9.98m of this money was repayment of a loan secured on a property purchased by Mr Cushnie in Kensington. Eventually, this fraud was discovered and VTFL was put into receivership. TPL also lost value as a result of VTFL's activities, and was also put into liquidation in July 2000.

LORD NEUBERGER OF ABBOTSBURY MR

The next case in time is a decision of the *House of Lords, Tyrrell v Bank of London (1862) 10 HL Cas 26*... The view of all three members of the Committee in the *Tyrrell* case was that a solicitor who bought a piece of land (which he knew that his client was interested in acquiring) (i) held that part of the land which his client then purchased on trust for his client (so that his client beneficially owned the profit which the solicitor made on that part), but (ii) did not hold the remainder of the land on trust for his client. In *Attorney General for Hong Kong v Reid* [1994] 1 AC 324 , 333 Lord Templeman seems to have thought that his conclusion that a bribe accepted by an agent was beneficially owned by his principal was inconsistent only with Lord Chelmsford's view. I find it hard to see how it is not also inconsistent with the view of all three members of the Committee in the Tyrrell case on point (ii)...

Lewison J followed the approach of the Court of Appeal in the *Heiron* 5 Ex D 319 and *Lister* 45 Ch D 1 cases, and accordingly held that TPL had no proprietary interest in the proceeds of sale of the shares. For TPL, Mr Miles (legal counsel) contends that this was wrong and that we should follow the decision of the Privy Council in the *Reid* case [1994] 1 AC 324 .

I would reject that contention. We should not follow the Privy Council decision in the Reid case in preference to decisions of this court, unless there are domestic authorities which show that the decisions of this court were *per incuriam* or at least of doubtful reliability. Save where there are powerful reasons to the contrary, the Court of Appeal should follow its own previous decisions, and in this instance there are five such previous decisions. It is true that there is a powerful subsequent decision of the Privy Council which goes the other way, but that of itself is not enough to justify departing from the earlier decisions of this court: see *In re Spectrum Plus Ltd* [2004] Ch 337 , para 58, per Lord Phillips of Worth Matravers MR and [2005] 2 AC 680, para 153, per Lord Walker of Gestingthorpe.

I do not suggest that it would always be wrong for this court to refuse to follow a decision of the Privy Council in preference to one of its own previous decisions, but the general rule is that we follow our previous decisions, leaving it to the Supreme Court to overrule those decisions if it is appropriate to do so. Two recent cases where this court preferred to follow a decision of the Privy Council rather than an earlier domestic decision which would normally be regarded as binding (in each case a decision of the House of Lords are *R v James* [2006] QB 588 and *Abou-Rahmah v Abacha* [2007] Bus LR 220 . In each case the decision was justified, based as it was on the proposition that it was a foregone conclusion that, if the case had gone to the House of Lords, they would have followed the Privy Council decision.

In the present instance Mr Miles invited us to take the view that it was a foregone conclusion that the Supreme Court would follow the Privy Council in the *Reid* case [1994] 1 AC 324 rather than the Court of Appeal in the *Heiron* 5 Ex D 319 and *Lister* 45 Ch D 1 cases, and therefore to follow the Privy Council approach rather than that of this court.

Although it is possible that the Supreme Court would follow the *Reid* case rather than the *Heiron* and *Lister* cases, I am far from satisfied that they would do so. In any event it does not seem to me right to follow the *Reid* case.

First, there are five decisions of this court (*Metropolitan Bank v Heiron* 5 Ex D 319, *Lister & Co v Stubbs* 45 Ch D 1, *Archer's Case* [1892] 1 Ch 322 , *Powell & Thomas v Evan Jones & Co* [1905] 1 KB 11 and *Attorney General's Reference (No 1 of 1985)* [1986] QB 491) spread over 95 years, all of which have reached the same conclusion on the point, and there is the reasoning of the House of Lords in *Tyrrell v Bank of London* 10 HL Cas 26 . Although it may be true that the reasoning in *Pearson's Case* 5 Ch D 336, which was not cited to the courts in the *Heiron* 5 Ex D 319 and *Lister* 45 Ch D 1 cases, is inconsistent with those cases, I am not persuaded that the point has any force: (i) the point does not appear to have been argued in *Pearson's Case* 5 Ch D 336, (ii) the *Tyrrell* case 10 HL Cas 26 was not cited in *Pearson's Case*, (iii) *Pearson's Case* and the *Lister* case 45 Ch D 1 were both cited in *Archer's Case* [1892] 1 Ch 322 and the latter authority was preferred, and (iv) in subsequent cases this court followed the *Lister* case.

Secondly, much of the reasoning of Lord Templeman in *Attorney General for Hong Kong v Reid* [1994] 1 AC 324 seems to me to beg the question, or to assume what it asserts (although I suppose that the same can be said about the views expressed in the *Heiron* 5 Ex D 319 and *Lister* 45 Ch D 1 cases). Thus before setting out to explain his reasoning, Lord Templeman asserts [1994] 1 AC 324, 331B–C that a bribe paid to a "false fiduciary" vests in him and he must pay and account for it to "the person to whom [the] duty is owed". But that is the very issue he then purports to decide.

Thirdly, the concern which Lord Templeman expressed at the end of the passage I have quoted in para 71 above might well be met by ordering an equitable account: there was apparently no argument before the Privy Council to that effect.

80 Fourthly, it seems to me that there is a real case for saying that the decision in the *Reid* case [1994] 1 AC 324 is unsound. In cases where a fiduciary takes for himself an asset which, if he chose to take, he was under a duty to take for the beneficiary, it is easy to see why the asset should be treated as the property of the beneficiary. However, a bribe paid to a fiduciary could not possibly be said to be an asset which the fiduciary was under a duty to take for the beneficiary. There can thus be said to be a fundamental distinction between (i) a fiduciary enriching himself by depriving a claimant of an asset and (ii) a fiduciary enriching himself by doing a wrong to the claimant. Having said that, I can see a real policy reason in its favour (if equitable accounting is not available), but the fact that it may not accord with principle is obviously a good reason for not following it in preference to decisions of this court.

Fifthly, not only has there been much academic commentary since the *Reid* case [1994] 1 AC 324 which supports the approach in the *Heiron* 5 Ex D 319 and *Lister* 45 Ch D 1 cases, but, at least from what I have seen, there is significantly more support for the approach for those cases in scholarly articles than there is for the *Reid* case...

Sixthly, it seems to me that Lord Templeman may have given insufficient weight to the potentially unfair consequences to the interests of other creditors, if his conclusion was right. His dismissal of their concerns on the basis that they should be in no better position than the defaulting fiduciary [1994] 1 AC 324, 331F–H stands in rather stark contrast with what was said in the *Lister* case 45 Ch D 1, 15, and in *Archer's Case* [1892] 1 Ch 322, 338, as well as more recently in *Westdeutsche Landesbank Girozentrale v Islington London Borough Council* [1996] AC 669, 716 E. In that case Lord Browne-Wilkinson disapproved of extending the reach of resulting trusts as it could produce "most unjust results", namely conferring "on the plaintiff a right to recover property from, or at the expense of [for example] the lender whose debt is secured by a floating charge and all other parties who have purchased an equitable interest only".

Seventhly, there are some relevant domestic decisions subsequent to the *Reid* case. In *Daraydan Holdings Ltd v Solland International Ltd* [2005] Ch 119, para 86 Lawrence Collins J (after referring, at para 81, to some other post-*Reid* first instance decisions which seemed to have gone in different ways) preferred to follow the *Reid* case, but (i) that was before the guidance given in *In re Spectrum Plus Ltd* [2004] Ch 337; [2005] 2 AC 680, referred to in para 73 above, (ii) as Lawrence Collins J pointed out [2005] Ch 119, paras 87–88, on the facts of that case the decision was not inconsistent with the reasoning in the *Lister* case 45 Ch D 1, and (iii) it was a first instance judgment and neither *Tyrrell v Bank of London* 10 HL Cas 26 nor *Archer's Case* [1892] 1 Ch 322 was cited to him...

In my view, Lewison J was right to reject TPL's proprietary claim to the proceeds of sale of the shares. It is true that the decisions in the *Reid* case [1994] 1 AC 324, *Sugden v Crossland* 3 Sm & G 192 and (at least arguably), *Pearson's Case* 5 Ch D 336 go the other way. However, there is a consistent line of reasoned decisions of this court (two of which were decided within the last ten years) stretching back into the late 19th century, and one decision of the House of Lords 150 years ago, which appear to establish that a beneficiary of a fiduciary's duties cannot claim a proprietary interest, but is entitled to an equitable account, in respect of any money or asset acquired by a fiduciary in breach of his duties to the beneficiary, unless the asset or money is or has been beneficially the property of the beneficiary or the trustee acquired the asset or money by taking advantage of an opportunity or right which was properly that of the beneficiary.

For the reasons I have given, previous decisions of this court establish that a claimant cannot claim proprietary ownership of an asset purchased by the defaulting fiduciary with funds which, although they could not have been obtained if he had not enjoyed his fiduciary status, were not beneficially owned by the claimant or derived from opportunities beneficially owned by the claimant. However, those cases also establish that in such a case a claimant does have a personal claim in equity to the funds. There is no case which appears to support the notion that such a personal claim entitles the claimant to claim the value of the asset (if it is greater than the amount of the funds together with interest), and there are judicial indications which tend to militate against that notion...

In these circumstances I cannot improve on Lewison J's conclusion on this part of the case [2011] 1 BCLC 202, para 81:

Lord Neuberger and the Court of Appeal left no doubt about their opinion of *Attorney General for Hong Kong v Reid* [1994] 1 AC 324 and its applicability to cases involving bribes or secret commissions. For various reasons, any such payments were not to be subject to a proprietary constructive trust remedy, but only a personal liability to account on the part of the fiduciary to their principal. Nevertheless, the Master of the Rolls was open to the issue being revisited by the Supreme Court.

FHR European Ventures LLP and others v Mankarious and others [2014] Ch. 1

Panel: Sir Terence Etherton C, Pill, Lewison LJJ

Facts: Cedar Capital Partners LLC (CCPL) had been established by the defendant, Ramsey Neil Mankarious, to provide consultancy services to the hotel industry. In this capacity, it entered into an agreement with the Monegasque owners of the Monte Carlo Grand Hotel to sell the property for them. In exchange, CCPL would receive a commission from Monte Carlo Grand Hotel Ltd; this arrangement was to be disclosed by CCPL to prospective purchasers. In breach, CCPL failed to disclose the arrangement to the eventual purchaser of the hotel, Fairmont Hotels and Resorts European Ventures LLP (FHR). Subsequently, FHR sought to recover the €10 million commission paid to CCPL by Monte Carlo Grand Hotel Ltd.

LEWISON LJ

Accordingly, the argument that [FHR] advances in this court is that the judge ought to have held that the investor group was entitled to a proprietary remedy against Cedar on one or both of the following bases. (i) Cedar received the commission in substance out of the sale proceeds. The money paid by the investor group was money that the investor group had beneficially owned. It does not matter that the money was not paid directly to Cedar. Thus the payment of the commission falls within the first of the two exceptions referred to in the *Sinclair* case. (ii) As the agent of the investor group Cedar had a duty to negotiate the lowest price that the vendors were willing to accept. In practical terms the vendors were willing to accept €10m less than the nominal purchase price. Accordingly the receipt by Cedar of the €10m commission was a benefit that Cedar ought to have acquired on behalf of its principal but instead diverted to itself. Thus the receipt of the €10m falls within the second of the two exceptions referred to in the *Sinclair* case.

I have no difficulty in accepting Mr Pymont's (legal counsel for FHR) submission that this case is factually different from the facts considered in the *Sinclair* case. In that case the connection between the breach of fiduciary duty and the profit was relatively remote. Mr Cushnie (the defaulting fiduciary in that case) made a profit by selling shares that he already owned before any question of relevant fiduciary duties arose. It was their value that was increased by reason of breaches of fiduciary duties. As Lord Neuberger of Abbotsbury MR pointed out the proprietary claim in that case was not a claim to funds in respect of which Mr Cushnie owed any relevant fiduciary duty, nor to any asset of the proceeds of any asset bought with those funds, nor to the proceeds of any right or opportunity which belonged to the principal. In our case the connection is much closer. But in the *Sinclair* case the principal legal debate was whether this court should follow on the one hand its own previous decisions in *Metropolitan Bank v Heiron* (1880) 5 Ex D 319 and *Lister & Co v Stubbs* 45 Ch D 1 or, on the other hand, the decision of the Privy Council in *Attorney General for Hong Kong v Reid* [1994] 1 AC 324... Accordingly this court affirmed the correctness (or at least the binding nature unless overruled by the Supreme Court) of the *Metropolitan Bank* and *Lister* cases...

Mr Collings (legal counsel for CCPL) submitted that: (i) the *Sinclair* case [2012] Ch 453 clearly equates bribes and secret commissions and treats them in precisely the same way; (ii) it also holds that there is a "fundamental difference" between (a) a fiduciary enriching himself by depriving the principal of an asset and (b) a fiduciary enriching himself by doing a wrong to the principal; (iii) since there is a fundamental difference between the two it is not possible for a single breach of duty to count as both; and the taking of a secret commission is plainly in the second of the two categories; (iv) the "lost" or "diverted" opportunity cases are equally clearly in the first of the two categories. It follows that the taking of a secret commission or bribe cannot fall within that category; (v) thus in the case of a bribe or secret commission the principal can only claim a proprietary interest if he can show that the payment of the bribe or secret commission was made out of his own money. Mr Collings thus accepted that in a case in which the principal could show that the fiduciary had acquired the principal's own money or property he could properly be described as a constructive trustee of that property or money...

Given that in the *Sinclair* case [2012] Ch 453 this court approved and followed the *Metropolitan Bank* case 5 Ex D 319 and the *Lister* case, we must do so too. Accordingly, in my judgment Mr Pymont's appeal must fail unless he can successfully distinguish those two cases as well as the *Sinclair* case...

In my judgment this group of cases shows that the principal can acquire a proprietary interest in an asset acquired by his agent, even though the principal had no pre-existing proprietary interest in the asset, and the asset was, in the first instance, acquired by the agent with his own money...

In my judgment there is no need to inquire whether the opportunity to acquire the hotel at a lower price can be characterised as an opportunity separate from the opportunity to acquire the hotel at all. I do not, therefore, agree with Newey J in *Cadogan Petroleum plc v Tolley* [2011] EWHC 2286 (Ch) that it is necessary to isolate the opportunity to acquire an asset at a lower price from the opportunity to acquire an asset at all. Nor is there any need to inquire whether the investor group can be said to have a proprietary interest, in the strict sense, in that opportunity. In my judgment the principle we must apply is that stated by Jonathan Parker LJ in *Bhullar v Bhullar* [2003] 2 BCLC 241: is the fiduciary's exploitation of the opportunity such as to attract the application of the rule? In the present case the exclusive brokerage agreement was part of the overall arrangement surrounding the purchase of the hotel. I cannot see that it is different in principle from the contract between Tyrrell and Read in so far as it concerned the target property (see the *Tyrrell* case 10 HL Cas 26) or the contract between Green and Smith: *Whaley Bridge Calico Printing Co v Green* 5 QBD 109. In my judgment the exploitation of the opportunity by Cedar was such as to attract the operation of the rule with the consequence that Cedar held the benefit of the contract on a constructive trust for the investor group. Thence it is possible to trace into the money paid under that contract which Cedar likewise held on a constructive trust for the investor group.

I would allow the appeal.

SIR TERENCE ETHERTON C

The constructive trust is a feature of equity which arises in many different areas of the law. They include, among others, contracts for the sale of land, the perfection of imperfect gifts, gifts in contemplation of death (donatio mortis causa), testamentary secret trusts, mutual wills, common intention constructive trusts, fraud and undue influence, estoppel, specific performance, joint ventures, breach of trust, and breach of fiduciary duty. Although it may be said at the most general level that the constructive trust is a feature of equity to prevent or remedy unconscionable conduct, there is no generally accepted set of principles governing the existence of a constructive trust across all the different areas of the law where it is to be found. Moreover, in some cases the constructive trust is a true institutional trust arising by operation of law at a particular moment and creating a property interest in the beneficiary from that time. In other cases, it simply connotes an obligation in equity of wrongdoers, who were not or are not in fact trustees, to account as though they were.

The present case is about the existence of a constructive trust, which is a true trust, of a benefit acquired by a fiduciary in breach of fiduciary duty. Short of a decision of the Supreme Court that the law of England and Wales recognises a remedial constructive trust, as is to be found in other common law countries, such as Australia, New Zealand and Canada, this court must proceed on the basis that in this jurisdiction the constructive trust of a benefit wrongly obtained by the fiduciary in breach of duty is an institutional trust arising at the moment the benefit is received and under which the principal obtains an immediate beneficial interest. Similarly, short of an express decision of the Supreme Court to the contrary, I do not consider it would be right to view the constructive trust in this area, as at least one leading academic commentator has urged, as a mere fiction for making orders of the court that the defendant pay a sum of money to the claimant or transfer a particular right to the claimant.

The issue in the present case arises because the decision of the *Court of Appeal in Sinclair Investments (UK) Ltd v Versailles Trade Finance Ltd* [2012] Ch 453, to follow *Lister & Co v Stubbs* 45 Ch D 1, in the Court of Appeal, rather than *Attorney General for Hong Kong v Reid* [1994] 1 AC 324, in the Privy Council, confirms that not all benefits wrongly obtained by a fiduciary in breach of fiduciary duty are subject to a constructive trust even though the fiduciary is still under a duty to account in equity. The problem is to identify when such a situation arises and specifically whether, as Simon J thought below [2011] EWHC 2999 (Ch), the facts of the present case are such a situation...

I entirely agree with Lewison LJ that it is not the function of this court to enter into the debate about whether or not the *Lister* case 45 Ch D 1 or the *Reid* case [1994] 1 AC 324 or the *Sinclair* case [2012] Ch 453 was correctly or incorrectly decided. At this level of the judicial hierarchy we are bound to accept the decision in the Sinclair case on its facts and also the conclusion in that case that the *Lister* case was correctly decided and should be followed by the courts of England and Wales in preference to the *Reid* case.

That leaves this court with the task of applying the decision and the analysis in the *Sinclair* case, and the case law which has not been overturned by or is not inconsistent with the *Sinclair* case, to the facts of this case. In order to do so, it is necessary to provide some coherence to the large body of relevant case law, not all of which was considered or even mentioned in the *Sinclair* case.

Lord Neuberger MR's analysis in paras 88 and 89 of the *Sinclair* case divides into three broad categories the situations in which a fiduciary obtains a benefit in breach of fiduciary duty. The first category ("category 1") is where the benefit is or was an asset belonging beneficially to the principal (most obviously where the fiduciary has gained the benefit by misappropriating or misapplying the principal's property). The second category ("category 2") is where the benefit has been obtained by the fiduciary by taking an advantage of an opportunity which was properly that of the principal. The third category ("category 3") is all other cases. According to the analysis and conclusion of Lord Neuberger MR, the situations in categories 1 and 2 give rise to a constructive trust, but those in category 3 do not. The issue in the present case arises out of the difficulty of ascertaining the borderline between category 2 and category 3.

The problem can be expressed in quite simple terms. It follows from the decision in the *Sinclair* case that the facts of that case and the bribe and secret commission situations exemplified by the facts in the Lister and Reid decisions fall within category 3. As a matter of ordinary language those were "opportunity" cases in the sense that the defendants in those cases wrongly obtained a benefit through the opportunity presented by their relationship to their principal. The cases, however, fall within category 3 rather than category 2 because the opportunity, in Lord Neuberger MR's words, was not "properly that of the beneficiary" (para 88) and was not "beneficially owned by the claimant": para 89. The question is what "opportunity" situations, apart from the precise factual situations in the decisions in *Sinclair* , *Lister* and *Reid* and those precisely analogous, fall within category 3 rather than category 2? The difficulty arises because the expressions "properly that of the beneficiary" and "beneficially owned by the claimant" are not to be found as legal expressions or tests in any of the reported cases. That is not surprising because opportunities are not a species of property capable of being held on trust. Moreover, in *Bhullar v Bhullar [2003] 2 BCLC 241* , which was not cited in the *Sinclair* case [2012] Ch 453, Jonathan Parker LJ, with whom the other members of the Court of Appeal agreed, expressly disapproved of those types of expressions and concepts. He said the following in relation to the rule, as formulated by Lord Cranworth LC in *Aberdeen Railway Co v Blaikie Bros* (1854) 1

Macq 461, 471, that "no one, having such [fiduciary] duties to discharge, shall be allowed to enter into engagements in which he has, or can have, a personal interest conflicting, or which may possibly conflict, with the interests of those whom he is bound to protect" ("the no conflict rule") [2003] 2 BCLC 241...

Lord Neuberger MR referred in the *Sinclair* case [2012] Ch 453, para 70, to the observation of the trial judge, Lewison J, that it was unclear whether the remedy granted in the *Phipps* case [1967] 2 AC 46 was proprietary or personal. Lord Neuberger MR also expressed his agreement with Lewison J that the question whether it should be proprietary or personal was never argued in the *Phipps* case and apparently did not matter. We have had the benefit of research by Mr Pymont, which demonstrates that Wilberforce J did indeed make a formal declaration of a constructive trust. Wilberforce J's judgment is reported [1964] 1 WLR 993; [1964] 2 All ER 187 . Both reports state that the writ claimed: (1) a declaration that first and second defendants held 5/18ths of 21,986 ordinary shares of £1 each in the company, or alternatively 5/18ths of the following holdings in the company, namely, 2,925 shares, 14,567 shares or 4,494 shares (or some one or more of such holdings) as constructive trustees for the plaintiff; (2) an account of the profits made by them from those holdings; and (3) an order that they should transfer to the plaintiff the shares which they held as constructive trustees for him and should pay to him 5/18ths of the profit. The report in the All England Law Reports records, at p 208H, that Wilberforce J made the declaration in (1) and ordered the account of profits in (2). That Wilberforce J made the declaration is supported by the express statements in the House of Lords to that effect by Lord Cohen [1967] 2 AC 46, 99C and Lord Guest at p 112G.

The misunderstanding in the *Sinclair* case about the declaration appears to have arisen as a result of the abbreviated record of Wilberforce J's order in the report in the Weekly Law Reports [1964] 1 WLR 993, 1018. It is misleading because it omitted reference to the declaration made by Wilberforce J, corresponding to the first head of the claim in the writ, but included reference to adjournment of the third head of relief, presumably until it had been worked out precisely how many shares should be transferred (corresponding to the percentages in the declaration) and after the taking of the account.

The declaration of a constructive trust was made in the *Phipps* case even though, as I have said, the shares could not have been purchased for the will trust without the sanction of the court since they were not an authorised investment under the testator's will. Furthermore, one of the trustees said in evidence that he would not consider the trustees buying the shares under any circumstances. Wilberforce J said [1964] 1 WLR 993, 1017 that, as was clear from the *Keech* case Sel Cas Ch 61 and *Regal (Hastings) Ltd v Guilliver* (Note) [1967] 2 AC 134, those impediments to any purchase of the shares by the trustees made no difference. The same point was made in the House of Lords [1967] 2 AC 46, per Lord Cohen at p 95G, and per Lord Guest at p 117G.

The *Phipps* case was plainly an "opportunity" case within Lord Neuberger MR's category 2. Indeed, in the House of Lords both Lord Cohen and Lord Hodson emphasised the misuse of "the opportunity" which presented itself to the first and second defendants...

The facts of the present case are in some important respects materially different from those in the *Sinclair* and *Lister* cases. Clause 3 of the exclusive brokerage agreement ("the commission agreement") provided that Cedar's €10m fee was to be paid within five working days of the vendor's receipt of the purchase price for the hotel. Mr Collings said that the commission paid to Cedar could not be identified as the claimants' money since, as a matter of law, their money ceased to be identifiable as their property the moment it was paid into the vendor's bank account. In a practical sense, however, it is plain that in reality the claimants' money funded the commission paid to Cedar. Unlike the *Sinclair* case [2012] Ch 453 and, possibly, the *Lister* case 45 Ch D 1, in both temporal and causative terms Cedar's receipt of the commission was the direct and immediate consequence of its breach of fiduciary duty.

Furthermore, as Simon J found in para 102 of his first judgment [2012] 2 BCLC 39 , the obligation of Cedar, which was the exclusive negotiator for the claimants, was to negotiate the best purchase price for them, that is to say the lowest possible price. In that context, it was material that the vendor was in fact prepared to receive a net sum of €201·5m from the sale (i.e. allowing for Cedar's €10m commission). That fact was not, however, made known to the claimants. Critically, Simon J made a finding of fact in para 106 of his first judgment that: "at the very least it is likely that they could have used the information to their financial advantage in the course of their negotiations."

If the claimants had known of the commission agreement, they might have deferred contracting to purchase the hotel until the commission agreement lapsed under the terms of clause 1 after 31 December 2005 and then negotiated the price with the vendor on the basis that the vendor was by that time free of an obligation to meet an expense of €10m. Furthermore, there was direct evidence that, if the claimants had known of the commission agreement, they would have changed their own fee arrangements with Cedar...

Do those facts bring the present case within category 2 rather than category 3? In my judgment, on the findings of the judge in the light of the evidence, they bring the case within category 2. On the basis of existing case law, that conclusion reflects both principle and precedent. It reflects principle because the commission agreement, and the fact that it was not disclosed by Cedar to the claimants, diverted from the claimants the opportunity to purchase the hotel at the lowest possible price, that is to say a price lower than the price they ultimately agreed to pay. That point remains a good one even if the claimants cannot show that the vendor would in fact have been willing to accept an amount precisely €10m less or indeed any specific amount less than the price actually paid by the claimants...

For those reasons, this case falls within category 2, and so I would allow the appeal. It throws into clear relief, however, the very considerable difficulties inherent in the analysis in the *Sinclair* case [2012] Ch 453 and the decision in *Lister* 45 Ch D 1 in marking the borderline between cases in category 2 and those in category 3. This has made the law more complex and uncertain and dependent on very fine factual distinctions. If the law is to be made simpler and more coherent, but the *Sinclair* case and the *Lister* case correctly represent the law, then that suggests a need to revisit the very many longstanding decisions in category 2 cases and to provide an overhaul of this entire area of the law of constructive trusts in order to provide a coherent and logical legal framework. If that can be done at all by the courts, rather than Parliament, it can only be accomplished by the Supreme Court. That indicates a need for informed debate and ultimately determination by the Supreme Court: (1) whether the Sinclair case was right to decide that the Lister case is to be preferred to the *Reid* case [1994] 1 AC 324 ; (2) in terms of constructive trusts and proprietary relief for breach of fiduciary duty, what are the principles to distinguish opportunity cases within category 2 and those within category 3; (3) what is the true jurisprudential nature of the constructive trust in this (and by necessity other) areas of the law, including whether it is—or should be—an institutional trust at all or something else. In considering those matters, there are important issues of policy, and the relative importance of different policies, to assess, including deterring fraud and corruption; the ability to strip the fiduciary of all benefits, including increases in the value of benefits, acquired by breach of duty, and vehicles or third parties through which those benefits have been channelled; the importance attached to the protection of those to whom fiduciary duties are owed; and the position of other creditors on the fiduciary's insolvency who may be prejudiced by a constructive trust or proprietary relief in favour of the fiduciary's principal but who, in the absence of such a trust and relief, would benefit from increases in value of assets acquired by the fiduciary's fraud, corruption or wrongdoing. It will also be necessary to bear in mind the international perspective applying to this area of trust law and equity, to which I have referred earlier in this judgment.

For the reasons I have given, I would allow this appeal.

The Court of Appeal, therefore, felt that there was enough justification in their case facts to distinguish the earlier authority of *Sinclair v Versailles*.

FHR European Ventures LLP and others v Cedar Capital Partners LLC [2014] UKSC 45

Panel: Lord Neuberger, Lord Mance, Lord Sumption, Lord Carnwath, Lord Toulson, Lord Hodge, Lord Collins

Facts: Cedar Capital Partners LLC (CCPL) had been established by the defendant, Ramsey Neil Mankarious, to provide consultancy services to the hotel industry. In this capacity, it entered into an agreement with the Monegasque owners of the Monte Carlo Grand Hotel to sell the property for them. In exchange, CCPL would receive a commission from Monte Carlo Grand Hotel Ltd; this arrangement was to be disclosed by CCPL to prospective purchasers. In breach, CCPL failed to disclose the arrangement to the eventual purchaser of the hotel, Fairmont Hotels and Resorts European Ventures LLP (FHR). Subsequently, FHR sought to recover the €10 million commission paid to CCPL by Monte Carlo Grand Hotel Ltd.

LORD NEUBERGER

This is the judgment of the Court on the issue of whether a bribe or secret commission received by an agent is held by the agent on trust for his principal, or whether the principal merely has a claim for equitable compensation in a sum equal to the value of the bribe or commission. The answer to this rather technical sounding question, which has produced inconsistent judicial decisions over the past 200 years, as well as a great deal of more recent academic controversy, is important in practical terms. If the bribe or commission is held on trust, the principal has a proprietary claim to it, whereas if the principal merely has a claim for equitable compensation, the claim is not proprietary. The distinction is significant for two main reasons. First, if the agent becomes insolvent, a proprietary claim would effectively give the principal priority over the agent's unsecured creditors, whereas the principal would rank pari passu, i.e. equally, with other unsecured creditors if he only has a claim for compensation. Secondly, if the principal has a proprietary claim to the bribe or commission, he can trace and follow it in equity, whereas (unless we develop the law of equitable tracing beyond its current boundaries) a principal with a right only to equitable compensation would have no such equitable right to trace or follow...

The following three principles are not in doubt, and they are taken from the classic summary of the law in the judgment of Millett LJ in *Bristol and West Building Society v Mothew* [1998] Ch 1 , 18. First, an agent owes a fiduciary duty to his principal because he is "someone who has undertaken to act for or on behalf of [his principal] in a particular matter in circumstances which give rise to a relationship of trust and confidence". Secondly, as a result, an agent "must not make a profit out of his trust" and "must not place himself in a position in which his duty and his interest may conflict" and, as Lord Upjohn pointed out in *Boardman v Phipps* [1967] 2 AC 46, 123, the former proposition is "part of the [latter] wider rule". Thirdly, "[a] fiduciary who acts for two principals with potentially conflicting interests without the informed consent of both is in breach of the obligation of undivided loyalty; he puts himself in a position where his duty to one principal *may* conflict with his duty to the other". Because of the importance which equity attaches to fiduciary duties, such "informed consent" is only effective if it is given after "full disclosure", to quote Sir George Jessel MR in *Dunne v English* (1874) LR 18 Eq 524, 533.

Another well-established principle, which applies where an agent receives a benefit in breach of his fiduciary duty, is that the agent is obliged to account to the principal for such a benefit, and to pay, in effect, a sum equal to the profit by way of equitable compensation. The law on this topic was clearly stated in *Regal (Hastings) Ltd v Gulliver* (Note) (1942) [1967] 2 AC 134. The principal's right to seek an account undoubtedly gives him a right to equitable compensation in respect of the bribe or secret commission, which is the quantum of that bribe or commission (subject to any permissible deduction in favour of the agent, e.g. for expenses incurred). That is because where an agent acquires a benefit in breach of his fiduciary duty, the relief accorded by equity is, again to quote Millett LJ in *Mothew* at p 18, "primarily restitutionary or restorative rather than compensatory". The agent's duty to account for the bribe or secret commission represents a personal remedy for the principal against the agent. However, the centrally relevant point for present purposes is that, at least in some cases where an agent acquires a benefit which came to his notice as a result of his fiduciary position, or pursuant to an opportunity which results from his fiduciary position, the equitable rule ("the Rule") is that he is to be treated as having acquired the benefit on behalf of his principal, so that it is beneficially owned by the principal. In such cases, the principal has a proprietary remedy in addition to his personal remedy against the agent, and the principal can elect between the two remedies.

Where the facts of a particular case are within the ambit of the Rule, it is strictly applied. The strict application of the Rule can be traced back to the well- known decision in *Keech v Sandford* (1726) Sel Cas Ch 61, where a trustee held a lease of a market on trust for an infant, and, having failed to negotiate a new lease on behalf of the infant because the landlord was dissatisfied with the proposed security for the rent, the trustee negotiated a new lease for himself. Lord King LC concluded at p 62 that, "though I do not say there is a fraud in this case" and though it "may seem hard", the infant was entitled to an assignment of the new lease and an account of the profits made in the meantime – a conclusion which could only be justified on the basis that the new lease had been beneficially acquired for the infant beneficiary.

Since then, the Rule has been applied in a great many cases. The question on this appeal is not so much concerned with the application of the Rule, as with its limits or boundaries. Specifically, what is in dispute is the extent to which the Rule applies where the benefit is a bribe or secret commission obtained by an agent in breach of his fiduciary duty to his principal…

The cases summarised in paras 13-17 above and the observations set out in paras 19-20 above are all consistent with the notion that the Rule should apply to bribes or secret commissions paid to an agent, so that the agent holds them on trust for his principal, rather than simply having an equitable duty to account to his principal. It is true that in many of those cases there was apparently no argument as to whether the benefit obtained by the fiduciary was actually held on trust for the principal. However, in some of the cases there was a dispute on the nature of the relief; in any event, the fact that it was assumed time and again by eminent barristers and judges must carry great weight.

However, there is one decision of the House of Lords which appears to go the other way, and several decisions of the Court of Appeal which do go the other way, in that they hold that, while a principal has a claim for equitable compensation in respect of a bribe or secret commission received by his agent, he has no proprietary interest in it. The House of Lords decision is *Tyrrell v Bank of London* (1862) 10 HL Cas 26…

Although there have been suggestions that, with the exception of Lord Chelmsford's obiter dicta about bribes, the decision of the House of Lords in *Tyrrell* was not inconsistent with the respondents' case on this appeal, it appears clear that it was. If, as the House held, the solicitor was liable to account to the client for the profit which he had made on the adjoining land, that can only have been because it was a benefit which he had received in breach of his fiduciary duty; and, once that is established, then, on the respondents' case, the Rule would apply, and that profit would be held on trust for the client (or, more accurately, his share of the adjoining land would be held on trust)...

More recently, in 1993, in *Attorney General for Hong Kong v Reid*, the Privy Council concluded that bribes received by a corrupt policeman were held on trust for his principal, and so they could be traced into properties which he had acquired in New Zealand. In his judgment on behalf of the Board, Lord Templeman disapproved the reasoning in *Heiron* , and the reasoning and outcome in Lister , and he thought his conclusion inconsistent with only one of the opinions, that of Lord Chelmsford, in *Tyrrell* . In *Daraydan Holdings Ltd v Solland International Ltd* [2005] Ch 119 , paras 75ff, Lawrence Collins J indicated that he would follow *Reid* rather than *Lister* , as did Toulson J in *Fyffes Group Ltd v Templeman* [2000] 2 Lloyd's Rep 643 , 668–672. But in *Sinclair Investments Ltd v Versailles Trade Finance Ltd* [2012] Ch 453, in a judgment given by Lord Neuberger MR, the Court of Appeal decided that it should follow *Heiron* and *Lister* , and indeed *Tyrrell* , for a number of reasons set out in paras 77ff, although it accepted that this Court might follow the approach in *Reid* . In this case, Simon J considered that he was bound by *Sinclair*, whereas the Court of Appeal concluded that they could and should distinguish it.

As mentioned above, the issue raised on this appeal has stimulated a great deal of academic debate. The contents of the many articles on this issue provide an impressive demonstration of penetrating and stimulating legal analysis. One can find among those articles a powerful case for various different outcomes, based on analysing judicial decisions and reasoning, equitable and restitutionary principles, and practical and commercial realities. It is neither possible nor appropriate to do those articles justice individually in this judgment, but the court has referred to them for the purpose of extracting the principle upon which the Rule is said to be based...

The respondents' formulation of the Rule, namely that it applies to all benefits received by an agent in breach of his fiduciary duty to his principal, is explained on the basis that an agent ought to account in specie to his principal for any benefit he has obtained from his agency in breach of his fiduciary duty, as the benefit should be treated as the property of the principal, as supported by many judicial dicta including those in para 19 above, and can be seen to be reflected in Jonathan Parker LJ's observations in para 14 above. More subtly, it is justified on the basis that equity does not permit an agent to rely on his own wrong to justify retaining the benefit: in effect, he must accept that, as he received the benefit as a result of his agency, he acquired it for his principal. Support for that approach may be found in Mellish LJ's judgment in *McKay's Case* at p 6, and Bowen J's judgment in *Whaley Bridge* at p 113.

The appellant's formulation of the Rule, namely that it has a more limited reach, and does not apply to bribes and secret commissions, has, as mentioned in para 10 above, various different formulations and justifications. Thus, it is said that, given that it is a proprietary principle, the Rule should not apply to benefits which were not derived from assets which are or should be the property of the principal, a view supported by the reasoning of Lord Westbury in *Tyrrell* . It has also been suggested that the Rule should not apply to benefits which could not have been intended for the principal and were, rightly or wrongly, the property of the agent, which seems to have been the basis of

Cotton LJ's judgment in *Heiron* at p 325 and *Lister* at p 12. In *Sinclair* , it was suggested that the effect of the authorities was that the Rule should not apply to a benefit which the agent had obtained by taking advantage of an opportunity which arose as a result of the agency, unless the opportunity "was properly that of the [principal]" – para 88...

Each of the formulations set out in paras 30 and 31 above have their supporters and detractors. In the end, it is not possible to identify any plainly right or plainly wrong answer to the issue of the extent of the Rule, as a matter of pure legal authority. There can clearly be different views as to what requirements have to be satisfied before a proprietary interest is created. More broadly, it is fair to say that the concept of equitable proprietary rights is in some respects somewhat paradoxical. Equity, unlike the common law, classically acts in personam (see eg Maitland, Equity , p 9); yet equity is far more ready to accord proprietary claims than common law. Further, two general rules which law students learn early on are that common law legal rights prevail over equitable rights, and that where there are competing equitable rights the first in time prevails; yet, given that equity is far more ready to recognise proprietary rights than common law, the effect of having an equitable right is often to give priority over common law claims – sometimes even those which may have preceded the equitable right. Given that equity developed at least in part to mitigate the rigours of the common law, this is perhaps scarcely surprising. However, it underlines the point that it would be unrealistic to expect complete consistency from the cases over the past 300 years. It is therefore appropriate to turn to the arguments based on principle and practicality, and then to address the issue, in the light of those arguments as well as the judicial decisions discussed above...

The notion that an agent should not hold a bribe or commission on trust because he could not have acquired it on behalf of his principal is somewhat inconsistent with the long-standing decision in *Keech*, the decision in *Phipps* approved by the House of Lords, and the Privy Council decision in *Bowes*. In each of those three cases, a person acquired property as a result of his fiduciary or quasi-fiduciary position, in circumstances in which the principal could not have acquired it: yet the court held that the property concerned was held on trust for the beneficiary. In *Keech*, the beneficiary could not acquire the new lease because the landlord was not prepared to let to him, and because he was an infant; in *Boardman*, the trust could not acquire the shares because they were not authorised investments; in *Bowes*, the city corporation would scarcely have been interested in buying the loan notes which it had just issued to raise money.

The respondents are also able to point to a paradox if the appellant is right and a principal has no proprietary right to his agent's bribe or secret commission. If the principal has a proprietary right, then he is better off, and the agent is worse off, than if the principal merely has a claim for equitable compensation. It would be curious...if a principal whose agent wrongly receives a bribe or secret commission is worse off than a principal whose agent obtains a benefit in far less opprobrious circumstances, e.g. the benefit obtained by the trustees' agents in *Boardman*. Yet that is the effect if the Rule does not apply to bribes or secret commissions.

Wider policy considerations also support the respondents' case that bribes and secret commissions received by an agent should be treated as the property of his principal, rather than merely giving rise to a claim for equitable compensation. As Lord Templeman said giving the decision of the Privy Council in *Attorney General for Hong Kong v Reid* [1994] 1 AC 324, 330H, "[b]ribery is an evil practice which threatens the foundations of any civilised society". Secret commissions are also objectionable as they inevitably tend to undermine trust in the commercial world. That has always been true, but concern about bribery and corruption generally has never been greater than it is now – see for instance, internationally, the OECD Convention on Combating Bribery of Foreign Public Officials in International Business Transactions 1999 and the United Nations Convention against Corruption 2003, and, nationally, the Bribery Acts 2010 and 2012. Accordingly, one would expect the law to be particularly stringent in relation to a claim against an agent who has received a bribe or secret commission...

Nonetheless, the appellant's argument based on potential prejudice to the agent's unsecured creditors has some force, but it is, as we see it, balanced by the fact that it appears to be just that a principal whose agent has obtained a bribe or secret commission should be able to trace the proceeds of the bribe or commission into other assets and to follow them into the hands of knowing recipients (as in *Reid*). Yet...tracing or following in equity would not be possible, at least as the law is currently understood, unless the person seeking to trace or follow can claim a proprietary interest. Common law tracing is, of course, possible without a proprietary interest, but it is much more limited than equitable tracing. Lindley LJ in *Lister* at p 15 appears to have found it offensive that a principal should be entitled to trace a bribe, but he did not explain why, and we prefer the reaction of Lord Templeman in *Reid*, namely that a principal ought to have the right to trace and to follow a bribe or secret commission.

Finally, on this aspect, it appears that other common law jurisdictions have adopted the view that the Rule applies to all benefits which are obtained by a fiduciary in breach of his duties...As overseas countries secede from the jurisdiction of the Privy Council, it is inevitable that inconsistencies in the common law will develop between different jurisdictions. However, it seems to us highly desirable for all those jurisdictions to learn from each other, and at least to lean in favour of harmonising the development of the common law round the world...

Were it not for the decision in *Tyrrell*, we consider that it would be plainly appropriate for this Court to conclude that the courts took a wrong turn in *Heiron* and *Lister* , and to restate the law as being as the respondents contend. Although the fact that the House of Lords decided *Tyrrell* in the way they did gives us pause for thought, we consider that it would be right to uphold the respondents' argument and disapprove the decision in *Tyrrell*. In the first place, *Tyrrell* is inconsistent with a wealth of cases decided before and after it was decided. Secondly, although *Fawcett* was cited in argument at p 38, it was not considered in any of the three opinions in *Tyrrell*; indeed, no previous decision was referred to in the opinions, and, although the opinions were expressed with a confidence familiar to those who read 19th century judgments, they contained no reasoning, merely assertion. Thirdly, the decision in *Tyrrell* may be explicable by reference to the fact that the solicitor was not actually acting for the client at the time when he acquired his interest in the adjoining land...in other words, it may be that their Lordships thought that the principal should not have a proprietary interest in circumstances where the benefit received by the agent was obtained before the agency began and did not relate to the property the subject of the agency.

Quite apart from these three points, we consider that, the many decisions and the practical and policy considerations which favour the wider application of the Rule and are discussed above justify our disapproving *Tyrrell*. In our judgment, therefore, the decision in *Tyrrell* should not stand in the way of the conclusion that the law took a wrong turn in *Heiron* and *Lister*, and that those decisions, and any subsequent decisions...at least in so far as they relied on or followed *Heiron* and *Lister*, should be treated as overruled.

In this case, the Court of Appeal rightly regarded themselves as bound by *Sinclair*, but they managed to distinguish it. Accordingly, the appeal is dismissed.

The Supreme Court was, therefore, unanimous that the appropriate remedy for property obtained as a bribe or secret commission was that of the constructive trust. It must be inferred, therefore, that the constructive trust will always be the appropriate remedy with respect to property obtained through breach of fiduciary duty.

Further Reading

Martin, Jill. Hanbury and Martin: *Modern Equity*. 17th edition. Sweet & Maxwell Ltd

Hayton and Mitchell. *Cases and Commentary on Trusts and Equitable Remedies* 12th edition

Birks, P. 'The content of fiduciary obligation' (2002) 16(1) Tru. L.I. 34

Conaglen, M. 'The Nature and Function of Fiduciary Loyalty' [2005] LQR 452

Finn, P. 'Fiduciary Law and the Modern Commercial World' in *Commercial Aspects of Trusts and Fiduciary Obligations*, McKendrick (ed) (Oxford: OUP, 1992)

Sealy, L. S. 'Fiduciary Obligations, Forty Years On' (1995) 9 JCL 37.

12

Maintenance and Advancement

Topic List

Introduction

The Trustee Act 1925 ss 31 and 32 contain powers to apply income and capital from a trust fund for the benefit of beneficiaries who would not otherwise be able to receive it because they are under 18 and/or have only a contingent interest. The statutory powers are intended as fall-back provisions where express powers have not been included in a trust deed or will, or where someone has died intestate. Section 69(2) allows statutory powers to be varied by express powers. It is common for express powers to be included and these are often wider than the statutory powers.

Some of the cases in this chapter concern the interpretation and application of express powers but, insofar as they relate to express wording which is similar to the statutory wording, they are also of relevance to the exercise of the statutory powers.

Note that many of the cases in this chapter were decided before the Family Law Reform Act 1969, which reduced the age of majority from 21 to 18 and altered the terminology for those under age from 'infant' to 'minor'.

12.1 Trustee Act 1925 s 31 – Payments from Income

Section 31 contains powers in relation to the income of the trust fund and sets out different rules according to whether the beneficiaries are under or over 18.

The following case concerned tax on income but is of general importance as it examined the effect of s 31 on the nature of a beneficiary's right to income.

Stanley v Inland Revenue Commissioners [1944] KB 255

Panel: Lord Greene MR, Mackinnon and Goddard LJJ

Facts: A beneficiary with a vested life interest was assessed to sur-tax (a higher rate tax that existed at the time) in respect of income from a trust which was accumulated while he was a minor and paid to him when he reached majority. The beneficiary appealed, first to the Special Commissioners of Income Tax and then to the court, but his appeals were dismissed. He further appealed to the Court of Appeal. It was held that the effect of Trustee Act 1925 s 31 was that the income was not income of the beneficiary and he could not be assessed to sur-tax on it.

LORD GREENE MR reading the judgment of the court

...In order that a person may be charged with sur-tax, the income in respect of which he is assessed must be his income. ... Apart from any special provision in the instrument under which an infant derives his interest and apart from statutory provisions, an infant who has a vested interest in possession is the person entitled to the income. It is his income although he cannot give a good receipt for it. On his death under twenty-one income which has accumulated during his minority goes to his legal personal representatives. In such a case there can be no doubt that the income accruing during minority is the income of the infant. He is, accordingly, chargeable with sur-tax in respect of it. ...If, on the other hand, the infant is only entitled contingently on his attaining twenty-one he has no title to any income until that event takes place. If the event does take place, he becomes entitled to future income and (in appropriate circumstances) to accumulations of past income, but that past income was not his income in the years in which it accrued, and no one suggests that he could be assessed to sur-tax in respect of it.

...By sub-s. 5 of [section 42 of the Conveyancing Act, 1881] the title of the infant to accumulations of his income was preserved in the sense that, if he died under twenty-one, they went (in the absence of special provision) to his legal personal representatives as part of his estate. Here again, there could have been no doubt that the income of such an infant was his income assessable to sur-tax. His title to it was absolute throughout, although his power to enjoy it was suspended during his infancy ... but s. 31 of the Trustee Act, 1925, has effected a radical change in the law. It declares statutory trusts which, in the case of an infant with a vested interest in income who dies during minority, destroy his title to the accumulations and direct them to be held, not as part of the infant's estate, but as an accretion to capital. The section applies to property of any description held in trust for any person for any interests whatsoever, whether vested or contingent. It provides that during the infancy of any such person income may be applied for his maintenance, education or benefit and any income not so applied is to be accumulated... . Sub-section 2, so far as relevant, proceeds as follows: The Trustees "shall hold those accumulations as follows: '(i.) If any such person (a) attains the age of twenty-one years, or marries under that age, and his interest in such income during his infancy or until his marriage is a vested interest; or (b)' (this is not relevant) .... the trustees shall hold the accumulations in trust for such person absolutely .... (ii.) In any other case the trustees shall, notwithstanding that such person had a vested interest in such income, hold the accumulations as an accretion to the capital of the property from which such accumulations arose ....'"

...It was said on behalf of the Crown that the infant has a vested interest in the surplus income as it accrues and that there is nothing in the section that deprives him of that interest during infancy – all that the section does is to divest him of his title to the accumulations of surplus income if he dies before attaining his majority. In other words, it was said, he has a vested interest in the accumulations which is defeasible in the event of his dying under twenty-one and, therefore, the surplus income is, during minority, income of the infant and as such is assessable year by year. It is necessary at this point to call attention to a distinction... . The expression "defeasible interest in income" may be used in two senses. In the case of an adult he receives and enjoys the income until the defeasance takes place. Until that event occurs the income is his income and he is assessable accordingly, but the same expression (if it be the correct one to use...) means, in the case of an infant in the situation of the appellant, something quite different. The infant does not during infancy enjoy the surplus income. It is not his in any real sense. The title to it is held in suspense to await the event, and if he dies under twenty-one his interest in it (whether or not it be truly described as a vested interest) is destroyed. He is, in fact, for all practical purposes in precisely the same position as if his interest in surplus income were contingent. If he attains twenty-one he takes the accumulations, if he dies under twenty-one he does not, but, as a matter of fact, the section itself does use words of contingency, since the trust of the accumulations is expressed to be for the infant "if he attains the age of twenty-one years or marries under that age." We are disposed to think that the effect of the section is better described, not as leaving the interest of the infant as a vested interest subject to defeasance, but as engrafting on the vested interest originally conferred on the infant by the settlement or other disposition a qualifying trust of a special nature which confers on the infant a title to the accumulations if and only if he attains twenty-one or marries. ... If this view is right, the interest of the appellant in the surplus income during his minority was a contingent interest only and he was not assessable.

Alert

...[T]he Crown's contention ... means ... that in respect of every year during his infancy the infant is assessable to sur-tax in respect of income which may never in truth be his. ... [I]f the infant were to be assessed during infancy ... [he] could be assessed to sur-tax in respect of income which, if he died under twenty-one, he would never receive. ...

The appeal is allowed... .

The case which follows concerned an express power to maintain which was in similar terms to s 31.

Fuller v Evans [2000] 1 All ER 636

Panel: Lightman J

Facts: The claimant (settlor) had created a settlement giving life interests to his children, with a provision that, until a beneficiary reached the age of 21 the trustees could pay or apply the whole or any part of the income of that beneficiary 'to or for the maintenance education or benefit of the Benficiary'. Clause 12 of the settlement provided that the trust fund and income were to be enjoyed to the entire exclusion of the settlor and of any benefit to him. The settlor and his wife divorced and, under a consent order, the settlor was obliged to pay an annual sum for the maintenance of the children and an amount to cover their school fees, until they reached the age of 17. There were two children. The trustees (defendants) asked the court for guidance as to a proposal to provide money from the trust income for the maintenance and education of the children, who were aged 14 and 12. It was held that the power could be exercised if it was in the best interests of the beneficiaries to do so, despite the exercise incidentally benefiting the settlor.

MR JUSTICE LIGHTMAN

The issue before me is whether the trustees may in their discretion exercise their power to provide monies out of the trust to pay for the childrens' maintenance and education, though the effect of such payment may be in whole or in part to relieve the settlor from the burden of his obligations under the consent order to pay for his children's maintenance and education. ...

The first stage is to consider what the position would have been if the settlement had not included Clause 12. In that situation in the exercise of the power in question in this case (as in the exercise of all other powers) the trustees would be required to have regard exclusively to the interests of the beneficiaries, and could not seek by the exercise or non-exercise of the power to promote the interests of anyone else, and most particularly the settlor. It would be open to the trustees to decide that the power be exercised though the effect would be to relieve the settlor in whole or in part of his obligations under the consent order, but they could not set out to benefit the settlor by affording him relief in this way. If the exercise of the power was in the best interests of the beneficiaries, the trustees might exercise the power though the exercise incidentally relieved the settlor in whole or in part from his obligation, but they could not allow the perceived advantage to the settlor to be a factor favouring its exercise.

I turn to the situation which arises where the settlement includes Clause 12. The obligation to have exclusive regard to the interests of the beneficiaries remains the same. The question raised is whether Clause 12 precludes the trustees exercising the power where the interests of the beneficiaries require its exercise if such exercise may incidentally benefit the settlor, and in particular may relieve the settlor from the actual or perceived need because of some legal or moral obligation (in this case an obligation arising under the consent order) to do at his own cost what the trustees are willing to do at the cost of the trust.

...I find it very difficult to read the settlement as paralysing the trustees in this situation, barring them from exercising the powers conferred on them merely because a by-product of their exercises is an advantage to the settlor. The power given by the settlement to apply the income for the maintenance, education and benefit of the settlor's children ... is calculated to provide for the discharge of legal or moral responsibilities of the settlor as father during the period in question and accordingly in whole or in part to relieve him of those responsibilities.

...[I]t seems to me that Clause 12 does little (if anything) more than vigorously reaffirm the duty of the trustees to have regard exclusively to the best interests of the beneficiaries and ignore those of the settlor. ...

This conclusion of course does no more than leave it open to the trustees to exercise a discretionary power to make provision for the education and maintenance of the two children out of the settlement funds. The trustees can only exercise that power if they consider that to do so is in the best interests of beneficiaries despite the existence of the consent order and the obligations of the settlor thereunder. The trustees must have regard to the obligation of the settlor to provide for the beneficiaries' maintenance and education when undertaking the decision-making process but the existence of that obligation is no more than a consideration to which due weight must be given (consider Section 31(1)(b)(i) of the Trustees Act 1925). If the trustees reach the conclusion that it is in the best interests of the beneficiaries to make such provision out of trust funds, they are free to do so.

Alert

See the similar view expressed in the case of *Pilkington v IRC* [1964] AC 612 in relation to the exercise of the power of advancement under s 32.

Alert

12.2 Trustee Act 1925 s 32 – Payments from Capital

This section gives trustees a discretion to advance up to half of a beneficiary's share of capital. The written consent of any person with a prior interest is required, so an advancement cannot be made to a remainder beneficiary without the life tenant's consent (unless an express power dispenses with the need for such consent). Express powers are often wider than the statutory power and may, for example, permit the whole share to be advanced. In a number of the cases below, there were express powers for the trustees to advance capital to a beneficiary who had only a life interest, which would not be possible under the statutory power. The first case is one such case.

In re Kershaw's Trusts (1868) LR 6 Eq 322

Panel: Sir R Malins V-C

Facts: A testator left his residuary estate in trust for his daughters for life in equal shares, with the remainder of each daughter's share to go to her issue or, in default, to the other daughters. The trust provided that the trustees could apply any part not exceeding half of the capital of any daughter's share for that daughter's advancement or benefit. The husband of one daughter needed capital to continue in a partnership and would otherwise have returned to the East to work. The trustees wished to know whether they should advance capital for this purpose. It was held that capital from the daughter's share could be advanced to the husband for this purpose.

SIR R MALINS V-C

The words of this power are very large; the trustees may apply any part not exceeding half the share at any period of the daughter's life for her advancement—that is a word appropriate to an early period of life—or otherwise for her benefit. The husband of one of the daughters requires a capital of £5000 for the purpose of carrying on a business which, in the opinion of the trustees, is likely to be successful, and if he cannot get this capital he must go abroad, and leave his wife and children. I think that in such a case what is for the benefit of the husband is for the benefit of the wife, and I shall answer the question in the affirmative, that the trustees may and ought to advance the money to the husband on the terms proposed by him. ...

The judge considered that the word 'advancement' was appropriate to an early period of life. He also took the view that a payment could, in appropriate circumstances, be made to someone else, if it was of benefit to the beneficiary. The next case considered the meaning of 'advancement or benefit' and also concerned a payment where someone other than the beneficiary would derive a benefit.

Lowther v Bentinck (1874-75) LR 19 Eq 166

Panel: Sir George Jessel MR

Facts: Under certain will trusts, Lowther was given a life interest, with remainder to his children. There was a power for the trustees to apply no more than half the capital towards Lowther's preferment or advancement or otherwise for his benefit. Lowther had incurred substantial debts, secured on his life interest. He was paying interest and did not have the funds to pay off the debts. It was held that paying his creditors would be for his benefit and the trustees could exercise the power to apply capital for this purpose.

> SIR GEORGE JESSEL MR
>
> ...The only question I have to decide is, whether a payment to the creditors of an adult who is unable to pay them himself, but whose life estate is mortgaged to secure the payment of those debts, is a payment for his benefit? ... The words which precede those which I have to construe are "preferment or advancement," both large words, but both words having, I may say, a well-known legal meaning. They are followed by the words "or otherwise for his benefit," which are the largest terms of all. The suggestion made is, that if it had been intended not to restrict the words to something *ejusdem generis*, why put in preferment or advancement at all? That is a question not very difficult to answer. ...[I]t is by no means uncommon (and it would be by no means improper were it not for this *ejusdem generis* doctrine) to indicate the primary objects desired by the testator, though he does not wish to restrict the power to those primary objects. The gentleman here was thirty years old at the time; it is difficult to see what his preferment could be, he being a commander in the Navy, except setting him up in business. It seems to me that the words "or otherwise for his benefit" are evidently put in for the purpose of not confining the trustees to preferment or advancement; and therefore, so far from finding any context which restricts the words, I think the context shews that the words could not mean something of the same kind. I must decide the case upon the words as they stand uncontrolled by any context. I do not think anybody can doubt that paying this money to the creditors of this gentleman will confer a very large benefit on him; the application is strictly within the terms of the power which leaves the propriety of the exercise of it to the discretion of the trustees. The ... opinion of the Court [is] that the trustees are entitled to apply ... funds ... towards the discharge of the incumbrances.

Although that case held that paying debts was an acceptable use of the power (even though, of course, the creditors could also be seen as benefiting), the next case shows that this would not be appropriate where the debts are owed to one of the trustees.

Molyneux v Fletcher and Clark [1898] 1 QB 648

Panel: Kennedy J

Facts: A testator left his estate to trustees on trust for his children for life, in equal shares, with remainder to their own children. He died leaving two daughters. There was a power for the trustees to apply a sum not exceeding £500 in or towards the advancement in life of each daughter, with a provision that the sum could be paid to the daughter 'if the trustees think fit' and that the trustees were to be the sole judges of the advisability of such payment and of what the term 'advancement in life' meant. The trustees advanced £500 to one daughter, Fanny Durant, and £250 to the other daughter, Amelia Molyneux. All the money was then given to Amelia's husband,

Daniel Molyneux, who used it to pay his business debts to Fletcher, who was one of the trustees. Amelia's children sued, claiming a breach of trust. It was held that there was a breach of trust by Fletcher.

MR JUSTICE KENNEDY

...The action is based on a claim that the moneys paid by Mr. Fletcher in December, 1887, were paid in breach of trust because they were not paid with a view to the advancement in life of the beneficiaries, but with a view to Mr. Fletcher's own interest. Mr. Fletcher was a large creditor of Mrs. Molyneux's husband, and was pressing him for payment, and it is alleged that this money, though nominally advanced for the purposes under the will of the advancement in life of the beneficiaries, was really only advanced in order that it might pass through the hands of the two ladies into those of Mr. Fletcher again. Before dealing with this allegation, I think that I ought to indicate my opinion upon another point... . According to my construction of the will, there was no power at the time this money was advanced for the trustees to make any such advance at all. It is clear on the authorities, one of which is the judgment of Jessel M.R. in *Lowther v Bentinck*, that a power to apply capital for the advancement in life of a child has a well-recognised meaning. Sometimes enlarging expressions, such as "or otherwise for the benefit," are used. In the absence of any such enlarging expression, the word "advancement," as pointed out by Malins V.-C. in *In re Kershaw's Trusts*, is to be read as a word appropriate to an early period of life. The cases cited shew that, in the opinion of the learned judges who decided them, the word "advancement," if standing by itself without the addition of larger words, has a narrow and restricted meaning. Here I have the words "advancement in life" alone... . [O]n the facts it seems to me that the advances made by Mr. Fletcher and his then co-trustee ... cannot be supported.

No doubt a large discretion is given to the trustees by the will, but I do not think that, large as that discretion is, it could be extended so as to cover these advances. ... I should doubt whether in the case of either daughter an advance to pay the debts of the husband of one of them could by any possibility be considered as an advance for her advancement in life. On the facts here, I am obliged to come to the conclusion that it was well understood that the moneys when advanced would be used for paying debts and liabilities in business of Mr. Molyneux in respect of part of which bills to fall due at various dates ahead had been given by Mr. Molyneux to Mr. Fletcher before the advances were made, and that moneys so provided cannot constitute a proper or justifiable advance under the will I have no doubt. The law was laid down in *Duke of Portland v Topham* that a person having a limited power must execute it without any ulterior object. He must act in good faith, and with a single view to the real purpose and object of the power. No doubt in this case Mr. Fletcher received a formal request from both Mrs. Molyneux and Miss Durant for the advancement of the money—500l. to Miss Durant and 250l. to Mrs. Molyneux; but it is quite clear to me that Mr. Fletcher knew that the money would be used by Mr. Molyneux. I ought in justice to Mr. Fletcher to say that, no doubt, he believed that whatever was done with the money would be done with the consent of Mrs. Molyneux and Miss Durant, and that, upon the evidence

Alert

Alert

before me, I have no doubt that they did consent to the use which was made of the moneys in question, and that Mrs. Molyneux, at all events, knew beforehand how they were going to be paid and employed.

But now comes the question as to the position of the plaintiffs, who are the infant children of Mrs. Molyneux. It is, I take it, the rule of equity that where a trustee has committed a breach of trust of this kind with the consent of the tenants for life he will be entitled as against them to an indemnity. ... [His Lordship explained that the plaintiffs did not have sufficient interest in the £500 advanced from Miss Durant's share to make a claim in respect of it and continued:] Therefore, as regards the 500l. I give no relief. As to the 250l., I must decree that there has been a breach of trust by Mr. Fletcher in regard to it, and that it shall be replaced for the benefit of the plaintiffs. If Mrs. Molyneux had been made a party to these proceedings, I could have given Mr. Fletcher liberty to apply in this action with a view to enforcing a right to indemnity against her ... But as she is not a party I cannot make that order. ... As to the other defendant, Mr. Clark, he has recently become a trustee, and he has had no part in the breach of trust committed by Mr. Fletcher. ...

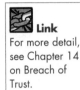

Link

For more detail, see Chapter 14 on Breach of Trust.

Note that, in this case, the power related only to 'advancement' and did not include the wider power to make payments for the 'benefit' of the beneficiaries. In the case that follows, the House of Lords gave its view on the meaning of the words 'advancement or benefit' in s 32. It is also authority for several other important principles regarding the exercise of the power to advance capital. (The perpetuity point is outside the scope of this course.) You will find that the key points are summarised in Lord Reid's speech and that Viscount Radcliffe expands on these.

Pilkington and Another v Inland Revenue Commissioners and Others [1964] AC 612

Panel: Lord Reid, Viscount Radcliffe, Lord Jenkins, Lord Hodson and Lord Devlin

Facts: Under the will of her great uncle, Penelope Pilkington (aged 5) had an interest in remainder after a life interest to her father, who was still alive. Her interest was contingent on her reaching 21 or marrying under that age. There were certain powers of appointment, which could be exercised in such a way that her interest might be reduced or excluded. The trustees proposed to resettle part of her presumptive share so that income could be used for her maintenance, education or benefit while she was under 21, the income would be paid to her between the ages of 21 and 30 and she would become absolutely entitled to the capital at 30. If she died before 30, her children, if any, would take her share. The judge approved the proposed exercise of the power. The Revenue, who were then added as parties, appealed and the Court of Appeal allowed the appeal. Penelope and her father further appealed to the House of Lords, who held that the advancement to resettle would be for her benefit and would be permissible except that, as proposed, it would infringe the perpetuity rules.

LORD REID

My Lords, I have had the advantage of reading the speech about to be delivered by my noble and learned friend Viscount Radcliffe. I entirely agree with what he says about the application of the rule against perpetuities; but I am only reluctantly persuaded by his reasoning to agree that section 32 of the Trustee Act, 1925, can be applied to the present case. I do not think that it is disputed that the main purpose of the appellants' scheme and its main benefit to the infant Penelope is avoidance of death duties and surtax. This is to be achieved by taking funds out of the testator's estate and resettling them on Penelope and any family she may have by means of a new trust with trust purposes different from those provided by the testator. It may be that one is driven step by step to hold that the power conferred by section 32 ... must be interpreted as including power to resettle such money on an infant in such a way as will probably confer considerable financial benefit on her many years hence if she survives. But that certainly seems to me far removed from the apparent purpose of the section and considerably beyond anything which it has hitherto been held to cover.

Nevertheless I am compelled to recognise that there is no logical stopping place short of that result. You cannot say that financial benefit from avoidance of taxation is not a benefit within the meaning of the section. Nor can you say that the section only authorises payments for some particular or immediate purpose or that the benefit must be immediate and certain and not future or problematical and again you cannot say that the beneficiary must consent to the course which the trustees have decided is for his benefit for that would rule out all payments where the beneficiary is under age.

I have more difficulty about the resettlement. My difficulty does not arise from the rule delegates non potest delegare for if the section authorises the creation of a new trust it must do so by writing into the testator's will authority to his trustees to do this: and new trust purposes almost inevitably mean that in certain events certain persons will take benefit who were not beneficiaries under the testator's will. But I think that the cases show that it is too late now to say that this power can never authorise trustees to convey funds to new trustees to hold for new trust purposes: to say that might endanger past transactions done on the faith of these authorities.

If that be so, then I must hold that, if trustees genuinely and reasonably believe that it is for the benefit of a beneficiary contingently entitled to a share of capital to resettle a sum not exceeding half of his prospective share, they are empowered to do so in ways which do not infringe the rule against perpetuities. ...

I agree that this appeal must be allowed.

VISCOUNT RADCLIFFE

...It is obvious, I think, that as things stand today and are likely to stand for some time to come, Miss Penelope is very far from having any certain or assured rights to any part of this trust fund. ...

Now what the trustees of the testator's will, the second respondents, are proposing to do, if they lawfully can, is to take a sum of about £7,600 ... out of Miss Penelope's expectant share ... and set it apart for her upon the trusts of a new settlement for her benefit... . The first trustees of this proposed new settlement are intended to be the same persons as the will trustees, but again I do not think that anything turns on this, nor has anyone suggested that it does. What matters is that there are new trusts, not that there are old trustees. ...

The trustees are satisfied that if money were thus raised out of her expectant share and settled on these trusts its disposition would be for her benefit. ... When one compares her situation under the proposed arrangement with her existing situation it is very natural to conclude that the give and take results to her advantage: but, apart from the actual variation of interests, the trustees have also to take into account the incidence of death duties... . [I]f this settlement is made, her fund will, it is thought, become free from duty on her father's death if he survives the making by five years. ...

It is necessary, therefore, to begin by saying something about the form and nature of what is known as the power of advancement.

No one doubts that such a power was frequently conferred upon trustees under settlements of personality (sic) and that its general purpose was to enable them in a proper case to anticipate the vesting in possession of an intended beneficiary's contingent or reversionary interest by raising money on account of his interest and paying or applying it immediately for his benefit. By so doing they released it from the trusts of the settlement and accelerated the enjoyment of his interest (though normally only with the consent of a prior tenant for life); and, where the contingency upon which the vesting of the beneficiary's title depended failed to mature or there was a later diffuseness or, in some cases, a great shrinkage in the value of the remaining trust funds, the trusts as declared by the settlement were materially varied through the operation of the power of advancement. This possibility was recognised and accepted as an incidental risk attendant upon the exercise of such a power, whose presence was felt on the whole to be advantageous in a system in which the possession of property interests was often deferred long beyond adult years.

No one disputes either that, when section 32 was framed and inserted in the Trustee Act of 1925 as a general enabling provision applying to trusts coming into existence after that date, it was expressed in terms that corresponded closely with the previous common form recommended in books of ... precedents and adopted in practice. I do not see any particular importance in this circumstance apart from the fact that it makes it the more natural to refer to what had been said in earlier reported decisions that bear upon the meaning and range of a power of advancement.

The word "advancement" itself meant in this context the establishment in life of the beneficiary who was the object of the power or at any rate some step that would contribute to the furtherance of his establishment. Thus it was found in such phrases as "preferment or advancement" (*Lowther v Bentinck*), "business, profession, or employment or ... advancement or preferment in the world" (*Roper-Curzon v Roper-Curzon*) and "placing out or advancement in life" (*In re Breeds' Will*). Typical instances of expenditure for such purposes under the social conditions of the nineteenth century were an apprenticeship or the purchase of a commission in the army or of an interest in

Alert

business. In the case of a girl there could be advancement on marriage (*Lloyd v Cocker*).

Advancement had, however, to some extent a limited range of meaning, since it was thought to convey the idea of some step in life of permanent significance, and accordingly, to prevent uncertainties about the permitted range of objects for which moneys could be raised and made available, such words as "or otherwise for his or her benefit" were often added to the word "advancement." It was always recognised that these added words were "large words" (see Jessel M.R. in *In re Breeds' Will* and indeed in another case (*Lowther v Bentinck*))... . This wide construction of the range of the power ... must have been carried into the statutory power created by section 32, since it adopts without qualification the accustomed wording "for the advancement or benefit in such manner as they may in their absolute discretion think fit."

So much for "advancement," which I now use for brevity to cover the combined phrase "advancement or benefit." It means any use of the money which will improve the material situation of the beneficiary. It is important, however, not to confuse the idea of "advancement" with the idea of advancing the money out of the beneficiary's expectant interest. ... The one refers to the operation of finding money by way of anticipation of an interest not yet absolutely vested in possession or, if so vested, belonging to an infant: the other refers to the status of the beneficiary and the improvement of his situation. The power to carry out the operation of anticipating an interest is not conferred by the word "advancement" but by those other words of the section which expressly authorise the payment or application of capital money for the benefit of a person... .

I think, with all respect to the commissioners, a good deal of their argument is infected with some of this confusion. To say, for instance, that there cannot be a valid exercise of a power of advancement that results in a deferment of the vesting of the beneficiary's absolute title (Miss Penelope, it will be remembered, is to take at 30 under the proposed settlement instead of at 21 under the will) is in my opinion to play upon words. The element of anticipation consists in the raising of money for her now before she has any right to receive anything under the existing trusts: the advancement consists in the application of that money to form a trust fund, the provisions of which are thought to be for her benefit. ...

I have not been able to find in the words of section 32, to which I have now referred, anything which in terms or by implication restricts the width of the manner or purpose of advancement. It is true that, if this settlement is made, Miss Penelope's children, who are not objects of the power, are given a possible interest in the event of her dying under 30 leaving surviving issue. But if the disposition itself, by which I mean the whole provision made, is for her benefit, it is no objection to the exercise of the power that other persons benefit incidentally as a result of the exercise. Thus a man's creditors may in certain cases get the most immediate advantage from an advancement made for the purpose of paying them off, as in *Lowther v Bentinck*; and a power to raise money for the advancement of a wife may cover a payment made direct to her husband in order to set him up in business (*In re Kershaw's Trusts*). The exercise will not be bad therefore on this ground.

Link
See the similar view expressed in *Fuller v Evans* in relation to payments from income.

Nor in my opinion will it be bad merely because the moneys are to be tied up in the proposed settlement. If it could be said that the payment or application permitted by section 32 cannot take the form of a settlement in any form but must somehow pass direct into or through the hands of the object of the power, I could appreciate the principle upon which the commissioners' objection was founded. But can that principle be asserted? Anyone can see, I think, that there can be circumstances in which, while it is very desirable that some money should be raised at once for the benefit of an owner of an expectant or contingent interest, it would be very undesirable that the money should not be secured to him under some arrangement that will prevent him having the absolute disposition of it. I find it very difficult to think that there is something at the back of section 32 which makes such an advancement impossible. ... Farwell J. authorised one in *In re Halsted's Will Trusts*, a case in which the trustees had left their discretion to the court. The trustees should raise the money and "have" it "settled," he said. So too, Harman J. in *In re Ropner's Settlement Trusts* authorised the settlement of an advance provided for an infant, saying that the child could not "consent or request the trustees to make the advance, but the transfer of a part of his contingent share to the trustees of a settlement for him must advance his interest and thus be for his benefit ..." All this must be wrong in principle if a power of advancement cannot cover an application of the moneys by way of settlement.

Alert

The truth is, I think, that the propriety of requiring a Settlement of moneys found for advancement was recognised as long ago as 1871 in *Roper-Curzon v Roper-Curzon* and, so far as I know, it has not been impugned since. Lord Romilly M.R.'s decision passed into the textbooks and it must have formed the basis of a good deal of subsequent practice. True enough, as counsel for the commissioners has reminded us, the beneficiary in that case was an adult who was offering to execute the post-nuptial settlement required: but I find it impossible to read Lord Romilly's words as amounting to anything less than a decision that he would permit an advancement under the power only on the terms that the money was to be secured by settlement. That was what the case was about. If, then, it is a proper exercise of a power of advancement for trustees to stipulate that the money shall be settled, I cannot see any difference between having it settled that way and having it settled by themselves paying it to trustees of a settlement which is in the desired form.

Alert

It is not as if anyone were contending for a principle that a power of advancement cannot be exercised "over the head" of a beneficiary, that is, unless he actually asks for the money to be raised and consents to its application. From some points of view that might be a satisfactory limitation, and no doubt it is the way in which an advancement takes place in the great majority of cases. But, if application and consent were necessary requisites of advancement, that would cut out the possibility of making any advancement for the benefit of a person under age, at any rate without the institution of court proceedings and formal representation of the infant: and it would mean, moreover, that the trustees of an adult could not in any Circumstances (sic) insist on raising money to pay his debts, however much the operation might be to his benefit, unless he agreed to that course. Counsel for the commissioners did not contend before us that the power of advancement was inherently limited in this way: and I do not think that such a limitation would accord with the general understanding. ...

[I]f it is part of the trusts and powers created by one settlement that the trustees of it should have power to raise money and make it available for a beneficiary upon new trusts approved by them, then they are in substance given power to free the money from one trust and to subject it to another.

In the same way I am unconvinced by the argument that the trustees would be improperly delegating their trust by allowing the money raised to pass over to new trustees under a settlement conferring new powers on the latter. In fact I think that the whole issue of delegation is here beside the mark. The law is not that trustees cannot delegate: it is that trustees cannot delegate unless they have authority to do so. If the power of advancement which they possess is so read as to allow them to raise money for the purpose of having it settled, then they do have the necessary authority to let the money pass out of the old settlement into the new trusts. No question of delegation of their powers or trusts arises. If, on the other hand, their power of advancement is read so as to exclude settled advances, cadit quaestio.

 Alert

...[T]he property effectually passes out of the old settlement into the new one, and it is of no relevance that, at any rate for the time being, the persons administering the new trust are the same individuals.

...I do not find it possible to import ... restrictions into the words of the statutory power which itself does not contain them. First, the suggested qualification, that the considerations or circumstances must be "personal" to the beneficiary, seems to me uncontrollably vague as a guide to general administration. What distinguishes a personal need from any other need to which the trustees in their discretion think it right to attend in the beneficiary's interest? And, if the advantage of preserving the funds of a beneficiary from the incidence of death duty is not an advantage personal to that beneficiary, I do not see what is. ...

I am of opinion that there is no maintainable reason for introducing into the statutory power of advancement a qualification that would exclude the exercise in the case now before us. It would not be candid to omit to say that, though I think that that is what the law requires, I am uneasy at some of the possible applications of this liberty, when advancements are made for the purposes of settlement or on terms that there is to be a settlement. It is quite true, as the commissioners have pointed out, that you might have really extravagant cases of resettlements being forced on beneficiaries in the name of advancement, even a few months before an absolute vesting in possession would have destroyed the power. I have tried to give due weight to such possibilities, but ... I do not believe that it is wise to try to cut down an admittedly wide and discretionary power, enacted for general use, through fear of its being abused in certain hypothetical instances; and moreover, as regards this fear, I think that it must be remembered that we are speaking of a power intended to be in the hands of trustees chosen by a settler because of his confidence in their discretion and good sense and subject to the external check that no exercise can take place without the consent of a prior life-tenant; and that there does remain at all times a residual power in the court to restrain or correct any purported exercise than (sic) can be shown to be merely wanton or capricious and not to be attributable to a genuine discretion. I think, therefore, that, although extravagant possibilities exist, they may be more menacing in argument than in real life.

The other issue … [is] that relating to the application of the rule against perpetuities… . On this issue … there are legal objections to the proposed settlement … placed before the court. …

LORD HODSON

My Lords, my noble and learned friends who are … unable to be present today, Lord Jenkins and Lord Devlin, are in full agreement with the opinion [of Lord Radcliffe] which I have just read and I am also in the same agreement.

This case provides House of Lords authority that the power of advancement can be applied in any way that improves the material situation of the beneficiary, including resettlement, and that incidental benefit to others does not matter, provided the advancement is made for the benefit of the beneficiary. Conflicting academic views have been expressed as to whether the resettlement can be made on discretionary or protective trusts or whether this could amount to an improper delegation.

Link
See Further Reading for reference to some discussion on this point.

The case which follows contains some key statements by the Court of Appeal on the duties of trustees in relation to advancements. The circumstances provide an interesting and useful illustration of the kinds of advancements which will be seen as improper and in breach of trust. In relation to some advancements, the trustees were able to rely on the defence of consent. (Detail on breach, liability and defences - including the effect of undue influence – can be found in Chapter 14 on Breach of Trust.)

In re Pauling's Settlement Trusts. Younghusband and Others v Coutts & Co [1964] Ch 303

Panel: Willmer, Harman and Upjohn LJJ

Facts: Under her marriage settlement, Mrs Younghusband had a life interest (with a power to appoint a life interest in half the fund to any surviving husband). The remainder was to go to her children. Over a period of years, advancements of capital were made, with her consent, to the children (under express powers in the trust) but the money was largely spent by the parents in funding their lifestyle and paying their debts. (Additional details of the facts appear in the extracts from the judgments.) The children, Francis, George, Ann and Anthony sued the trustees for breach of trust. Some of their claims succeeded but others failed and they appealed to the Court of Appeal. It was held that the advancements were made in breach of trust and, except insofar as there were valid consents (obtained free from the undue influence of the parents), the trustees were liable.

LORD JUSTICE WILLMER

The judgment which I am about to read is the judgment of the court... .

This is indeed a sorry story, and one which reflects no credit at all on any of the parties to it. When Miss Pauling, the plaintiffs' mother (and we shall refer to her throughout as "the mother") married their father (to whom we shall refer as "the commander") she was a young lady of considerable fortune. She was marrying a naval officer who had almost no fortune at all, and by the wisdom, no doubt, of her parents, it was decided to vest her fortune in trustees on the trusts of a marriage settlement. The whole object of this transaction was to prevent the use (or rather misuse) of the lady's capital for the very purposes for which in fact it has been very largely frittered away, that is, in the ordinary living expenses of the family. ...

In June, 1948, the trust funds were intact, and amounted to over £70,000. By June, 1954, the bank (the trustees of the settlement) had raised and paid away over £29,000 from the capital of these funds in purported exercise of a power of advancement, and there was nothing whatever left to show for it. ... It was in part due to a misunderstanding of a power of advancement contained in the settlement, which was in rather unusual form, and later on to its plain misuse, but also was largely due to the charm of manner and powers of persuasion of the commander. ...

The defendants, Coutts & Co (to whom we shall refer as "the bank"), have all along been the sole trustees. ... Charles Russell & Co were nominated as solicitors to the trust with permission to the bank to consult its own solicitors in any case in which it should think fit. ... [A]t all material times the mother had an account with the bank. The commander did not have any separate bank account with the bank, but he was authorised to draw on the mother's account, and it appears that it was he who largely controlled it. During most of the time with which we are concerned this account was substantially overdrawn.

...Apart from ... small additional sources of income, the family were wholly dependent on the income derived from the marriage settlement. The evidence shows that ... the available income was always over-spent so that the commander was always hard up for money.

...[T]he power in clause 11 ... has been accepted as containing two limbs, first a power with the consent of the mother in her lifetime to raise any part or parts not exceeding in the whole one-half of the ... share of any child, and to pay the same to him or her for his or her absolute use, and, secondly, the more usual power to pay or apply the same for his or her advancement or otherwise for his or her benefit in such manner as the bank might think fit. It was argued that the power contained in the first limb was wider than that in the second, although it was conceded on both sides that in both cases the power was fiduciary. Having regard to the very wide interpretation given to the statutory power (which approximates to the second limb in Pauling's settlement) by their Lordships' House in In re Pilkington's Will Trusts, we cannot see that the ambit of the first limb of the power substantially differs from that of the second limb. But, as all the advances were made in purported exercise of the first limb, we must examine the argument upon it. Being a fiduciary power, it seems to us quite clear that the power can be exercised only if it is for the benefit of the child or remoter issue to be advanced. ... That this must be so ... follows from ... the fact that the parties to a settlement intend the normal trusts to take effect, and that a power of advancement be exercised only if there is some good reason for it. That good reason must be beneficial to the person to be advanced; it cannot be exercised capriciously or with some other benefit in view. The trustees, before exercising the power, have to weigh on the one side the benefit to the proposed advancee, and on the other hand the rights of those who are or may hereafter become interested under the trusts of the settlement. We reject Sir Milner Holland's argument on behalf of the bank to the effect that an advancement can be made under the first limb which is not for the benefit of the advanced person. Furthermore, it is clear that the power under the first limb may be exercised, if the circumstances warrant it, either by making an out-and-out payment to the person to be advanced, or for a particular purpose specified by the trustees. Thus in argument an example was given that when George was called to the Bar the trustees might have quite properly advanced to him a sum of capital quite generally for his living expenses to support him while starting to practise, provided they thought that this was a reasonable thing to do, and that he was a type of person who could reasonably be trusted to make proper use of the money. On the other hand, if the trustees make the advance for a particular purpose which they state, they can quite properly pay it over to the advancee if they reasonably think they can trust him or her to carry out the prescribed purpose. What they cannot do is to prescribe a particular purpose, and then raise and pay the money over to the advancee leaving him or her entirely free, legally and morally, to apply it for that purpose or to spend it in any way he or she chooses, without any responsibility on the trustees even to inquire as to its application.

Failure to appreciate this was one of the root causes of the trouble, for in the first opinion of counsel in 1948 ... he advised that the trustees could make an advancement out and out for the purpose of a purchase of a house in the Isle of Man, but he said ..."So far as the trustees are concerned, they will be paying the money to the children for their own absolute use." This, we think, was the wrong approach. At that time both Francis and George were studying at university, and it was not suggested that they required any sum for their maintenance there; the only possible justification for advancing the very substantial sum of £5,000 to each of the two boys, one of them 27 and the other just 22, who had no other possible proper use for this money, was to invest it in a house in the Isle of Man ... and the advancement could be justified only for that purpose. This error was perpetuated later by the children's solicitor, who got into the habit of advising them that, although purported advancements were, for example, for the repair of a house or for the purchase of furniture, they were sums which the children could "blue," for example, on a horse.

This was wrong and misleading advice. If money was advanced for an express purpose by the bank, the advanced person was under a duty to carry that purpose out, and he could not properly apply it to another. We are not concerned with the question whether in such circumstances the bank could recover money so misapplied, but this much is plain, that if such misapplication came to their notice, they could not safely make further advances for particular purposes without making sure that the money was in fact applied to that purpose, since the advancee would have shown him or herself quite irresponsible. ...

The first question, therefore, that arises in relation to each of the advances ... is whether there was a proper exercise of the power under either limb. No question arises as to the consent of the mother, for that was given in every case. If the advance were proper in any particular case, the question of the children's consent, although adult, would not arise; that has been made quite clear in *In re Pilkington's Will Trusts*. ...[I]it would not be necessary to obtain that consent, though no doubt any trustee intending to advance an adult beneficiary would normally do so only with his consent and probably only at his request. But, if any advance were an improper exercise of the power in clause 11 (and they all were in the judge's view) what is the position? Prima facie, having improperly exercised the power, the bank would be guilty of breach of trust and must replace the money misapplied.

...[I]n this action each beneficiary is suing to recover only the advances purported to have been made to him or her, or for his or her benefit. This is not a case where any beneficiary is seeking to compel the trustees to replace trust funds wrongly applied, or paid away to some other beneficiary. Had that been the case, different considerations would, no doubt, have applied. But in the circumstances of this case it is clear to us that if the bank can establish a valid request or consent by the advanced beneficiary to the advance in question, that is a good defence on the part of the bank to the beneficiary's claim, even though it be plain that the advance was made in breach of trust. ...

[A] trustee dealing in breach of trust with a beneficiary who has just attained the age of 21 years must realise the danger that such beneficiary may be acting under the influence of a parent. ...

[T]he bank knew ... the ages of each of the children, and ... that as each child attained 21, that child received advances from the bank which went straight into the banking account of the mother. ...[I]f it can be established that the presumption [of undue influence] exists in any given case, the bank are fixed with notice of it and cannot rely on any consents given under such influence. ...

We now deal with the impugned transactions seriatim. ...[T]he two eldest children, Francis and George, were over 21, and counsel advised that if they were agreeable, advances could be made to them of sums sufficient to enable a house to be bought, which they could then settle voluntarily on their mother for life with remainder to themselves. ...Francis and George joined in signing a memorandum, ... the material part of which was in the following terms: "We ... hereby authorise and request you to apply such sums as may be made available for our advancement ... in purchasing a property in the Isle of Man, which it is our intention to settle in accordance with the suggestion contained in the opinion of counsel ... in a settlement in which you are to be the trustee." ...[A] house ... in the Isle of Man ... was duly purchased ... for £8,450 and became the family home for the next seven years.

...On October 22, 1948, the bank were writing to Francis about completion of the purchase in the joint names of "you and your brother." Yet on October 26 they wrote this to the Isle of Man solicitors acting for them in connection with the conveyance:

"...Oakhill is being purchased with money being taken out of the above-mentioned trust and placed at the disposal of the two eldest sons ... but Commander Younghusband has told us this morning that it is their wish that the conveyance should be in favour of himself and Mrs. Younghusband." Not one word of protest was raised by the bank at this complete reversal of the scheme envisaged by counsel. They quite calmly applied the money raised for the benefit of the sons in the purchase of a house for the commander and the mother. They never obtained the consent of the sons to this, and the evidence was that the sons never did consent. The subsequent history of the house was that shortly afterwards it was mortgaged by the commander for £5,000, which sum was apparently spent as income. When financial disaster overtook the commander in 1956 (as a result of which he was made bankrupt in the Isle of Man), the house was sold for less than the amount of the mortgage, so that in the event Francis and George lost the whole of their £8,450.

 Alert

Making all due allowance for the fact that the bank may have misunderstood the effect of clause 11, it does not explain their complete laxity in permitting this transaction to go forward. Even at this early stage they wholly failed to exercise any powers or duties as trustees, and thought only of themselves as bankers to the commander and the mother. We doubt whether the original advance, if counsel's advice had been carried out, would have been a proper exercise of the power, but no harm could come of it, for the new settlement would replace the old, and the position would be safeguarded. But having regard to the way in which the transaction was in fact carried out, they have no defence to the claim to replace this sum... . Any relief under section 61 [Trustee Act 1925] is out of the question.

 Link
For more detail on this, see Chapter 14 on Breach of Trust.

...On the same day on which the deposit was paid is found the first payment made direct into the mother's account, then heavily overdrawn. This was a sum of £1,000. The payment arose out of advice given ... by the bank's solicitors to the effect that it would be proper, in addition to advancing money on the house ... to advance a sum for the purpose of furnishing it. The first mention of amount emanated from the commander, who fixed it arbitrarily at £1,000, a sum to which he obtained his sons (sic) assent... . The trustees accepted this without inquiry, no doubt upon the footing that the house would be conveyed to the sons and their consent was given only on that footing. ... [W]hen the bank realised that the house was not going to belong to the boys, but to their parents, the impropriety of purchasing furniture with the boys' money became obvious. Yet they took no steps to remedy the situation. The bank never even took any steps to see whether any furniture was in fact purchased, and none (or almost none) in fact was. All that happened was that the mother's overdraft was reduced by £1,000. The bank was in a delicate position. Their interest as bankers conflicted with their duties as trustees... . The bank acted in plain breach of their duty most unreasonably, and no question of relief under section 61 of the Trustee Act, 1925, can arise. The appeal is allowed so far as this advance is concerned.

 Alert

...It was calculated that each child's presumptive share ... would be about £14,000. The commander therefore embarked upon a plan for raising approximately £7,000 to be advanced nominally to each child on attaining the age of twenty-one. ...[T]he commander, early in 1948, suggested to the bank that further sums be advanced to

Francis and George up to a total of approximately £14,000 with the object of paying off (a) a loan of £2,600 which the bank, as trustees of another settlement (by a Mrs. Hodson) had advanced to the mother, and (b) the overdraft on the mother's account, which then stood at about £3,000. ...

This ... led to another lamentable and indeed inexplicable transaction. The bank ... at first ... expressed doubt as to whether this would be a proper exercise of their power under clause 11 ... . They took advice from Charles Russell & Co., whose advice was no more encouraging. The commander, however, was importunate and apparently very persuasive. ...In due course Charles Russell & Co advised that ... this [paying off the Hodson loan] might be a proper exercise of the power ... provided that Francis and George received an adequate quid pro quo. ...

The scheme as advised by Charles Russell & Co might at a pinch be justified as an exercise of the power ... but as carried out the transaction was disastrously different. ...[I]n due course, at the request of the mother, and with the consent of Francis and George, a sum of £2,600 was raised and paid over to the mother, who applied it for paying off the Hodson loan. ...All the sons got in return for the expenditure of £2,600 extracted from their expectancies and paid to the bank in release of their mother's debt were policies with a surrender value of £650, and probably an implied covenant to keep up payment of the premiums.

The payment of this sum was a clear breach of trust. In this case the sons did have separate advice, but what they approved was the proposed, not the actual, transaction, of which latter they never knew, and to which they never consented. ...As carried out, the transaction plainly could not be justified ..., and, of course, the bank cannot hide behind the negligence of their own advisers for whose neglect they must, as between them and their beneficiaries, assume full responsibility. The payment being, therefore, a plain breach of trust ... [t]he bank must show that the boys consented to the breach of trust; this on the evidence they cannot do. ...

 Alert

LORD JUSTICE UPJOHN

continuing reading the judgment of the court: Later ... the commander returned to the suggestion of raising another £2,000 so as to bring the total advanced to Francis and George up to approximately £14,000. The bank was not at first prepared to make this further advance, and in this it was supported by the advice of Charles Russell & Co The commander, however, continued to press his request, and alleged that the money was needed to pay for improvements to the recently purchased house in the Isle of Man. At the request of the bank he promised to submit accounts in respect of the improvements, showing what had been or had to be paid, but in fact this was never done. Eventually, ... Francis and George signed a document drafted by the bank in the following terms: "With reference to the further sum of not exceeding £2,000 ... by way of advancement, we hereby authorise and request you to place the money when raised to the account in your books of Mrs. R. Violet Younghusband. We fully appreciate that the money in question has been or is being used for the purpose of making improvements to the property in the Isle of Man belonging to Mrs. Younghusband." As a result, £2,000 was raised and ... paid into the mother's account. It will be seen that in this

 Alert

case there was no pretence that the money raised was being used for the benefit of Francis and George.

...[T]hough this was the plainest breach of trust, we agree with the judge that the bank have a good defence, for they obtained consents from the two children concerned, and they were emancipated.

...The next victim on the list was the daughter Ann. Even before she attained 21 ... her father was looking about for ways of spending her money... . He very soon seems to have concluded that, having acquired a country residence at the expense of his sons, it would now be a good plan to get a town house at the expense of his daughter. It is indeed fortunate for her that the proposed house ... was put into her name, probably to preserve the fiction that the parents were living in the Isle of Man. ...Why the bank should entertain this proposal passes our comprehension. The girl was in her first year at oxford (sic), and there was no reason at all why her expectant share should be spent in buying a house and furnishing it for her family's use. A family in these comparatively straitened circumstances had no justification for having two houses. This project, in our judgment, was clearly an improper use of the power, made in order to suit the father, and without any proper regard to the benefit of the daughter. Having regard to her age, it is clear that the presumption of undue influence applies to this transaction. ...Luckily for the bank, property in Chelsea of whatever sort has appreciated very much in value. When Ann married in 1952 the house became in truth hers, and she has since disposed of it to advantage and recognises that, having had the money once, she cannot claim it again. ...[U]nder her father's influence a further sum of £3,260 was advanced to the father or the mother nominally for the further improvement and furnishing of the Chelsea house, but in fact spent on the Isle of Man house, or used to support her mother's overdraft. ...

 Alert

[T]he commander ... asked for ... £1,000 to cover furniture. ... [His Lordship then listed various payments made to the father or mother and continued:] In the intervals between these payments the bank made a few ineffectual protests and asked to see bills, but never insisted, and it is evident that they exercised no discretion at all as to the amount needed for furniture first stated to be £1,000, and gradually increased to reach £3,260.

There is no doubt that Ann asked for each of these sums to be advanced ... well knowing in fact that only about £300 was expended on the purchase of furniture from start to finish. The rest went in the family living expenses through the mother's account. ...The judge refused to give relief to Ann in these respects. ...[T]he bank ... could have no more than a pious hope, which they did not dare to test by pressing to see receipts for the purchase of this vast quantity of furniture, that most of it was being invested in furniture. A moment's study of the mother's account at this time would have shown that even this was improbable. They merely wanted some document which, as they thought, would give legal justification for making the payments.

Further, it seems to us that these very untrue statements [by Ann] must be treated as issuing out of the presumed undue influence of her father, made, as they were, either to the bank in his presence, or by arrangement with him. Finally, we do not consider that these statements, if true, would, as the judge held, have justified the advances, though furniture bought and taken by Ann and retained by her might have afforded some defence to the breach of trust. The bank at this stage ought to have had their eyes wide open to the situation and insisted on calling a halt to this reckless expenditure apparently for furniture. Ann by her counsel concedes that she must give credit for £300 of furniture actually purchased. Subject to that, we feel constrained to come to the conclusion that, without separate advice, the bank cannot rely on the assent of this young girl to gifts direct into her mother's and father's pockets, and we hold the bank liable in respect of [those] advances ... and ... allow the appeal accordingly. Having behaved unreasonably, the bank cannot rely on section 61.

Alert

Ann's portion had now been fully used, but there remained one chicken to be plucked, a younger brother, Anthony... . He attained 21 on June 15, 1951... .

Burrell [a solicitor] wrote a most perfunctory letter to the young man ... which he agreed in the witness-box could not constitute proper separate advice ... and between July 11, 1951, and February 7, 1952, £6,500 was paid straight into the mother's account. There is one payment which is characteristic. The father had succeeded to the tune of £1,000 in raising the wind by a charge on Ann's house, and half the first payment to Anthony was used to repay the bank this amount, thus robbing Anthony to pay Ann. There was not even a pretence ... of ... countervailing benefit to Anthony... . We do not feel any doubt that the bank is liable on these payments, as the judge held. Relief under section 61 is out of the question.

The story does not end there. In 1953 and 1954 the bank revalued the assets in the trust. Accordingly, when the father in June, 1953, "called to inquire whether he could borrow a few hundred pounds," the bank (whose words these are) ... without any inquiry whatever as to the purpose except that the father was in what he called "an awful hole," cheerfully agreed to advance to him a further £1,200, and suggested that it should be taken out of the shares of Francis, George and Ann in shares designed to make their advances equal. Fortunately for him, Anthony escaped this raid. Between September, 1953, and June, 1954, the advances ... were made direct to the father or mother; they aggregated the grand total of £5,350. Nobody pretends that these were not breaches of trust, but they were assented to by each of the three children. We have already concluded that Francis and George must be taken to be emancipated by this time, and so, we hold, was Ann. She had been married in 1952 and was living in her Chelsea house with her husband. In these circumstances, the judge rightly held that these sums were not recoverable. ...

Alert

The outcome of this case shows that, even though the word 'benefit' has been given a wide interpretation, an advancement can never be a proper one if it is not genuinely made for the benefit of the beneficiary whose share is being advanced. If it is not for his benefit, or it is not used for the agreed purpose, the fact that the beneficiary requests or consents to this does not, of itself, make it proper but may, if the consent is valid, afford a defence for the trustees.

The next two cases consider the extent to which advancements, made to fulfil a moral obligation felt by a beneficiary, can be seen to be proper as conferring a benefit on him or her. Both cases related to donations to charity.

In re Clore's Settlement Trusts Sainer and Others v Clore and Others [1966] 1 WLR 955

Panel: Pennycuick J

Facts: Charles Clore created a settlement in favour of his children, under which they would be entitled to capital if they reached the age of 30. There was an express provision that up to two-thirds of each beneficiary's presumptive share of capital could be advanced, once that beneficiary was over 21, for his advancement or benefit. The son Alan Clore, on reaching 21, wanted one-seventh of his very substantial share to be advanced as a donation to charity. The trustees, as plaintiffs, wished to know if they were authorised to pay money to the charity or to the beneficiary for this purpose. The judge held that this was permissible.

MR JUSTICE PENNYCUICK

...Mr. Brightman, who appears for the trustees, formulated his argument ... in the form of five propositions. The first is that payment or application for the advancement or benefit of a person means "any use of the money which will improve the material situation of the beneficiary." That expression is taken from the speech of Lord Radcliffe in *In re Pilkington's Will Trusts*. The proposition is well established and requires no further elaboration.

The second proposition is that the improvement of the material situation of a beneficiary is not confined to his direct financial advantage. That may be amplified, I think, by saying that it includes the discharge, at any rate, of certain moral or social obligations on the part of the beneficiary, for example towards dependants. In support of that, Mr. Brightman cites a series of cases in which the court has held that trustees can properly exercise such a power by paying money to the trustees of a settlement for the benefit of the beneficiary and the members of his family. There is no doubt that that is so. *In re Pilkington's Will Trust* is an example and there have been many others. In such a case the interest which the beneficiary would take on attaining the age at which the interest would vest absolutely is reduced from an absolute interest to a more limited interest, normally a life interest, but nonetheless the court treats the settlement as being for his benefit, that is, as improving his material situation.

Alert

The third proposition is the crux of the present application: it is that the court has always recognised that a wealthy person has a moral obligation to make appropriate charitable donations. The court has certainly recognised this in several cases, although, generally, it has been concerned with relatively small sums of income: see, in particular, *In re Walker*. It seems to me that a beneficiary under a settlement may indeed in many cases be reasonably entitled to regarded himself as under a moral obligation to make donations towards charity. The nature and amount of those donations must depend upon all the circumstances, including the position in life of the beneficiary, the amount of the fund and the amount of his other resources. Once that proposition is accepted, it seems to me that it must lie within the scope of a power such as that contained in clause 8 of this settlement for the trustees to raise capital for the purpose of relieving the beneficiary of his moral obligation towards whatever charity he may have in mind. If the obligation is not to be met out of the capital of the trust fund, he would have to meet it out of his own pocket, if at all. Accordingly, the discharge of the obligation out of the capital of the trust fund does improve his material situation. The precise amount which the trustees can in any given case apply for this purpose must depend, I think, on the particular circumstances, and in this respect quantum is a necessary ingredient in the proper exercise of the power. It is difficult, for example, to see how the trustees under a power such as that in clause 8 could validly pay over the whole authorised two-thirds to charitable purposes. On the other hand, it is certainly not for the court to say precisely where the line is to be drawn. In the present case, having regard to all the circumstances, I think the proposed proportion of one-seventh can fairly be regarded as on the right side of the line. It appears from the evidence that Alan Clore recognises that he is under a moral obligation to make payments to charity. He has not yet been subjected to any public or social pressure in this respect, though he believes that it may come about in the future. Once he recognises this obligation the trustees may properly regard it as improving his material situation to discharge the obligation out of the trust fund... .

Link

See the further discussion of these issues in *X v A* [2006] 1 WLR 741.

Mr. Brightman added in his formulation two further propositions: fourthly, that a wealthy person can discharge his moral obligation at less cost to himself if he makes a charitable settlement and, fifthly, it follows that any advance of an appropriate sum under the settlement is capable of improving his material situation by enabling him to discharge his moral obligation without undue burden upon himself. It is certainly true that by making a capital settlement Alan Clore can confer the same benefit upon the charity at much less expense to himself than if he were to make a corresponding payment to the charity personally out of income, which at the present rate of income tax it would be impossible for him to do. This last consideration emphasises the desirability of making the proposed advance, but I do not think it is essential to the power of the trustees to make the advance.

Mr. Walton, in his argument against the power of the trustees to make the proposed advance, cited a number of authorities and contended that the advance must be for the direct material advantage of the beneficiary concerned. That requirement may be said to be satisfied if it can be shown that public pressure would be such that it would be seriously detrimental to the material position of the beneficiary not to make a charitable donation; that, however, does not arise in the present case. I think that that is too narrow a view of what represents a benefit in a material sense to the beneficiary. Once the beneficiary himself regards the payment as a moral obligation, then it may be for his benefit to be relieved of it.

To avoid misunderstanding, it seems to me that in the case of a transaction of this kind, i.e., an advance of capital in discharge of a moral obligation towards charity, it is essential to a valid exercise of the power that the beneficiary himself should recognise the moral obligation. It is not open to the trustees to pay away the beneficiary's

Alert

See also the discussion of this point in *X v A*.

prospective capital over his head or against his will in discharge of what they consider to be his moral obligations.

...[T]aking his present position in life and his social outlook, it must be said that he [Alan Clore] does consider it to be his moral obligation to make a contribution on this scale to this charity.

I propose, accordingly, to answer the question ... declaring that the plaintiffs as trustees of the settlement ... with the consent of Charles Clore, which consent he is willing to give,

"are at liberty in exercise of the power conferred upon them by clause 8 of the settlement to pay out of the trust fund [the amount specified] and to apply the same for the benefit of the defendant Alan Evelyn Clore by ... paying the same to the trustees of the charity ...". ...

X and another v A and others [2006] 1 WLR 741

Panel: Hart J

Facts: Under a marriage settlement, certain powers of appointment were exercisable and, subject to these, there was a life interest for the wife, with remainder to the children and remoter issue. There was an express power for the trustees to advance the whole or part of the capital to or for the benefit of the wife. Two advancements were made and the sums advanced were given to charity. She now wanted the trustees to advance a considerable part of the remaining capital so that it could be donated to charity. She was motivated by a strong feeling of moral obligation and also a view that inhereted wealth was likely to have adverse consequences. The judge held that, although a donation to charity could in principle be made if for the benefit of the wife, the particular proposal was not an appropriate exercise of the power of advancement.

MR JUSTICE HART

...[T]he power to benefit the wife ... is not subject to any wording (such as is sometimes seen) making it clear that it can be exercised without regard to the interests of those entitled in reversion... . The power in the settlement can, by express words, be exercised in favour of one beneficiary to the exclusion of all the others but that does not mean (nor was it contended that it does) that in exercising the power the trustees are free to ignore their interests.

Benefit

In *In re Pilkington's Will Trusts* [1964] AC 612, 635 Viscount Radcliffe, construing the phrase "advancement or benefit" in section 32 of the Trustee Act 1925, said that it covered "any use of the money which will improve the material situation of the beneficiary".

At first sight those words might be thought to be an obstacle to the advance which is here proposed since its purpose has nothing whatever to do with improving the wife's material situation but rather the reverse. It is designed to enable her to deprive herself of the material benefit currently available to her in the form of income from the substantial assets which she now wishes should be devoted to charitable causes. The justification for nevertheless regarding that as a benefit to her is founded on a line of cases of which the earliest (and closest to the present) is *In re Clore's Settlement Trusts* [1966] 1 WLR 955. ...[His Lordship explained the facts of that case and the findings of Pennycuick J, and cited passages from the judgment. He continued:]

Subsequent cases have further illustrated the width of the word "benefit" in this context: *In re C L* [1969] 1 Ch 587 (where the transaction involved the extinction of the beneficiary's interest in favour of her adopted children and a consequent saving of estate duty on her death with no real detriment to the material position of the beneficiary), *In re Hampden's Settlement Trusts* [2001] WTLR 195 (where it involved a settlement on the beneficiary's children relieving him of the "considerable obligation in respect of making provision for their future" which he would otherwise have owed) and *In re Leigh's Settlement Trusts* (1980) 19 Tru LI 109 (which concerned a substantial application to a charity founded to maintain the stately home the preservation of which within the family had been one of the stated motivations behind the discretionary settlement out of which the funds had been advanced).

...*In re Hampden's Settlement Trusts* is ... pertinent since it contains a useful summary of the propositions to be derived from the cases in the submissions there recorded as having been made by Mr Browne-Wilkinson QC on behalf of the beneficiary, namely: (i) that a power to apply capital for the benefit of somebody is the widest possible formulation of such power; (ii) that under such a power the trustees can deal with capital in any way which, viewed objectively, can fairly be regarded as being to the benefit of the object of the power, and subjectively they believe to be so; and (iii) such benefit need not consist of a direct financial advantage to the person who is being benefited. It may be that he is benefited by benefiting a near relation or by relieving him of moral responsibilities.

 Alert

In re Hampden's Settlement Trusts is also pertinent since it contains a passage in the judgment of Walton J which seeks to indicate what is meant by "viewed objectively" in the second of the above propositions: see p 202:

"the figures are such that it is quite possible to regard this provision for the children, although generous, as being for the benefit of [the beneficiary]. By way of reductio ad absurdum if [the beneficiary] had himself no resources whatever then I do not think it would be possible objectively to regard the making of a provision of half a million pounds or thereabouts for his children as realistically conferring a benefit upon him ... here he is himself ... very well provided for, and that makes all the difference. In every case the question must be one of degree, but there are no such difficulties in the present case."

Building on those authorities, and in particular on *In re Clore's Settlement Trusts* [1966] 1 WLR 955, Mr Le Poidevin submitted that the only questions to be answered were whether the wife was reasonably entitled to regard herself as being under a moral obligation to make or procure the making of the proposed gift to charity and whether she did in fact recognise the obligation. As to the latter it was plain on the evidence (he submitted) that she did recognise the obligation and, as to the former, that it was not for the trustees or the court to decide whether they would take the same view. It was enough, he submitted, that the wife's view was one she could reasonably take. ...

In my judgment these submissions place a greater weight on the personal views of the beneficiary than is justified by the authorities. In *In re Clore's Settlement Trusts* itself the references made in the judgment to the sense of obligation felt by the beneficiary himself are made with the view of imposing a requirement additional to the initial requirement that there should be an existing moral obligation capable of being recognised by the court. In *In re Clore's Settlement Trusts* the court acknowledged that earlier examples of charitable gifts had been on a very different scale from that proposed before it ... but said that the question of the size of the particular gift must depend on "all the circumstances, including the position in life of the beneficiary, the amount of the fund and the amount of his other resources" and added ...: "If the obligation is not to be met out of the capital of the trust fund, he would have to meet it out of his own pocket, if at all. Accordingly, the discharge of the obligation out of the capital of the trust fund does improve his material situation."

That passage emphasised the potentially limiting effect of the requirement (from which none of the authorities have departed) that there be some sense in which the beneficiary's material situation can be said to be improved by the situation. The same point is made by Walton J's reductio ad absurdum in *In re Hampden's Settlement Trusts* : see ... above. In the present case I find it impossible to see how this requirement can be satisfied. It cannot be said that the proposed advance is relieving the wife of an obligation she would otherwise have to discharge out of her own resources if only because the amount proposed to be advanced exceeds the amount of her own free resources. In any event the court has no reason to suppose that, in relation to her free assets, she will regard the advance as having discharged her moral obligation. The moral imperative informing her request to the trustees might logically be thought to apply to her own assets regardless of whether or not an advance is made out of the trust fund.

...No ... case goes anywhere near recognising the existence of a moral obligation of the extent in question here.

For those reasons I do not think that I can conclude that it is open to the trustees to make the proposed advance.

...[T]o the question whether the power can in principle (ie as a matter of construction) be exercised by advancing money to or for the benefit of the wife so that she may discharge a moral obligation to charity my answer is affirmative. To the question whether the exercise actually proposed can properly be said to be for her benefit the answer is negative.

...Assuming (contrary to the view at which I have arrived) that it was in principle open to them to make the appointment proposed, the trustees should have asked themselves whether it was proper to make it given the fact that it would severely cut down ... the interests of those entitled to capital under the settlement. In considering that question general views about the evils of inherited wealth would in my judgment have been

Link

Contrast this with the position in *Re Clore*.

irrelevant. I am not entirely satisfied that the trustees did, in their deliberations, properly discount this inadmissible consideration.

I am also not entirely satisfied on the evidence that those deliberations gave as full a consideration as they should have done to the impact of the proposed exercise on the beneficiaries other than the wife herself. The trustees formed the view that the financial interests of those other beneficiaries were "generously catered for" by the interests and expectations they had under other family settlements... .

...Suffice to say that in the context of an exercise of a power in favour of one beneficiary which would confer no material benefit on her and her family, it behoved the trustees to look in a very detailed way into the individual circumstances of those in existence who would otherwise be entitled to consideration under the trusts and to consider what might be the potential future calls on the trust from them and those yet unborn. They may well have done so but I cannot be sure on the evidence before me that they did... .

Accordingly, the order which I propose to make is that the trustees are not at liberty to enter into the proposed transaction... .

This case stressed that there must always be some sense in which the beneficiary's material situation is improved. It also emphasised the need to take account of the interests of other beneficiaries whose rights could be affected by a proposed advancement. It is always important to consider the effect that the exercise of the power of advancement might have on all potential beneficiaries.

The next case conisdered whether a beneficiary, in whose favour the power had been exercised to the full extent, could seek further advancements if the remaining fund later increased in value.

In re Marquess of Abergavenny's Estate Act Trusts, Marquess of Abergavenny v Ram and Another [1981] 1 WLR 843

Panel: Goulding J

Facts: Under a settlement created by a private Act of Parliament, the trustees had power in their discretion to raise and pay up to one half of the value of the settled fund to a tenant for life for the time being in possession, for his own use and benefit. In 1965, they exercised their power to its full extent in favour of Lord Abergavenny. During the next 15 years, the remaining fund increased in value very considerably and it was suggested that the trustees consider exercising their discretion to pay him sufficient to bring the amounts he had received up to half of the present value of the fund. The trustees were prepared to consider some further payment if they had power to do this. The judge held that once the beneficiary had received assets to the prescribed limit, no further exercise of the power is possible.

MR JUSTICE GOULDING

The point is a short one. It is not, so far as the researches of counsel have revealed, the subject of any express judicial authority. Mr. Buckley for the plaintiff, Lord

Abergavenny, has referred me to cases that he submits are applicable by analogy, namely, cases where ... a partial appropriation has been made in the first place. There the approved practice is, when the balance of the share comes to be appropriated, to require the beneficiary to bring in what he has previously received at a money valuation as at the date when it was previously allocated to him. That is brought into account and the fund still retained by the trustees or other holders of the fund is valued as at the date of the further appropriation. The cases cited to illustrate that principle are *In re Richardson* [1896] 1 Ch 512, a decision of North J., and *In re Gollin's Declaration of Trust* [1969] 1 WLR 1858, decided by Buckley J. ... Mr. Buckley says that it really should make no difference whether a limit has been completely reached or nearly reached. If the remainder of the fund appreciates, why should the person previously paid out be entitled to get his benefit from it if he has had almost the whole of his share and yet be debarred from reopening the matter just because the limit has been reached? ... I put to Mr. Buckley an illustration... : supposing that a testator gives his residue, half to his son absolutely and half in settlement for his daughter and her children, and the son's share is fully paid out in one operation shortly after the testator's death, would anyone suppose that he could at any time thereafter during his sister's life require a valuation of the half retained for her and her children and, if it had appreciated since the original appropriation, require some more? I think that Mr. Buckley did not feel able to resist my suggestion that in such a case the son could not reopen the appropriation, but he did draw a distinction between a simple appropriation case and one like the present where there is a continuing discretionary power, intended to be available for repeated exercise during the whole of a life. ...

Mr. Hedley Marten for the trustees ... suggests, and I agree, that the only true conclusion from the evidence is that Lord Abergavenny received a full one half of the trust fund as valued in 1965. Then, Mr. Hedley Marten says, as a matter of law, that amounted to an exhaustive exercise of the power which ceased to be exercisable for the future, whatever might happen to the retained assets, that is, whether they went up or down in value. In my judgment that is right. I do not think that the authorities on a partial appropriation followed by a supplemental appropriation really assist in the present matter one way or the other. ...

[W]here there is a power to make successive payments to a person up to a limit of a certain fraction of a fund and at a certain date, he, the beneficiary, has received assets then fully reaching the prescribed limit, thereafter no further exercise of the power is possible. ... It would be to my mind strange and unexpected if the object of the power as such retained an interest or possibility of interest in the fund still in settlement, so that he could require accounts from the trustees and demand reconsideration of his position whenever there should be an appreciation of assets. It is perfectly true that even in the partial appropriation cases the beneficiary who has received something early may do very well because he may keep what has been given to him in some asset that appreciates while he only has to bring a cash sum, fixed once for all, into account; it may of course go the other way. But some such possibility of good or ill fortune is inherent in the very nature of payments made under a duty or a power on successive occasions up to an aggregate limit. There is no reason that I can see why such

Alert

Alert

inequality, or exposure to fortune, should be continued to the possible disadvantage of other beneficiaries after the limit has been reached.

...I must answer the question asked by the originating summons by declaring that ... in the events which have happened the power has already been exercised to the full. ...

This case suggests that, once the maximum amount permitted has been advanced (one half of the beneficiary's capital under s 32), there is no scope for further advancements, at any rate if this could affect the rights of other beneficiaries who are, or might be, entitled to a share of capital.

The next case concerned a situation where the trust instrument did not extend the power of advancement beyond the half share permitted under the Trustee Act 1925 s 32. As the power had already been exercised to the full extent, an application was made to vary the terms of the trust. Under the Variation of Trusts Act 1958, the court can sanction a proposed variation on behalf of beneficiaries who cannot consent in person, for example, because they are under 18 or not yet born. In this case the application was made to allow more than half to be advanced to a minor beneficiary. As she had a vested interest, no other beneficiary would be prejudiced by such payments.

CD (A Child) v O [2004] 2 P & CR DG13

Panel: Lloyd J

Statute: Variation of Trusts Act 1958

Facts: A trust fund (consisting of the proceeds of two life insurance policies) was held on trust for three minors in equal shares. The income of one beneficiary's share and part of her capital had been used for her school fees. There was an application to the court so that the whole of her capital could be applied for this purpose. The judge held that a variation of the trusts to allow this should be approved.

MR JUSTICE LLOYD

...In practice, though the fund ... has not yet been divided, it is treated, for reasons which do not matter, as if there were separate funds for each beneficiary. This application is concerned with C's Fund.

The income of C's Fund has in fact been applied to meet her school bills, but it is already inadequate. Part of the capital has also been advanced, under section 32 of the Trustee Act 1925, to be used for the same purposes.

The application is intended to secure that, if necessary, the whole capital can be applied for this purpose.

I have come to the conclusion that I should approve the extension of the statutory power of advancement as being for C's benefit. This point does, however, raise legal issues which may be of some wider interest and on which different views have been expressed. ...

The trusts applying to the policies incorporate a number of provisions such as a wide investment clause, but nothing that bears on the application of the income or capital.

There is an express power to revoke, vary or add administrative provisions of the trusts. The power of advancement is not an administrative power and the desired result cannot be achieved by using this power.

C is absolutely entitled to her Fund and, but for her being under age, she could call for it, give the trustee a good receipt for it and spend it as she chooses. Since she is only 12 years old she cannot do so. Section 31 of the Trustee Act 1925 applies to the fund and enables the income to be applied for her maintenance education or benefit even though she cannot give a receipt for it. That section applies "where any property is held by trustees in trust for any person for any interest whatsoever", which clearly includes property held on trust for a minor absolutely.

Section 32 of the 1925 Act is in different terms. ... [His Lordship quoted from s 32 and continued:] The references to the use of the power in relation to a beneficiary who is already absolutely entitled leave me in no doubt that the section applies to the present trusts of the proceeds of the policies. ...

However, by virtue of proviso (a) to section 32(1), no more than half of the presumptive or vested share or interest of the beneficiary may be paid or applied by way of advancement. That limit is commonly relaxed in modern trust deeds, but there is nothing to that effect in the documents in the present case.

On the evidence I am satisfied that it would be for C's benefit for the limit imposed by section 32 on the application of the capital of the fund for her education to be lifted. The question is whether and on what basis the court has power to achieve this result. There are two possible sources of jurisdiction.

The Court of Chancery had an ancient jurisdiction to authorise the application of income and, in more limited circumstances, capital, for the maintenance of a minor even if this was not authorised by the terms of the trust. This jurisdiction is recognised in the speeches in *Chapman v Chapman* [1954] AC 429... . As to the application of capital, Lewin on Trusts, 17th ed., refers to a number of cases at paragraph 32–06. One of them, in which specific reference was made to the court's ability to authorise the expenditure of capital to which a minor was absolutely entitled for his or her maintenance, is *Worthington v M'Craer* (1856) 23 Beav 81. It seems to me that this would be a possible basis on which the court could proceed in the present circumstances.

However, since the decision in *Chapman v Chapman*, the relevant area of law has been transformed by the Variation of Trusts Act 1958. While this Act does not take away any jurisdiction that the court already had, it seems to me that it would be more appropriate to proceed under the Act if that is possible.

The 1958 Act applies "where property ... is held on trusts arising ... under any will settlement or other disposition". ...[T]he proceeds of the insurance policies are held on trusts arising under a settlement, albeit that they are held for the three children in equal shares absolutely. The idea of varying a bare trust might perhaps seem a little odd, and but for the beneficiary not being of full legal capacity it is difficult to imagine how the question could arise. Given that lack of capacity, and the constraints on the extent of the statutory provisions which do authorise the trustees to act in certain ways, it does not seem to me so surprising that the Act should apply to property held on a bare trust, at least for a minor.

...What is proposed in the present case would have the effect ... of accelerating the benefit for C, by allowing the whole of the fund to be used for her benefit while she is still under age. ...

In my judgment ... [i]t is ... open to the court to exercise the powers conferred by the 1958 Act in relation to the funds, so long as it is satisfied that the proposed variation of the trusts is for the benefit of the relevant beneficiary. I am satisfied that it is for C's benefit to vary the trusts applying to her fund so that the whole fund, not merely one half, may be applied pursuant to section 32 of the Trustee Act 1925. I have therefore approved on her behalf a variation of the trusts applying to C's Fund so as to permit the powers under section 32 to be exercised in relation to the whole, not only half, of the fund.

 Alert

Further Reading

Hassall, Natasha, 'Powers of advancement: how far can Pilkington be stetched?' at (2007) 4 PCB 282

Halsbury's *Laws of England*, Vol 42 (Reissue) para 626

13

Investment

Introduction

Trustees must invest the trust fund during the lifetime of the trust for the benefit of the beneficiaries. The primary source of their obligations in this regard will be the trust instrument. However, regardless of whether or not the trust instrument contains express powers in relation to investment, both common law and statute (principally the Trustee Act 2000) also apply in relation to the trustees' duty to invest.

As is discussed in more detail below, the common law duty is one of 'prudence', whereas the 2000 Act s 1 imposes a statutory duty of care. However, the statutory duty only relates to certain aspects of the trustees' obligations in relation to investment, so the common law duty of prudence remains relevant to those obligations to which the Act does not apply.

13.1 The Common Law Duty of Prudence

Speight v Gaunt (1883) 9 App Cas 1

Panel: Earl of Selborne LC, Lord Blackburn, Lord Watson and Lord Fitzgerald

Facts: A trustee gave a broker the entirety of a trust fund to invest in municipal stocks, which was an authorised investment under the trust deed. The broker failed to make the intended investment but instead used the money for his own purposes. He became insolvent, whereupon the beneficiaries brought proceedings against the trustee for breach of trust for having used the services of a broker rather than having made the investment himself. The House of Lords dismissed the claim.

LORD BLACKBURN

...The case is of importance to the parties as involving a very considerable sum of money. It is also of general importance, so far as the application of the principles, on which the Court acts in respect to the liability of trustees to make good losses of trust funds, to the facts disclosed by the evidence, will be an authority in future cases. After some consideration, and reading the evidence, I have come to the conclusion that the judgment appealed against is right, and should be affirmed. ...

The authorities cited ... shew that as a general rule a trustee sufficiently discharges his duty if he takes in managing trust affairs all those precautions which an ordinary prudent man of business would take in managing similar affairs of his own. There is one exception to this: a trustee must not choose investments other than those which the terms of his trust permit, though they may be such as an ordinary prudent man of business would select for his own money; and it may be that however usual it may be for a person who wishes to invest his own money, and instructs an agent, such as an attorney, or a stockbroker, to seek an investment, to deposit the money at interest with the agent till the investment is found, that is in effect lending it on the agent's own personal security, and is a breach of trust. No question as to this arises here, for [the trustee] did nothing of that kind. Subject to this exception, as to which it is unnecessary

 Alert

to consider further, I think the case of *Ex parte Belchier* Amb 218 establishes the principle that where there is a usual course of business the trustee is justified in following it, though it may be such that there is some risk that the property may be lost by the dishonesty or insolvency of an agent employed.

The transactions of life could not be carried on without some confidence being bestowed. When the transaction consists in a sale where the vendor is entitled to keep his hold on the property till he receives the money, and the purchaser is entitled to keep his money till he gets the property, it would be in all cases inconvenient if the vendor and purchaser were required to meet and personally exchange the one for the other; when the parties are, as is very often the case, living remote from each other, it would be physically impossible. ...

Judges and lawyers who see brought before them the cases in which losses have been incurred, and do not see the infinitely more numerous cases in which expense and trouble and inconvenience are avoided, are apt to think men of business rash. I think that the principle ... is that, while the course is usual, a trustee is not to be blamed if he honestly, and without knowing anything that makes it exceptionally risky in his case, pursues that usual course. ... It would be both unreasonable and inexpedient to make a trustee responsible for not being more prudent than ordinary men of business are.

The House of Lords therefore held that a trustee did not breach his duty to exercise reasonable care and prudence in the performance of his duties as trustee if he employed an apparently reputable agent to carry out certain tasks, if those tasks were then apparently carried out in the usual way.

Re Whiteley, Whiteley v Learoyd (1886) 33 Ch D 347

Panel: Lord Halsbury LC, Lord Watson and Lord Fitzgerald

Facts: The defendants were trustees under a will of a sum of £5,000, with power to invest in 'real securities' in England and Wales. They invested £3,000 on the mortgage of freehold brickworks, having first obtained a valuation that the property would be good security for £3,500 before certain projected improvements. In fact, the business failed and the security proved to be insufficient. The beneficiaries sought to hold the trustees liable in respect of the loss arising from that investment. The House of Lords held that the trustees had failed to invest the trust fund prudently and hence were liable to the beneficiaries.

LORD WATSON

My Lords: I also am of opinion that the order of the Court of Appeal must be affirmed. As a general rule, the law requires of a trustee no higher degree of diligence in the execution of his office than a man of ordinary prudence would exercise in the management of his own private affairs. Yet he is not allowed the same discretion, in investing the moneys of the trust, as if he were a person 'sui juris' dealing with his own estate. Business men of ordinary prudence may and frequently do select investments which are more or less of a speculative character; but it is the duty of a trustee to confine himself to the class of investments which are permitted by the trust, and likewise

 Alert

to avoid all investments of that class which are attended with hazard. So long as he acts in the honest observance of these limitations the general rule already stated will apply. The courts of equity in England have indicated and given effect to certain general principles for the guidance of trustees in lending money upon the security of real estate. Thus it has been laid down that, in the case of ordinary agricultural land, the margin ought not to be less than one-third of its value; whereas in cases where the subject of the security derives its value from buildings erected upon the land, or its use for trade purposes, the margin ought not to be less than one-half. I do not think these have been laid down as hard-and-fast limits up to which trustees would be invariably safe, and beyond which they could never be in safety to lend, but as indicating the lowest margins which, in ordinary circumstances, a careful investor of trust funds ought to accept. It is manifest that, in cases where the subject of the security is exclusively or mainly used for the purposes of trade, no prudent investor could be in a position to judge of the amount of margin necessary to make a loan for a term of years reasonably secure until he had ascertained, not only their present market price, but their intrinsic value, apart from those trading considerations which gave them a speculative, and, it might be, a temporary value. Upon the general law applicable to this case I have only to observe further that, while trustees cannot delegate the execution of the trust, they may, as was held by this House in *Speight v Gaunt* (1883) 9 App Cas 1), avail themselves of the services of others, wherever such employment is according to the usual course of business. If they employ a person of competent skill to value a real security, they may, so long as they act in good faith, safely rely upon the correctness of his valuation. But the ordinary course of business does not justify the employment of a valuator for any other purpose than obtaining the data necessary in order to enable the trustees to judge of the sufficiency of the security offered. They are not in safety to rely upon his bare assurance that the security was sufficient, in the absence of information which would enable them to form, and without forming, an opinion for themselves. At all events, if they chose to place reliance upon his opinion without the means of testing its soundness they could not, should the security prove defective, escape from personal liability, unless they proved that the security was such as would have been accepted by a trustee of ordinary prudence, fully informed of its character, and having in view the principles to which I have already adverted. ...

The trustees' fault, therefore, was in investing a significant sum of money on a parcel of land which depended ultimately for the greater part of its value upon the continuing success of the manufacturing business which was carried out upon it, as to which there could be no certainty. Whilst a commercial businessman might legitimately take the view that that constituted an acceptable risk for him to take with his own money, the House of Lords considered that the trustees should have been more prudent, because they were not investing their own money on such a 'hazard', and so had a greater 'moral' obligation to be prudent.

It seems that the common law duty applies not only to the decision to make an investment, but also to the decision whether to retain an investment in its current form or to sell it and find an alternative form of investment. The decision to retain/sell is, therefore, predicated upon a duty to review the current state of the trust's investments periodically with a view to deciding whether retention constitutes the best investment decision at the relevant time.

Nestle v National Westminster Bank plc [1993] 1 WLR 1260

Panel: Dillon, Staughton and Leggatt LJJ

Facts: Between 1922 and 1986 the defendant bank was the trustee of a trust fund, the substantial part of which was invested in bank and insurance company shares. On the death of the last surviving life tenant, the plaintiff became entitled to the entire fund absolutely. She complained that the fund, which was worth some £269,000, would have been worth over £1million if the bank had periodically reviewed the performance of the shares and had adopted a different investment strategy. It was common ground that the bank had erroneously believed that it was only entitled to invest in bank and insurance company shares under the terms of the trust instrument. The Court of Appeal held that the bank had not failed in its duty of prudence.

LORD JUSTICE LEGGATT

...There is no dispute about the nature of the bank's duty. It was, as Lindley LJ has expressed it, a duty 'to take such care as an ordinary prudent man would take if he were minded to make an investment for the benefit of other people for whom he felt morally bound to provide' (see *Re Whiteley, Whiteley v Learoyd* (1886) 33 Ch D 347 at 355). The trustee must have regard 'not only to the interests of those who are entitled to the income, but to the interests of those who will take in future' (at 350 per Cotton LJ). 'A trustee must not choose investments other than those which the terms of his trust permit' (see *Speight v Gaunt* (1883) 9 App Cas 1 at 19 per Lord Blackburn). So confined, the trustee must also 'avoid all investments of that class that are attended with hazard' (see *Learoyd v Whiteley* (1887) 12 App Cas 727 at 733 per Lord Watson). The power of investment-

'must be exercised so as to yield the best return for the beneficiaries, judged in relation to the risks of the investments in question; and the prospects of the yield of income and capital appreciation both have to be considered in judging the return from the investment.' (See *Cowan v Scargill* [1984] 2 All ER 750 at 760, [1985] Ch 270 at 287 per Megarry VC.)

Since the Trustee Investments Act 1961 came into force a trustee has been required by s 6(1)(a) to have regard in the exercise of his powers of investment-

'to the need for diversification of investments of the trust, in so far as is appropriate to the circumstances of the trust ...'

It is common ground that a trustee with a power of investment must undertake periodic reviews of the investments held by the trust. In relation to this trust, that would have meant a review carried out at least annually, and whenever else a reappraisal of the trust portfolio was requested or was otherwise requisite. ...

The appellant alleges that the bank is in breach of trust because over the years since her grandfather set up the trust the bank has supposed that its power of investment was

Link

See *Cowan v Scargill* below

more limited than it was, has failed to carry out periodic reviews of the portfolio and to maintain a proper balance between equities and gilts and to diversify the equity investments, and has unduly favoured the interests of her father and her uncle as life tenants at the expense of her own interest as remainderman. She says that in consequence the trust fund was worth less in 1986 than it should have been.

The essence of the bank's duty was to take such steps as a prudent businessman would have taken to maintain and increase the value of the trust fund. Unless it failed to do so, it was not in breach of trust. A breach of duty will not be actionable, and therefore will be immaterial, if it does not cause loss. In this context I would indorse the concession of Mr Nugee QC for the bank that 'loss' will be incurred by a trust fund when it makes a gain less than would have been made by a prudent businessman. A claimant will therefore fail who cannot prove a loss in this sense caused by breach of duty. So here, in order to make a case for an inquiry, the appellant must show that loss was caused by breach of duty on the part of the bank.

 Alert

On the appellant's behalf Mr Lyndon-Stanford QC seeks to rely on a presumption against a wrongdoing trustee. He invokes Brightman LJ's dictum in *Bartlett v Barclays Bank Trust Co Ltd (No 2)* [1980] 2 All ER 92 at 96, [1980] Ch 515 at 545 that 'The trustee's obligation is to restore to the trust estate the assets of which he has deprived it'. But that presupposes deprivation.

 Link
See *Bartlett v Barclays Bank Trust Co Ltd (No 2)* below.

The appellant alleges, and I am content to assume, that the bank was at all material times under a misapprehension about the meaning of the investment clause in the will, with the result that the bank believed that the scope of its powers of investment was more confined than it was. I also regard it as unlikely that the bank conducted any reviews of the portfolio between 1922 and 1959. If any were conducted, they were unplanned, sporadic and indecisive. Mr Lyndon-Stanford argues that it should be presumed that, had there been a better balance between gilts and equities and had the equity investment been more diversified, the fund would ultimately have been worth more than it was. The fallacy is that it does not follow from the fact that a wider power of investment was available to the bank than it realised either that it would have been exercised or that, if it had been, the exercise of it would have produced a result more beneficial to the bank than actually was produced. Loss cannot be presumed if none would necessarily have resulted. Until it was proved that there was a loss, no attempt could be made to assess the amount of it. ...

In my judgment, either there was a loss in the present case or there was not. Unless there was a loss, there was no cause of action. It was for the appellant to prove on balance of probabilities that there was, or must have been, a loss. If proved, the court would then have had to assess the amount of it, and for the purpose of doing so might have had recourse to presumptions against the bank. In short, if it were shown that a loss was caused by breach of trust, such a presumption might avail the appellant in quantifying the loss. The appellant's difficulty is in reaching that stage.

The appellant therefore had to prove that a prudent trustee, knowing of the scope of the bank's investment power and conducting regular reviews, would so have invested the trust funds as to make it worth more than it was worth when the appellant inherited it.

That was a matter for expert evidence. In the result, there was evidence which the judge was entitled to accept and did accept that the bank did no less than expected of it up to the death of the testator's widow in 1960. ...

After 1960 investment of the trust funds preponderantly in tax-exempt gilts for the benefit of life tenants resident abroad is not shown to have produced a less satisfactory result for the remainderman than an investment in equities after taking into account savings in estate duty and capital transfer tax, because this policy had the effect of preserving the capital. ...

No testator, in the light of this example, would choose this bank for the effective management of his investments. But the bank's engagement was as a trustee, and, as such, it is to be judged not so much by success as by absence of proven default. The importance of preservation of a trust fund will always outweigh success in its advancement. Inevitably, a trustee in the bank's position wears a complacent air, because the virtue of safety will in practice put a premium on inactivity. Until the 1950s active management of the portfolio might have been seen as speculative, and even in these days such dealing would have to be notably successful before the expense would be justified. The very process of attempting to achieve a balance, or (if that be old fashioned) fairness, as between the interests of life tenants and those of a remainderman inevitably means that each can complain of being less well served than he or she ought to have been. But by the undemanding standard of prudence the bank is not shown to have committed any breach of trust resulting in loss.

I am therefore constrained to agree that the appeal must be dismissed.

Lord Justice Leggatt, whose reasoning mirrored that of the other two members of the Court, was content to assume that one aspect of a trustee's duty in relation to investment was the obligation to review the state of the trust's investments. And yet, the outcome in this case is perhaps rather surprising. Although the trustee bank had manifestly failed to fulfil its duty to review, and had been wrong about the extent of its investment powers, it avoided liability to the plaintiff because she was unable to prove that the trustees had made decisions they should not have made or had failed to make decisions they should have made. This seems to set an extremely low bar for a trustee to overcome – or, as Leggatt LJ put it, the standard of prudence is 'undemanding'.

13.1.1 Investment criteria

There have been two cases of note as to the factors which the trustees must take into account and, equally, what factors they must ignore when deciding where to invest trust funds.

Cowan and Others v Scargill and Others [1985] Ch 270

Panel: Sir Robert Megarry V-C

Facts: The five plaintiffs and the five defendants comprised all the trustee members of the management committee of the mineworkers' pension scheme. The defendants, all of whom had been appointed by the National Union of Mineworkers, objected to certain proposed investment decisions ('the 1982 plan') on the grounds that they conflicted with union policy. The management committee was therefore deadlocked and unable to implement the 1982 plan. On the application of the remaining (non-union) trustees, the court held that the interests of the pension scheme beneficiaries rather than those of the union were paramount, and that accordingly the union trustees were in breach of their duties as members of the management committee by refusing to concur in the adoption of the 1982 plan.

SIR ROBERT MEGARRY V-C

...The main issue (and I put it very shortly) is whether the defendants are in breach of their fiduciary duties in refusing approval of an investment plan for the [Mineworkers' Pension Scheme] unless it is amended so as to prohibit any increase in overseas investment, to provide for the withdrawal of existing overseas investments at the most opportune time, and to prohibit investment in energies which are in direct competition with coal ... which I shall call the "1982 plan". ...

[Having reviewed the evidence at length, the judge continued]

I turn to the law. The starting point is the duty of trustees to exercise their powers in the best interests of the present and future beneficiaries of the trust, holding the scales impartially between different classes of beneficiaries. This duty of the trustees towards their beneficiaries is paramount. They must, of course, obey the law; but subject to that, they must put the interests of their beneficiaries first. When the purpose of the trust is to provide financial benefits for the beneficiaries, as is usually the case, the best interests of the beneficiaries are normally their best financial interests. In the case of a power of investment, as in the present case, the power must be exercised so as to yield the best return for the beneficiaries, judged in relation to the risks of the investments in question; and the prospects of the yield of income and capital appreciation both have to be considered in judging the return from the investment. ...

In considering what investments to make trustees must put on one side their own personal interests and views. Trustees may have strongly held social or political views. They may be firmly opposed to any investment in South Africa or other countries, or they may object to any form of investment in companies concerned with alcohol, tobacco, armaments or many other things. In the conduct of their own affairs, of course, they are free to abstain from making any such investments. Yet under a trust, if investments of this type would be more beneficial to the beneficiaries than other investments, the trustees must not refrain from making the investments by reason of the views that they hold.

 Alert

Trustees may even have to act dishonourably (though not illegally) if the interests of their beneficiaries require it. Thus where trustees for sale had struck a bargain for the sale of trust property but had not bound themselves by a legally enforceable contract, they were held to be under a duty to consider and explore a better offer that they received, and not to carry through the bargain to which they felt in honour bound: *Buttle v Saunders* [1950] 2 All ER 193. In other words, the duty of trustees to their beneficiaries may include a duty to "gazump," however honourable the trustees. As

Wynn-Parry J said at p 195, trustees "have an overriding duty to obtain the best price which they can for their beneficiaries." ...

Third, by way of caveat I should say that I am not asserting that the benefit of the beneficiaries which a trustee must make his paramount concern inevitably and solely means their financial benefit, even if the only object of the trust is to provide financial benefits. Thus if the only actual or potential beneficiaries of a trust are all adults with very strict views on moral and social matters, condemning all forms of alcohol, tobacco and popular entertainment, as well as armaments, I can well understand that it might not be for the "benefit" of such beneficiaries to know that they are obtaining rather larger financial returns under the trust by reason of investments in those activities than they would have received if the trustees had invested the trust funds in other investments. The beneficiaries might well consider that it was far better to receive less than to receive more money from what they consider to be evil and tainted sources. "Benefit" is a word with a very wide meaning, and there are circumstances in which arrangements which work to the financial disadvantage of a beneficiary may yet be for his benefit: see, for example, *In re T's Settlement Trusts* [1964] Ch 158 and *In re CL* [1969] 1 Ch 587. But I would emphasise that such cases are likely to be very rare, and in any case I think that under a trust for the provision of financial benefits the burden would rest, and rest heavy, on him who asserts that it is for the benefit of the beneficiaries as a whole to receive less by reason of the exclusion of some of the possibly more profitable forms of investment. Plainly the present case is not one of this rare type of cases. ...

Fourth, the standard required of a trustee in exercising his powers of investment is that he must:

"take such care as an ordinary prudent man would take if he were minded to make an investment for the benefit of other people for whom he felt morally bound to provide:"

per Lindley LJ in *In re Whiteley* (1886) 33 Ch D 347, 355; see also at pp 350, 358; and see *Learoyd v Whiteley* (1887) 12 App Cas 727. That duty includes the duty to seek advice on matters which the trustee does not understand, such as the making of investments, and on receiving that advice to act with the same degree of prudence. This requirement is not discharged merely by showing that the trustee has acted in good faith and with sincerity. Honesty and sincerity are not the same as prudence and reasonableness. Some of the most sincere people are the most unreasonable; and Mr Scargill [for himself and the other defendants] told me that he had met quite a few of them. Accordingly, although a trustee who takes advice on investments is not bound to accept and act on that advice, he is not entitled to reject it merely because he sincerely disagrees with it, unless in addition to being sincere he is acting as an ordinary prudent man would act.

Fifth, trustees have a duty to consider the need for diversification of investments. By section 6(1) of the Trustee Investments Act 1961:

"In the exercise of his powers of investment a trustee shall have regard - (a) to the need for diversification of investments of the trust, in so far as is appropriate to the circumstances of the trust; (b) to the suitability to the trust of investments of the description of investment proposed and of the investment proposed as an investment of that description."

The reference to the "circumstances of the trust" plainly includes matters such as the size of the trust funds: the degree of diversification that is practicable and desirable for a large fund may plainly be impracticable or undesirable (or both) in the case of a small fund.

In the case before me, it is not in issue that there ought to be diversification of the investments held by the fund. The contention of the defendants, put very shortly, is that there can be a sufficient degree of diversification without any investment overseas or in oil, and that in any case there is no need to increase the level of overseas investments beyond the existing level. Other pension funds got on well enough without overseas investments, it was said, and in particular the NUM's own scheme had, in 1982, produced better results than the scheme here in question. ...

Even if other funds in one particular year, or in many years, had done better than the scheme which is before me, that does not begin to show that it is beneficial to this scheme to be shorn of the ability to invest overseas. ...

Sixth, there is the question whether the principles that I have been stating apply, with or without modification, to trusts of pension funds. Mr Stamler [for the plaintiffs] asserted that they applied without modification, and that it made no difference that some of the funds came from the members of the pension scheme, or that the funds were often of a very substantial size. Mr Scargill did not in terms assert the contrary. ...

I shall refer to the authorities in a moment, and consider the question of principle first. I can see no reason for holding that different principles apply to pension fund trusts from those which apply to other trusts. Of course, there are many provisions in pension schemes which are not to be found in private trusts, and to these the general law of trusts will be subordinated. But subject to that, I think that the trusts of pension funds are subject to the same rules as other trusts. The large size of pension funds emphasises the need for diversification, rather than lessening it, and the fact that much of the fund has been contributed by members of the scheme seems to me to make it even more important that the trustees should exercise their powers in the best interests of the beneficiaries. In a private trust, most, if not all, of the beneficiaries are the recipients of the bounty of the settlor, whereas under the trusts of a pension fund many (though not all) of the beneficiaries are those who, as members, contributed to the funds so that in due time they would receive pensions. It is thus all the more important that the interests of the beneficiaries should be paramount, so that they may receive the benefits which in part they have paid for. I can see no justification for holding that the benefits to them should run the risk of being lessened because the trustees were pursuing an investment policy intended to assist the industry that the pensioners have left, or their union.

I turn to the authorities. *Evans v London Co-operative Society Ltd* The Times, 6 July 1976 is a decision of Brightman J which has apparently achieved a considerable measure of renown among those concerned with pension funds as being the only English authority on the subject. I do not think that I need discuss the details of the case, because it seems to me to be perfectly clear that it is a decision upon a particular rule of the pension fund there in question, rule 7, and not upon the general law. ... I find it impossible to read pp 17-20 of the transcript without reaching the conclusion that the judge was deciding the case on the extent to which rule 7 took the case out of the ordinary law of trusts, and that but for rule 7 the ordinary law of trusts would have been applied to the case. In my judgment, the case does nothing to support the contentions of the defendants. Instead, I think it provides some support for the plaintiffs.

Blankenship v Boyle (1971) 329 F Supp 1089 was a case heard in the US District Court for the District of Columbia by Judge Gesell. The trustees of a pension fund had allowed large sums of money to remain in bank accounts bearing no interest at a bank controlled by the union. Over an 18-year period, varying sums between $14 million and $75 million, representing between 14 per cent and 44 per cent of the fund's total resources, had been left in this way. The fund was established for the benefit of employees of coal operators, their families and dependants, and over 95 per cent of the members of the fund were also members of the union. It was contended that the trustees could properly consider not only the interests of the beneficiaries but also collateral matters such as increasing the tonnage of union-mined coal; but this was rejected. The court re-affirmed the duty of undivided loyalty to the beneficiaries that a trustee owes, and did not accept that regard should also be paid to the union or its members who generated some of the income of the fund, or to the industry as a whole. That seems to me to be plainly right.

Withers v Teachers' Retirement System of the City of New York (1978) 447 F Supp 1248 arose out of the impending insolvency of the City of New York in 1975. The Teachers' Retirement System ("TRS") and four other New York pension funds agreed to purchase $2,530 million unmarketable and highly speculative New York City bonds over the next two and a half years in an attempt to stave off the imminent bankruptcy of the city; the share contributed by TRS was $860 million. TRS was an unfunded scheme, and the evidence was that if the city ceased to make its massive contributions to the scheme, the reserves would be exhausted in some 8 to 10 years, even if the contributions by employees continued and there was a constant rate of retirement of teachers. In the US District Court for the Southern District of New York, Judge Conner considered and accepted *Blankenship v Boyle* ... and the traditional rules of equity, but held that the trustees had been justified in purchasing the bonds since they had done so in the best interests of the beneficiaries, and not out of concern for the general public welfare or the protection of the jobs of city teachers. The object of the trustees, who had imposed stringent conditions in an attempt to protect the TRS, had been to ensure the continuance of the city's major contributions to the scheme, and preserve the city's position as the ultimate guarantor of the payment of pension benefits; and this was in the best interests of the beneficiaries. This differed from the position in *Blankenship v Boyle*, where

"the trustees pursued policies which may incidentally have aided the beneficiaries of the fund but which were intended, primarily, to enhance the position of the union and the welfare of its members, presumably, through the creation and/or preservation of jobs in the coal industry": p 1256.

Apart from the expression "and/or," I would agree.

The American cases do not, of course, bind me; but they seem, if I may say so, to be soundly based on equitable principles which are common to England and most jurisdictions in the United States, and they accord with the conclusion that I would have reached in the absence of authority. Accordingly, on principle, on the *Evans* case, and on the two American cases, I reach the unhesitating conclusion that the trusts of pension funds are in general governed by the ordinary law of trusts, subject to any contrary provision in the rules or other provisions which govern the trust. In particular, the trustees of a pension fund are subject to the overriding duty to do the best that they can for the beneficiaries, the duty that in the United States is known as "the duty of undivided loyalty to the beneficiaries": see *Blankenship v Boyle* ... .

In considering that duty, it must be remembered that very many of the beneficiaries will not in any way be directly affected by the prosperity of the mining industry or the union. Miners who have retired, and the widows and children of deceased miners, will continue to receive their benefits from the fund even if the mining industry shrinks: for the scheme is fully funded, and the fund does not depend on further contributions to it being made. If the board fell on hard times, it might be unable to continue its voluntary payments to meet cost-of-living increases ... [but] the impact of that remote possibility falls far short of the imminent disaster facing the City of New York and TRS in the *Withers* case ... ; and I cannot regard any policy designed to ensure the general prosperity of coal mining as being a policy which is directed to obtaining the best possible results for the beneficiaries, most of whom are no longer engaged in the industry, and some of whom never were. The connection is far too remote and insubstantial. Further, the assets of even so large a pension fund as this are nowhere near the size at which there could be expected to be any perceptible impact from the adoption of the policies for which Mr Scargill contends.

I turn to consider the grounds on which the prohibitions put forward by the defendants have been supported. First, there are the reasons put forward during the discussions by the trustees. ... Put shortly, these were that the prohibitions were NUM policy: the union, as a matter of principle, was totally and unequivocally opposed to investment overseas. These views were put forward in various ways on various occasions, but the substance was unvarying. However, ... [at] no stage did [Mr Scargill] explain how or why it was for the benefit of the beneficiaries to put union policy into force under the scheme by imposing the prohibitions. ...

I can see no escape from the conclusion that the NUM trustees were attempting to impose the prohibitions in order to carry out union policy; and mere assertions that their sole consideration was the benefit of the beneficiaries do not alter that conclusion. If the NUM trustees were thinking only of the benefit of the beneficiaries, why all the references to union policy instead of proper explanations of how and why the prohibitions would bring benefits to the beneficiaries? No doubt some trustees with strong feelings find it irksome to be forced to submerge those feelings and genuinely put the interests of the beneficiaries first. Indeed, there are some who are temperamentally unsuited to being trustees, and are more fitted for campaigning for changes in the law. This, of course, they are free to do; but if they choose to become trustees they must accept it that the rules of equity will bind them in all that they do as trustees. ...

I therefore reject any ... assertion that prior to the commencement of these proceedings the benefit of the beneficiaries was the sole consideration that the union trustees had: that ... is untrue. The union trustees were mainly, if not solely, actuated by a desire to pursue union policy, and they were not putting the interests of the beneficiaries first, as they ought to have done. ... They were adamant in their determination to impose the restrictions, whether or not they harmed their beneficiaries. ...

This conclusion, however, does not end the matter. If trustees make a decision upon wholly wrong grounds, and yet it subsequently appears, from matters which they did not express or refer to, that there are in fact good and sufficient reasons for supporting their decision, then I do not think that they would incur any liability for having decided the matter upon erroneous grounds; for the decision itself was right. ...

Some of the evidence filed by the defendants tended to show that the prohibitions would not be harmful to the beneficiaries, or jeopardise the aims of the fund, and that some pension funds got along well enough without any overseas investments. Such evidence misses the point. Trustees must do the best they can for the benefit of their beneficiaries, and not merely avoid harming them. I find it impossible to see how it will assist trustees to do the best they can for their beneficiaries by prohibiting a wide range of investments that are authorised by the terms of the trust. Whatever the position today, nobody can say that conditions tomorrow cannot possibly make it advantageous to invest in one of the prohibited investments. It is the duty of trustees, in the interests of their beneficiaries, to take advantage of the full range of investments authorised by the terms of the trust, instead of resolving to narrow that range.

There was other evidence filed by the defendants which was more to the point; and it was met by countervailing evidence of the plaintiffs. This evidence was directed to economics and investment strategy. At the outset I must say that I found the plaintiffs' evidence the more cogent and practical, and more directly related to what was in issue. The general thrust of the defendants' evidence in support of the restrictions that they seek to impose was along the following lines. Pensions funds in Britain have enormous assets. If all, or nearly all, of these assets were invested in Britain, and none, or few, were invested overseas, this would do much to revive this country's economy and so benefit all workers, especially if the investments were in the form not of purchasing established stocks and shares but of "real" investment in physical assets and new ventures. For the mineworkers' scheme, the prosperity of the coal industry would aid the prosperity of the scheme, and so lead to benefits for the beneficiaries under the scheme. This point was put in various ways, and a short summary necessarily omits many facets; but in the end the approach seems to me to have been along these general lines.

I readily accept that a case, and perhaps a strong case, can be made for legislation or other provisions that in the general public interest would restrict the outflow of large funds from this country and put the money to work here. ... But I am not concerned with changes in the law or in the scheme for any pension fund, whether this fund or any other. I have to deal with this fund under the scheme as it now stands. I am concerned with a fund under which there are many beneficiaries who no longer have any financial interest in the welfare of the coal industry. They may well be "interested" in it in the sense that they remember the years that they spent in it with affection or the reverse, and they may well find it "interesting" to know what is going on in it, in the sense of gratifying a natural curiosity and concern about the industry and the people in it. But apart from such matters, they are not affected by the industry and its success.

In my view, therefore, the broad economic arguments of the defendants provide no justification for the restrictions that they wish to impose. Any possible benefits from imposing the restrictions that would accrue to the beneficiaries under the scheme (as distinct from the general public) are far too speculative and remote. Large though the fund is, I cannot see how the adoption of the restrictions can make any material impact on the national economy, or bring any appreciable benefit to the beneficiaries under the scheme. There is nothing whatever to suggest that the board will be in any difficulty in making its payments under the scheme unless the restrictions are adopted. There is not a shred of evidence to suggest that the board is in a state of imminent disaster like that which faced the City of New York in the *Withers* case ... , or that even if it were the imposition of the restrictions would save it; and in any case the scheme, unlike that in the *Withers* case, is fully funded. As for diversification, I can see that the risks inherent in an individual investment can be met by a modest degree of diversification; but where the risks are not merely for one particular investment but for a whole sector of the market, such as mining or tea, a wider degree of diversification will be needed. In any case, the question is one of excluding a very large sector of the market, and preventing diversification into investments in other countries which may do well at a time when the whole British market is depressed; and I can see no possible benefit in such an exclusion, especially in the case of a very large fund with highly skilled investment expertise.

Accordingly, on the case as a whole, in my judgment the plaintiffs are right and the defendants are wrong. ... [Subject] to what may be said when I have concluded this judgment, I propose to make suitable declarations, and to give liberty to apply for directions or other appropriate relief if the declarations are not duly acted upon. ...

So, except in very rare circumstances, trustees must not allow political or economic considerations to influence their investment decision-making. Nor may they take account of ethical or moral considerations.

Harries (Bishop of Oxford) and Others v The Church Commissioners for England and Another [1992] 1 WLR 1241

Panel: Sir Donald Nicholls V-C

Facts: The plaintiffs were concerned that the investment policy of the Church Commissioners in their administration of trust funds of the Church of England attached undue importance to financial considerations and failed to take into account the underlying purpose for which the assets were held. They therefore applied for declarations that in the management of their assets the Church Commissioners were obliged to have regard to the object of promoting the Christian faith through the established Church of England and might not act in a manner which would be incompatible with that object. The court declined to make those declarations.

SIR DONALD NICHOLLS V-C

The Church Commissioners for England administer vast estates and large funds. At the end of 1990 their holdings of land were valued at about £1.7bn, their mortgages and loans at about £165m, and their stock exchange investments at about £780m. In 1990 these items yielded altogether an investment income of £164m. The commissioners' income included also some £66m derived principally from parish and diocesan contributions to clergy stipends. So the commissioners' total income last year was £230m.

The needs which the commissioners seek to satisfy out of this income are daunting. In 1990 they provided almost one half of the costs of the stipends of the Church of England serving clergy, much of their housing costs, and almost all their pension costs. These items absorbed over 85 per cent of the commissioners' income: that is, a sum of almost £200m. Unfortunately, this does not mean that the clergy are well remunerated or that the retired clergy receive good pensions. Far from it. The commissioners' income has to be spread widely, and hence thinly, over 11,400 serving clergy and 10,100 clergy pensioners and widows. So, as is well known, the amount each receives is not generous. In 1990–1991 the national average stipend of incumbents was only £11,308. The full-service pension from April 1991 was £6,700 per year.

For some time there have been voices in the Church of England expressing disquiet at the investment policy of the commissioners. They do not question either the good faith or the investment expertise of the commissioners. Their concern is not that the commissioners have failed to get the best financial return from their property and investments. Their concern is that, in making investment decisions, the commissioners are guided too rigorously by purely financial considerations, and that the commissioners give insufficient weight to what are now called "ethical" considerations. They contend, moreover, that the commissioners have fallen into legal error. The commissioners attach overriding importance to financial considerations, and that is a misapprehension of the approach they ought property to adopt when making investment decisions. The commissioners ought to have in mind that the underlying purpose for which they hold their assets is the promotion of the Christian faith through the Church of England. The commissioners should not exercise their investment functions in a manner which would be incompatible with that purpose even if that involves a risk of incurring significant financial detriment. So these proceedings, seeking declaratory relief, were launched ... . I understand that by an ethical investment policy is meant an investment policy which is not guided solely by financial criteria but which takes into account non-financial considerations deduced from Christian morality. ...

Before going further into the criticism made of the commissioners I will consider the general principles applicable to the exercise of powers of investment by charity trustees. It is axiomatic that charity trustees, in common with all other trustees, are concerned to further the purposes of the trust of which they have accepted the office of trustee. That is their duty. To enable them the better to discharge that duty, trustees have powers vested in them. Those powers must be exercised for the purpose for which they have been given: to further the purposes of the trust. That is the guiding principle applicable to the issues in these proceedings. Everything which follows is no more than the reasoned application of that principle in particular contexts.

Broadly speaking, property held by charity trustees falls into two categories. First, there is property held by trustees for what may be called functional purposes. The National Trust owns historic houses and open spaces. The Salvation Army owns hostels for the destitute. And many charities need office accommodation in which to carry out essential administrative work. Second, there is property held by trustees for the purpose of generating money, whether from income or capital growth, with which to further the work of the trust. In other words, property held by trustees as an investment. Where property is so held, prima facie the purposes of the trust will be best served by the trustees seeking to obtain therefrom the maximum return, whether by way of income or capital growth, which is consistent with commercial prudence. That is the starting point for all charity trustees when considering the exercise of their investment powers. Most charities need money; and the more of it there is available, the more the trustees can seek to accomplish.

 Alert

In most cases this prima facie position will govern the trustees' conduct. In most cases the best interests of the charity require that the trustees' choice of investments should be made solely on the basis of well-established investment criteria, having taken expert advice where appropriate and having due regard to such matters as the need to diversify, the need to balance income against capital growth, and the need to balance risk against return.

In a minority of cases the position will not be so straightforward. There will be some cases, I suspect comparatively rare, when the objects of the charity are such that investments of a particular type would conflict with the aims of the charity. Much-cited examples are those of cancer research companies and tobacco shares, trustees of temperance charities and brewery and distillery shares, and trustees of charities of the Society of Friends and shares in companies engaged in production of armaments. If, as would be likely in those examples, trustees were satisfied that investing in a company engaged in a particular type of business would conflict with the very objects their charity is seeking to achieve, they should not so invest. Carried to its logical conclusion the trustees should take this course even if it would be likely to result in significant financial detriment to the charity. The logical conclusion, whilst sound as a matter of legal analysis, is unlikely to arise in practice. It is not easy to think of an instance where in practice the exclusion for this reason of one or more companies or sectors from the whole range of investments open to trustees would be likely to leave them without an adequately wide range of investments from which to choose a properly diversified portfolio.

There will also be some cases, again I suspect comparatively rare, when trustees' holdings of particular investments might hamper a charity's work either by making potential recipients of aid unwilling to be helped because of the source of the charity's money, or by alienating some of those who support the charity financially. In these cases the trustees will need to balance the difficulties they would encounter, or likely financial loss they would sustain, if they were to hold the investments against the risk of financial detriment if those investments were excluded from their portfolio. The greater the risk of financial detriment, the more certain the trustees should be of countervailing disadvantages to the charity before they incur that risk. Another circumstance where trustees would be entitled, or even required, to take into account non-financial criteria would be where the trust deed so provides.

No doubt there will be other cases where trustees are justified in departing from what should always be their starting point. The instances I have given are not comprehensive. But I must emphasise that of their very nature, and by definition, investments are held by trustees to aid the work of the charity in a particular way: by generating money. That is the purpose for which they are held. That is their raison d'être. Trustees cannot properly use assets held as an investment for other, viz, non-investment, purposes. To the extent that they do they are not properly exercising their powers of investment. This is not to say that trustees who own land may not act as responsible landlords or those who own shares may not act as responsible shareholders. They may. The law is not so cynical as to require trustees to behave in a fashion which would bring them or their charity into disrepute (although their consciences must not be too tender: see *Buttle v Saunders* [1950] 2 All ER 193). On the other hand, trustees must act prudently. They must not use property held by them for investment purposes as a means for making moral statements at the expense of the charity of which they are trustees. Those who wish may do so with their own property, but that is not a proper function of trustees with trust assets held as an investment.

 Alert

I should mention one other particular situation. There will be instances today when those who support or benefit from a charity take widely different views on a particular type of investment, some saying that on moral grounds it conflicts with the aims of the charity, others saying the opposite. One example is the holding of arms industry shares by a religious charity. There is a real difficulty here. To many questions raising moral issues there are no certain answers. On moral questions widely differing views are held by well-meaning, responsible people. This is not always so. But frequently, when questions of the morality of conduct are being canvassed, there is no identifiable yardstick which can be applied to a set of facts so as to yield one answer which can be seen to be "right" and the other "wrong." If that situation confronts trustees of a charity, the law does not require them to find an answer to the unanswerable. Trustees may, if they wish, accommodate the views of those who consider that on moral grounds a particular investment would be in conflict with the objects of the charity, so long as the trustees are satisfied that course would not involve a risk of significant financial detriment. But when they are not so satisfied trustees should not make investment decisions on the basis of preferring one view of whether on moral grounds in investment conflicts with the objects of the charity over another. This is so even when one view is more widely supported than the other.

I have sought above to consider charity trustees' duties in relation to investment as a matter of basic principle. I was referred to no authority bearing directly on these matters. My attention was drawn to *Cowan v Scargill* [1985] Ch 270, a case concerning a pension fund. I believe the views I have set out accord with those expressed by Sir Robert Megarry VC in that case, bearing in mind that he was considering trusts for the provision of financial benefits for individuals. In this case I am concerned with trusts of charities, whose purposes are multifarious. ...

The commissioners' investment policy is set out in their annual report for 1989 in terms I should quote in full:

"The primary aim in the management of our assets is to produce the best total return, that is capital and income growth combined. While financial responsibilities must remain of primary importance (given our position as trustees), as responsible investors we also continue to take proper account of social, ethical and environmental issues. As people became increasingly aware of the many factors which can adversely affect both their own and other people's lives, so we must be responsive to these areas of concern. As regards our Stock Exchange holdings this means that we do not invest in companies whose main business is armaments, gambling, alcohol, tobacco and newspapers: it also means that we must continue to be vigilant in our monitoring of the activities of those companies where we do have a shareholding. Our practice is to follow up with senior management any major criticisms of a particular company's activities through confidential correspondence and, where appropriate, direct discussions. Our aim is to establish facts, to see whether there is any basis for the criticism and to evaluate what action the company has taken or is prepared to take if the criticism is justified. Each case is considered on its merits. The ultimate pressure we can bring to bear is that of disinvestment. The paradox of doing so is that we then lose any opportunity to use our influence for good. Our policy with regard to investment and South Africa remains unchanged. We do not invest in any South African company nor in any other company where more than a small part of their business is in South Africa. Where we do invest in a company with a small stake in South Africa we try to ensure that it follows enlightened social and employment policies, so far as is possible within the system of apartheid of which we have repeatedly expressed our abhorrence. In common with the rest of the Church, we welcome the important political developments since the end of 1989 and hope that the momentum will be sustained. On the property side, although we shall continue to seek out development possibilities so as to discharge our duties as trustees, we are conscious of the effect of our actions upon local communities and their perceptions of the Church as a whole. We shall therefore continue to ensure that environmental considerations are properly taken into account when development schemes arise. In particular, during the year we have introduced new procedures for keeping bishops, incumbents and local church members informed whenever we are involved in a scheme affecting their community. We are also keen to find investments which respond positively to specific areas of concern in our society. We were glad therefore that our development of four small light industrial units at Walsall was completed during 1989. We believe that in direct property investments such as this we can set an example of what help can be given to small businesses wishing to expand, particularly in urban priority areas, although only a small proportion of our total funds can be invested in this way. However, if we can influence others to respond in a similar way it will do much to improve the quality of life of those living in areas of high unemployment."

It will be seen, therefore, that the commissioners do have an "ethical" investment policy. They have followed such a policy for many years. Indeed they have done so ever since they were constituted in 1948. Let me say at once that I can see nothing in this statement of policy which is inconsistent with the general principles I have sought to expound above.

The statement of policy records that the commissioners do not invest in companies whose main business is in armaments, gambling, alcohol, tobacco or newspapers. Of these, newspapers fall into a category of their own. The commissioners' policy regarding newspapers is based on the fact that many newspapers are associated, to a greater or lesser extent, with a particular political party or political view. Leaving aside newspapers, the underlying rationale of the commissioners' policy on these items is that there is a body of members of the Church of England opposed to the businesses in question on religious or moral grounds. There are members who believe these business activities are morally wrong, and that they are in conflict with Christian teaching and its moral values. But this list has only to be read for it to be obvious that many committed members of the Church of England take the contrary view. To say that not all members of the Church of England eschew gambling, alcohol or tobacco would be an understatement. As to armaments, the morality of war, and the concepts of a "just war," [these] are issues which have been debated for centuries. These are moral questions on which no single view can be shown to be "right" and the others "wrong." As I understand the position, the commissioners have felt able to exclude these items from their investments despite the conflicting views on the morality of holding these items as investments because there has remained open to the commissioners an adequate width of alternative investments.

I have already indicated that at the heart of the plaintiffs' case is a contention that the commissioners' policy is erroneous in law in that the commissioners are only prepared to take non-financial considerations into account to the extent that such considerations do not significantly jeopardise or interfere with accepted investment principles. I think it is implicit, if not explicit, in the commissioners' evidence that they do regard themselves as constrained in this way. So far as I have been able to see, this is the only issue identifiable as an issue of law raised in these proceedings. In my view this self-constraint applied by the commissioners is not one which in practice has led to any error of law on their part, nor is it likely to do so. I have already indicated that the circumstances in which charity trustees are bound or entitled to make a financially disadvantageous investment decision for ethical reasons are extremely limited. I have noted that it is not easy to think of a practical example of such a circumstance. There is no evidence before me to suggest that any such circumstance exists here.

 Alert

So the duty of trustees when exercising their powers of investment is, save in the very rare cases identified both by Sir Robert Megarry V-C and Sir Donald Nicholls V-C, to secure the maximum income and/or capital return, consistent with the exercise of prudence.

13.1.2 Controlling shareholdings

The trust fund may consist of shares which give the trustees a controlling interest over a company. In this situation, the common law duty of prudence in relation to such an investment requires the trustees to do more than simply keep themselves appraised of the company's affairs, eg by reading the material which is sent by the company to shareholders from time to time or by taking account of such information about the company as is in the public domain.

In re Lucking's Will Trusts [1968] 1 WLR 866

Panel: Cross J

Facts: A trust fund held nearly 70 per cent of the shares in a small private company. There were two trustees of the fund (L and B). The remaining shares were owned or controlled by L. The directors were L, his wife and a third party (D), who was the manager of the business. D wrongfully withdrew some £15,000 from the company's bank account and later became bankrupt, as a result of which the money was lost. L had been aware of the overdrawings but had accepted D's assurances that the money would be repaid. The beneficiaries brought proceedings for breach of trust, and Cross J held that L (but not B) was liable to make good the loss.

MR JUSTICE CROSS

... The conduct of the defendant trustees is, I think, to be judged by the standard applied in *Speight v Gaunt*, namely, that a trustee is only bound to conduct the business of the trust in such a way as an ordinary prudent man would conduct a business of his own.

Now what steps, if any, does a reasonably prudent man who finds himself a majority shareholder in a private company take with regard to the management of the company's affairs? He does not, I think, content himself with such information as to the management of the company's affairs as he is entitled to as shareholder, but ensures that he is represented on the board. He may be prepared to run the business himself as managing director or, at least, to become a non-executive director while having the business managed by someone else. Alternatively, he may find someone who will act as his nominee on the board and report to him from time to time as to the company's affairs. In the same way, as it seems to me, trustees holding a controlling interest ought to ensure so far as they can that they have such information as to the progress of the company's affairs as directors would have. If they sit back and allow the company to be run by the minority shareholder and receive no more information than shareholders are entitled to, they do so at their risk if things go wrong.

 Alert

In this case, of course, the trust was represented on the board by [L]. But, as I see it, one ought not to regard him as performing a duty to the trust which it was incumbent on the trustees to perform personally, so that [B] became automatically responsible for any deficiencies in [L], as does a passive trustee who allows his co-trustee to exercise alone discretions which it is their duty to exercise jointly.

If these trustees had decided, as they might have done, to be represented on the board by a nominee they would have been entitled to rely on the information given them by that nominee as to the way in which the company's affairs were being managed even though such information was inaccurate or inadequate, unless they had some reason to suspect that it was inaccurate or inadequate. [B], as I see it, cannot have been in a worse position because his co-trustee was the trust's representative on the board than he would have been if their representative had not been a trustee at all. The position of [L], on the other hand, as I see it, was much different. He cannot say that what he knew, or ought to have known, about the company's affairs he knew, or ought to have known, simply as a director with a duty to the company and no one else. He was in the position he was partly as a representative of the trust and if and so far as he failed in his duty to the company he also failed in his duty to the trust. ...

Finally, I must ask myself how these principles are to be applied to the facts of this case. It is not suggested that it was not proper for the company to appoint [D] to be manager of its business on the terms contained in the service agreement, nor can it be suggested that [L] failed to follow the fortunes of the company under [D's] management. ... [But] this position changed altogether when [L] realised ... that [D] was overdrawing at a rate of some £1,400 a year on top of his salary and his expenses and travel allowance. I do not say that he ought to have leaped there and then to the conclusion that [D] was dishonest and that he would be unable to pay what he owed ... but [L] saw - or if he did not, ought to have seen - that [D] was very careless in matters of account, and in my judgment it was negligent of him to retain [him] as manager without imposing any check on his drawings. ... With his own property a man may well say: "I will trust my friend even though there are circumstances which might make some stranger suspicious of him. I would rather be cheated than spy on him." But a trustee cannot take that line ... . Although I have sympathy for [L], I feel bound to hold that he is liable to the other beneficiaries for such loss as was suffered by the trust shareholding for his falling adequately to supervise [D]'s drawings ... .

Bartlett & others v Barclays Bank Trust Co Ltd (No 2) [1980] Ch 515

Panel: Brightman J

Facts: The defendant bank was the trustee of a fund which held 99.8 per cent of the shares in a property company. The company's directors decided upon a change of investment policy, which led it to undertake various speculative property development projects with third parties, none of which was challenged or questioned by the bank. Ultimately, those projects brought about the company's insolvency, whereupon the beneficiaries brought proceedings against the bank to recover the losses which they had suffered. The bank was held liable.

MR JUSTICE BRIGHTMAN

...What, then, was the duty of the bank and did the bank fail in its duty? It does not follow that because a trustee could have prevented a loss it is therefore liable for the loss. The questions which I must ask myself are (1) What was the duty of the bank as the holder of 99.8 per cent of the shares ... ? (2) Was the bank in breach of duty in any and if so what respect? (3) If so, did that breach of duty cause the loss which was suffered by the trust estate? (4) If so, to what extent is the bank liable to make good that loss? ...

The cases establish that it is the duty of a trustee to conduct the business of the trust with the same care as an ordinary prudent man of business would extend towards his own affairs: *In re Speight* (1883) 22 Ch D 727, per Sir George Jessel MR at p 739 and Bowen LJ at p 762; affirmed on appeal, *Speight v Gaunt* (1883) 9 App Cas 1, and see Lord Blackburn at p 19. In applying this principle, Lindley LJ (who was the third member of the court in the *Speight* case) added in *In re Whiteley* (1886) 33 Ch D 347, 355:

"... care must be taken not to lose sight of the fact that the business of the trustee, and the business which the ordinary prudent man is supposed to be conducting for himself, is the business of investing money for the benefit of persons who are to enjoy it at some future time, and not for the sole benefit of the person entitled to the present income. The duty of a trustee is not to take such care only as a prudent man would take if he had only himself to consider; the duty rather is to take such care as an ordinary prudent man would take if he were minded to make an investment for the benefit of other people for whom he felt morally bound to provide. That is the kind of business the ordinary prudent man is supposed to be engaged in; and unless this is borne in mind the standard of a trustee's duty will be fixed too low; lower than it has ever yet been fixed, and lower certainly than the House of Lords or this Court endeavoured to fix it in *Speight v Gaunt*."

See on appeal *Learoyd v Whiteley* (1887) 12 App Cas 727, where Lord Watson added, at p 733:

"Business men of ordinary prudence may, and frequently do, select investments which are more or less of a speculative character; but it is the duty of a trustee to confine himself to the class of investments which are permitted by the trust, and likewise to avoid all investments of that class which are attended with hazard."

That does not mean that the trustee is bound to avoid all risk and in effect act as an insurer of the trust fund: see Bacon VC in *In re Godfrey* (1883) 23 Ch D 483, 493:

"No doubt it is the duty of a trustee, in administering the trusts of a will, to deal with property intrusted into his care exactly as any prudent man would deal with his own property. But the words in which the rule is expressed must not be strained beyond their meaning. Prudent businessmen in their dealings incur risk. That may and must happen in almost all human affairs."

The distinction is between a prudent degree of risk on the one hand, and hazard on the other. Nor must the court be astute to fix liability upon a trustee who has committed no more than an error of judgment, from which no business man, however prudent, can expect to be immune: see Lopes LJ in *In re Chapman* [1896] 2 Ch 763, 778:

"A trustee who is honest and reasonably competent is not to be held responsible for a mere error in judgment when the question which he has to consider is whether a security of a class authorized, but depreciated in value, should be retained or realized, provided he acts with reasonable care, prudence, and circumspection."

If the trust had existed ... [in such a way] ... that the bank held the freehold and leasehold properties and other assets [of the company] directly upon the trusts of the settlement, it would in my opinion have been a clear breach of trust for the bank to have hazarded trust money upon the Old Bailey development project with Stock Conversion. The Old Bailey project was a gamble, because it involved buying into the site at prices in excess of the investment values of the properties, with no certainty or probability, with no more than a chance, that planning permission could be obtained for a financially viable redevelopment, that the numerous proprietors would agree to sell out or join in the scheme, that finance would be available upon acceptable terms, and that the development would be completed, or at least become a marketable asset, before the time came to start winding up the trust. However one looks at it, the project was a hazardous speculation upon which no trustee could properly have ventured without explicit authority in the trust instrument. I therefore hold that the entire expenditure in the Old Bailey project would have been incurred in breach of trust, had the money been spent by the bank itself. The fact that it was a risk acceptable to the board of a wealthy company like Stock Conversion has little relevance.

I turn to the question, what was the duty of the bank as the holder of shares in [the company]? I will first answer this question without regard to the position of the bank as a specialist trustee, to which I will advert later. The bank, as trustee, was bound to act in relation to the shares and to the controlling position which they conferred, in the same manner as a prudent man of business. The prudent man of business will act in such manner as is necessary to safeguard his investment. He will do this in two ways. If facts come to his knowledge which tell him that the company's affairs are not being conducted as they should be, or which put him on inquiry, he will take appropriate action. Appropriate action will no doubt consist in the first instance of inquiry of and consultation with the directors, and in the last but most unlikely resort, the convening of a general meeting to replace one or more directors. What the prudent man of business will not do is to content himself with the receipt of such information on the affairs of the company as a shareholder ordinarily receives at annual general meetings. Since he has the power to do so, he will go further and see that he has sufficient information to enable him to make a responsible decision from time to time either to let matters proceed as they are proceeding, or to intervene if he is dissatisfied. This topic was considered by Cross J in *In re Lucking's Will Trusts* [1968] 1 WLR 866 ...

 Alert

I do not understand Cross J to have been saying that in every case where trustees have a controlling interest in a company it is their duty to ensure that one of their number is a director or that they have a nominee on the board who will report from time to time on the affairs of the company. He was merely outlining convenient methods by which a prudent man of business (as also a trustee) with a controlling interest in a private company, can place himself in a position to make an informed decision whether any action is appropriate to be taken for the protection of his asset. Other methods may be equally satisfactory and convenient, depending upon the circumstances of the individual case. Alternatives which spring to mind are the receipt of copies of the agenda and minutes of board meetings if regularly held, the receipt of monthly management accounts in the case of a trading concern, or quarterly reports. Every case will depend on its own facts. The possibilities are endless. It would be useless, indeed misleading, to seek to lay down a general rule. The purpose to be achieved is not that of monitoring every move of the directors, but of making it reasonably probable, so far as circumstances permit, that the trustee or (as in the *Lucking* case) one of them will receive an adequate flow of information in time to enable the trustees to make use of their controlling interest should this be necessary for the protection of their trust asset, namely, the shareholding. The obtaining of information is not an end in itself, but merely a means of enabling the trustees to safeguard the interests of their beneficiaries. ...

So far, I have applied the test of the ordinary prudent man of business. Although I am not aware that the point has previously been considered, except briefly in *In re Waterman's Will Trusts* [1952] 2 All ER 1054, I am of opinion that a higher duty of care is plainly due from someone like a trust corporation which carries on a specialised business of trust management. A trust corporation holds itself out in its advertising literature as being above ordinary mortals. With a specialist staff of trained trust officers and managers, with ready access to financial information and professional advice, dealing with and solving trust problems day after day, the trust corporation holds itself out, and rightly, as capable of providing an expertise which it would be unrealistic to expect and unjust to demand from the ordinary prudent man or woman who accepts, probably unpaid and sometimes reluctantly from a sense of family duty, the burdens of a trusteeship. Just as, under the law of contract, a professional person possessed of a particular skill is liable for breach of contract if he neglects to use the skill and experience which he professes, so I think that a professional corporate trustee is liable for breach of trust if loss is caused to the trust fund because it neglects to exercise the special care and skill which it professes to have. The advertising literature of the bank was not in evidence (other than the scale of fees) but counsel for the defendant did not dispute that trust corporations, including the bank, hold themselves out as possessing a superior ability for the conduct of trust business, and in any event I would take judicial notice of that fact. Having expressed my view of the higher duty required from a trust corporation, I should add that the bank's counsel did not dispute the proposition.

 Alert

In my judgment the bank wrongfully and in breach of trust neglected to ensure that it received an adequate flow of information concerning the intentions and activities of the boards of [the company]. It was not proper for the bank to confine itself to the receipt of the annual balance sheet and profit and loss account, detailed annual financial statements and the chairman's report and statement, and to attendance at the annual general meetings and the luncheons that followed, which were the limits of the bank's regular sources of information. Had the bank been in receipt of more frequent information it would have been able to step in and stop, and ought to have stopped [the company] embarking on the Old Bailey project. That project was imprudent and hazardous and wholly unsuitable for a trust whether undertaken by the bank direct or through the medium of its wholly owned company. Even without the regular flow of information which the bank ought to have had, it knew enough to put it upon inquiry. There were enough obvious points at which the bank should have intervened and asked questions. Assuming, as I do, that the questions would have been answered truthfully, the bank would have discovered the gamble upon which [the company was] about to embark in relation to the Old Bailey site, and it could have, and should have, stopped the initial move towards disaster, and later on arrested further progress towards disaster. I have indicated in the course of this judgment a number of obvious points at which the bank should have intervened, and it would be repetitive to summarise them.

I hold that the bank failed in its duty whether it is judged by the standard of the prudent man of business or of the skilled trust corporation. The bank's breach of duty caused the loss which was suffered by the trust estate. If the bank had intervened as it could and should have that loss would not have been incurred. By "loss," I mean the depreciation which took place in the market value of the ... shares, by comparison with the value which the shares would have commanded if the loss on the Old Bailey project had not been incurred, and reduction of dividends through loss of income. The bank is liable for the loss so suffered by the trust estate ... .

13.2 The Statutory Duty of Care

As mentioned above, trustees may be subject to the statutory duty contained in Trustee Act 2000 s 1.

The statutory duty of care applies to the specified functions whether they are conferred upon the trustees expressly by the terms of the trust instrument or by implication under the Act. They apply regardless of whether the trust was created before or after the Act came into effect.

Further Reading

Le Poidevin, Nicholas. 'The worried trustee', T & T 2009, 15(7), 596-601

Halpern, David. 'Negligent investment: claims against trustees and agents', T & T 2009, 15(7), 602-610

Thornton, Rosy. 'Ethical investments: a case of disjointed thinking', CLJ 2008, 67(2), 396-422

Scanlan, Charles. 'Socially responsible investment by charities and pension schemes', CL & PR 2006, 9(1), 39-72

Harris, David. 'Investments by professional trustees in private companies and partnerships', PCB 2005, 3, 167-175

14

Breach of Trust

Topic List

Introduction

As has been shown in previous chapters, trustees have numerous duties with regard to how they deal with beneficiaries and trust property. A potential consequence of these duties existing is the possibility of a breach taking place. This possibility of a breach taking place is made more likely by the fact that a breach can be made inadvertently as well as deliberately. Furthermore, a breach of trust can take many forms and can lead to a variety of remedies to rectify the breach.

14.1 Causation

Due to the nature of how trust assets are used whilst the trust is up and running, it would be unfair to find a trustee liable for every single event that touches on the assets themselves. We therefore have to find a link between the trustee and what has happened to the asset to justify finding the trustee in breach of trust. The following two cases show the casual link to the breach that is required, firstly when the trustee does something he is not authorised to do with the trust property, and secondly where the trustee does something which he is authorised to do with the trust property.

Target Holdings Ltd v Redferns (A Firm) and Another Appellants [1996] AC 421

Panel: Lord Keith of Kinkel, Lord Ackner, Lord Jauncey of Tilluchettle, Lord Browne-Wilkinson and Lord Lloyd of Berwick

Facts: Target Holdings was a finance company that entered into a mortgage arrangement for £1,525,000 with a company, Crowngate Ltd, for the acquisition of commercial property. Redferns was the firm of solicitors acting on the part of both Target Holdings and Crowngate Ltd, as well as Kohli Ltd and Panther Ltd, two sister companies to Crowngate, for the facilitation of the mortgage.

Unfortunately Target Holdings was the victim of a cunning mortgage fraud. Target Holdings knew nothing of these events, and thought that it was providing a mortgage for a property worth more than the amount of money that was lent. The sum of £1,525,000 was duly transferred from Target Holdings to Redferns, who held the money on bare trust subject to instructions from Target Holdings. In breach of trust Redferns transferred the money to Crowngate Ltd one month before the charges were actually executed. Crowngate Ltd subsequently defaulted upon the mortgage and Target Holdings were only able to sell the commercial property at its true value of £500,000. Target Holdings sued Redferns for breach of trust

LORD BROWNE-WILKINSON

Before considering the technical issues of law which arise, it is appropriate to look at the case more generally. Target allege, and it is probably the case, that they were defrauded by third parties (Mr. Kohli and Mr. Musafir and possibly their associates) to advance money on the security of the property. If there had been no breach by Redferns of their instructions and the transaction had gone through, Target would have suffered a loss in round figures of £1.2m. (i.e. £1.7m. advanced less £500,000 recovered on the realisation of the security). Such loss would have been wholly caused by the fraud of the third parties. The breach of trust committed by Redferns left Target in exactly the same position as it would have been if there had been no such breach: Target advanced the same amount of money, obtained the same security and received the same amount on the realisation of that security. In any ordinary use of words, the breach of trust by Redferns cannot be said to have caused the actual loss ultimately suffered by Target unless it can be shown that, but for the breach of trust, the transaction would not have gone through, e.g. if Panther could not have obtained a conveyance from Mirage otherwise than by paying the purchase money to Mirage out of the moneys paid out, in breach of trust, by Redferns to Panther on 29 June. ...

The argument both before the Court of Appeal and your Lordships concentrated on the equitable rules establishing the extent and quantification of the compensation payable by a trustee who is in breach of trust. In my judgment this approach is liable to lead to the wrong conclusions in the present case because it ignores an earlier and crucial question, viz., is the trustee who has committed a breach under any liability at all to the beneficiary complaining of the breach? There can be cases where, although there is an undoubted breach of trust, the trustee is under no liability at all to a beneficiary. For example, if a trustee commits a breach of trust with the acquiescence of one beneficiary, that beneficiary has no right to complain and an action for breach of trust brought by him would fail completely. Again there may be cases where the breach gives rise to no right to compensation. Say, as often occurs, a trustee commits a judicious breach of trust by investing in an unauthorised investment which proves to be very profitable to the trust. A carping beneficiary could insist that the unauthorised investment be sold and the proceeds invested in authorised investments: but the trustee would be under no liability to pay compensation either to the trust fund or to the beneficiary because the breach has caused no loss to the trust fund. ...

The basic right of a beneficiary is to have the trust duly administered in accordance with the provisions of the trust instrument, if any, and the general law. Thus, in relation to a traditional trust where the fund is held in trust for a number of beneficiaries having different, usually successive, equitable interests, (e.g. A for life with remainder to B), the right of each beneficiary is to have the whole fund vested in the trustees so as to be available to satisfy his equitable interest when, and if, it falls into possession. Accordingly, in the case of a breach of such a trust involving the wrongful paying away of trust assets, the liability of the trustee is to restore to the trust fund, often called 'the trust estate,' what ought to have been there.

The equitable rules of compensation for breach of trust have been largely developed in relation to such traditional trusts, where the only way in which all the beneficiaries' rights can be protected is to restore to the trust fund what ought to be there. In such a case the basic rule is that a trustee in breach of trust must restore or pay to the trust estate either the assets which have been lost to the estate by reason of the breach or compensation for such loss. Courts of Equity did not award damages but, acting in personam, ordered the defaulting trustee to restore the trust estate... . If specific restitution of the trust property is not possible, then the liability of the trustee is to pay sufficient compensation to the trust estate to put it back to what it would have been had the breach not been committed... . Even if the immediate cause of the loss is the dishonesty or failure of a third party, the trustee is liable to make good that loss to the trust estate if, but for the breach, such loss would not have occurred...

[A]s I have sought to show a beneficiary becoming absolutely entitled to a trust fund has no automatic right to have the fund reconstituted in all circumstances. Thus, even applying the strict rules so developed in relation to traditional trusts, it seems to me very doubtful whether Target is now entitled to have the trust fund reconstituted. But in my judgment it is in any event wrong to lift wholesale the detailed rules developed in the context of traditional trusts and then seek to apply them to trusts of quite a different kind. In the modern world the trust has become a valuable device in commercial and financial dealings. The fundamental principles of equity apply as much to such trusts as they do to the traditional trusts in relation to which those principles were originally formulated. But in my judgment it is important, if the trust is not to be rendered commercially useless, to distinguish between the basic principles of trust law and those specialist rules developed in relation to traditional trusts which are applicable only to such trusts and the rationale of which has no application to trusts of quite a different kind.

...I have no doubt that, until the underlying commercial transaction has been completed, the solicitor can be required to restore to client account moneys wrongly paid away. But to import into such trust an obligation to restore the trust fund once the transaction has been completed would be entirely artificial. The obligation to reconstitute the trust fund applicable in the case of traditional trusts reflects the fact that no one beneficiary is entitled to the trust property and the need to compensate all beneficiaries for the breach. That rationale has no application to a case such as the present. ...

But the fact that there is an accrued cause of action as soon as the breach is committed does not in my judgment mean that the quantum of the compensation payable is ultimately fixed as at the date when the breach occurred. The quantum is fixed at the date of judgment at which date, according to the circumstances then pertaining, the compensation is assessed at the figure then necessary to put the trust estate or the beneficiary back into the position it would have been in had there been no breach. I can see no justification for 'stopping the clock' immediately in some cases but not in others: to do so may, as in this case, lead to compensating the trust estate or the beneficiary for a loss which, on the facts known at trial, it has never suffered.

 Alert

For these reasons I reach the conclusion that, on the facts which must currently be assumed, Target has not demonstrated that it is entitled to any compensation for breach of trust. Assuming that moneys would have been forthcoming from some other source to complete the purchase from Mirage if the moneys had not been wrongly provided by Redferns in breach of trust, Target obtained exactly what it would have obtained had no breach occurred, i.e. a valid security for the sum advanced. ...

I would therefore allow the appeal, set aside the order of the Court of Appeal and restore the order of Warner J.

There are two important aspects to take from Lord Browne-Wilkinson's speech. Firstly, whilst a breach of trust might exist, if it is rectified before the trust suffers any loss, then the trustees cannot be held liable for the subsequently corrected breach. Secondly, the quantification of liability with regard to the specific breach does not stop at the moment the breach takes place, but instead will be assessed at the date of the trial.

On both of these factors Redferns was therefore not liable for the losses Target Holdings suffered. They had ensured charges were executed over the commercial property and therefore Target Holdings was in exactly the same situation they would have been in had the charges been executed before the money was transferred to Crowngate Ltd. Secondly, whilst Redferns was liable for the whole sum of money at the moment it was paid to Crowngate Ltd in breach of trust, the obtaining of the charges executed over the property meant that the valid substitute for the money was obtained. From that stage onwards, Redferns' liability was reduced to nothing.

Bartlett v Barclays Bank Trust Co Ltd [1980] Ch 515

Panel: Brightman J

Statute: Trustee Act 1925 s 61

Link
See Chapter 13, where the case is also extracted under 'controlling shareholders'.

Facts: Barclays Bank was trustee of a family trust that had a majority of shares in a private company, Bartletts Trust Ltd ('BTL'). BTL subsequently became a subsidiary of Bartlett Trust Holdings ('BTH'), in which the trust had 99.8% of the shareholding. Barclays Bank took no role in the management nor exercised any form of control of the company from 1960. During this time period BTH altered its investment programme to go into property development. Barclays Bank made no objection to this change.

BTH then embarked upon two hazardous property transactions without any consultation or interaction with Barclays Bank. Although the first project in Guildford was profitable, the second project at the Old Bailey in London involved the purchase of land for more than the market rate, with only a slight chance of obtaining planning permission on the land. Planning permission was subsequently not forthcoming and the land could not be developed. BTH subsequently suffered a loss of £500,000 from this transaction and the beneficiaries subsequently sued the trustees for failing to exercise proper supervision and management of BTH.

It was held that Barclays were in breach of their duties as trustee to manage BTH prudently. However, since the profit from the Guildford project and the loss from the Old Bailey project stemmed from the same breach, a set-off of the loss from the Old Bailey project against the profit from the Guildford project was allowed.

MR JUSTICE BRIGHTMAN

The situation may be summed up as follows. Bartlett Trust (Holdings) Ltd. (BTH) made a large loss as a result of the involvement of itself and BTL in the Old Bailey project. This loss reduced the value of the BTH shares and thereby caused a loss to the trust fund of the 1920 settlement. The bank, had it acted in time, could by reason of its shareholding have stopped the board of BTL embarking upon the Old Bailey project; and, had it acted in time, could have stopped the board of BTL and later the board of

BTH (it is unnecessary to differentiate) from continuing with the project; and could, had it acted in time, have required BTH to sell its interest in Far Investments Ltd. (Far) to Stock Conversion on the no-loss or small-loss terms which (as I find) were available for the asking.

What, then, was the duty of the bank and did the bank fail in its duty? It does not follow that because a trustee could have prevented a loss it is therefore liable for the loss. The questions which I must ask myself are (1) What was the duty of the bank as the holder of 99.8 per cent of the shares in BTL and BTH? (2) Was the bank in breach of duty in any and if so what respect? (3) If so, did that breach of duty cause the loss which was suffered by the trust estate? (4) If so, to what extent is the bank liable to make good that loss? In approaching these questions, I bear in mind that the attack on the bank is based, not on wrongful acts, but on wrongful omissions, that is to say, non-feasance not misfeasance.

 Alert

The cases establish that it is the duty of a trustee to conduct the business of the trust with the same care as an ordinary prudent man of business would extend towards his own affairs... .

If the trust had existed without the incorporation of BTL, so that the bank held the freehold and leasehold properties and other assets of BTL directly upon the trusts of the settlement, it would in my opinion have been a clear breach of trust for the bank to have hazarded trust money upon the Old Bailey development project in partnership with Stock Conversion. The Old Bailey project was a gamble, because it involved buying into the site at prices in excess of the investment values of the properties, with no certainty or probability, with no more than a chance, that planning permission could be obtained for a financially viable redevelopment, that the numerous proprietors would agree to sell out or join in the scheme, that finance would be available upon acceptable terms, and that the development would be completed, or at least become a marketable asset, before the time came to start winding up the trust. However one looks at it, the project was a hazardous speculation upon which no trustee could properly have ventured without explicit authority in the trust instrument. I therefore hold that the entire expenditure in the Old Bailey project would have been incurred in breach of trust, had the money been spent by the bank itself. The fact that it was a risk acceptable to the board of a wealthy company like Stock Conversion has little relevance.

I turn to the question, what was the duty of the bank as the holder of shares in BTL and BTH? I will first answer this question without regard to the position of the bank as a specialist trustee, to which I will advert later. The bank, as trustee, was bound to act in relation to the shares and to the controlling position which they conferred, in the same manner as a prudent man of business. The prudent man of business will act in such manner as is necessary to safeguard his investment. He will do this in two ways. If facts come to his knowledge which tell him that the company's affairs are not being conducted as they should be, or which put him on inquiry, he will take appropriate action. Appropriate action will no doubt consist in the first instance of inquiry of and consultation with the directors, and in the last but most unlikely resort, the convening of a general meeting to replace one or more directors. What the prudent man of business will *not* do is to content himself with the receipt of such information on the affairs of the company as a shareholder ordinarily receives at annual general meetings. Since he has the power to do so, he will go further and see that he has sufficient information to enable him to make a responsible decision from time to time either to let matters proceed as they are proceeding, or to intervene if he is dissatisfied. …

So far, I have applied the test of the ordinary prudent man of business. …I am of opinion that a higher duty of care is plainly due from someone like a trust corporation which carries on a specialised business of trust management. A trust corporation holds itself out in its advertising literature as being above ordinary mortals. With a specialist staff of trained trust officers and managers, with ready access to financial information and professional advice, dealing with and solving trust problems day after day, the trust corporation holds itself out, and rightly, as capable of providing an expertise which it would be unrealistic to expect and unjust to demand from the ordinary prudent man or woman who accepts, probably unpaid and sometimes reluctantly from a sense of family duty, the burdens of a trusteeship. Just as, under the law of contract, a professional person possessed of a particular skill is liable for breach of contract if he neglects to use the skill and experience which he professes, so I think that a professional corporate trustee is liable for breach of trust if loss is caused to the trust fund because it neglects to exercise the special care and skill which it professes to have. The advertising literature of the bank was not in evidence (other than the scale of fees) but counsel for the defendant did not dispute that trust corporations, including the bank, hold themselves out as possessing a superior ability for the conduct of trust business, and in any event I would take judicial notice of that fact. Having expressed my view of the higher duty required from a trust corporation, I should add that the bank's counsel did not dispute the proposition.

Alert

In my judgment the bank wrongfully and in breach of trust neglected to ensure that it received an adequate flow of information concerning the intentions and activities of the boards of BTL and BTH. It was not proper for the bank to confine itself to the receipt of the annual balance sheet and profit and loss account, detailed annual financial statements and the chairman's report and statement, and to attendance at the annual general meetings and the luncheons that followed, which were the limits of the bank's regular sources of information. Had the bank been in receipt of more frequent information it would have been able to step in and stop, and ought to have stopped, Mr Roberts and the board embarking on the Old Bailey project. That project was imprudent and hazardous and wholly unsuitable for a trust whether undertaken by the bank direct or through the medium of its wholly owned company. Even without the regular flow of information which the bank ought to have had, it knew enough to put it upon inquiry. There were enough obvious points at which the bank should have intervened and asked questions. Assuming, as I do, that the questions would have been answered truthfully, the bank would have discovered the gamble upon which Mr Roberts and his board were about to embark in relation to the Old Bailey site, and it could have, and should have, stopped the initial move towards disaster, and later on arrested further progress towards disaster. I have indicated in the course of this judgment a number of obvious points at which the bank should have intervened, and it would be repetitive to summarise them.

I hold that the bank failed in its duty whether it is judged by the standard of the prudent man of business or of the skilled trust corporation. The bank's breach of duty caused the loss which was suffered by the trust estate. If the bank had intervened as it could and should have that loss would not have been incurred. By "loss," I mean the depreciation which took place in the market value of the BT shares, by comparison with the value which the shares would have commanded if the loss on the Old Bailey project had not been incurred, and reduction of dividends through loss of income. The bank is liable for the loss so suffered by the trust estate, except to the extent that I shall hereafter indicate.

The bank also relies on clauses 18 and 26 of the settlement. Clause 18 entitled the bank to

"act in relation to the Bartlett Trust Ltd. or any other company and the shares securities and properties thereof in such way as it shall think best calculated to benefit the trust premises and as if it was the absolute owner of such shares, securities and property."

In my judgment this is a clause which confers on the bank power to engage in a transaction which might otherwise be outside the scope of its authority; it is not an indemnity protecting the bank against liability for a transaction which is a breach of trust because it is one that a prudent man of business would have eschewed. ...

There remains this defence, which I take from paragraph 26 of the amended pleading:

"In about 1963 [BTL] purchased a site at Woodbridge Road, Guildford, pursuant to the policy pleaded in paragraph 19 hereof, for the sum of £79,000, and re-sold the same for £350,000 to MEPC Ltd. in 1973. The net profit resulting from such sale was £271,000. If, which is denied, the defendant is liable for breach of trust whether as alleged in the amended statement of claim or otherwise, the defendant claims credit for such sum of £271,000 or other sum found to be gained in taking any accounts and inquiries."

The general rule as stated in all the textbooks, with some reservations, is that where a trustee is liable in respect of distinct breaches of trust, one of which has resulted in a loss and the other in a gain, he is not entitled to set off the gain against the loss, unless they arise in the same transaction: see *Halsbury's Laws of England*, 3rd ed., vol. 38 (1962), p. 1046; *Snell's Principles of Equity* , 27th ed. (1973), p. 276; Lewin on the Law of Trusts, 16th ed. (1964), p. 670 and *Underhill's Law of Trusts and Trustees*, 12th ed. (1970), p. 634. The relevant cases are, however, not altogether easy to reconcile. All are centenarians and none is quite like the present. The Guildford development stemmed from exactly the same policy and (to a lesser degree because it proceeded less far) exemplified the same folly as the Old Bailey project. Part of the profit was in fact used to finance the Old Bailey disaster. By sheer luck the gamble paid off handsomely, on capital account. I think it would be unjust to deprive the bank of this element of salvage in the course of assessing the cost of the shipwreck. My order will therefore reflect the bank's right to an appropriate set-off.

This case is extremely useful in revealing the methodology judges use when ascertaining whether a breach of trust has occurred when trustees have dealt with trust property in a manner authorised by the trust instrument. Furthermore, quantification of loss in such circumstances will be quantified in relation to what the value of the trust fund would have been but for the breach taking place.

It is also important to realise Brightman J's judgment covers other important aspects of breach of trust. Firstly, the duty of a trustee is to deal with the trust to the same standard as the ordinary prudent man of business. However, where the 'professional' trustee has specialist experience or skills that would go beyond that of the ordinary 'lay' trustee, then the duty of care should be of a higher standard than the ordinary prudent man of business. This higher standard also extends to the situations where the court can forgive a trustee for breach under the Trustee Act 1925 s 61. Where a professional trustee is seeking relief from liability under s 61, there is also a higher standard to pass before the court will excuse the breach than if a lay trustee was asking to be excused for the same breach.

Link
see "Defences to Breach of Trust" below.

The final point of interest is the set-off itself. It is submitted that Brightman J's statement of the principles for when a set-off should be allowed are correct. However, it is questionable whether these principles have been correctly applied to this case. It must be remembered that Barclays' course of dealings throughout was not to run the company, in other words to be passive instead of playing an active role. If Barclays had been active in running BTH then a set-off would be clearly justifiable. Yet, since Barclays in essence did nothing, it is submitted that this is different from pursuing a constant course of action; it is not pursuing a course of action at all. Therefore, a set-off should not have been allowed in this case.

14.2 Liability Between Trustees

As a general principle, trustees are jointly and severably liable for breach of trust. This means that a beneficiary can claim against any of the trustees in the event of a breach, and trustees share the liability between them. This is even the case where the breach has only been undertaken by one of the trustees.

Bahin v Hughes (1886) 31 Ch D 390

Panel: Cotton, Bowen and Fry LJJ

Facts: A testator, Robert Hughes, bequeathed £2,000 to his daughters Eliza Hughes, Sarah Hughes (who subsequently became Sarah Burden) and Frances Hughes (who subsequently became Frances Edwards), to hold on trust to invest in specified securities in England and Wales. Mrs Bahin was the life tenant of this trust. It is important to note at the time of this case married women were not allowed to own property and therefore Mr Burden and Mr Edwards would have to perform trustee functions upon their behalf.

Eliza Hughes, being unmarried, was able to actively manage the trust with Mr Burden. They invested in unauthorised leasehold properties. Frances Edwards was informed of this at the time but subsequently agreed to investing in unauthorised assets. Mrs Bahin found out about the breach and sued the trustees. By this time Frances Edwards had died and Mr Edwards was sued instead. Mr Edwards claimed an indemnity from liability, as Frances Edwards was the trustee and any investments were made solely through the instigation or subsequent consent of Frances Edwards, not him.

It was held that, despite Mr Edwards being entirely passive and only having trustee duties as a consequence of his marriage to Frances Edwards, he was still liable for the breach of trust and could not claim an indemnity.

LORD JUSTICE COTTON

As regards this first question, namely, whether Mr Edwards is answerable for the default of his wife in committing such a breach of trust as this, as much as if she had misspent the money, in my opinion he is altogether answerable. It was an action brought for the loss of the fund, occasioned by a breach of trust, being negligence, on the part of the trustees. We feel no doubt that the *cestui que trust* is entitled to redress as against the trustees, and therefore consider both that the wife of Mr Edwards and himself, as well as Mr and Mrs Burden, were answerable. ...and in my opinion it would be wrong to raise a distinction as regards the liability of Mr Edwards. He is answerable for the same breach of trust, and is not to be differently treated from the other trustees in the matter. The husband is acting and administering on the part and in the right of his wife the duty of trusteeship, who cannot act in the matter without him; therefore he is liable for the breaches of trust committed by her, without drawing any minute distinctions, as might have been done if the case had come within a recent Act, the Married Women's Property Act. But that Act does not apply to this case.

But then we come to another and more difficult question, namely, how far Mr Edwards can, as against Miss Hughes, have indemnity for the loss, on the ground that she was the acting trustee, that she and Mrs Burden took upon themselves to invest this money, and that although both she and Mr Edwards are liable to the beneficiaries, she is liable to Mr Edwards, who left the matter in her hands. On going into the authorities, there are very few cases in which one trustee, who has been guilty with a co-trustee of breach of trust and held answerable, has successfully sought indemnity as against his co-trustee. ...Of course where one trustee has got the money into his own hands, and made use of it, he will be liable to his co-trustee to give him an indemnity. Now I think it wrong to lay down any limitation of the circumstances under which one trustee would be held liable to the other for indemnity, both having been held liable to the *cestui que trust*; but so far as cases have gone at present, relief has only been granted against a trustee who has himself got the benefit of the breach of trust, or between whom and his co-trustees there has existed a relation, which will justify the Court in treating him as solely liable for the breach of trust. Here, when Miss Hughes got the money, she handed it over to the mortgagor... The Appellant, Mr Edwards, relies on the fact that she sent him a letter with the cheque for him and his wife to indorse, saying that nothing should be done with the money without consulting him... Miss Hughes was the active trustee and Mr Edwards did nothing, and in my opinion it would be laying down a wrong rule to hold that where one trustee acts honestly, though erroneously, the other trustee is to be held entitled to indemnity who by doing nothing neglects his duty more than the acting trustee. That Miss Hughes made an improper investment is true, but she acted honestly, and intended to do the best she could, and believed that the property

 Alert

was sufficient security for the money, although she made no inquiries about their being leasehold houses. In my opinion the money was lost just as much by the default of Mr Edwards as by the innocent though erroneous action of his co-trustee, Miss Hughes. All the trustees were in the wrong, and everyone is equally liable to indemnify the beneficiaries.

Therefore a trustee cannot escape liability by stepping back from the trust and letting other trustees breach their duties. Indeed, by doing so a trustee is breaching the duty to safeguard trust property. This case does show, however, that it is possible for a trustee to obtain an indemnity against the breach by another trustee.

Head v Gould [1898] 2 Ch 250

Panel: Kekewich J

Facts: Robert Head created a marriage settlement for his wife and himself successively for life, remainder to their children. The original trustees were Mr Clapp and Mr Houlditch. After Robert Head died his widow obtained advances out of the capital of the fund up to her maximum share. Clapp and Houlditch were unwilling to advance any more capital. They wrote a letter to Mrs Head which contained the following phrase 'The only way we can assist you is by handing the trust over to others, as we are most desirous of doing.' Clapp and Houlditch were subsequently replaced with Mr Gould, a solicitor who was a family friend, and Miss Head, one of the children and a remainderman to the settlement.

The new trustees sold a house in breach of trust and surrendered some life insurance polices on the life of Mrs Head, with Mrs Head's agreement. The proceeds went to Mrs Head.

The trustees were sued for breach of trust by one of the children, whose share in the trust had been given to his mother Mrs Head.

MR JUSTICE KEKEWICH

It will be convenient here at once to deal with the claim made by Miss Head against her co-trustee Gould. By her third-party notice she seeks to be indemnified by him against loss by reason of the breaches of trust, on the ground that the loss and misapplication (if any) of the trust funds, or any part thereof, were occasioned entirely by his acts or defaults, and that he assumed to act as solicitor to the trust estate and as sole trustee thereof, and exercised control of the administration of the trust funds, and that whatever was done by herself in connection with the trust was at his instigation and in reliance upon his advice.

This is a serious charge, and if it had been proved would have entitled her to the relief claimed according to well-known and well-recognised principles. ... My conclusion from such evidence as there is before the Court is distinctly adverse to the claim. I know that, before the appointment of herself and Gould as trustees, Miss Head was an active party to the importunities of her mother which induced the former trustees to commit a breach of trust for their benefit, and that she looked to the change of trustees as a means of, in some way or other, obtaining further advances. I know further that she was well acquainted with the position of the trust, and that it was all-important to maintain the policies and to appropriate the rents of the house to that purpose. She now affects to ignore all that has been done since her appointment, and professes not to remember having executed the several instruments which must have been executed by her for the sale of the house and the surrender of the policies, or the receipt of moneys arising therefrom. With regret and under a painful sense of duty, I am bound to say that I do not credit her testimony. True it is that the defendant Gould is a solicitor, and that he was appointed a trustee for that very reason. True no doubt, also, that the legal business was managed by him, and I do not propose to absolve him from any responsibility attaching to him on that ground; but I do not myself think that … any other judge ever intended to hold that a man is bound to indemnify his co-trustee against loss merely because he was a solicitor, when that co-trustee was an active participator in the breach of trust complained of, and is not proved to have participated merely in consequence of the advice and control of the solicitor. …

 Alert

A key issue is the fact Miss Head was unable to obtain an indemnity merely because Mr Gould was a solicitor and handled the legal aspects of trusteeship. This reasoning is undoubtedly correct; even if the lay trustee does not understand all the legal consequences of administering the trust, it is always possible to run some rudimentary checks to ensure the expert trustee is doing what is supposed to be done.

This scenario can be distinguished from the situation where the expert trustee uses his/her influence to in effect deprive the lay trustee from being able to perform various trust duties. This can be seen from the case of *Re Partington* (1887) 57 LT 654. In this case the trustees, which included Mr Allen, a solicitor trustee and Mrs Partington, the widow of the testator, were found liable for investing in an unauthorised mortgage. Mrs Partington subsequently applied for an indemnity against Mr Allen. In his judgment Stirling J held that when Mr Allen made the investment he did so in such a way that Mrs Partington was unable to exercise her judgment upon this investment. To make a judgment upon the mortgage Mrs Partington relied upon Mr Allen to give her information surrounding the transaction. On the evidence Stirling J held that Mr Allen neither communicated the real state of the property that was going to be subject to the mortgage nor that investing in such a mortgage would be an improper investment. This situation was distinguishable from *Bahin v Hughes* (1886) 31 Ch D 390 because Mrs Partington was not merely standing by whilst Mr Evans committed the breach, but instead had been actively misinformed by Mr Evans. In essence, her will to act properly as trustee had been overborne. Consequently, it was held that Mrs Partington was entitled to an indemnity and Mr Allen was primarily liable for this breach of trust.

14.3 Defences to Breach of Trust

With the wide range of possibilities in which a breach of trust can exist, it is unsurprising that there are circumstances where it is unsuitable to find a trustee liable. Consequentially a number of defences have been created, both judicially and through statute. The defences of consent, acquiescence, and the Trustee Act 1925 s 61 were considered in *Re Pauling's Settlement Trusts* [1964] Ch 303.

Re Pauling's Settlement Trusts [1964] Ch 303

Panel: Willmer, Harman and Upjohn LJJ

Statute: Trustee Act 1925 s 61

Facts: The facts of this case are fully covered in Chapter 13 on Maintenance and Advancement, as are most of the relevant breaches of trust. The following extract focuses firstly upon the nature of undue influence, which was one of the factors relevant to the breaches of trust. The extract then considers the various defences to breach of trust.

LORD JUSTICE WILLMER delivering the judgment of the court

Where the presumption of undue influence exists, a gift by a child cannot be retained by a parent unless he or she can show, first, that the gift was the spontaneous act of the child, and, secondly, that the child knew what his rights were. Thirdly, it is desirable, though not essential, that a child should have independent, and, if possible, professional, advice before making a gift. "In such a case the court," said Cotton LJ in *Allcard v Skinner*, "sets aside the voluntary gift, unless it is proved that in fact the gift was the spontaneous act of the donor acting under circumstances which enabled him to exercise an independent will and which justifies the court in holding that the gift was the result of a free exercise of the donor's will." ...

The question of the duration of the presumption has also been much discussed. ... In our judgment the question is one of fact and degree. One begins with a strong presumption in the case of a child just 21 living at home, and this will grow less and less as the child goes out in the world and leaves the shelter of his home. Nevertheless, the presumption normally lasts only a "short" time after the child has attained 21 (see *Lancashire Loans Ltd v Black*, per Greer LJ, and it seems impossible and undesirable to define it further. A married daughter with a separate establishment of her own may be emancipated directly she attains 21, whereas a spinster who has never left home might be able to rely on the presumption for a longer period. We reject, however, Mr Bagnall's submission that this presumption continues indefinitely until it is proved that the undue influence has ceased to exist. That is to confuse a case of actual undue influence with the presumption. On the other hand, it may not be difficult for a spinster daughter living at home to prove a case of actual undue influence for many years after she has attained the age of 21. In the present case it is important to remember that only the presumption is relied on; no actual undue influence is alleged.

Then Sir Milner argued that trustees who have obtained no benefit from payments induced by undue influence could not be held liable, and that the only person who could be sued would be the parent presumed to have exercised the undue influence, or any person (short of a bona fide purchaser for value) who received the benefit of the payments. On the other hand, Mr Bagnall argued that the bank were in the position of volunteers, and therefore could not escape the consequences of dealing in breach of trust with a beneficiary presumed to have been actuated by the undue influence of a third party; they were at risk just as any other volunteer who takes the property acquired in breach of trust. In the circumstances of this case, we do not think it necessary to express a concluded opinion upon this matter except to say that we reject Sir Milner Holland's argument that the bank cannot be made liable unless they received some benefit from the breach of trust. It seems to us in principle that a trustee dealing in breach of trust with a beneficiary who has just attained the age of 21 years must realise the danger that such beneficiary may be acting under the influence of a parent. We do not see how a trustee can possibly escape the consequences of that knowledge. ... Without expressing a final opinion, we think that the true view may be that a trustee carrying out a transaction in breach of trust may be liable if he knew, or ought to have known, that the beneficiary was acting under the undue influence of another, or may be presumed to have done so, but will not be liable if it cannot be established that he so knew, or ought to have known.

 Alert

That is sufficient for the purposes of the present case, for, of course, the bank knew very exactly the ages of each of the children, and they knew further that as each child attained 21, that child received advances from the bank which went straight into the banking account of the mother. Indeed, in Ann's case plans were made to effect this unhappy result even before the child attained 21. Accordingly, it seems to us clear that if it can be established that the presumption exists in any given case, the bank are fixed with notice of it and cannot rely on any consents given under such influence.

The bank also rely for relief from the consequences of any breach of trust upon section 61 of the Trustee Act, 1925. At this stage all we propose to say is that it would be a misconstruction of the section to say that it does not apply to professional trustees, but, as was pointed out in the Judicial Committee of the Privy Council in National Trustees Company of Australasia Ltd v General Finance Company of Australasia Ltd., "... without saying that the remedial provisions of the section should never be applied to a trustee in the position of the appellants, their Lordships think it is a circumstance to be taken into account ..." Where a banker undertakes to act as a paid trustee of a settlement created by a customer, and so deliberately places itself in a position where its duty as trustee conflicts with its interest as a banker, we think that the court should be very slow to relieve such a trustee under the provisions of the section. ...

 Alert

LORD JUSTICE UPJOHN

Continuing reading the judgment of the court: ...

It seems to us that the whole picture must be looked at, and it is from the documents that a fairly clear view can be had. It does not appear that the mother, the source of the money was more than a cypher willing to sign whatever her husband put before her. He controlled the family fortune by his right to draw on the family banking account, and he assumed throughout that what he said would go. As we have already said, he was the originator of all the transactions complained of here. His method was to cajole the bank into going as far as they thought they dared, and then to prepare what he called "chits" (or sometimes got them prepared by the bank) and send them to his wife or the child or children concerned for signature. So far this looks like a typical case where undue influence ought to be presumed, but the judge, who saw the witnesses, was chary of acting upon the presumption. The impression he got was of a united family determined to extract from the bank by hook or by crook the money necessary to continue its extravagant way of life. On this view of it, the passage we have quoted about the sons being willing to sign anything bears a less sinister aspect. At the time of this advance the son George was twenty-three years old. He had done his military service, and was up at Cambridge. The judge thought him an exceptionally able young man, well acquainted with his rights, and able to take care of himself. He had no separate advice about this £2,000 advance, but he had been advised about the Hodson loan transaction, and in the course of receiving the explanations then offered he must have realised what the power was which the trustees were purporting to exercise. ...

The case of the other son, Francis, is quite different. He was at this time 28 years old, and was apparently living for the most part with his grandmother, so that he was removed from immediate parental control. On the other hand, we now know that he was a schizophrenic. This diagnosis had been made in 1940 when he found one day of life in the Royal Air Force altogether too much for him, and was repeated by a doctor who saw him in 1951. He was not called by either side, it being agreed that his memory was not at all to be trusted. Consent to this, as to other transactions in which he was involved, was written out and sent to him by his father. There is no letter from him anywhere in the correspondence. No representative of the bank ever saw him. He was obviously left purposely in the background. On the other hand, he was capable of teaching in a boys school, which he did for two years towards the end of the war, and was accepted for entry to Edinburgh University after the war, where also he continued for two years as a student. Further, when he went with his brother to be advised over the Hodson loan, the partner in Farrer & Co who saw him thought him capable of understanding the transaction. Moreover, it has never been alleged that he was at any material time incapacitated from contracting or conducting business affairs by reason of his mental health, though we cannot think that if the bank had known of his history of ill-health they would have acted on the consents he returned signed to his father. But the bank did not know the facts. We have considered anxiously whether, before making an advance, they should have made some inquiry into his circumstances. ... On the whole, we do not feel able to say that the presumption of undue influence must be held to exist between Francis and his parents having regard to his age and his absence from home, and we conclude that the bank were not bound to make inquiries as to his state of mind or fitness as an object of the power they were affecting to exercise. Accordingly, though this was the plainest breach of trust, we agree with the judge that the bank have a good defence, for they obtained consents from the two children concerned, and they were emancipated. ...

 Alert

The next victim on the list was the daughter Ann. ...

There is no doubt that Ann asked for each of these sums to be advanced, and it is clear that on each such occasion that Ann requested these advances she did so in writing, and represented that they were required for furniture, etc., well knowing in fact that only about £300 was expended on the purchase of furniture from start to finish. The rest went in the family living expenses through the mother's account. Of course, Ann appreciated that these representations were untrue; "silly lies," as she said in the witness-box. The judge refused to give relief to Ann in these respects. He carefully set out the details of the payments. We think it is to be inferred that he did not believe that Ann was so innocent as she pretended in the witness-box, saying that she always regarded the money as her mother's. Nevertheless, the judge was clearly of opinion that a presumption of undue influence applied in Ann's case because he stated it was essential that she should have independent advice on the transaction. Independent advice she did have on the purchase of the house, but none upon the expenditure on furniture, which was quite a separate matter, and this the judge overlooked. The judge says that the bank acted on the faith of untrue statements by Ann, and refused Ann relief on this ground. We cannot agree with this. If the judge meant no more than that the bank required some document signed by Ann stating that the money was required for furniture, we agree with him, but we do not think that the bank can have really acted on a sincere belief in the truth of the representations; their supine conduct shows that they really could have no more than a pious hope, which they did not dare to test by pressing to see receipts for the purchase of this vast quantity of furniture, that most of it was being invested in furniture. A moment's study of the mother's account at this time would have shown that even this was improbable. They merely wanted some document which, as they thought, would give legal justification for making the payments.

Further, it seems to us that these very untrue statements must be treated as issuing out of the presumed undue influence of her father, made, as they were, either to the bank in his presence, or by arrangement with him. Finally, we do not consider that these statements, if true, would, as the judge held, have justified the advances... . The bank at this stage ought to have had their eyes wide open to the situation and insisted on calling a halt to this reckless expenditure apparently for furniture. Ann by her counsel concedes that she must give credit for £300 of furniture actually purchased. Subject to that, we feel constrained to come to the conclusion that, without separate advice, the bank cannot rely on the assent of this young girl to gifts direct into her mother's and father's pockets, and we hold the bank liable in respect of advances numbered 8, 10, 12, 17, 18, half of 20 and 22 as set out in the statement of claim, and pro tanto allow the appeal accordingly. Having behaved unreasonably, the bank cannot rely on section 61.

 Alert

Ann's portion had now been fully used, but there remained one chicken to be plucked, a younger brother, Anthony... . He attained 21 on June 15, 1951, and three days after that event there is recorded an interview with the father, the terms of which are too important to omit. "Date June 18, 1951. Interview with Commander Younghusband. They want £2,000 to be raised for the youngest son. Mr Burrell is to write to the boy explaining that the money will be his to do as he likes with and when that has been done and we receive Mrs Younghusband's formal request we are to raise the money and get the boy's directions for its disposal."

As the judge said, the process had become streamlined. So long as Burrell could write a letter telling the boy the money was his, all else would be automatic. This is exactly what happened. Burrell wrote a most perfunctory letter to the young man in Germany which he agreed in the witness-box could not constitute proper separate advice, and in fairness to him was not intended to be more than a pipe opener to a lawyer's relationship with a potential client, and between July 11, 1951, and February 7, 1952, £6,500 was paid straight into the mother's account. There is one payment which is characteristic. The father had succeeded to the tune of £1,000 in raising the wind by a charge on Ann's house, and half the first payment to Anthony was used to repay the bank this amount, thus robbing Anthony to pay Ann. There was not even a pretence in any instance of any countervailing benefit to Anthony except as mentioned later. We do not feel any doubt that the bank is liable on these payments, as the judge held. Relief under section 61 is out of the question.

 Alert

… As to acquiescence, we think that this must be looked at rather broadly. … In this case it would be wrong, we feel, to place any disability upon the beneficiaries because it so happened that George was a member of the bar, and had been in well-known chambers. He had not been in Chancery chambers where it may be said that these things are better understood; but the real truth of the matter is that a party cannot be held to have acquiesced unless he knew, or ought to have known, what his rights were. On the facts of this case we cannot criticise any of the plaintiffs for failing to appreciate their rights until another junior counsel, whom they consulted on a far-fetched and futile scheme of George's for avoiding estate duty on his mother's death, advised that the advances might be improper That was in 1954, and thereupon the family, headed, of course, by George, took immediate steps to explore this matter. This is a most complicated action, and many matters had to be explored before an action for breach of trust could properly be mounted. The writ was issued in 1958, and we do not think it right to hold that the plaintiffs were debarred by acquiescence from bringing an action which otherwise, to the extent we have indicated, is justified. …

In my judgment, therefore, the only question that arises is whether the bank should be relieved from the consequences of their breach of trust under section 61 of the Trustee Act, 1925, to any, and if so, what extent. This, I think, is a very difficult question. The judgment of the court has already pointed out that the bank were personally innocent, but they were ill-advised by their own solicitors; but the bank must accept responsibility for such negligence, and section 61 cannot possibly be invoked to relieve them from its consequences without more. The circumstance that seems to me to make the application of the section possible is that the bank received the letter quoted in the judgment of the court written by Burrell on behalf of Francis and George saying that the matter was in a satisfactory state. Thereafter it would have been quite unreasonable for the bank to take any further step to assure themselves that the transaction had been properly carried out, and they were lulled into a false sense of security. Section 61 is purely discretionary, and its application necessarily depends on the particular facts of each case. I think, in the circumstances of this case, that I am prepared to hold that the bank acted honestly (that is not in dispute) and reasonably and ought fairly to be excused to the extent of the surrender value of the policies transferred to the boys at the date of the transaction, about £650, but no doubt the exact figure can be ascertained. I do not see how the bank can properly be relieved to any greater extent. …

 Alert

In this case there were numerous breaches that took place over an extended period, which means the full facts of the case are extremely complicated. However, the general principles applied to the case are clear. Firstly, where the trustee knows or ought to have known that the beneficiary was giving trust property to another as a consequence of undue influence, then the trustee will be in breach of trust. Furthermore, if the beneficiary is a child then undue influence from a parent can be rebuttably presumed where the child is not emancipated from parental control. When emancipation will take place will depend upon the facts of the case.

Secondly, the defence of consent from a beneficiary would appear to only be present where the beneficiary is *sui juris*, gives consent free of any external pressure or undue influence, and at least understands the nature of the proposed breach. Subsequent acquiescence to a breach can also only take place where the beneficiary knew or ought to have known their rights under the trust and the breach of these rights which the beneficiary has forgiven.

Thirdly, whilst the Trustee Act 1925 s 61 was held to apply to both lay and professional trustees, the courts will look at the trustee's acts to see if the trustee has acted honestly, fairly, and ought reasonably to be excused from liability. If any of the criteria are missing, particularly acting in a reasonable way, then the court will not apply s 61. It is important to also note that s 61 is a last resort defence for a trustee and the general body of caselaw suggests it will only ever be applied by the court in truly meritorious circumstances. The fact that the trustee breached the trust as a consequence of incorrect legal advice is not a sufficiently meritorious circumstance, as held in *Re Pauling's Settlement Trusts*.

Another statutory defence within the court's discretion is the ability to impound a beneficiary's interest to be used by the trustee as an indemnity to the extent that the beneficiary's interest can replace any loss suffered by the trust.

Re Pauling's Settlement Trusts (No 2) [1963] Ch 576

Panel: Wilberforce J

Statute: Trustee Act 1925 s 62

Facts: After judgment was given in the High Court decision of *Re Pauling's Settlement Trusts*, the claimants took out a summons to appoint new trustees. The trustees, Coutts Bank, refused the new appointment on the ground that they were entitled to the interest of the life tenant, Mrs Younghusband, and that their removal as trustees would imperil their right to impound this interest. It was held that the trustees did not have a right to remain as trustees until they had impounded Mrs Younghusband's equitable interest, as s 62 could be exercised by the court in favour of a former trustee. However, in the circumstance it was not suitable to appoint new trustees.

MR JUSTICE WILBERFORCE

... What is said by the defendants is that that right to impound would be prejudiced if new trustees were appointed now and the trust fund handed over to them. That involves a consideration as to what is the nature of the right to impound which exists in favour of a trustee who has committed a breach of trust at the instigation of a beneficiary. I have to consider both the ordinary right which exists in equity apart from statute and also the further statutory right which has been conferred by section 62 of the Trustee Act, 1925, both of which are invoked by the defendants as plaintiffs in the Chancery action now pending. It seems to me that it is not possible to maintain, as is the defendants' contention here, that a trustee, having committed a breach of trust, is entitled to remain as a trustee until it has exercised its right to impound the income of the beneficiary in order to recoup itself. That seems to me an impossible proposition. It is quite true that, in the reported authorities, there is no case where the right to impound has been exercised by a former trustee as distinct from an existing trustee, but it seems to me in principle that it is impossible to contend that the right to impound is limited to the case where the trustee seeking the right is an actual trustee. The nature of the right to impound seems to me to turn on two things: first, that the money paid back to capital is in its origin the money of the trustee, and that when it comes to considering who should get the income of it, the trustee who has provided the money has a better right to it than the tenant for life who has instigated the breach of trust. The alternative way of putting the matter is that the trustee in breach of trust is in some way subrogated to the rights of the beneficiary. He stands in his position in order that he may be indemnified. …

It is said that the defendants have a right to control the investment of the trust fund, so that it is not invested in such a way as to prejudice their right to recoup out of income. That point seems to me to be completely misconceived. It is, of course, the duty of any trustee to exercise his powers of investment in such a way as to hold the balance properly between capital and income. If the fund were transferred to new trustees they would be under that duty and it is to be observed… in place of the life tenant, and the plaintiffs who are in the position of those entitled to capital. The new trustees would be under the normal duty of preserving an equitable balance, and if at any time it was shown they were inclining one way or the other, it would not be a difficult matter to bring them to account.

It is clear from Wilberforce J's judgment that s 62 is not meant to replace the court's inherent power to impound a beneficiary's interest under the trust but is in addition to this power. However it must be noted that defences under ss 61 and 62 will only be allowed by the court in truly meritorious circumstances.

Further Reading

Chambers R 'Liability' in P Birks and A Pretto (eds) *Breach of Trust* (2002) Hart Publishing, Chapter 1.

Hayton D and Mitchell C, *Hayton & Marshall Commentary and Cases on The Law of Trusts and Equitable Remedies*, 12th edition, pp 705-711

Penner J E, *The Law of Trusts*, 6th edition, pp 311-327

Mitchell C 'Equitable Rights and Wrongs' (2006) 59 CLP 267

15

Tracing

Topic List

Introduction

Tracing is used as a generic term to describe two processes: following and tracing. Following is the process of identifying the same asset as it moves from person to person. Tracing is the term used when one asset is exchanged for another and is the process of identifying the new asset as a substitute for the original. Lord Millett outlined the nature of tracing very clearly in the House of Lords decision below.

Foskett v McKeown and Others [2001] 1 AC 102

Panel: Lord Browne-Wilkinson, Lord Steyn, Lord Hoffmann, Lord Hope of Craighead and Lord Millett

Facts: The appellants had entered into contracts with a Mr Murphy to purchase land in Portugal. It was agreed that Murphy would hold the appellants' money on trust until the land was developed and transferred. Murphy used the money to pay some annual premiums on his life insurance policy. He held this policy for the benefit of the defendants. Murphy then committed suicide and the policy paid out £1 million. The appellants sought to trace their money into the money paid out on Murphy's death. At first instance they were held to be entitled to 53.46%, being the proportion of the premiums paid with their money. The Court of Appeal held that they were merely entitled to a charge over the proceeds of the policy to recover their money, together with interest thereon. The appeal was successful and the House of Lords held them to be entitled to the same proportion of the payment as the proportion of the premiums which had been paid with their money.

LORD MILLETT

My Lords, this is a textbook example of tracing through mixed substitutions. At the beginning of the story the plaintiffs were beneficially entitled under an express trust to a sum standing in the name of Mr Murphy in a bank account. From there the money moved into and out of various bank accounts where in breach of trust it was inextricably mixed by Mr Murphy with his own money. After each transaction was completed the plaintiffs' money formed an indistinguishable part of the balance standing to Mr Murphy's credit in his bank account. The amount of that balance represented a debt due from the bank to Mr Murphy, that is to say a chose in action. At the penultimate stage the plaintiffs' money was represented by an indistinguishable part of a different chose in action, viz, the debt prospectively and contingently due from an insurance company to its policyholders, being the trustees of a settlement made by Mr Murphy for the benefit of his children. At the present and final stage it forms an indistinguishable part of the balance standing to the credit of the respondent trustees in their bank account.

Tracing and following

The process of ascertaining what happened to the plaintiffs' money involves both tracing and following. These are both exercises in locating assets which are or may be taken to represent an asset belonging to the plaintiffs and to which they assert ownership. The processes of following and tracing are, however, distinct. Following is the process of following the same asset as it moves from hand to hand. Tracing is the process of identifying a new asset as the substitute for the old. Where one asset is exchanged for another, a claimant can elect whether to follow the original asset into the hands of the new owner or to trace its value into the new asset in the hands of the same owner. In practice his choice is often dictated by the circumstances. In the present case the plaintiffs do not seek to follow the money any further once it reached the bank or insurance company, since its identity was lost in the hands of the recipient (which in any case obtained an unassailable title as a bona fide purchaser for value without notice of the plaintiffs' beneficial interest). Instead the plaintiffs have chosen at each stage to trace the money into its proceeds, viz, the debt presently due from the bank to the account holder or the debt prospectively and contingently due from the insurance company to the policy holders.

Alert

Having completed this exercise, the plaintiffs claim a continuing beneficial interest in the insurance money. Since this represents the product of Mr Murphy's own money as well as theirs, which Mr Murphy mingled indistinguishably in a single chose in action, they claim a beneficial interest in a proportionate part of the money only. The transmission of a claimant's property rights from one asset to its traceable proceeds is part of our law of property, not of the law of unjust enrichment. There is no "unjust factor" to justify restitution (unless "want of title" be one, which makes the point). The claimant succeeds if at all by virtue of his own title, not to reverse unjust enrichment. Property rights are determined by fixed rules and settled principles. They are not discretionary. They do not depend upon ideas of what is "fair, just and reasonable". Such concepts, which in reality mask decisions of legal policy, have no place in the law of property.

A beneficiary of a trust is entitled to a continuing beneficial interest not merely in the trust property but in its traceable proceeds also, and his interest binds every one who takes the property or its traceable proceeds except a bona fide purchaser for value without notice. In the present case the plaintiffs' beneficial interest plainly bound Mr Murphy, a trustee who wrongfully mixed the trust money with his own and whose every dealing with the money (including the payment of the premiums) was in breach of trust. It similarly binds his successors, the trustees of the children's settlement, who claim no beneficial interest of their own, and Mr Murphy's children, who are volunteers. They gave no value for what they received and derive their interest from Mr Murphy by way of gift.

Tracing

We speak of money at the bank, and of money passing into and out of a bank account. But of course the account holder has no money at the bank. Money paid into a bank account belongs legally and beneficially to the bank and not to the account holder. The bank gives value for it, and it is accordingly not usually possible to make the money itself the subject of an adverse claim. Instead a claimant normally sues the account holder rather than the bank and lays claim to the proceeds of the money in his hands. These consist of the debt or part of the debt due to him from the bank. We speak of tracing money into and out of the account, but there is no money in the account. There is merely a single debt of an amount equal to the final balance standing to the credit of the account holder. No money passes from paying bank to receiving bank or through the clearing system (where the money flows may be in the opposite direction). There is simply a series of debits and credits which are causally and transactionally linked. We also speak of tracing one asset into another, but this too is inaccurate. The original asset still exists in the hands of the new owner, or it may have become untraceable. The claimant claims the new asset because it was acquired in whole or in part with the original asset. What he traces, therefore, is not the physical asset itself but the value inherent in it.

 Alert

Tracing is thus neither a claim nor a remedy. It is merely the process by which a claimant demonstrates what has happened to his property, identifies its proceeds and the persons who have handled or received them, and justifies his claim that the proceeds can properly be regarded as representing his property. Tracing is also distinct from claiming. It identifies the traceable proceeds of the claimant's property. It enables the claimant to substitute the traceable proceeds for the original asset as the subject matter of his claim. But it does not affect or establish his claim. That will depend on a number of factors including the nature of his interest in the original asset. He will normally be able to maintain the same claim to the substituted asset as he could have maintained to the original asset. If he held only a security interest in the original asset, he cannot claim more than a security interest in its proceeds. But his claim may also be exposed to potential defences as a result of intervening transactions. Even if the plaintiffs could demonstrate what the bank had done with their money, for example, and could thus identify its traceable proceeds in the hands of the bank, any claim by them to assert ownership of those proceeds would be defeated by the bona fide purchaser defence. The successful completion of a tracing exercise may be preliminary to a personal claim (as in *El Ajou v Dollar Land Holdings plc* [1993] 3 All ER 717) or a proprietary one, to the enforcement of a legal right (as in *Trustees of the Property of F C Jones & Sons v Jones* [1997] Ch 159) or an equitable one.

15.1 When is Tracing Possible?

Re Diplock [1948] Ch 465

Panel: Lord Greene MR, Wrottesley and Evershed LJJ

Facts: Caleb Diplock had left the residue of his estate 'for such charitable institution or institutions or other charitable or benevolent object or objects in England as my acting executors or executor may in their or his absolute discretion select'. His executors had paid out a large amount of the residue to various charities before his next-of-kin challenged the validity of the clause. The House of Lords held the gift to be void as it was not for exclusively charitable purposes. This case concerned the next of kin's claims to recover the money wrongly paid out to the charities.

15.1.1 Into whose hands can property be traced?

Property cannot be traced into the hands of a bone fide purchaser for value without notice.

> LORD GREENE MR
>
> Where the moneys are handed by way of transfer to a person who takes for value without notice, the claim of the owner of the moneys is extinguished just as all other equitable estates or interests are extinguished by a purchase for value without notice.
>
> In the case, however, of a volunteer who takes without notice, e.g., by way of gift from the fiduciary agent, if there is no question of mixing, he holds the money on behalf of the true owner whose equitable right to the money still persists as against him. On the other hand, if the volunteer mixes the money with money of his own, or receives it mixed from the fiduciary agent, he must admit the claim of the true owner, but is not precluded from setting up his own claim in respect of the moneys of his own which have been contributed to the mixed fund. The result is that they share pari passu. It would be inequitable for the volunteer to claim priority for the reason that he is a volunteer: it would be equally inequitable for the true owner of the money to claim priority over the volunteer for the reason that the volunteer is innocent and cannot be said to act unconscionably if he claims equal treatment for himself. The mutual recognition of one another's rights is what equity insists upon as a condition of giving relief

Lord Greene MR also cited the situation where a fiduciary mixes property acquired from two different funds, and noted Lord Parker's conclusions on this in *Sinclair v Brougham* [1914] AC 398.

> The first of Lord Parker's own two illustrations is the case where a person standing in a fiduciary relation to two different persons acquires property by means of a mixed fund of money part of which had belonged to one and part to the other. In such a case each has an equal equity. Each is entitled to a charge and neither is entitled to priority over the other. The explanation of this result lies in the fact that each has an equitable right of property and that right of property can be traced by each into the asset purchased. Equity gives effect to this right by means of the equitable remedy of a declaration of charge.

15.1.2 Property cannot be traced if it has been dissipated

Much of the wrongly paid out money had been spent on unsecured debts or to pay general expenses. Lord Greene MR held that this money could not be traced.

> The equitable remedies pre-suppose the continued existence of the money either as a separate fund or as part of a mixed fund or as latent in property acquired by means of such a fund. If, on the facts of any individual case, such continued existence is not

established, equity is as helpless as the common law itself. If the fund, mixed or unmixed, is spent upon a dinner, equity, which dealt only in specific relief and not in damages, could do nothing.

It is, therefore, a necessary matter for consideration in each case where it is sought to trace money in equity, whether it has such a continued existence, actual or notional, as will enable equity to grant specific relief.

He considered the specific case of money spent on a pre-owned asset by an innocent volunteer.

In the present cases, however, the charities have used the Diplock money, not in combination with money of their own to acquire new assets, but in the alteration and improvement of assets which they already owned. The altered and improved asset owes its existence, therefore, to a combination of land belonging to the charity and money belonging to the Diplock estate. The question whether tracing is possible and if so to what extent, and also the question whether an effective remedy by way of declaration of charge can be granted consistently with an equitable treatment of the charity as an innocent volunteer, present quite different problems from those arising in the simple case above stated. In the case of the purchase of an asset out of a mixed fund, both categories of money are, as we have said, necessarily present throughout the existence of the asset in an identifiable form. In the case of adaptation of property of the volunteer by means of trust money, it by no means necessarily follows that the money can be said to be present in the adapted property. The beneficial owner of the trust money seeks to follow and recover that money and claims to use the machinery of a charge on the adapted property in order to enable him to do so. But in the first place the money may not be capable of being followed. In every true sense, the money may have disappeared. A simple example suggests itself. The owner of a house who, as an innocent volunteer, has trust money in his hands given to him by a trustee uses that money in making an alteration to his house so as to fit it better to his own personal needs. The result may add not one penny to the value of the house. Indeed, the alteration may well lower its value; for the alteration, though convenient to the owner, may be highly inconvenient in the eyes of a purchaser. Can it be said in such cases that the trust money can be traced and extracted from the altered asset? Clearly not, for the money will have disappeared leaving no monetary trace behind: the asset will not have increased (or may even have depreciated) in value through its use.

But the matter does not end here. What, for the purposes of the inquiry, is to be treated as "the charity property"? Is it to be the whole of the land belonging to the charity? or is it to be only that part of it which was altered or reconstructed or on which a building has been erected by means of Diplock money? If the latter, the result may well be that the property, both in its original state and as altered or improved, will, when taken in isolation, have little or no value. What would be the value of a building in the middle of Guy's hospital without any means of access through other parts of the hospital property? If, on the other hand, the charge is to be on the whole of the charity land, it might well be thought an extravagant result if the Diplock estate, because Diplock money had been used to reconstruct a corner of it, were to be entitled to a charge on the entirety.

15.2 The Remedies Available as a Result of Tracing

Foskett v McKeown and Others [2001] 1 AC 102

Panel: Lord Browne-Wilkinson, Lord Steyn, Lord Hoffmann, Lord Hope of Craighead and Lord Millett

Having described tracing as a process (see the nature of tracing above) Lord Millett then identified the remedies available as a result of tracing. He noted that any remedy would depend on property rights rather than unjust enrichment.

LORD MILLETT

The cause of action

As I have already pointed out, the plaintiffs seek to vindicate their property rights, not to reverse unjust enrichment. The correct classification of the plaintiffs' cause of action may appear to be academic, but it has important consequences. The two causes of action have different requirements and may attract different defences.

A plaintiff who brings an action in unjust enrichment must show that the defendant has been enriched at the plaintiff's expense, for he cannot have been unjustly enriched if he has not been enriched at all. But the plaintiff is not concerned to show that the defendant is in receipt of property belonging beneficially to the plaintiff or its traceable proceeds. The fact that the beneficial ownership of the property has passed to the defendant provides no defence; indeed, it is usually the very fact which founds the claim. Conversely, a plaintiff who brings an action like the present must show that the defendant is in receipt of property which belongs beneficially to him or its traceable proceeds, but he need not show that the defendant has been enriched by its receipt. He may, for example, have paid full value for the property, but he is still required to disgorge it if he received it with notice of the plaintiff's interest.

15.2.1 A straightforward substitution

Here the beneficiary can chose between claiming the property and a personal claim against the wrongdoer, which could be enforced by a lien or charge on the property.

The simplest case is where a trustee wrongfully misappropriates trust property and uses it exclusively to acquire other property for his own benefit. In such a case the beneficiary is entitled at his option either to assert his beneficial ownership of the proceeds or to bring a personal claim against the trustee for breach of trust and enforce an equitable lien or charge on the proceeds to secure restoration of the trust fund. He will normally exercise the option in the way most advantageous to himself. If the traceable proceeds have increased in value and are worth more than the original asset, he will assert his beneficial ownership and obtain the profit for himself. There is nothing unfair in this. The trustee cannot be permitted to keep any profit resulting from his misappropriation for himself, and his donees cannot obtain a better title than their donor. If the traceable proceeds are worth less than the original asset, it does not usually matter how the beneficiary exercises his option. He will take the whole of the proceeds on either basis. This is why it is not possible to identify the basis on which the claim succeeded in some of the cases.

Both remedies are proprietary and depend on successfully tracing the trust property into its proceeds. A beneficiary's claim against a trustee for breach of trust is a personal claim. It does not entitle him to priority over the trustee's general creditors unless he can trace the trust property into its product and establish a proprietary interest in the proceeds. If the beneficiary is unable to trace the trust property into its proceeds, he still has a personal claim against the trustee, but his claim will be unsecured. The beneficiary's proprietary claims to the trust property or its traceable proceeds can be maintained against the wrongdoer and anyone who derives title from him except a bona fide purchaser for value without notice of the breach of trust. The same rules apply even where there have been numerous successive transactions, so long as the tracing exercise is successful and no bona fide purchaser for value without notice has intervened.

15.2.2 The property being traced has been mixed with other property

The beneficiary can choose between claiming a proportion of the property equivalent to the proportion his contribution bore to the purchase price or a lien or charge on the property for the amount of his contribution.   Alternatively he would have a personal claim against the wrongdoer.

A more complicated case is where there is a mixed substitution. This occurs where the trust money represents only part of the cost of acquiring the new asset. As James Barr Ames pointed out in "Following Misappropriated Property into its Product" (1906) 19 HarvLRev 511, consistency requires that, if a trustee buys property partly with his own money and partly with trust money, the beneficiary should have the option of taking a proportionate part of the new property or a lien upon it, as may be most for his advantage. In principle it should not matter (and it has never previously been suggested that it does) whether the trustee mixes the trust money with his own and buys the new asset with the mixed fund or makes separate payments of the purchase price (whether simultaneously or sequentially) out of the different funds. In every case the value formerly inherent in the trust property has become located within the value inherent in the new asset.

The rule, and its rationale, were stated by Samuel Williston in "The Right to Follow Trust Property when Confused with other Property" (1888) 2 HarvLRev 28, 29:

"If the trust fund is traceable as having furnished in part the money with which a certain investment was made, and the proportion it formed of the whole money so invested is known or ascertainable, the cestui que trust should be allowed to regard the acts of the trustee as done for his benefit, in the same way that he would be allowed to if all the money so invested had been his; that is, he should be entitled in equity to an undivided share of the property which the trust money contributed to purchase—such a proportion of the whole as the trust money bore to the whole money invested. The reason in the one case as in the other is that the trustee cannot be allowed to make a profit from the use of the trust money, and if the property which he wrongfully purchased were held subject only to a lien for the amount invested, any appreciation in value would go to the trustee."

If this correctly states the underlying basis of the rule (as I believe it does), then it is impossible to distinguish between the case where mixing precedes the investment and the case where it arises on and in consequence of the investment. It is also impossible to distinguish between the case where the investment is retained by the trustee and the case where it is given away to a gratuitous donee. The donee cannot obtain a better title than his donor, and a donor who is a trustee cannot be allowed to profit from his trust.

In *In re Hallett's Estate; Knatchbull v Hallett* (1880) 13 ChD 696 , 709 Sir George Jessel MR acknowledged that where an asset was acquired exclusively with trust money, the beneficiary could either assert equitable ownership of the asset or enforce a lien or charge over it to recover the trust money. But he appeared to suggest that in the case of a mixed substitution the beneficiary is confined to a lien. Any authority that this dictum might otherwise have is weakened by the fact that Sir George Jessel MR gave no reason for the existence of any such rule, and none is readily apparent. The dictum was plainly obiter, for the fund was deficient and the plaintiff was only claiming a lien. It has usually been cited only to be explained away: see for example In *re Tilley's Will Trusts* [1967] Ch 1179, 1186, per Ungoed-Thomas J; Burrows, The Law of Restitution (1993), p 368. It was rejected by the High Court of Australia in *Scott v Scott* (1963) 109 CLR 649: see the passage at pp 661-662 cited by Morritt LJ below [1998] Ch 265, 300-301. It has not been adopted in the United States: see the American Law Institute, Restatement of the Law, Trusts, 2d (1959) at section 202(h). In *Primeau v Granfield* (1911) 184 F 480 , Learned Hand J expressed himself in forthright terms: "On principle there can be no excuse for such a rule."

In my view the time has come to state unequivocally that English law has no such rule. It conflicts with the rule that a trustee must not benefit from his trust. I agree with Burrows that the beneficiary's right to elect to have a proportionate share of a mixed substitution necessarily follows once one accepts, as English law does, (i) that a claimant can trace in equity into a mixed fund and (ii) that he can trace unmixed money into its proceeds and assert ownership of the proceeds.

Accordingly, I would state the basic rule as follows. Where a trustee wrongfully uses trust money to provide part of the cost of acquiring an asset, the beneficiary is entitled at his option either to claim a proportionate share of the asset or to enforce a lien upon it to secure his personal claim against the trustee for the amount of the misapplied money. It does not matter whether the trustee mixed the trust money with his own in a single fund before using it to acquire the asset, or made separate payments (whether

 Alert

simultaneously or sequentially) out of the differently owned funds to acquire a single asset.

Two observations are necessary at this point. First, there is a mixed substitution (with the results already described) whenever the claimant's property has contributed in part only towards the acquisition of the new asset. It is not necessary for the claimant to show in addition that his property has contributed to any increase in the value of the new asset. This is because, as I have already pointed out, this branch of the law is concerned with vindicating rights of property and not with reversing unjust enrichment. Secondly, the beneficiary's right to claim a lien is available only against a wrongdoer and those deriving title under him otherwise than for value. It is not available against competing contributors who are innocent of any wrongdoing. The tracing rules are not the result of any presumption or principle peculiar to equity. They correspond to the common law rules for following into physical mixtures (though the consequences may not be identical). Common to both is the principle that the interests of the wrongdoer who was responsible for the mixing and those who derive title under him otherwise than for value are subordinated to those of innocent contributors. As against the wrongdoer and his successors, the beneficiary is entitled to locate his contribution in any part of the mixture and to subordinate their claims to share in the mixture until his own contribution has been satisfied. This has the effect of giving the beneficiary a lien for his contribution if the mixture is deficient.

15.2.3 The property has been mixed with property of innocent contributors

Where the beneficiary's property is mixed with that of an innocent contributor, a lien will not be available. The property must be shared rateably, that is proportionately.

Innocent contributors, however, must be treated equally inter se. Where the beneficiary's claim is in competition with the claims of other innocent contributors, there is no basis upon which any of the claims can be subordinated to any of the others. Where the fund is deficient, the beneficiary is not entitled to enforce a lien for his contributions; all must share rateably in the fund.

The primary rule in regard to a mixed fund, therefore, is that gains and losses are borne by the contributors rateably. The beneficiary's right to elect instead to enforce a lien to obtain repayment is an exception to the primary rule, exercisable where the fund is deficient and the claim is made against the wrongdoer and those claiming through him. It is not necessary to consider whether there are any circumstances in which the beneficiary is confined to a lien in cases where the fund is more than sufficient to repay the contributions of all parties. It is sufficient to say that he is not so confined in a case like the present.

15.2.4 Innocent volunteers who are not contributors

It is not enough that those defending the claim are innocent of any wrongdoing if they are not themselves contributors but, like the trustees and Mr Murphy's children in the present case, are volunteers who derive title under the wrongdoer otherwise than for value. On ordinary principles such persons are in no better position than the wrongdoer, and are liable to suffer the same subordination of their interests to those of the claimant as the wrongdoer would have been. They certainly cannot do better than the claimant by confining him to a lien and keeping any profit for themselves.

Similar principles apply to following into physical mixtures: see *Lupton v White* (1808) 15 Ves 432; and *Sandeman & Sons v Tyzack* and *Branfoot Steamship Co Ltd* [1913] AC 680,695 where Lord Moulton said: "If the mixing has arisen from the fault of 'B,' 'A' can claim the goods." There are relatively few cases which deal with the position of the innocent recipient from the wrongdoer, but *Jones v De Marchant* (1916) 28 DLR 561 may be cited as an example. A husband wrongfully used 18 beaver skins belonging to his wife and used them,(sic) together with four skins of his own, to have a fur coat made up which he then gave to his mistress. Unsurprisingly the wife was held entitled to recover the coat. The mistress knew nothing of the true ownership of the skins, but her innocence was held to be immaterial. She was a gratuitous donee and could stand in no better position than the husband. The coat was a new asset manufactured from the skins and not merely the product of intermingling them. The problem could not be solved by a sale of the coat in order to reduce the disputed property to a divisible fund, since (as we shall see) the realisation of an asset does not affect its ownership. It would hardly have been appropriate to require the two ladies to share the coat between them. Accordingly it was an all or nothing case in which the ownership of the coat must be assigned to one or other of the parties. The determinative factor was that the mixing was the act of the wrongdoer through whom the mistress acquired the coat otherwise than for value.

The rule in equity is to the same effect, as Sir William Page Wood V-C observed in *Frith v Cartland* (1865) 2 H & M 417 ,420: "if a man mixes trust funds with his own, the whole will be treated as the trust property, except so far as he may be able to distinguish what is his own". This does not, in my opinion, exclude a pro rata division where this is appropriate, as in the case of money and other fungibles like grain, oil or wine. But it is to be observed that a pro rata division is the best that the wrongdoer and his donees can hope for. If a pro rata division is excluded, the beneficiary takes the whole; there is no question of confining him to a lien. *Jones v De Marchant* 28 DLR 561 is a useful illustration of the principles shared by the common law and equity alike that an innocent recipient who receives misappropriated property by way of gift obtains no better title than his donor, and that if a proportionate sharing is inappropriate the wrongdoer and those who derive title under him take nothing.

15.2.5 The beneficiary's money is spent by a volunteer on a pre-owned asset

This situation was considered by Lord Browne Wilkinson who stated that the only remedy available would be a lien.

LORD BROWNE-WILKINSON

The question of tracing which does arise is whether the rules of tracing are those regulating tracing through a mixed fund or those regulating the position when moneys of one person have been innocently expended on the property of another. In the former case (mixing of funds) it is established law that the mixed fund belongs proportionately to those whose moneys were mixed. In the latter case it is equally clear that money expended on maintaining or improving the property of another normally gives rise, at the most, to a proprietary lien to recover the moneys so expended. In certain cases the rules of tracing in such a case may give rise to no proprietary interest at all if to give such interest would be unfair: see *In re Diplock; Diplock v Wintle* [1948] Ch 465 , 548.

Lord Browne-Wilkinson then noted that the Court of Appeal considered what had happened in this case as being akin to an innocent volunteer spending trust money on pre-owned land.

Cases where the money of one person has been expended on improving or maintaining the physical property of another raise special problems. The property left at the end of the day is incapable of being physically divided into its separate constituent assets, ie the land and the money spent on it. Nor can the rules for tracing moneys through a mixed fund apply: the essence of tracing through a mixed fund is the ability to re-divide the mixed fund into its constituent parts pro rata according to the value of the contributions made to it.

15.2.6 Money is spent paying secured debts

Where the claimant's money is spent to pay off secured debts, the remedy available to him is called subrogation. This allows him to step into the creditor's shoes and become a secured creditor. The rule on subrogation was dealt with in *Bowcawen v Bajwa* [1996] 1 WLR 328.

Boscawen v Bajwa [1996] 1 WLR 328

Panel: Stuart-Smith, Waite and Millett LJJ

Facts: Abbey National, one of the defendants, had advanced money to purchase a house. They were to receive the first legal charge on that house. Before the sale was completed, the money was paid to the vendors and used to discharge the existing mortgage with the Halifax Building Society. The sale then fell through. The plaintiffs were the vendor's creditors who were claiming the house. Abbey National claimed to be subrogated to the position of the Halifax Building Society and thereby to have a charge over the house. The judge held this to be the case. The Court of Appeal dismissed an appeal, holding that Abbey National's money had been held on trust first by the purchaser's solicitors and then the vendor's solicitors, pending completion. The Abbey National therefore had an equitable interest in the money which paid off the Halifax mortgage.

LORD JUSTICE MILLETT

If the plaintiff succeeds in tracing his property, whether in its original or in some changed form, into the hands of the defendant, and overcomes any defences which are put forward on the defendant's behalf, he is entitled to a remedy. The remedy will be fashioned to the circumstances. The plaintiff will generally be entitled to a personal remedy; if he seeks a proprietary remedy he must usually prove that the property to which he lays claim is still in the ownership of the defendant. If he succeeds in doing this the court will treat the defendant as holding the property on a constructive trust for the plaintiff and will order the defendant to transfer it in specie to the plaintiff. But this is only one of the proprietary remedies which are available to a court of equity. If the plaintiff's money has been applied by the defendant, for example, not in the acquisition of a landed property but in its improvement, then the court may treat the land as charged with the payment to the plaintiff of a sum representing the amount by which the value of the defendant's land has been enhanced by the use of the plaintiff's money. And if the plaintiff's money has been used to discharge a mortgage on the defendant's land, then the court may achieve a similar result by treating the land as subject to a charge by way of subrogation in favour of the plaintiff.

Subrogation, therefore, is a remedy, not a cause of action: see Goff & Jones, Law of Restitution, 4th ed. (1993), pp. 589 et seq.; *Orakpo v Manson Investments Ltd* [1978] AC 95,104, per Lord Diplock and *In re T. H. Knitwear (Wholesale) Ltd* [1988] Ch 275,284. It is available in a wide variety of different factual situations in which it is required in order to reverse the defendant's unjust enrichment. Equity lawyers speak of a right of subrogation, or of an equity of subrogation, but this merely reflects the fact that it is not a remedy which the court has a general discretion to impose whenever it thinks it just to do so. The equity arises from the conduct of the parties on well settled principles and in defined circumstances which make it unconscionable for the defendant to deny the proprietary interest claimed by the plaintiff. A constructive trust arises in the same way. Once the equity is established the court satisfies it by declaring that the property in question is subject to a charge by way of subrogation in the one case or a constructive trust in the other.

Accordingly, there was nothing illegitimate in the deputy judge's invocation of the two doctrines of tracing and subrogation in the same case. They arose at different stages of the proceedings. Tracing was the process by which the Abbey National sought to establish that its money was applied in the discharge of the Halifax's charge; subrogation was the remedy which it sought in order to deprive Mr. Bajwa (through whom the appellants claim) of the unjust enrichment which he would thereby otherwise obtain at the Abbey National's expense.

15.3 Payments In and Out of Bank Accounts Representing Mixed Funds

Rules have been developed concerning payments in and out of bank accounts containing mixed funds.

15.3.1 The Claimant and the wrongdoer

Very often a claimant's money will have been paid into the wrongdoer's own bank account. As seen above, the claimant will then have a charge over the wrongdoer's bank account for the value of that money.

15.3.2 Payments out

The general rule is that the first payments out of such a mixed fund are deemed to be of the wrongdoer's own money. This arises from a presumption of honesty. The wrongdoer is deemed to intend to spend his own money before that of the trust.

In re Hallett's Estate, Knatchbull v Hallett (1879-80) LR 13 Ch D 696

Panel: Sir George Jessel MR, Baggallay and Thesiger LJJ

Facts: Hallett was a solicitor who looked after some Russian bonds for his client, Mrs Cotterill. He sold the bonds and paid the proceeds into his bank account, which contained some of his own money. He then withdrew money from his account and used it for his own purposes. The Court held that this money was Hallett's and Mrs Cotterill's money was left in the account. There was enough money in the account for her claim to be met in full.

SIR GEORGE JESSEL MR

Now, first upon principle, nothing can be better settled, either in our own law, or, I suppose, the law of all civilised countries, than this, that where a man does an act which may be rightfully performed, he cannot say that that act was intentionally and in fact done wrongly. A man who has a right of entry cannot say he committed a trespass in entering. A man who sells the goods of another as agent for the owner cannot prevent the owner adopting the sale, and deny that he acted as agent for the owner. It runs throughout our law, and we are familiar with numerous instances in the law of real property. A man who grants a lease believing he has sufficient estate to grant it, although it turns out that he has not, but has a power which enables him to grant it, is not allowed to say he did not grant it under the power. Where ever it can be done rightfully, he is not allowed to say, against the person entitled to the property or the right, that he has done it wrongfully. That is the universal law.

When we come to apply that principle to the case of a trustee who has blended trust moneys with his own, it seems to me perfectly plain that he cannot be heard to say that he took away the trust money when he had a right to take away his own money. The simplest case put is the mingling of trust moneys in a bag with money of the trustee's own. Suppose he has a hundred sovereigns in a bag, and he adds to them another hundred sovereigns of his own, so that they are commingled in such a way that they cannot be distinguished, and the next day he draws out for his own purposes £100, is it tolerable for anybody to allege that what he drew out was the first £100, the trust money, and that he misappropriated it, and left his own £100 in the bag? It is obvious he must have taken away that which he had a right to take away, his own £100. What difference does it make if, instead of being in a bag, he deposits it with his banker, and then pays in other money of his own, and draws out some money for his own purposes? Could he say that he had actually drawn out anything but his own money? His money was there, and he had a right to draw it out, and why should the natural act of simply drawing out the money be attributed to anything except to his ownership of money which was at his bankers.

The presumption that the first payment out is of the wrongdoer's money does not apply when there is no money left in the account to represent the claimant's money. This was held in the case below.

In re Oatway, Hertslet v Oatway [1903] 2 Ch 356

Panel: Joyce J

Facts: Oatway received £7,000 in breach of trust which he paid into his own bank account. He paid out about £5,000 for his own purposes and then paid in £3,000 of his own money. He then bought some shares in the Oceana Company for approximately £2,000. Later the rest of the money in the account was dissipated, but he owned the shares on his death. It was held that the trust could claim the proceeds of the shares.

MR JUSTICE JOYCE

...[I]f money held by any person in a fiduciary capacity be paid into his own banking account, it may be followed by the equitable owner, who, as against the trustee, will have a charge for what belongs to him upon the balance to the credit of the account. If, then, the trustee pays in further sums, and from time to time draws out money by cheques, but leaves a balance to the credit of the account, it is settled that he is not entitled to have the rule in Clayton's Case applied so as to maintain that the sums which have been drawn out and paid away so as to be incapable of being recovered represented pro tanto the trust money, and that the balance remaining is not trust money, but represents only his own moneys paid into the account. Brown v Adams to the contrary ought not to be followed since the decision in In re Hallett's Estate. It is, in my opinion, equally clear that when any of the money drawn out has been invested, and the investment remains in the name or under the control of the trustee, the rest of the balance having been afterwards dissipated by him, he cannot maintain that the investment which remains represents his own money alone, and that what has been spent and can no longer be traced and recovered was the money belonging to the trust. In other words, when the private money of the trustee and that which he held in a fiduciary capacity have been mixed in the same banking account, from which various payments have from time to time been made, then, in order to determine to whom any remaining balance or any investment that may have been paid for out of the account ought to be deemed to belong, the trustee must be debited with all the sums that have been withdrawn and applied to his own use so as to be no longer recoverable, and the trust money in like manner be debited with any sums taken out and duly invested in the names of the proper trustees. The order of priority in which the various withdrawals and investments may have been respectively made is wholly immaterial. I have been referring, of course, to cases where there is only one fiduciary owner or set of cestuis que trust claiming whatever may be left as against the trustee. In the present case there is no balance left. The only investment or property remaining which represents any part of the mixed moneys paid into the banking account is the Oceana shares purchased for 2137l. Upon these, therefore, the trust had a charge for the 3000l. trust money paid into the account. That is to say, those shares and the proceeds thereof belong to the trust.

It was objected that the investment in the Oceana shares was made at a time when Oatway's own share of the balance to the credit of the account (if the whole had been then justly distributed) would have exceeded 2137l., the price of the shares; that he was therefore entitled to withdraw that sum, and might rightly apply it for his own purposes; and that consequently the shares should be held to belong to his estate. To this I answer that he never was entitled to withdraw the 2137l. from the account, or, at all events, that he could not be entitled to take that sum from the account and hold it or the investment made therewith, freed from the charge in favour of the trust, unless or until the trust money paid into the account had been first restored, and the trust fund reinstated by due investment of the money in the joint names of the proper trustees, which never was done.

The investment by Oatway, in his own name, of the 2137l. in Oceana shares no more got rid of the claim or charge of the trust upon the money so invested, than would have been the case if he had drawn a cheque for 2137l. and simply placed and retained the amount in a drawer without further disposing of the money in any way. The proceeds of the Oceana shares must be held to belong to the trust funds under the will of which Oatway and Maxwell Skipper were the trustees

The question remains whether a claimant can claim property bought with an earlier payment out of the account when there is enough money left in the account to satisfy his claim. This has been referred to as 'cherry picking'. Mr Justice Joyce in *Re Oatway* saw the claimant's charge on the whole account lasting only until the trust money had been restored. Lord Millett in *Foskett v McKeown* reiterated this but later left the matter open.

The High Court in *Shalson v Russo* suggested, obiter, that cherry picking might be allowed against the wrongdoer.

Shalson and Others v Russo and Others (Mimran and Another, Part 20 Claimants) [2003] EWHC 1637 [2005] Ch 281

Panel: Rimer J

Facts: This case arose from the business dealings of Russo, an Italian, who had fraudulently obtained money from the claimants and several others, including Mimran, one of the defendants. Mimran was attempting to trace his money into a yacht owned jointly by Shalson and Russo. The court held he was unable to do so, but Mr Justice Rimer stated the following, obiter.

> MR JUSTICE RIMER
>
> 144 This method is a "cherry-picking" exercise, as Mr Smith recognised. But in a case in which the only contest is between the claimant seeking to trace (Mr Mimran) and the wrongdoer (WIB/Mr Russo), there is, he says, every reason why the latter's interests should be subordinated to the claimant's. Normally, it is presumed that if a trustee uses money from a fund in which he has mixed trust money with his own, he uses his own money first: In re Hallett's Estate (1880) 13 Ch D 696. But Mr Smith submits that this is not an inflexible rule and that if the trustee can be shown to have made an early application of the mixed fund into an investment, the beneficiary is entitled to claim that for himself. He says, and I agree, that this is supported by In re Oatway [1903] 2 Ch 356. The justice of this is that, if the beneficiary is not entitled to do this, the wrongdoing trustee may be left with all the cherries and the victim with nothing. The limitation referred to in the penultimate sentence of the previous paragraph is the "lowest intermediate balance" rule, illustrated by James Roscoe (Bolton) Ltd v Winder [1915] 1 Ch 62.

However, in a subsequent case, the High Court refused to allow the claimant to cherry pick. In this case there were unusual facts which meant that, had the claimant been able to cherry pick, she would have acquired the money twice.

Turner v Jacob [2006] EWHC 1317 (Ch), [2008] WTLR 307

Panel: Patten J

Facts: Mrs Turner was a stuntwoman who had appeared in eight James Bond films, as well as Batman, Superman and Robin Hood. Mrs Jacob was the child of her first marriage. Mrs Turner's second husband considered himself as a father to Mrs Jacob, and after he separated from Mrs Turner gave her £75,000 to pay off a mortgage on a property on the understanding that it be given to Mrs Jacob. This was not done. The court held that the £75,000 from the sale of the property was held on trust for Mrs Jacob. Mrs Turner paid the money into her bank account and then dissipated all but £10,399. She later paid her own money into her bank account and bought several properties. When she died she left the residue of her estate, which included the bank account, to Mrs Jacob. Mrs Jacob claimed that, instead of locating her £10,399 in her mother's bank account, she should be able to trace it into a property called Clarkfield which had been bought with money from that bank account.

MR JUSTICE PATTEN

87 On my findings Mrs Jacob was beneficially entitled to a substantial interest in the proceeds of sale of Fleetwood corresponding to the amount paid by Mr Hutchison to redeem the mortgage on the property. That amounted to £75,000 which was the sum retained by Mrs Turner and transferred to her deposit account. Where the trust asset consists of a sum of money which is paid into an account and mixed with other funds belonging to the trustee various rules apply which are designed to give the beneficial owner the benefit of any doubts as to whose assets have been utilised in any subsequent dealings affecting the mixed fund. So the onus is on the trustee in the first place to distinguish his own assets from the trust assets and a failure to do so will result in the assets being presumed to be trust property. Similarly, any withdrawals from a mixed fund are presumed to be of the trustee's own money rather than trust money.

88 A point may, however, be reached when it is clear in arithmetical terms that some or all of the trust money must have been expended. Subsequent deposits in the same account are not presumed to have been intended to replace the lost fund and the tracing claim is therefore limited to what was the lowest intermediate balance prior to the deposit of the trustee's own money: see Snell's Equity (31st ed) para 28–37 and the cases cited therein.

89 In this case there is no need for Mrs Jacob to resort to a tracing claim in order to recover what is due to her in respect of the proceeds of sale of Fleetwood. Her mother's estate would be liable to account for the £75,000 regardless of how the money has been spent but that would reduce the value of the residuary estate and therefore of Mrs Jacob's own share of it. She has not therefore sought recovery of the monies from the estate. Instead she has asserted a beneficial interest in Clarkfield on the basis that the trust monies were used to purchase it. She must therefore show (on an application of the principles I have referred to) that the trust monies were preserved by Mrs Turner and then applied towards the purchase. Although Mr Turner gave no consideration for Clarkfield he is only bound by the same equities as would have affected the property in the hands of his late wife.

Mr Justice Patten then noted the amounts of money paid in and out of the account containing the trust money, and continued:

97 This analysis indicates that the low point was reached in early May 1995 when on any view no more than £10,339.21 of the £75,000 remained. Applying the principles referred to earlier, the tracing claim is therefore limited to identifying what became of that sum without regard to the deposits which were subsequently made from other sources. Those other funds are relevant only insofar as they allow the Court to presume that they would have been used first to meet any subsequent withdrawals from the deposit account and there was no time after May 1995 when the relevant credit balance was less than £10,339.21.

98 On this basis it is possible to trace this sum through to March 1998 when the Diamond Reserve account was closed and the new Crown Reserve account opened. By the same exercise, one can treat the £10,339.21 as retained in the Crown Reserve

account until May 2002 when the £30,000 was paid into the Reserve Reward account. Again, at no time between March 1998 and May 2002 was the credit balance on the Crown Reserve account less than that sum. The Reward Reserve account remained substantially in credit both up to and after the purchase of Clarkfield.

99 Mrs Jacob's case is that she is entitled to treat at least the £10,339.21 as having been used to purchase Clarkfield and Mr Callman's analysis concentrated on the £30,000 transferred into the Reward Reserve account. But it is not clear to me why I should under the rules of tracing described earlier, assume that in 2002 the £10,339.21 was invested in the purchase of Clarkfield rather than being retained in the Reward Reserve account yet should also assume that it was not used for investment in property at a much earlier stage. The point arises because in July 1997 the Diamond Reserve account was used to fund the purchase of Merry Acres. This left a balance on the account of £18,335.09. On Mrs Jacob's case I have to assume that her money was not used as part of the £110,000 transferred to buy that property but was kept in the account as part of the £18,355.09. If the money was used as part of the purchase price of Merry Acres then clearly it was not used to purchase Clarkfield.

100 The rules of tracing which govern a beneficiary's right to follow trust money in a mixed running account are technical rules based on presumptions which are designed to allow the recovery in specie of the trust monies by deeming the trustee to have preserved the trust fund at the expense of his own money regardless of the time at which his own funds were paid into the account. This is the result of the decision in *Re Hallett's Estate* (1880) 13 Ch D 696 which disapplied the rule in *Clayton's case* to accounts in which the only funds were those of the beneficiary and the trustee. The trustee is effectively disabled from asserting that the money withdrawn from the account was trust money if the expenditure can be attributed to his own funds in the account. If, however, the credit balance on the account falls below the amount of the trust monies the presumption can no longer apply and the lowest intermediate balance is, as explained earlier, then taken as the limit of the trust fund for all subsequent purposes. But part of the rationale behind the operation of these rules has to be the requirement that the trustee will preserve the fund and not utilise it for purposes unauthorised by the beneficiary. This principle is on the authorities modified where part of a mixed fund is used for an investment in property or in some other form of security (including another account) and the remaining credit balance is then dissipated. In this case the trustee is not permitted to treat the monies remaining in the account and dissipated as the trust monies. The beneficiary is entitled to assert a lien over the new asset acquired with monies from the mixed account: see *Re Oatway* [1903] 2 Ch 356.

101 In his judgment in *Re Oatway* (at p.361) Joyce J explained the reasoning behind the reversal of the general rule in cases where the monies remaining in the account have been dissipated.

Mr Justice Patten then quoted from the judgment and continued:

102 It seems to me that in a case (such as the present) where the trustee maintains in the account an amount equal to the remaining trust fund, the beneficiary's right to trace is limited to that fund. It is not open to the beneficiary to assert a lien against an

Alert

investment made using monies out of the mixed account unless the sum expended is of such a size that it must have included trust monies or the balance remaining in the account after the investment is then expended so as to become untraceable. That is not the position here. From May 1995 onwards there was always at least £10,339.21 remaining in the successive deposits and that remained the position even after Clarkfield had been purchased. I take the view that under the rules of tracing, Mrs Jacob's lien remained attached to this fund and not to Clarkfield. If I am wrong about that and one has to assume that the trust monies were invested in property then it must follow that they were used to purchase Merry Acres, which was the first property purchase made using the mixed funds. Either way, the claim to an interest in Clarkfield under a resulting trust is not made out.

15.3.3 Payments in – the lowest intermediate balance rule

Once the claimant's money has been paid out of the wrongdoer's bank account, it is not replaced by money subsequently paid in by the wrongdoer. This later money will only be subject to a trust if the wrongdoer shows an intention that it should replace the earlier money.

James Roscoe (Bolton), Limited v Winder [1915] 1 Ch 62

Panel: Sargant J

Facts: The plaintiff company was in voluntary liquidation and the defendant was the trustee in bankruptcy of William Wigham (W). The company had been sold to W and it had been agreed that W would collect the existing debts and pay them to the company. He collected over £6,000 in existing debts, but paid it into his own bank account. The court decided that he was thus holding this money on trust for the company. W spent all but £25 18s of the money. He later paid money into his account. The Court held that the later money did not replace the company's money. It would only have done so if W had shown that a clear intention that he was to hold the later money on trust for the company and he had not done this.

MR JUSTICE SARGANT

But there is a further circumstance in the present case which seems to me to be conclusive in favour of the defendant as regards the greater part of the balance of 358l. 5s. 5d. It appears that after the payment in by the debtor of a portion of the book debts which he had received the balance at the bank on May 19, 1913, was reduced by his drawings to a sum of 25l. 18s. only on May 21. So that, although the ultimate balance at the debtor's death was about 358l. there had been an intermediate balance of only 25l. 18s. The result of that seems to me to be that the trust moneys cannot possibly be traced into this common fund, which was standing to the debtor's credit at his death, to an extent of more than 25l. 18s., because, although prima facie under the second rule in *In re Hallett's Estate* any drawings out by the debtor ought to be attributed to the private moneys which he had at the bank and not to the trust moneys, yet, when the drawings out had reached such an amount that the whole of his private money part had been exhausted, it necessarily followed that the rest of the drawings must have been against trust moneys. There being on May 21, 1913, only 25l. 18s., in all, standing to the credit of the debtor's account, it is quite clear that on that day he must have denuded his account of all the trust moneys there – the whole 455l. 18s. 11d. – except to the extent of 25l. 18s.

Practically, what Mr. Martelli and Mr. Hansell have been asking me to do – although I think Mr. Hansell in particular rather disguised the claim by the phraseology he used – is to say that the debtor, by paying further moneys after May 21 into this common account, was impressing upon those further moneys so paid in the like trust or obligation, or charge of the nature of a trust, which had formerly been impressed upon the previous balances to the credit of that account. No doubt, Mr. Hansell did say "No. I am only asking you to treat the account as a whole, and to consider the balance from time to time standing to the credit of that account as subject to one continual charge or trust." But I think that really is using words which are not appropriate to the facts. You must, for the purpose of tracing, which was the process adopted in *In re Hallett's Estate*, put your finger on some definite fund which either remains in its original state or can be found in another shape. That is tracing, and tracing, by the very facts of this case, seems to be absolutely excluded except as to the 25l. 18s.

Then, apart from tracing, it seems to me possible to establish this claim against the ultimate balance of 358l. 5s. 5d. only by saying that something was done, with regard to the additional moneys which are needed to make up that balance, by the person to whom those moneys belonged, the debtor, to substitute those moneys for the purpose of, or to impose upon those moneys a trust equivalent to, the trust which rested on the previous balance. Of course, if there was anything like a separate trust account, the payment of the further moneys into that account would, in itself, have been quite a sufficient indication of the intention of the debtor to substitute those additional moneys for the original trust moneys, and accordingly to impose, by way of substitution, the old trusts upon those additional moneys. But, in a case where the account into which the moneys are paid is the general trading account of the debtor on which he has been accustomed to draw both in the ordinary course and in breach of trust when there were trust funds standing to the credit of that account which were convenient for that purpose, I think it is impossible to attribute to him that by the mere payment into the account of further moneys, which to a large extent he subsequently used for purposes of his own, he intended to clothe those moneys with a trust in favour of the plaintiffs.

Certainly, after having heard *In re Hallett's Estate* stated over and over again, I should have thought that the general view of that decision was that it only applied to such an amount of the balance ultimately standing to the credit of the trustee as did not exceed the lowest balance of the account during the intervening period. That view has practically been taken, as far as I can make out, in the cases which have dealt with *In re Hallett's Estate*. *In re Oatway*, a decision of Joyce J., was cited to me in support of the plaintiffs' case, but I do not find anything in it to help them. All that Joyce J. did in that case was to say that, if part of the mixed moneys can be traced into a definite security, that security will not become freed from the charge in favour of the trust, but

Alert

will, together with any residue of the mixed moneys, remain subject to that charge. I am sure that nothing which he said was intended to mean that the trust was imposed upon any property into which the original fund could not be traced. The head-note to the decision of North J. in *In re Stenning* (which accurately represents the effect of the case) is stated in such terms as to indicate that the application of the doctrine in *In re Hallett's Estate* implied that there should be a continuous balance standing to the credit of the account equal to the balance against which the charge is sought to be enforced. And certainly in the recent case of *Sinclair v Brougham* I can see nothing in any way to impeach the doctrine as to tracing laid down in *In re Hallett's Estate*.

In my opinion, therefore, the only part of the balance of 358l. 5s. 5d. which can be made available by the plaintiffs is the sum of 25l. 18s., being the smallest amount to which the balance, to the credit of the account had fallen between May 19, 1913, and the death of the debtor.

15.3.4 Payments out – Two claimants or a claimant and an Innocent Volunteer

Where the money of one claimant is mixed in a bank account with the money of another claimant, or that of an innocent volunteer, they share the mixture rateably. The general rule is that payments out of the account will be in proportion to their share of the mixed fund. However a special rule was developed for active current accounts in *Re Clayton's Case* (1816) 1 Mer 572. This rule states that payments out of the account will be made in the same order that they were made into the account, so the first payment in will be the first payment out. This rule has been criticised. The Court of Appeal has confirmed that the rule is still good law, but is subject to a contrary intention.

Barlow Clowes International Ltd (in liq) and others v Vaughan and others [1992] 4 All ER 22

Panel: Dillon, Woolf and Leggatt LJJ

Facts: Barlow Clowes International had fraudulently acquired money from numerous investors which it was meant to invest on their behalf. Instead the directors appropriated and spent most of the money on themselves. This case concerned the method of distribution amongst the creditors of the money which remained in the Company's bank accounts after it went into liquidation. The judge appointed a defendant to represent the early investors and another defendant to represent the later investors. At first instance the rule in *Re Clayton's Case* was applied. The defendant representing the earlier investors appealed.

LORD JUSTICE WOOLF

...[T]he rule in *Clayton's Case, Devaynes v Noble* (1816) 1 Mer 572, [1814–23] All ER Rep 1. That case was authority for the principle that, when sums are mixed in a bank account as a result of a series of deposits, withdrawals are treated as withdrawing the money in the same order as the money was deposited.

Lord Justice Woolf then noted the alternative ways in which it had been suggested the money could be allocated and continued:

...[I]t is settled law that the rule in *Clayton's Case* can be applied to determine the extent to which, as between each other, equally innocent claimants are entitled in equity to moneys which have been paid into a bank account and then subject to the movements within that account. However, it does not, having regard to the passages from the judgments in the other authorities cited, follow that the rule has always to be applied for this purpose. In a number of different circumstances the rule has not been applied. The rule need only be applied when it is convenient to do so and when its application can be said to do broad justice having regard to the nature of the competing claims. *Re Hallett's Estate* shows that the rule is displaced where its application would unjustly assist the trustee to the disadvantage of the beneficiaries. In *Re Diplock's Estate* the rule would have been displaced by the trustee subsequently earmarking the beneficiary's funds. It is not applied if this is the intention or presumed intention of the beneficiaries. The rule is sensibly not applied when the cost of applying it is likely to exhaust the fund available for the beneficiaries.

Lord Justice Woolf then noted other instances in which the rule was not applied, and concluded:

For the reasons I have expressed, the approach, in summary, which I would adopt to resolving the issues raised by this appeal are as follows.

(1)   While the rule in *Clayton's Case* is prima facie available to determine the interests of investors in a fund into which their investments have been paid, the use of the rule is a matter of convenience and if its application in particular circumstances would be impracticable or result in injustice between the investors it will not be applied if there is a preferable alternative.

(2)   Here the rule will not be applied because this would be contrary to either the express or inferred or presumed intention of the investors. If the investments were required by the terms of the investment contract to be paid into a common pool this indicates that the investors did not intend to apply the rule. If the investments were intended to be separately invested, as a result of the investments being collectively misapplied by BCI a common pool of the investments was created. Because of their shared misfortune, the investors will be presumed to have intended the rule not to apply.

15.4 Defences

15.4.1 Inequitable

The Court of Appeal in *Re Diplock* allowed the defence of inequitability to many of the claims against the charities. However, later cases suggest that this defence should be used sparingly. In *Re Diplock,* two of the charities had used money from the Diplock estate to redeem mortgages on their properties, but it was said to be inequitable to allow a claim of subrogation.

Re Diplock **[1948] Ch 465**

LORD GREENE MR

If equity is now to create a charge (and we say "create" because there is no survival of the original charge) in favour of the judicial trustee, it will be placing him in a position to insist upon a sale of what was contributed by the charity. The case, as it appears to us, is in effect analogous to the cases where Diplock money is expended on improvements on charity land. The money was in this case used to remove a blot on the title; to give the judicial trustee a charge in respect of the money so used would, we think, be equally unjust to the charity who, as the result of such a charge, would have to submit to a sale of the interest in the property which it brought in. We may point out that if the relief claimed were to be accepted as a correct application of the equitable principle, insoluble problems might arise in a case where in the meanwhile fresh charges on the property had been created or money had been expended upon it.

The use of the defence in such circumstances has attracted criticism, both academic and judicial.

Boscawen and Others v Bajwa and Another **[1996] 1 WLR 328**

Panel: Stuart-Smith, Waite and Millett LJJ

LORD JUSTICE MILLETT

Taken as a whole, however, the passage cited [from Re Diplock , see above] is an explanation of the reasons why, in the particular circumstances of that case, it was considered unjust to grant the remedy of subrogation. The hospital had changed its position to its detriment. It had in all innocence used the money to redeem a mortgage held by its bank, which, no doubt, was willing to allow its advance to remain outstanding indefinitely so long as it was well secured and the interest was paid punctually. The next of kin were seeking to be subrogated to the bank's security in order to enforce it and enable a proper distribution of the estate to be made. This would have been unjust to the hospital. It may be doubted whether in its anxiety to avoid injustice to the hospital the court may not have done an even greater injustice to the next of kin, who were denied even the interest on their money. Justice did not require the withholding of any remedy, but only that the charge by subrogation should not be enforceable until the hospital had had a reasonable opportunity to obtain a

Link
see Martin in 'Handbury & Martin Modern Equity', Further Reading.

fresh advance on suitable terms from a willing lender, perhaps from the bank which had held the original security.

The House of Lords decision in *Foskett v McKeown* casts doubt on inequitability being a defence to subrogation.

Foskett v McKeown and Others [2001] 1 AC 102

Panel: Lord Browne-Wilkinson, Lord Steyn, Lord Hoffmann, Lord Hope of Craighead and Lord Millett

LORD BROWNE-WILKINSON

If, as a result of tracing, it can be said that certain of the policy moneys are what now represent part of the assets subject to the trusts of the purchasers trust deed, then as a matter of English property law the purchasers have an absolute interest in such moneys. There is no discretion vested in the court. There is no room for any consideration whether, in the circumstances of this particular case, it is in a moral sense "equitable" for the purchasers to be so entitled. The rules establishing equitable proprietary interests and their enforceability against certain parties have been developed over the centuries and are an integral part of the property law of England. It is a fundamental error to think that, because certain property rights are equitable rather than legal, such rights are in some way discretionary. This case does not depend on whether it is fair, just and reasonable to give the purchasers an interest as a result of which the court in its discretion provides a remedy. It is a case of hard-nosed property rights

LORD MILLETT

Property rights are determined by fixed rules and settled principles. They are not discretionary. They do not depend upon ideas of what is "fair, just and reasonable". Such concepts, which in reality mask decisions of legal policy, have no place in the law of property.

Despite the above, the House of Lords recognised two occasions when it would be inequitable to allow a remedy as a result of tracing. The first of these was the bone fide purchaser for value without notice.

LORD MILLETT

A beneficiary of a trust is entitled to a continuing beneficial interest not merely in the trust property but in its traceable proceeds also, and his interest binds every one who takes the property or its traceable proceeds except a bona fide purchaser for value without notice.

The second was an innocent volunteer who has spent money on a pre-owned asset

> **LORD BROWNE -WILKINSON**
>
> In certain cases the rules of tracing in such a case may give rise to no proprietary interest at all if to give such interest would be unfair: see *In re Diplock; Diplock v Wintle* [1948] Ch 465, 548.

15.4.2 Change of position

The House of Lords introduced the defence of change of position in *Lipkin Gorman v Karpnale* [1991] 2 AC 548   (see below) and suggested that it could apply to both personal and proprietary claims in equity. In the light of *Foskett v McKeown*, it looks unlikely that this is available as a defence to an equitable *proprietary* claim. This is implied in this extract from that case.

> **LORD MILLETT**
>
> Furthermore, a claim in unjust enrichment is subject to a change of position defence, which usually operates by reducing or extinguishing the element of enrichment. An action like the present [an equitable proprietary claim] is subject to the bona fide purchaser for value defence, which operates to clear the defendant's title.

Further, Lord Millett, having stated in *Boscawen v Bajwa*, when he was Millett LJ, that change of position could be a defence to a proprietary claim, has now stated expressly, extra-judicially in 'Equity in Commercial Law' eds S.Degeling and J. Edelman, that this is not so.

15.5 Personal Claims in Equity

There will be personal claims against recipients of trust property whose knowledge makes it unconscionable for them to receive the property free of trust (see Chapter 16). However there is no general claim in equity against innocent recipients: *Re Montagu's Settlement* [1987] 1 Ch 264.   An exception is where money is wrongly paid out in the administration of an estate.

Ministry of Health v Simpson and Others **[1951] AC 251**

Panel: Lord Simonds, Lord Normand, Lord Oaksey, Lord Morton of Henryton and Lord Macdermott

Facts: This was an appeal from the case of *Re Diplock*. The only issue was whether there was a personal claim against the charities.

> **LORD SIMONDS**
>
> The problem for determination can be simply stated and it is perhaps surprising that the sure answer to it is only to be found by examination of authorities which go back nearly 300 years. Acting under a mistake the personal representatives of a testator whose residuary disposition is invalid distribute his residuary estate upon the footing that it is valid. Have the next of kin a direct claim in equity against the persons to

whom it has been wrongfully distributed? I think that the authorities clearly establish that, subject to certain qualifications which I shall state, they have such a claim.

I think that it is important in the discussion of this question to remember that the particular branch of the jurisdiction of the Court of Chancery with which we are concerned relates to the administration of assets of a deceased person. While in the development of this jurisdiction certain principles were established which were common to it and to the comparable jurisdiction in the execution of trusts, I do not find in history or in logic any justification for an argument which denies the possibility of an equitable right in the administration of assets because, as it is alleged, no comparable right existed in the execution of trusts. I prefer to look solely at the authorities which are strictly germane to the present question: it is from them alone that the nature and extent of the equity are to be ascertained.

Before I turn back to the 17th century when the Court of Chancery was gradually wresting from the Spiritual Courts the jurisdiction in administering the assets of deceased persons and framing apt rules to that end, I will first refer to a statement made by Lord Davey early in this century, which, as I think, illuminates the position. In *Harrison v Kirk*. Lord Davey says this: "But the Court of Chancery, in order to do justice and to avoid the evil of allowing one man to retain what is really and legally applicable to the payment of another man, devised a remedy by which, where the estate had been distributed either out of court or in court without regard to the rights of a creditor, it has allowed the creditor to recover back what has been paid to the beneficiaries or the next of kin who derive title from the deceased testator or intestate".

The importance of this statement is manifold. It explains the basis of the jurisdiction, the evil to be avoided and its remedy: its clear implication is that no such remedy existed at common law: it does not suggest that it is relevant whether the wrong payment was made under error of law or of fact: it is immaterial whether those who have been wrongly paid are beneficiaries under the will or next of kin, it is sufficient that they derive title from the deceased. It is true that Lord Davey expressly dealt with the case of a claimant creditor not a beneficiary or next of kin. I shall show your Lordships that what he said of the one might equally well be said of the other. It would be strange if a court of equity, whose self-sought duty it was to see that the assets of a deceased person were duly administered and came into the right hands and not into the wrong hands, devised a remedy for the protection of the unpaid creditor but left the unpaid legatee or next of kin unprotected

The judgment of the Court of Appeal was therefore upheld. The Court of Appeal had allowed the remedy subject to two limitations. The claim was limited to the amount the beneficiaries could not recover from the personal representatives and it was for the principal sum only, no interest being payable.

The charities had no defence to this claim, but since then the defence of change of position has emerged and it is generally accepted that this will apply to such a personal claim.

Lipkin Gorman (A Firm) v Karpnale Ltd [1991] 2 AC 548

Panel: Lord Bridge of Harwich, Lord Templeman, Lord Griffiths, Lord Ackner and Lord Goff of Chieveley

Facts: Cass was a partner in Lipkin Gorman, a firm of solicitors. He was also a compulsive gambler. He took cheques, belonging to the firm and used them to get chips at The Playboy Club, the defendant's casino. It was held that, because gaming contracts were unenforceable, the casino had not given consideration, so was not a bone fide purchaser for value without notice. Therefore a claim was available against it for money had and received. A defence of change of position was allowed for the amount it had paid out in winnings.

LORD GOFF OF CHIEVELY

Whether change of position is, or should be, recognised as a defence to claims in restitution is a subject which has been much debated in the books. It is however a matter on which there is a remarkable unanimity of view, the consensus being to the effect that such a defence should be recognised in English law. I myself am under no doubt that this is right.

In these circumstances, it is right that we should ask ourselves: why do we feel that it would be unjust to allow restitution in cases such as these? The answer must be that, where an innocent defendant's position is so changed that he will suffer an injustice if called upon to repay or to repay in full, the injustice of requiring him so to repay outweighs the injustice of denying the plaintiff restitution. If the plaintiff pays money to the defendant under a mistake of fact, and the defendant then, acting in good faith, pays the money or part of it to charity, it is unjust to require the defendant to make restitution to the extent that he has so changed his position. Likewise, on facts such as those in the present case, if a thief steals my money and pays it to a third party who gives it away to charity, that third party should have a good defence to an action for money had and received. In other words, bona fide change of position should of itself be a good defence in such cases as these.

Lord Goff then noted the various countries where the defence exists. He continued:

The time for its recognition in this country is, in my opinion, long overdue.

I am most anxious that, in recognising this defence to actions of restitution, nothing should be said at this stage to inhibit the development of the defence on a case by case basis, in the usual way. It is, of course, plain that the defence is not open to one who has changed his position in bad faith, as where the defendant has paid away the money with knowledge of the facts entitling the plaintiff to restitution; and it is commonly accepted that the defence should not be open to a wrongdoer. These are matters which can, in due course, be considered in depth in cases where they arise for consideration. They do not arise in the present case. Here there is no doubt that the respondents have acted in good faith throughout, and the action is not founded upon any wrongdoing of the respondents. It is not however appropriate in the present case to attempt to identify all those actions in restitution to which change of position may be

Alert

a defence. A prominent example will, no doubt, be found in those cases where the plaintiff is seeking repayment of money paid under a mistake of fact; but I can see no reason why the defence should not also be available in principle in a case such as the present, where the plaintiff's money has been paid by a thief to an innocent donee, and the plaintiff then seeks repayment from the donee in an action for money had and received. At present I do not wish to state the principle any less broadly than this: that the defence is available to a person whose position has so changed that it would be inequitable in all the circumstances to require him to make restitution, or alternatively to make restitution in full. I wish to stress however that the mere fact that the defendant has spent the money, in whole or in part, does not of itself render it inequitable that he should be called upon to repay, because the expenditure might in any event have been incurred by him in the ordinary course of things. I fear that the mistaken assumption that mere expenditure of money may be regarded as amounting to a change of position for present purposes has led in the past to opposition by some to recognition of a defence which in fact is likely to be available only on comparatively rare occasions. In this connection I have particularly in mind the speech of Lord Simonds in *Ministry of Health v Simpson* [1951] AC 251, 276.

Alert

I wish to add two further footnotes. The defence of change of position is akin to the defence of bona fide purchase; but we cannot simply say that bona fide purchase is a species of change of position. This is because change of position will only avail a defendant to the extent that his position has been changed; whereas, where bona fide purchase is invoked, no inquiry is made (in most cases) into the adequacy of the consideration. Even so, the recognition of change of position as a defence should be doubly beneficial. It will enable a more generous approach to be taken to the recognition of the right to restitution, in the knowledge that the defence is, in appropriate cases, available; and while recognising the different functions of property at law and in equity, there may also in due course develop a more consistent approach to tracing claims, in which common defences are recognised as available to such claims, whether advanced at law or in equity.

Alert

Lord Goff concluded that the casino should have the defence to prevent restitution of the amount it had paid out on winning bets.

Further Reading

Martin 'Tracing Fraud and Ultra Vires' (1993) Conv 372

Stevens 'Vindicating the Proprietary Nature of Tracing' (2001) Conv 94

Pawlowski 'The Demise of the rule in Clayton's Case' (2003) Conv 339

Hanbury & Martin 'Modern Equity' edited Martin 18th edition. (2009) pp 715-748

16

Liability of Strangers

Introduction

This topic concerns third parties (ie non-trustees) who are somehow implicated in a breach of trust or fiduciary duty and so become personally liable for any loss caused by the breach. There are two main heads of liability, traditionally referred to as 'knowing assistance' (now often called 'dishonest assistance') and 'knowing receipt'. There has been much judicial and academic debate about the basis of liability under either head. This has centred around the kind of knowledge necessary to make the third party personally liable, whether it is necessary to show that he was dishonest, the meaning of dishonesty in the context of liability for assistance and whether the requirements for the two heads of liability are the same or different.

Many of the cases refer to a five-scale categorisation of knowledge from *Baden v Société Générale pour Favoriser le Développement du Commerce et de l'Industrie en France SA* [1993] 1 WLR 509 (the *Baden* scale of knowledge): (i) actual knowledge; (ii) wilfully shutting one's eyes to the obvious; (iii) wilfully and recklessly failing to make such inquiries as an honest and reasonable man would make; (iv) knowledge of circumstances which would indicate the facts to an honest and reasonable man; (v) knowledge of circumstances which would put an honest and reasonable man on inquiry. The first three categories are generally treated as actual knowledge (or its equivalent) and the last two as constructive knowledge.

A knowing recipient is someone who held the trust property for his own benefit, rather than merely as an agent. To the extent that he still holds it or its traceable proceeds, a proprietary claim can be made. To the extent that he no longer holds it, the liability is personal liability for knowing receipt. A dishonest assistant can be liable even if he never held trust property. It is sometimes said that third parties become liable as 'constructive trustees', although this terminology is not really apt in relation to third parties who never held trust property. What it really means is that they are liable to the beneficiaries in the same way as if they had been trustees.

16.1 Knowing/Dishonest Assistance

Royal Brunei Airlines Sdn. Bhd. v Philip Tan Kok Ming [1995] 2 AC 378

Panel: Lord Goff of Chieveley, Lord Ackner, Lord Nicholls of Birkenhead, Lord Steyn and Sir John May

Facts: The plaintiff airline appointed a travel agent, Borneo Leisure Travel (BLT), to sell airline tickets. The agreement expressly provided that the ticket money would be held on trust for the airline until accounted for, although BLT could deduct its commission. BLT paid the ticket money into its ordinary account, not a separate one, and used it for ordinary business purposes, in breach of trust. It fell behind with payments to the airline and became insolvent. The airline brought an action for unpaid money against Tan, the managing director and principal shareholder of BLT. The judge upheld the claim against Tan for knowingly assisting a breach of trust. Tan appealed to the Court of Appeal of Brunei Darussalam which allowed the appeal on the basis that dishonesty by the trustee BLT had not been established. The airline appealed to the Privy Council which advised that Tan had acted dishonestly in causing or permitting BLT to commit a breach of trust and so was liable.

> LORD NICHOLLS OF BIRKENHEAD delivering the advice of the Board
>
> The proper role of equity in commercial transactions is a topical question. Increasingly plaintiffs have recourse to equity for an effective remedy when the person in default, typically a company, is insolvent. Plaintiffs seek to obtain relief from others who were involved in the transaction, such as directors of the company, or its bankers, or its legal or other advisers. They seek to fasten fiduciary obligations directly onto the company's officers or agents or advisers, or to have them held personally liable for assisting the company in breaches of trust or fiduciary obligations.
>
> This is such a case. An insolvent travel agent company owed money to an airline. The airline seeks a remedy against the travel agent's principal director and shareholder. Its claim is based on the much-quoted dictum of Lord Selborne L.C., sitting in the Court of Appeal in Chancery, in *Barnes v Addy* (1874) LR 9 Ch App 244, 251-252:
>
> "[The responsibility of a trustee] may no doubt be extended in equity to others who are not properly trustees, if they are found ... actually participating in any fraudulent conduct of the trustee to the injury of the cestui que trust. But ... strangers are not to be made constructive trustees merely because they act as the agents of trustees in transactions within their legal powers, transactions, perhaps of which a court of equity may disapprove, unless those agents receive and become chargeable with some part of the trust property, or unless they assist with knowledge in a dishonest and fraudulent design on the part of the trustees."
>
> In the conventional shorthand, the first of these two circumstances in which third parties (non-trustees) may become liable to account in equity is "knowing receipt," as distinct from the second, where liability arises from "knowing assistance." ...[T]he first limb ... is concerned with the liability of a person as a recipient of trust property or its traceable proceeds. The second limb is concerned with what ... can be called the liability of an accessory to a trustee's breach of trust. Liability as an accessory is not dependent upon receipt of trust property. ...It is a form of secondary liability... . In the present case the plaintiff airline relies on the accessory limb. ...
>
> [T]he issue on this appeal is whether the breach of trust which is a prerequisite to accessory liability must itself be a dishonest and fraudulent breach of trust by the trustee.
>
> ## The honest trustee and the dishonest third party
>
> ...Take a case where a dishonest solicitor persuades a trustee to apply trust property in a way the trustee honestly believes is permissible but which the solicitor knows full well is a clear breach of trust. The solicitor deliberately conceals this from the trustee. ...[T]he case for liability of the dishonest third party seems stronger where the trustee is innocent, because in such a case the third party alone was dishonest and that was the cause of the ... misapplication of the trust property. ...

[W]hat matters is the state of mind of the third party..., not the state of mind of the trustee. The trustee will be liable in any event for the breach of trust, even if he acted innocently, unless excused by an exemption clause ... or relieved by the court. ... If the liability of the third party is fault-based, what matters is the nature of his fault, not that of the trustee. ...[D]ishonesty on the part of the third party would seem to be a sufficient basis for his liability, irrespective of the state of mind of the trustee who is in breach of trust. ...The alternative view would mean that ... if the trustee did not act dishonestly that ... would excuse a dishonest third party from liability. That would make no sense.

Alert

Earlier authority

...In *Eaves v Hickson* (1861) 30 Beav. 136 trustees, acting in good faith, paid over the fund to William Knibb's adult children on the strength of a forged marriage certificate produced to them by William Knibb. Sir John Romilly M.R. held that William Knibb was liable to replace the fund, to the extent that it was not recovered from his children, and to do so in priority to the liability of the trustees. Far from this being a case of fraud by the trustees, Sir John Romilly M.R. ... described it as a very hard case on the trustees, who were deceived by a forgery which would have deceived anyone who was not looking out for forgery or fraud. ...

What has gone wrong? ...[T]here has been a tendency to cite and interpret and apply Lord Selborne L.C.'s formulation in *Barnes v Addy* ... as though it were a statute. This has particularly been so with the accessory limb... . [T]he courts have found themselves wrestling with the interpretation of the individual ingredients, especially "knowingly" but also "dishonest and fraudulent design on the part of the trustees," without examining the underlying reason why a third party who has received no trust property is being made liable at all. ...

To resolve this issue it is necessary to take an overall look at the accessory liability principle. ...It is not necessary ... [to] consider ... recipient liability. ...Different considerations apply to the two heads of liability. Recipient liability is restitution-based; accessory liability is not.

Link
For further discussion on Lord Nicholls's views on recipient liability, see the reference to them in *BCCI v Akindele* (below).

No liability

The starting point for any analysis must be to consider the extreme possibility: that a third party who does not receive trust property ought never to be liable directly to the beneficiaries merely because he assisted the trustee to commit a breach of trust or procured him to do so. This possibility can be dismissed summarily. ...[T]he beneficiary should be able to look for recompense to the third party as well as the trustee. Affording the beneficiary a remedy against the third party serves the dual purpose of making good the beneficiary's loss should the trustee lack financial means and imposing a liability which will discourage others from behaving in a similar fashion. ...

Strict liability

The other extreme possibility can also be rejected out of hand. This is the case where a third party deals with a trustee without knowing, or having any reason to suspect, that he is a trustee. Or the case where a third party is aware he is dealing with a trustee but has no reason to know or suspect that their transaction is inconsistent with the terms of the trust. The law has never gone so far as to give ... a remedy against a non-recipient third party in such circumstances. Within defined limits, proprietary rights ... endure against third parties who were unaware of their existence. But accessory liability is concerned with the liability of a person who has not received any property. ...Beneficiaries could not reasonably expect that third parties should deal with trustees at their peril, to the extent that they should become liable ... even when they received no trust property and even when they were unaware and had no reason to suppose that they were dealing with trustees.

Fault-based liability

...[T]he next step is to seek to identify the touchstone of liability. By common accord dishonesty fulfils this role. Whether, in addition, negligence will suffice is an issue on which there has been a well-known difference of judicial opinion. ...[His Lordship cited a number of cases and continued:]

[T]he tide in England has flowed strongly in favour of the test being one of dishonesty... Most, but not all, commentators prefer the test of dishonesty...

Dishonesty

...[I]t will be helpful to define the terms being used by looking more closely at what dishonesty means in this context. Whatever may be the position in some criminal or other contexts (see, for instance, *Reg. v Ghosh [1982] QB 1053*), in the context of the accessory liability principle acting dishonestly, or with a lack of probity, which is synonymous, means simply not acting as an honest person would in the circumstances. This is an objective standard. At first sight this may seem surprising. Honesty has a connotation of subjectivity, as distinct from the objectivity of negligence. Honesty, indeed, does have a strong subjective element in that it is a description of a type of conduct assessed in the light of what a person actually knew at the time, as distinct from what a reasonable person would have known or appreciated. Further, honesty and its counterpart dishonesty are mostly concerned with advertent conduct, not inadvertent conduct. Carelessness is not dishonesty. Thus for the most part dishonesty is to be equated with conscious impropriety. However, these subjective characteristics of honesty do not mean that individuals are free to set their own standards of honesty in particular circumstances. The standard of what constitutes honest conduct is not subjective. ...If a person knowingly appropriates another's property, he will not escape a finding of dishonesty simply because he sees nothing wrong in such behaviour.

 Alert

In most situations there is little difficulty in identifying how an honest person would behave. Honest people do not intentionally deceive others to their detriment. Honest people do not knowingly take others' property. Unless there is a very good and compelling reason, an honest person does not participate in a transaction if he knows it involves a misapplication of trust assets to the detriment of the beneficiaries. Nor does an honest person in such a case deliberately close his eyes and ears, or deliberately not ask questions, lest he learn something he would rather not know, and then proceed regardless. ...

Taking risks

...Imprudence is not dishonesty, although imprudence may be carried recklessly to lengths which call into question the honesty of the person making the decision. This is especially so if the transaction serves another purpose in which that person has an interest of his own. ...

The individual is expected to attain the standard which would be observed by an honest person placed in those circumstances. It is impossible to be more specific. ...Acting in reckless disregard of others' rights or possible rights can be a tell-tale sign of dishonesty. ...Ultimately, in most cases, an honest person should have little difficulty in knowing whether a proposed transaction, or his participation in it, would offend the normally accepted standards of honest conduct.

Likewise, when called upon to decide whether a person was acting honestly, a court will look at all the circumstances known to the third party at the time. The court will also have regard to personal attributes of the third party, such as his experience and intelligence, and the reason why he acted as he did.

 Alert

...To inquire ... whether a person dishonestly assisted in ... a breach of trust is to ask a meaningful question... . This is not always so if the question is posed in terms of "knowingly" assisted. Framing the question in the latter form all too often leads one into tortuous convolutions about the "sort" of knowledge required, when the truth is that "knowingly" is inapt as a criterion when applied to the gradually darkening spectrum where the differences are of degree and not kind.

Negligence

It is against this background that the question of negligence is to be addressed. This question ... is directed at whether an honest third party who receives no trust property should be liable if he procures or assists in a breach of trust of which he would have become aware had he exercised reasonable diligence. Should he be liable to the beneficiaries for the loss they suffer... ?

...[T]heir Lordships consider that dishonesty is an essential ingredient here. ...As a general proposition, ... beneficiaries cannot reasonably expect that all the world dealing with their trustees should owe them a duty to take care lest the trustees are behaving dishonestly.

Unconscionable conduct

Mention, finally, must be made of the suggestion that the test for liability is that of unconscionable conduct. Unconscionable is a word of immediate appeal to an equity lawyer. ...It must be recognised, however, that unconscionable is not a word in everyday use by non-lawyers. If ... it is to be the touchstone for liability as an accessory, it is essential to be clear on what, *in this context*, unconscionable *means*. If unconscionable means no more than dishonesty, then dishonesty is the preferable label. If unconscionable means something different, it must be said that it is not clear what that something different is. Either way, therefore, the term is better avoided in this context.

 Link
Note the adoption of 'unconscionability' as the basis of liability for knowing receipt in *BCCI v Akindele*.

The accessory liability principle

Drawing the threads together, their Lordships' overall conclusion is that dishonesty is a necessary ingredient of accessory liability. It is also a sufficient ingredient. A liability in equity to make good resulting loss attaches to a person who dishonestly procures or assists in a breach of trust or fiduciary obligation. It is not necessary that, in addition, the trustee or fiduciary was acting dishonestly, although this will usually be so where the third party who is assisting him is acting dishonestly. "Knowingly" is better avoided as a defining ingredient of the principle, and in the context of this principle the Baden [1993] 1 W.L.R. 509 scale of knowledge is best forgotten.

Conclusion

From this statement of the principle it follows that this appeal succeeds. The money paid to B.L.T. on the sale of tickets ... was held by B.L.T. upon trust for the airline. ...B.L.T. committed a breach of trust by using the money instead of simply deducting its commission and holding the money intact until it paid the airline. The defendant ... caused or permitted his company to apply the money in a way he knew was not authorised by the trust of which the company was trustee. Set out in these bald terms, the defendant's conduct was dishonest. ...

The Court of Appeal held that it was not established that B.L.T. was guilty of fraud or dishonesty in relation to the amounts it held for the airline. Their Lordships understand that by this the Court of Appeal meant that it was not established that the defendant intended to defraud the airline. The defendant hoped, maybe expected, to be able to pay the airline, but the money was lost in the ordinary course of a poorly-run business with heavy overhead expenses. These facts are beside the point. The defendant had no right to employ the money in the business at all. That was the breach of trust. The company's inability to pay the airline was the consequence of that breach of trust. ...

[T]his appeal should be allowed... .

> **Link**
>
> For further discussion of the relevance of the Baden scale, see per Nourse LJ in *BCCI v Akindele*.

Although only of persuasive authority, the Privy Council's decision in *Tan* was generally seen as bringing clarity in relation to this head of liability. For that reason, the majority in the House of Lords in the next case purported to adopt the reasoning from *Tan*. However, they appeared to give a different interpretation to the subjective element of dishonesty.

Twinsectra Ltd v Yardley and others [2002] 2 AC 164

Panel: Lord Slynn of Hadley, Lord Steyn, Lord Hoffmann, Lord Hutton and Lord Millett

Facts: Twinsectra lent money to Yardley and received an undertaking from Yardley's solicitor, Sims, that the money would be used solely for the acquisition of property on Yardley's behalf and for no other purpose and would be retained by Sims until so applied. In breach of the undertaking, Sims transferred the money to Leach, another solicitor acting for Yardley. Leach was aware of the terms of the undertaking but paid the money out on Yardley's instructions without ensuring that it would be used for acquiring property. Some of the money was used for other purposes. When the loan was not repaid, Twinsectra brought a number of claims, including a claim against

Leach for dishonestly assisting in a breach of trust. The judge held that the money was not subject to a trust and that Leach was not dishonest. The Court of Appeal allowed Twinsectra's appeal, holding that the terms of the undertaking created a trust for Twinsectra and that Leach was dishonest and therefore liable. Leach appealed to the House of Lords which held unanimously that the money was subject to a trust but, Lord Millett dissenting, that Leach was not liable for dishonest assistance.

LORD SLYNN OF HADLEY

...The first main issue is whether the moneys ... were held in trust. The judge found that they were not; the Court of Appeal held that they were. ...I agree firmly with the Court of Appeal.

The second issue I have found more difficult. The judge found that Mr Leach had shut his eyes to the problems or the implications of what happened, yet he acquitted him of dishonesty. The Court of Appeal ... concluded that deliberately shutting his eyes in this way was dishonesty within the valuable analysis by Lord Nicholls of Birkenhead in *Royal Brunei Airlines Sdn Bhd v Tan...* .

There are conflicting arguments. Prima facie shutting one's eyes to problems or implications ... may well indicate dishonesty; on the other hand prima facie it needs a strong case to justify the Court of Appeal reversing the finding as to dishonesty of the trial judge who has heard the witness...

In the end I am not satisfied that the Court of Appeal were entitled to substitute their assessment for that of the trial judge. Despite my doubts ... it seems to me clear that the judge was very conscious of Lord Nicholls's analysis and I do not think he can possibly have left out of account the question whether Mr Leach knew or realised that what he was doing fell below the required standards when he deliberately shut his eyes eg to the implications of the undertaking given by Mr Sims. Mr Leach may have been naive or misguided but I accept that the judge after hearing lengthy evidence from Mr Leach was entitled to conclude that he had not been dishonest.

...[F]or these brief reasons and the reasons given by Lord Hutton I would allow the appeal.

LORD STEYN

...I agree that the law is as stated in the judgments of ... Lord Hoffmann and Lord Hutton. In particular I agree with their interpretation of the decision in Royal Brunei Airlines... . I agree that a finding of accessory liability against Mr Leach was only permissible if, applying what Lord Hutton has called the combined test, it were established on the evidence that Mr Leach had been dishonest.

...I agree with Lord Hutton's reasons for concluding that the Court of Appeal was not entitled to reverse the judge on the central issue of dishonesty. I too would allow the appeal.

Link
For the meaning of 'the combined test' see the speech of Lord Hutton.

LORD HOFFMANN

...The terms of the trust upon which Sims held the money must be found in the undertaking which ... made it clear that the money was not to be at the free disposal of Mr Yardley. ...

The ... question is whether Mr Leach, in receiving the money and paying it to Mr Yardley without concerning himself about its application, could be said to have acted dishonestly. The judge found that in so doing he was "misguided" but not dishonest. He had "shut his eyes" to some of the problems but thought he held the money to the order of Mr Yardley without restriction. The Court of Appeal reversed this finding and held that he had been dishonest.

...Lord Millett considers that the Court of Appeal was justified in taking this view because liability as an accessory to a breach of trust does not depend upon dishonesty in the normal sense of that expression. It is sufficient that the defendant knew all the facts which made it wrongful for him to participate in the way in which he did. In this case, Mr Leach knew ... all the facts... .

I do not think that it is fairly open to your Lordships to take this view of the law without departing from the principles laid down by the Privy Council in *Royal Brunei*... . For the reasons given by ... Lord Hutton, I consider that those principles require more than knowledge of the facts which make the conduct wrongful. They require a dishonest state of mind, that is to say, consciousness that one is transgressing ordinary standards of honest behaviour. I also agree ... that the Court of Appeal was not entitled ... to make a finding of dishonesty which the judge ... did not.

Alert

...I do respectfully think it was unfortunate that the judge three times used the expression "shut his eyes" to "the details", or "the problems", or "the implications". The expression produces in judges a reflex image of Admiral Nelson at Copenhagen and the common use of this image by lawyers to signify a deliberate abstinence from inquiry in order to avoid certain knowledge of what one suspects to be the case... . But ... there were in this case no relevant facts of which Mr Leach was unaware. What I think the judge meant was that he took a blinkered approach to his professional duties as a solicitor, or buried his head in the sand... . But neither of those would be dishonest.

Mr Leach believed that the money was at the disposal of Mr Yardley. He thought that whether Mr Yardley's use of the money would be contrary to the assurance he had given Mr Sims or put Mr Sims in breach of his undertaking was a matter between those two gentlemen. Such a state of mind may have been wrong. It may have been, as the judge said, misguided. But if he honestly believed, as the judge found, that the money was at Mr Yardley's disposal, he was not dishonest. ...

A person may dishonestly assist in ... a breach of trust without any idea of what a trust means. The necessary dishonest state of mind may be found to exist simply on the fact that he knew perfectly well that he was helping to pay away money to which the recipient was not entitled. But that was not the case here. I would therefore allow the appeal... .

Link
Lord Millett also refers to this point in his dissenting speech (and see the concurrence with both in *Barlow Clowes v Eurotrust*).

LORD HUTTON

...I agree that the undertaking ... created a trust...

[W]hether the Court of Appeal was right to hold that Mr Leach had acted dishonestly depends on the meaning to be given to that term in the judgment ... in *Royal Brunei Airlines Snd Bhd v Tan*...

[T]here are three possible standards which can be applied to determine whether a person has acted dishonestly. There is a purely subjective standard, whereby a person is only regarded as dishonest if he transgresses his own standard of honesty, even if that standard is contrary to that of reasonable and honest people. This has been termed the "Robin Hood test" and has been rejected... .

Secondly, there is a purely objective standard whereby a person acts dishonestly if his conduct is dishonest by the ordinary standards of reasonable and honest people, even if he does not realise this. Thirdly, there is a standard which combines an objective test and a subjective test, and ... requires that before there can be a finding of dishonesty it must be established that the defendant's conduct was dishonest by the ordinary standards of reasonable and honest people and that he himself realised that by those standards his conduct was dishonest. I will term this "the combined test".

There is a passage in ... the judgment in *Royal Brunei* which suggests that Lord Nicholls considered that dishonesty has a subjective element. Thus in discussing the honest trustee and the dishonest third party ... he stated: " ...[W]hat matters is the state of mind of the third party... ."

...Lord Nicholls went on ... to discuss the meaning of dishonesty:

" ...Whatever may be the position in some criminal or other contexts (see, for instance, *R v Ghosh* [1982] QB 1053), in the context of the accessory liability principle acting dishonestly ... means simply not acting as an honest person would in the circumstances. This is an objective standard."

...Lord Millett ... is of the opinion that Lord Nicholls used the term "dishonesty" in a purely objective sense so that ... a person can be held to be dishonest even though he does not realise that what he is doing is dishonest by the ordinary standards of honest people. This leads Lord Millett on to the conclusion that ... dishonesty is not necessary and that liability depends on knowledge.

In *R v Ghosh*... , Lord Lane CJ held that in the law of theft dishonesty required that the defendant himself must have realised that what he was doing was dishonest by the ordinary standards of reasonable and honest people. The three sentences in Lord Nicholls's judgment ... which appear to draw a distinction between the position in criminal law and the position in equity, do give support to Lord Millett's view. But considering those sentences in the context of the remainder of the paragraph and taking account of other passages in the judgment, I think that in referring to an objective standard Lord Nicholls was contrasting it with the purely subjective standard whereby a man sets his own standard of honesty and does not regard as dishonest what upright and responsible people would regard as dishonest. Thus after stating that

Link

See the speech of Lord Steyn who accepted this as the correct test.

dishonesty is assessed on an objective standard he continued... : [His Lordship quoted the passage from *Tan* (extracted above) beginning "At first sight this may seem surprising." and ending "will not escape a finding of dishonesty simply because he sees nothing wrong in such behaviour." and continued:] Further ... Lord Nicholls said:

"Ultimately, in most cases, an honest person should have little difficulty in knowing whether a proposed transaction, or his participation in it, would offend the normally accepted standards of honest conduct. Likewise... , a court will look at all the circumstances known to the third party at the time. The court will also have regard to personal attributes of the third party, such as his experience and intelligence, and the reason why he acted as he did."

The use of the word "knowing" in the first sentence would be superfluous if the defendant did not have to be aware that what he was doing would offend the normally accepted standards of honest conduct, and the need to look at the experience and intelligence of the defendant would also appear superfluous if all that was required was a purely objective standard of dishonesty. Therefore I do not think that Lord Nicholls was stating that in this sphere of equity a man can be dishonest even if he does not know that what he is doing would be regarded as dishonest by honest people.

Then ... Lord Nicholls stated the general principle that dishonesty is a necessary ingredient of accessory liability and that knowledge is not an appropriate test...

There is, in my opinion, a further consideration which supports the view that ... the defendant must himself appreciate that what he was doing was dishonest by the standards of honest and reasonable men. A finding by a judge that a defendant has been dishonest is a grave finding, and it is particularly grave against a professional man, such as a solicitor. Notwithstanding that the issue arises in equity law and not in a criminal context, I think that it would be less than just for the law to permit a finding that a defendant had been "dishonest" in assisting in a breach of trust where he knew of the facts which created the trust and its breach but had not been aware that what he was doing would be regarded by honest men as being dishonest.

It would be open to your Lordships to depart from the principle stated by Lord Nicholls that dishonesty is a necessary ingredient ... and to hold that knowledge is a sufficient ingredient. But the statement of that principle by Lord Nicholls has been widely regarded as clarifying this area of the law and, as he observed, the tide of authority in England has flowed strongly in favour of the test of dishonesty. Therefore I consider that the courts should continue to apply that test and that your Lordships should state that dishonesty requires knowledge by the defendant that what he was doing would be regarded as dishonest by honest people, although he should not escape a finding of dishonesty because he sets his own standards of honesty and does not regard as dishonest what he knows would offend the normally accepted standards of honest conduct. ...

 Alert

At the trial Mr Leach was cross-examined very closely and at length about his state of mind when he paid to Mr Yardley the moneys transferred to him by Mr Sims. The tenor of his replies was that he paid the moneys to his client because his client instructed him to do so. ...

Carnwath J stated... :

"I do not find Mr Leach to have been dishonest, but he was certainly misguided. ...When asked to give the undertaking himself, he regarded it as a very unusual request, and one outside the normal course of a solicitor's practice. This did not lead him to advise Mr Yardley against it, but rather to distance himself from any responsibility for its terms. He told Mr Sims that they were a matter for him. This unease ought to have put him on notice of the need for caution when dealing with the money received under the undertakings. He was clearly aware of their terms. ...Yet, in evidence, he frankly admitted that he had regarded the money as held simply to the order of Mr Yardley, without restriction. Again, I have to conclude that he simply shut his eyes to the problems. As far as he was concerned, it was a matter solely for Mr Sims to satisfy himself whether he could release the money to Mr Yardley's account. ...In Mr Leach's case, I have found that he was not dishonest, but that he did deliberately shut his eyes to the implications of the undertaking. ..."

It would have been open to the judge to hold that Mr Leach was dishonest... . But the experienced judge who was observing Mr Leach being cross-examined at length found that Mr Leach, although misguided, was not dishonest in carrying out his client's instructions.

The judge did not give reasons for this finding or state what test he applied to determine dishonesty, but I think it probable that he applied the combined test and I infer that he considered that Mr Leach did not realise that in acting on his client's instructions in relation to the moneys he was acting in a way which a responsible and honest solicitor would regard as dishonest. ...

It is only in exceptional circumstances that an appellate court should reverse a finding by a trial judge on a question of fact (and particularly on the state of mind of a party)... . Therefore I do not think that it would have been right for the Court of Appeal in this case to have come to a different conclusion from the judge and to have held that Mr Leach was dishonest in that ... he knew that his conduct was dishonest by the standards of responsible and honest solicitors. ...

I agree ... that it is unfortunate that Carnwath J referred to Mr Leach deliberately shutting his eyes... but like Lord Hoffmann I do not think it probable that having cited the passage from the judgment of Lord Nicholls ... the judge then over-looked the issue of Nelsonian dishonesty in finding that Mr Leach was not dishonest. ...[T]his was not a case where Mr Leach deliberately closed his eyes and ears, or deliberately did not ask questions ... - he already knew all the facts, but the judge concluded that nevertheless he had not been dishonest. I also think that Potter LJ applied too strict a test when he stated... : "It seems to me that, save perhaps in the most exceptional circumstances, it is not the action of an honest solicitor knowingly to assist or encourage another solicitor in a deliberate breach of his undertaking." This test does not address the vital point whether Mr Leach realised that his action was dishonest by the standards of responsible and honest solicitors. ...

I would allow Mr Leach's appeal and set aside the judgment of the Court of Appeal.

LORD MILLETT

My Lords, there are two issues in this appeal. The first is concerned with the nature of the so-called "Quistclose trust" and the requirements for its creation. The second ... is whether his [the appellant's] conduct rendered him liable for having assisted in a breach of trust. This raises two questions of some importance. One concerns the extent of the knowledge of the existence of a trust which is required before a person can be found civilly liable for having assisted in its breach. ...The other, which has led to a division of opinion among your Lordships, is whether, in addition to knowledge, dishonesty is required and, if so, the meaning of dishonesty in this context. ...

[His Lordship concluded that the undertaking created a *Quistclose* trust. He continued:] Twinsectra parted with the money to Mr Sims, relying on him to ensure that the money was properly applied or returned to it. Mr Sims' act in paying the money over to Mr Leach was a breach of trust... .

Link
For more detail on this, see Chapter 9 on Resulting Trusts.

Knowing (or dishonest) assistance

...Liability for "knowing receipt" is receipt-based. ...There is no basis for requiring actual knowledge of the breach of trust, let alone dishonesty, as a condition of liability. Constructive notice is sufficient, and may not even be necessary. There is powerful academic support for the proposition that the liability of the recipient is the same as in other cases of restitution, that is to say strict but subject to a change of position defence.

Link
See the discussion of this point in *BCCI v Akindele*.

Mr Leach received sums totalling £22,000 in payment of his costs for his own use and benefit, and Twinsectra seek their repayment on the ground of knowing receipt. But he did not receive the rest of the money for his own benefit at all. He never regarded himself as beneficially entitled to the money. He held it to Mr Yardley's order... . Twinsectra cannot and does not base its claim in respect of these moneys in knowing receipt, not for want of knowledge, but for want of the necessary receipt. It sues in respect of knowing (or dishonest) assistance.

Link
See the requirement for 'beneficial' receipt referred to in *BCCI v Akindele*, citing *El Ajou v Dollar Land Holdings*.

The accessory's liability for having assisted in a breach of trust is quite different. It is fault-based, not receipt-based. ..[T]he claimant seeks compensation for wrongdoing. ...Liability is not restricted to the person whose breach of trust or fiduciary duty caused [the] original diversion [of funds]. His liability is strict. Nor is it limited to those who assist him in the original breach. It extends to everyone who consciously assists in the continuing diversion of the money. Most of the cases have been concerned, not with assisting in the original breach, but in covering it up afterwards by helping to launder the money. Mr Leach's wrongdoing is not confined to the assistance he gave Mr Sims to commit a breach of trust by receiving the money from him knowing that Mr Sims should not have paid it to him (though this is sufficient to render him liable for any resulting loss); it extends to the assistance he gave in the subsequent misdirection of the money by paying it out to Mr Yardley's order without seeing to its proper application.

The ingredients of accessory liability

...Since ...[*Royal Brunei Airlines Sdn Bhd v Tan*] it has been clear that actual knowledge is necessary; the question is whether it is sufficient, or whether there is an additional requirement of dishonesty in the subjective sense in which that term is used in criminal cases.

Prior to the decision in *Royal Brunei Airlines Sdn Bhd v Tan* the equitable claim was described as "knowing assistance". ...The accessory was liable if he knew all the relevant facts... . ...[J]udges embarked on sophisticated analyses of the kind of knowledge required to found liability.

...Despite a divergence of judicial opinion, by 1995 the tide was flowing strongly in favour of rejecting negligence. It was widely thought that the accessory should be liable only if he actually knew the relevant facts. It should not be sufficient that he ought to have known them or had the means of knowledge if he did not in fact know them.

There was a gloss on this. It is dishonest for a man deliberately to shut his eyes to facts which he would prefer not to know. ...Such knowledge has been described as "Nelsonian knowledge", meaning knowledge which is attributed to a person as a consequence of his "wilful blindness"... . But a person's failure through negligence to make inquiry is insufficient to enable knowledge to be attributed to him: see *Agip (Africa) Ltd v Jackson* [1990] Ch 265, 293.

In ... *Royal Brunei Airlines* ... Lord Nicholls firmly rejected negligence as a sufficient condition of accessory liability. ...Dishonesty, he said, was a necessary ... ingredient... ."Knowingly" was better avoided as a defining ingredient... . His purpose ... was to get away from the refinements which had been introduced into the concept of knowledge in the context of accessory liability.

The meaning of dishonesty in this context

In taking dishonesty to be the condition of liability, however, Lord Nicholls used the word in an objective sense. He did not employ the concept of dishonesty as it is understood in criminal cases. ... [His Lordship cited the passage beginning "Whatever may be the position in some criminal or other contexts" and ending "and then proceed regardless." and continued:]

Alert

Dishonesty as a state of mind or as a course of conduct?

In *R v Ghosh* [1982] QB 1053, Lord Lane CJ drew a distinction between dishonesty as a state of mind and dishonesty as a course of conduct, and held that dishonesty in section 1 of the Theft Act 1968 referred to dishonesty as a state of mind. The question was not whether the accused had in fact acted dishonestly but whether he was aware that he was acting dishonestly. ...

The same test of dishonesty is applicable in civil cases where, for example, liability depends upon intent to defraud, for this connotes a dishonest state of mind. ...But it is not generally an appropriate condition of civil liability, which does not ordinarily require a guilty mind. Civil liability is usually predicated on the defendant's conduct rather than his state of mind; it results from his negligent or unreasonable behaviour or, where this is not sufficient, from intentional wrongdoing. ...

Lord Nicholls rejected a dishonest state of mind as an appropriate condition of liability. This is evident from the opening sentence of the passage cited above, from his repeated references ... to the defendant's conduct in "acting dishonestly" and "advertent conduct", and from his statement that "for the most part" (ie not always) it involves "conscious impropriety". "Honesty," he said, "is a description of a type of conduct assessed in the light of what a person actually knew at the time." Usually ("for the most part"), no doubt, the defendant will have been guilty of "conscious impropriety"; but this is not a condition of liability. ...There is no trace in Lord Nicholls' opinion that the defendant should have been aware that he was acting contrary to objective standards of dishonesty. In my opinion, in rejecting the test of dishonesty adopted in *R v Ghosh* ... Lord Nicholls was using the word to characterise the defendant's conduct, not his state of mind.

...[H]is approach to dishonesty is premised on the belief that it is dishonest for a man consciously to participate in the misapplication of money. This is ... most clearly evident in the way in which Lord Nicholls described the conduct of the defendant in the case under appeal. ...:

" ...[H]e caused or permitted his company to apply the money in a way he knew was not authorised by the trust... . Set out in these bald terms, the defendant's conduct was dishonest."

There was no evidence and Lord Nicholls did not suggest that the defendant realised that honest people would regard his conduct as dishonest. ...

In my opinion Lord Nicholls was adopting an objective standard of dishonesty by which the defendant is expected to attain the standard which would be observed by an honest person placed in similar circumstances. Account must be taken of subjective considerations such as the defendant's experience and intelligence and his actual state of knowledge at the relevant time. But it is not necessary that he should actually have appreciated that he was acting dishonestly...

 Alert

The only subjective elements are those relating to the defendant's knowledge, experience and attributes. ...The question is whether an honest person would appreciate that what he was doing was wrong or improper, not whether the defendant himself actually appreciated this. The third limb of the test established for criminal cases in *R v Ghosh* ... is conspicuously absent. ...

The modern tendency is to deprecate the use of words like "fraud" and "dishonesty"... . There is much to be said for ... changing the language while retaining the incidents of equitable liability; but there is nothing to be said for retaining the language and giving it the meaning it has in criminal cases so as to alter the incidents of equitable liability.

Should subjective dishonesty be required?

The question for your Lordships is ... whether a plaintiff should be required to establish that an accessory to a breach of trust had a dishonest state of mind (so that he was subjectively dishonest in the *R v Ghosh* sense); or whether it should be sufficient to establish that he acted with the requisite knowledge (so that his conduct was objectively dishonest). ...[W]e are free to resolve it either way.

I would resolve it by adopting the objective approach. I would do so because:

(1) Consciousness of wrongdoing is an aspect of mens rea and an appropriate condition of criminal liability: it is not an appropriate condition of civil liability. ...For ... civil liability, it should not be necessary that the defendant realised that his conduct was dishonest; it should be sufficient that it constituted intentional wrongdoing.

(2) The objective test is in accordance with Lord Selborne's statement in *Barnes v Addy*... and traditional doctrine. This taught that a person who knowingly participates in the misdirection of money is liable to compensate the injured party. While negligence is not a sufficient condition of liability, intentional wrongdoing is. Such conduct is culpable and falls below the objective standards of honesty adopted by ordinary people. ...

Link
See the similar view expressed by Arden LJ in *Abou-Rahmah v Abac*.

If we were to reject subjective dishonesty as a requirement of civil liability in this branch of the law, the remaining question is merely a semantic one. Should we return to the traditional description of the claim as "knowing assistance", reminding ourselves that nothing less than actual knowledge is sufficient; or should we adopt Lord Nicholls' description of the claim as "dishonest assistance", reminding ourselves that the test is an objective one?

For my own part, I have no difficulty in equating the knowing mishandling of money with dishonest conduct. But the introduction of dishonesty is ... conducive to error. Many judges would be reluctant to brand a professional man as dishonest where he was unaware that honest people would consider his condut to be so. If the condition of liability is intentional wrongdoing and not conscious dishonesty as understood in the criminal courts, I think that we should return to the traditional description of this head of equitable liability as arising from "knowing assistance".

Alert

Knowledge

...It is sufficient that he knows that the money is not at the free disposal of the principal. In some circumstances it may not even be necessary that his knowledge should extend this far. It may be sufficient that he knows that he is assisting in a dishonest scheme.

...[K]nowledge of the arrangements which constitute the trust is sufficient; it is not necessary that the defendant should appreciate that they do so. Of course, if they do not create a trust, then he will not be liable for having assisted in a breach of trust. But he takes the risk that they do.

...[T]he accessory is ... assisting a person ... entrusted with the control of a fund to dispose of the fund in an unauthorised manner. He should be liable if he knows of the arrangements by which that person obtained control of the money and that his authority to deal with the money was limited, and participates in a dealing with the money in a manner which he knows is unauthorised. I do not believe that the man in the street would have any doubt that such conduct was culpable. ...

Link
Lord Hoffmann also refers to this point in his speech (and see the concurrence with both in *Barlow Clowes v Eurotrust*).

Conclusion

I do not think that this was a case of wilful blindness, or that the judge overlooked the possibility of imputed knowledge. There was no need to impute knowledge to Mr Leach, for there was no relevant fact of which he was unaware. ...He knew of the terms of the undertaking, that the money was not to be at Mr Yardley's free disposal. ...There were no enquiries which Mr Leach needed to make to satisfy himself that the money could properly be put at Mr Yardley's free disposal. He knew it could not. The only thing that he did not know was that the terms of the undertaking created a trust...

Yet ... he treated it as held to Mr Yardley's order and at Mr Yardley's free disposition. He did not shut his eyes to the facts, but to ... the impropriety of putting the money at Mr Yardley's disposal. His explanation was that this was Mr Sims' problem, not his.

Mr Leach knew that Twinsectra had entrusted the money to Mr Sims with only limited authority to dispose of it; that Twinsectra trusted Mr Sims to ensure that the money was not used except for the acquisition of property; that Mr Sims had betrayed the confidence placed in him by paying the money to him (Mr Leach) without seeing to its further application; and that by putting it at Mr Yardley's free disposal he took the risk that the money would be applied for an unauthorised purpose and place Mr Sims in breach of his undertaking. But all that was Mr Sims's responsibility.

In my opinion this is enough to make Mr Leach civilly liable as an accessory ... for assisting in a breach of trust. It is unnecessary to consider whether Mr Leach realised that honest people would regard his conduct as dishonest. His knowledge that he was assisting Mr Sims to default in his undertaking to Twinsectra is sufficient.

Knowing receipt

Each of the sums which Mr Leach received for his own benefit was paid in respect of an acquisition of property, and as such was a proper disbursement. He thus received trust property, but not in breach of trust. This was very properly conceded by counsel for Twinsectra before your Lordships.

Conclusion

I would reduce the sum for which judgment was entered ... and subject thereto dismiss the appeal.

The general view of this decision was that the majority had misinterpreted the subjective element of dishonesty as set out in *Tan* and had introduced an additional requirement that the defendant must realise that his conduct would be regarded as dishonest by ordinary people. Lord Millett was viewed as correctly interpreting the meaning given to dishonesty in *Tan* and his view on this appears to have been vindicated in subsequent decisions (see below). However, his suggestion that the terminology should revert to 'knowing' assistance, and the label of dishonesty be dropped, has not been adopted.

Barlow Clowes International Ltd (in liquidation) and others v Eurotrust International Ltd and others [2006] 1 WLR 1476

Panel: Lord Nicholls of Birkenhead, Lord Steyn, Lord Hoffmann, Lord Walker of Gestingthorpe and Lord Carswell

Facts: Barlow Clowes Ltd (a company in Gibraltar) fraudulently promised UK investors high returns from investments in UK gilt-edged securities. In fact, the money was mainly spent by Peter Clowes and his associate Cramer on speculative personal investments and extravagant living. Some of the investors' money was paid through bank accounts of companies administered by ITC, an Isle of Man company. The principal directors of ITC, including Mr Henwood, were sued (in the Isle of Man High Court) by Barlow Clowes Ltd (in administration) for dishonestly assisting Mr Clowes. They were found liable by the Acting Deemster (Isle of Man equivalent of High Court judge). Mr Henwood's appeal to the Staff of Government Division of the High Court (Isle of Man appeal court) was allowed. Barlow Clowes then appealed to the Judicial Committee of the Privy Council, which held that the Acting Deemster's decision should be restored.

LORD HOFFMANN delivering the advice of the Board

...The judge stated the law in terms largely derived from the advice of the Board ... in *Royal Brunei Airlines Sdn Bhd v Tan*... . In summary, she said that liability for dishonest assistance requires a dishonest state of mind on the part of the person who assists in a breach of trust. Such a state of mind may consist in knowledge that the transaction is one in which he cannot honestly participate (for example, a misappropriation of other people's money), or it may consist in suspicion combined with a conscious decision not to make inquiries which might result in knowledge... . Although a dishonest state of mind is a subjective mental state, the standard by which the law determines whether it is dishonest is objective. If by ordinary standards a defendant's mental state would be characterised as dishonest, it is irrelevant that the defendant judges by different standards. The Court of Appeal held this to be a correct statement of the law and their Lordships agree.

 Alert

The judge found that during and after June 1987 Mr Henwood strongly suspected that the funds passing through his hands were moneys which Barlow Clowes had received from members of the public who thought that they were subscribing to a scheme of investment in gilt-edged securities. If those suspicions were correct, no honest person could have assisted Mr Clowes and Mr Cramer to dispose of the funds for their personal use. But Mr Henwood consciously decided not to make inquiries because he preferred in his own interest not to run the risk of discovering the truth.

Their Lordships consider that by ordinary standards such a state of mind is dishonest. The judge found that Mr Henwood may well have lived by different standards and seen nothing wrong in what he was doing. He had an: 'exaggerated notion of dutiful service to clients, which produced a warped moral approach that it was not improper to treat carrying out clients' instructions as being all important. Mr Henwood may well have thought this to be an honest attitude, but, if so, he was wrong.'

Lord Neill of Bladen QC, who appeared for Mr Henwood, submitted to their Lordships that such a state of mind was not dishonest unless Mr Henwood was aware that it would by ordinary standards be regarded as dishonest. Only in such a case could he be said to be consciously dishonest. But the judge made no finding about Mr Henwood's opinions about normal standards of honesty. The only finding was that by normal standards he had been dishonest but that his own standard was different.

...Lord Neill relied upon a statement by Lord Hutton in *Twinsectra Ltd v Yardley...* , with which the majority of their Lordships agreed... .

Their Lordships accept that there is an element of ambiguity in these remarks which may have encouraged a belief, expressed in some academic writing, that the *Twinsectra* case had departed from the law as previously understood and invited inquiry not merely into the defendant's mental state about the nature of the transaction in which he was participating but also into his views about generally acceptable standards of honesty. But they do not consider that this is what Lord Hutton meant. The reference to 'what he knows would offend normally accepted standards of honest conduct' meant only that his knowledge of the transaction had to be such as to render his participation contrary to normally acceptable standards of honest conduct. It did not require that he should have had reflections about what those normally acceptable standards were.

 Alert

Similarly in the speech of Lord Hoffmann, the statement ... that a dishonest state of mind meant 'consciousness that one is transgressing ordinary standards of honest behaviour' was in their Lordships' view intended to require consciousness of those elements of the transaction which make participation transgress ordinary standards of honest behaviour. It did not also require him to have thought about what those standards were.

On the facts of the *Twinsectra* case, neither the judge who acquitted Mr Leach of dishonesty nor the House undertook any inquiry into the views of ... Mr Leach about ordinary standards of honest behaviour. ...The judge found that he was not dishonest because he honestly believed that the undertaking did not, so to speak, run with the money and that, as between him and his client, he held it for his client unconditionally. He was therefore bound to pay it upon his client's instructions without restriction on its use. The majority in the House of Lords considered that a solicitor who held this view of the law, even though he knew all the facts, was not by normal standards dishonest.

Their Lordships therefore reject Lord Neill's submission that the judge failed to apply the principles of liability for dishonest assistance which had been laid down in the *Twinsectra* case. In their opinion they were no different from the principles stated in *Royal Brunei Airlines Sdn Bhd v Tan* ... which were correctly summarised by the judge. ...

Alert

Their Lordships consider that ... it was not necessary ... that Mr Henwood should have concluded that the disposals were of moneys held in trust. It was sufficient that he should have entertained a clear suspicion that this was the case. ...[I]t is quite unreal to suppose that Mr Henwood needed to know all the details ... before he had grounds to suspect that Mr Clowes and Mr Cramer were misappropriating their investors' money. The money in Barlow Clowes was either held on trust for the investors or else belonged to the company and was subject to fiduciary duties on the part of the directors. In either case, Mr Clowes and Mr Cramer could not have been entitled to make free with it as they pleased. In *Brinks Ltd v Abu-Saleh (No 3)* [1996] CLC 133 at 151 Rimer J expressed the opinion that a person cannot be liable for dishonest assistance in a breach of trust unless he knows of the existence of the trust or at least the facts giving rise to the trust. But their Lordships do not agree. Someone can know, and can certainly suspect, that he is assisting in a misappropriation of money without knowing that the money is held on trust or what a trust means: see *Twinsectra Ltd v Yardley* ... (Lord Hoffmann) and ... (Lord Millett). And it was not necessary to know the 'precise involvement' of Mr Cramer in the group's affairs in order to suspect that neither he nor anyone else had the right to use Barlow Clowes money for speculative investments of their own.

 Alert

...[T]here was abundant evidence on which the judge was entitled to make the findings of fact which she did... . The Staff of Government Division should not have set them aside.

By the time of the later transactions, Mr Henwood had even more reason to be suspicious. In particular, he had been told on 2 July 1987 by two employees in the Geneva office that Mr Clowes and Mr Cramer were misappropriating clients' money. Mr Clowes had subsequently persuaded the employees to say that they had been misunderstood, but Mr Henwood knew he had understood them perfectly well. The Staff of Government nevertheless found that even in these circumstances, the judge was not entitled to find that he must have entertained suspicions which he chose not to investigate. They said that he might have thought his suspicions would somehow be disabused or that he might have relied upon the word of Mr Clowes that all was well.

...Mr Henwood's evidence, which the judge found to be untruthful, was that he knew nothing and had no reason to suspect anything. A state of mind in which suspicion had been allayed was entirely the invention of the Staff of Government Division. There was no evidence that Mr Henwood had tried to seek any explanation whatever and their Lordships consider that the judge was fully justified in concluding that this was the result of a deliberate and dishonest decision.

Their Lordships will therefore humbly advise Her Majesty that the appeal should be allowed and the decision of the Acting Deemster restored. ...

This case returned to the meaning of dishonesty set out in *Tan*. However, like *Tan*, it is only of persuasive authority, whereas the decision of the House of Lords in *Twinsectra* is binding. In the next case, Arden LJ, in the Court of Appeal, took the view that the decision of the Privy Council in *Barlow Clowes v Eurotrust* should be followed. The other two Lords Justices preferred not to commit themselves on the subject of the relationship between that case and the case of *Twinsectra*.

Abou-Ramah and another v Abacha and others [2007] 1 All ER (Comm) 827

Panel: Pill, Rix and Arden LJJ

Facts: Abou-Rahmah (a lawyer in Kuwait) was asked by fraudsters to assist in investing a large sum in an Arab country. He was told that it was money from a trust but that the money was in Benin and could only be transferred out if certain payments were made. On the fraudsters' instructions, he made payments to a London-based account of City Express Bank, a Nigerian bank. The Bank transferred it to the account in Nigeria of Trusty International, a company run by Ibrahim and Saminu, who were accomplices in the fraud. The fraudsters disappeared. Abou-Rahmah sued City Express Bank for dishonest assistance in a breach of trust. The judge found that the fraud amounted to a breach of trust and that the Bank's local manager, Mr Farobi, who dealt with the opening of the Trusty International account, had suspected that Ibrahim and Saminu might sometimes assist corrupt politicians to launder money, but did not have any particular suspicions about the transactions involved in the case. The judge found that the bank did not act dishonestly, so the claim failed. The claimant appealed to the Court of Appeal which upheld the judge's decision.

LORD JUSTICE RIX

...Knowing/dishonest assistance

The Privy Council's decision in Barlow Clowes emerged only after trial, pending judgment. The judge invited, and received, further written submissions in the light of that decision. ...

It would seem that a claimant in this area needs to show three things: first, that a defendant has the requisite knowledge; secondly, that, given that knowledge, the defendant acts in a way which is contrary to normally acceptable standards of honest conduct (the objective test of honesty or dishonesty); and thirdly, possibly, that the defendant must in some sense be dishonest himself (a subjective test of dishonesty which might, on analysis, add little or nothing to knowledge of the facts which, objectively, would make his conduct dishonest).

It is the third element which raises a problem of definition in the light of Twinsectra and Barlow Clowes. In commenting on Twinsectra before Barlow Clowes, Snell's Equity, 31st ed, 2005, at 692/3 (para 28-46) put the matter in this way:

"The Defendant must be proved to have been dishonest in giving his assistance to the trustee's breach. In applying this standard the Defendant is not free to be judged according to his standards of dishonesty. Nor is he to be judged by a purely objective standard of whether an ordinary honest person in his position would regard his conduct as dishonest. Rather, it must be established that he knew that ordinary honest people would regard his assistance as dishonest in all the circumstances."

In commenting on the subject-matter after Barlow Clowes, however, Snell ... has replaced the above paragraph with the following:

"The Defendant must be proved to have been dishonest in giving his assistance to the trustee's breach. In applying this standard, it is clear that the Defendant is not free to be judged according to his own standards of honesty. He is judged according [to] the standard of ordinary honest people (Royal Brunei Airlines Sdn Bhd v Tan...). The authorities have in the past been uncertain about whether the trustee [sic] also needs to be aware that his conduct would be regarded as dishonest by this standard. The better view is that it is unnecessary for the Defendant to take a view on the propriety of his conduct. (Compare Twinsectra Ltd v Yardley ... with Barlow Clowes v Eurotrust International Ltd...). A finding that the Defendant was dishonest need only involve an assessment of his participation in the light of his knowledge of the facts of the transaction."

In Twinsectra the House of Lords split ... on the question whether the dishonesty spoken of in Tan was objective or subjective. The majority ... were in favour of a subjective test. ...

Lord Millett, however, was for adopting an objective approach as being more apposite to civil as distinct from criminal liability... . He would therefore have placed particular weight on the requirement of knowledge...

In Barlow Clowes ... [t]he single judgment was delivered by Lord Hoffmann. There are passages in the judgment which have raised academic controversy (see for instance LQR 2006 171, JIBLR 2006 377) as to whether the Privy Council has in Barlow Clowes rowed back towards Lord Millett's views in Twinsectra... . [His Lordship cited the passage where Lord Hoffmann commented on his own speech in Twinsectra and continued:]

I do not need to enter into that controversy for the purposes of this appeal. It is sufficient to concentrate on what was said in Barlow Clowes about the element of knowledge required to set up an investigation of the subsequent element of dishonesty. For in this respect, the Privy Council underlined that there may be sufficient knowledge (a) in suspicion and (b) despite ignorance that money is held on trust at all. ...

[O]nce Mr Faronbi suspected Trusty International's directors of participating in money laundering, ... the distinction which the judge then drew between Mr Faronbi's suspicions of the business in general and his ignorance about the particular transactions in question ... becomes a thin line... . It is one thing to be negligent in failing to spot a possible money launderer, providing the negligence does not extend to shutting one's eyes to the truth. It is another thing ... to have good grounds for suspecting money laundering and then to proceed as though one did not. ...I do not see why a bank which has, through its managers, a clear suspicion that a prospective client indulges in money laundering, can be said to lack that knowledge...

However, ...where the trial judge has nevertheless acquitted Mr Faronbi of any dishonesty ... I do not consider it ... possible to reverse the judge's finding on appeal so as to conclude that Mr Faronbi or the bank was dishonest in the Twinsectra sense, even as clarified in Barlow Clowes. ...

LADY JUSTICE ARDEN

...The dishonest assistance issue

I agree with Rix LJ that the appeal on this issue fails. In Barlow Clowes International Ltd (in liquidation) v Eurotrust International Ltd... , the Privy Council considered the case law of England and Wales on the issue of the element of dishonesty necessary for liability under this head. Its interpretation of that case law was that it is unnecessary to show subjective dishonesty in the sense of consciousness that the transaction is dishonest. It is sufficient if the defendant knows of the elements of the transaction which make it dishonest according to normally accepted standards of behaviour. ...[I]n my judgment this court should follow the decision of the Privy Council. ...

The decision of the Privy Council in Royal Brunei Airlines Sdn Bhd v Tan ... had been taken to establish for the purposes of English law that dishonesty was required before liability for assisting in a breach of trust could be imposed... . Indeed, in the Twinsectra case, Lord Hutton accepted that the House should follow ... the Royal Brunei case... . Lord Nicholls ... [in Royal Brunei] held that "the standard of what constitutes honest conduct is not subjective" ... and gave other indications that consciousness of wrongdoing was not required for accessory liability for breach of trust.

The subsequent decision of the House of Lords in *Twinsectra Ltd v Yardley* ... was widely interpreted as requiring both an objective and subjective test to be applied... . In the case of the subjective test, that would mean that the Defendant would not be guilty of dishonesty unless he was conscious that the transaction fell below normally acceptable standards of conduct. The Privy Council in the *Barlow Clowes* case has now clarified that this is a wrong interpretation of the Twinsectra decision. It is not a requirement of the standard of dishonesty that the defendant should be conscious of his wrongdoing. *Snell's Equity* now refers to this as the "better view"... .

 Alert

On the basis of this interpretation, the test of dishonesty is predominantly objective: did the conduct of the defendant fall below the normally acceptable standard? But there are also subjective aspects of dishonesty. As Lord Nicholls said in the *Royal Brunei* case, honesty has:

"a strong subjective element in that it is a description of a type of conduct assessed in the light of what a person actually knew at the time, as distinct from what a reasonable person would have known or appreciated"... .

In this case, the judge applied the Barlow Clowes decision without asking himself, on the basis that Twinsectra was binding on him under the doctrine of precedent and the Barlow Clowes case ... was only persuasive authority, whether the interpretation in that case was one he would himself have come to... . Adherence to the doctrine of precedent is important... . On the other hand special factors can arise with respect to decisions of the Privy Council...

[B]efore this court ... decides to follow a decision of the Privy Council in place of a decision of the House of Lords the circumstances must be quite exceptional and the court must be satisfied that in practice the result would be a foregone conclusion. In my judgment, the circumstances of this case are ... exceptional and justify the course which the judge took for the following reasons:

i. The decision in Twinsectra is of course binding on this court and the judge. But the *Barlow Clowes* decision does not involve a departure from, or refusal to follow, the *Twinsectra* case. Rather, the *Barlow Clowes* case gives guidance as to the proper interpretation to be placed on it as a matter of English law. It shows how the *Royal Brunei* case and the *Twinsectra* case can be read together to form a consistent corpus of law.

 Alert

ii. The meaning of dishonesty in the Twinsectra case appeared to involve an additional subjective element, namely an awareness on the part of the accessory that his conduct was dishonest. ...The approach of the Privy Council [in Barlow Clowes] was both striking and bold: one writer has referred to it as taking judicial re-interpretation "to new heights" (Virgo, Mapping the Law, Essays in memory of Peter Birks, ed Burrows and Rodger (2006)(Oxford) ch 5 p 86). The decision in the Barlow Clowes case could probably have been reached without consideration of the Twinsectra decision... , and it is significant that the Privy Council took another course.

iii. ...[T]he approach in Barlow Clowes was to clarify the meaning of the speeches of Lord Hutton and Lord Hoffmann in the Twinsectra case. The view expressed by Lord Hutton represented the view of the majority. Two members of the constitution of the Appellate Committee which sat in Twinsectra (Lord Steyn and Lord Hoffmann) were parties to the decision in Barlow Clowes. It is difficult to see that another constitution of the Appellate Committee would itself come to a different view as to what the majority in Twinsectra had meant. ...I do not see how in these particular circumstances this court could be criticised for adopting the interpretation of the Twinsectra decision unanimously adopted by the Privy Council... .

iv. There is no overriding reason why in respect of dishonesty in the context of civil liability ... the law should take account of the Defendant's views as to the morality of his actions.

For all the above reasons, I consider that the judge was right to proceed on the basis that the law as laid down in the Twinsectra case, as interpreted ... in Barlow Clowes, represented the law... .

 Link
See the similar view expressed by Lord Millett in his dissenting speech in *Twinsectra v Yardley.*

In considering the decision in the Barlow Clowes case, I would acknowledge in addition to the articles to which Rix LJ referred in para 22 of his judgment the case note entitled Dishonesty in the Context of Assistance – again [2006] 65 CLJ 18 by Conaglen & Goymour.

I now turn to consider the application of the test of dishonesty as established in the Barlow Clowes case to the present case. ...The highest that it can be put is that the bank had suspicions about TI's possible involvement in the money-laundering of money at the instance of corrupt politicians. But it had no knowledge of any specific act of dishonesty by TI and it had no grounds for believing that the Appellants were, or were associates of, politicians and it had no particular suspicions about the transactions in question. There was no finding that in those circumstances a bank would normally raise additional inquiries ... or decline to act. Thus, the lack of particular suspicions about the transactions in question ... diminished Mr Faronbi's general suspicions ... to an extent that it was no longer commercially unacceptable for the bank to implement the instructions that [it] had received.

...I would thus dismiss the appeal on the dishonest assistance issue. ...

LORD JUSTICE PILL

...I do not consider that the disputed question whether subjective dishonesty is necessary to establish dishonest assistance ... has any bearing upon the outcome of the appeal. If viewed objectively, the conduct in relation to the relevant transactions, of Mr Faronbi, the Bank's local manager, were to be held to have fallen below normally acceptable standards, it can readily be inferred that he knew it did so that his conduct would have amounted to dishonest assistance. I would expect that to be the position in the great majority of ordinary commercial transactions.

I agree with Rix LJ that it is not necessary in this appeal to resolve the question of the impact of *Barlow Clowes* ... upon *Twinsectra* ... . The case does not turn upon it and we have heard argument, though very fairly presented, from only one party.

 Alert

Putting it at its highest, however, it will not exclude the need, in some cases, to consider the Defendant's state of mind. [His Lordship cited the commentary of Lord Hoffmann in Barlow Clowes on Twinsectra and continued:]

The Privy Council in Barlow Clowes did not find that the decision of the House of Lords in Twinsectra was, on its facts, wrong. What determined the outcome in that case was, in the view of the majority, as described by Lord Hoffmann in Barlow Clowes, ... the honest belief of the Defendant solicitor in a certain view of the law. ...The case turned, it appears to me, on the view taken of the honesty of the Defendant's conduct in the transaction. The majority all took the view that the trial judge's conclusion that the Defendant had not been dishonest should be upheld. Whether a Defendant's belief is honest or dishonest involves an assessment of his mental state.

Both Rix LJ ... and Arden LJ, when using the expression "predominantly objective"... , acknowledge the possibility of the presence of a subjective element. I fully and respectfully acknowledge the value of Barlow Clowes in its explanation of Twinsectra but the implications are in my view best considered in a case in which a real issue arises on its impact.

...I agree with Rix LJ that it would not be right to reverse the judge's findings. ... I agree that the appeal based on dishonest assistance must be dismissed. ...

It seems likely from Arden LJ's judgment that the courts will adopt the interpretation of *Twinsectra* given in *Barlow Clowes v Eurotrust* but the matter cannot be regarded as settled beyond doubt.

16.2 Knowing Receipt

Bank of Credit and Commerce International (Overseas) Ltd and another v Akindele [2001] Ch 437

Panel: Nourse, Ward and Sedley LJJ

Facts: Akindele, a Nigerian businessman, entered an agreement in 1985 with ICIC, a Cayman Islands company controlled by BCCI, under which he was to buy BCCI shares and hold them for at least two years. If he decided to sell them after two years, but before five years had elapsed, he would be guaranteed a return of 15% per annum on his investment. The shares would not actually be transferred to his name unless he held them for more than five years. The agreement was part of a fraudulent scheme devised by BCCI directors who were acting in breach of their fiduciary duties. By late 1987, there were press rumours of irregularities within BCCI and, in 1988, the defendant found out that certain BCCI officials had been arrested in connection with money laundering. He decided to end his agreement and received his money back, with the agreed interest, under a divestiture agreement. BCCI went into liquidation and the liquidators sued Akindele for knowing assistance and knowing receipt. The judge held that Akindele was unaware of the fraud and had not acted dishonestly. The liquidators appealed and the Court of Appeal upheld the judge's decision.

LORD JUSTICE NOURSE

Introduction

This is a claim by liquidators under both the knowing assistance and knowing receipt heads of constructive trust. The argument in this court has been mainly directed to two questions arising in relation to liability under the latter head. What must be the recipient's state of knowledge? Must he be dishonest? ...

Dishonesty: the judge's findings

...The judge ... considered the defendant's credibility... . He said... :

"I am satisfied that he did not himself see it as a dishonest transaction. He saw it simply as an arm's-length business transaction with a major bank... ." ...

The claimants' case in this court

The judge ... identified the two main issues ... as being, first, was the defendant liable for dishonestly assisting or participating in breaches of trust ... (knowing assistance) and, secondly, was the defendant liable for receiving the divestiture payment with knowledge of the breaches of trust (knowing receipt). ...The defendant not having acted dishonestly, the case in knowing assistance is bound to fail. If the claim is to succeed at all, it can only be in knowing receipt.

Knowing receipt

The essential requirements of knowing receipt were stated by Hoffmann LJ in *El Ajou v Dollar Land Holdings plc* [1994] 2 All ER 685, 700:

"For this purpose the plaintiff must show, first, a disposal of his assets in breach of fiduciary duty; secondly, the beneficial receipt by the defendant of assets which are traceable as representing the assets of the plaintiff; and thirdly, knowledge on the part of the defendant that the assets he received are traceable to a breach of fiduciary duty."

In the present case the first two requirements were satisfied in relation to the defendant's receipt of the US$16.679m paid to him pursuant to the divestiture agreement. But the satisfaction of the third requirement ... is problematical.

So far as the law is concerned, ... there are two questions which, though closely related, are distinct: first, what, in this context, is meant by knowledge; second, is it necessary for the recipient to act dishonestly? [T]he convenient course is to deal with the second of those questions first.

Knowing receipt-dishonesty

...Carnwath J proceeded on an assumption that dishonesty in one form or another was the essential foundation of the claimants' case, whether in knowing assistance or knowing receipt. That was no doubt caused by the acceptance before him (though not at any higher level) ... that the thrust of the recent authorities at first instance was that the recipient's state of knowledge must fall into one of the first three categories listed by Peter Gibson J in *Baden v Société Générale pour Favoriser le Développement du Commerce et de l'Industrie en France SA* [1993] 1 WLR 509, 575-576, on which basis, said Carnwath J, it was doubtful whether the test differed materially in practice from that for knowing assistance. However, the assumption on which the judge proceeded, derived as I believe from an omission to distinguish between the questions of knowledge and dishonesty, was incorrect in law. While a knowing recipient will often be found to have acted dishonestly, it has never been a prerequisite of the liability that he should.

An authoritative decision on this question ... is *Belmont Finance Corpn Ltd v Williams Furniture Ltd (No 2)* [1980] 1 All ER 393... . [T]hough the claim in knowing assistance failed because the directors of Belmont did not act dishonestly, the claim in knowing receipt succeeded. ...

Belmont Finance Corpn Ltd v Williams Furniture Ltd (No 2) [1980] 1 All ER 393 is clear authority for the proposition that dishonesty is not a necessary ingredient of liability in knowing receipt. There have been other, more recent, judicial pronouncements to the same effect. ...

Knowing receipt--the authorities on knowledge

...[T]here has been a sustained judicial and extrajudicial debate as to the knowledge on the part of the recipient which is required in order to found liability in knowing receipt. Expressed in its simplest terms, the question is whether the recipient must have actual knowledge (or the equivalent) that the assets received are traceable to a breach of trust or whether constructive knowledge is enough. The instinctive approach of most equity judges, especially in this court, has been to assume that constructive knowledge is enough. But there is now a series of decisions of eminent first instance judges who,

Link
on the need for 'beneficial' receipt, see the discussion by Lord Millett in *Twinsectra v Yardley*.

Alert

after considering the question in greater depth, have come to the contrary conclusion, at all events when commercial transactions are in point. In the Commonwealth, on the other hand, the preponderance of authority has been in favour of the view that constructive knowledge is enough. ...

In *Belmont Finance Corpn Ltd v Williams Furniture Ltd (No 2)* [1980] 1 All ER 393, 405 Buckley LJ ... [said]:

"So, if the directors of a company in breach of their fiduciary duties misapply the funds of their company so that they come into the hands of some stranger to the trust who receives them with knowledge (actual or constructive) of the breach, he cannot conscientiously retain those funds ... . He becomes a constructive trustee for the company of the misapplied funds." ...

Sir Robert Megarry V-C in *In re Montagu's Settlement Trusts* [1987] Ch 264 ... first plumbed the distinction between notice and knowledge. It was he who, building on a passage in the judgment of this court in *In re Diplock* [1948] Ch 465, 478-479, first emphasised the fundamental difference between the questions which arise in respect of the doctrine of purchaser without notice on the one hand and the doctrine of constructive trusts on the other. Reading from his earlier judgment in the same case, ... he said:

"The former is concerned with the question whether a person takes property subject to or free from some equity. The latter is concerned with whether or not a person is to have imposed upon him the personal burdens and obligations of trusteeship. I do not see why one of the touchstones for determining the burdens on property should be the same as that for deciding whether to impose a personal obligation on a [person]. The cold calculus of constructive and imputed notice does not seem to me to be an appropriate instrument for deciding whether a [person's] conscience is sufficiently affected for it to be right to bind him by the obligations of a constructive trustee." ...

Sir Robert Megarry V-C summarised his conclusions in eight subparagraphs... . I read the first three:

"(1) The equitable doctrine of tracing and the imposition of a constructive trust by reason of the knowing receipt of trust property are governed by different rules and must be kept distinct. Tracing is primarily a means of determining the rights of property, whereas the imposition of a constructive trust creates personal obligations that go beyond mere property rights. (2) In considering whether a constructive trust has arisen in a case of the knowing receipt of trust property, the basic question is whether the conscience of the recipient is sufficiently affected to justify the imposition of such a trust. (3) Whether a constructive trust arises in such a case primarily depends on the knowledge of the recipient, and not on notice to him; and for clarity it is desirable to use the word 'knowledge' and avoid the word 'notice' in such cases."

 Alert

The effect of Sir Robert Megarry V-C's decision, broadly stated, was that, in order to establish liability in knowing receipt, the recipient must have actual knowledge (or the equivalent) that the assets received are traceable to a breach of trust and that constructive knowledge is not enough. ...

[His Lordship referred to three decisions in New Zealand and one in Canada, all cases of commercial transactions, where the view was that constructive knowledge was enough. He cited a passage from the judgment in *Westpac Banking Corpn v Savin* [1985] 2 NZLR 41 in which Richardson J, having expressed a provisional preference for the view that constructive knowledge was enough, said that "courts would not readily import a duty to inquire in the case of commercial transactions" and continued:]

The Baden case

It will have been observed that up to this stage I have made no more than a passing reference to the fivefold categorisation of knowledge accepted by Peter Gibson J in *Baden v Société Générale pour Favoriser le Développement du Commerce et de l'Industrie en France SA* [1993] 1 WLR 509, 575-576: (i) actual knowledge; (ii) wilfully shutting one's eyes to the obvious; (iii) wilfully and recklessly failing to make such inquiries as an honest and reasonable man would make; (iv) knowledge of circumstances which would indicate the facts to an honest and reasonable man; (v) knowledge of circumstances which will put an honest and reasonable man on inquiry. Reference to the categorisation has been made in most of the knowing receipt cases to which I have referred from *In re Montagu's Settlement Trusts* [1987] Ch 264 onwards. In many of them it has been influential in the decision. In general, the first three categories have been taken to constitute actual knowledge (or its equivalent) and the last two constructive knowledge.

Two important points must be made about the *Baden* categorisation. First, it appears to have been propounded by counsel for the plaintiffs, accepted by counsel for the defendant and then put to the judge on an agreed basis. Secondly, though both counsel accepted that all five categories of knowledge were relevant and neither sought to submit that there was any distinction for that purpose between knowing receipt and knowing assistance (a view with which the judge expressed his agreement...), the claim in constructive trust was based squarely on knowing assistance and not on knowing receipt... . In the circumstances ... it is natural to assume that the categorisation was not formulated with knowing receipt primarily in mind. ...

Knowing receipt--the recipient's state of knowledge

In *Royal Brunei Airlines Sdn Bhd v Tan...* , which is now the leading authority on knowing assistance, Lord Nicholls ... said ... that "knowingly" was better avoided as a defining ingredient of the liability, and that in that context the *Baden* categorisation was best forgotten. Although my own view is that the categorisation is often helpful in identifying different states of knowledge which may or may not result in a finding of dishonesty for the purposes of knowing assistance, I have grave doubts about its utility in cases of knowing receipt. Quite apart from its origins in a context of knowing assistance ... any categorisation is of little value unless the purpose it is to serve is adequately defined, whether it be fivefold, as in the *Baden* case... , or twofold, as in the classical division between actual and constructive knowledge, a division which has itself become blurred... .

Link
Compare this with the view expressed in *Royal Brunei Airlines v Tan*.

What then, in the context of knowing receipt, is the purpose to be served by a categorisation of knowledge? It can only be to enable the court to determine whether, in the words of Buckley LJ in *Belmont Finance Corpn Ltd v Williams Furniture Ltd (No 2)* ... the recipient can "conscientiously retain [the] funds against the company" or, in the words of Sir Robert Megarry V-C in *In re Montagu's Settlement Trusts...* , "[the recipient's] conscience is sufficiently affected for it to be right to bind him by the obligations of a constructive trustee". But, if that is the purpose, there is no need for categorisation. All that is necessary is that the recipient's state of knowledge should be such as to make it unconscionable for him to retain the benefit of the receipt.

For these reasons I have come to the view that, just as there is now a single test of dishonesty for knowing assistance, so ought there to be a single test of knowledge for knowing receipt. The recipient's state of knowledge must be such as to make it unconscionable for him to retain the benefit of the receipt. A test in that form, though it cannot, any more than any other, avoid difficulties of application, ought to avoid those of definition and allocation to which the previous categorisations have led. Moreover, it should better enable the courts to give commonsense decisions in the commercial context in which claims in knowing receipt are now frequently made...

Knowing receipt--a footnote

We were referred in argument to "Knowing Receipt: The Need for a New Landmark", an essay by Lord Nicholls of Birkenhead in *Restitution Past, Present and Future* (1998) p 231, a work of insight and scholarship... . Most pertinent for present purposes is the suggestion ... at p 238, in reference to the decision of the House of Lords in *Lipkin Gorman v Karpnale Ltd* [1991] 2 AC 548:

"In this respect equity should now follow the law. Restitutionary liability, applicable regardless of fault but subject to a defence of change of position, would be a better-tailored response to the underlying mischief of misapplied property than personal liability which is exclusively fault-based. Personal liability would flow from having received the property of another, from having been unjustly enriched at the expense of another. It would be triggered by the mere fact of receipt, thus recognising the endurance of property rights. But fairness would be ensured by the need to identify a gain, and by making change of position available as a defence in suitable cases when, for instance, the recipient had changed his position in reliance on the receipt."

Lord Nicholls goes on to examine the *In re Diplock* [1948] Ch 465 principle, suggesting, at p 241, that it could be reshaped by being extended to all trusts but in a form modified to take proper account of the decision in *Lipkin Gorman v Karpnale Ltd* [1991] 2 AC 548.

No argument before us was based on the suggestions made in Lord Nicholls's essay. Indeed, at this level of decision, it would have been a fruitless exercise. ...While in general it may be possible to sympathise with a tendency to subsume a further part of our law of restitution under the principles of unjust enrichment, I beg leave to doubt whether strict liability coupled with a change of position defence would be preferable to fault-based liability in many commercial transactions, for example where, as here,

Link
Note the rejection of unconscionability as the basis of liability for dishonest assistance in *Royal Brunei Airlines v Tan*.

Link
See the brief *obiter* comment on recipient liability made by Lord Nicholls in *Royal Brunei Airlines v Tan* and the view on this expressed *obiter* by Lord Millett in *Twinsectra v Yardley*.

the receipt is of a company's funds which have been misapplied by its directors. Without having heard argument it is unwise to be dogmatic, but in such a case it would appear to be commercially unworkable ... that, simply on proof of an internal misapplication of the company's funds, the burden should shift to the recipient to defend the receipt either by a change of position or perhaps in some other way. ...

 Alert

Knowing receipt – the facts of the present case

I return to the facts of the present case, in order to determine whether the defendant is liable in knowing receipt to repay (together with interest) US$6.679m of the sum received by him pursuant to the divestiture agreement, being the excess over the US$10m he paid to ICIC Overseas pursuant to the 1985 agreement. ...

I start with the defendant's state of knowledge at the date of the 1985 agreement. As to that, the judge found that there was no evidence that anyone outside BCCI had reason to doubt the integrity of its management at that time. More specifically, it is clear that the judge was of the view that the defendant had no knowledge of the underlying frauds within the BCCI group either in general or in relation to the 1985 agreement. ...Moreover, he was not prepared to draw the conclusion that the high rate of interest and the artificial nature of the agreement were sufficient to put an honest person in the defendant's position on notice that some fraud or breach of trust was being perpetrated. He said that the defendant would have had no reason to question the form of the transaction.

Those findings, expressed in language equally appropriate to an inquiry as to constructive notice, appear to me to be consistent only with the view that the defendant's state of knowledge at the date of the 1985 agreement was not such as to make it unconscionable for him to enter into it. However, ...[w]e have also to consider the defendant's state of knowledge at the date of the divestiture agreement, by which time ... he did have suspicions as to the conduct of BCCI's affairs. ...

There having been no evidence that the defendant was aware of the internal arrangements within BCCI which led to the payment to him of the US$16.679m pursuant to the divestiture agreement, did the additional knowledge which he acquired between July 1985 and December 1988 make it unconscionable for him to retain the benefit of the receipt? In my judgment it did not. The additional knowledge went to the general reputation of the BCCI group from late 1987 onwards. It was not a sufficient reason for questioning the propriety of a particular transaction entered into more than two years earlier, at a time when no one outside BCCI had reason to doubt the integrity of its management and in a form which the defendant had no reason to question. The judge said that the defendant was entitled to take steps to protect his own interest, and that there was nothing dishonest in his seeking to enforce the 1985 agreement. Nor was there anything unconscionable in his seeking to do so. Equally, had I thought that that was still the appropriate test, I would have held that the defendant did not have actual or constructive knowledge that his receipt of the US$6.79m was traceable to a breach or breaches of fiduciary duty... .

Conclusion

For these reasons, though by a different route in relation to knowing receipt, I have come to the conclusion that Carnwath J's decision to dismiss the action was correct. I would affirm it and dismiss the claimants' appeal.

LORD JUSTICE WARD

I agree.

LORD JUSTICE SEDLEY

I also agree.

Further Reading

Hunter Robert, 'The Honest Truth about Dishonesty', PCB (Private Client Business) 2002, 6, 390-393

Ryan Desmond, *Royal Brunei* 'Dishonesty: A Clear Welcome' for *Barlow Clowes*, Conv. 2007, Mar/Apr, pp 168-175

Dishonest Assistance: restatement from the Privy Council Yeo T.M, LQR 2006, 122(Apr), pp 171-174

Dishonesty in the context of assistance – again Conaglen and Goymour, CLJ 2006, 65(1), pp 18-21

Knowing Receipt: 'The Need for a New Landmark' Lord Nicholls in Cornish, Nolan, O'Sullivan and Virgo (eds) *Restitution Past, Present and Future* 1998, published by Hart

''Goodbye' Knowing Receipt. 'Hello' Unconscientious Receipt', Susan Barkehall Thomas, OJLS June 2001.21(239) – read the Introduction and Part 1

17

Equitable Remedies

Topic List

Introduction

The limitations of the common law remedy of damages had become acutely apparent during the historical development of equity, particularly to those seeking solutions to their legal problems. In many cases damages were simply inadequate and it was in these situations that equity was, and continues to be, of such tremendous value by offering more appropriate alternatives.

In this chapter we shall look at equitable remedies, particularly those of specific performance, freezing injunctions and search orders. These remedies often arise as a result of contract or tort claims but we will not examine these claims in any great detail as they are dealt with in other modules and casebooks on your course.

17.1 Specific Performance

17.1.1 Sale of Goods

The general principle that the court will apply, when looking at whether or not specific performance is appropriate, is the adequacy of damages to the claimant. If damages are sufficient to compensate the claimant then it is very unlikely that specific performance will be granted as per Sir John Leech V-C in *Adderley v Dixon* (1824) 1 S & S 607.

Cohen v Roche [1927] 1 KB 169

Panel: McCardie J

Statutes: Sale of Goods Act 1893 ss 4, 18 and 52

Facts: The claimant was an antiques dealer who had visited an auction house at which the defendant, an auctioneer, had been conducting a sale. In the course of the auction a lot of 8 Hepplewhite chairs, the personal property of the defendant, was sold to the claimant for an agreed price. The defendant made a note in his book next to the description of the chairs indicating the final sale price. When the claimant sought delivery of the chairs, having provided the agreed sale price, the defendant refused and the claimant sought specific performance of the contract. It was held that the court would not allow specific performance but instead awarded the claimant damages for breach of contract. While valuable antiques in and of themselves the Hepplewhite chairs were not extraordinary and nor were they exceptional in any way. They had been purchased for the sole purpose of profit in the everyday business of the claimant.

MR JUSTICE MCCARDIE

...For the reasons given I am of opinion that there is in the case now before me a sufficient and duly signed memorandum within s 4 of the Sale of Goods Act, 1893, and that an enforceable contract exists between the parties.

I now take the final point in the case. The plaintiff sued in detinue only. The writ and statement of claim contain no alternative demand for damages for breach of contract. They ask (a) for delivery up of the chairs or payment of their value, and (b) damages for detention. I have however allowed an amendment whereby the statement of claim asks damages for breach of contract. The plaintiff vigorously contends that he is entitled as of right, once a binding contract is established, to an order for the actual delivery of the chairs, and that he is not limited to damages for breach of bargain. This point raises a question of principle and practice. Here I may again state one or two of the facts. The Hepplewhite chairs in lot 145 possessed no special features at all. They were ordinary Hepplewhite furniture. The plaintiff bought them in the ordinary way of his trade for the purpose of ordinary resale at a profit. He had no special customer in view. The lot was to become a part of his usual trade stock. ...

It seems clear that the discretionary provisions of s 52 cannot be consistent with an absolute right of a plaintiff to an order for compulsory delivery under a detinue judgment in such a case as the present. How, then, does the law stand as to detinue? In my view the power of the Court in an action of detinue rests upon a footing which fully accords with s 52 of the Sale of Goods Act, 1893. In *Whiteley, Ltd v Hilt* (an action of detinue) Swinfen Eady M.R. said:

> "The power vested in the Court to order the delivery up of a particular chattel is discretionary, and ought not to be exercised when the chattel is an ordinary article of commerce and of no special value or interest, and not alleged to be of any special value to the plaintiff, and where damages would fully compensate. In equity, where a plaintiff alleged and proved the money value of the chattel, it was not the practice of the Court to order its specific delivery: see *Dowling v Betjemann*."

The law is thus, I am glad to find, consistent in its several parts. In the present case the goods in question were ordinary articles of commerce and of no special value or interest, and no grounds exist for any special order for delivery. The judgment should be limited to damages for breach of contract. The plaintiff in his evidence said that the chairs were worth from 70l. to 80l. With this I agree. I assess the damages at the sum of 15l.

For the reasons given I therefore enter judgment for the plaintiff for 15l. damages for breach of contract with costs on scale "C" of county court costs.

 Alert

Contrasting this case is the situation where the property is not an ordinary article or does have a special value, interest, or significance to the claimant.

Falcke v Gray (1859) 62 ER 250

Panel: Sir R T Kindersley V-C

Facts: The claimant was a tenant of the defendant, from whom he was granted the option to purchase a pair of Chinese Ming Dynasty vases for a specified sum. A contract was drawn up but, in breach of this, the defendant then sold the jars to a third party. The value of the jars was assessed as much greater than that contracted for between the claimant and defendant, who argued that the sale of chattels could not be the subject of specific performance. It was held that specific performance was available

SIR R T KINDERSLEY V-C

Upon what principle does the Court decree specific performance of any contract whatever? Lord Redesdale in *Harnett v Yeilding* (2 Sch & Lef 549) says: "Whether Courts of Equity in their determinations on this subject have always considered what was the original foundation for decrees of this nature I very much doubt. I believe that from something of habit, decrees of this kind have been carried to an extent which has tended to injustice. Unquestionably the original foundation of these decrees was simply this, that damages at law would not give the party the compensation to which he was entitled; that is, would not put him in a situation as beneficial to him as if the agreement were specifically performed." So that the principle on which a Court of Equity proceeds is this. A Court of law gives damages for the non-performance, but a Court of Equity says "that is not sufficient-justice is not satisfied by that remedy;" and, therefore, a Court of Equity will decree specific performance, because a mere compensation in damages is not a sufficient remedy and satisfaction for the loss of the performance of the contract.

Now why should that principle apply less to chattels? If in a contract for chattels damages will be a sufficient compensation, the party is left to that remedy. Thus if a contract is for the purchase of a certain quantity of coals, stock, &c., this Court will not decree specific performance, because a person can go into the market and buy similar articles, and get damages for any difference in the price of the articles in a Court of law. But if damages would not be a sufficient compensation, the principle, on which a Court of Equity decrees specific performance, is just as applicable to a contract for the sale and purchase of chattels, as to a contract for the sale and purchase of land.

In the present case the contract is for the purchase of articles of unusual beauty, rarity and distinction, so that damages would not be an adequate compensation for non-performance; and I am of opinion that a contract for articles of such a description is such a contract as this Court will enforce; and, in the absence of all other objection, I should have no hesitation in decreeing specific performance. ...

 Alert

Behnke v Bede Shipping Company, Limited [1927] 1 KB 649

Panel: Wright J

Statutes: Sale of Goods Act 1893 ss 4, 52 and 62

Facts: The claimant was a German national who had contracted with the defendants to purchase a steamship from them for an agreed price. The ship was currently 35-years old and available at a large discount. The boilers and engines on the ship were almost new, however, and were thus able to comply with German maritime regulations. As a result the German owner could have placed the ship onto the German register at once. Negotiations were protracted but the claimant accepted the defendant's offer. Shortly thereafter the defendant retracted the offer and the claimant sued for specific performance.

It was held that a ship fell within the definition of 'goods' under the Sale of Goods Act 1893 and a contract existed between the parties for its sale at an agreed price. The ship was of particular importance to the claimant and unique given its specific characteristics and the requirements of the claimant. As such the discretionary award of specific performance was available as damages would not be adequate to the claimant: a replacement ship was not available at the same price.

> MR JUSTICE WRIGHT
>
> ...It remains to consider what is the proper remedy. The plaintiff claims a decree of specific performance. This claim is strongly contested on behalf of the defendants. It is curious how little guidance there is on the question whether specific performance should be granted of a contract for the sale of a ship. Sect. 52 of the Sale of Goods Act gives the Court a discretion, if it think fit, in any action for breach of contract to deliver specific or ascertained goods, to direct that the contract shall be performed specifically. I think a ship is a specific chattel within the Act. In Fry on Specific Performance, 6th ed., p. 37, note 4, it is said a ship is probably within the general principle and reference is made to *Claringbould v Curtis*, which, however, is the case of a barge and contains no discussion of principle. *Hart v Herwig* seems to imply that a man who has contracted to purchase a ship is prima facie entitled to have it - that is, by an order for specific performance.
>
> In the present case there is evidence that the City was of peculiar and practically unique value to the plaintiff. She was a cheap vessel, being old, having been built in 1892, but her engines and boilers were practically new and such as to satisfy the German regulations, and hence the plaintiff could, as a German shipowner, have her at once put on the German register. A very experienced ship valuer has said that he knew of only one other comparable ship, but that may now have been sold. The plaintiff wants the ship for immediate use, and I do not think damages would be an adequate compensation. I think he is entitled to the ship and a decree of specific performance in order that justice may be done. What is the position between the defendants and the other buyers, whose contract was later in time than that of the plaintiff, is irrelevant in this action. ...

 Alert

The position on the availability of specific performance of a contract for the sale of goods is fairly stable, therefore, following the guidance provided by the above cases. When dealing with contracts for the provision of services, however, additional considerations and authorities must be addressed.

17.1.2 Contracts for Services

De Francesco v Barnum (1890) LR 45 Ch D 430

Panel: Fry LJ

Facts: A contract was entered into between the claimant, two infant girls and the mother of the girls. The claimant operated a school at which the girls were to be taught stage dance for a period of seven years, during which term they were not allowed to enter into other professional employment or marry without the consent of the claimant. The defendant was an entertainer who contracted with the girls in their professional capacity for the purposes of dancing at a show that he was putting on in London. The claimant sued for specific performance of the employment contract.

It was held that the employment contract between the claimant and the girls was unenforceable. The terms of the contract were unreasonable; the girls could also not sue the claimant due to their age and so the contract should not be enforced against them. As a result the claim against the defendant also failed as there was no breach of contract and he had not acted improperly in enticing the girls away from the claimant.

LORD JUSTICE FRY

...In the first place, with regard to the two infants, the case appears to me to have been determined by Mr. Justice Chitty when it came before him on the motion. I say that for this reason, that he pointed out in his judgment, that so far back as the reign of *Charles I.* it had been determined that an infant could not be sued at law upon an apprenticeship indenture; that there are other remedies which the master may have recourse to, but that he cannot sue the apprentice at law, and, furthermore, that there is no case in which the apprentice has been sued in equity; and he came to the conclusion that that authority was binding on him, unless after the various statutes, the statute of *Elizabeth* and the subsequent statutes, with regard to apprenticeship were all examined, there were some explanation given of that authority... For my own part, I should be very unwilling to extend decisions the effect of which is to compel persons who are not desirous of maintaining continuous personal relations with one another to continue those personal relations. I have a strong impression and a strong feeling that it is not in the interest of mankind that the rule of specific performance should be extended to such cases. I think the Courts are bound to be jealous, lest they should turn contracts of service into contracts of slavery; and therefore, speaking for myself, I should lean against the extension of the doctrine of specific performance and injunction in such a manner. ...

 Alert

In addition to the danger of turning contracts of personal services into contracts of servitude the courts will also look at other considerations including the adequacy of damages.

Verrall v Great Yarmouth Borough Council [1981] QB 202

Panel: Lord Denning MR, Roskill and Cumming-Bruce LJJ

Facts: The defendant borough council contracted with the claimant, on behalf of a political party known as the National Front, to hire out their hall on Wellington Pier, Great Yarmouth. The hall was to be used by the National Front for their annual conference in October of the same year. Following elections, however, the political balance of the defendant council shifted and they sought to repudiate their contract with the claimant and his party. The claimant and the National Front subsequently sued for specific performance of the contract so that they might use the hall for their conference.

It was held that given the advanced arrangements made by the National Front in reliance upon the contract, the knowledge of the defendant borough council, the difficulties faced by the National Front in procuring another venue and the inadequacy of damages, specific performance was appropriate and the appeal by the defendant was dismissed.

LORD DENNING MR

... The National Front has been in existence for some years. At the end of 1978 it made arrangements for its annual conference to be held this year, 1979, in Great Yarmouth at the Wellington Pier Pavilion on October 26 and 27, 1979. To that end it entered, by its officers, into negotiations with the officers of the Great Yarmouth Borough Council. The council was at that time controlled by a Conservative majority. They were fully aware of all the difficulties which might ensue - even the tumults and disturbances - if the conference were held there. In the course of the negotiations, there was much discussion in the council. The public in the gallery made their voices heard against any such conference being held. Nevertheless, after two or three meetings, the council deliberately decided to allow the National Front to hold its conference there. ...

[A]fter hearing arguments on both sides, on March 27, 1979, the council approved the letting of the halls for the conference. They referred the details to a committee. There was a substantial fee for the hire of the halls. There were also to be safeguards by way of insurance. Arrangements were made with the police so as to ensure security during the conference.

The contract was concluded on April 4, 1979, by a letter from the Chief Executive Officer's Department, saying: "... the council have now agreed to let you have the accommodation on the following terms." The letter set out the terms. Over £6,000 was to be paid down by the National Front for the facility of holding their conference in the Wellington Pier Pavilion: and this sum was paid down at once. ...

... On May 3 the Labour Party came into control at Great Yarmouth. One of the first things the new council did was to hold a special meeting on May 15. It passed a resolution that the approval for the use of the conference halls by the National Front be rescinded, the offer of facilities be withdrawn, and any payment sent back. So there it was. The new Labour-controlled council put everything into reverse.

Faced with this difficulty, the National Front tried to find a place elsewhere in which to hold their conference. They tried both in England and Wales. They are trying even now. No other town or city will receive them. So they have brought proceedings in the courts by a writ issued on August 6, 1979. They claim that a contract was made for the use of this conference hall for those two days, that it has been repudiated, and they claim specific performance of that contract.

The matter has come speedily before the courts. It came before Watkins J. After hearing the case argued for a day and a half, Watkins J. (and I would like to pay tribute to his judgment, which was prepared very quickly) came to the conclusion that the National Front should be entitled to go ahead with their conference and hold it in the Wellington

Pier Pavilion. He granted a decree of specific performance accordingly, ordering the council to hold to their contract and allow the National Front to come in. …

If [a man] has a contractual right to enter, and the licensor refuses to let him come in, then he can come to the court and in a proper case get an order for specific performance to allow him to come in. An illustration was taken in the course of the argument. Supposing one of the great political parties – say, the Conservative Party – had booked its hall at Brighton for its conference in September of this year: it had made all its arrangements accordingly: it had all its delegates coming: it had booked its hotels, and so on. Would it be open to the local council to repudiate that agreement, and say that the Conservative Party could not go there? Would the only remedy be damages? Clearly not. The court would order the council in such a case to perform its contract. It would be the same in the case of the Labour Party, or whoever it may be. When arrangements are made for a licence of this kind of such importance and magnitude affecting many people, the licensors cannot be allowed to repudiate it and simply pay damages. It must be open to the court to grant specific performance in such cases. …

Alert

All technical objections being on one side, we come to the real point in the case: whether or not, as a matter of discretion, we should order specific performance of this contract.

Watkins J. ordered the new council to perform the contract. He did so because of the importance of freedom of speech and freedom of assembly. These are among our most precious freedoms. Freedom of speech means freedom not only for the views of which you approve, but also freedom for the views you most heartily disapprove. This is a land, in the words of the poet:

> "where a man may speak the things he will. A land of settled government.
> A land of just and old renown where freedom broadens slowly down from
> precedent to precedent."

But, mark you, freedom of speech can be abused. It can be used so as to promote violence; to propagate racial hatred and class warfare; and to undermine the structure of society itself. History provides examples. Such as when Hitler led the Germans to believe that they were the master race, and inflamed them so that they expelled and massacred the Jews. Or when the communists have used their freedom to destroy the freedom of others. If there were any evidence that the National Front were abusing this freedom, it might turn the scale. But there is no evidence of it here.

Freedom of assembly is another of our precious freedoms. Everyone is entitled to meet and assemble with his fellows to discuss their affairs and to promote their views: so long as it is not done to propagate violence or do anything unlawful. On this point I would stress - and it is very important that it should be stressed - that this is a private meeting of this political party. I will read what the plaintiff said in his affidavit:

> "The conference which is to be held in Great Yarmouth is a private
> meeting. It is open to members and to invited members of the press only.

> Each person attending the meeting will be required to produce a current membership card validated by a regional officer of the National Front. A panel of senior members of the National Front will scrutinise the credentials of every person seeking entry to the meeting. There have been 12 such conferences in the past. There has never been any trouble inside such a meeting."

That is the meeting which is contemplated. It is essential under the constitution of this party that it should hold the meeting; that it should elect its officers and members for the ensuing year and the like; and that it should do all such things as are done at an annual conference of this kind. ...

In this case, in April the Great Yarmouth Borough Council made a deliberate decision. They took everything into account. They had all information before them. They must have decided that the dangers were not such as to lead them to withhold the use of their halls for the conference. The dangers are just the same now. The newly constituted council is bound by what the old constituted council did. The newly constituted council must honour the contract. I see no sufficient reason for not holding the council to their contract. In the interests of our fundamental freedoms - freedom of speech, freedom of assembly, and the importance of holding people to their contracts - we ought to grant specific performance in this case, as the judge did.

I would therefore dismiss the appeal.

In a similar manner as with pure personal property, the courts will, therefore, look at the adequacy of damages to the claimant given the facts of the particular case.

We shall now go on to look at other considerations that the court may look at when deciding whether or not to grant specific performance.

17.1.3 Supervision

Ryan v Mutual Tontine Westminster Chambers Association [1893] 1 Ch 116

Panel: Lord Esher MR, Lopes and Kay LJJ

Facts: A block of flats was let to a number of tenants and an agreement was entered into between the lessors (the defendants) and the lessees (one of whom was the claimant) to provide a resident porter for the purposes of carrying out a number of duties. The porter hired was, however, also employed elsewhere and was required to be away from the flats for long periods of time. During these absences he delegated his responsibilities to various individuals. The claimant sued for specific performance of these duties as required by his contract of service as a resident porter.

It was held that the contract of employment could not be the subject of an order for specific performance or an injunction to prevent its breach. As the only way that compliance with such an order could be guaranteed was through constant supervision of the porter in the fulfilment of his duties there was no way for the court to enforce it.

An order of specific performance, therefore, would be in vain and the claimant's remedy was limited to damages.

LORD ESHER MR

…The contract sought to be enforced here is not a contract with a person employed as a servant. It is a contract between a person who has to employ a servant and a person for whose benefit the employment of such servant is to take place. It is a contract between a landlord and his tenant, by which the former undertakes to employ a porter to perform certain services for the benefit of the latter. The contract, therefore, is not merely that the landlord shall employ a porter, but that he shall employ a porter who shall do certain specified work for the benefit of the tenant. That is, in my opinion, one indivisible contract. The performance of what is suggested to be the first part of the contract, viz., the agreement to employ a porter, would be of no use whatever to the tenant unless he performed the services specified. The right of the tenant under the contract is really an entirety, viz., to have a porter employed by whom these services shall be performed; and the breach of the contract substantially is that these services were not performed. The contract is that these services shall be performed during the whole term of the tenancy; it is therefore a long-continuing contract, to be performed from day to day, and under which the circumstances of non-performance might vary from day to day. I apprehend, therefore, that the execution of it would require that constant superintendence by the Court, which the Court in such cases has always declined to give. Therefore, if the contract is regarded as a whole, there is good ground for saying that it is not one of which the Court could compel specific performance. It was contended that the Court could grant specific performance of the Defendants' obligation to appoint a porter. But then the case is brought within another rule, viz., that, when the Court cannot compel specific performance of the contract as a whole, it will not interfere to compel specific performance of part of a contract. That clearly appears to be a rule of Chancery practice on the subject. Therefore, if it is urged that what the Judge has ordered to be performed is merely the obligation to appoint a porter, the case falls within that rule, and on that ground his decision must be reversed. It was argued that the case of *Rigby v Great Western Railway Company*, shewed (sic) that a contract such as this might be severed, and that performance of part of it could be enforced. But that is not what the case appears to have decided. It decided that, where in one contract there were really several wholly independent stipulations, the Court could grant specific performance of one of them. It is no authority for the proposition that the Court can separate part of what is really one single indivisible contract and grant specific performance of that part. …It appears to me that the appeal must be allowed, and the judgment for the Plaintiff must stand only for the damages found by the learned Judge.

 Alert

Where the effect of specific performance would be to necessitate constant supervision, therefore, the courts will not grant such a remedy and damages will be awarded in lieu. However, one may contrast this authority with a much more recent but very similar case below.

17.1.4 Supervision, Equity Acting in Vain, and Sufficiently Clear Definition

Posner and Others v Scott-Lewis and Others [1987] Ch 25

Panel: Mervyn Davies J

Facts: The defendants owned a block of flats that was let out to the claimants. Under the terms of the leases between them the defendants were obligated to employ a resident porter to carry out a number of specific tasks. At a later date, the person hired for this role moved out of the flats but contracted with the defendants to continue to return and fulfil his contractual duties. The claimants sued the defendants for specific performance of their obligation to hire a resident porter as the current porter did not satisfy this contractual requirement.

Ryan v Mutual Tontine was distinguished. An order of specific performance was granted. The duties of the resident porter were sufficiently well-defined to allow specific performance and the effect would not have been to enforce a contract of employment. The effect of specific performance was a one-off event, requiring the lessors to employ a resident porter rather than enforce the contract of employment against the current porter.

MR JUSTICE MERVYN DAVIES

...There are also covenants by the lessor. These covenants include: clause 3 (2), where the lessor promises to maintain etc. the main hall, staircases, lift, the central heating system and the internal telephone system (which connects with the porter's flat); clause 3 (7), a promise by the lessor to see that the common parts are kept clean and lighted and – see clause 3 (1) – to supply and maintain hot water and central heating. There is a lessor's covenant that I must quote in full. Clause 3 (11) reads:

> "To employ (so far as in the lessor's power lies) a resident porter for the following purposes and for no other purposes:- (a) To keep clean the common staircases and entrance hall landings and passages and lift (b) To be responsible for looking after and stoking the central heating and domestic hot water boilers (c) To carry down rubbish from the properties to the dustbins outside the building every day." ...

The writ claims specific performance of the lessor's covenant m clause 3 (11) of the plaintiffs' respective leases of their respective flats that is to say the plaintiffs seek to compel the defendants to employ a resident porter for the purposes itemised in 3 (11). There is also a claim for damages by reason of the defendants' failure to employ a resident porter since 1 June 1985. ...

The plaintiffs' principal claim, pursuant to R.S.C., Ord. 14 , is in these terms:

> "(1) Specific performance of the lessors' covenant in clause 3 (11) of the plaintiffs' respective leases of their respective flats (and garages in the case of the third and fifth plaintiffs) in Danes Court, nos. 1-5, St. Edmunds

Terrace, London N.W.8 to employ (so far as in the defendants' power lie) a resident porter for the purposes more particularly set forth in the said clause 3 (11)."...

Since I am of the view that the defendants are in breach of clause 3 (11), the question arises whether or not clause 3 (11) is a provision susceptible of specific performance. I was referred to *Ryan v Mutual Tontine Westminster Chambers Association* [1893] 1 Ch. 116. That is a case where the Court of Appeal considered a contract between a landlord and his tenant by which the landlord undertook to employ a porter to perform certain services for the benefit of the tenant. The contract was held to be not specifically enforceable. One ground of the decision was that the execution of the contract would require "constant superintendence by the court."

A close examination of the facts in the Ryan case [1893] 1 Ch 116, 117-120 shows the situation in that case differs in some respects from the situation before me. For example, in the Ryan case the porter was to "be and act as the servant of the tenants." That is not so at Danes Court. Again the Danes Court lease has, but the Ryan lease has not, covenants by the lessor whereby the porter's duties are, at any rate as to clause 3 (11) (a) and (b), elsewhere in the lease seen as direct obligations; also the fact that the scheme of apportioning service charges between the Danes Court tenants involves taking account of the costs of maintaining and repairing the porter's flat: see clause 3 (12).

Alert

Drawing attention to these differences between *Ryan v Mutual Tontine Westminster Chambers Association* [1893] 1 Ch 116 and the present case, Mr. Tager for the plaintiffs submitted that the *Ryan* case should be distinguished. In short, he said that since the resident porter's functions at Danes Court were already obligations of the lessor to the lessees, there were no duties on the part of the porter towards the tenants that the tenants were seeking to enforce. All that was required was the appointment of a resident porter, whereas in the *Ryan* case the plaintiff was in effect seeking to enforce performance of duties said to be owed by the porter to the plaintiff. I do not accept or reject Mr. Tager's able argument. I suspect that it is difficult to distinguish the *Ryan* case. However that may be, the *Ryan* case has been remarked upon in many later authorities.

In *C. H. Giles & Co Ltd v Morris* [1972] 1 WLR 307 Megarry J., after referring to *Ryan's* case, said, at p. 318:

"One day, perhaps, the courts will look again at the so-called rule that contracts for personal services or involving the continuous performance of services will not be specifically enforced. Such a rule is plainly not absolute and without exception, nor do I think that it can be based on any narrow consideration such as difficulties of constant superintendence by the court. Mandatory injunctions are by no means unknown, and there is normally no question of the court having to send its officers to supervise the performance of the order of the court. Prohibitory injunctions are common, and again there is no direct supervision by the court.

Performance of each type of injunction is normally secured by the realisation of the person enjoined that he is liable to be punished for contempt if evidence of his disobedience to the order is put before the court; and if the injunction is prohibitory, actual committal will usually, so long as it continues, make disobedience impossible. If instead the order is for specific performance of a contract for personal services, a similar machinery of enforcement could be employed, again without there being any question of supervision by any officer of the court. The reasons why the court is reluctant to decree specific performance of a contract for personal services (and I would regard it as a strong reluctance rather than a rule) are, I think, more complex and more firmly bottomed on human nature. If a singer contracts to sing, there could no doubt be proceedings for committal if, ordered to sing, the singer remained obstinately dumb. But if instead the singer sang flat, or sharp, or too fast, or too slowly, or too loudly, or too quietly, or resorted to a dozen of the manifestations of temperament traditionally associated with some singers, the threat of committal would reveal itself as a most unsatisfactory weapon: for who could say whether the imperfections of performance were natural or self-induced? To make an order with such possibilities of evasion would be vain; and so the order will not be made. However, not all contracts of personal service or for the continuous performance of services are as dependent as this on matters of opinion and judgment, nor do all such contracts involve the same degree of the daily impact of person upon person. In general, no doubt, the inconvenience and mischief of decreeing specific performance of most of such contracts will greatly outweigh the advantages, and specific performance will be refused. But I do not think that it should be assumed that as soon as any element of personal service or continuous services can be discerned in a contract the court will, without more, refuse specific performance. Of course, a requirement for the continuous performance of services has the disadvantage that repeated breaches may engender repeated applications to the court for enforcement. But so may many injunctions; and the prospects of repetition, although an important consideration, ought not to be allowed to negative a right. As is so often the case in equity, the matter is one of the balance of advantage and disadvantage in relation to the particular obligations in question; and the fact that the balance will usually lie on one side does not turn this probability into a rule. The present case, of course, is a fortiori, since the contract of which specific performance has been decreed requires not the performance of personal services or any continuous series of acts, but merely procuring the execution of an agreement which contains a provision for such services or acts."

Those observations do not of themselves enable me to disregard *Ryan v Mutual Tontine Westminster Chambers Association* [1893] 1 Ch 116. But then one comes to *Shiloh Spinners Ltd v Harding* [1973] AC 691. At p. 724C-D Lord Wilberforce seems to say that "the impossibility for the courts to supervise the doing of work" may be rejected as a reason against granting relief. Finally there is *Tito v Waddell* (No 2) [1977] Ch 106. Sir Robert Megarry V-C said, at p. 321:

"In cases of this kind it was at one time said that an order for the specific performance of the contract would not be made if there would be difficulty in the court supervising its execution: see, e.g., *Ryan v Mutual Tontine Westminster Chambers Association* [1893] 1 Ch 116, especially at pp. 123, 125, 128. Sir Archibald Smith M.R. subsequently found himself unable to see the force of this objection (see *Wolverhampton Corporation v Emmons* [1901] 1 QB 515, 523); and after it had been discussed and questioned in *C. H. Giles & Co Ltd v Morris* [1972] 1 WLR 307, 318, the House of Lords disposed of it (I hope finally) in *Shiloh Spinners Ltd v Harding* [1973] AC 691, 724. The real question is whether there is a sufficient definition of what has to be done in order to comply with the order of the court. That definition may be provided by the contract itself, or it may be supplied by the terms of the order, in which case there is the further question whether the court considers that the terms of the contract sufficiently support, by implication or otherwise, the terms of the proposed order."

Alert

In the light of those authorities it is, I think, open to me to consider the making of an order for specific performance in this case; particularly since the order contemplated is in the a fortiori class referred to by Megarry J. in the last sentence of the extract from *C. H. Giles & Co Ltd v Morris* [1972] 1 WLR 307 quoted above. Damages here could hardly be regarded as an adequate remedy.

Whether or not a specific performance order should be made seems to me to depend on the following considerations: (a) is there a sufficient definition of what has to be done in order to comply with the order of the court? (b) Will enforcing compliance involve superintendence by the court to an unacceptable degree? (c) What are the respective prejudices or hardships that will be suffered by the parties if the order is made or not made?

Alert

As to (a), one may in this case sufficiently define what has to be done by the defendants by ordering the defendants, within say two months, to employ a porter to be resident at Danes Court for the purpose of carrying out the clause 3 (11) duties. It is to be borne in mind that there is still a vacant flat available for a resident porter. As to (b), I do not see that such an order will occasion any protracted superintendence by the court. If the defendants without good cause fail to comply with the order in due time, then the plaintiffs can take appropriate enforcement proceedings against the defendants. As to (c), I see no hardship or prejudice resulting to the defendants from the order. They will simply be performing what they have promised to do and what has been carried out by the lessors over the past 20 years. On the other hand I see considerable inconvenience, if not exactly hardship, for the plaintiffs if, having bargained for a resident porter and paid a premium and having enjoyed his presence for 20 years, they are to be expected for the future to be content with a porter who simply walks up and down the stairs for two hours only during the day doing his cleaning and refuse collection. It follows that there should be an order for specific performance.

Posner v Scott-Lewis is a particularly helpful case as it not only helps to clarify and distinguish *Ryan v Mutual Tontine* but also addresses numerous issues in other cases, which are also important when looking at the availability of specific performance.

17.2 Interim Injunctions

17.2.1 Prohibitory Injunctions

Often it is not practical to wait for a full trial, as damage may occur to a party long before the matter comes to trial. In situations such as these one may try to secure an *interim* remedy, which may include an injunction against another party. We shall first look at the prohibitory injunction.

American Cyanamid Co v Ethicon Ltd [1975] AC 396

Panel: Lord Diplock, Viscount Dilhorne, Lord Cross of Chelsea, Lord Salmon and Lord Edmund-Davies

Facts: The claimants were an American company in the business of supplying medical products; the defendants were also an American company in the same business. The claimants possessed a patent over a certain type of sterile absorbable surgical suture. The defendants launched a suture onto the British market that the claimants alleged infringed their patent. At first instance the claimants were successful in their application for an interim prohibitory injunction. On appeal this was overturned and the matter then came before the House of Lords.

The appeal was allowed. The Court of Appeal had incorrectly determined that it was necessary to present a prima facie case for infringement before an interim injunction application could be successful. The proper requirement for suitability was the balance of convenience and the appropriateness of damages to the claimant and defendant. Should this prove to be inconclusive then the courts should seek to preserve the status quo.

LORD DIPLOCK

Both Graham J. and the Court of Appeal felt constrained by authority to deal with Cyanamid's claim to an interlocutory injunction by considering first whether, upon the whole of the affidavit evidence before them, a prima facie case of infringement had been made out. As Russell L.J. put it in the concluding paragraph of his reasons for judgment with which the other members of the court agreed [1974] F.S.R. 312 , 333:

'... if there be no prima facie case on the point essential to entitle the plaintiffs to complain of the defendants' proposed activities, that is the end of the claim to interlocutory relief.'

'Prima facie case' may in some contexts be an elusive concept, but the sense in which it was being used by Russell L.J. is apparent from an earlier passage in his judgment. After a detailed analysis of the conflicting expert testimony he said, at p. 330:

> 'I am not satisfied on the present evidence that on the proper construction
> of this specification, addressed as it is to persons skilled in the relevant art
> or science, the claim extends to sterile surgical sutures produced not only
> from a homopolymer of glycolide but also from a copolymer of glycolide
> and up to 15 per cent. of lactide. That is to say that I do not consider that
> a prima facie case of infringement is established.'

In effect what the Court of Appeal was doing was trying the issue of infringement upon the conflicting affidavit evidence as it stood, without the benefit of oral testimony or cross-examination. They were saying:

> 'If we had to give judgment in the action now without any further evidence
> we should hold that Cyanamid had not satisfied the onus of proving that
> their patent would be infringed by Ethicon's selling sutures made of XLG.'

The Court of Appeal accordingly did not find it necessary to go into the questions raised by Ethicon as to the validity of the patent or to consider where the balance of convenience lay. ...

The grant of an interlocutory injunction is a remedy that is both temporary and discretionary. It would be most exceptional for your Lordships to give leave to appeal to this House in a case which turned upon where the balance of convenience lay. In the instant appeal, however, the question of the balance of convenience, although it had been considered by Graham J. and decided in Cyanamid's favour, was never reached by the Court of Appeal. They considered that there was a rule of practice so well established as to constitute a rule of law that precluded them from granting any interim injunction unless upon the evidence adduced by both the parties on the hearing of the application the applicant had satisfied the court that on the balance of probabilities the acts of the other party sought to be enjoined would, if committed, violate the applicant's legal rights. In the view of the Court of Appeal the case which the applicant had to prove before any question of balance of convenience arose was 'prima facie' only in the sense that the conclusion of law reached by the court upon that evidence might need to be modified at some later date in the light of further evidence either detracting from the probative value of the evidence on which the court had acted or proving additional facts. It was in order to enable the existence of any such rule of law to be considered by your Lordships' House that leave to appeal was granted.

My Lords, when an application for an interlocutory injunction to restrain a defendant from doing acts alleged to be in violation of the plaintiff's legal right is made upon contested facts, the decision whether or not to grant an interlocutory injunction has to be taken at a time when ex hypothesi the existence of the right or the violation of it, or both, is uncertain and will remain uncertain until final judgment is given in the action. It was to mitigate the risk of injustice to the plaintiff during the period before that uncertainty could be resolved that the practice arose of granting him relief by way of interlocutory injunction; but since the middle of the 19th century this has been made subject to his undertaking to pay damages to the defendant for any loss sustained by reason of the injunction if it should be held at the trial that the plaintiff had not been entitled to restrain the defendant from doing what he was threatening to do. The object of the interlocutory injunction is to protect the plaintiff against injury by violation of his right for which he could not be adequately compensated in damages recoverable in the action if the uncertainty were resolved in his favour at the trial; but the plaintiff's need for such protection must be weighed against the corresponding need of the defendant to be protected against injury resulting from his having been prevented from exercising his own legal rights for which he could not be adequately compensated under the plaintiff's undertaking in damages if the uncertainty were resolved in the defendant's favour at the trial. The court must weigh one need against another and determine where 'the balance of convenience' lies. ...

In those cases where the legal rights of the parties depend upon facts that are in dispute between them, the evidence available to the court at the hearing of the application for an interlocutory injunction is incomplete. It is given on affidavit and has not been tested by oral cross-examination. The purpose sought to be achieved by giving to the court discretion to grant such injunctions would be stultified if the discretion were clogged by a technical rule forbidding its exercise if upon that incomplete untested evidence the court evaluated the chances of the plaintiff's ultimate success in the action at 50 per cent. or less, but permitting its exercise if the court evaluated his chances at more than 50 per cent. ...

Graham J. and the Court of Appeal in the instant appeal [left] intact the supposed rule that the court is not entitled to take any account of the balance of convenience unless it has first been satisfied that if the case went to trial upon no other evidence than is before the court at the hearing of the application the plaintiff would be entitled to judgment for a permanent injunction in the same terms as the interlocutory injunction sought.

Your Lordships should in my view take this opportunity of declaring that there is no such rule. The use of such expressions as 'a probability,' 'a prima facie case,' or 'a strong prima facie case' in the context of the exercise of a discretionary power to grant an interlocutory injunction leads to confusion as to the object sought to be achieved by this form of temporary relief. The court no doubt must be satisfied that the claim is not frivolous or vexatious, in other words, that there is a serious question to be tried.

It is no part of the court's function at this stage of the litigation to try to resolve conflicts of evidence on affidavit as to facts on which the claims of either party may ultimately depend nor to decide difficult questions of law which call for detailed argument and mature considerations. These are matters to be dealt with at the trial. One of the reasons for the introduction of the practice of requiring an undertaking as to damages upon the grant of an interlocutory injunction was that 'it aided the court in doing that which was its great object, viz. abstaining from expressing any opinion upon the merits of the case until the hearing': *Wakefield v Duke of Buccleugh* (1865) 12 LT 628, 629. So unless the material available to the court at the hearing of the application for an interlocutory injunction fails to disclose that the plaintiff has any real prospect of succeeding in his claim for a permanent injunction at the trial, the court should go on to consider whether the balance of convenience lies in favour of granting or refusing the interlocutory relief that is sought.

 Alert

As to that, the governing principle is that the court should first consider whether, if the plaintiff were to succeed at the trial in establishing his right to a permanent injunction, he would be adequately compensated by an award of damages for the loss he would have sustained as a result of the defendant's continuing to do what was sought to be en joined between the time of the application and the time of the trial. If damages in the measure recoverable at common law would be adequate remedy and the defendant would be in a financial position to pay them, no interlocutory injunction should normally be granted, however strong the plaintiff's claim appeared to be at that stage. If, on the other hand, damages would not provide an adequate remedy for the plaintiff in the event of his succeeding at the trial, the court should then consider whether, on the contrary hypothesis that the defendant were to succeed at the trial in establishing his right to do that which was sought to be enjoined, he would be adequately compensated under the plaintiff's undertaking as to damages for the loss he would have sustained by being prevented from doing so between the time of the application and the time of the trial. If damages in the measure recoverable under such an undertaking would be an adequate remedy and the plaintiff would be in a financial position to pay them, there would be no reason upon this ground to refuse an interlocutory injunction.

It is where there is doubt as to the adequacy of the respective remedies in damages available to either party or to both, that the question of balance of convenience arises. It would be unwise to attempt even to list all the various matters which may need to be taken into consideration in deciding where the balance lies, let alone to suggest the relative weight to be attached to them. These will vary from case to case.

Where other factors appear to be evenly balanced it is a counsel of prudence to take such measures as are calculated to preserve the status quo. If the defendant is enjoined temporarily from doing something that he has not done before, the only effect of the interlocutory injunction in the event of his succeeding at the trial is to postpone the date at which he is able to embark upon a course of action which he has not previously found it necessary to undertake; whereas to interrupt him in the conduct of an established enterprise would cause much greater inconvenience to him since he would have to start again to establish it in the event of his succeeding at the trial.

Save in the simplest cases, the decision to grant or to refuse an interlocutory injunction will cause to whichever party is unsuccessful on the application some disadvantages which his ultimate success at the trial may show he ought to have been spared and the disadvantages may be such that the recovery of damages to which he would then be entitled either in the action or under the plaintiff's undertaking would not be sufficient to compensate him fully for all of them. The extent to which the disadvantages to each party would be incapable of being compensated in damages in the event of his succeeding at the trial is always a significant factor in assessing where the balance of convenience lies, and if the extent of the uncompensatable disadvantage to each party would not differ widely, it may not be improper to take into account in tipping the balance the relative strength of each party's case as revealed by the affidavit evidence adduced on the hearing of the application. This, however, should be done only where it is apparent upon the facts disclosed by evidence as to which there is no credible dispute that the strength of one party's case is disproportionate to that of the other party. The court is not justified in embarking upon anything resembling a trial of the action upon conflicting affidavits in order to evaluate the strength of either party's case.

I would reiterate that, in addition to those to which I have referred, there may be many other special factors to be taken into consideration in the particular circumstances of individual cases. ...

17.2.2 Mandatory Injunctions

Shepherd Homes Ltd v Sandham [1971] Ch 340

Panel: Megarry J

Facts: The claimant was a development company that had divided a particular piece of land into a number of plots. One of these was owned by the defendant. The defendant had entered into a covenant with the claimant not to erect any fence or boundary on his plot as it would interfere with the building lines of the claimant. In breach of this covenant he did so and the defendant claimed a mandatory injunction to have it taken down. However the claimant delayed for four months before bringing their application for an interim injunction.

It was held that the granting of a mandatory injunction was not subject to the same requirements as a prohibitory injunction; the court was less likely to grant a mandatory injunction. The usual requirement for such an injunction would be a high degree of assurance that at trial it will appear that the injunction was rightly granted. In the present case the requirements were not met by the claimant.

MR JUSTICE MEGARRY

As it seems to me, there are important differences between prohibitory and mandatory injunctions. By granting a prohibitory injunction, the court does no more than prevent for the future the continuance or repetition of the conduct of which the plaintiff complains. The injunction does not attempt to deal with what has happened in the past; that is left for the trial, to be dealt with by damages or otherwise. On the other hand, a mandatory injunction tends at least in part to look to the past, in that it is often a means of undoing what has already been done, so far as that is possible. Furthermore, whereas a prohibitory injunction merely requires abstention from acting, a mandatory injunction requires the taking of positive steps, and may (as in the present case) require the dismantling or destruction of something already erected or constructed. This will result in a consequent waste of time, money and materials if it is ultimately established that the defendant was entitled to retain the erection. As Kindersley V-C said in *Gale v Abbot* (1862) 10 WR 748, 750, an interlocutory application for a mandatory injunction was one of the rarest cases that occurred, "for the court would not compel a man to do so serious a thing as to undo what he had done except at the hearing."

Even if today the degree of rarity of such applications is not quite so profound, the seriousness of such an order remains as an important factor. Another aspect of the point is that if a mandatory injunction is granted on motion, there will normally be no question of granting a further mandatory injunction at the trial; what is done is done, and the plaintiff has on motion obtained, once and for all, the demolition or destruction that he seeks. Where the injunction is prohibitory, however, there will often still be a question at the trial whether the injunction should be dissolved or continued; except in relation to transient events, there will usually be no question of the plaintiff having obtained on motion all that he seeks. ...

...I may summarise my conclusions as follows. First, Lord Cairns's statement of principle prima facie [in *Doherty v Allman*, 3 App.Cas. 709, 710, 720] applies to mandatory injunctions; but it does not apply in its full width. The matter is tempered by a judicial discretion which will be exercised so as to withhold an injunction more readily if it is mandatory than if it is prohibitory. Even a blameless plaintiff cannot as of right claim at the trial to enforce a negative covenant by a mandatory injunction. Second, although it may not be possible to state in any comprehensive way the grounds upon which the court will refuse to grant a mandatory injunction in such cases at the trial, they at least include the triviality of the damage to the plaintiff and the existence of a disproportion between the detriment that the injunction would inflict on the defendant and the benefit that it would confer on the plaintiff. The basic concept is that of producing a "fair result," and this involves the exercise of a judicial discretion.

 Alert

Third, on motion, as contrasted with the trial, the court is far more reluctant to grant a mandatory injunction than it would be to grant a comparable prohibitory injunction. In a normal case the court must, inter alia, feel a high degree of assurance that at the trial it will appear that the injunction was rightly granted; and this is a higher standard than is required for a prohibitory injunction. Fourth, it follows that the statement in *Halsbury* founded on *Morris v Grant*, 24 WR 55. namely: "If the defendant, after express notice, has committed a clear violation of an express contract ... a mandatory injunction will be granted on an interlocutory application," is too wide. Both the case itself and the statement founded on it have to be qualified in the light of the other authorities to which I have referred, especially *Bowes v Law*, LR 9 Eq. 636 and *Kilbey v Haviland*, 19 WR 698 (which, though decided earlier, do not seem to have been cited), and *Sharp v Harrison* [1922] 1 Ch 502. No doubt a mandatory injunction may be granted where the case for one is unusually sharp and clear; but it is certainly not a matter of course. ...

 Alert

...Looking at the case as a whole, it seems to me plain that it would be quite wrong on motion to grant the mandatory injunction sought. This is a delayed motion in a case where it is very far from clear that a mandatory order would be granted at the trial. ...

17.2.3 Search Orders

Anton Piller KG v Manufacturing Processes Ltd and Others [1976] Ch 55

Panel: Lord Denning MR, Ormrod and Shaw LJJ

Facts: The defendants were an English company and the agents of the claimants, who operated out of Germany and produced power converters for computers. Information came to the claimants that the defendants were in discussions with other German companies regarding the disclosure of confidential information about a new type of converter that would cause great damage to the claimants should the information be disposed of.

It was held that under exceptional circumstances it was permissible to order the defendants to allow a party into their premises to search for and seize information. In this particular case the claimants were permitted to enter the premises of the defendants for the purposes of claiming the information sought.

LORD DENNING MR

During the last 18 months the judges of the Chancery Division have been making orders of a kind not known before. They have some resemblance to search warrants. Under these orders, the plaintiff and his solicitors are authorised to enter the defendant's premises so as to inspect papers, provided the defendant gives permission.

Now this is the important point: The court orders the defendant to give them permission. The judges have been making these orders on ex parte applications without prior notice to the defendant. None of the cases have been reported except the one before Templeman J. on December 3, 1974, *E.M.I. Ltd v Pandit* [1975] 1 WLR 302 . ...

Let me say at once that no court in this land has any power to issue a search warrant to enter a man's house so as to see if there are papers or documents there which are of an incriminating nature, whether libels or infringements of copyright or anything else of the kind. No constable or bailiff can knock at the door and demand entry so as to inspect papers or documents. The householder can shut the door in his face and say "Get out." That was established in the leading case of *Entick v Carrington* (1765) 2 WilsKB 275. None of us would wish to whittle down that principle in the slightest. But the order sought in this case is not a search warrant. It does not authorise the plaintiffs' solicitors or anyone else to enter the defendants' premises against their will. It does not authorise the breaking down of any doors, nor the slipping in by a back door, nor getting in by an open door or window. It only authorises entry and inspection by the permission of the defendants. The plaintiffs must get the defendants' permission. But it does do this: It brings pressure on the defendants to give permission. It does more. It actually orders them to give permission - with, I suppose, the result that if they do not give permission, they are guilty of contempt of court. ...

It seems to me that such an order can be made by a judge ex parte, but it should only be made where it is essential that the plaintiff should have inspection so that justice can be done between the parties: and when, if the defendant were forewarned, there is a grave danger that vital evidence will be destroyed, that papers will be burnt or lost or hidden, or taken beyond the jurisdiction, and so the ends of justice be defeated: and when the inspection would do no real harm to the defendant or his case.

 Alert

Nevertheless, in the enforcement of this order, the plaintiffs must act with due circumspection. On the service of it, the plaintiffs should be attended by their solicitor, who is an officer of the court. They should give the defendants an opportunity of considering it and of consulting their own solicitor. If the defendants wish to apply to discharge the order as having been improperly obtained, they must be allow to do so. If the defendants refuse permission to enter or to inspect, the plaintiffs must not force their way in. They must accept the refusal, and bring it to the notice of the court afterwards, if need be on an application to commit.

You might think that with all these safeguards against abuse, it would be of little use to make such an order. But it can be effective in this way: It serves to tell the defendants that, on the evidence put before it, the court is of opinion that they ought to permit inspection - nay, it orders them to permit - and that they refuse at their peril. It puts them in peril not only of proceedings for contempt, but also of adverse inferences being drawn against them; so much so that their own solicitor may often advise them to comply. We are told that in two at least of the cases such an order has been effective. We are prepared, therefore, to sanction its continuance, but only in an extreme case where there is grave danger of property being smuggled away or of vital evidence being destroyed. ...

LORD JUSTICE ORMROD

...I agree with all that Lord Denning M.R. has said. The proposed order is at the extremity of this court's powers. Such orders, therefore, will rarely be made, and only when there is no alternative way of ensuring that justice is done to the applicant.

There are three essential pre-conditions for the making of such an order, in my judgment. First, there must be an extremely strong prima facie case. Secondly, the damage, potential or actual, must be very serious for the applicant. Thirdly, there must be clear evidence that the defendants have in their possession incriminating documents or things, and that there is a real possibility that they may destroy such material before any application inter partes can be made.

 Alert

The form of the order makes it plain that the court is not ordering or granting anything equivalent to a search warrant. The order is an order on the defendant in personam to permit inspection. It is therefore open to him to refuse to comply with such an order, but at his peril either of further proceedings for contempt of court - in which case, of course, the court will have the widest discretion as to how to deal with it, and if it turns out that the order was made improperly in the first place, the contempt will be dealt with accordingly - but more important, of course, the refusal to comply may be the most damning evidence against the defendant at the subsequent trial. Great responsibility clearly rests on the solicitors for the applicant to ensure that the carrying out of such an order is meticulously carefully done with the fullest respect for the defendant's rights, as Lord Denning M.R. has said, of applying to the court, should he feel it necessary to do so, before permitting the inspection.

In the circumstances of the present case, all those conditions to my mind are satisfied, and this order is essential in the interests of justice.

I agree, therefore, that the appeal should be allowed.

17.2.4 Freezing Injunctions

Mareva Compania Naviera S.A. v International Bulkcarriers S.A. [1975] 2 Lloyd's Rep 509

Panel: Lord Denning MR, Roskill and Ormrod LJJ

Facts: The claimants were ship owners who had let their motor vessel *Mareva* to the defendants for a time charter-party. The ship was then delivered to the defendants, who sub-chartered it to the President of India. The defendants paid two instalments of the hire but the third was not received by the claimants, who then became aware that the defendants were unable to pay. The contract was repudiated by the claimants and an injunction sought to stop the defendants removing or disposing of their assets.

It was held that if a debt was owed and there was a danger that the defendants might remove or dispose of assets so as to defeat it then the court had the right to grant an interim injunction to prevent this. If the court did not intervene then the claimants would be in a position to suffer a grave injustice and suffer losses as a result. The injunction was, therefore, granted until trial or judgment or further order.

LORD DENNING MR

...Now Mr Rix has been very helpful. He has drawn our attention not only to *Lister v Stubbs* but also to s.45 of the Judicature Act, which repeats s 25 (8) of the Judicature Act, 1875. It says:

> A mandamus or an injunction may be granted or a receiver appointed by an interlocutory order of the court in all cases in which it shall appear to the court to be just or convenient.

In *Beddow v Beddow*, (1878) 9 ChD 89, Sir George Jessel, the then Master of the Rolls, gave a very wide interpretation to that section. He said:

> "I have unlimited power to grant an injunction in any case where it would be right or just to do so."

There is only one qualification to be made. The Court will not grant an injunction to protect a person who has no legal or equitable right whatever. That appears from *North London Railway Co v Great Northern Railway Co*, (1883) 11 QBD 30. But, subject to that qualification, the statute gives a wide general power to the Courts. It is well summarized in Halsbury's Laws of England, vol. 21, 3rd ed., p. 348, par. 739:

> . . . now, therefore, whenever a right, which can be asserted either at law or in equity, does exist, then, whatever the previous practice may have been, the Court is enabled by virtue of this provision, in a proper case, to grant an injunction to protect that right. ...

...In my opinion that principle applies to a creditor who has a right to be paid the debt owing to him, even before he has established his right by getting judgment for it. If it appears that the debt is due and owing —and there is a danger that the debtor may dispose of his assets so as to defeat it before judgment—the Court has jurisdiction in a proper case to grant an interlocutory judgment so as to prevent him disposing of those assets. It seems to me that this is a proper case for the exercise of this jurisdiction... In face of this danger, I think this Court ought to grant an injunction to restrain the defendants from disposing of these moneys now in the bank in London until the trial or judgment in this action. If the defendants have any grievance about it when they hear of it, they can apply to discharge it. But meanwhile the plaintiffs should be protected. It is only just and right that this Court should grant an injunction. I would therefore continue the injunction. ...

This case established the basic principle, therefore, that an injunction of this type could be awarded by the court although traditionally it had always been refused. The words of the court are indeed helpful but a case following this elucidated the requirements even further while approving of the earlier approach of the Court of Appeal.

Derby & Co Ltd and Others v Weldon and Others (No 1) [1990] Ch 48

Panel: May, Parker and Nicholls LJJ

Facts: The claimant and a number of others in a particular group of companies applied for *Mareva* injunctions against two former directors of another company in that group. The ex parte application concerned assets worth £25m situated worldwide and for disclosure of all such assets. The defendants denied the existence of any assets outside the UK or EU and questioned the court's authority to grant such an injunction outside the jurisdiction.

It was held that, given the position of the defendants' assets in the UK compared to the high value of the claim, the existence of the defendants' foreign assets, and the likelihood that the defendants would remove or dissipate such assets, an extra-territorial *Mareva* injunction was just and convenient. It was granted together with a UK *Mareva* injunction over the defendants' domestic assets.

LORD JUSTICE PARKER

...I agree that this appeal should be allowed and I also agree with the judgments of May L.J. and Nicholls L.J. which I have had the opportunity to read in draft. I desire however to add some observations of my own on two matters.

(1) It was submitted for the defendants (i) that if a worldwide *Mareva* could be granted on no more than a good arguable case and a risk of dissipation of assets it would follow that such an order could be made in the vast majority of commercial cases in which material existed for the grant of an internal *Mareva*, and (ii) that this would conflict with statements in *Ashtiani v Kashi* [1987] QB 888; *Babanaft International Co S.A. v Bassatne*, and *Republic of Haiti v Duvalier* , that an extraterritorial *Mareva*, albeit effective only in personam would only rarely be granted and would require exceptional circumstances.

I do not accept the first of the above submissions. The mere fact that the plaintiff shows a good arguable case and a real risk of disposal or hiding of English assets - the requisites for an internal Mareva – clearly cannot by itself be sufficient to justify an extraterritorial Mareva either worldwide or at all. Such a Mareva would clearly be unjustified if, for example, there were sufficient English assets to cover the appropriate sum, or if the court were not satisfied that there were foreign assets or that there was a real risk of disposal of the same, or if it would in all the circumstances be oppressive to make the order.

Alert

Here, however, it is accepted that there are foreign assets. The judge has found, correctly in my view, that there is a high risk of disposal of such assets. The English assets are wholly insufficient to afford protection. The defendants are clearly sophisticated operators who have amply demonstrated their ability to render assets untraceable and a determination not to reveal them. In those circumstances it appears to me that there is every justification for a worldwide *Mareva*, so long as, by undertaking or proviso or a combination of both, (a) oppression of the defendants by way of exposure to a multiplicity of proceedings is avoided, (b) the defendants are protected against the misuse of information gained from the ordinary order for disclosure in aid of the *Mareva*, and (c) the position of third parties is protected. Whether, ultimately, the order *in personam* will be converted into an order attaching some or all of the assets disclosed will of course depend on (i) the court here giving the plaintiffs leave to proceed in a jurisdiction in which assets have been found and (ii) the decision of the court in such jurisdiction whether to make an order. ...

There are in essence only three issues; (i) has the plaintiff a good arguable case; (ii) has the plaintiff satisfied the court that there are assets within and, where an extraterritorial order is sought, without the jurisdiction; and (iii) is there a real risk of dissipation or secretion of assets so as to render any judgment which the plaintiff may obtain nugatory. Such matters should be decided on comparatively brief evidence. In *American Cyanamid Co v Ethicon Ltd* [1975] AC 396, 407-408, Lord Diplock, dealing in that case with an application for an interlocutory injunction, said:

Alert

> "It is no part of the court's function at this stage of the litigation to try to resolve conflicts of evidence on affidavit as to facts on which the claims of either party may ultimately depend nor to decide difficult questions of law which call for detailed argument and mature considerations. These are matters to be dealt with at the trial. One of the reasons for the introduction of the practice of requiring an undertaking as to damages upon the grant of an interlocutory injunction was that 'it aided the court in doing that which was its great object, viz. abstaining from expressing any opinion upon the merits of the case until the hearing': *Wakefield v Duke of Buccleugh* (1865) 12 LT 628, 629."

In my view the difference between an application for an ordinary injunction and a *Mareva* lies only in this, that in the former case the plaintiff need only establish that there is a serious question to be tried, whereas in the latter the test is said to be whether the plaintiff shows a good arguable case. This difference, which is incapable of definition, does not however affect the applicability of Lord Diplock's observations to *Mareva* cases. ...

It is to be hoped that in future the observations of Lord Diplock and Lord Templeman will be borne in mind in applications for a *Mareva* injunction, that they will take hours not days and that appeals will be rare. I do not mean by the foregoing to indicate that argument as to the principles applying to the grant of a *Mareva* injunction should not be fully argued. With a developing jurisdiction it is inevitable and desirable that they should be. What, however, should not be allowed is (1) any attempt to persuade a court to resolve disputed questions of fact whether relating to the merits of the underlying claim in respect of which a *Mareva* is sought or relating to the elements of the *Mareva* jurisdiction such as that of dissipation or (2) detailed argument on difficult points of law on which the claim of either party may ultimately depend. If such attempts are made they can and should be discouraged by appropriate orders as to costs. ...

LORD JUSTICE NICHOLLS

...In my view each case must depend on its own facts. An order restraining a defendant from dealing with any of his assets overseas, and requiring him to disclose details of all his assets wherever located, is a draconian order. The risk of prejudice to which, in the absence of such an order, the plaintiff will be subject is that of the dissipation or secretion of assets *abroad*. This risk must, on the facts, be appropriately grave before it will be just and convenient for such a draconian order to be made. It goes without saying that before such an order is made the court will scrutinise the facts with particular care. In the instant case there are present the special factors to which May and Parker L.JJ. have referred. I do not think that it is correct that, if an order is made in the present case regarding overseas assets, such an order will become, or should become, the norm in cases where a restraint order is made regarding assets within the jurisdiction. ...

 Alert

17.3 Conclusion

From the above authorities and discussions we have seen how the courts assess the availability and appropriateness of equitable remedies. Each is governed by its own particular set of guidelines or restrictions and these are applied by the courts against the particular facts of any case.

Equity provides a large amount of freedom and flexibility to the court and also to those seeking remedies to their particular legal problems. In many cases damages will be inadequate and so equity may be called upon to step in and provide an alternative.

Further Reading

Berryman, Jeff: *'Recent Developments in Anton Piller Orders'*.   Oxford Intellectual Property Research Centre, 2001.

Civil Procedure Rules Part 25: Interim Applications

Gaskell, Nicholas: *'The Mareva Injunction and Maritime Creditors'*.   University of Southampton, 1992.

Gillard, Richard and Thomas, Simon: *'Interim Injunctions: Recent UK Patents Case Law'*. Elkington and Fife, April 2005

Pettit, Philip H.   Equity and the Law of Trusts: Eleventh Edition. Oxford University Press, 2009. Chapters 25 – 29.

Notes

Notes

Notes

Notes

Notes

Notes